Objective ENGLISH

FOR COMPETITIVE EXAMINATIONS

Fifth Edition

About the Authors

Dr. Hari Mohan Prasad, presently Director, Academy of Foreign Languages was formerly Professor and Head, Department of English and Dean Faculty of Humanities, Magadh University, Bodh Gaya, Bihar. An erudite scholar, he is an author of outstanding repute whose books have been published by world-class publishers like Oxford University Press, Macmillan India Ltd., Arnold Heinemann, Lucas, McGraw Hill Education, Motilal Banarasidas and some others. He has contributed research papers to almost all important journals published in India. He has worked on several UGC financed projects and has delivered expert lectures at UGC sponsored Refresher Courses at several Universities across the states. He has guided D.Litt. and Ph.D dissertations of more than two dozen research scholars. He was also a nominee of Government of India, MHRD on the Board of Governors, NIT, Kurukshetra, as well as Vice Chairman in Board of Management JSS, Gaya.

Uma Rani Sinha is a freelance writer and an Educational Advisor. She is also Chairman, Language Forum, Gaya and the Secretary of the Council of Academic Development, a centre of excellence for research, innovative teaching, career counseling and personality development programmes.

Objective ENGLISH

FOR COMPETITIVE EXAMINATIONS

Fifth Edition

Hari Mohan Prasad
Director, Academy of Foreign Languages
(Formerly) Prof and Head, Department of English
Dean, Faculty of Humanities
Magadh University, Bodh Gaya

Uma Rani Sinha
Educational Consultant

McGraw Hill Education (India) Private Limited

NEW DELHI

McGraw Hill Education Offices

New Delhi New York St Louis San Francisco Auckland Bogotá Caracas
Kuala Lumpur Lisbon London Madrid Mexico City Milan Montreal
San Juan Santiago Singapore Sydney Tokyo Toronto

McGraw Hill Education (India) Private Limited

Published by McGraw Hill Education (India) Private Limited
P-24, Green Park Extension, New Delhi 110 016

Objective English for Competitive Examinations, 5e

Ninth reprint 2016
DDARRRQQRBAQD

ISBN (13 digits): 978-93-329-0177-3
ISBN (10 digits): 93-329-0177-5

Managing Director: *Kaushik Bellani*
Deputy General Manager—Test Prep and School: *Tanmoy Roychowdhury*
Assistant Sponsoring Editor: *Bhavna Malhotra*
Asstt Manager—Production: *Medha Arora*
Production Executive: *Dharmender Sharma*
General Manager—Production: *Rajender P. Ghansela*
Production Manager: *Reji Kumar*

Typeset at Kaushik Laser Point & Printers, Tis Hazari Court, Delhi 110 053 and text and cover printed at SDR Printers, A-7, Sector- B3, Tronica City, Ghaziabad, U.P. 201 103

Cover Design: K. Anoop

Visit us at: www.mheducation.co.in

Preface to The Fifth Edition

Nothing gives a writer more satisfaction than the success of his book. We are grateful for the growing popularity of ***Objective English***, and thank the readers for using it for their examination preparation. New and revised editions of this book which come at short intervals keep it updated, exam-oriented, and suited to the current requirement of the students. A revised edition also helps us in providing our readers with new concepts and techniques to equip them even better to tackle the various questions in their competitive examinations.

Who can Use this Book?

This book is aimed at aspirants of various jobs in banks, defence and insurance sector, government offices, private companies, embassies, ministries, non-Governmental organisations, and public undertakings. This book will also help those aspirants who compete for admission to prestigious professional and vocational institutes.

Coverage of the Book

This book starts by giving general information about different examinations and then organises the text in the following ways:

- **Section A** provides reading materials, concepts, techniques, tips, figures, illustrations, and drilling exercises.
- **Section B** contains practice test papers comprising the latest types of questions set in various examinations.
- **Section C** contains more than forty previous years' papers of various examinations.

Main Features of the Book

This book has the unique distinction of being the first text designed to help students in solving English language questions in an objective format. It imparts in a planned, systematic, and comprehensive way, the knowledge, concepts, and techniques required to successfully solve the English questions appearing in various competitive examinations.

Unlike other books in the market which either deal with one or two types of questions or are purely grammar-based, this book approaches the objective English of examination papers in a comprehensive manner in the following ways:

- It has been prepared after a careful scrutiny and analyses of the syllabi and questions of different competitive examinations and the basic principles behind such tests.
- In order to tackle objective English questions of competitive examinations, a candidate requires a sound understanding of comprehension, applied grammar, vocabulary in usage, and logical application of language. These topics are thoroughly covered in this book.

- This book also covers secondary units like *phrases, substitution, preposition, voice*, and *analogy* which will help the candidates enhance their understanding of English language.
- Each chapter has drilling exercise sets at the end to help the students master their learning.

Highlights of this Edition

Exhaustive changes and additions have been incorporated in the fifth edition of this book keeping in view the changing trends of the examinations. Section A which comprises the staple of the book, i.e. the basic units, has been retained and revised. The chapter on *Voice* in this section has been made more comprehensive. Two new chapters on *Spelling* and *Narration* have been added. All concepts and techniques have been maintained and improved wherever necessary.

Sections B and C have been extensively revised in the following ways:

- Completely fresh practice test papers prepared on the latest pattern of various examinations have been added in Section B.
- Section C has been thoroughly revamped. This section has five units now and each contains questions of previous years up to 2014 . The answers have also been provided along with the analysis, trends, and variations in question types. This section also includes suggestions to help the students gain confidence, surety, and swiftness in dealing with the questions. Comments included in this section will help students in designing the strategy required to tackle the questions in the examination. About 40 examination papers from sectors like Banking, Insurance, Defence, Business Management etc., have been included in this section.

We hope this book in its present form and format will be immensely useful to the aspiring candidates. We also acknowledge all those who have extended cooperation in the preparation of this new edition.

Hari Mohan Prasad
Uma Rani Sinha

PREFACE TO THE FIRST EDITION

I have been writing research papers and books of explanatory nature on literature, which were meant only for a select audience. With this book, I hope to reach a much wider section of the student community and others, trying relentlessly to compete for various jobs in Government and Public sectors.

Objective English forms a part of the syllabi of different competitive examinations. It is basically a string of three units: Grammar, Comprehension, Vocabulary. There is certainly a dearth of good and reliable books, which completely cover all three units. A majority of the books available are mere compilation of questions asked over the years. Keeping this in mind, I have tried to explain the concepts behind every possible kind of test and have also endeavoured to develop simple techniques possible. In addition to these, practice sets at the end of every unit and 30 model test papers have been provided, with a view to helping the student develop competence and confidence in tackling communication and language tests. Consequently, the book has become both comprehensive and innovative.

While preparing this book, my sons Rajnish and Soujanya, my daughter Swetali, my nephew Bablu came out with various magazines, questions and self-developed problems, which helped me in the formulation of techniques. I am grateful to them for their keen interest in my book. I am also thankful to Dr Satguru Prasad my friend, who joyfully shared the painful task of proof-reading with me. I shall be remiss, if I fail to mention my wife Rani, who extended her help in various invisible ways. I sincerely hope the book will meet a good response. I shall greatly appreciate suggestions for further improvement of the book.

HARI MOHAN PRASAD
UMA RANI SINHA

How to use this Book

Optimise Your Learning

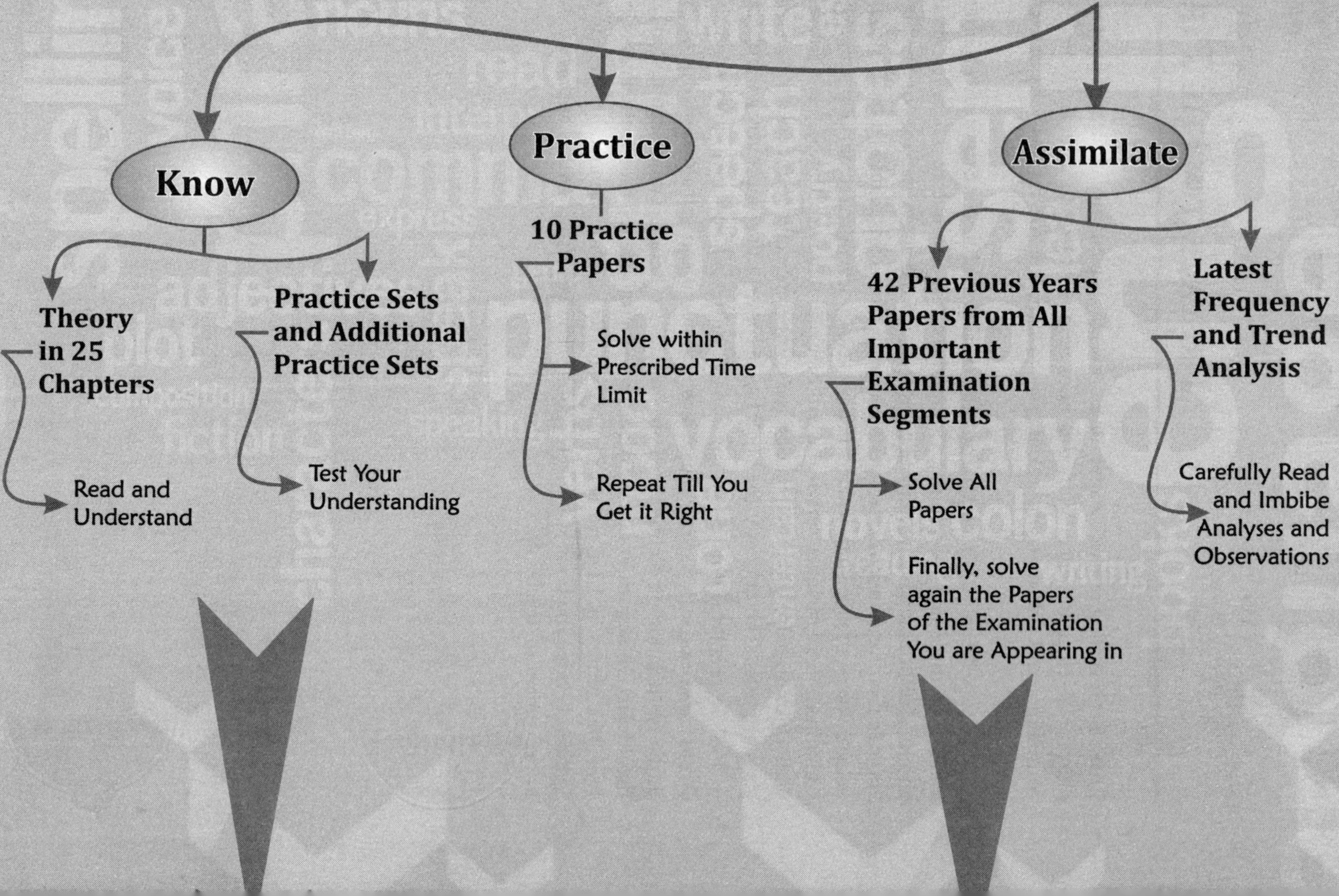

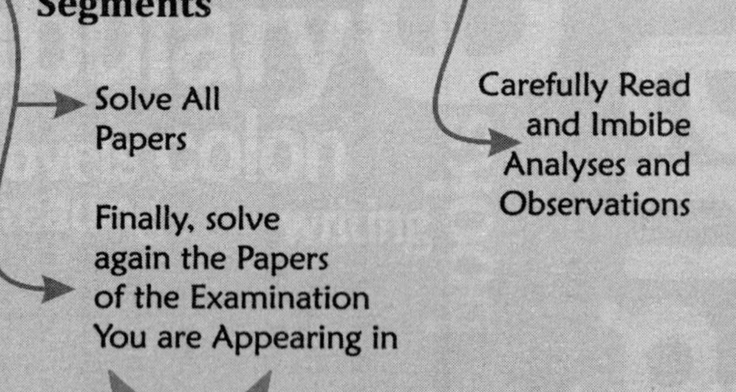

Know

- **Theory in 25 Chapters**
  - Read and Understand
- **Practice Sets and Additional Practice Sets**
  - Test Your Understanding

Practice

- **10 Practice Papers**
  - Solve within Prescribed Time Limit
  - Repeat Till You Get it Right

Assimilate

- **42 Previous Years Papers from All Important Examination Segments**
  - Solve All Papers
  - Finally, solve again the Papers of the Examination You are Appearing in
- **Latest Frequency and Trend Analysis**
  - Carefully Read and Imbibe Analyses and Observations

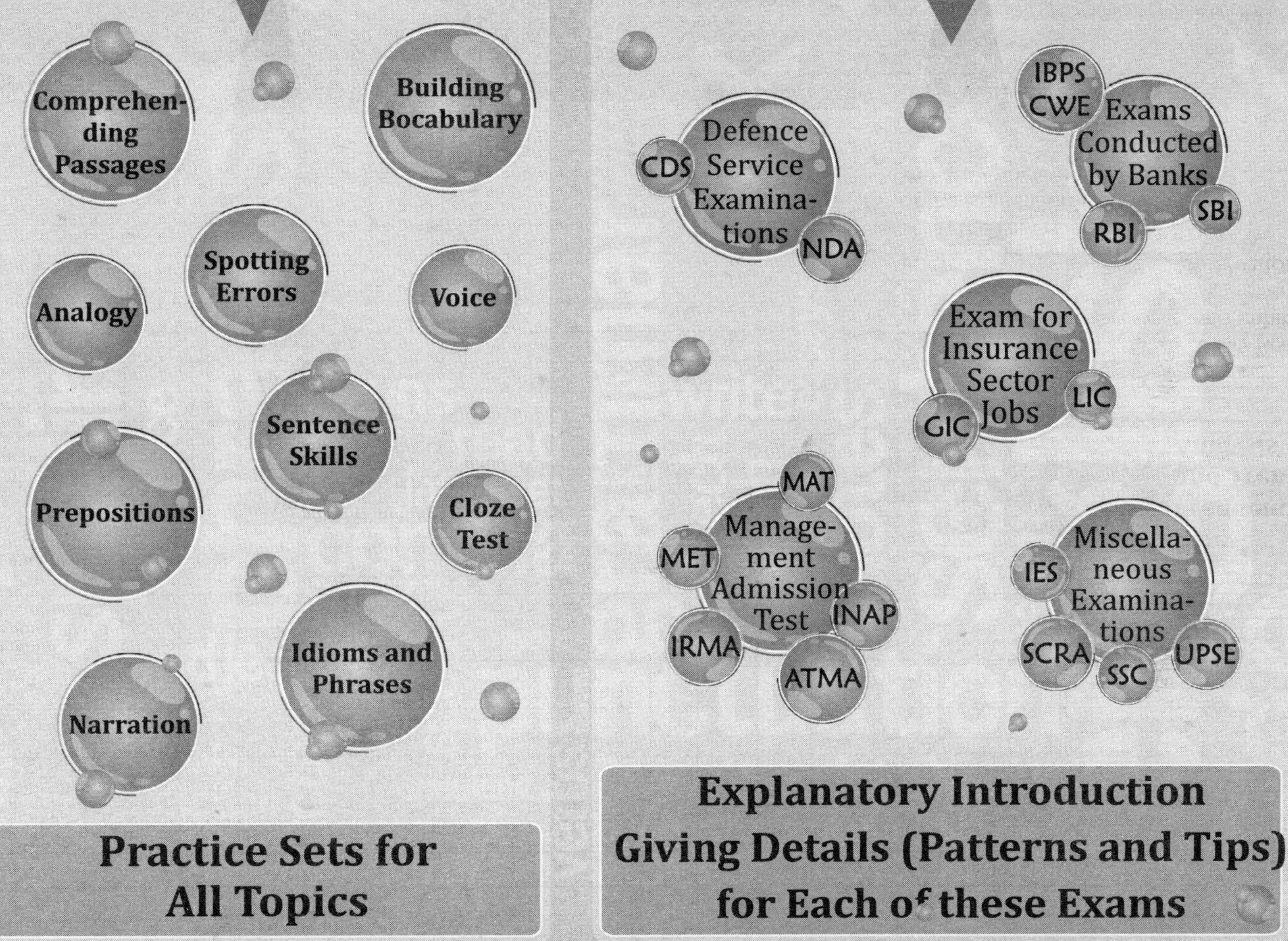
Comprehending Passages
Building Bocabulary
Analogy
Spotting Errors
Voice
Sentence Skills
Prepositions
Cloze Test
Narration
Idioms and Phrases
Practice Sets for All Topics
Defence Service Examinations
CDS
NDA
Exams Conducted by Banks
IBPS CWE
RBI
SBI
Exam for Insurance Sector Jobs
GIC
LIC
Management Admission Test
MAT
MET
INAP
IRMA
ATMA
Miscellaneous Examinations
IES
SCRA
SSC
UPSE
Explanatory Introduction Giving Details (Patterns and Tips) for Each of these Exams

FREQUENCY ANALYSIS OF QUESTIONS ASKED IN VARIOUS EXAMINATIONS* (TILL 2007)

	Comprehension	Spotting Error	Synonym	Antonym	Vocabulary	New Type Vocab	Cloze Test	Substitution	Sentence Improvement	Phrases	Idiom	Sentence Completion	Sentence Completion New Style	Ordering of Words in Sentence	Ordering of Sentence in Paragraphs	Selecting Words and Paragraphs
(1)	(2)	(3)	(4)	(5)	(6)	(7)	(8)	(9)	(10)	(11)	(12)	(13)	(14)	(15)	(16)	(17)
RBI	10			5		10		10			5					
ANDHRA BANK	13	5			3				10						5	
UCO BANK	11	10	2	2			10		10						5	
CENTRAL BANK	9	10			6				15						10	
INDIAN OVERSEAS BANK	10	10			5		10		5			5			5	
BANK OF MAHARASHTRA	15	10			5		10		5						5	
SBI	15	5					10		15						5	
CORPORATION BANK	10	5			5		10		15						5	
BANK OF BARODA	10	10			5		10					5			5	
PNB	9				6		10		5			10			10	
CDS	27		11	11					15		10	16		10	5	15
NDA	12	6	5	5			5		6					5	5	
GIC	5	5	5	5								5		5		
NEW INDIA ASSURANCE	5	5	5	5								10				
L I C	15	5					10			10		5			5	
ORIENTAL INSURANCE	5	5				5	10		5		5					
ASSISTANT PROVIDENT FUND COMMIS-SIONEERS	5	5	4	3		5				5		3				

* The numbers have been collated as per the latest trends in the examinations

Contd..

FREQUENCY ANALYSIS OF QUESTIONS ASKED IN VARIOUS EXAMINATIONS* (TILL 2007)

	Comprehension	Spotting Error	Synonym	Antonym	Vocabulary	New Type Vocab	Cloze Test	Substitution	Sentence Improvement	Phrases	Idiom	Sentence Completion	Sentence Completion New Style	Ordering of Words in Sentence	Ordering of Sentence in Paragraphs	Selecting Words and Paragraphs
(1)	(2)	(3)	(4)	(5)	(6)	(7)	(8)	(9)	(10)	(11)	(12)	(13)	(14)	(15)	(16)	(17)
SO AUDIT	10	10	5	5			10	10	10	10		10			10	
TAX ASSISTANT	10	10	10	10			10	5	5	10		10			5	
STATICAL INVESTIGATOR		10	10	10				10	10	10						
SPACIAL CLASS RAILWAY APPRENCE	15	10	5	5			10		10				5			
INDIAN ENGINEERING SERVICE	15	10	5	5			5		10				5			
IIT	12		8			2		8		8		4				
DIPLOMA PROGRAMME IN FASHION TECHNOLOGY	10		3	3							3					
PROGRAMME IN FASHION TECHNOLOGY	15	5	5	5								5				
PROGRAMME IN FASHION MANGEMENT	15		4	4						4		4				
JEE FOR DIPLOMA IN HOTEL MANAGEMENT	5	10					10					15	10			
INDIAN INSTITUTE OF TRAVEL AND TOURISM	10		4	4								8				
OPEN MAT IGNOU	10	10	5	5					5			5				
ICFAI HYDRABAD	20		12	10												
FMS, DELHI	45	4	8	4								4				

* The numbers have been collated as per the latest trends in the examinations

Contd..

FREQUENCY ANALYSIS OF QUESTIONS ASKED IN VARIOUS EXAMINATIONS* (TILL 2007)

	Comprehension	Spotting Error	Synonym	Antonym	Vocabulary	New Type Vocab	Cloze Test	Substitution	Sentence Improvement	Phrases	Idiom	Sentence Completion	Sentence Completion New Style	Ordering of Words in Sentence	Ordering of Sentence in Paragraphs	Selecting Words and Paragraphs
(1)	(2)	(3)	(4)	(5)	(6)	(7)	(8)	(9)	(10)	(11)	(12)	(13)	(14)	(15)	(16)	(17)
SO AUDIT	10	10	5	5			10	10	10	10		10			10	
IIFT	12	4	6	5								5				
CAT	15															
IRMA	10	10	3	2			10								5	
MAT	20	4							8			5			4	

* The numbers have been collated as per the latest trends in the examinations

UPDATED CHART FOR FREQUENCY ANALYSIS
Based on Questions of Different Examinations from 2008 to 2013

Exams	Compre-hension	Spotting Error	Sentene Improve-ment	Sentence ompletion	Sentence Completion with Vari-ation	Synonym	Antonym	Vocabulary with Vari-ation	Sentence Arrang-ment	Substitution	Cloze Test	Phreses / Idioms	Spelling	Misc
IBPS CWE / PO + MT 2012	8	10	5	5		4	3		5		10			
IBPS Specilist Officers CWE 2012	8	15	5			5	2		5		10			
RBI Gr-B Offic-ers 2009	15	5	5	5							10			
RBI/GR-B Offic-ers 2012	6		5	5	5	2	2		5					
SBI / PO 2013	9	10		5		3	3		5		10			
SBI / Clerk 2012	10	5	5	5		3	2				10			
SBI / Associate PO 2011	18		5	5		4	3		5		10			
LIC AAO-2013	5		10	5		5	5	5		5			10	
LIC ADO-2010	7	5		5		3			5					
New India As-surance AAO-2011		4		4+3		3+4	4	4						
Oriental Ins. A.O. 2010	5	5		5+5		5	5				10			
Indian Engg. Services-2011	10		10	10			9		10		11			
SCRA 2012	10	10		10		10	10		10					
CDS-2012	17	18	14	21		15	14		11+10					
NDA-2012 NA	10	10				10	10		10					

Contd..

UPDATED CHART FOR FREQUENCY ANALYSIS

Based on Questions of Different Examinations from 2008 to 2013

Exams	Compre-hension	Spotting Error	Sentene Improve-ment	Sentence ompletion	Sentence Completion with Vari-ation	Synonym	Antonym	Vocabulary with Vari-ation	Sentence Arrang-ment	Substitution	Cloze Test	Phreses / Idioms	Spelling	Misc
I.I.T. -2012	8	5	3	10+5		5	5		5			4	5	
MAT-2011	5	5		5		3	3				5			
SNAP-2010	5			4+6+8								2+5		
IRMA-2012	7+8			5		4+5	3+2		6		10			
MET Punjab Univ.-2010						5	5	5+5		5+5	10	5	5	
SSC Grd. Level TR-I	5	5		5		5	5				10	5		
Assistant Provident Fund Commissoner	10					1	1							
SSC Grd. Level TR-II	30	20	10+20	5		5	5		20	10	25		5	20
CPO-2010	5	5	5	5		5	5		5	5			5	5
Indian Nevy SSR-2010	5	5		5		5	5							
Cabinet Secreteriat As-sistant-2010	15	10	10	5		5	5		5		20	5		
SSC Tax As-sistant 2009	10	10	5	10		10	10		5	5	10	10	10	5
Total	251	162	117	168	5	134	126	19	127	35	166	36	40	10
	25/27	19/27	14/27	23/27	2/27	23/27	24/27	4/27	16/27	5/27	15/27	6/27	6/27	10/27
	1	5	8	3	14	4	2	13	6	12	7	11	10	9

No. of Exam 27 Highest Frequency:

1 — Comprenhension
2 — Sentence Completion
3 — Vocabulary
4 — Spotting Errors

CONTENTS

SECTION-A THEORY

Part One: Comprehending Passages

Part Two: Spotting Errors

Part Three: Filling in Paragraph Gaps

Part Four: Sentence Skills

Part Five: Building Vocabulary

Part Six: Other Important Topics

SECTION-B PRACTICE TEST PAPERS

SECTION-C PREVIOUS YEARS' QUESTION PAPERS

Part One: Examinations Conducted by Banks

Reserve Bank of India Examination Papers

State Bank of India Examination Papers

IBPS Common Written Examination Papers

Part Two: Examinations for Insurance Sector Jobs

LIC (AAO) Examination Papers

GIC Officers' Examination Papers

Part Three: Defence Services Examinations

National Defence Academy Examination Papers

Combined Defence Service Examination Papers

Part Four: Management Admission Tests

Part Five: Miscellaneous Examinations

Union Public Service Commission (UPSC) Examination Papers

Staff Selection Commission (SSC) Examination Papers

SECTION A

Part One
Comprehending Passages

Part Two
Spotting Errors

Part Three
Filling in Paragraph Gaps

Part Four
Sentence Skills

Part Five
Building Vocabulary

Part Six
Other Important Topics

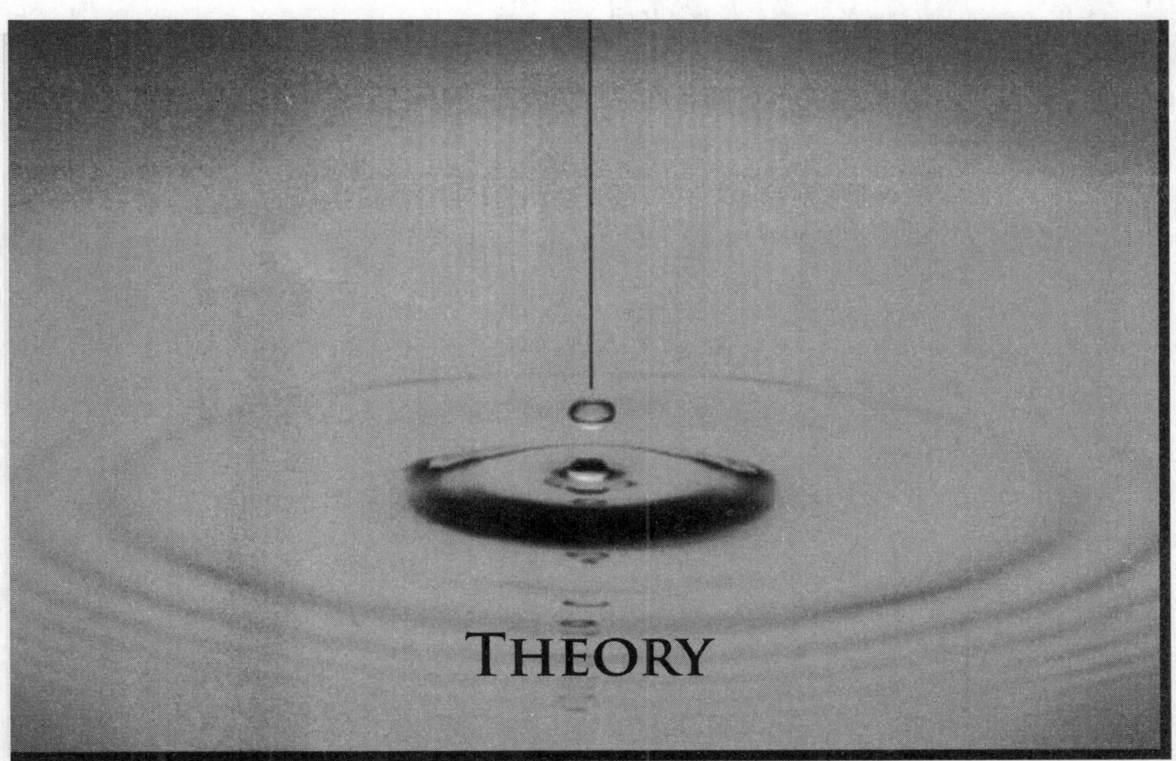

Section A, which covers concepts, techniques, and tips of the theory of English language, intends to make the candidates competent enough to tackle any question on English language in the objective format. This section will help candidates in acquiring the complete know-how for solving any type of question—whatever the format, howsover innovative the pattern of question, however the mingling of applied grammar, vocabulary, and reading comprehension. Drilling exercise at the end of each chapter will help the candidates get a deeper understanding of the concerned topic.

PART ONE

COMPREHENDING PASSAGES

'Comprehension' is a compulsory part of every competitive examination. It is a complex mental process, which requires reading, understanding, inference and judgment. Chapter One analyses the concept of 'comprehension' in a detailed manner. The IEI formula, which will help the students tackle this section with greater efficiency is also discussed in this chapter. Chapter Two provides the MLE technique that helps in solving comprehension questions pertaining to short passages. In some exams, one-line passages are set with several similar and near-correct answers to options. Chapter Three provides the MIEI formula to solve such questions.

CHAPTER 1

Objective Comprehension-I

Comprehension is an important test in most competitive examinations. Some of them have separate sections for comprehension where candidates have to work on several passages. Hence, it is important that due attention is paid to comprehension exercises.

Concept Summary

The word 'comprehend' means 'to understand'. You are required to go through a passage, grasp its gist, and then answer the questions based on it. It involves the use of your vocabulary, your sense of language, your ability to locate meanings, your intelligence to assess the real spirit of the passage, and your capability infer conclusions from the given content. You should remember that your answers must be based on and confirmed by the information given in the passage and not by any outside source. Only in certain cases, the inference may take you outside the boundary of the passage but even then your answer must be a logical consequence of the information in the passage.

It is advisable to improve your sense of language and stock of words by reading regularly and bringing new words in your day-to-day usage of language. Though regular practice helps, while adopting the IEI (Information-Elimination-Inference) formula, the following tips may prove useful.

IEI Formula

The words—*information*, *elimination*, and *inference*—may be used as the main keys.

Information

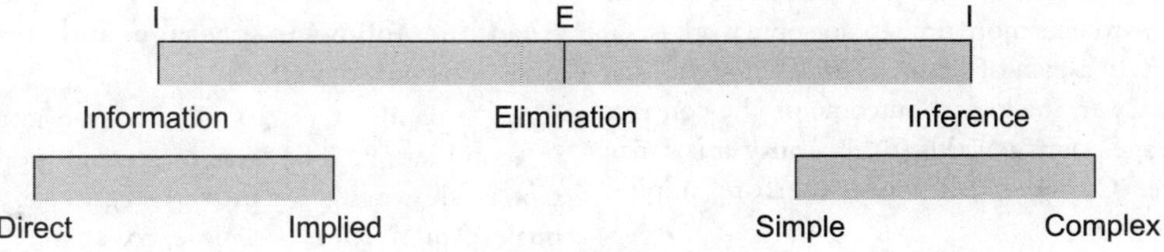

Fig 1.1 IEI Formula

Every passage offers you some 'information'. Some questions are straightforward and they may be answered from the information within the passage itself. In the two passages taken up for illustration below, refer to Questions 3 and 5 in Passage 1 and Questions 1, 2, 4, 5, and 6 in Passage 2. These questions can be answered on the basis of the information given in the passage.

The information in the passage may be *direct* or *implied*. For example, in Passage 1, Question 5 is based on direct information, and Question 3 on implied information.

Elimination

The process of 'elimination' entails saying no to alternatives on justifiable grounds until you have a positive answer. Question 9 in Passage 2 is one such example. Usually, this process helps in answering questions of the 'true or false' category.

Inference

The word 'inference' means 'to arrive at a logical conclusion'. Some questions which cannot be answered by information or elimination require the process of inference. Refer to Questions 3 and 7 in Passage 2.

There are times when you may have tocom-bine two of these keys together. For example, see Question 4 in Passage 1. A and D can be eliminated in the first reading, B and C appear to be correct, but, if you combine 'elimination' with 'inference', you find the clue in the description that the lady takes a whole day in writing the postcard. Thus, B is eliminated and C becomes the correct choice.

Inference may be either simple or complex. For example, Question 1 requires simple inference. A statement is made right in the beginning of the passage and the story of the lady illustrates the fact in the statement that whatever time is available for work, people tend to use up. But Question 2 requires complex inference. The person likely to take more time to do some work is: (a) a busy man (b) a man of leisure. Though it seems that (a) is the answer, the logical outcome of the contents in the passage points towards (b). The answer is a man of leisure. Complex inference therfore implies reasoning.

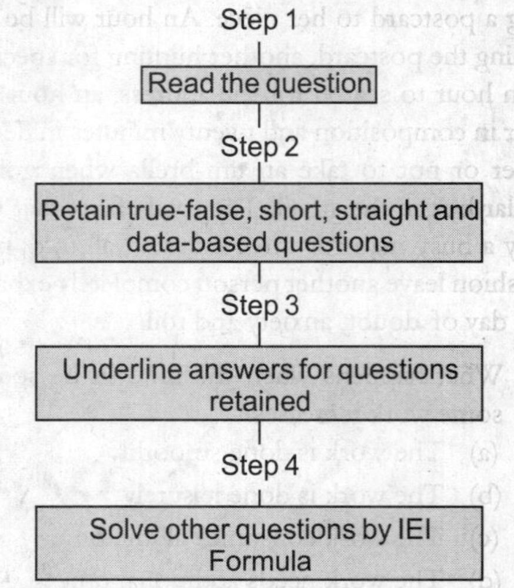

Fig 1.2 Time-saver IEI Formula

Thus it is now evident that different questions of a comprehension passage can be answered by any of the three clues separately and sometimes by combining them.

Further Tips

The IEI formula helps every candidate. However, those who have a sharp memory and can retain certain facts on the first reading may work a little differently to save further time. Instead of reading the passage first, you read the questions and try to retain some of them in your memory. Then while reading the passage you will be able to underline the answer and later tick the correct choice in a flash.

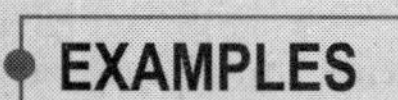

(A) By IEI Formula

Passage 1

Read the following passage and answer the questions based on it.

Work expands so as to fill the time available for its completion. The general recognition of this fact is shown in the proverbial phrase, 'It is the busiest man who has time to spare.' Thus, an elderly lady at leisure can spend the entire day writing a postcard to her niece. An hour will be spent in finding the postcard, another hunting for spectacles, half an hour to search for the address, an hour and a quarter in composition and twenty minutes in deciding whether or not to take an um-brella when going to the pillar box in the street. The total effort that would occupy a busy man for three minutes, all told, may in this fashion leave another person completely exhausted after a day of doubt, anxiety and toil.

1. What happens when the time to be spent on some work increases?
   (a) The work is done smoothly
   (b) The work is done leisurely
   (c) The work consumes all the time
   (d) The work needs additional time
2. Explain the sentence: 'Work expands so as to fill the time available for its completion'.
   (a) The more work there is to be done, the more the time needed.
   (b) Whatever time is available for a given amount of work, all of it will be used.
   (c) If you have more time, you can do more work.
   (d) If you have some important work to do, you should always have some additional time.
3. Who is the person likely to take more time to do work:
   (a) A busy man
   (b) A man of leisure
   (c) An elderly person
   (d) An exhausted person
4. What is the total time spent by the elderly lady in writing a postcard?
   (a) Three minutes
   (b) Four hours and five minutes
   (c) Half an hour
   (d) A full day
5. What does the expression 'pillar box' stand for?
   (a) A box attached to the pillar
   (b) A box in the pillar
   (c) Box office
   (d) A Pillar-type post box

ANSWERS TO PASSAGE 1

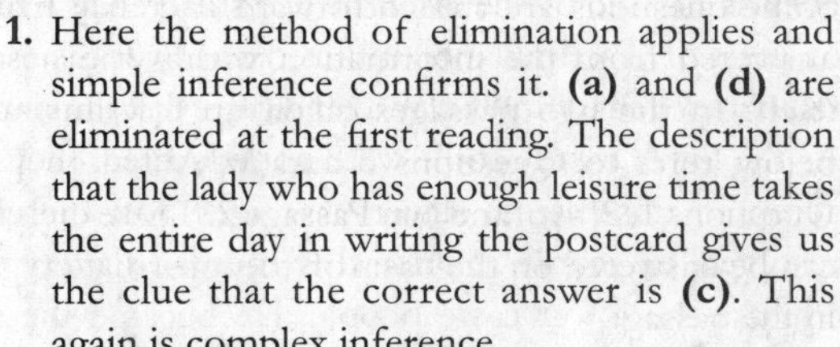

1. Here the method of elimination applies and simple inference confirms it. **(a)** and **(d)** are eliminated at the first reading. The description that the lady who has enough leisure time takes the entire day in writing the postcard gives us the clue that the correct answer is **(c)**. This again is complex inference.
2. The answer here is **(b)**. This can be found out through simple inference. A statement is made right in the beginning of the passage and the story of the lady illustrates the fact that whatever time is available for a work, people tend to use all of it.
3. Here, the answer is **(b)**. It requires inference. The answer is to be inferred from the facts given in the passage that the more time you have, the more you will need. Therefore, the answer is arrived at through complex inference.
4. The answer is **(d)** and it is based on the information given in the passage.
5. The answer is **(d)**. It can be derived through implied information. The lady has to go to the pillar box to drop her letter.

(B) By Time-Saver IEI Formula

Passage 2

Joti, a gardener's son, was once invited to attend the marriage ceremony of a Brahmin friend. As he loved his friend dearly, he attended the function. The bridegroom was being led in a procession to the bride's house. The procession consisted of men, women and children mostly Brahmins. Joti was also walking along with the procession.

One orthodox Brahmin recognised him and was annoyed at the sight of a low caste boy walking with the Brahmins in the marriage procession. Unable to contain himself, he shouted, "How dare you walk along with us? You are not our equal. Get behind! Otherwise, go away." Joti felt insulted. He left the procession and returned home.

He narrated the whole incident to his father with anger in his eyes. However, his father advised him to observe old customs. That night Joti could not sleep. He was assailed by the insult he had suffered as a result of years of discrimination inflicted on lower castes. He felt compelled to find a way to end caste discrimination. As the lower caste people were not educated, they had accepted this mental slavery for ages. Joti therefore resolved to revolt against this mental slavery and educate the lower caste people. He became the first Indian to start a school for the untouchables as well as a girls' school in Maharashtra. We recongnise him today as Mahatma Phule.

1. According to the passage, what has made low caste people accept mental slavery?
   (a) Poverty
   (b) Old customs
   (c) Apathy of change
   (d) Lack of education
   (e) Supremacy of the Brahmins

2. What kind of a man was Joti's father?
   (a) A man of revolutionary ideas
   (b) One who advised him to start a school for the untouchables
   (c) A man who did not want Joti to break old traditions
   (d) A man not in favour of Joti attending the marriage ceremony
   (e) One who was also present in the mar-riage procession

3. What did Joti do after he was insulted?
   (a) Left the procession and went to his friend
   (b) Tried to take a revenge on his friend
   (c) Decided not to join any such marriage processions in future
   (d) Involved himself actively in the freedom movement
   (e) Engaged himself in social service

4. Why did Joti attend the marriage?
   (a) On the advice of his father
   (b) He was invited by the father of the bride
   (c) The bridegroom was a good friend of Joti
   (d) Not mentioned in the passage
   (e) None of these

5. Why could Joti not sleep that night?
   (a) He had to attend the marriage of his friend
   (b) He wanted to do something for the lower caste people
   (c) The Brahmin insulted his friend
   (d) His father was sick
   (e) He was not getting any help for his school

6. Why was the Brahmin annoyed with Joti?
   (a) He left the marriage procession abruptly
   (b) He insulted his friend
   (c) He did not invite the Brahmin for the marriage procession
   (d) He was an uninvited guest
   (e) He was walking along with other Brahmins in the marriage procession

7. According to the passage, why did Joti quit the marriage procession?
   (a) He was asked accordingly by his friend
   (b) He could not tolerate his insult
   (c) He had to see his ailing father
   (d) His father warned him against attending that marriage
   (e) He had no faith in such customary rituals

8. What does the author highlight in this passage?
   (a) Joti's contribution to the upliftment of the people of lower classes
   (b) Poverty of lower class people in India
   (c) Need for separate schools for girls
   (d) Merits of caste system in India
   (e) Need for unity among different sections of people in India

9. Which of the following statement is true according to the passage?
   (a) The bridegroom was Joti's classmate
   (b) Joti's father was also invited to the marriage
   (c) Mahatma Phule started a school for the untouchables
   (d) Joti did not say anything about the incident to his father
   (e) The Brahmin who insulted Joti was the bride's father

Here, when you read the questions, you may retain numbers 1, 4, 5 and 6. You can remember as such:

Question 1. the cause of mental slavery,

Question 4. the case of Joti attending the marriage,

Question 5. why couldn't Joti sleep that night; and

Question 6. why the Brahmin was annoyed with Joti.

Now, while reading the passage you can under-line the answer to

Question 1 : 'no education';

Question 4: 'a Brahmin friend';

Question 5 : 'what could he do for the equality of human beings'; and

Question 6 : 'How dare you walk along with us'.

When you read the alternatives, you will immediately tick the correct answers.

The answers to the rest of the questions are listed below:

Question 2: The correct answer is **(c)**, on the basis of the information in the passage.

Question 3: The correct answer **(e)** can be identified by simple inference. The last lines help you locate the answer.

Question 7: The correct answer **(b)** can be arrived at through simple infer-ence.

Question 8: The correct answer is **(e)** which could be arrived at by inference. Alternative **(a)** may also be an answer, but **(e)** is logically more viable.

Question 9: The correct answer is **(c)**—arrived at through the process of elimination. **(a)**, **(b)**, **(d)** and **(e)** are eliminated on the basis of the information given in the passage.

Passage 3

The last half of my life was spent at one of those painful epochs of human history, during which the world seemed to be getting worse; where past victories which had seemed to be definitive have turned out to be only temporary. When I was young, Victorian optimism was taken for granted. It was thought that freedom and prosperity would spread gradually throughout the world through an orderly process, and it was hoped that cruelty, tyranny, and injustice would continually diminish. Hardly anyone was haunted by the fear of great wars. Hardly anyone thought of the nineteenth century as a brief interlude between past and future barbarism.

1. The author felt sad about the latter part of his life because:

(a) He was nostalgic about his childhood

(b) The world had not become prosperous

(c) The author had not won any further victories

(d) The world was painfully disturbed during that period of time

2. The victories of the past:

(a) Brought permanent peace and prosperity

(b) Ended cruelty, tyranny and injustice

(c) Proved to be temporary events

(d) Filled men with a sense of pessimism

3. The word 'definitive' used in the passage means:

(a) Defined (b) Final

(c) Temporary (d) Incomplete

4. During the Victorian age people believed that:

(a) Strife would increase

(b) There would be unlimited freedom

(c) Wars would be fought on a bigger scale

(d) Peace would prevail and happiness would engulf the whole world

5. "A brief interlude between past and future barbarism" can be interpreted as:

(a) A short period of time between past and future acts of savagery

(b) A short interlude between two great events

(c) An interval between cruel wars

(d) A dramatic performance during wars

ANSWERS TO PASSAGE 3

1. The answer is **(d)**. You can hit at the answer through inference. The clue is in the first sentence itself—'the world is getting worse'. The whole passage also implies that the last half of the life of the author was a period of turmoil.

2. The answer is **(c)** and it can be based on the information given in the passage: 'the nineteenth century was a brief interlude'.

3. The answer is **(b)**. Both information and simple inference suggest this answer.
4. The answer is **(d)**. It is based on information that can be inferred from the last two lines.
5. The answer is **(a)**. The information is implied in the question itself through the word 'barbarism'. The passage also confirms it.

Passage 4

It is not luck but labour that makes a man. Luck, says an American writer, is ever waiting for something to turn up; labour with keen eyes and strong will always turns up something. Luck lies in bed and wishes the postman would bring him news of a legacy; labour turns out at six and with busy pen and ringing hammer lays the foundation of competence. Luck whines, labour watches. Luck relies on chance, labour on character. Luck slips downwards to self-indulgence; labour strides upwards and aspires to independence. The conviction, therefore, is extending that diligence is the mother of good luck. In other words, that a man's success in life will be proportionate to his efforts, to his industry, to his attention to small things.

1. Which one of the following statements sums up the meaning of the passage ?
   (a) Luck waits without exertion, but labour exerts without waiting
   (b) Luck waits and complains without working while labour achieves success although it complains
   (c) Luck is self-indulgent, but labour is selfless
   (d) Luck often ends in defeat, but labour produces luck.
2. Which one of the following words in the passage indicate that the writer does not ultimately reject the element of Luck?
   (a) 'Luck...is ever waiting'
   (b) 'Luck whines'
   (c) 'Diligence is the mother of good luck'
   (d) 'Luck... wishes the postman would bring him news.'
3. Which one of the statements is true about the passage?
   (a) Luck is necessary for success
   (b) Success depends only on hard luck
   (c) Expectation of good luck always meets with disappointment
   (d) Success is exactly proportionate to hard work.
4. "... Labour turns out at six and with busy pen and ringing hammer lays the foundation of competence." What does this statement mean?
   (a) Hard work of all kinds makes people efficient
   (b) Labour lays the foundation of the building
   (c) The writer and the labourer are the true eyes of the society
   (d) There is no worker who works so hard as the labourer who begins his day at six in the morning.

ANSWERS TO PASSAGE 4

1. The answer is **(d)**. It can be derived through inference. Elimination will also help. **(a)** and **(b)** are eliminated easily on the basis of information. **(c)** and **(d)** are of a general nature, but you may come to the right conclusion by arguing that labour is not always selfless. One does hard labour for a purpose. Again, remember the general hint that you should prefer a choice in such cases which includes the largest possibility.
2. The answer is **(c)**. The answer can be arrived at by simple inference. This is the implication of the passage as well.
3. The answer is **(d)**. The information is in the last sentence.
4. The answer is **(a)**. The information given in the middle of the passage and simple inference will help. The reference to both pen and hammer implies that the meaning here includes all kinds of work. The pen stands for mental work and the hammer for the physical labour.

Passage 5

The news that the Indian Railways are going to incur a shortfall of Rs 1000 crore in their resources generation—and will, therefore, have to seek budgetary support to that extent—will not surprise many. That's a scenario that has been *played out* for years now, and the outcome, too, has been predictable—with the railway budget doing its duty by doling out public money. But it's time to look at the problem differently, in view of the current concerns of the government in economising its charity and the feeling that the railways have to stand on their own legs.

The Railways have, over the last few months, continued to experience a shortfall of Rs 85 crore per month, a feature that could add to their woes if it continues. Fall in expected goods traffic, in the rate per tonne and also a *dip* in passenger traffic have contributed to the shortfall. All these may not be new concerns for the Railways; the relevant point, however, is how the system and the government hope to tackle it.

Clearly, budgetary support should be considered only in the last instance, after various measures to both reduce expenditure and raise resources have been tried out. Consider subsidies on passenger traffic—the expenditure which really *digs* into the government's coffers. In fact, passenger traffic subsidy accounted for nearly 90 per cent of the railways' losses in 1992/93, with freight traffic subsidies taking up the rest.

Freight traffic subsidy cuts should prove more easy if this year's budget exercise is any indication. Till now, sixteen commodities were subsidised. In 1993/94, budget subsidy on four commodities were removed. Prices did not rise, there was little protest and now the Railways ought to be emboldened to do more. Reduction in passenger subsidies is more *tricky* given the dependence of such a large population, mostly poor, on the system and most governments have been reluctant to do much. In fact, passenger rates have been hiked very few times and that, too, only in recent years.

One area where the Railways could do a lot more *pruning* is in shutting uneconomic branch lines. For instance, in 1992/93 it was found that 114 branch lines contributed a loss of Rs 121 crore.

To its credit, however, the railways have been looking around for sources of funds other than the budget.

1. Which of the following has the ***same*** meanings as phrase *played out* as it has been used in the passage?
   (a) Enacted (b) Repeated
   (c) Dramatised (d) Done
   (e) Predicted

2. Which of the following is ***false*** regarding the railway operation?
   (a) Reduction in goods traffic is not a new phenomenon
   (b) Passenger traffic has shown an increase in recent years
   (c) Rates per tonne of goods carried has come down
   (d) Railways are aware of the problem of reduction in income
   (e) None of these

3. How does the cut in freight traffic affect the shortfall?
   (a) By increasing the income
   (b) By reducing the expense
   (c) Simultaneously increasing income and reducing expense
   (d) By reducing dependence on the Central Government
   (e) None of these.

4. Which of the followinjg is ***correct*** regarding the shortfall in the Railways' resource generation?
   (a) It was higher than earlier years
   (b) It is happening for the first time
   (c) It was anticipated by most people
   (d) This is the largest shortfall ever to happen
   (e) None of these

5. How does the government expect to 'economise its charity'?
   (a) By requiring the railways to be self-sufficient
   (b) By stopping the budget support
   (c) By showing its concern through the Railway ministry
   (d) By not doling out public money
   (e) By reducing the overall operation of the Railways

6. Which of the following has the ***same*** meaning as the word *dip* as it has been used in the passage?
   (a) Drift (b) Slowness
   (c) Plunge (d) Reduction
   (e) Tardiness

7. Which of the following seems to be the major contributing factor towards the losses of the Railways?
   (a) Passenger subsidies
   (b) Freight subsidies
   (c) Uneconomical lines
   (d) All of the three are at the same level
   (e) None of these

8. According to the author, what should the Railways do as regards freight subsidy?
   (a) It should introduce subsidy for more items
   (b) It should be very courageous
   (c) It should remove or reduce subsidies of more items
   (d) Author's views are not explicit
   (e) None of these

9. Which of the following is ***true*** regarding the passenger fare charged by the Railways?
   (a) It is excessively high now
   (b) First class passengers are not given any subsidy
   (c) Only second class passengers get subsidy
   (d) Poor people alone get subsidy
   (e) None of these

10. What seems of be the ultimate consideration for allowing freight subsidy by the Railways?
   (a) Keeping the freight charges low
   (b) Keeping the railways in losses
   (d) Keeping the prices of commodities low
   (d) Cannot be made out from the passage
   (e) None of these

11. Why do the government and Railways not raise the passenger fares?
   (a) It is anyway subsidised
   (b) It does not affect the railways very much
   (c) It is anyway making losses
   (d) It would affect a large number of people
   (e) None of these

12. Which of the following has the ***same*** meaning as the word *pruning* as it has been used in the passage?
   (a) Stopping (b) Economising
   (c) Spending (d) Profiteering
   (e) Cancelling

13. Which of the following has the ***same*** meaning as the word *tricky* as it has been used in the passage?
   (a) Foolish (b) Deceitful
   (c) Useless (d) Needless
   (e) Difficult

14. Which of the following has the ***opposite*** meaning to the word *digs* as it has been used in the passage?
   (a) Donates (b) Constructs
   (c) Levels (d) Contributes
   (e) Shares

15. How many freight items are now subsidised by the Railways?
   (a) Sixteen (b) Four
   (c) Ten (d) Twenty
   (e) None of these

EXPLANATION OF PASSAGE 5

1. The answer is **(b)**—repeated. The word 'scenario' may suggest the word 'enacted' but here the emphasis is on 'four years now' and thus the real implication is repetition. Information and inference work together here.
2. The answer is **(b)**. It can be located by eliminating the alternatives one after another on the basis of information given in the passage.
3. The answer is **(e)**. The process of elimination will help you find it.
4. The answer is **(c)**. The answer can be located by information and may be confirmed by the process of elimination.
5. The answer is **(a)**. You can arrive at the answer through the process of complex inference only.
6. The answer is **(d)**. You can get it by simple inference. It is implied in the context.
7. The answer is **(a)**. You can base it on information. However, you may also confirm it by simple inference.
8. The answer is **(c)**. There is sufficient information in Paragraph 4.
9. The answer is **(e)**. You can reach the answer through elimination.
10. The answer, **(c)**, can be located by complex inference.

11. See paragraph 4. You have the full information for the answer **(d)**.

12. The correct answer, **(b)**, can be reached at through inference.

13. By elimination you get the answer—**(e)**.

14. By elimination you get the answer—**(d)**.

15. On the basis of information you can find out that the correct number is 16 – 4 = 12 and thus the answer is **(e)**.

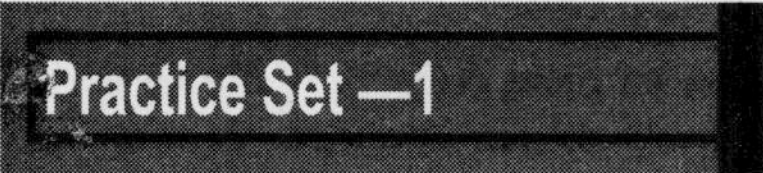

Practice Set —1

Read the following passage and answer the following questions on the basis of information provided in the passage.

Our body is a wondrous mechanism and when subjected to unusual stress over a period of time, it adapts itself to deal more effectively with that stress. Therefore, when you exert your muscles against resistance, they are forced to adapt and deal with this extraordinary work load. This is the principle of weight training. Strands of muscle fibres become thicker and stronger in response to the demands placed on them.

One of the great merits of weight training is the strength of your heart. During weight training, your heart is forced to beat faster and stronger in order to pump sufficient blood to the muscles being worked. In time, your heart, like your body, will adapt to this extra-workload by becoming stronger and more efficient. Since your body needs a given amount of blood to perform its daily tasks your heart will now need fewer beats to pump the same quantity of blood. Sounds good? There's more. Your entire circulatory system is given a thorough workout everytime you exercise, which increases its overall efficiency. Even the neural paths from your brain's command centres to each individual muscle become more effective, enabling easier recruitment of muscle fibres for carrying out physical tasks. In essence, your body becomes a well-oiled and finely-tuned piece of machinery, whirring along without any break-down. In today's stress filled world, you need all help you can get.

1. What is the principal training of weight lifting?

(a) Adapting the body to muscle force
(b) Adapting muscles to force implied on them
(c) Disposing extra-workload
(d) Mechanised response to external conditions

2. What affects the nature of muscle fibres?

(a) Intensity of workload
(b) Alimentary system
(c) Nutrition
(d) Stress imposed on them

3. How does the heart become stronger owing to physical exercise?

(a) Thorough acclimatisation
(b) Naturalisation
(c) Adapting to excessive workload
(d) By accelerating the circulation of blood

4. How much blood does the heart pump at the same number of heartbeats, when exposed to excessive stress?

(a) Same quantity
(b) Less than before
(c) More than normal
(d) None of these

5. What happens to our body due to physical exercise?

(a) More efficient
(b) Less efficient
(c) Efficiency of the body remains the same
(d) None of these

6. What does the term 'well-oiled' in the passage denote?

(a) Healthy (b) Efficient
(c) Massaged (d) None of these

7. Which one of the following is the most appropriate title for the passage?

(a) Health is wealth
(b) Exercise—its benefits
(c) The mechanics of weight training
(d) How to retain your health

8. In the present world, the importance of physical exercise has

(a) Increased
(b) Decreased
(c) Remained at the same level
(d) None of these

9. What, according to the passage, is the function of the heart?
(a) Oxygenation of blood
(b) Pumping the blood to the muscles
(c) Pumping the blood to capillaries
(d) Accelerating the circulation of blood

10. What does the above passage suggest?
(a) We should carry out physical exercise as a routine
(b) Physical exercise is necessary occasionally
(c) We should ignore physical exercise
(d) We should subject our body to as much exercise as it can withstand.

Practice Set —2

The task which Gandhiji undertook was not only the achievement of political freedom but also the establishment of a social order based on truth and non-violence, unity and peace, equality and universal brotherhood, and maximum freedom for all. This unfinished part of his experiment was perhaps even more difficult to achieve than the achievement of political freedom. Political struggle involved fight against a foreign power and all one could do was either join it or wish it success and give it his moral support. In establishing the social order of this pattern, there was a lively possibility of a conflict arising between groups and classes of our own people. Experience shows that man values his possessions even more than his life because in the former he sees the means for perpetuation and survival of his descendants even after his body is reduced to ashes. A new order cannot be established without radically changing the mind and attitude of men towards property and, at some stage or the other, the 'haves' have to yield place to the 'have-nots'. We have seen, in our time, attempts to achieve a kind of egalitarian society and the picture of it after it was achieved. But this was done, by and large, through the use of physical force.

In the ultimate analysis, it is difficult, if not impossible, to say that the instinct to possess has been rooted out or that it will not reappear in an even worse form under a different guise. It may even be that, like a gas kept confined within containers under great pressure, or water held by a big dam, once a barrier breaks, the reaction will one day sweep back with a violence equal in extent and intensity to what was used to establish and maintain the outward egalitarian form. This enforced egalitarianism contains, in its bosom, the seed of its own destruction.

The root cause of class conflict is possessiveness or the acquisitive instinct. So long as the ideal that is to be achieved is one of securing the maximum material satisfaction, possessiveness can neither be suppressed nor eliminated but will grow on what it feeds. Nor will it cease to be such—it is possessiveness, still, whether it is confined to only a few or is shared by many.

If egalitarianism is to endure, it has to be based not on the possession of the maximum material goods by a few or by all but on voluntary, enlightened renunciation of those goods which cannot be shared by others or can be enjoyed only at the expense of others. This calls for substitution of spiritual values for purely material ones. The paradise of material satisfaction, that is sometimes equated with progress these days neither spells peace nor progress. Mahatma Gandhi has shown us how the acquisitive instinct inherent in man could be transmuted by the adoption of the ideal of trusteeship by those who 'have' for the benefit of all those who 'have not' so that, instead of leading to exploitation and conflict, it would become a means and incentive for the amelioration and progress of society, respectively.

1. According to the passage, egalitarianism will not survive if
(a) It is based on voluntary renunciation
(b) It is achieved by resorting to physical force
(c) Underprivileged people are not involved in its establishment
(d) People's outlook towards it is not radically changed
(e) None of these

2. According to the passage, why does man value his possessions more than his life?

(a) He has an inherent desire to share his possessions with others
(b) He is endowed with the possessive instinct
(c) Only his possessions help him earn love and respect from his descendants
(d) Through his possessions he can preserve his name even after his death
(e) None of these

3. According to the passage, which was the unfinished part of Gandhiji's experiment ?
(a) Educating people to avoid class conflict
(b) Achieving total political freedom for the country
(c) Establishment of an egalitarian society
(d) Radically changing the mind and attitude of men towards truth and non-violence
(e) None of these

4. Which of the following statements is 'not true' in the context of the passage?
(a) True egalitarianism can be achieved by giving up one's possessions under compulsion
(b) Man values his life more than his possessions
(c) Possessive instinct is a natural part of the human being
(d) In the political struggle, the fight was against the alien rule
(e) The root cause of class conflict is possessiveness

5. According to the passage, true egalitarianism will last if
(a) It is thrust upon people
(b) It is based on truth and non-violence
(c) People inculcate spiritual values along with material values
(d) 'Haves' and 'have-nots' live together peacefully
(e) None of these

6. According to the passage, people ultimately overturn the form of a social order
(a) Which is based on coercion and oppression
(b) Which does not satisfy their basic needs
(c) Which is based upon conciliation and rapprochement
(d) Which is not congenial to the spiritual values of the people
(e) None of these

7. According to the passage, the root cause of class conflict is
(a) The paradise of material satisfaction
(b) Dominant inherent acquisitive instinct in man
(c) Exploitation of the 'have-nots' by the 'haves'
(d) A social order where the unprivileged are not a part of the establishment
(e) None of these

8. Which of the following statements is *not* true in the context of the passage?
(a) A new order can be established by radically changing the outlook of peo-ple towards it
(b) Adoption of the ideal of trusteeship can minimise possessive instinct
(c) Enforced egalitarianism can be the cause of its own destruction
(d) Idea of new order is to secure maximum material satisfaction
(e) None of these

9. According to the passage, which of the following statements is true?
(a) A social order based on truth and non-violence alone can help the achievement of political freedom
(b) In establishing the social order of Gandhiji's pattern, the possibility of a conflict between different classes of society hardly exists
(c) It is difficult to change the mind and attitude of men towards property
(d) In an egalitarian society, material satisfaction can be enjoyed only at the expense of others
(e) None of these

10. According to the passage, what does adop-tion of the ideal of trusteeship mean?

(a) Equating peace and progress with material satisfaction
(b) Adoption of the ideal by the 'haves' for the benefit of the society
(c) Voluntary, enlightened renunciation of the possessive instinct by the privileged class
(d) Substitution of spiritual values by material ones by those who live in the paradise of material satisfaction
(e) None of these

Practice Set —3

The first thing the children wanted to do at the zoo was to ride the elephant. They were frightened as they climbed the ladder to take their seats on the swaying back of the huge beast. Elephants seem awkward creatures as they move along heavily, their legs covered with loose folds of tough skin and their trunk swinging from side to side in search of food or drink. An elephant has great strength in its trunk, and can drag heavy loads with ropes, but it can also use its trunk to pick up small articles such as coins or nuts from the ground.

After their ride on the elephant, the children went to see the lions and tigers. Crowds of people stood watching, protected from the cruel beasts by the strong metal bars of the cages.

From there, they went to see the monkeys. Those merry creatures were jumping about the rocks, swinging on the wires of their cages, or begging for nuts from the passers-by. If anyone annoyed them, they would scold him angrily and beat their chests with their hands.

In the end, they saw some curious creatures like the giraffe with its long neck and the camel with its short beard.

1. Which of the following is the reaction of monkeys when they get irritated?
(a) They jump about the rock
(b) They swing on the wire of the cage
(c) They beat their chest
(d) They beg from visitors
(e) They keep quiet

2. The cages of lions are made of strong metals bars in order to
(a) Protect visitors from the lions
(b) Protect lions from other animals
(c) Ensure the durability of the cages
(d) Enable the visitors to see the lions
(e) Enable lions to get fresh air

3. Which of the following is the chief function of the trunk of the elephants?
(a) Picking up small articles like coins from the ground
(b) Swaying from side to side
(c) Dragging heavy loads
(d) Eating food and drinking water
(e) Creating fear among other animals

4. The children were afraid of riding on the elephant as
(a) The elephant looked awkward
(b) The back of the elephant was swaying
(c) The trunk of the elephant was swinging
(d) The elephant was dragging heavy loads
(e) Its legs were covered with loose folds

5. Which of the following is a ferocious animal?
(a) Giraffe (b) Elephant
(c) Camel (d) Monkey
(e) None of these

6. Which of the following does not make the elephant awkward in appearance?
(a) Its long trunk
(b) Its swinging trunk
(c) Its heavy movement
(d) Loose folds on its legs
(e) None of these

7. Which of the following is typical of the giraffe?
(a) Hump on the back
(b) Short beard
(c) Tough skin
(d) Swaying back
(e) Long neck

Practice Set —4

To those who do listen, the desert speaks of things with an emphasis quite different from that of the shore, the mountain, the valley, or the plains. Whereas these invite action and suggest limitless opportunity and exhaustless resources, the implications and the mood of the desert are something different. For one thing, the desert is conservative, not radical. It is more likely to provide awe than to invite conquest. The heroism which it encourages is the heroism of the endurance, not that of conquest. It brings man up against his limitation, turns him in upon himself and suggests values which more indulgent regions suppress. Sometimes it induces contemplation in men who have never contemplated before. And of all the answers to the question—what is a desert good for—'contemplation' is perhaps the best.

1. In order to receive the desert's message, the beholder needs to be
(a) Courageous in his reaction
(b) Conservative in his responses
(c) A good listener
(d) Sensitive to nature

2. The desert is unique among landscapes in that it encourages only
(a) Contemplation
(b) Indolence
(c) Heroic endeavour
(d) Adventurous spirit

3. If one responds with insight to the mood of the desert, it evokes
(a) An inclination for deep thought
(b) The possibility of unending resources
(c) The desire for heroic conquest
(d) A sense of intense revulsion

4. The writer calls the desert 'conservative' rather than 'radical' because it provides an environment that
(a) Inspires man to explore it
(b) Offers unlimited opportunity to conquer
(c) Tests one's endurance
(d) Makes one gloomy

5. What does the phrase "it brings man up against his limitations", mean?
(a) It makes man feel hopeless about his limitations
(b) It makes man aware of his limitations
(c) It compels man to fight against his limitations
(d) It persuades man to overcome his limitations

Practice Set —5

The best way of understanding our own civilisation is to take an ordinary sort of day in the life of an ordinary sort of man, myself for instance, and to see what he does. My home is in London. I get up in the morning when an alarm clock rings on the table by my bed. It is quite a complicated machine and works perfectly. I get into a hot bath, the water for which has been heated by gas. The gas is supplied by the Gas Board for the area in which I live; it is part of a national system. The water is supplied by the City Water Board. After bathing, I shave—the water for my shave comes from a kettle which has been heated by electricity. As far as I am concerned, what happens is very simple: I put a plug in the wall and put on the switch and the electricity does the rest. I use a safety razor, the blade of which, made of very finely tempered steel, has been cut, together with millions of other blades, by machines. The clothes which I put on have also been spun and woven largely by steam or electrically driven machines.

1. The 'I' in this passage represents:
(a) A common man
(b) A rich person
(c) An automation
(d) A robot

2. The ideal way of understanding a civilisation is
(a) To read its literature
(b) To see how the people shave, bathe and dress
(c) To assess its technological progress
(d) To study the daily routine of an ordinary person

3. The 'complicated machine' in the passage refers

to
(a) An electric kettle
(b) A safety razor
(c) An alarm clock
(d) Gas

4. The gas being 'supplied by a national sys-tem' means that
(a) It is supplied by a nationalist goverment
(b) It is supplied only nationally and not internationally
(c) It is supplied all over the country by a central agency
(d) It is supplied to only those who believe in a national system

5. The kind of life experienced by the writer is representative of
(a) An advanced urban society
(b) A rural society
(c) A semi-urbanised society
(d) A socialist society

Practice Set —6

The idea of evolution (which is a gradual change) was not a new one. The Greeks had thought of it, so had Erasmus Darwin, the grandfather of Charles Darwin, and also the Frenchman, Lamarck. It is one thing to have an idea; we can all guess and sometimes make a lucky guess. It is quite another thing to produce a proof of the correctness of that idea. Darwin thought he had that proof in his notebooks. He saw that all animals had to struggle to survive. Those which were best at surviving their environment passed on the good qualities which helped them to their descendants. This was called 'the survival of the fittest'. For example, in a cold climate, those who have the warmest fur will live. Darwin believed that this necessity for an animal to deal with its environment explained the immense variety of creatures.

1. At the time that Darwin arrived on the scene, the idea of evolution
(a) Was an idea unheard of
(b) Had already been proved beyond doubt
(c) Had been thought of but not proved
(d) Was not thought fit for exploration

2. According to Darwinian thought, the world of animals is marked by
(a) Peaceful coexistence
(b) A struggle for survival
(c) Indifference towards each other
(d) Love and friendship

3. The expression 'the survival of the fittest' means that—
(a) The strong will survive while the weak will perish
(b) The strong and the weak will live peacefully
(c) The strong will help the weak survive
(d) Both the strong and the weak will survive

4. In colder climates
(a) All animals can survive
(b) No animal can survive
(c) Only animals with fur can survive
(d) Animals are hard to come by

5. Darwin thought that the environment
(a) Has no effect on animals
(b) Has lot of effect on animals
(c) Has a marginal effect on animals
(d) Has an effect on man but not on animals

Practice Set —7

Mikhail Gorbechev's ouster, though dramatic in every respect, is on no account a surprise. Both his foes and his closest friends had been warning him of it with a heightening sense of urgency for the past several months. Its consequences, however, are wholly unpredictable. The Soviet Union could well witness protracted violence on a mass scale should the reformists and supporters of the republic, those who have sought varying degrees of sovereignty for themselves, choose to defy the central author-ity. It is possible that the country after an initial period of uncertainty, and perhaps even violence, could revert to the pre-Perestroika system. Equally uncertain is the course of East-West relations. These are bound to deteriorate though the extent of deterioration must remain a matter of conjecture. Hailed abroad as a leader who had dared to free Soviet citizens from fear, who had enabled the countries of Eastern Europe to become democracies even as they regained their full sovereign status, who had paved the way for the reunification of Germany and who had exposed the moribund and totalitarian character of communism, he appeared, at home, to come under fire from all sides.

1. Under Gorbachev's term, the Soviet people were
   (a) Afraid to speak
   (b) Indisciplined and lazy
   (c) Committed to communism
   (d) Not afraid to criticise
2. The relations between the Soviet Union and Western countries
   (a) Are likely to remain unaffected
   (b) May improve considerably
   (c) Will definitely get worse
   (d) Will fluctuate
3. The post-Gorbachev era may witness
   (a) A more open economy
   (b) Reversal of Perestroika
   (c) Greater role for reformers
   (d) Sovereignty for republics
4. As a result of his policies, the countries of Eastern Europe became
   (a) Democratic and truly independent
   (b) Authoritarian and inhuman
   (c) United and totalitarian
   (d) Democratic but with a monarchy
5. The removal of Mikhail Gorbachev from power is
   (a) Vivid and shocking
   (b) Dramatic but expected
   (c) Thrilling and extraordinary
   (d) Strange and cruel

Practice Set —8

Bansilal's train was late and it reached Bombay a little after midnight. It was his first visit to the city, and he didn't know where to go. He thought he would go to a *choultry* where he would not have to pay rent, but he did not know how to find one at that hour. He asked a porter to get him a cheap room. The porter asked him for three rupees to take him to one. But Bansilal waved him away and walked out of the station. He wandered through the streets and asked a number of people, but could not find a room cheap enough for him.

He sat down on a park bench to think of what he should do next. He was very tired and fell asleep on the bench. He woke up the next morning, stiff in every limb; but he smiled when he realised that it was the cheapest night's lodging that he had ever had.

1. Bansilal could not get any accommodation for the night as
   (a) All the hotels in the city were closed
   (b) All the hotel rooms were booked
   (c) The hotels were too expensive for him to afford
   (d) He wanted to spend the night in the open
2. In the passage, the word 'choultry' should mean
   (a) An expensive hotel
   (b) A highway hotel
   (c) A roadside eatery
   (d) A free resting place
3. The porter refused to help Bansilal because
   (a) He was rude to the porter
   (b) He had no previous acquaintance with the porter
   (c) He spoke a language which the porter could not understand
   (d) He refused to pay the porter any tip
4. The night in the open
   (a) Refreshed Bansilal
   (b) Gave him aches all over his body
   (c) Made his limbs stronger
   (d) Did not affect him at all
5. From the passage, Bansilal emerges as
   (a) A thrifty person
   (b) An extravagant spender
   (c) An adventurous person
   (d) A fun loving person

Practice Set —9

Most of us use the products of science—railways, aeroplanes, electricity, wireless and thousands of others—without thinking how they came into existence. We take them for granted, as if we were entitled to them as a matter of right. We are very proud of the fact that we live in an advanced age and are ourselves very advanced. Now, there is no doubt that our age is very different from previous ages and I think it is perfectly correct to say that it is far more advanced. But it is a different thing from saying that we, as individuals or groups, are more advanced. It would be the height of absurdity to say that because an engine driver can run an engine and Plato or Socrates could not, the engine driver is more advanced than, or is superior to, Plato or Socrates. But it would be perfectly correct to say that the engine itself is a more advanced method of locomotion than Plato's chariot was.

1. Which one of the following statements is true?
(a) An engine driver is cleverer than Plato or Socrates
(b) Plato or Socrates are in no way inferior to the engine driver
(c) Plato and Socrates surpassed the engine driver in every respect
(d) The engine driver cannot be compared to Plato or Socrates

2. In this passage, the author mentions Plato and Socrates to emphasise that
(a) They were men of great scholarship
(b) People as individuals in the modern age are not more advanced than their predecessors
(c) The engine is a better mode of locomotion than Plato's chariot
(d) Plato and Socrates had greater respect for learning

3. According to the author, the present age is far more advanced than
(a) All the previous ages in some respects
(b) The age of Plato and Socrates in some respects
(c) Some of the previous ages in all respects
(d) All the previous ages in all respects

4. Many of us make use of machines
(a) With very little knowledge of their mechanism
(b) Without any knowledge of their historical significance
(c) With full knowledge of their genesis
(d) Without knowing how they were invented

5. People today are very proud because they live
(a) In a philosophically advanced age
(b) In a materially advanced age
(c) In a scientifically advanced age
(d) In a spiritually advanced age

Practice Set —10

Economists, ethicists and business experts persuade us that honesty is the best policy, but their evidence is weak. We hoped to find data that would support their theories and thus, perhaps, encourage higher standards of business behaviour. To our surprise, their pet theories failed to stand up. Treachery, we found, can pay. There is no compe-lling economic reason to tell the truth or keep one's word. Punishment for the treacherous in the real world is neither swift nor sure.

Honesty is, in fact, primarily a moral choice. Business people do tell themselves that, in the long run, they will do well by doing good. But there is little factual or logical basis for this conviction. Without values, without a basic preference of right over wrong, trust based on such delusion would crumble in the face of temptation. Most of us choose virtue because we want to believe in ourselves and because others respect and believe us.

And due to this, we should be happy. We can be proud of a system in which people are honest because they want to be, not because they have to be. Materially, too, trust based on morality provides great advantages. It allows us to join in great and exciting enterprises that we could never undertake if we relied on economic incentives alone.

Economists tell us that trust is enforced in the market place through retaliation and reputation. If you violate a trust, your victim is apt to seek revenge and others are likely to stop doing business with you, at least under favourable terms. A man or woman with a reputation for fair dealing will prosper. Therefore, profit maximisers are honest. This sounds plausible enough until you look for concrete examples. Cases that apparently demonstrate the awful consequences of trust turn out to be few and weak, while evidence that treachery can pay seems compelling.

1. According to the passage, what do economists and ethicists, want us to believe?
(a) Businessmen should always be honest
(b) Businessmen cannot always be honest
(c) Businessmen turn dishonest at times
(d) Businessmen are honest only at times

2. What did the author find out about the theory that 'honesty is the best policy'?
(a) It is correct on many occasions
(b) It is correct for all businesses
(c) It is a useless theory
(d) It is a theory which seems to be correct only occasionally

3. Why are businessmen, according to the author, honest in their dealings?
(a) Businessmen are God-fearing
(b) Businessmen choose to be honest
(c) Businessmen are honest by nature
(d) All businessmen are caught if they are dishonest

4. According to the author, which of the following, is the reason for being honest in business?
(a) It gives no immediate benefits
(b) It gives no long-term benefits
(c) It makes a person self-seeking
(d) None of the above

5. Why does the author say that one can be proud of the present situation?
(a) People are self-respecting
(b) People are respect-seekers
(c) People are unselfish
(d) People are honest without compulsion

6. What is the material advantage which the author sees in being honest?
(a) It permits one to undertake activities which may not be economically attractive
(b) It permits one to be honest for the sake of honesty alone
(c) It permits one to be make a lot of profit in various areas
(d) It permits one to form various trusts to make profits

7. Why do businessmen, according to economists, remain honest?
(a) Dishonest businessmen can make more money
(b) Dishonest businessmen make money in the long run
(c) Dishonest businessmen cannot stay in business for long
(d) Dishonest businessmen are flogged in the market place

8. Which of the following phrases is most nearly the same in meaning as the word 'persuade' as it has been used in the passage?
(a) Give an assurance
(b) Give an opinion
(c) Try to convince
(d) Cheat

9. Which of the following is *false* according to the passage?
(a) Economists believe that all businessmen are dishonest
(b) Generally people are honest so as to earn self-respect
(c) Virtuous behaviour earns the respect of others
(d) All dishonest men are not caught

10. Which of the following best describes what the author is trying to point out through the last sentence of the passage, ' Cases that... compelling'?
(a) The consequences of dishonesty
(b) Theories do not seem to be true
(c) Economists predict correctly
(d) The contradictions in the real world

Practice Set —11

The greatest enemy of mankind, as people have discovered, is not science, but war. Science merely reflects the prevailing social forces. It is found that, when there is peace, science is constructive; when there is war, science is perverted to destructive ends. The weapons which science gives us do not necessarily cause war; they make war increasingly terrible. Till now, it has brought us to the doorstep of doom. Our main problem, therefore, is not to curb science, but to stop war—to substitute law for force, and international government for anarchy in the relations of one nation with another. That is a job in which everybody must participate, including the scientists. But the bombing of Hiroshima suddenly woke us up to the fact that we have very little time. The hour is late and our work has scarcely begun. Now we are face to face with an urgent question—Can education and tolerance, understanding and creative intelligence run fast enough to keep us abreast with our own mounting capacity to destroy? That is the question which we shall have to anwer one way or the other in this generation. Science must help us in arriving at the answer, but the main decision lies within ourselves.

1. According to the writer, the real enemy of mankind is not science but war, because
   (a) Science merely invents the weapons with which war is fought
   (b) Science during wars becomes destructive
   (c) The weapons that science invents necessarily lead to war
   (d) The weapons invented by science do not cause war, though these make it more destructive
2. War can be stopped if
   (a) Science is not allowed to lead us to utter destruction
   (b) We replace force and lawlessness by law and international government
   (c) Science is restricted to be utilised only during war time
   (d) Weapons invented by science are not used to launch a war.
3. According to the writer, the main problem we are faced with is to
   (a) Stop science from reflecting social forces
   (b) Stop scientific activities everywhere
   (c) Abolish war
   (d) Prevent scientists from participating in destructive activities
4. Our mounting sagacity to destroy can be kept under control by
   (a) Encouraging social forces
   (b) Education and broad-mindedness
   (c) Insight and constructive thinking
   (d) Both (b) and (c) (as above) together
5. The expression 'bring to the doorstep of doom' means
   (a) Carry close to death and destruction
   (b) Lead to the threshold of a new destiny
   (c) Indulge in a ruinous activity
   (d) Introduces to an unpredictable destiny
6. Which one of the following statements is not implied in the passage?
   (a) People needlessly blame science for war
   (b) Science is misused for destructive purposes
   (c) Neither science nor the weapons it invents add to the horrors of war
   (d) The role of science in ensuring world peace is subsidiary to that of man
7. Which of the following is opposite in mean-ing to the word 'anarchy' in the passage?
   (a) Law and order
   (b) Political dominance
   (c) Economic prosperity
   (d) Communal harmony
8. The phrase 'our work has scarcely begun' implies that our work
   (a) Has not yet begun
   (b) Has only just begun
   (c) Has been half-way through
   (d) Has begun, but not yet completed
9. The expression 'keep us abreast' in the passage means
   (a) Keep at a distance
   (b) Keep side by side
   (c) Hold out a challenge
   (d) Prevent from escaping
10. Which of the following would be the most suitable title for the passage:
    (a) Science and social forces
    (b) Science and the horrors of war
    (c) Science and world peace
    (d) Science and the new generation

Practice Set —12

We develop the vital bond of attachment between a mother and her child through a smiling response. As a visual stimulus, the smile has attained its unique configuration principally by the simple act of turning up the corners of the mouth. The mouth is opened to some extent and the lips pulled back, as in the expresssion of fear, but with the curling-up of the corners, the character of the expression of radically changed. This development has in turn led to the possibility of another and contrasting facial posture—that of the down-turned mouth. By adopting a mouthline that is the complete opposite of the smile it is possible to signal an anti-smile. Just as laughing, 50 also the unfriendly face has evolved by a pendulum swing from the friendly face.

But there is more to smiling than a line of the mouth. As adults, we may be able to convey our mood by a mere twist of the lips, but the infant throws much more into the battle. When smiling at full intensity, it also kicks and waves its arms about, stretches its hands out towards the stimulus and moves them about, produces babbling sounds, tilts back its head and protrudes its chin, leans its trunk forward or rolls it to one side and exaggerates its respiration. Its eyes become brighter and may close slightly; wrinkles appear underneath or along the eye and sometimes also on the bridge of the nose; the fold of the skin between the sides of the nose and the side of the mouth becomes more accentuated, and the tongue may be slightly protruded. The body movements seem to indicate a stuggle on the infant's part to make contact with the mother. With its clumsy physique, the baby is probably showing us all that remains of the ancestral primate's clinging response.

1. We recognise a smile by
   (a) The turning up of the corners of the mouth
   (b) Opening the mouth, stretching the lips making them longer and curling up the corners
   (c) Stretching the lips and turning down the corners while at the same time opening the mouth a little
   (d) Kicking and moving the arms and stretching the hands towards the opposite person
   (e) By closing the eyes and making them brighter
2. An adult can convey his smile by
   (a) A mere twist of his lips
   (b) Twisting his lips upwards
   (c) Kicking his arms about, producting babbling noises and breathing hard
   (d) Adopting a mouth line completely opposite the anti-smile shape
3. Which statement is TRUE?
   (a) A baby's smile is more vigorous than that of an adult
   (b) When compared to adults, a baby smiles more quietly
   (c) It is not possible to speak when one is smiling, especially when the person is a baby
   (d) Babies make babbling noises, tilt their heads back and protrude their chin before they can smile
4. Smiling is an effort on the infant's part to show
   (a) That it is happy
   (b) Its mother is happy
   (c) That it is struggling to make contact with its mother
   (d) It attempts to develop a vital bond of attachment which its ape-like ancestors tried to do by clinging to the mother
5. Match the following with words factually opposite in meaning

(a) Laughing	(a) Smile
(b) Anti-smile	(b) Crying
(c) Curling up	(c) Frown
	(d) Down-turned

Practice Set —13

A vexed problem facing us is the clamour to open more colleges and to reserve more seats for backward classes. But it will be a sheer folly to expand such facilities recklessly without giving any thought to the quality of education imparted. If admissions are made far more selective, it will automatically reduce the number of entrants. This should apply particularly to new colleges, many of which are little more than degree factories. Only then can the authorities hope to bring down the teacher-student ratio to manageable proportion. What is more, teachers should be given refresher courses every summer to brush up their knowledge. Besides, if college managements increase their library budget it will help both the staff and the students a great deal.

At the same time, however, it will be unfair to deny college education to thousands of young men and women, unless employers stop insisting on degrees even for clerical jobs. For a start, why cannot the government disqualify graduates from securing certain jobs, say Class III and IV posts? Once the link between degrees and jobs is severed, at least in some important departments, it will make young people think twice before joining college.

1. What can automatically help to reduce admissions?
   (a) Tough entrance tests
   (b) Discouragement to open new colleges
   (c) Selective admissions
   (d) Abolishing reservation
2. How can the standards of education be raised?
   (a) By admitting only the best students
   (b) By opening model institutions
   (c) By discouraging dull students
   (d) By reducing the number of new entrants
3. How can teachers be helped to brush up their knowledge?
   (a) By providing better library facilities
   (b) By arranging refresher courses
   (c) By providing them more leisure
   (d) By persuasive measures
4. The author is not in favour of restricting admissions
   (a) Unless degree are delinked from jobs
   (b) Unless alternative opportunities are provided
   (c) Unless other incentives are offered
   (d) Unless the teacher-student ratio is changed
5. What does the phrase 'vexed problem' mean?
   (a) An extraordinary problem
   (b) A problem which is being discussed at length
   (c) A difficult problem
   (d) An irritating problem

Practice Set —14

Once upon a time there was a shy and quiet octopus. He nearly always went about on his own because, although he wanted to have lots of friends, he was too self-conscious.

One day, the octopus was trying to catch a very slippery oyster. Before he knew it, he had tied himself into one massive knot, and he couldn't move. He tried with all his strength to wriggle free, but it was no good. In the end, despite the great embarrassment he felt at being seen in such a tangle, he had to ask for help from the passing fish. Many fish swam past, ignoring him, but one very kind little, fish offered to help untie all those tentacles from all those suckers.

The octopus felt heartily relieved; when he was finally set free, but he was so shy that he didn't dare talk to the fish and make friends with him. He simply thanked the fish, and quickly swam off. Later, the octopus spent the whole night thinking that he had wasted, a great opportunity to make friends with that very kind little fish.

A couple of days later the octopus was resting between some rocks, when he noticed that everyone around was hurriedly swimming past. He looked into the distance and saw an enormous fish coming over to feed in that area. The octopus quickly hid then, peeping an eye out from his hiding place, he saw that the huge fish was chasing the kind little fish who had untied him, That little fish really needed urgent help, but the big fish was so dangerous looking that no one dared to go near. The octopus, remembering how the little fish had helped him, felt that he had to do whatever he could to come to his aid.

Without hesitating, the octopus shot out from the rocks, like a ray. He put himself right in the path of the giant fish, and before the .fish could do anything about it, the octopus had shot out the biggest jet of ink of his life. He grabbed the little fish, and swam off back to hide in the rocks. Everything happened so fast that the big fish had no time to react. However, he soon recovered from the surprise. Off he went to the rocks, looking for the octopus and the little fish. Now he. really wanted to gobble them down!

Soon, though, he began feeling a terrible itch; first in his gills, and then in his fins, and then all over his body. It turned out that this giant fish had a very sensitive skin and the octopus's dark ink had given him a terrible allergy!! So the big fish swam away, irritated all over.

As soon as he was gone, all the fish that had been hiding came and congratulated the octopus for being so brave. Then the little fish told them all how he had helped the octopus a few days earlier, but he had never known anyone to end up doing something so dangerous. Hearing this, the other fish discovered how nice the shy octopus was, and everyone around was keen to be friends with such a brave and honourable octopus.

1. How did the octopus save the little fish?
   (a) By asking the little fish to hide before the big fish could see him.
   (b) By putting himself between the big fish and the little fish and shooting a jet of ink at the big fish.
   (c) By shooting a jet of ink at the big fish and thus managing to kill it.
   (d) By calling out for help from all the other fish and carrying the little fish to safety.
   (e) By offering his life to the big fish instead of the life of the little fish.

2. Why did the octopus nave to ask for help from the passing fish?
   (a) He was bored of swimming alone and thus asked the fish to accompany him.
   (b) He desperately needed to make friends and thus needed the fish to help him.
   (c) Someone had tied him up in a knot and he could not get himself untied.
   (d) He needed help in order to escape from the big fish that had come to eat him.
   (e) He had gotten himself tied up in a knot trying to catch an oyster.

3. He nearly always went about on his own because, although he wanted to have lots of friends, he was too self-conscious. How can this sentence be best reframed without changing its meaning?
   (a) Having many friends, he was self-conscious despite being alone.
   (b) Being alone, he had many friends despite being self-conscious.
   (c) Being self-conscious, he went about alone despite wanting to have many friends.
   (d) Being alone, he was self-conscious despite wanting to have many friends.
   (e) Having many friends, he went about alone despite being self-conscious.

4. Which of the following characteristics can be attributed to the little fish from the story?
   (A) Kind
   (B) Persuasive
   (C) Shy
   (a) Only (A) and (C)
   (b) Only (A)
   (c) All (A), (B) and (C)
   (d) Only (B)
   (e) Only (B) and (C)

5. 'The octopus, remembering how the little fish had helped him, feel that he had to do whatever he could to come to his aid.' What feeling of the octopus towards the little fish does his line signify?
   (a) Revenge (b) Suspicion
   (c) Gratitude (d) Compassion
   (e) Repentance

6. 'Now he really wanted to gobble them down!' What emotion of the big fish does this sentence convey?
   (a) Happiness (b) Pleasure
   (c) Anger (d) Helplessness
   (e) Fear

7. Why did all the fish congratulate the octopus?
   (a) He had bravely saved the little fish from being eaten by the big fish.
   (b) He had successfully gotten himself untied all by himself.

(c) He had managed to kill the big fish all along and thus saved the lives of all the other fish.
(d) He had finally managed to make a large number of friends in the ocean.
(e) He had saved the little fish from the clutches of the oyster.

8. Which of the following can be the most appropriate title for the passage/story?
(a) The Brave But Shy Octopus
(b) The Tiniest Fish
(c) The Fishes of the Ocean
(d) The Big Hungry Fish
(e) The Dumb Octopus

9. Which of the following characteristics can be attributed to the octopus from the story?
(A) Troublesome
(B) Noble
(C) Brave (A) Only (B)
(b) Only (A)
(c) Only (A) and (B)
(d) Only (B) and (C)
(e) All (A), (B) and (C)

10. Why did the big fish swim away?
(a) He got scared looking at the huge octopus and decided not to attack the little fish.
(b) He was driven away by the other fish.
(c) He was unable to locate the octopus and the fish.
(d) He got a terrible itch all over his body from the octopus ink.
(e) He decided that he would not be able to handle both the octopus and the fish together.

Practice Set —15

It was in the offing. With shortages mounting across the board for water as they are for energy, it was only inevitable that the Central government would be stirred into starting a Bureau of Water Efficiency (BWE), much like the Bureau of Energy Efficiency (BEE) that was launched some years ago.

Early reports suggest that the draft norms for various sectors consuming water will be created by the BWE soon. The alarm bells have been ringing for some years now. Water availability per capita in India has fallen from about 5 million litres in the 1950s to 1.3 million litres in 2010- that's a staggering 75 per cent drop in 50 years. Nearly 60 per cent of India's aquifers have slumped to critical levels in just the last 15 years. The rate at which borewells are being plunged in every city with no law to ban such extraction, groundwater tables have depleted alarmingly.

The BEE's efforts in the last seven years have only been cosmetic. The bureau has looked at efficiency rating systems for white goods in the domestic sector, and has not paid attention to the massive consumption of energy in metals manufacture, paper and textiles. These sectors are very intense in both energy and water consumption. But very little attention has been paid to the water and energy used per tonne of steel or cement or aluminum that we buy, and without significant changes in these areas, the overall situation is unlikely to change.

Use of water is inextricably interlinked with energy. One does not exist without the other. The BWE should steer clear of the early mistake of BEE- of focusing on the softer target's in the domestic sector. Nearly 80 per cent of fresh water is used by agriculture, with industry coming a close second. The domestic sector's consumption of fresh water is in single digit. So the BWE's priority should be to look at measures that will get farmers and industrialists to follow good practices in water use. Water resources have to be made, by law, an indivisible national asset. The protection and withdrawal of this resource, as well as its sustainable development are of general importance and therefore in the public interest. This will mean that individuals and organizations may own land but not water or the other resources that lie below the first 20 metres of the surface of those lands. Drilling of borewells into such national assets will have to be banned or at the very least they must be regulated. What would be more sensible for the new water bureau to do would be to look at some of the low hanging fruits that can be plucked and pretty quickly with laws that can emantate from the centre, without the risk of either dilution or inaction from state administrations. The other tactical approach that the BWE can adopt is to devise a policy that addresses the serious water challenge in industry segments across a swathe of companies this will be easier than taking on the more disparate domestic sector which hurts the water crisis less than industry. Implementing a law is more feasible when the concentration is dense and identifiable. Industry offers this advantage more than the domestic or the commercial sector of hotels and offices.

As for agriculture, though the country's water requirement is as high as 80 per cent, the growing of water within the loop in agriculture de-risks the challenge of any perceived deficit. Rice, wheat, sugarcane are crops that need water-logging, which ensures groundwater restoration. Surface water evaporation doesn't amount to any more than 7-8 per cent and only strengthens precipitation and rainfall.

Agriculture and water need is not quite as much a threat as industry and domestic sectors that account for the rest of the 20 per cent.

The primary challenge in industry and the building sector is that no conscious legal measures have been enacted that stipulate 'growing your own water' with measures that will 'put all water in a loop' in any residential or commercial building. This involves treating all used water to a grade that it can be 'upcycle' for use in flush tanks and for gardens across all our cities with the polluter owning the responsibility for treating and for reuse. The drop in fresh water demand can be dramatic with such upcycle, reuse, and recycle of treated water. Water by itself in industry and the domestic sector, is not as much a challenge as pollution of water. Not enough measures exist yet to ensure that such polluters shift the water back for reuse. If legislation can ensure that water is treated and reused for specific purposes within industry as well as in the domestic sector, this will make all the difference to the crisis on fresh water.

So is the case in industry, especially in sectors like textiles, aluminium and steel. Agriculture offers us the amusing irony of the educated ur-banites dependent on cereals like rice and wheat that consume 4000 litres of water for every Kilogramme, while the farmer lives on the more nutritious millets that consume less than half the quantity. Sugarcane consumes as much as 12,000 litres of water for a kilo of cane that you buy!

A listing of such correlations of water used by every product that we use in our daily lives will make much better sense than any elaborate rating system from the newly formed BWE. Such sensitizing with concerted awareness campaigns that the new Bureau drives will impact the urban consumer more than all the research findings that experts can present. What is important for us is to understand the life-cycle impact in a way that we see the connect between a product that we use and the resources it utilizes up to the point where we bring the visible connect to destruction of natural resources of our ecosystems.

1. How, according to the author, can the bureau sensitize the urban consumer about careful utilization of water?
   (a) By encouraging them to consume more rice instead of millets daily and thereby reduce the amount of water consumption.
   (b) By providing them more insight into the water consumption cycle of the textile, aluminium and steel industries.
   (c) By making them aware of the linkages between water consumption for daily activities and the resource utilization and subsequent ecological destruction associated with it.
   (d) By publishing research findings of experts in popular media whereby people gain awareness on the impact of water misuse.
   (e) By conducting elaborate drives which notify the urban population about the penalties levied on misuse of water resources.

2. Why, according to the-author, is the water consumption for agricultural activities the least risky?
   (a) Proportion of water consumed for agricultural activities is much less as compared to that consumed for domestic and industrial purposes,
   (b) Most farmers are aware of the popular methods of water conservation and hence do not allow wastage of water.
   (c) Water is fairly recycled through groundwater restoration due to water-logging and surface water evaporation.
   (d) Farmers in India mostly cultivate crops that require less amount of water.
   (e) None of these

3. Which of the following is possibly the most appropriate title for the passage?
   (a) Water Challenges in the New Millennium
   (b) The Bureau of Water Efficiency Vs the Bureau of Energy Efficiency
   (c) Unchecked Urban Consumption of Water
   (d) Challenges of the Agricultural Sector and Water Resources
   (e) The Route to Conservation of Water Resources

4. What does low-hanging fruits that can be plucked, and pretty quickly' mean in the context of the passage?
   (a) The bureau should employ the cheapest methods possible to effectively control the current situation of improper usage of water resources.
   (b) The bureau should target the industrial sector as well as the domestic sector to reduce water wastage.
   (c) The bureau should target the agricultural sector only for producing quick results in reducing wastage of water.
   (d) The bureau should ensure that all the state officials concerned with the measures are actively involved.
   (e) The bureau should start with adopting measures which are simple to execute and produce immediate results in reducing water wastage.

5. Which of the following, according to the author, is/are the indications of a water crisis?
   (A) Many agrarian areas in the country are facing a drought-like situation.
   (B) Almost three-fifth of the naturally available water has been reduced to a very critical level in a relatively short span of time.
   (C) There has been a significant drop in the availability of water over the past fifty years
   (a) Only (B)
   (b) Only (A) and (C)
   (c) Only (C)
   (d) Only (B) and (C)
   (e) All (A), (B) and (C)

6. The author suggests that the Bureau of Water Efficiency devises a strategy or makes laws to meet water challenges in the industrial segments rather than the domestic segments because
   (a) The industrial sector is the only one that is in a position to reduce its water consumption by a significant margin.
   (b) There is comparatively less serious water misuse in the domestic sector
   (c) It would be easy to identify the consumption patterns in the industrial sector because of its density and visibility.
   (d) The industrial sector would be capable of paying the fines levied by the Bureau for water misuse whereas the domestic sector would be in no such position.
   (e) The industrial sector would be easier to manage in terms of making them understand the importance of water conservation.

7. Which of the following, according to the author, is/are the step/s that the Bureau of Water Efficiency can take to ensure proper utilization of water resources?
   (A) Put in place measures that ensure proper water usage.
   (B) Concentrate on the water consumption patterns of the domestic sector alone.
   (C) Monitor carefully the activity of digging borewells.
   (a) Only (A) and (C)
   (b) Only (A; and (B)
   (c) Only (A)
   (d) Only (B) and (C)
   (e) All (A), (B) and (C)

8. Which of the following is true about the Bureau of Energy Efficiency, in the context of the passage?
   (A) It failed to pay adequate attention to industries like met-al. textiles. Etc., in terms of energy consumption.
   (B) It focused on rating systems for efficient use of goods in the domestic sector.
   (C) It mostly focused on the energy consumption in the domestic sector.

(a) Only (A) and (C)
(b) Only (A) and (B)
(c) Only (A)
(d) Only (B) and (C)
(e) All (A), (B) and (C)

Directions (9- 12): Choose the word/group of words which is most similar in meaning to the word/group of words printed in **bold** as used in the passage.

9. COSMETIC
(a) enhancive (b) beauty
(c) augmentative (d) superficial
(e) aesthetic

10. STAGGERING
(a) weaving (b) astounding
(c) lurching (d) stumbling
(e) unsteady

11. CONSCIOUS
(a) unknown (b) mindful
(c) self-aware (d) awake
(e) alert

12. DRAMATIC
(a) remarkable (b) moving
(c) theatrical (d) histrionic
(e) staged

Directions (188-190): Choose the word/group of words which is MOST OPPOSITE, in meaning to the word/group of words printed in BOLD as used in the passage.

13. INTENSE
(a) smooth (b) serious
(c) low (d) diluted
(e) jovial

14. TACTICAL
(a) unplanned (b) uniform
(c) devious (d) premeditated
(e) deformed

15. INEVITABLE
(a) certain (b) unforeseeable
(c) unavoidable (d) inescapable
(e) predictable

ANSWER KEY

Set 1	Set 2	Set 3	Set 4	Set 5
1. (b)	1. (d)	1. (c)	1. (d)	1. (a)
2. (d)	2. (d)	2. (a)	2. (a)	2. (d)
3. (c)	3. (d)	3. (d)	3. (a)	3. (c)
4. (b)	4. (b)	4. (b)	4. (c)	4. (c)
5. (a)	5. (c)	5. (e)	5. (d)	5. (a)
6. (a)	6. (a)	6. (e)		
7. (c)	7. (b)	7. (e)		
8. (a)	8. (d)			
9. (b)	9. (b)			
10. (a)	10. (b)			

Set 6	Set 7	Set 8	Set 9	Set 10
1. (c)	1. (d)	1. (c)	1. (d)	1. (a)
2. (b)	2. (c)	2. (d)	2. (b)	2. (b)
3. (a)	3. (b)	3. (d)	3. (a)	3. (b)
4. (c)	4. (a)	4. (b)	4. (d)	4. (d)
5. (b)	5. (b)	5. (a)	5. (c)	5. (d)
				6. (c)
				7. (c)
				8. (c)
				9. (a)
				10. (d)

Set 11

1. (d)
2. (b)
3. (c)
4. (d)
5. (a)
6. (c)
7. (b)
8. (b)
9. (b)
10. (c)

Set 12

1. (b)
2. (d)
3. (a)
4. (d)
5. (a) : (b)
   (b) : (a)
   (c) : (d)

Set 13

1. (c)
2. (a)
3. (b)
4. (a)
5. (d)

Set 14

1. (b)
2. (e)
3. (c)
4. (b)
5. (c)
6. (c)
7. (a)
8. (a)
9. (d)
10. (d)
11. (b)

Set 15

1. (c)
2. (c)
3. (e)
4. (e)
5. (d)
6. (b)
7. (a)
8. (b)
9. (d)
10. (b)
11. (b)
12. (a)
13. (c)
14. (a)
15. (b)

CHAPTER 2

OBJECTIVE COMPREHENSION-II

Short Paragraphs

Of late, a new trend has set in with respect to comprehension. Earlier, the comprehension passages were of a moderate size in case of CDS, NDA and lengthy in case of CAT and some other examinations conducted by management institutes. Now a one line passage or very short passages comprising only two or three sentences are set. Students have need not become unduly answers; they must keep their cool. In fact, the work has become easier than before because it is more convenient to recollect ideas contained in two or three lines than those from a long passage. Candidates should read the passage and compute the points in their minds. On the basis of the points they can locate the main idea or the motive around which these points have been illustrated. Normally, in a short passage there is a basic idea and all points are given to illustrate or analyse, or prove the central idea. The answer must confirm to the central idea. The accessory or secondary points may be true but they have a partial identity only and thus they cannot be the correct answers. We may illustrate it through the MLE (Motive, Location, Elimination), technique. Let us understand the technique through an example (Example1) from the Bank PO Examination, Madras, March 1996.

MLE (Motive Location Elimination (Techniques

EXAMPLE – 1

One of the important humanitarian by-products of technology is the greater dignity and value that it imparts to human labour. In a highly industrialised society, there is no essential difference between Brahmin and Dalit, Muslim and Hindu; they are equally useful and hence equally valuable, for in the industrial society individual productivity fixes the size of the pay cheque and this fixes the social status.

This paragraph best supports the statement that—

1. There are numerous side-effects of technology
2. Labour force is treated well in modern day industries
3. Division of labour based on caste was justified
4. There are individual differences in industrial productivity

5. Size of the pay and social status contradict each other

Points that illustrate the motive are:

1. Industry makes no difference between caste and religion
2. In industrial society social status comes from individual performance

In fact both points reinforce the motive of the passage. Refer to Fig. 2.1.

EXAMPLE – 2

The only true education comes through the stimulation of the child's powers by the demands of the social situations in which he finds himself. Through these demands he is stimulated to act as a member of a unit, to emerge from his original narrowness of action and feeling, and to conceive himself from the standpoint of the welfare of the group to which he belongs.

The paragraph best supports the statement that real education

1. Is not provided in our schools today
2. Comes from the self-centred approach of the students
3. Comes through the interaction with social situations
4. Will take place if the children are physically strong
5. Will take place if the children imbibe action and feeling

On reading the passage carefully we locate that the motive of the author is to say that the interaction between child and society gives true education. Other points are secondary in identifying and reinforcing this basic idea or motive.

Now let us eliminate incorrect responses through MLE Technique.

Alternative **1:** It is wrong as this is not the motive of the author

Alternative **2:** It is wrong

Alternative **3:** It is the right answer as it is the main idea or motive

Alternative **4:** It is wrong because it is a partial fact

Alternative **5:** It is wrong as it is also a partial fact

Practice Set —1

Throughout the ages the businessman has helped build civilisation's great cities, provide people with luxuries and artists with patronage, and lift his fellow-citizens to understand the standard of living. In the last few centuries the businessman has seeded the Industrial Revolution around the world.

Q. The paragraph best supports the statement that the businessman—

(a) Is accountable to the society

(b) Is the beneficiary of the Industrial Revolution

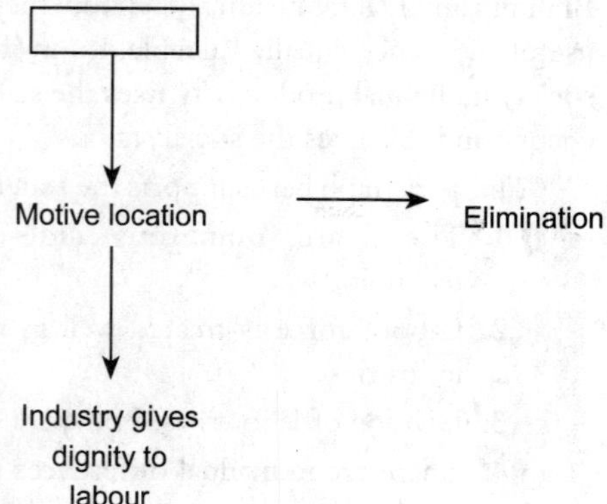

Fig 2.1 MLE Technique

(c) Has contributed to the growth of civilisation
(d) Is capable of raising his standard of living
(e) Lives a luxurious and comfortable life

Practice Set —2

Through advertising, manufacturers exercise a high degree of control over consumer's desires. However, the manufacturer assumes enormous risks in attempting to predict what consumers will want and in producing goods in quantity and distributing them in advance of the final selection by the consumers.

Q. The paragraph best supports the statement that manufacturers—
(a) Can eliminate the risk of overproduction by advertising
(b) Distribute goods directly to the consumers
(c) Can predict with great accuracy the success of any product they put on the market
(d) Must depend finally upon the consumers for the success of their undertakings
(e) Always take moderate and calculated risk

Practice Set —3

The school has always been the most important means of transferring the wealth of tradition from one generation to the next. This applies today in an even higher degree than in former times for, through the modern development of economic life, the family's role as the bearer of tradition and education has become weak.

Q. The paragraph best supports the statement that for transferring the wealth of tradition from one generation to the next—
(a) Economic development plays a crucial role
(b) There are means other than the school
(c) Family, as ever, is the most potent means
(d) Several different sources must be tried
(e) Modern technology must be put to use

Practice Set —4

The attainment of individual and organisational goals is mutually interdependent and linked by a common denominator—employee work motivation. Organisation members are motivated to satisfy their personal goals, and they contribute their efforts to the attainment of organisational objectives as means of achieving these personal goals.

Q. The paragraph best supports the statement that motivation—
(a) Is crucial for the survival of an individual and organisation
(b) Is the external force which induces an individual to contribute his efforts
(c) Makes organisation and society inseparable
(d) Is the product of an individual's physical and mental energy
(e) Encourages an individual to give priority to personal goals over organisational goals

Practice Set —5

The prevention of accidents makes it necessary that not only safety devices be used to guard exposed machinery but also that mechanics be instructed in safety rules which they must follow for their own protection, and that the lighting in the plant be adequate.

Q. The paragraph best supports the statement that industrial accidents—
(a) May be due to ignorance
(b) Can be eliminated with the help of safety rules
(c) Usually result from inadequate machinery
(d) Cannot be entirely overcome
(e) Are always avoidable

Practice Set —6

To forgive an injury is often considered to be a sign of weakness; it is actually a sign of strength. It is easy to allow oneself to be carried away by resentment and hate into an act of vengeance; but it takes a strong character to restrain those natural passions. The man who forgives an injury proves himself to be superior to the man who wronged him and puts the wrong-doer to shame.

Q. This paragraph best supports the statement that—

(a) A person of calm and composed nature has depth of thought and vision
(b) People tend to forgive the things that happened in the past
(c) Natural passions are difficult to suppress
(d) The sufferer alone knows the intensity of his sufferings
(e) Mercy is the noblest form of revenge

Practice Set —7

The consumption of harmful drugs by the people can be prevented not only by banning their sale in the market but also by instructing users about their dangerous effects which they must understand for their safety. Also the drug addicts may be provided with proper medical facilities for their rehabilitation. This will help in scaling down the use of drugs.

Q. The paragraph best supports the statement that consumption of harmful drugs—

(a) May be channelised through a proper system
(b) Can be eliminated with the help of banning their sale
(c) Are on an increase in the society
(d) Are due to lack of medical facilities
(e) Can always be reduced

Practice Set —8

The virtue of art is that it does not allow the work to be interfered with or immediately ruled by anything other than itself. It insists that it alone shall touch the work in order to bring it into being. Art requires that nobody shall attain the work except through art itself.

Q. The paragraph best supports the statement that—

(a) Art is for the sake of art and life
(b) Art is for the sake of art alone
(c) The artist should use his art for the sake of society
(d) Art is governed by external rules and conditions
(e) The artist realises his dreams through his artistic creation

Practice Set —9

One of the important humanitarian by-products of technology is the greater dignity and value that it imparts to human labour. In a highly industrialised society, there is no essential difference between Brahmin and Dalit, Muslim and Hindu; they are equally useful and hence equally valuable, for in the industrial society individual productivity fixes the size of the pay cheque and this fixes social status.

1. The paragraph best supports the statement that—

(a) Industrial society is a great leveller of men
(b) Technology decides the individual's social status
(c) All individuals, irrespective of caste and creed, and born equal
(d) Castes and religions are man-made
(e) Human labour has dignity and value

Practice Set —10

There is a shift in our economy from a manufacturing one to a service-oriented one. The increase in the service sector will require the managers to work more with people rather than with objects and things from the assembly line.

Q. The paragraph best supports the statement that—

(a) Inter-Personal skills will become more important in the future workplace

(b) Service organisations will not deal with objects and things
(c) Manufacturing organisations ignore the importance of people
(d) Assembly line will exist in service organisations
(e) Managers should have a balanced mind

Practice Set —11

Satisfaction with co-workers, promotion opportunities, the nature of work, and pay go with high performance. Among those with weak growth needs, no such relationship is present and, in fact, satisfaction with promotion opportunities goes with low performance.

Q. This paragraph best supports the statement that—
(a) High performance is essential for organisational effectiveness
(b) Every organisation has few employees having weak growth needs
(c) Relationship between job satisfaction and performance is moderated by growth need
(d) Job satisfaction and performance are directly and closely related
(e) Satisfaction is an inevitable organisational variable

Practice Set —12

People need to determine whether or not their opinions are correct and to obtain an accurate appraisal of their abilities. The individual's opinions and beliefs, as well as his evaluation of his abilities are important determinants of his behaviour. Correct opinions and accurate appraisals of ability from others are likely to lead to satisfying or rewarding behaviour; incorrect beliefs and/or inaccurate appraisals of ability lead to unpleasant consequences.

Q. This paragraph best supports the statement that—
(a) People need to depend on others to satisfy their needs
(b) Every individual has some ability and some emotions
(c) Most individuals are not correct in their opinions and beliefs
(d) There exists a drive among individuals to evaluate their opinions and abilities
(e) Appraisal of abilities is a continuous activity

Practice Set —13

Among the elite of metropolitan India, things are gradually changing. Women are being recognised by employers, particularly in the corporate sector, as temperamentally suited to the information age. Visit any advertising agency or ad-film maker's office and the male-female ratio leans heavily towards the female population.

Q. This paragraph best supports the statement that—
(a) Women are heading most of the agencies or ad-film makers' offices
(b) Women are believed to be more equipped to handle infotech
(c) Only elite women join the corporate sector
(d) Male-Female ratio in the society is gradually changing
(e) Women have advantage of their sex in employment

Practice Set —14

Moral education centres upon this conception of the school as a mode of social life, that the best and the deepest moral training is precisely that which one gets through having to enter into proper relations with others in a unity of work and thought. The present educational systems, so far as they destroy or neglect this unity, render it difficult or impossible to get any genuine, regular moral training.

Q. This paragraph best supports the statement that—
(a) Society survives on moral values

(b) Mortality is based on proper relations with others

(c) Schools must teach the basic principles of social life

(d) Morality differs from place to place and is situation bound

(e) It is the responsibility of any education system to impart moral education

Practice Set —15

The school is primarily a social institution. Education being a social process, the school is simply that form of community life in which all those agencies are concentrated which will be most effective in bringing the child to share in the inherited resources of the race, and to use his/her own powers for social ends.

Q. This paragraph best supports the statement that—

(a) Education is a process of living and not a preparation for future living

(b) Education in the real sense is not provided in our schools today

(c) Education teaches how to share the inherited treasures

(d) The school, as an institution, should simplify existing social life

(e) Children are endowed with immense powers

Practice Set —16

Accidents on roads can be prevented, provided the quality of roads is improved and the drivers are instructed in safety rules which they must follow for their own protection. It is also necessary that the illumination on the roads is adequate so as to prevent accidents at night.

Q. This paragraph best supports the statement that—

(a) Road accidents are solely due to improper illumination

(b) Road accidents result in large number of deaths

(c) Road accidents are man-made and are always avoidable

(d) Safety rules are not taught properly to all drivers

(e) Safety must be the uppermost in the minds of road drivers

Practice Set —17

In the final analysis, the wealth of a country is based upon its power to develop and to effectively utilise the innate capacities of its people. It takes skilled human agents to discover and exploit natural resources, to mobilise capital, to develop technology, to produce goods, and to carry out trade. Indeed, if a country is unable to develop its human resources, it cannot build anything else, whether it be a modern political system, a sense of national unity, or a prosperous economy.

Q. This paragraph best supports the statement that—

(a) The wealth of a country resides in several types of resources

(b) Natural resources play a vital role in human development

(c) Human resources constitute the ultimate basis for the wealth of nations

(d) Capital and natural resources are active factors of production

(e) The economic development of nations is ultimately the result of proper and effective planning and coordination

Practice Set —18

People need to determine whether or not their opinions are correct and to obtain an accurate appraisal of their abilities. The individual's opinions and beliefs, as well as his evaluation of his abilities are important determinants of his behaviour. Correct opinions and accurate appraisals of ability from others are likely to lead to satisfying or rewarding behaviour; incorrect beliefs and/or inaccurate appraisals of ability lead to unpleasant consequences.

Q. This paragraph best supports the statement that—

(a) Individuals seek feedback from others to evaluate the correctness of their opinions and beliefs

(b) All human behaviour has certain antecedents

(c) All human behaviour is purposive and goal-oriented

(d) All individuals want rewards and avoid punishments

(e) An individual's personality determines his social behaviour

ANSWER KEY

1. (c)	4. (e)	7. (b)	10. (a)	13. (b)	16. (c)
2. (a)	5. (b)	8. (b)	11. (c)	14. (b)	17. (c)
3. (a)	6. (e)	9. (e)	12. (a)	15. (c)	18. (a)

CHAPTER 3

OBJECTIVE COMPREHENSION-III

There is still another variation in which the passage is short, comprising one or two sentences, but the questions are many. This variation is also easier than the longer passages because it is easy to read and comprehend the passage and recall the points. You can glean the points separately and mark them on a rough page or keep them in memory. On the basis of Information Elimination and Inference formula the correct answers can be located. Let us take an example from the practice set itself:

EXAMPLES

The surprisingly abundant life of the Indian Ocean is confined to the upper layers; the deeper and especially the bottom waters are devoid of oxygen and are often permeated with hydrogen sulphide.

1. The passage gives the information about

1. The life of the people near the Indian Ocean

2. The reason why life exists in particular water layers

3. The reason why oxygen is not found in the bottom layers

4. The reason why hydrogen sulphide is found in the bottom layers

5. The life of the people who sail across the Indian Ocean

Now we may glean the points:

(a) Life exists in the upper layers of the ocean

(b) Deeper/bottom layers have no oxygen

(c) They have hydrogen sulphide

These three points have been made in this passage. Now let us apply our elimination technique.

(a) This is outside the boundary of the passage. Thus it is wrong.

(b) This is correct because the writer explains why life does not exist in deeper layers (Simple Inference).

(c) This is wrong as no reason has been given.

(d) This is wrong as no reason has been given

(e) Not relevant and thus it is wrong

I may like to add that locating the motive of the writer as we have done in variation 2 will further help even in this case. The motive of the writer is to communicate that life exists only in the upper layers of the ocean as the deeper layers have no oxygen. The motive helps us hit the choice B most immediately.

2. The bottom waters of the Indian Ocean
(a) Have no oxygen
(b) Have large amounts of oxygen
(c) Contain a lot of sea plants and animals
(d) Have no hydrogen sulphide
(e) Contain oxygen and hydrogen sulphide

Alternative: **(a)** Yes **(b)** No. **(c)** No. **(d)** No. **(d)** No.

Alternatives **(b)**, **(c)**, **(d)** and **(e)** are easily eliminated in accordance with the information available in this passsage.

This process can be illustrated by this figure:

Step 1

Locate motive

Step 2

Glean points

Step 3

Solve the questions by IEI formula

Fig. 3.1 MIEI Formula

Practice Set —1

The surprisingly abundant life of the Indian Ocean is confined to the upper layers; the deeper and especially the bottom waters are devoid of oxygen and are often permeated with hydrogen sulphide.

1. The passage gives the information about
(a) The life of the people near the Indian Ocean
(b) The reason why life exists in particular water layers
(c) The reason why oxygen is not found in the bottom layers
(d) The reason why hydrogen sulphide is found in the bottom layers
(e) The life of the people who sail across the Indian Ocean

2. The bottom waters of the Indian Ocean
(a) Have no oxygen
(b) Have large amounts of oxygen
(c) Contain a lot of sea plants and animals
(d) Have no hydrogen sulphide
(e) Contain hydrogen sulphide

3. The waters of the Indian Ocean
(a) Are devoid of life
(b) Are always permeated with hydrogen sulphide
(c) Have life only in the lower layers
(d) Lack life and it is very surprising
(e) Have life only in the upper layers

4. Which of the following is the most **opposite** of the word ABUNDANT, as used in the passage?
(a) Plentiful
(b) Minute
(c) insufficient
(d) Meagre
(e) Tiny

5. The passage suggests which one of the following:
(a) Observers are surprised at abundant life exists in the Indian Ocean
(b) Hydrogen sulphide is necessary to life
(c) Both oxygen and hydrogen sulphide are necessary to life
(d) Oxygen is not necessary for marine life
(e) There are different layers of waters in the ocean

Practice Set —2

Although a smiling face often disguises the mind and heart of a villain, an indiscriminate generalisation of this phenomenon will do injustice to the innocent children whose faces bloom like flowers.

1. The intention of the author seems to be
   (a) To point out to an exception to the general rule
   (b) To argue in favour of children who are sometimes guilty
   (c) To forcefully defend the kind acts of villains
   (d) To give justice to the generous actions of everyone
   (e) To create a favourable opinion about people with smiling faces
2. The author of the sentence accepts the fact that
   (a) All the things that appear most beautiful are the ugliest within
   (b) The faces of innocent children disguise ill acts
   (c) The faces of innocent children are as pleasing as the flowers in bloom
   (d) An indiscriminate generalisation is justifiable in this case
   (e) The faces of the villains are never smiling
3. The author feels that an indiscriminate generalisation of the phenomenon
   (a) Would brand all people with smiling faces as villains
   (b) Would do justice to the children who are guilty
   (c) May lead good people to involve in ill actions
   (d) Would prevent villains from committing ill acts
   (e) Should be done in all cases except children and flowers
4. Which of the following is most nearly the same in meaning as the word DISGUISES, as used in the sentence?
   (a) Reflects
   (b) Proves
   (c) Conceals
   (d) Reveals
   (e) Discloses
5. Which of the following is most opposite of the word INDISCRIMINATE as used in the sentence?
   (a) Promiscuous
   (b) Selective
   (c) Undistinguished
   (d) Broad
   (e) Conspicuous

Practice Set —3

A man of disarming candour and unexpected wit delivered in those unmistakable Rameshwaram cadences, Kalam Saheb and his team epitomise perseverance and pride in things Indian when it is no longer the flavour of the times. His stewardship of the Integrated Guided Missile Development Programme (IGMDP) and the vision that underpins it could well define the kind of profile the nation is likely to acquire in the global comity in the next century.

1. 'It is no longer the flavour of the times' in this context means
   (a) A picture of the food habits of the modern people
   (b) A picture of the habits of the youth of modern India
   (c) An idea of the habits and likings of modern Indians
   (d) A picture of the true Indian
2. The vision in this passage stands for
   (a) Kalam's stewardship
   (b) Target of IGMDP
   (c) The dream of the global comity
   (d) The picture of the next century
3. The passage reveals that perseverance
   (a) Has always been in Indian character
   (b) Was a trait of Indian character earlier
   (c) Is a trait of Indian character now
   (d) Has never been a trait of Indian Character

Practice Set —4

The current political turmoil in India is more or less synonymous with the turmoil in Hindu society arising out of conflicting global ideologies and the obsolescence of the Manu code of behaviour for Hindus. Hinduism owed its survival not only to the phenomenon of enlightened gurus and seers over the centuries—from Adi Shankara and Ramanuja to Ramakrishna Paramhansa; Vivekananda and Maharshi Ramana—but also because Hindu society was quick to adjust itself to the changing times and people and believed in assimilation and absorption rather than exclusivist faith.

1. The passage hints a similarity
   (a) Between Vivekananda and Rama-krishna
   (b) Between Hinduism and current political crisis
   (c) Between current political crisis and the turmoil in Hindu society
   (d) Global ideologies and obsolescence of the Manu code

2. Hinduism survived
   (a) Only because of enlightened gurus
   (b) Only because of its quality to adjust itself to the changing times
   (c) Only because of its assimilative quality
   (d) Because it has synthesised its assimilative absorbing quality with the enlightenment of its thinkers over a long time

3. The passage suggests that
   (a) The elightened gurus have done harm to Hinduism
   (b) The current political turmoil in India is the consequence of Guru's teachings
   (c) The obsolescence of the Manu code of behaviour has come in conflict with global ideologies
   (d) Hinduism is the cause of current political turmoil

Practice Set —5

Following chaotic scenes in the Lok Sabha—with a clamorous Congress sticking to its demands for dropping the DMK from the UF and the DMK responding by calling for a debate on the Thakkar Commission's controversial findings—an anguished Speaker PA Sangma had little option but to adjourn the House *sine die.* With Parliament having been put into cold storage, the politics of durbar manoeuvring—at which the Congress, in particular, is a pastmaster—will inevitably come to the fore. While wheeling—dealing will be the order of the day, when the scene shifts to Rashtrapati Bhavan, the President assuredly will exercise his prerogative in the best interest of the country.

1. The passage expresses the fear that
   (a) The politics of wheeling-dealing will prevail
   (b) The politics of manoeuvring will come to an end
   (c) The President may not work in the interest of the people
   (d) The Speaker's act might have been prompted by ordinary factors

2. The passage suggest that
   (a) Congress was very weak in political strategy
   (b) Congress was a pastmaster in politics of manoeuvring
   (c) P.A. Sangma had many options
   (d) The President will have no choice

3. The author is of the opinion
   (a) That Congress party has behaved very well
   (b) That P.A. Sangma has done what many would have done
   (c) That the President will use discretion
   (d) That DMK should have been dropped

ANSWER KEY

Set 1	Set 2	Set 3	Set 4	Set 5
1. (d)	1. (a)	1. (c)	1. (c)	1. (a)
2. (e)	2. (c)	2. (c)	2. (d)	2. (b)
3. (e)	3. (a)	3. (b)	3. (c)	3. (c)
4. (d)	4. (c)			
5. (a)	5. (b)			

PART TWO

SPOTTING ERRORS

Spotting an error requires a good grasp of grammer, usage and nuançes of expressions. Chapters 4–8 provide 100 select rules that cover almost all important types of errors that are frequently aksed in various types of examinations.

CHAPTER 4

Spotting Errors: Important Rules

Spotting errors is a common test and forms a part of almost all the important examinations that have objective English test on their syllabi. It requires an awareness of the basic rules of grammar—parts of speech, noun, pronoun, adjective, adverb, preposition, conjunction, genders, infinitives, participles, subject-verb accord, form of tenses, use of articles and certain exceptional usages.

Hence, it is necessary that all candidates taking up these examinations brush up their essentials of grammar with the help of the grammar books that they have read at their intermediate level. After this initial exercise they should learn or revise the following rules that are given below in the form of practical tips with illustrative examples. The practice test must be done carefully and repeatedly to ensure full competence and confidence.

Rules and Examples

1. Some nouns always take a singular verb.
Scenery, advice, information, machinery, stationery, furniture, abuse, fuel, rice, gram, issue, bedding, repair, news, mischief, poetry, business, economics, physics, mathematics, classics, ethics, athletics, innings, gallows.

(a) The scenery of Kashmir are enchanting. *(Incorrect)*

(b) The scenery of Kashmir is enchanting. *(Correct)*

(a) He has given advices. *(Incorrect)*

(b) He has given advice. *(Correct)*

(a) The Indian team defeated the English by innings. *(Incorrect)*

(b) The Indian team defeated the English by an innings. *(Correct)*

(a) Mathematics are a difficult subject. *(Incorrect)*

(b) Mathematics is a difficult subject. (Correct)

Note: If you have to indicate that the number of news, advice, information or furniture is more than one, the examples listed can be followed.

(a) I have a lot of news to tell you.

(b) He has sold many pieces of his furniture.

2. Some nouns are singular in form, but they are used as plural nouns and always take a plural verb.
Cattle, gentry, vermin, peasantry, artillery, people, clergy, company, police.

(a) The cattle is grazing in the ground*(Incorrect)*

(b) The cattle are grazing in the ground *(Correct)*

(a) The clergy is in the church *(Incorrect)*
(b) The clergy are in the church (Correct)

3. Some nouns are always used in a plural form and always take a plural verb.

Trousers, scissors, spectacles, stockings, shorts, measles, goods, alms, premises, thanks, tidings, annals, chattels, etc.

(a) Where is my trousers? *(Incorrect)*
(b) Where are my trousers? *(Correct)*
(a) Spectacles is now a costly item *(Incorrect)*
(b) Spectacles are now a costly item *(Correct)*

4. There are some nouns that indicate length, measure, money, weight or number. When they are preceded by a numeral, they remain unchanged in form.

Foot, metre, pair, score, dozen, head, year, hundred, thousand, million.

(a) It is a three-years degree course *(Incorrect)*
(b) It is a three-year degree course *(Correct)*
(a) I have ten dozens of shoes. *(Incorrect)*
(b) I have ten dozen of shoes. *(Correct)*

5. Collective nouns such as jury, public, team, committee, government, audience, orchestra, company, etc. are used both as singular and plural depending on the meaning. When these words indicate a unit, the verb is singular, otherwise the verb will be plural.

(a) The jury was divided in this case. *(Incorrect)*
(b) The jury were divided in this case. *(Correct)*
(a) The team have not come as yet. *(Incorrect)*
(b) The team has not come as yet. *(Correct)*

6. Some nouns have one meaning in the singular and another in the plural:

advice = counsel, advices = information,
air = atmosphere, airs = proud,
authority = command, authorities = persons in power
good = wise, goods = property
iron = metal, irons = fetters, chains,
force = strength, forces = army,
content = satisfaction, contents = things contained,
physic = medicine, physics = physical sciences,
respect = regards, respects = compliments
work = job, works = compositions, factories,
earning = income, earnings = sowings,
quarter = one-fourth, quarters = houses.

Examples

(a) Air is necessary for human life.
(b) It is bad to put on airs.
(a) I have eaten one quarter of the cake.
(b) I live in the government quarters.

7. People are often confused or they commit mistakes in the use of certain nouns.

(a) **Lecturership is wrong; lectureship is correct**

(i) There are twenty candidates for lecturership *(Incorrect)*
(ii) There are twenty candidates for lectureship *(Correct)*

(b) **Freeship is wrong; free-studentship is correct.**

(i) Ramesh has applied for freeship *(Incorrect)*
(ii) Ramesh has applied for free-studentship *(Correct)*

(c) **Boarding is wrong; boarding house is correct**

(i) Mohan lives in a boarding. *(Incorrect)*
(ii) Mohan lives in a boarding house. *(Correct)*

(d) **Family members is wrong; members of the family is correct.**

(i) Vivek and Ramesh are my family members *(Incorrect)*
(ii) Vivek and Ramesh are the members of my family. *(Correct)*

(e) **English teacher is wrong; the teacher of English is correct.**

(i) Dr Raina is our English teacher. *(Incorrect)*
(ii) Dr Raina is our teacher of English. *(Correct)*

(f) **Cousin-brother or sister is wrong; only cousin is correct**

(i) Geeta is my cousin sister. *(Incorrect)*
(ii) Geeta is my cousin. *(Correct)*

(g) **Room in a compartment or a bench means unoccupied seat.**

There is no room on this bench. *(Correct)*

(h) **Ours, yours, hers, theirs are correct**

(i) This house is our's. *(Incorrect)*

(ii) This house is ours. *(Correct)*

Note: The same principle applies to 'yours', 'hers' and 'theirs'.

(i) Wages means punishment when used in singular.

(i) The wages of sin is death.

(j) It also means charges for the labour when used in plural sense.

(i) The wages of daily workers have been raised.

8. Also remember the subtle differences in the usage of these pairs of nouns.

(a) **The noun 'habit' applies only to an individual whereas 'custom' applies to a society or country.**

(i) Poor children often become a victim of bad habits.

(ii) Tribals in India have many interesting customs.

(b) **'Cause' produces a result, while 'reason' explains or justifies a cause.**

(i) Scientists try to find out the cause of a phenomenon.

(ii) You have a good reason to be pleased with your students.

(c) **'Man' is used in ordinary sense while 'gentleman' is a man of character.**

(i) Man is mortal.

(ii) He is a gentleman at large.

(d) **'Men'—Plural of man; 'people' is used for persons.**

(i) There are five men in the room

(ii) The people of Bihar are simple

(e) **'Shade'—a place sheltered from the Sun; 'shadow'—the shade of a distinct form or object**

(i) The villagers sat under the shade of trees.

(ii) He is even afraid of his own shadow

(f) **'Cost'—amount paid by the shopkeeper; 'price'— amount paid by the customer.**

(i) The cost of production of automobile items has gone up.

(ii) Sometimes the buyers have to pay higher price for necessary items.

(g) **'House'—a building to live in; 'Home'—one's native place.**

(i) Quarters are houses allotted to us for a definite period.

(ii) My home town is Muzaffarpur.

(h) **'Customer'—a buyer of goods; 'Client'—one who avails oneself of a service.**

(i) The shopkeepers welcome customers with smiles.

(ii) The lawyer discusses the cases of his clients.

9. A pronoun must agree with its antecedent in person, number and gender.

For example:

Every *man* must bring *his* luggage.

All students must do *their* home work.

Each of the girls must carry *her* own bag.

Each *student* must bring *their* books. *(Incorrect)*

Each *student* must bring *his* books. *(Correct)*

10. While using 'everybody', 'anyone', 'anybody', and 'each' the pronoun of the masculine or the feminine gender is used according to the content.

I shall be happy to help each of the boys in this practice.

But when the sex is not mentioned, we use the pronoun of the masculine gender.

Anyone can do this job if *he* tries.

Each of the six boys in the class has finished their task. *(Incorrect)*

Each of the six boys in the class has finished *his* task. *(Correct)*

11. The pronoun 'one' must be followed by 'one's'.

One must finish his task in time *(Incorrect)*

One must finish *one's* task in time *(Correct)*

12. Enjoy, apply, resign, acquit, drive, exert, avail, pride, absent, etc. when used as transitive verbs, always take a reflexive pronoun after them. When 'self' is added to 'my', 'your', 'him', 'her' and 'it' and 'selves' to 'our' and 'them'—they are known as reflexive pronouns.

He absented from the class. *(Incorrect)*

He absented *himself* from the class. *(Correct)*

13. 'Who' denotes the subjects and 'whom' is used for the object.

Whom do you think won the award? *(Incorrect)*

Who do you think won the award? *(Correct)*

Who are you taking to? *(Incorrect)*

Whom are you talking to? *(Correct)*

14. When two or more singular nouns are joined together by 'either or'; 'neither nor'; and 'or', the pronoun is singular.

Either Ram or Shyam will give their book. *(Incorrect)*

Either Ram *or* Shyam will give *his* book. *(Correct)*

Neither Ramesh nor Rajendra has done their work. *(Incorrect)*

Neither Ramesh *nor* Rajendra has done *his* work. *(Correct)*

15. When a singular and a plural noun are joined by 'or', 'nor', the pronoun must be plural.

Either the engineer or his mechanics failed in his duty. *(Incorrect)*

Either the *engineer* or his *mechanics* failed in *their* duty. *(Correct)*

16. 'Whose' is used for living persons and 'which' for lifeless objects.

Which photograph is lying there? *(Incorrect)*

Whose photograph is lying there? *(Correct)*

What book do you read? (Incorrect)

Which book do you read? *(Correct)*

17. 'Each other' is used when there are two subjects or objects and 'one another' when there are more than two.

Romeo and Juliet loved *each* other.

Those five friends, who are sitting there, love *one another.*

All the students of the class are friendly; they love *each other.* *(Incorrect)*

All the students of the class are friendly; they love *one another.* *(Correct)*

18. When a pronoun stands for a collective noun, it must be in the singular number and in the neuter gender if the collective noun is viewed as a whole.

The jury gave '*its*' verdict.

Here the '*jury*' gives the idea of one whole.

If the collective noun conveys the idea of separate individuals comprising the whole, the pronoun standing for it must be plural.

The jury were divided in *their* opinions.

Here the 'jury' gives the idea of several individuals.

The team are divided in this opinion about playing on Sunday. *(Incorrect)*

The team are divided in their opinion about playing on Sunday. *(Correct)*

19. If pronouns of different persons are to be used together in a sentence, the serial order of persons should be as follows: second person + third person + first person in a good normal sentence. But if a fault is to be confessed, the order will be: first person + second person + third person.

You, *he* and *I* have finished the work. (Normal sentence)

I, *you* and he are to blame. (Confession)

Ram, I and you have finished our studies. *(Incorrect)*

You, Ram and I have finished our studies. *(Correct)*

20. 'Some' is used in affirmative sentences to express quantity or degree. 'Any' is used in negative or interrogative sentences.

I shall buy some apples.

I shall not buy any apples.

Have you bought any apples?

But 'some' may be correctly used in interrogative sentences which are, in fact, requests.

Will you please give me some milk?

I shall read any book. *(Incorrect)*

I shall read some book. *(Correct)*

Have you bought some apples? *(Incorrect)*

Have you bought any apples? *(Correct)*

21. The use of 'few', 'a few', and 'the few' should be used with care. They denote 'number'.

'Few' means 'not many'. It is the opposite of many. A 'few' is positive and means 'some at least'. It is the opposite of none. 'The few' means 'whatever there is'.

A few men are free from fault. *(Incorrect)*

Few men are free from fault. *(Correct)*

Here the sense is negative and thus 'a few' is wrong.

Few boys will pass in the examination. *(Incorrect)*

A few boys will pass in the examination. *(Correct)*

Here the sense is positive and thus 'few' is incorrect.

I have already read a few books that are on the bookshelf. *(Incorrect)*

I Have already read the few books that are on the bookshelf. *(Correct)*

Here the sense is 'whatever there is'

22. Use of 'less' and 'fewer'.

'Less' denotes quantity and 'fewer' denotes number.

No less than fifty persons were killed. *(Incorrect)*

No fewer than fifty person were killed. *(Correct)*

There are no fewer than five litres of water in the jug. *(Incorrect)*

There are no less than five litres of water in the jug. *(Correct)*

23. Use of little, a little, the little.

'Little' means 'hardly any'.

There is a little hope of his recovery. *(Incorrect)*

There is little hope of his recovery. *(Correct)*

'A little' means 'some', though not much

Little knowledge is a dangerous thing. *(Incorrect)*

A little knowledge is a dangerous thing. *(Correct)*

'The little' means 'not much but all there is'.

A little milk that is in the pot may be used for the patient. *(Incorrect)*

The little milk that is in the pot may be used for the patient. *(Correct)*

24. Use of elder, older.

'Older' refers to persons as well as things and is followed by 'than'.

Ram is elder than all other boys of this area. *(Incorrect)*

Ram is *older than* all other boys of this area. *(Correct)*

'Elder' is used for members of the family.

Suresh is my older brother. *(Incorrect)*

Suresh is my elder brother. *(Correct)*

25. Normally 'than' is used in the comparative degree, but with words like superior, inferior, senior, junior, prior, anterior, posterior and prefer 'to' is used.

Shelley is junior than Wordsworth. *(Incorrect)*

Shelley is *junior to* Wordsworth. *(Correct)*

I prefer reading than sleeping. *(Incorrect)*

I prefer *reading to* sleeping. *(Correct)*

26. When a comparison is made by using a comparative followed by 'than', the word 'other' must be used to exclude the thing compared from the class of things with which it is compared.

He is stronger than any man. (Incorrect)

He is *stronger* than any *other* man. *(Correct)*

'Any man' includes the man himself and thus the sentence will be absurd.

27. In some cases, the comparison is subtle and must be given proper attention.

The climate of Ranchi is better than Gaya. *(Incorrect)*

Here the comparison should be between the climate of Ranchi and the climate of Gaya.

The climate of Ranchi is better than the climate of Gaya. *(Correct)*

or

The climate of Ranchi is better than that of Gaya. *(Correct)*

The scenery of Kashmir is better than Shimla. *(Incorrect)*

The scenery of Kashmir is better than that of Shimla. *(Correct)*

'That of' means 'the climate of'.

Note: If the traits are in plural, it will be 'those of'.

The clothes of DCM are better than *those of* Mafatlal.

28. 'Many a' is always followed by the singular verb.

Many a man were drowned in the sea. *(Incorrect)*

Many a man *was* drowned in the sea. *(Correct)*

29. If the subject is 'the number of' the singular verb is used.

The number of students are very small. *(Incorrect)*

The *number* of students is very small. *(Correct)*

If the subject is 'a number of', the plural verb is used.

A number of books is missing. *(Incorrect)*

A number of books *are* missing. *(Correct)*

30. When 'as well as', 'along with', 'together with', 'no less than', 'in addition to', and 'not' and 'with' join two subjects, the verb will be according to the first subject.

Ram, as well as his ten friends, are going. *(Incorrect)*

Ram, as well as his ten friends, is going. *(Correct)*

The teacher, along with the students, were going *(Incorrect)*

The teacher, along with the students, was going *(Correct)*

31. 'A great many' is always followed by a plural noun and a plural verb.

A great many student has been declared successful. *(Incorrect)*

A great many students *have* been declared successful. *(Correct)*

32. If two subjects are joined by 'either or', 'neither nor', the verb agrees with the subject that is near.

Either Ramesh or I are to do this work. *(Incorrect)*

Either Ramesh *or I am* to do this work. *(Correct)*

Neither he nor his friends is reading. *(Incorrect)*

Neither he *nor* his *friends are* reading. *(Correct)*

33. When two singular nouns joined by 'and' point out the same thing or person, the verb will be singular.

Bread and butter make a good breakfast. *(Incorrect)*

Bread and butter makes a good breakfast. *(Correct)*

The Collector and the District Magistrate are on leave. *(Incorrect)*

The Collector and the District Magistrate is on leave. *(Correct)*

34. 'One of' always takes a plural noun after it.

It is one of the important day in my life. *(Incorrect)*

It is *one of* the important *days* in my life. *(Correct)*

35. Use of 'not only' and 'but also': Examine the sentences given below.

He not only comes for swimming but also for coaching the learners. *(Incorrect)*

He comes not only for swimming but also for coaching the learners. *(Correct)*

Here the error is due to misplacement.

The expression 'not only' must be placed before the right word, otherwise the meaning changes. Here this expression is meant for swimming and not for coming.

36. 'Scarcely' and 'hardly' are followed by 'when' and not by 'than'.

I had scarcely entered the room than the phone rang. *(Incorrect)*

I had *scarcely* entered the room *when* the phone rang. *(Correct)*

37. 'Though' is followed by 'yet' and not by 'but'.

Though he is poor but he is honest. *(Incorrect)*

Though he is poor, *yet* he is honest. *(Correct)*

38. 'No sooner' is followed by 'than'.

No sooner had I entered the class when the students stood up. *(Incorrect)*

No sooner had I entered the class *than* the students stood up. *(Correct)*

Attention must also be given to the verb form while using 'no sooner than'. The correct forms are past perfect or past indefinite.

No sooner had I entered the class than the students stand up. *(Incorrect)*

No sooner had I entered the class *than* the students *stood up*. *(Correct)*

39. 'Lest' must be followed by 'Should'.

Read regularly lest you will fail. *(Incorrect)*

Read regularly *lest* you *should* fail. *(Correct)*

40. 'Such' is followed by 'as'.

He is such a writer that everybody should read his books. *(Incorrect)*

He is *such* a writer *as* everybody should read his books. *(Correct)*

'Such' is also followed by 'that' if we emphasise the degree of something by mentioning the result.

The extent of the disaster was *such that* the authorities were quite unable to cope.

41. 'So' is followed by 'that'.

Sarita was popular with her classmates that she always had some people coming to her for advice. *(Incorrect)*

Sarita was *so* popular with her classmates *that* she always had some people coming to her for advice. *(Correct)*

42. 'Unless' expresses a condition. It is always used in the negative sense. Thus 'not' is never used with 'unless'.

Unless you do not labour hard, you will not pass. *(Incorrect)*

Unless you labour hard, you will not pass. *(Correct)*

43. Until expresses time. It has a negative sense and thus 'not' should never be used with it.

Wait here until I do not return. *(Incorrect)*

Wait here until I return. *(Correct)*

44. 'Since' indicates a point of time and 'for' stands for the length of time.

He has been reading the book since two hours. *(Incorrect)*

He has been reading the book *for two hours. (Correct)*

Two hours is a length of time and thus 'for' is correct

It has been raining for Monday last. *(Incorrect)*

It has been raining *since Monday last. (Correct)*

45. 'As if' is used to convey the sense of pretension. When 'as if' is used in this sense, 'were' is used in all cases, even with third person singular.

He behaves as if he was a king. *(Incorrect)*

He behaves *as if* he *were a* king. *(Correct)*

Note: The *sense of time* and tense is also very important. Certain important rules are listed below.

46. A past tense in the principal clause is followed by a past tense in the subordinate clause.

He saw that the clock has stopped. *(Incorrect)*

He saw that the clock has stopped. *(Correct)*

There are, however, two exceptions to this rule:

(1) A past tense in the principal clause may be followed by a present tense in the subordinate clause, when it expresses a universal truth.

The teacher observed that the Earth moved round the Sun. *(Incorrect)*

The teacher observed that the Earth moves round the Sun. (Correct)

(2) When the subordinate clause is introduced by 'than', even if there is past tense in the principal clause, it may be followed by any tense required by the sense in the subordinate clause.

He helped him more than he helped his own children. (Incorrect)

He helped him more than he helps his own children. (Correct)

47. If two actions in a sentence are shown happening in the past, one after the other; the tense of the action happening first should be past perfect and that of the second should be past indefinite.

The patient died before the doctor arrived. *(Incorrect)*

The patient *had died* before the doctor *arrived. (Correct)*

48. Two actions in the past, one depending on the other, should have the sequence as follows:

Past perfect + Future perfect

Had + past participle + would + have + past participle

If you *had worked* hard, you *would have succeeded* in the examination.

Or

Had you *worked* hard, you *would have succeeded* in the examination.

If you would have practised regularly, you would win the match. *(Incorrect)*

If you *had practised* regularly, you *would have* won the match. *(Correct)*

49. If, in a sentence, two actions are indicated and both are to take place in future, the sequence of tenses will be as follows:

The principal clause in present indefinite; and the subordinate clause in future indefinite.

If I go to Delhi, I shall attend the seminar.

Note: 'If I go to Delhi' is the principal clause and 'I shall attend the seminar' is the subordinate clause.

If it will rain, I shall not attend the meeting. *(Incorrect)*

If it rains, I shall not attend the meeting. *(Correct)*

50. When an action has taken place in two clauses of a sentence, it is used in both the clauses according to the requirement.

My brother has and is still doing excellent work for his organisation. *(Incorrect)*

My brother *has done* and *is still doing* excellent work for his organisation. *(Correct)*

51. When there is a sense of continuity, that is, when a thing has taken place in the past and still continues in the present, the perfect continuous tense form of the verb should be used.

India is independent for the last forty-six years. *(Incorrect)*

India *has been independent* for the last forty-six years *(Correct)*

Note: The use of *articles* is also an important matter and one must be careful about it.

52. Before a consonant 'a' is used.

A boy, a horse, a woman.

But 'a' is also used before words like university, useful, unicorn, union, European, and one, etc., because these words begin with a consonant sound.

Here is an University. *(Incorrect)*

Here is *a* University. *(Correct)*

An European lives in my area. *(Incorrect)*

A European lives in my area. *(Correct)*

It is an one-rupee note. *(Incorrect)*

It is *a* one-rupee note. *(Correct)*

53. Similarly, words like 'hour', 'honest', 'heir', etc. take 'an' before them as they begin with a vowel sound.

I have been waiting for him for a hour. *(Incorrect)*

I have been waiting for him for *an* hour. *(Correct)*

54. Some important points to remember regarding the omission of a/an/the:

1. **Before a common noun used in its widest sense, e.g.,**

   Man is mortal.

2. **Before names of materials.**

   Bronze is a useful metal.

3. **Usually before proper names.**

   Patna is the capital of Bihar.

4. **Before abstract nouns used in general sense.**

   Beauty fascinates people.

5. **Before languages**

   English is a very popular language in the Delhi University.

6. **Before 'school', 'college', 'church', 'bed', 'table', 'hospital', 'market', and 'prison', when these places are visited or used for their common purpose.**

   My Christian friends go to the church every Sunday.

7. **Before names of relations, like 'father', 'mother', 'aunt', 'uncle', 'cook', and 'nurse'.**

   Father is very happy today.

8. **Before predicative nouns denoting a unique position that is normally held at one time by one person only.**

   He was elected chairman of the Board.

Note: But 'the' is used with these words when we refer to them as a definite place, building, or object rather than to the normal activity that goes on there.

I met my friend at the church.

55. Uses of 'the'

1. **When the object is unique**

   The earth, the sky, the equator

2. **Before superlatives**

   The best, the finest, the most

3. **With proper nouns like 'seas', 'rivers', 'group of islands', 'chains of mountains', 'deserts', 'newspapers', 'buildings', 'religious books', 'gulfs'.**

   The Arabian sea, The Ganges, The Taj Mahal,

   The Times of India, The Ramayana

4. **Before a proper noun, when it is qualified by an adjective.**

   The immortal Kalidas.

5. **Before an adjective, when the noun is hidden.**

   The rich should be kind and helping.

6. **Before musical instruments.**

   I know how to play the harmonium.

7. **With a class of things.**

   The crow is a clever bird.

8. **'The' should be used before both comparative degrees when they are used in a sentence for proportion.**

   Higher we go, cooler we feel. *(Incorrect)*

   The Higher we go, *the* cooler we feel. *(Correct)*

56. 'What to speak of' is incorrect; the correct expression is 'not to speak of'.

What to speak of running, he cannot even walk. *(Incorrect)*

Not to speak of running, he cannot even walk. *(Correct)*

57. When there is the sense of dislike, hesitation, risk, etc., in a sentence, we should use a gerund instead of a verb. A gerund is that form of the verb which ends in 'ing' and can be used in the place of a noun.

I dislike to see a film late in the night. *(Incorrect)*

I dislike *seeing a* film late in the night. *(Correct)*

Young girls hesitate to talk to strangers. *(Incorrect)*

Young girls hesitate *talking to* strangers. *(Correct)*

58. 'Cent per cent' and 'word by word' are wrong. 'Hundred per cent' and 'word for word' are correct expressions.

You are never cent per cent sure of your success in a competitive examination. *(Incorrect)*

You are never *hundred per cent* sure of your success in a competitive examination. *(Correct)*

I can reproduce this lesson word by word. *(Incorrect)*

I can reproduce this lesson *word for word.* *(Correct)*

59. 'Since', 'because', 'as', and 'for',—all mean 'because', but there is a difference in their degree. 'Since' and 'because' are used for stronger cases and 'as' and 'for' for weak cases.

I respect him as he is my teacher. *(Incorrect)*

I respect him because he is my teacher. *(Correct)*

I could not attend the meeting because it was very hot today. *(Incorrect)*

I could not attend the meeting as it was very hot today. *(Correct)*

60. Use of 'when' and 'while': Proper attention must be paid to these words. 'When' indicates a general sense and 'while' implies a time during the process of doing a work.

When learning to swim, one of the most important things is to relax. *(Incorrect)*

While learning to swim, one of the most important things is to relax. *(Correct)*

61. Sometimes the error lies in the use of words. Proper attention must, therefore, be given to the appropriateness of words.

Prakash was leading a happy and leisurely life after his retirement from his service. *(Incorrect)*

Prakash was living a happy and leisurely life after his retirement from his service. *(Correct)*

Here the word 'leading' is inappropriate. One does not lead life, one lives life. One leads a group, team, movement, etc.

62. If in a sentence an apposition has been used, the verb will follow not the apposition

but the noun or pronoun preceding it.

You, my son, is a good boy. *(Incorrect)*

You, my son, are a good boy. *(Correct)*

63. Proper, abstract and material nouns have no plural except when they are used as common nouns.

The house is built of bricks. *(Incorrect)*

The house is built of brick. *(Correct)*

Note: When such nouns are used in the plural, they become common nouns with changed meanings; as

Coppers = Copper coins;

Iron = fetters.

Tins = cans made of tin;

Woods = forest.

He lives in the woods.

It means he lives in a forest.

64. Clauses in a sentence beginning with a relative pronoun (who, which, that) take a verb according to the noun or pronoun preceding the relative pronoun.

It is I who has done it. *(Incorrect)*

It is *I* who *have* done it. *(Correct)*

65. The relative pronoun should be placed as near as possible to its antecedent so that no ambiguity arises.

The boy is my cousin who stood first in the mile race. *(Incorrect)*

The boy, who stood first in the mile race, is my cousin. *(Correct)*

66. When two singular nouns joined by 'and' are preceded by 'each' or 'every' the pronoun used for them is singular.

Each Man and each boy is responsible for their action. *(Incorrect)*

Each Man and *each boy* is responsible for his action. *(Correct)*

67. Sometimes a pronoun is used where it is not required at all.

He being an M.A., he is qualified for the post. *(Incorrect)*

He, being an M.A., is qualified for the post. *(Correct)*

68. If a pronoun comes after a preposition it should be used in the objective case.

Between you and I neither of us is correct. *(Incorrect)*

Between you and *me* neither of us is correct. *(Correct)*

69. When a pronoun comes after 'like' and 'unlike' it takes an objective case.

A man like I will not do it. *(Incorrect)*

A man *like me* will not do it. *(Correct)*

70. A pronoun takes an objective case after 'let'.

Let I do it. *(Incorrect)*

Let me do it. *(Correct)*

71. Pronouns joined by 'and' remain in the same case.

He and her are brother and sister. *(Incorrect)*

He and she are brother and sister. *(Correct)*

He and me are friends. *(Incorrect)*

He and I are friends. *(Correct)*

72. When pronouns of second person and third person are used as subjects, the pronoun following them will be according to the second person pronoun.

You and he must bring his books. *(Incorrect)*

You and *he* must bring *your* books. *(Correct)*

73. When pronouns of second person and first person are used as subjects, the pronoun following them will be first person plural form.

You and I must finish your work in time. *(Incorrect)*

You and *I* must finish *our* work in time. *(Correct)*

74. 'But' is also used as a relative pronoun. When a sentence has a negative noun or pronoun, 'but' can be used with it. In this case 'but' means: who not; that not.

Here was none but laughed to see the joker.

There is no bird but flies.

Note: Here the meaning of 'but laughed' is 'who did not laugh'.

'But flies' means 'that does not fly'.

75. The relative pronoun 'that' is used in preference to 'who' or 'which' after adjectives in the superlative degree.

The wisest man who ever lived made mistakes. *(Incorrect)*

The *wisest* man *that* ever lived made mistakes. *(Correct)*

This is the best which we can do. *(Incorrect)*

This is *the best that* we can do. *(Correct)*

76. The relative pronoun 'that' is also used in preference to 'who' and 'which' after words 'all', 'same', 'any', 'none', 'nothing', and (the) 'only'.

He is the same man who he has seen. *(Incorrect)*

He is *the same* man *that* he has seen. *(Correct)*

Man is the only animal who can talk. *(Incorrect)*

Man is *the only* animal *that* can talk. *(Correct)*

77. The same rule applies after interrogative pronouns 'who' and 'what'.

What is there which I do not know? *(Incorrect)*

What is there *that* I do not Know? *(Correct)*

78. When there are two antecedents, a man and an animal or two things before the relative pronoun, we should use 'that'.

The man and his dog which passed through this road were killed. *(Incorrect)*

The *man and his dog that* passed through this road were killed. *(Correct)*

79. The case of the noun or pronoun preceding or succeeding the verb 'to be' should be the same.

It is him who came to see us. *(Incorrect)*

It is he who came to see us. *(Correct)*

It is me who caught the thief. *(Incorrect)*

It is I who caught the thief. *(Correct)*

80. When two qualities of a person or thing are compared 'more' or 'less' is used before the adjective and the adjective following them takes positive degree.

Suman is better than brave. *(Incorrect)*

Suman is more good than brave. *(Correct)*

81. When two or more adjectives are used to show the qualities of the same man or thing, all the adjectives must be in the same degree.

Sita is more intelligent and wise than Rita. *(Incorrect)*

Sita is *more intelligent* and *wiser* than Rita. *(Correct)*

Ramesh is the wisest and strong boy of the class. *(Incorrect)*

Ramesh is *the wisest* and *the strongest* boy of the class. *(Correct)*

82. 'Very' is used with adjectives in the positive degree and with present participles.

He is a much strong man. *(Incorrect)*

He is a *very strong* man. *(Correct)*

It is a much interesting book. *(Incorrect)*

It is *very interesting* book. *(Correct)*

Note: 'Much' is used with adjectives in the comparative degree and with past participles.

He is very stronger than I am. *(Incorrect)*

He is very much stronger than I am. *(Correct)*

I am very obliged to my friend. *(Incorrect)*

I am very much obliged to my friend. *(Correct)*

83. To show equality 'as' is used before and after the adjective.

I can run as fast, if not faster, than you. *(Incorrect)*

I can run *as fast as*, if not faster, than you. *(Correct)*

84. Certain adjectives do not admit of comparison and thus they always remain in the positive degree:

'Absolute', 'annual', 'chief', 'circular', 'complete', 'entire', 'extreme', 'excellent', 'full', 'impossible', 'perfect', 'right', 'round', 'unique', 'universal', 'whole', etc.

This is the most unique building that I have seen. *(Incorrect)*

This is the unique building that I have seen. *(Correct)*

85. 'More than one' indicates a plural sense, but it is treated as a sort of compound of one. Thus it agrees with a singular noun and takes a singular verb.

More than one employees were killed in the accident. *(Incorrect)*

More than one employee *was* killed in the accident. *(Correct)*

86. A verb must agree with its subject and not with the complement.

Our only guide at night were the stars. *(Incorrect)*

Our *only guide* at night *was* the stars. *(Correct)*

87. If the plural subject denotes a definite amount or quantity taken as a whole, the verb is singular.

Forty miles are a good distance. *(Incorrect)*

Forty miles is a good distance. *(Correct)*

Two-thirds of the book were rubbish. *(Incorrect)*

Two-thirds of the book was rubbish. *(Correct)*

88. The plural 'heaps' and 'lots' used colloquially for a great amount take a singular verb unless a plural noun with 'of' is added.

There are lots of book. *(Incorrect)*

There is lots of book. *(Correct)*

There is lots of books to read. *(Incorrect)*

There are lots of books to read. *(Correct)*

89. When qualified by 'each' or 'every' two singular subjects, even if connected by 'and', take a singular verb.

Each boy and every girl were given rewards. *(Incorrect)*

Each boy and *every girl was* given rewards. *(Correct)*

90. The following verbs are always followed by an infinitive:

'decide', 'plan', 'expect', 'fail', 'hope', 'intend', 'learn', 'promise', 'refuse', 'want', 'agree', 'consent', 'try', 'love', etc.

I refuse meeting him. *(Incorrect)*

I *refuse to meet* him. *(Correct)*

91. The following verbs and phrases should be followed by a gerund which is verbal noun: 'enjoy', 'admit', 'deny', 'appreciate', 'regret', 'avoid', 'help', 'consider', 'stop', 'looking forward to', 'accustomed to', 'is used to', 'do not mind', 'object to', etc.

I am looking forward to receive your reply. *(Incorrect)*

I am *looking forward to receiving* your reply. *(Correct)*

He is used to work hard. *(Incorrect)*

He *is used to working* hard. *(Correct)*

92. The word 'to' is frequently used with the infinitive, but it is not an essential part of it. For example, after certain verbs ('bid', 'let', 'make', 'need', 'dare', 'see', 'hear') we use the infinitive without 'to'.

Bid him to go there. *(Incorrect)*

Bid him *go* there. *(Correct)*

Make him to stand. *(Incorrect)*

Make him *stand.* *(Correct)*

I saw him to cry *(Incorrect).*

I *saw* him *cry* *(Correct).*

93. The infinitive is used without 'to' after 'had better', 'had rather', 'would rather', 'sooner than' and 'rather than'.

You had better to ask permission from him. *(Incorrect)*

You *had better ask* permission from him. *(Correct)*

94. 'Than' should be used after 'no other'.

I met no other man but Mr. Roy. *(Incorrect)*

I met *no other* man *than* Mr. Roy. *(Correct)*

Ram has no other claim except his degrees. *(Incorrect)*

Ram has *no other* claim *than* his degrees. *(Correct)*

95. After the word 'know', 'how', or 'when' should be used before using an infinitive.

I know to write French. *(Incorrect)*

I know how to write French. *(Correct)*

96. A verb may take an infinitive or a gerund according to its implication. If the verb indicates a purpose, an infinitive should be used and if the verb indicates a cause, a gerund should be used.

He went to school for seeing the principal. *(Incorrect)*

He went to school to see the principal. *(Correct)*

He was turned out to copy answers. *(Incorrect)*

He was turned out for copying answers. *(Correct)*

97. Adverb 'as' is not used with verbs like 'appointed', 'elected', 'considered', 'called' but it is used with 'regard'.

He was elected as President of our society. *(Incorrect)*

He was *elected President* of our society. *(Correct)*

I regard Ramesh my friend. *(Incorrect)*

I *regard Ramesh as* my friend. *(Correct)*

98. After the verb 'doubt' 'that' should not be used. 'If' or 'whether' should be used in its place.

I doubt that Ravi will come. *(Incorrect)*

I *doubt if* Ravi will come. *(Correct)*

99. Often a mistake is committed in the use of adjectives and adverbs. An adjective is correctly used with the verb when some quality of the subject, rather than of the action of the verb, is to be expressed.

The flowers smelt sweetly. *(Incorrect)*

The flowers smelt *sweet.* *(Correct)*

100. It is a common practice in conversation to make a statement and ask for confirmation; as, 'It's very hot, isn't it?' Two points are to be kept in mind. If the statement is positive, the pattern will be

Auxiliary + n't + subject.

If the statement is negative, the pattern will be

Auxiliary + subject

It is raining, is it? *(Incorrect)*

It is raining isn't it? *(Correct)*

You are not busy, aren't you? *(Incorrect)*

You are not busy, are you? *(Correct)*

Note: The point to note here is that the question tag will always have the same verb form which we have in the main statement:

I have finished my work, didn't I? *(Incorrect)*

I have finished my work, haven't I? *(Correct)*

101. There are certain **common errors** which should be avoided.

(a) 'The two first' is a meaningless expression for it implies that two things may be first. We should say 'the first two'.

The two first chapters of the novel are dull. *(Incorrect)*

The *first two* chapters of the novel are dull. *(Correct)*

(b) 'Only' should be placed immediately before the word it qualifies.

He only lost his ticket in the stampede. *(Incorrect)*

Only he lost his ticket in the stampede. *(Correct)*

(c) An infinitive verb should not be split.

I request you to kindly help me. *(Incorrect)*

I request you kindly *to help* me. *(Correct)*

(d) Care should be taken in the use of verbs.

The doctor saw the pulse of the patient. *(Incorrect)*

The doctor felt the pulse of the patient. *(Correct)*

He told the truth. *(Incorrect)*

He spoke the truth. *(Correct)*

Do not speak a lie. *(Incorrect)*

Do not tell a lie. *(Correct)*

Our team made a goal. *(Incorrect)*

Our team scored a goal. *(Correct)*

He is taking a bath. *(Incorrect)*

He is having a bath. *(Correct)*

I tell my prayers in the morning. *(Incorrect)*

I say my prayers in the morning. *(Correct)*

Illustrations

Bank Probationary Officers'/Trainee Officers' Examination, Guwahati, 1990

Find out error, if at all, in any part of the sentence.

1. Peoples above seventy-five (a)/ years of age (b)/ are not allowed to travel (c)/ by air (d)/ No error (e)

Here the error is in (a). See Rule 2. 'People' is used in plural.

2. She counted the books (a)/ to make sure that (b)/ none of them (c)/ were missing (d)/ No error (e)

Here the error is in (d). See Rule 9.

3. To make him succeed (a)/ the correct thing to do (b)/ is to punish him (c)/ until he does not try (d)/No error (e)

Here the error is in (d). See Rule 43.

4. It being a holiday (a)/ every student wanted (b)/ to leave (c)/ for their hometown (d)/ No error (e).

   Here the error is in (D). See Rule 9.

5. The invigilator asked him (a)/ that why he had (b)/ not brought (c)/ his call letter (d)/ No error (e)

   Here the error is in (b). See Rules of narration.

6. Now I understand (a)/ why Vishnu did not (b)/ told me the reason (c)/ why he was late (d)/ No error.

   Here the error is in (c). See Rule of narration.

7. There is no doubt (a)/ that the Pacific is (b)/ the largest of all other oceans (c)/ No error (d)

   Here the error is in (c). See Rule 26.

8. Taking pity (a)/ on the mouse (b)/ the sage transformed it (c)/ into a cat (d)/ No error (e)

   Here the answer is (E). No error.

9. With each academic year (a)/ the number of applicants (b)/ are increasing (c)/ in all colleges (d)/ No error (e)

   Here the error is in (C). See Rule 29.

10. With a lot of persuasion (a)/ the villagers agreed to (b)/ participate in the (c)/ family welfare programme (d)/ No error (e)
    Here the error is in (A). 'After' should be used in place of 'with'.

IBPS 2012 CWE for PO/MT: Solved English Language Question Paper

Read each sentence to find out whether there is any grammatical error or idiomatic error in it. The error, if any, will be in one part of the sentence. The alphabet of that part is the answer, If there is 'No error', the answer is 'e'. (ignore errors of punctuation, if any).

1. The Government has asked individuals (a)/ with income of over Rs. 10 lakhs to (b)/ electronic file tax returns for the year 2011-12, (c)/ something which was optional till last year (d). No error (e)

   No error

2. The power tariff had already (a)/ been increased twice in (b)/ the last 15 months and the Electricity Board had also (c)/ levied additional monthly charges to consigners (d). No error (e)

   No error

3. Despite of curfew (a)/ in some areas, minor (b)/ communal incidents were reported (c)/ from different areas of the walled city (d)/. No error (e)

   Error is in (a) 'Despite of' is wrong. 'Despite' is right.

4. This comes (a)/ at a time (b)/ when fund allocation (c)/ is been doubled (d)/. No error (e)

   Error is in (d) 'is been doubled' is wrong 'Is being doubled' will be right.

5. As the prison will get (a)/ an official telephone facility soon, the prisoners (b)/ won't have to make calls in discreet manner (c)/ through smuggled mobile phones(d)/. No error (e)

   Error is in (a) 'As the prison will get' is wrong 'As the prison gets' will be correct see the rules of tense.

6. The area was plunged into (a)/ darkness mid a wave of (b)/ cheering and shouting (c)/ Slogans like 'Save The Earth'(d)/. No error (e)

   Error is in (b) 'mid a wave of' is incorrect 'Amidst a wave' is correct.

7. The poll contestants approached (a)/ the commission complaining that the hoardings (b)/ violated the code of conduct (c)/ and influenced public perception (d)/. No error (e)

   Error is in (c) 'Violated the code of conduct' is wrong. 'Had violated the code of conduct' is right.

8. The country has (a)/ adequate laws but problems (b)/ arise when these are not (c)/ implemented in letter and spirit (d)/. No error (e)

   Error is in (a) Here the country should show a plural sense and thus the country have may be right

9. The Management feels that)(a)/ the employees of the organisation are (b)/ non-productive, and do not want (c)/ to work hard (d)/. No error (e)

   No error:

Practice Set —1

Read each sentence to find if there is any grammatical error in it. If there is any error, it will be only in one part of the sentence. The number or alphabet of that part is your answer. (Disregard punctuation errors, if any).

1. I shall(a)/ ring him (b)/ tomorrow (c)/ in the afternoon. (d)/ No error
2. I enjoyed (a)/ during my (b)/ stay in (c)/ England. (d)/ No error (e)
3. The clothes (a)/ were neatly (b)/ hanged (c)/ on the cloth line. (d)/No error (e)
4. The Major (a)/ along with (b)/ his soldiers (c)/ were killed in the field. (d)/ No error
5. The film show (a)/began (b)/when we arrived (c)/ in the hall. (d)/No error
6. I believe (a)/ that respect (b)/ is more preferable than/money. (d)/ No error (e)
7. I never have (a)/ visited (b)/ or intend to visit (c)/ foreign countries. (d)/ No error (e)
8. In this way nuclear fission, (a)/or the splitting (b)/ of the atom, (c)/have been achieved. (d)/ No error (e)
9. Modern film techniques (a)/are far superior (b)/ than that (c)/employed in the past. (d)/No error (e)
10. No sooner the news appeared in the paper (a)/ than (b)/there was a rush (c)/in the counter. (d)/ No error (e)

Practice Set —2

1. John's salary (a)/ is much (b)/larger than (c)/ Tom. (d)/ No error (e)
2. Ramesh helped (a)/ not only me (b)/ but also my brother (c)/when he was in need. (d)/ No error (e)
3. Give me (a)/ three thousands (b)/rupees,)(c)/ please. (d)/ No error (e)
4. More than (a)/ two boys (b)/ were present (c)/ in the class. (d)/ No error (e)
5. More than one (a)/ person (b)/ have found it (c)/ correct. (d)/ No error (e)
6. Only three-fourths (a)/ of the work (b)/ are complete (c)/ and we are left with no time. (d)/ No error (e)
7. The English (a)/ defeated (b)/ French (c)/ in the battle of Waterloo. (d)/ No error (e)
8. The three last chapters (a)/ of this (b)/ book (c)/ are very interesting. (d)/ No error
9. In summer, (a)/ days are (b)/ warm than (c)/ nights. (d)/ No error (e)
10. A large number (a)/ of houses (b)/are coming up (c)/ in our town. (d)/ No error (e)

Practice Set —3

1. They appointed (a)/ him as a manager (b)/as he is (c)/ efficient. (d)/ No error (e)
2. The reason (a)/ of his (b)/ failure (c)/ is due to his intelligence. (d)/ No error (e)
3. The prices of (a)/ his article (b)/ considerably varies (c)/ in different (d)/ parts of the country. (e)/No error
4. Mr. Sharma is planning (a)/to settle in Delhi (b)/ as soon as (c)/ he will retire in April next year. (d)/ No error (e)
5. One should (a)/ always (b)/ take care (c)/ of his health. (d)/ No error (e)
6. Mary is smarter (a)/ than (b)/ anybody (c)/ in her class. (d)/ No error (e)
7. I lived (a)/ in a three-hundred-years (b)/ old house (c)/ in Bombay. (d)/ No error (e)
8. He is (a)/the strongest and very tall (b)/boy in the (c)/ whole college. (d)/ No error (e)
9. I was (a)/born (b)/on the August 3 1947 in Bihar. (c)/ No error (d)
10. The Principal (a)/ offered me (b)/ tea but (c)/I denied it. (d)/No error (e)

Practice Set —4

1. Even though he was over ninety (a)/ he still enjoyed reading novels (b)/ and sometimes

spend (c)/ an evening at the cinema. (d)/ No error (e)

2. Up to the time the last vote was recorded (a)/ it was difficult (b)/ to decide whether victory lay with theruling party (c)/ or the opposition. (d)/ No error (e)
3. We should always (a)/ side with those who (b)/ are true and unselfish (c)/ and work for other. (d)/ No error (e)
4. I will now deal with him (a)/ in a manner different (b)/ from the one I have adopted so far. (c)/ No error (d)
5. His manners indicate (a)/ that he has no other intention (b)/ than (c)/ to steal his money. (d)/ No error (e)
6. Page after page (a)/ of Gita were read (b)/ and it gave great consolation (c)/ to his mind. (d)/ No error (e)
7. He was unanimously (a)/ elected (b)/ the General Secretary (c)/ of our Association. (d)/ No error (e)
8. Before giving (a)/ the mixture (b)/ to the child, (c)/ shake it thoroughly. (d)/ No error (e)
9. The short story (a)/ should not exceed (b)/ more than (c)/ two hundred words. (d)/ No error (e)
10. He looks at everything (a)/ from (b)/ their (c)/ best side. (d)/ No error (e)

Practice Set —5

1. Our teacher (a)/ often emphasises on (b)/ the need for (c)/ a lot of oral practice. (d)/ No error (e)
2. As he was feeling very thirsty (a)/ after the long journey, (b)/ he went into a bar (c)/ and ordered a cold drink. (d)/ No error (e)
3. He told me that (a)/ he couldn't buy the paintings, (b)/ which he wanted very much, (c)/ because he hadn't enough money. (d)/ No error (e)
4. Neither Mr Jones (a)/ nor Mr Smith (b)/ were able to give me (c)/ any advice. (d)/ No error (e)
5. A tallest man (a)/ I have seen (b)/ lives near the village (c)/ where I was born. (d)/ No error (e)
6. Although he had worked hard (a)/ and was understanding as much about the subject (b)/ as I did (c)/ he failed to get a second class in the examination. (d)/No error (e)
7. If you do not agree (a)/ to my request (b)/ then I shall be (c)/ forced to take drastic measures. (d)/No error (e)
8. She has told me that her brother might have done much better (a)/ at the university last year (b)/ had he not given so much time (c)/ to the students Union. (d)/No error (e)
9. He hesitated to accept the post (a)/ as he did not think (b)/ that the salary was enough (c)/ for a man with a family of six. (d)/No error (e)
10. The Headmaster advised the student (a)/ who had failed in the examination twice (b)/ that not to attempt it again (c)/ until he had time to prepare for it properly. (d)/ No error (e)

Practice Set —6

1. Surekha was trying for admission (a)/ in the engineering college (b)/ even though her parents wanted (c)/ her to take up medicine. (d)/ No error (e)
2. There is no book (a)/ in English language (b)/ which is as interesting (c)/ as this. (d)/ No error (e)
3. There is no other book (a)/ in the English language (b)/ which is as interesting (c)/ as this. (d)/ No error (e)
4. Even after working in the office (a)/ for several years (b)/ Suresh had (c)/ hardly mastered any job at all. (d)/ No error (e)
5. It is a job (a)/ wherein (b)/ neither knowledge nor skill (c)/ are needed. (d)/ No error (e)
6. Orders have been placed (a)/ so far as (b)/ painting the walls of the (c)/ classrooms are concerned. (d)/ No error (e)
7. No decision can be made (a)/ unless (b)/ firm data is available (c)/ to the committee. (d)/ No error (e)

8. There was (a)/ a number of conferences (b)/ which produced little (c)/ of practical value. (d)/ No error (e)

9. There was no play (a)/ on the fourth day (b)/ of the test match (c)/ due to the heavy rain. (d)/ No error (e)

10. Sushma persuaded (a)/ her sister (b)/ to go with her (c)/ on the trip. (d)/ No error (e)

Practice Set —7

1. Sarita was popular (a)/ with her classmates that (b)/ she always had some or (c)/ the other coming to her house. (d)/ No error (e)

2. The programme which (a)/ came on television (b)/ These days in the evenings (c)/ is very interesting. (d)/ No error (e)

3. Prakash was leading (a)/ a happy and leisurely life (b)/ after his retirement (c)/ from service. (d)/ No error (e)

4. 'Yavanika' is one (a)/ of the latest (b)/ addition to good drama (c)/ which appeared in recent times. (d)/ No error (e)

5. Children visiting the (a)/ park are amused (b)/ by the monkeys (c)/ play in the cages. (d)/ No error (e)

6. The car flew off the road (a)/ and fell into the valley (b)/ because Amit (c)/ was driving faster. (d)/ No error (e)

7. Sadhana was the one person (a)/ who could somehow manage (b)/ to working in the section (c)/ for such a long time. (d)/ No error (e)

8. In spite of the late hour (a)/ and the bad weather (b)/ Naveen decided to brave it out (c)/ and drink at bar. (d)/ No error (e)

9. Sooner than he had arrived (a)/ his friends arranged a reception (b)/ in his honour in (c)/ the best hotel in town. (d)/ No error (e)

10. The number of people (a)/ applying were so large (b)/ that the college had to (c)/ stop issuing application forms. (d)/ No error (e)

Practice Set —8

1. If you will (a)/ follow my instructions (b)/ you will get (c)/ a suitable reward for that. (d)/ No error (e)

2. He obtained good marks (a)/ not only in English essay (b)/ but also in Arithmetic which was (c)/ full of complicated calculations. (d)/ No error (e)

3. As soon as the Principal (a)/ entered the school (b)/ all the students approached him (c)/ and report the matter. (d)/ No error (e)

4. It is raining (a)/ very heavily since (b)/ last night. (c)/ No error (d)

5. He asked me (a)/ when could I finish (b)/ the work. (c)/ No error (d)

6. My younger brother and (a)/ I am interested (b)/ in music. (c)/ No error (d)

7. If you would try sincerely (a)/ you would get (b)/ good results certainly. (c)/ No error (d)

8. Does he really believe (a)/ that he is more intelligent than all the boys (b)/ in the class. (c)/ No error (d)

9. Hari was unhappy (a)/ that he would (b)/ not attend the marriage (c)/ of his friend yesterday. (d)/ No error (e)

10. Rama could not (a)/ go to the picnic (a)/ for his mother (b)/ was not well. (c)/ No error (d)

Practice Set —9

1. My friend did not see me (a)/ for many years (b)/ when I met him last week. (c)/ No error (d)

2. It is incumbent (a)/ with all the students (b)/ to abide by the college rules. (c)/ No error (d)

3. The bus collided (a)/ but nobody was hurt (b)/ in the accident. (c)/ No error (d)

4. by all standards (a)/ he is a best soldier (b)/ our military school (c)/ has produced so far. (d)/ No error (e)

5. While going to his office yesterday (a)/ Bhola remembered that (b)/ he had not taken (c)/ one important office file. (d)/ No error (e)

6. Why you don't told him (a)/ and (b)/ clarify all (c)/ pending matters. (d)/ No error (e)

7. He very promptly (a)/ withdrew the marks (b)/ made by him (c)/ on my office note. (d)/ No error (e)

8. No one will deny (a)/ that Sarla is one (b)/ of the most well-dressed girl (c)/ in our office. (d)/ No error (e)

9. He was extremely annoyed (a)/ when I reported (b)/ the matter to him (c)/ and has fired me. (d)/ No error (e)

10. The director, along with (a)/ the staff members (b)/ were present for (c)/ the annual day celebrations. (d)/ No error (e)

Practice Set —10

1. It is our duty (a)/ to put off our shoes (b)/ before entering the sanctum sanctorum of any temple or mosque. (c)/ No error (d)

2. The only good thing (a)/ about these pens (b)/ are their colour and their size. (c)/ No error (d)

3. My brother-in-laws (a)/ who live in Mumbai (b)/ have come to stay with us. (c)/ No error (d)

4. I advised my son (a)/ to engage two coolies instead of one (b)/ because the luggage was too much heavyfor a single coolie. (c)/ No error (d)

5. Raman was one of those great sons of India (a)/ who has earned everlasting fame (b)/ for scientific researches. (c)/ No error (d)

6. No sooner did the thief see the policeman (a)/ that he jumped over the wall (b)/ and ran away. (c)/ No error (d)

7. On entering the room (a)/ she was found hanging (b)/ from the ceiling. (c)/ No error (d)

8. If I were (a)/ in his shoes (b)/ I would die with shame. (c)/ No error (d)

9. I am vexed (a)/ at him about what (b)/ he has done. (c)/ No error (d)

10. He laid for half an hour unconscious (a)/ until he was seen (b)/ by a passing vehicle. (c)/ No error (d)

Practice Set —11

1. The teacher (a)/ together with his (b)/ wife and daughter (c)/ were drowned. (d)/ No error (e)

2. The taxi was (a)/ hired by (b)/ the ladies for (c)/ its picnic. (d)/ No error (e)

3. Having been found guilty (a)/ on murder (b)/ the accused was (c)/ sentenced to death. (d)/ No error (e)

4. The father as well (a)/ as the sons were (b)/ mysteriously missing (c)/ from the house. (d)/ No error (e)

5. The issues are (a)/ complex and (b)/ has been obscured (c)/ by other factors. (d)/ No error (e)

6. Neither the size (a)/ nor the colour (b)/ of the gloves (c)/ were right. (d)/ No error (e)

7. It is in 1929 (a)/ that we first (b)/ flew to (c)/ the United States. (d)/ No error (e)

8. Hardly had (a)/ I left the house (a)/ than it began (a)/ to rain. (a)/ No error (a)

9. A more irrational world (a)/ to this one in which (a)/ we presently live (a)/ could hardly be conceived. (a)/ No error (a)

10. He hoped to finish (a)/ the work in the last week (a)/ but in fact (a)/ he could not. (a)/ No error (a)

Practice Set —12

1. He not only comes there (a)/ for swimming (b)/ but also for coaching (c)/ new swimmers. (d)/ No error (e)

2. He could not cut (a)/ the grass today because (b)/ the handle of the machine (c)/ has broken a fewdays ago. (d)/ No error (e)

3. His ability to (a)/ talk to strangers (b)/ is one of his (c)/ stronger points. (d)/ No error (e)

4. My brother said (a)/ that he preferred (b)/ the white shirt (c)/ than the black one. (d)/ No error (e)

5. She was the daughter (a)/ of a working farmer (b)/ who was one of the (c)/ headman of his village. (d)/ No error (e)

6. No king in that period (a)/ was so intensely involved (b)/ in the welfare of his people (c)/ as king Ashoka. (d)/ No error (e)

7. What to talk of charity (a)/ Rajan does not practice (b)/ even (c)/ ordinary humanity. (d)/ No error (e)

8. I have hunted and (a)/ shot myself (b)/ so I know what (c)/ it is like. (d)/ No Error (e)

9. He only wrote (a)/ on one side of (b)/ the paper. (c)/ No error (d)

10. The two sisters (a)/ struck (b)/ one another (c)/ at the platform. (d)/ No error (e)

Practice Set —13

1. I am very thirsty, (a)/ give me (b)/ little water (c)/ to drink. (d)/ No error (e)

2. Everybody was (a)/ in the garden (b)/ amusing (c)/ themselves. (d)/ No error (e)

3. If I was you (a)/ I would not (b)/ attend (c)/ the function. (d)/ No error (e)

4. These organisations (a)/ work lest (b)/ their activities (c)/ may be banned. (d)/ No error (e).

5. Avinash and his friend (a)/ were walking towards (b)/ the station when (c)/ they met this common friend. (d)/ No error (e)

6. Priyamvada was unhappy (a)/ to hear the news (b)/ of her son's failing (c)/ in the final examination. (d)/ No error (e)

7. For expecting the company to pay (a)/ for the transport (b)/ of the personal furniture of the employee (c)/ was not fair. (d)/ No error (e)

8. Aditi was unable (a)/ to support her parent (b)/ even though both of them (c)/ had no income of their own. (d)/ No error (e)

9. Tax evaders should (a)/ be heavily fined (b)/ as they are doing (c)/ it intentionally. (d)/ No error (e)

10. The idea that shook (a)/ the whole world was (b)/ published in one (c)/ of the unknown journal. (d)/ No error (e)

Practice Set —14

1. The information supplied (a)/ to us were not as (b)/ useful as we first (c)/ thought it would be. (d)/ No error (e)

2. The man (a)/ appears to have seen (b)/ more happier days. (c)/ No error (d)

3. Have you read (a)/ this book (b)/ farther than I? (c)/ No error (d)

4. The production of different kinds of artificial materials (a)/ are essential to the conservation of (b)/ our natural resources. (c)/ No error (d)

5. My brother-in-law with his wife (a)/ now in Singapore (b)/ were present at the function. (c)/ No error (d)

6. She (a)/ eagerly wishes (b)/ to help me. (c)/ No error (d)

7. The sun is shining good (a)/ about (b)/ the horizon. (c)/ No error (d)

8. To lead a well-balanced life (a)/ you need (b)/ to have other interests besides studying. (c)/ No error (d)

9. Nehru was (a)/ a great politician (b)/ and a great statesman. (c)/ No error (d)

10. The disclosure of the synopsis of (a)/ the Thakkar Commission Report (b)/ on the assassination of Mrs. Gandhi has raised several vital questions. (c)/ No error (d)

Practice Set —15

1. Her (a)/ knowledge of English are (b)/ very limited. (c)/ No error (d)

2. There are so many filths (a)/ all around (b)/ the place. (c)/ No error (d)

3. Do you really believe (a)/ that she has blamed us (b)/ for the accident, especially you and I? (c)/ No error (d)

4. Nobody offered to give up (a)/ their seat to the lady (b)/ holding her child in her arms. (c)/ No error (d)

5. He labours (a)/ hard lest (b)/ he may fail (c)/ No error (d)

6. You have (a)/ no (b)/ excuse (c)/ to be late. (d)/ No error (e)

7. The flowers smell sweetly (a)/ and (b)/ are (c)/ of great value. (d)/ No error (e)

8. His all daughters (a)/ are ugly so (b)/ they cannot be married. (c)/ No error (d)

9. Two men have (a)/ been arrested (b)/ by the police who are believed (c)/ to be involved in the robbery. (d)/ No error (e)

10. The price (a)/ of his car is (b)/ higher (c)/ than your car. (d)/ No error (e)

Practice Set —16

1. He suggested (a)/ that I should (b)/ see him (c)/ in his letter. (d)/ No error (e)

2. I am hardly pressed (a)/ for time, (b)/ I can not (c)/ accompany you. (d)/ No error (e)

3. Even so great a poet (a)/ like Shakespeare (b)/ has his (c)/ faults. (d)/ No error (e)

4. I have great pleasure (a)/ move (b)/ this resolution (c)/ for your consent. (d)/ No error (e)

5. Did not the teacher (a)/ instruct you (b)/ to revise your answer (c)/ if time was available? (d)/ No error (e)

6. No sooner the bell rang (a)/ than the teacher entered the class (b)/ No error (c)

7. Wearing a costly suit (b)/ and flaunting a foreign accent (b)/ does not make (c)/ one respectable. (e)/ No error (e)

8. I have pleasure (a)/ to certify (b)/ that Shamim worked meritoriously (c)/ for the last three years in our organisation. (d)/ No error (e)

9. Pappu was happy that Jyoti and (a)/ his sister was going (b)/ on the same train (c)/ next day. (d)/ No error (e)

10. The manager tested (a)/ the peon to see (b)/ if he could (c)/ read English. (d)/ No error (e)

Practice Set —17

1. It was difficult (a)/ to persuade Subas to agree (b)/ to read the book (c)/ to the blind man. (d)/ No error (e)

2. How to solve the problems (a)/ is the main concern (b)/ of the organisers (c)/ at the moment. (d)/ No error (e)

3. Upon arrival (a)/ at any place of posting (b)/ I found it greatly different than (c)/ what I had imagined. (d)/ No error (e)

4. Neither the speaker (a)/ nor his secretary (b)/ were informed (c)/ of the cancellation. (d)/ No error (e)

5. When learning to swim (a)/ one of the most important things (b)/ is to relax. (c)/ No error (d)

6. Each girl (a)/ was given a bunch of flowers (b)/ which pleased her very much. (c)/ No error (d)

7. He says he (a)/ is going to (b)/ cut down his smoking. (c)/ No error (d)

8. The Department of Modern Indian Langauges (a)/ is running a course in Comparative Literature (b)/ for the last fifteen years. (c)/ No error (d)

9. After you will return (a)/ from Shimla (b)/ I will come and see you. (c)/ No error (d)

10. Had he follow (a)/ the directions carefully (b)/ he would have felt (c)/ better much quicker. (d)/ No error (e)

Practice Set —18

1. Once he realised (a)/ that he has committed a mistake (b)/ he admits it (c)/ and arrected it without delay. (d)/ No error (e)

2. Since we do not accept cheques (a)/ you will have to buy (b)/ a draft so that to pay (c)/ for you tickets. (d)/ No error (e)

3. The parents scolded the child (a)/ for having broke the windows (b)/ but their words fell (c)/ on deaf ears. (d)/ No error (e)

4. Each cigarette which (a)/ a person smokes some (b)/ does (c)/ harm to him. (d)/ No error (e)

5. He hoped to finish (a)/ the work in the last week (b)/ but in fact (c)/ he could not. (d)/ No error (e)

6. It was apparent to (a)/ everyone present that (b)/ he would die (c)/ if doesn't receive time help. (d)/ No error (e)

7. The speech he made (a)/ on his visit to our college (b)/ concerning our society's needs (c)/ have bothered me greatly. (d)/ No error (e)

8. The driver tried his best (a)/ to avert the accident by (b)/ bringing the car (c)/ to a suddenly stop. (d)/ No error (e)

9. The lecture to be held (a)/ in the auditorium tomorrow (b)/ was open to the public (c)/ and free of charge. (d)/ No error (e)

10. There appears to be (a)/ very little liaison (b)/ among the two of (c)/ the various wings of the party. (d)/ No error (e)

Practice Set —19

1. Everyone of the survivors (a)/ of the ill-fated aircraft (b)/ have told (c)/ the same story. (d)/ No error (e)

2. My neighbour along with his children (a)/ are going tonight (b)/ to see the Taj Mahal (c)/ at Agra. (d)/ No error (e)

3. But for his cousin's help (a)/ he would have been (b)/ at the height (c)/ of his career. (d)/ No error (e)

4. He would not have (a)/ written this letter (b)/ if he would not have (c)/ heard the news. (d)/ No error (e)

5. Soon after their child was born (a)/ he went off (b)/ leaving her (c)/ in the lurch. (d)/ No error (e).

6. She was able (a)/ to free herself (b)/ with her debts (c)/ by working very hard. (d)/ No error (e)

7. Hardly had we (a)/ settled down for the night's rest (b)/ when we were started by (c)/ loud noises outside the house. (d)/ No error (e)

8. No sooner did (a)/ the train arrived at the station (b)/ than the passengers (c)/ rushed towards it. (d)/ No error (e)

9. I have worked (a)/ in this office for six years (b)/ but I now work (c)/ in a different office. (d)/ No error (e)

10. A first European sailor (a)/ to come to India (b)/ in modern times (c)/ was Vasco Da Gama. (d)/ No error (e)

Practice Set —20

1. All we could find (a)/ from his neighbours are (b)/ that he has (c)/ a job in the competition. (d)/ No error (e)

2. None of the rooms (a)/ are available (b)/ for occupation (c)/ at present. (d)/ No error (e)

3. Drawing water from the well (a)/ is preferable (b)/ than depending on (c)/ the erratic tap-water supply. (d)/ No error (e)

4. May I know (a)/ whom (b)/ you wish (c)/ to see now? (d)/ No error (e)

5. Sumitra appealed (a)/ to the managing committee (b)/ that she may be (c)/ allowed to join the volunteer force. (d)/ No error (e)

6. Being a short vacation (a)/ Vanita had to return (b)/ without visiting (c)/ many of the places. (d)/ No error (e)

7. An uncle of mine (a)/ who is a lawyer (b)/ gave me a useful advice (c)/ when I went to see him there weeks ago. (d)/ No error (e)

8. An old man in the crowd (a)/ warned Julius Caesar (b)/ from the danger of death (c)/ on a certain day. (d)/ No error (e)

9. If John had told me (a)/ last Thursday (b)/ I will have given him the money (c)/ but now it is too late. (d)/ No error (e)

10. Never I have listened (a)/ to such beautiful music (b)/ as the piece we heard on the radio (c)/ last night. (d)/ No error (e)

ANSWER KEY

Set 1	Set 2	Set 3	Set 4	Set 5
1. (b)	1. (d)	1. (b)	1. (c)	1. (c)
2. (a)	2. (e)	2. (d)	2. (c)	2. (c)
3. (c)	3. (b)	3. (a)	3. (d)	3. (c)
4. (d)	4. (e)	4. (d)	4. (c)	4. (c)
5. (b)	5. (c)	5. (d)	5. (c)	5. (a)
6. (c)	6. (c)	6. (b)	6. (b)	6. (c)
7. (c)	7. (c)	7. (b)	7. (e)	7. (c)
8. (d)	8. (a)	8. (b)	8. (d)	8. (a)
9. (c)	9. (c)	9. (c)	9. (c)	9. (a)
10. (a)	10. (e)	10. (d)	10. (c)	10. (c)

Set 6	Set 7	Set 8	Set 9	Set 10
1. (c)	1. (a)	1. (a)	1. (a)	1. (b)
2. (a)	2. (b)	2. (a)	2. (b)	2. (c)
3. (b)	3. (a)	3. (d)	3. (a)	3. (a)
4. (a)	4. (c)	4. (a)	4. (b)	4. (c)
5. (d)	5. (d)	5. (b)	5. (a)	5. (b)
6. (d)	6. (d)	6. (b)	6. (a)	6. (b)
7. (c)	7. (c)	7. (a)	7. (a)	7. (b)
8. (a)	8. (a)	8. (b)	8. (c)	8. (c)
9. (d)	9. (a)	9. (b)	9. (d)	9. (b)
10. (c)	10. (b)	10. (c)	10. (c)	10. (a)

Set 11	Set 12	Set 13	Set 14	Set 15
1. (d)	1. (a)	1. (c)	1. (b)	1. (b)
2. (d)	2. (d)	2. (d)	2. (c)	2. (a)
3. (b)	3. (d)	3. (a)	3. (c)	3. (c)
4. (b)	4. (d)	4. (d)	4. (b)	4. (b)
5. (c)	5. (d)	5. (d)	5. (c)	5. (c)
6. (d)	6. (a)	6. (c)	6. (b)	6. (d)
7. (a)	7. (a)	7. (a)	7. (a)	7. (a)
8. (c)	8. (b)	8. (b)	8. (a)	8. (a)
9. (b)	9. (a)	9. (c)	9. (c)	9. (c)
10. (a)	10. (c)	10. (d)	10. (a)	10. (d)

Set 16	Set 17	Set 18	Set 19	Set 20
1. (d)	1. (b)	1. (c)	1. (c)	1. (b)
2. (a)	2. (e)	2. (c)	2. (b)	2. (b)
3. (a)	3. (c)	3. (b)	3. (b)	3. (c)
4. (b)	4. (c)	4. (a)	4. (c)	4. (b)
5. (a)	5. (a)	5. (a)	5. (b)	5. (c)
6. (a)	6. (c)	6. (d)	6. (c)	6. (a)
7. (c)	7. (a)	7. (d)	7. (e)	7. (c)
8. (c)	8. (b)	8. (d)	8. (b)	8. (c)
9. (b)	9. (a)	9. (c)	9. (a)	9. (c)
10. (b)	10. (a)	10. (c)	10. (a)	10. (a)

EXPLANATIONS

Set I

1. (b) 'Ring him up' in place of 'ring him'. 'Ring up' is the correct idiom.
2. (a) 'I enjoyed myself' in place of 'I enjoyed'. Some verbs take reflexive pronouns after them. See Rule 12.
3. (c) 'Hung' in place of 'hanged'. 'Hanged' is used for living beings and 'hung' is used for other objects.
4. (d) 'Was killed' in place of 'were killed'. Already explained. See Rule 30.
5. (b) 'Had begun' in place of 'began'. See the Rules of tense.
6. (c) 'Preferable to' in place of 'more preferable than'. 'Preferable' is a word indicating a comparative sense and thus 'more' is superfluous. Secondly, 'prefer' is followed by 'to'.
7. (c) 'Nor' in place of 'or'. 'Nor' is used after 'neither'.
8. (d) 'Has been' in place of 'have been'. When two subjects are joined by 'or', it is treated as singular.
9. (c) 'To those' in place of 'than that'. 'Superior' is followed by 'to'. Techniques is a plural subject and thus the pronoun for it must be plural. Thus 'those' in place of 'that.
10. (a) 'No sooner had the news appeared' in place of 'No sooner the news appeared'. Already discussed earlier. 'No sooner' is used in two forms: (I) 'No sooner had' and (ii) 'No sooner did'.

Set 2

1. (d) 'That of Tom' in place 'Tom'. See Rule 27.
2. (e) No Error
3. (b) 'Three thousand' in place of 'Three thousands'. Some nouns, when preceded by a numeral, remain unchanged in form. See Rule 4.
4. (e) No error
5. (c) 'Has found' in place of 'have found'. 'More than one' is singular.
6. (c) 'Is' in the place of 'are'. 'Three-fourths' make one unit and thus it is singular.
7. (c) 'The French' in place of 'French'. 'The French' means 'the French people'.
8. (a) 'The last three' in place of 'The three last'. Explained earlier. See Rule 35.
9. (c) 'Warmer in place of 'warm'. Here the sentence is in the comparative degree and thus 'warmer' is appropriate.
10. (e) No Error.

Set 3

1. (b) 'Manager' in place of 'as a manager'.
2. (d) 'Due to' should be deleted. The reason is sufficient. 'Due to' is a duplication and thus is superfluous.
3. (a) 'The price' in place of 'The prices'.
4. (d) 'He retires' in place of 'he will retire'.
5. (d) 'Of one's' in place of 'his'. 'One' is followed by 'one's'. See Rule 11.
6. (c) 'Anybody else' in place of 'Anybody'. See Rule 26.
7. (b) 'Three hundred year' in place of 'three hundred years'. See Rule 4.
8. (b) 'The stronger and tallest' in place of 'very tall'. A word showing superlative degree should not be joined by a word showing comparative or the assertive degree. Both qualifiers must be of the same degree.
9. (c) 'On 3rd August' in place of 'the 3rd August'. When the letter or the number form is used, the article is not required. When it is in the word form, the article will be used. Thus we can say '3rd August' and 'the third August'.
10. (d) 'Declined' in place of 'denied'.

Set 4

1. (c) 'Spent' in place of 'spend'. The reporting verb is in the past tense and thus all other clauses must be in the past tense.
2. (c) 'Till' in place of 'up to'.
3. (d) 'Who work for others' in place of 'work for others'. One form of the verb pattern should

be used with one subject. If the verb pattern changes the subject must be mentioned. Here the subject is 'those who' and the verb is 'are'. It is an auxiliary verb. But, in the next clause, the verb is main verb or action verb. Thus there must be a subject.

4. (c) 'I have been adopting' in place of 'I have'. Here the tense should be in continuous sense.

5. (c) 'But' in the place of 'than'.

6. (b) 'The Gita was' in place of 'Gita were'.

7. e.

8. (d) 'It' is confusing; it is not clear whether 'it' is for the mixture or for the child. Thus better to use the word 'the mixture'.

9. (c) 'More than' should be deleted. Double comparatives are to be avoided. 'Exceed' is sufficient.

10. (c) 'Its' in place of 'their'. See the Rules of pronouns. The pronoun for 'everything' is 'its'.

Set 5

1. (c) 'Of' in place of 'for'. Here the correct preposition will be 'of'.

2. (c) 'In' should be used in place of 'into'.

3. (c) 'Which he had wanted' in place of 'which he wanted'.

4. (c) 'Was' in place of 'were'. Explained earlier. See Rule 14.

5. (a) 'The tallest' in place of 'a tallest'. Here the definite article should be used.

6. (b) 'Understood' in place of 'was understanding'. See the Rules of tense.

7. (c) Delete 'then'. 'Then' is not required when 'if' is used.

8. (a) 'She told me' in place of 'she has told me'. See the Rules of tense.

9. (a) 'In accepting' in place of 'to accept'. See Rule 56.

10. (c) Delete 'that'. It is unnecessary here.

Set 6

1. (c) 'Had wanted' in place of 'wanted'. See the Rules of tense and see Rule 47.

2. (a) 'No other book' in place of 'no book'. See Rule 26.

3. (b) The article is not required here. It has to be deleted. See Rule 53.

4. (a) 'After having worked' in place of 'After working'. In such sentences the past perfect is used.

5. (d) 'Is needed' in place of 'are needed'. See Rule 14.

6. (d) 'Is concerned' in place of 'are concerned'. Has been explained earlier. See the rules of subject-verb accord. The verb should be in accordance with 'painting' which is the subject and is singular.

7. (c) 'Full data' or 'confirmed data' in place of 'firm'. The word 'firm' is inappropriate here.

8. (a) 'There were' in place of 'there was'.

9. (d) 'Because of' in place of 'due to'. 'Due to' always takes an abstract noun after it.

10. (d) 'To come' in place of 'to go'. Look at the sense in the sentence. Sushma, who is going asks her sister. Thus she has to say 'come'.

Set 7

1. (a) 'Sarita was so popular' in place of 'Sarita was popular'. 'That' is preceded by 'so'. See Rule 41.

2. (b) 'Comes on television' in place of 'came on television'. See the Rules of tense.

3. (a) 'Was leaving' in place of 'was leading'. 'Leading' is not an appropriate word.

4. (c) 'Additions' in place of 'addition'. See Rule 34.

5. (d) 'Playing' in place of 'play'

6. (d) 'Fast' in place of 'faster'. This is a simple sentence and thus 'faster' which indicates a comparative sense is inappropriate.

7. (c) 'To work' in place of 'to working'.

8. (a) 'Despite' in place of 'in spite of'. The meaning of 'in spite of' is not appropriate here.

9. (a) 'No sooner had he arrived than' in place of 'sooner than he had arrived'. This is the correct form of sentence structure in case of using 'no sooner than' or 'sooner than'. See Rule 38.

10. (b) 'Was' in place of 'were', in case the number of the verb is singular. See Rule 29.

Set 8

1. (a) 'If you' in place of 'if you will'. When two parts of a sentence are in the future tense, the reporting verb will be in the present indefinite. See Rule 49.
2. (a) 'He had obtained good marks' in place of 'He obtained good marks'. See Rule 48.
3. (d) 'And reported the matter' in place of 'and report the matter'. See Rule 46
4. (a) 'It has been raining' in place of 'It is raining'. The perfect continuous tense is required here. See Rule 51.
5. (b) 'I could' in place of 'could I'. See narration Rules.
6. (b) 'Are' in place of 'am'.
7. (a) 'If you try' in place of 'If you would try'. Already explained earlier. See Rule 49.
8. (b) 'Than all the other boys' in place of 'than all the boys'. See Rule 26.
9. (b) 'That he could' in place of 'that he would'. See the Rules of tense.
10. (c) 'Because' in place of 'for'. See Rule 58.

Set 9

1. (a) 'My friend had not seen me' in place of 'my friend did not see me'. See Rule 47.
2. (b) 'Upon' in place of 'with'. See the Rules of preposition.
3. (a) There should be an object after 'collided' to make the meaning clear.
4. (b) 'The' in place of 'a'. 'The' is used to show the superlative degree. See Rule 54.
5. (a) 'While he was going to his office' in place of 'while going to his office'. In sentences beginning with 'while', 'when', 'this', 'it', or similar conjunctions, you should be careful to see that the meaning is clear. There should be no confusion in the first part.
6. (a) 'Why don't you tell him' in place of 'why you don't told him'. see the rules of tense and forms of interrogative sentences.
7. (a) 'Very promptly he' in place of 'He very promptly'. Words have been misplaced here. See Rule 35.
8. (c) 'Girls' in place of 'girl'. 'One of' is followed by a plural object. See Rule 34.
9. (d) 'And fired him' in place of 'and has fired me'. The reporting verb is in the past tense and thus other clauses must be in the past tense.
10. (c) 'Was present' in place of 'were present'. In the case of 'along with', the verb is in accordance with the first object. See Rule 46.

Set 10

1. (b) 'Pull off' in place of 'put off'.
2. (c) 'Is' in place of 'are'. The subject 'the only good thing' is singular and thus the verb will be singular.
3. (a) 'Brothers-in-law' in place of 'brother-in-laws'. For the plural 's' is added to the root word.
4. (c) 'Too heavy' in place of 'too much'.
5. (b) 'who have' in place of 'who has'. 'Who' has been used here for 'sons' and as this is plural, the verb should also be in accordance with that.
6. (b) 'Than' in place of 'that. See Rule 38.
7. (b) 'Found hanged' in place of 'found hanging'. See the Rules of tense.
8. (c) 'I would have died' in place of 'I would die'. This is the form of structure. If two parts of a sentence are in the past tense, one part will be in the past indefinite and another in the past perfect. See Rule 48.
9. (b) 'With' in place of 'at'. See the Rules of preposition.
10. (a) 'Lay' in place of 'laid'. 'Lay' is the past indefinite form of 'lie'.

Set 11

1. (d) 'Was' in place of 'were'. The verb will be in accordance with the first subject in case of 'together with'. See Rule 30.
2. (d) 'Their' in place of 'its'. The pronoun must be in accordance with 'ladies'. See Rule 9.

3. (b) 'Of' in place of 'on'. See Prepositions.

4. (b) 'Was' in place of 'were'. See Rule 30.

5. (c) 'Have' in place of 'has'. The simple rule of subject-verb accord should be taken care of.

6. (d) 'Was' in place of 'were'. When two singular subjects are joined by neither-nor, the verb is singular. See Rule 14.

7. (a) 'Was' in place of 'is'. See Rules of tense.

8. (c) 'When' in place of 'than'. See Rule 36.

9. (b) 'Than' in place of 'to'. 'Than' is normally used in comparative degree. See Rule 25.

10. (a) 'He had hoped' in place of 'he hoped'. See Rules of tense.

Set 12

1. (a) 'He comes there not only' in place of 'he not only comes there'. The error is in placement of words. See Rule 35.

2. (d) 'Had broken' in place of 'has broken'. See Rules of tense.

3. (d) 'Strong points' in place of 'stronger points'. No need of the comparative degree. See Rules of degree.

4. (d) 'To the' in place of 'than the'. See Rule 25.

5. (d) 'Headmen' in place of 'headman'. 'One of' is followed by a plural noun. See Rule 11.

6. (a) 'No other king' in place of 'no king'. It is an important rule. Try to understand it carefully. See Rule 26.

7. (a) 'Not to talk of' in place of 'what to talk of'. See Rule 55.

8. (b) 'Myself' is unwanted. It confuses the meaning.

9. (a) 'He wrote only' in place of 'he only wrote'. See Rule 35.

10. (c) 'Each other' in place of 'one another'. See Rule 17.

Set 13

1. (c) 'A little water' in place of 'little water'. See Rule 23.

2. (d) 'Himself' in place of 'themselves'. See Rule 10.

3. (a) 'If I were' in place of 'if I was'. In sentences showing condition 'were' is used. See Rule 45.

4. (d) 'Should be' in place of 'may be'. 'Lest' is followed by 'should'. See Rule 39.

5. (d) 'There common' in place of 'his common'. The pronoun must be in accordance with the subject. Here the subject is plural. See Rule 9.

6. (c) 'Son failing' in place of 'son's failing'. The use of the apostrophe is not required here.

7. (a) 'To expect' in place of 'For expecting'.

8. (b) 'Parents' in place of 'parent' parents is a plural noun and is always used in plural form.

9. (c) 'They have been doing' in place of 'they are doing'. The sentence is in perfect continuous tense. See Rules of tense.

10. (d) 'Journals' in place of 'journal'. 'One of' is always followed by a plural object. See Rule 34.

Set 14

1. (b) 'Was not' in place of 'were not'. Information is always used in singular. See Rule 1.

2. (c) 'Happier' in place of 'more happier'. Double comparatives should be avoided.

3. (c) 'Further' in place of 'Farther'. 'Farther' is used to denote a sense of distance and 'further' is used to indicate more.

4. (b) 'Is essential' in place of 'are essential'. The subject is production, not materials. As the subject is singular, the verb will be singular. Be careful about the subject-verb accord.

5. (c) 'Was' in place of 'were'. In case of 'along with' or 'with', the verb is in accordance with the first subject. See Rule 30.

6. (b) 'Wishes eagerly' in place of 'eagerly wishes'. See Rule 35.

7. (a) 'Good' is inappropriate. It is an adjective. An adverb should be used, say, 'fine' or 'brightly'.

8. (a) 'To live' in place of 'to lead'. The word is inappropriate.

9. (c) 'And great statesman.' When the same article is to be used with two successive subjects, the first works for the next also.

10. (c) 'Vital questions' in place of 'vital question'.

Set 15

1. (b) 'English is' in place of 'English are'. See the Rules on the subject-verb accord.
2. (a) 'There is so much filth' in place of 'There are so many filths.' Filth is uncountable and thus 'much' should be used in place of 'many'.
3. (c) 'You and me' in place of 'you and I'.
4. (b) 'His seat' in place of 'their seat'. The pronoun for 'nobody' is singular, his or her. See Rule 9.
5. (c) 'Should' in place of 'may'. 'Lest' is followed by 'should'. See Rule 39.
6. (d) 'For being late' in place of 'to be late'.
7. (a) 'Sweet' in place of 'sweetly'. Sweetly is an adverb and an adjective should be used here.
8. (a) 'All his daughters' in place of 'His all daughters'. Here the error is in placement of words. See Rule 35.
9. (c) Here the words 'who are' create confusion. It is not clear whether the words are for the police or for the men who have been arrested. Such tags cause confusion and should be avoided.
10. (d) 'Than that of' in place of 'than your'. Here the comparison is between the price of the two cars. Thus 'that of' or 'the price of' should be used. See Rule 27.

Set 16

1. (d) 'In his letter', is inappropriate. This tag should come after 'he suggested'. It is an error of misplacement of words, causing confusion. See Rule 35.
2. (a) 'I am hard pressed' in place of 'hardly pressed'. See the usage of adverbs.
3. (a) 'As' in place of 'so'. 'Like' is preceded by 'as'.
4. (b) 'In moving' in place of 'to move'.
5. (a) 'Did the teacher not' in place of 'Did not the teacher'. Here the error is of misplacement of words. See Rule 35.
6. (a) 'No sooner did the bell ring' in place of 'no sooner the bell rang'. 'No sooner' is used in two forms in the past tense: (1) No sooner did; (2) No sooner had. See Rule 38.
7. (c) 'Do not' in place of 'does not'. The two subjects have been joined by 'and'. Thus the verb should be plural.
8. (c) 'Has been working' in place of 'worked'. The sentence is in the continuous tense. See Rule 51.
9. (b) 'Were going' in place of 'was going'. See the rules of the subject-verb accord.
10. (b) 'To see' is redundant. It should be deleted. 'Tested' and 'to see' both mean the same thing.

Set 17

1. (b) 'To agree' is redundant. 'To persuade' and 'to agree' mean the same thing.
2. (e) No error
3. (c) 'From' in place of 'that'. 'Different' takes 'from' after it.
4. (c) 'Was' in place of 'were'. See Rule 14.
5. (a) 'While' in place of 'when'.
6. (c) Here the pronoun should be 'them' as the meaning implied here is for the whole lot.
7. (a) 'He says that' in place of 'He says'.
8. (b) 'Has been running' in place of 'is running'. See Rule 51.
9. (a) 'You return' in place of 'you will return'. Future tense cannot be used twice in two different parts of a sentence. See Rule 49.
10. (a) 'Had he followed' in place of 'had he follow'. The correct past perfect form is 'followed'. See Rules of tense.

Set 18

1. (c) 'He admitted' in place of 'He admits'. The reporting verb is in the past tense and thus all other clauses of the sentence must be in the past tense. See Rule 46.
2. (c) 'To pay' or 'so that you may pay' in place of 'so that to pay'. It makes the structure faulty and clumsy.
3. (b) 'For having broken' in place of 'for having broke'. This is the correct form of verb. See the rules of tense.

4. (a) 'That' in place of 'which'. The correct word in such cases is 'that', not 'which'.

5. (a) 'He had hoped' in place of 'He hoped'. When there are two parts of a sentence and both are in the past form, one part will be in the past perfect form and the other in the past indefinite form. The part showing the first incident will be in the perfect form. See Rule 47.

6. (d) 'Did not' in place of 'doesn't'. As the reporting verb is in the past tense, other clauses have also to be in the past tense. See Rule 46.

7. (d) 'Has bothered' in place of 'have bothered'. The subject is the speech he made. It is singular and thus the verb will be 'has'.

8. (d) 'Sudden' in place of 'suddenly'. Here an adjective is required, not an adverb.

9. (c) 'Is Open' in place of 'was open'. The rule that future tense cannot appear twice in a sentence will be applicable. See Rule 49.

10. (c) 'Between' in place of 'among'. For two persons 'between' is used and for more than two persons 'among' is used.

Set 19

1. (c) 'Has told' in place of 'have told'. The verb will be in accordance with 'everyone'. See Rule 10.

2. (b) 'Is going' in place of 'are going'. In case of 'along with' the verb will be in accordance with the first subject. See Rule 30.

3. (b) 'He would not have been' in place of 'he would have been'. In an expression beginning with 'but for', the next part should contain a negative to make the meaning.

4. (c) 'If he had not heard the news' in place of 'if he would not have'. 'Would not have', cannot be used twice in the same sentence. If one part is 'would' the other part should be 'had'. See Rule 48.

5. (b) 'Went out' in place of 'went off'. For a living man, the correct expression is 'went out'. 'Went off' may be used in cases like 'The light went off'.

6. (c) 'From' in place of 'with'. See the Rules of preposition.

7. (e) No Error.

8. (b) 'Arrive' in place of 'arrived'. After 'no sooner did' the verb will be in the present tense. 'Did' is followed by the present form of verb: Did he 'go'? He did not 'come' on time.

9. (a) 'I have been working' in place of 'I have worked'. 'Six years' indicate that the work began in the past and has been continuing. Thus the perfect continuous tense is required.

10. (a) 'The' in place 'a'. Here as it is the case of the first European, it is a definite case and thus the definite article 'the' should be used. See Rule 54.

Set 20

1. (b) 'Is' in place of 'are'. 'All we could find' is singular and thus the verb will be singular.

2. (b) 'None of the rooms' here indicates a singular sense and thus the verb will be singular. Usually 'none' is used in singular.

3. (c) 'To' in place of 'than'. 'Prefer' takes 'to' after it. See Rule 25.

4. (b) 'Who, in place of 'whom'.

5. (c) 'Might' in place of 'may'. The reporting verb is appealed. It is in the past tense and thus all other clauses will be in the past tense. See Rule 46.

6. (a) 'It being a short vacation' in place of 'being a short vacation' There should be a subject here.

7. (c) A piece of useful advice

8. (c) 'Against' in place of 'from'. See the Rules of preposition.

9. (c) 'I would have' in place of 'I will have'. See Rule 48.

10. (a) 'Never have I' in place of 'Never I have'.

Additional Practice Sets

Direction for Questions 1- 40

Read each sentence to find out whether there is any grammatical error in it. The error, if any, will be in one part of the sentence. The alphabet of that part is the answer. If there is no error, the answer is (e) i.e. 'No error'. (Ignore the errors of punctuation, if any).

1. As they watched (a)/ the football match (b)/ the huge crowd (c)/ chant in unison (d). No error (e).

2. The noise was (a)/ so faintly that/ (b) one had to strain (c)/ one's ears to hear it (d). No error (e).

3. When he found out that (a)/ the girl had escaped (b)/ he was absolute (c)/ irritated and furious. (d). No error (e).

4. The weather is (a)/ much more warmer (b)/ than it was (c)/ a few days ago (d). No error (e).

5. A vast numbers (a)/ of people greeted (b)/ the film star on his arrival (c)/ at the airport (d). No error (e)

6. Time the concert ended, (a)/ the crowd clapped (b)/ and cheered/ enthusiastically (d). No error (e)

7. The students blamed (a)/ their professor for (b)/ their late arrival (c)/ in the concert. (d). No error (e)

8. We have many rooms (a)/ in our house, (b)/ several of which (c)/ have not been in use for years .No error (e)

9. When I heard (a)/ footsteps behind me (b)/ I was being scared (c)/ that I would be attacked (d).No error (e)

10. The Manager said that (a)/ he wanted to known (b)/ the pros and cons (c)/ of the issue. (d). No error (e)

11. We have recently began (a)/ the process of recruiting (b)/ insurance agents for (c)/ our North-Eastern branches. (d)/ No error (e)

12. Inspite that organisations are aware (a)/ of the importance of IT (b)/ they often do not know (c)/ how to deploy it effectively. (d)/ No error (e)

13. Although interlinking of rivers will (a)/ help tackle drought, the government (b)/ has not paid much (c)/ attention to this project. (d)/ No error (e)

14. Keeping in mind that India (a)/ is one of the world's fastest (b)/ growing economies many international (c)/ companies are invested in India. (d)/ No error (e)

15. Despite the merger, (a)/ the airline has reported (b)/ sizeable losses and is unable (c)/ to pay their employees. (d)/ No error (e)

16. The company's decision to issue (a)/ bonus shares clearly indicates (b)/ the management's confident (c)/ about the future. (d)/ No error (e)

17. RBI is in favour (a)/ of amending currently (b)/ policies governing operations of (c)/ foreign banks in India. (d)/ No error (e)

18. These recently upgraded branch offices (a)/ have been fully computerised (b)/ and are connected to headquarters (c)/ to ensure proper monitoring. (d)/ No error (e)

19. The rise in prices of food items is (a)/ likely the cause of inflation (b)/ to exceed eight percent (c)/ during the next quarter. (d)/ No error (e)

20. Many people believe that (a) the nationalisation of banks in (b) the 1960s have protected India (c)/ from the current financial crisis. (d)/ No error (e)

21. To begun with (a)/ three agencies were/ (b) retained to study/ (c) and submit recommendations. (d)/ No error (e)

22. To clamp down on illegal mining (a)/ that loses money for the exchequer,/ (b) local people need to empowered/ (c) to vet and oversee operations. (d)/ No error (e)

23. In real terms, it (a)/ means passing up on/ (b) opportunities that presents/ (c) themselves to us. (d)/ No error (e)

24. The failure to control (a)/ losses or increase revenues/ (b)in a market growing/ (c) in double digit is significantly. (d)/ No error (e)

25.. There have been (a)/ marked changes/ (b) but social rather/ (c) then economic. (d)/ No error (e)

26. Not withstand his (a)/ frequent indisposition,/ (b) he has diligently attended/ (c) every single court hearing. (d)/ No error (e)

27. The administration continued to (a)/ improve bilateral relations, (b)/ while deepening and/ (c) formalizing the economic dialogue. (d)/ No error (e)

28. The cause of rising crimes (a)/ against women has its roots/ (b) in the skewed sex ratio which/ (c) males outnumber females. (d)/ No error (e)

29. Now that more and more (a)/ internet sites are tailored/ (b) their services to the requirements of individual users,/ (3) queries may yield different outcomes for different people. (d)/ No error (e)

30. These are among (a)/ the many contentious points/ (b) that the author make/ (c) in his controversial book. (d)/ No error (e)

31. As they watched (a) the football match '(b)/ the huge crowd (c)/ chant in unison (d). No error (e).

32. The noise was (a)/ so faintly that (b)/ one 'had to strain (c)/ one's ears !o hear it (d). No error (e).

33. When, he found out that (a)/ the girl had escaped (b)/ he was absolute (c)/ irritated and furious. (d). No error (e).

34. My cousin's wedding provided (a)/ me with the chance (b)/ to meet with relatives (c)/ had not met for a long time (d) No error (e).

35. There are floods in this (a)/ region last year but (b)/ many of victims have (c)/ not yet been compensated (d). No error (e).

36. We must ensure that (a)/ all our records (b)/ are computrised (c) for next year (d) No error (e)

37. In order to impart (a)/ training to bank employees (b)/ we are seting up (c)/ centers of various locations. (d). No error (e)

38. When Rahul reached (a)/ the office there was so (b)/ he sat down to wait. (d)/ No error (e)

39. The completion (a)/ of the tunnel 2/ has been held (c)/ up owing to the strike (d). No error (e)

40. The Director (a)/ spoke clearly and distinctly (b)/ therefore the audience (c)/ Directions (d). No error (e)

Directions for Questions 41 to 60

Read each sentence to find out whether there isany grammatical error in it.The error, if any, will be in one part of the sentence. The alphabet of that part is the answer. If there is no error the answer is(d) i.e. No error. (Ignore the errors of punctuation, if any).

41. When I entered the bedroom, (a)/ I saw a snake crawling (b)/ on the ground, (c)/ No error (d)

42. He was debarred (a)/ to appear (b)/ at the examination, (c)/ No error (d)

43. It is not (a)/ I who is (b)/ to blame, (c)/ No error (d)

44. Shyam is telling (a)/ that I have (b)/ stolen his pen. (c)/ No error (d)

45. The timid creature was driven (a)/ into a narrow lane (b)/ where it was slewed by the kidnapper. (c)/ No error (d)

46. The river is in spate (a)/ and it has overflow (b)/ its banks, (c)/ No error (d)

47. It is a truth that (a)/ those who are jealous of others (b)/ never get peace in life. (c)/ No error (d)

48. I was having a holiday (a)/ by seaside last summer (b)/ when I ran into captain Robinson. (c)/ No error (d)

49. The driver showed (a)/ great talent in keeping (b)/ the damaged car under control. (c)/ No error (d)

50. He described about (a)/ the unpleasant experiences (b)/ he had in the jail. (c)/ No error (d)

51. The G.M. (a)/ of the company (b)/ dispensed the Manager's services. (c)/ No error (d)

52. If it were possible to get near when (a)/ one of the volcanic eruptions take place (b)/ we should see a grand sight. (c)/ No error (d)

53. Engines used in space shuttles (a)/ are much larger (b)/ and more strong than the ones used in jet planes. (c)/ No error (d)

54. Walking along (a)/ the bank of the river (b)/ the road begins to rise. (c)/ No error (d)

55. A rise in rents and wages (a)/ have been found (b)/ to go together. (c)/ No error (d)

56. Remember that a (a)/ stitch at a time (b)/ saves nine. (c)/ No error (d)

57. If I got rich (a)/ I would travel (b)/ around the world. (c)/ No error (d)

58. I shall avail (a)/ of this opportunity (b)/ to meet you there. (c)/ No error (d)

59. Tea grows (a)/ both in Assam (b)/ and Ceylon. (c)/ No error (d)

60. Of the two great cities (a)/ the former is (b)/ biggest. (c)/ No error (d)

Directions for Questions 61 to 70

Read each sentence to find out whether there isany grammatical error in it.The error, if any, will be in one part of the sentence. The alphabet of that part is the answer. If there is no error the answer is(d) i.e. No error. (Ignore the errors of punctuation, if any).

61. As you know(a)/ by my visiting card(b)/ I am now(c)/ in Mumbai(d)/ No error(e).
62. With a fresh coat(a)/ of paint(b)/ the school can(c)/ look much nice(d)/ No error(e)
63. I asked the salesman(a)/ If I could exchanged (b)/ the faulty camera (c)/ with another one(d)/ No error(e)
64. I took me(a)/ almost a hour(b)/ to fill the(c)/ application form(d)/ No error(e)
65. She insists(a)/ you stay(b)/ until her husband(c)/ comes home(d)/ No error(e)
66. I don't understand! (a)/ how she could(b)/ treat him(c)/ so bad(d)/ No error(e)
67. At any arrival! (a)/ in Delhi(b)/ I went straight(c)/ to the nearest hospital. (d)/ No error(e)
68. It is more better (a)/ if one of the parents(b)/ stays at home(c)/ to look after the children(d)/ No error (e)
69. These reports have (a)/ deterred some(b)/ women to have(c)/ the operation(d)/ No error(e)
70. I answered (a)/ the questions (b)/ as best as (c)/ I could(d)/ No error/ (e)

Directions for Questions 71 to 90

Read each sentence to find out whether there isany grammatical error in it.The error, if any, will be in one part of the sentence. The alphabet of that part is the answer. If there is no error the answer is(d) i.e. No error. (Ignore the errors of punctuation, if any).

71. We had a lot of difficulty (a)/ to find (b)/ the house.(c)/ No error. (d).
72. Patience as well as perseverance (a)/ are necessary (b)/ for success. (c)/ No error/ (d).
73. The passer-by told us (a)/ where was the marriage hall (b)/ and even led us to it. (c)/ No error (d).
74. The increase in consumption is directly (a)/ proportional to the increase (b)/ in income. (c)/ No error. (d).
75. In Singapore (a)/ my brother-in- law with his wife (b)/ were present at the function. (c)/ No error. (d).
76. Scarcely had (a)/ I arrived than (b)/ the train left. (c)/ No error. (d).
77. The reason why (a)/ he was rejected (b)/ was because he was too young. (c)/ No error. (d).
78. Teachers of various schools (a)/ met to discuss about (b)/ how to improve the standard of English.(c)/ No error. (d).
79. His tradition-bound attitude (a)/ had to be a constant source of dissatisfaction (b)/ among the younger members of the family.(c)/ No error. (d).
80. The two first to arrive (a)/ were the lucky recipients (b)/ of a surprise gift. (c)/ No error (d)
81. He thinks that he (a)/ knows his subject well (b)/ and can taught this to others also. (c)/ No error (d)
82. Sita and her children feels (a)/ that they have been (b)/ given a raw deal by the society in general. (c)/ No error (d)
83. Either he nor his brother (a)/ was informed about (b)/ the venue of the meeting of our society. (c)/ No error (d)
84. Enough is enough (a)/ I cannot now (b)/ tolerate this working any much. (c)/ No Error (d)
85. Given a choice (a)/ I will prefer working (b)/ in field to working in office. (c)/ No error (d)
86. Inspite trying (a)/ our best we could not (b)/ reach an agreement on any of the issues. (c)/ No error (d)
87. What was his response (a)/ when you tried (b)/ to got some information from him? (c)/ No error (d)
88. Ever since (a)/ I joined (b)/ he has not been attend office. (c)/ No error (d)

89. This time election (a)/ did not had (b)/ heat and dust usually associated with it. (c)/ No error (d)

90. I along with my family (a)/ were planning to (b)/ go for a picnic on this weekend. (c)/ No error (d)

Directions for Questions 91 to 100

Read each sentence to find out whether there isany grammatical error in it.The error, if any, will be in one part of the sentence. The alphabet of that part is the answer. If there is no error the answer is(d) i.e. No error. (Ignore the errors of punctuation, if any).

91. The martyrdom (a)/ about Sardar Bhagat (b)/ Singh created (c)/ a stir. (d)/ No error (e)

92. He is well (a)/ known in Hindi, (b)/ Urdu and (c)/ Arabic languages. (d)/ No error (e)

93. Ruskin had postulated (a)/ the concept of social affection (b)/ as the founding principle (c)/ of a humanity economy. (d) No error (e)

94. His only motive (a)/ was to finding (b)/ the truth and (c)/ follow it. (d)/ No error (e)

95. On the surfacing (a)/ she presented herself (b)/ as someone in supreme (c)/ control of her life. (d)/ No error (e)

96. Motivating the youth of (a)/ the nation is (b)/ the central theme (c)/ of the book.(d)/ No error (e)

97. He have faced (a)/ failures and (b)/ disappointments without(c)/ feeling defeated. (d)/ No error (e)

98. Since time immemorial (a)/ , India's spiritual (b)/ wisdom has being (c)/ its strength. (d)/ No error (e)

99. Courage is an (a)/ inner fortress which (b)/ no enemy can (c)/ ever destruction. (d)/ No error (e)

100. Boldness has (a)/ genius, power and (b)/ magic in it along (c)/ with infinite possibilities. (d)/ No error (e)

ANSWER KEY

1. (d)	2. (b)	3. (c)	4. (b)	5. (a)
6. (a)	7. (c)	8. (e)	9. (c)	10. (b)
11. (a)	12. (a)	13. (e)	14. (d)	15. (d)
16. (c)	17. (e)	18. (c)	19. (c)	20. (c)
21. (a)	22. (c)	23. (c)	24. (d)	25. (d)
26. (a)	27. (a)	28. (c)	29. (c)	30. (c)
31. (c)	32. (b)	33. (c)	34. (c)	35. (a)
36. (d)	37. (d)	38. (e)	39. (a)	40. (a)
41. (c)	42. (b)	43. (b)	44. (a)	45. (c)
46. (b)	47. (b)	48. (c)	49. (a)	50. (a)
51. (c)	52. (c)	53. (c)	54. (d)	55. (b)
56. (b)	57. (a)	58. (a)	59. (a)	60. (c)
61. (b)	62. (d)	63. (b)	64. (a)	65. (a)
66. (d)	67. (a)	68. (a)	69. (c)	70. (c)
71. (b)	72. (b)	73. (b)	74. (d)	75. (c)
76. (b)	77. (c)	78. (b)	79. (b)	80. (a)
81. (c)	82. (a)	83. (a)	84. (c)	85. (d)
86. (a)	87. (c)	88. (c)	89. (b)	90. (b)
91. (a)	92. (b)	93. (d)	94. (b)	95. (a)
96. (e)	97. (a)	98. (c)	99. (d)	100. (b)

CHAPTER 5

SPOTTING ERRORS VARIATION PATTERN-I

In recent years some variations have been made in the format of the questions on spotting errors. Candidates must remain calm when there is a deviation from the previous pattern. A thorough understanding of the rules of grammar and an alert application of these rules will help them solve these questions irrespective of their format. Let us solve some questions.

Illustrations

State Bank P. O. Examination November, 1995.

Directions: In each of the following questions, five sentences are given which are on the same theme. Decide which sentence is the preferable one with respect to grammar and usage suitable for formal writing in English and mark the number of that sentence on the answersheet.

Set 1

1. If you would have told me that you were in Bombay I would have certainly contacted you instead of getting bored there.
2. If you would have told me that you were in Bombay I had certainly contacted you to instead of getting bored there.
3. If you had told me that you were in Bombay I would have certainly contacted you instead of getting bored there.
4. If you had told me that you were in Bombay I would have certainly contacted you despite getting bored there.
5. If you had told me that you were in Bombay I had certainly contacted by you instead of getting bored there.

Set 2

1. The receptionist must answer courteously the questions of all them callers.
2. The receptionist must answer courteously the question what are asked by the callers.
3. There would have been no trouble if the receptionist have always answered courteously.
4. The receptionist courteously should answer the questions of all callers.
5. The receptionist should answer courteously the questions of all callers.

Set 3

1. The supervisors reprimanded the typist whom he believed had made careless errors.
2. The typists would have corrected the errors had they of known that the supervisors would see the report.
3. Many errors were found in the report which they typed and could not disregarded them.
4. The errors in the typed reports were so numerous that they could hardly be overlooked.
5. The typist had corrected the errors had they known that the supervisors would have seen the reports.

Set 4

1. Since the report lacked needed information it was of no use to them.
2. The report was useless to them because there were no needed information in it.
3. Since the report did not contain the needed information, it was not real useful to them.
4. Being that the report lacked the needed information, they could not use it.
5. Since the report lacked needed information it would have not been useful to them.

Set 5

1. The company had hardly declared the dividend till the notices were prepared for mailing.
2. No sooner had the dividend been declared than the notices were prepared for mailing.
3. They had no sooner declared the dividend when they sent the notices to the stockholders.
4. Scarcely had the dividend been declared than the notices were sent out.
5. Since the dividend being declared than the notices were prepared for mailing.

Let us apply our rules.

ANSWERS AND EXPLANATION

1. (1) There is error in *if you would have*. It should be *had you*. See Rule 48. (2) There are errors in both first and second clauses. (3) It is correct according to Rule 48 and the meaning is also clear. (4) The structure is correct but the use of *despite* disturbs the meaning of the sentence. (5) There is error in the second clause. Thus the answer is 3.
2. (1) *Them* is wrong (error of pronoun). (2) *What* is wrong (error of conjunction). (3) *Have* is wrong (error of verb form). (4) *Courteously* should is wrong (error of adverb). (5) It has no error and thus this is the answer.
3. (1) *Whom* is wrong (error of pronoun). (2) *they of known* is wrong (error of preposition). (3) *Could not disregarded* is wrong (error of verb form). (4) No error. (5) There are errors in both clauses. Thus the answer is 4.
4. (1) No error. (2) *Were* is wrong (error of verb). (3) *Real* is wrong (error of adverb). (4) There is error in the first clause. (5) There is error in the second clause. Thus the answer is 1.
5. (1) The first clause is wrong. (2) No error. (3) *When* is wrong (than should be used). (4) *Than* is wrong (when should be sued). (5) The first clause is wrong. Thus the correct answer is 2.

Practice Set

Directions: In each of the following questions, five sentences are given which are on the same theme. Decide which sentence is the preferable one with respect to grammar and usage suitable for formal writing in English and mark the number of that sentence on the answersheet.

1. (a) Being worked for the whole day, you should have taken some rest and started the work tomorrow.
   (b) Working for the whole day, you should have taken some rest and started the work tomorrow.
   (c) After being worked for the whole day, you should have taken some rest and started the work tomorrow.
   (d) Having worked for the whole day, you should have taken some rest and started the work tomorrow.
   (e) After having work the whole day, you should have taken some rest and started the work tomorrow.
2. (a) Have you not reached in time, we would have lost our lives.

(b) If you have not reached in time, we would have lost our lives.

(c) Had you not reach in time, we would have lost our lives.

(d) Had you not reach in time, we would have lost our lives.

(e) If you would not have reached in time, we would have lost our lives.

3. (a) The various practices and norms for bank's transactions are laid down by the Reserve Bank of India.

(b) The various practices and norms for banks' transactions are led down by the Reserve Bank of India.

(c) The various practices and norms for banks' transactions have been lay down by the Reserve Bank of India.

(d) The various practices and norms for banks' transactions are lead up by the Reserve Bank of India.

(e) The various practices and norms for banks' transactions are laid up by the Reserve Bank of India.

4. (a) Your statement that you were through ignorant of the consequences cannot be trusted.

(b) Your statement that you were thorough ignorant of the consequences cannot be trusted.

(c) Your statement that you were thoroughly ignorant of the consequences cannot be trusted.

(d) Your statement that you were thorough of ignorance of the consequences cannot be trusted.

(e) Your statement that you were thoroughly in ignorance of the consequences cannot be trusted.

5. (a) He was extremely unhappy because of inordinately delay.

(b) He was extremely unhappy because of the inordinate delay.

(c) He was extremely unhappy because of the inordinately delay.

(d) He was extremely unhappy because of the inordinately delaying.

(e) He was extremely unhappy because of the inordinate delaying.

6. (a) I am remembering you telling me that you are having two cars.

(b) I do remember your telling me that you have two cars.

(c) I do remember your telling me that you were having two cars.

(d) I am remembering your telling me that you are having two cars.

(e) I remember your telling me that you are having two cars.

7. (a) A community is like a ship, everyone should be prepared to take the helm.

(b) A community is like a ship, as everyone should be prepared to take the helm.

(c) A community is like a ship, since everyone should be prepared to take the helm.

(d) A community is like a ship, so everyone should be prepared to take the helm.

(e) A community is like a ship, hence everyone should be prepared to take the helm.

8. (a) My wife and I do not worry about AIDS since we practise monogamy.

(b) My wife and I do not worry about AIDS even if we practise monogamy.

(c) My wife and I do not worry about AIDS as we practise monogamy.

(d) My wife and I do not worry about AIDS though we practise monogamy.

(e) My wife and I do not worry about AIDS even though we practise monogamy.

9. (a) Such thing does not happen to you and I, isn't it?

(b) Such a thing does not happen to you and me, isn't it?

(c) Such things do not happen to you and me, don't they?

(d) Such things do not happen to you and I, do they?

(e) Such things do not happen to you and me, do they?

10. (a) Had I been older and wiser, I would have not acted on your advise and made a fool of me.

(b) Had I been older and wiser, I wouldn't act on your advice and made a fool of me.

(c) Had I been older and wiser, I would not have acted on your advice and made a fool of me.

(d) Had I been older and wiser, I would not have acted on your advice and made a fool of myself.

(e) Had I been older and wiser, I would have not acted on your advice and make a fool of myself.

11. (a) The more they earn, more they spend.

(b) More they earn, more they spend.

(c) More they earn, the more they spend.

(d) The more they earn, the more they spend.

12. (a) The old man felled some trees in the garden with hardly no effort at all.

(b) The old man felled some trees in the garden with hard effort at all.

(c) The old man felled some trees in the garden with hardly any effort at all.

(d) The old man felled some trees in the garden with a hardly any effort at all.

13. (a) She says she's already paid me back, but I can't 'remember, so I'll have to take her word.

(b) She says she's already paid me back, but I can't remember, so I'll have to take her word true.

(c) She says she's already paid me back, but I can't remember, so I'll have to take her at her word.

(d) She says she's already paid me back, but I can't remember, so I'll have to take her word for it.

14. (a) The workers are hell bent at getting what is due to them.

(b) The workers are hell bent on getting what is due to them.

(c) The workers are hell bent for getting what is due to them.

(d) The workers are hell bent upon getting what is due to them.

15. (a) While we would like that all Indian children to go to school, we need to ponder why they do not.

(b) While we would like that all the Indian children to go to school, we need to ponder why they do not.

(c) While we would like if all the Indian children of India to go to school, we need to ponder why they do not.

(d) While we would like all Indian children to go to school, We need to ponder why they do not.

ANSWER KEY

1. (d)	6. (b)	11. (d)
2. (d)	7. (d)	12. (c)
3. (a)	8. (a)	13. (d)
4. (c)	9. (e)	14. (d)
5. (b)	10. (d)	15. (d)

CHAPTER 6

SPOTTING ERRORS VARIATION PATTERN-II

In this format four parts of each sentence are given as A, B, C, D. These are in a sequence. One has to point out which part is not acceptable in standard English. In other words we can say that it is spotting error in vertical form.

EXAMPLE

(a) We are three
(b) But you have ordered
(c) Only for
(d) Two drinks

The answer is (c) because the word *for* is wrong. No preposition is used after *order.*

Practice Set

1. (a) many a man
(b) have realised that real happiness
(c) lies in making sacrifices
(d) and not in personal gains.

2. (a) honestly speaking
(b) I like him not because
(c) he is handsome but that
(d) he is kind.

3. (a) the teacher
(b) emphasised on
(c) the point
(d) again and again.

4. (a) the students
(b) will be giving
(c) their final
(d) examination shortly.

5. (a) you arrived
(b) here this morning.
(c) didn't you?
(d) where are you living?

6. (a) He accepted
(b) all the things
(c) which providence gave him
(d) with thankful good humour.

7. (a) Nothing has
(b) or could be
(c) more unfortunate
(d) than his departure.

8. (a) They were quarrelling between themelves
(b) when all of a sudden it
(c) occurred to them that someone was watching
(d) all the five of them.

9. (a) when at last we got to
(b) the theatre, the much
(c) publicised play
(d) was already begun.

10. (a) one of the biggest
(b) industrial houses
(c) in Maharashtra
(d) are declaring a lock out.

ANSWER KEY

1. (b)
2. (c)
3. (b)
4. (a)
5. (d)
6. (b)
7. (a)
8. (a)
9. (d)
10. (d)

CHAPTER 7

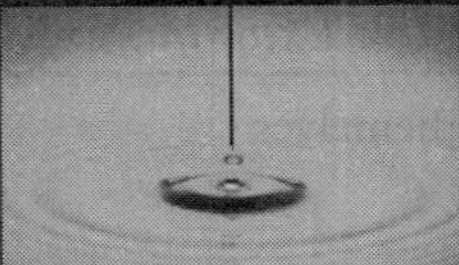

SPOTTING ERRORS VARIATION PATTERN-III

In this format sentences with one or more errors are given. One has to locate the number of errors and mark one of the following alternatives.

(a) only one mistake;
(b) only two mistakes;
(c) only three mistakes;
(d) only four mistakes;
(e) more than four mistakes;

EXAMPLES

1. The visitors complained at the poor accommodation they were given.
   The answer is (a) because there is only one error—at. The correct preposition will be about.
2. One of the biggest industrial house in Maharashtra are declaring a lockout.
   The answer is (b) because there are two errors—(1) house should be *houses*, (2) *are* should be *is*.
3. Work hard in English lest you may not fail in this subject.
   The answer is (c) because there are three errors—(1) *In* should be *at*, (2) *may* should be *should*, (3) *not* should be deleted.

Practice Set

1. He not only helped me but my brother when he was in trouble.
2. Every man, woman and child in this country are aware that smoking is injurious to health.
3. He had hardly leave the room than it begun to rain.
4. Mary is more smarter to anybody in her class.
5. John's salary is very larger than Bobby.
6. The old man no longer believe that money was the most important thing in life.
7. Nights after nights he used to pore over his books with patient determination of a scholar.
8. Ram is better than all boys of his class.
9. Many Indian states have hardly no dearth of talent.
10. He resigned from the directorship and took up teaching with a view ultimately to become a consultant.

ANSWER KEY

1. (b)
2. (c)
3. (b)
4. (c)
5. (a)
6. (a)
7. (c)
8. (a)
9. (a)
10. (b)

CHAPTER 8

Spotting Errors Variation Pattern-IV

In this format four sentences are given. Three of the four sentences contain some type of grammatical error. One has to spot the correct sentence.

EXAMPLE

1. The answer is given line fifteen on page four.
2. She has so much problems that she could not concentrate.
3. He had such bad a headache that he could not sleep well at all.
4. Gopa is very sick to come to school everyday.

In sentence no. 2 *much* should be *many*, in sentence no. 3 *that* should be *as* and in sentence no. 4 *very* should be *too*. Only sentence no. 1 has no error.

Practice Set —1

1. (a) John, as well as his brothers, are coming today.
(b) Is the old always more wiser than the young?
(c) More than two boys were present in the class.
(d) The wages of sin are death.

2. (a) This book does not have their cover.
(b) He gave me many wrong informations.
(c) He is one of the bright students of the class.
(d) Did you apply for lecturership?

3. (a) I am not at all satisfied by my new apartment.
(b) He never says a lie.
(c) I am looking forward to see you once again.
(d) I cannot agree to write the letter for you.

4. (a) As an artist he is as good if not better than Ramesh.
(b) Mohan does not know to swim.
(c) He is blind with one eye.
(d) One of the rooms has been closed for a week.

5. (a) It is time you decide about your next course of action.
(b) What I did say was that just as meteorologists have classified clouds, so they have classified winds.
(c) Whatever the solution to the problems may be we should consider them carefully before we decide to take any action.
(d) No one can help admiring a person who does not complain about their problems.

6. (a) Ram disappointed his mother in that he didn't write to her very often.
(b) In a hour's time when I had finished the work I got up and slipped out unnoticed.

(c) I walked on as fastly as I could until I reached the road which led to my house.

(d) I am surprised at not having saw her even though she was standing in front of me.

7. (a) Our life may be compared to a flower.

(b) We left the place with bag and baggage.

(c) The reason of his absence is due to his illness.

(d) He bought a fresh basket of fruits.

8. (a) I have some milk but I do not have some sugar.

(b) The teacher asked him to explain why had he been absent for such a long time.

(c) One of our most serious problems are the growing menace of terrorism.

(d) My brother has been ill for a long time.

9. (a) It has been reported by the chairman of the committee that all possible efforts have made to reach the target.

(b) You are required to explain your conduct within two days of the receipt of this letter.

(c) This room would be much improved if you have put a furniture in the corner near the window.

(d) I remember to having read somewhere that the first satellite was launched by Russians.

10. (a) The Major along with his soldiers were killed in the battlefield today.

(b) The movie began when we arrived.

(c) The economical condition of the country is very bad.

(d) In my opinion respect is preferable to money.

ANSWER KEY

1. (c)
2. (c)
3. (d)
4. (d)
5. (c)
6. (a)
7. (a)
8. (d)
9. (b)
10. (d)

Appendix

SPOTTING ERROSS: QUESTIONS FROM VARIOUS COMPETITIVE EXAMINATIONS WITH FREQUENCY ANALYSIS

Set I

1. (a) Now that she is living in her own flat, /(b) she cleans the windows, /(c) twice a week in the summer and once a week in the winter. /(d) No error *(CDS)*
2. (a) This town isn't very well know (b)/and there isn't much to see, /(c) so a few tourists come here /(d) No error *(MBA)*
3. (a) The reason we have not been able to pay income tax /(b) is due to fact /(c) that we did not receive pay one time. /(d) No error *(SSC)*
4. (a) All the furniture have been /(b) sent to the new house /(c) located in a village /(d)No error *(Section Officers' Exam)*
5. (a) My brother-in-laws /(b) who live in Bombay /(c) have come to stay with us. /(d) No error *(NDA)*
6. (a) He could not plan his strategy /(b) until he knew /(c) whom his opponents could be. /(d) No error *(Railways)*
7. (a) The downfall of this kind /(b) is to be attributed to /(c) nothing else than pride. (d) No error *(CBI)*
8. (a) Neither the famine /(b) or the subsequent fire /(c) was able to destroy the spirit of the people. /(d) No error *(Stenographers)*
9. (a) The child /(b) picked up a burned paper /(c) from the street. /(d) No error *(Section Officers' Exam)*
10. (a) One of the drawbacks /(b) of modern education are /(c) that it does not encourage original thinking /(d) No error *(Stenographers' Exam)*
11. (a) If I knew /(b) that my friend had planned to visit the town today, /(c) I would have made his stay comfortable. /(d) No error *(SCRA)*
12. (a) Sharad was entrusted with /(b) the task of coordinating yesterday's programme, /(c) but due to certain difficulties /(d) he does not do it. /(e) No error *(Bank PO)*
13. (a) How long /(b) were you /(c) learning English for? /(d) No error *(Central Excise)*
14. (a) Coffee seeds /(b) is dried and roasted /(c) before they are ground into powder. /(d) No error *(Income Tax)*
15. (a) The technician reminded /(b) them to have a /(c) thoroughly cleaning of the /(d) machine after each use. /(e) No error *(Bank, PO)*
16. (a) If I were /(b) in his shoes /(c) I would die with shame. /(d) No error *(CBI)*
17. (a) Even many people /(b) carry an infection /(c) without showing its symptoms. /(d) No error *(SSC)*

Set 2

1. (a) My Father is /(b) in bad mood /(c) today. /(d) No error *(Stenographer's Exam.)*
2. (a) The majority of the /(b) computer professionals recommends /(c) that effective measures /(d) should be taken against software piracy. /(e) No error *(Bank, PO)*
3. (a) A person I met /(b) in the theatre /(c) was the playwright himself. /(d) No error *(UDC)*
4. (a) As he had taken only a few sips /(b) there was still little water /(c) left in the glass. /(d) No error *(Central Excise, 1994)*
5. (a) To perform this experiment, /(b) drop little sugar /(c) into a glass of water. /(d) No error *(SSC)*
6. (a) The recent study has /(b) indicated that there /(c) is perceptible change in /(d) the attitudes of the people. /(e) No error *(Bank PO)*
7. (a) The bus could not /(b) ascend the steep hill /(c) because it was in the wrong gears. /(d) No error *(IES, 1994)*

8. (a) Had I come /(b) to know about /(c) his difficulties /(d) I would have certainly helped. /(e) No error *(Bank PO)*
9. (a) Our laxity in duty /(b) increases with our /(c) aversion for work. /(d) No error *(Income Tax)*
10. (a) The trust plans /(b) to set on /(c) a special school for /(d) dumb and deaf children. /(e) No error *(BSRB, 1994)*
11. (a) We never buy any jam in the shops, /(b) because my wife makes all our jam from the fruit in our garden /(c) and it tastes much better than the jam from the shops, we think /(d) No error *(CDS)*
12. (a) He won't return the money /(b) that he borrowed, /(c) will he? /(d) No error *(Income Tax)*
13. (a) The statement made by the writer /(b) appears to be incorrect /(c) as Gandhijee was never born in Ahmedabad. /(d) No error *(NDA)*
14. (a) I can't /(b) afford to pay /(c) that much for it. /(d) No error *(UDC)*
15. (a) He makes it clear in the very first novel /(b) of this period that /(c) he sees his life and work on dramatic terms. /(d) No error *(NDA)*
16. (a) Even though the shirt is rather expensive /(b) but I wish to /(c) purchase it with my own money. /(d) No error *(IES)*
17. (a) While going /(b) through the report /(c) yesterday I find /(d) several factual mistakes. /(e) No error *(SS)*

Set 3

1. (a) The road /(b) to famous monument /(c) passes through a forest. /(d) No error *(Stenographer's Exam.)*
2. (a) According to the Bible /(b) it is meek and humble /(c) who shall inherit the earth. /(d) No error *(CBI)*
3. (a) Troy was taken by Greeks /(b) this formed the basis of a story /(c) which has become famous. /(d) No error *(Central Excise)*
4. (a) He was fascinated by insects /(b) and the more he studied their habits /(c) greater was his fascination. /(d) No error *(Clerks' Grade)*
5. (a) The polling was marred /(b) at many a place /(c) by attempts at rigging. /(d) No error *(CBI)*
6. (a) Mr. Sunil Pawar, our representative, /(b) he will attend the meeting /(c) on our behalf. /(d) No error *(NDA)*
7. (a) If the teacher is good /(b) the students /(c) will respond /(d) positively to them. /(e) No error *(BSRB)*
8. (a) Whatever work /(b) that which you undertake /(c) put your best efforts /(d) in it. (e)/No error *(BSRB, 1995)*
9. (a) It is the duty of every right thinking citizen /(b) to try to make the whole world /(c) a happier place to live. /(d) No error *(Asstt. Grade)*
10. (a) After opening the door /(b) we entered into the room /(c) next to the kitchen. /(d) No error *(CDS)*
11. (a) They walked /(b) besides each other /(c)in silence. /(d) No error *(Asstt. Grade)*
12. (a) The students were /(b) awaiting for /(c) the arrival of the chief guest. /(d) No error *(CDS)*
13. (a) He fixed a metal ladder /(b) for the wall below his window /(c) so as to be able to /(d) escape if there was a fire. /(e) No error *(Bank PO)*
14. (a) I offered him part-time work /(b) but he turned it over /(c) saying that he would /(d) rather wait for a full-time job. /(e) No error *(Bank PO)*
15. (a) The Hindi and the Marathi are /(b) different forms of the Sanskrit language, /(c) which were once spoken /(d) in almost every part of India. /(e) No error *(Bank PO)*
16. (a) After toiling very hardly /(b) over a long period of time /(c) he found that people rewgnised him as a successful person. /(d) No error *(MBA)*
17. (a) He speaks /(b) not only Tamil /(c) but Telugu as well. /(d) No error *(Central Excise)*

Set 4

1. (a) I have been travelling by local trains /(b)since last several years /(c) but had never

experienced /(d) such a horrible situation as this. /(e) No error *(Bank PO Exam)*

2. (a) If I would have realised /(b) what a bad shape our library is in /(c) I would have done something /(d) to arrest the deterioration. /(e) No error *(Bank PO Exam)*

3. (a) May I /(b) know who you want /(c) to see please. /(d) No error *(Hotel Management)*

4. (a) It is not difficult to believe that a man /(b) who has lived in this city for a long time /(c) he will never feel at home anywhere else in the world. /(d) No error *(NDA)*

5. (a) The party chief made it a point to state that /(b) the Prime Minister and the Union Home Minister should also come /(c) and they see what his partymen had seen. /(d) No error *(Asstt. Grade)*

6. (a) Myself and Gopalan /(b) will take care of /(c) the function on Sunday. /(d) No error *(Hotel Management)*

7. (a) On a holiday /(b) Madhu prefers reading /(c) than going out visiting friends /(d) No error *(Hotel Management)*

8. (a) A large scale exchange of nuclear weapons /(b) will produce unprecedented amo-unts of radiation /(c) that can penetrate into the biological tissue. /(d) No error *(Asstt. Grade)*

9. (a) Considering about these facts /(b) the principal has offered /(c) him a seat. /(d) No error *(NDA)*

10. (a) The student /(b) answered to /(c) the question /(d) asked by the inspector of school. /(e) No error *(Railways, 1996)*

11. (a) All the boys /(b) returned back home /(c) well in time for lunch. /(d) No error *(NDA)*

12. (a) A group of friends /(b) want to visit /(c) the new plant as early as possible. /(d) No error *(Hotel Management)*

13. (a) One of the members /(b) expressed doubt if /(c) the Minister was an atheist. /(d) No error *(Asstt. Grade)*

14. (a) The reason why /(b) he was rejected /(c) was because he was too young. /(d) No error *(Asstt. Grade)*

15. (a) Although we reached his house on time /(b) he was left /(c) for the airport. /(d) No error *(NDA)*

16. (a) He has seen /(b) the picture /(c) yesterday. /(d) No error *(Railways)*

17. (a) If a thing /(b) is worth doing at all /(c) it is worth done well. /(d) No error *(NDA)*

Set 5

1. (a) Our system of assigning /(b) different jobs to different people /(c) should be based on /(d) their strengths and weaknesses. /(e) No error *(Bank PO, Mumbai)*

2. (a) Reasonable ambition, if supported /(b) at president efforts, /(c) is likely to yield /(d) the desired results. /(e) No error *(Bank PO, Mumbai)*

3. (a) This is an important difference in /(b) that it marks the first move towards /(c) profess-ionalising the sport and turning it into /(d) an institution money-earning proposition. /(e) No error *(MBA)*

4. (a) All three products help wean smokers /(b) from cigarettes by providing small doses /(c) of nicotine designed to replace the basic level /(d) of average smoker's day's nicotine con-sumption *(MBA)*

5. (a) The ultimate problem of physics /(b) is to reduce matter by analysis /(c) to its lowest condition of divisibility. /(d) No error *(CDS)*

6. (a) As a nation we neither impress the belligerent /(b) or inspire the lovers of peace, /(c) the speaker added. /(d) No error *(CDS)*

7. (a) If the by-stander had not been /(b) familiar with first-aid techniques, /(c) the driver which had met /(d) with the accident would have died. /(e) No error *(Bank PO, Hyderabad)*

8. (a) By arresting the local criminals /(b) and encouraging good people, /(c) we can end /(d) hostilities of the area /(e) No error *(Bank PO, Hyderabad)*

9. (a) We admired the way /(b) he had completed all his work /(c) and appreciating the method /(d) adopted by him. /(e) No error *(Bank PO, Mumbai)*

10. (a) Not only judges acquitted / (b) him of all the charges / (c) levelled against him, but / (d) also commended all his actions. / (e) No error *(Bank PO, Mumbai)*

11. (a) We do not know where he was educated / (b) or what did he do to earn his bread at that time / (c) because history is silent about his early life. / (d) No error *(NDA)*

12. (a) Under the present circumstances, / (b) sanctioning another post for the organisation / (c) is out of question. / (d) No error *(NDA)*

13. (a) If you permit me to speak the truth, / (b) I shall say without hesitation / (c) that you have done a mistake. / (d) No error *(CDS)*

14. (a) By the time / (b) she finished typing / (c) it was not hardly ten / (d) No error *(CDS)*

15. (a) A picture of / (b) one of the progenitors / (c) of the founder / (d) of the company hanged / (e) on the wall. / (f) No error *(MBA)*

16. (a) Lost in thought, / (b) with a vacant look / (c) in his eyes, / (d) he laid / (e) on the couch. / (f) No error *(MBA)*

17. (a) In spite of toiling / (b) very hardly he / (c) realised that he had / (d) not earned anything substantial. / (e) No error *(BSRB, Patna)*

18. (a) We have observed that / (b) many good programmers / (c) suffer of shortage / (d) of funds and other resources. / (e) No error *(BSRB, Patna)*

19. (a) The principal indicated that / (b) the issue of improved quality of teaching / (c) in the college were high / (d) in his list of priorities. / (e) No error *(BSRB, Calcutta)*

20. (a) Unless you take / (b) interest into the studies / (c) you will not succeed / (d) in the examination / (e) No error *(BSRB, Calcutta)*

ANSWER KEY

Set 1		Set 2		Set 3		Set 4		Set 5	
1. (c)	11. (d)	1. (b)	11. (a)	1. (b)	11. (b)	1. (b)	11. (b)	1. (d)	11. (b)
2. (a)	12. (d)	2. (b)	12. (c)	2. (b)	12. (b)	2. (a)	12. (b)	2. (b)	12. (b)
3. (b)	13. (b)	3. (a)	13. (c)	3. (a)	13. (b)	3. (b)	13. (b)	3. (d)	13. (c)
4. (a)	14. (b)	4. (b)	14. (d)	4. (c)	14. (b)	4. (c)	14. (c)	4. (d)	14. (c)
5. (a)	15. (c)	5. (b)	15. (a)	5. (d)	15. (a)	5. (c)	15. (b)	5. (b)	15. (d)
6. (c)	16. (c)	6. (c)	16. (b)	6. (b)	16. (a)	6. (a)	16. (a)	6. (b)	16. (d)
7. (c)	17. (a)	7. (c)	17. (c)	7. (d)	17. (c)	7. (c)	17. (c)	7. (c)	17. (b)
8. (b)		8. (e)		8. (b)		8. (c)		8. (d)	18. (c)
9. (b)		9. (c)		9. (c)		9. (a)		9. (c)	19. (c)
10. (b)		10. (b)		10. (b)		10. (b)		10. (a)	20. (b)

Table Spotting Error: Frequency Analysis

Items	*1993* No. of exams covered 11 No. of questions = 17	*1994* No. of exams covered 11 No. of questions = 17	*1995* No. of exams covered 11 No. of questions = 17	*1996* No. of exams covered 9 No. of questions = 17	*1997* No. of exams covered 7 No. of questions = 17	Total
Verb and Tense form	8	5	1	8	6	28
Article	1	3	4	—	—	8
Noun	2	1	1	—	—	4
Pronoun	1	—	3	4	1	9
Adjective/Adverb Degree	1	3	3	—	2	9
Conjunction	2	1	1	—	2	6
Preposition	—	2	3	3	4	12
Wrong word	1	—	1	1	2	5
Repetition	1	—	—	1	—	2
No error	—	2	—	—	—	2

Observation: Highest frequency — Verb and tense form
Next — Preposition
Next — Pronoun
Next — Adjective/Adverb degree

Table Trends in Spotting Error Questions (2001–2004)

Examinations	*Items*									
Examinations	*Noun*	*Pronoun*	*Adjective*	*Connector*	*Article*	*Preposition*	*Idioms*	*Miscellaneous wrong word misplaced 1*	*No error*	*Verb tense related 4*
Indian Overseas Bank PO Exam 2004										
PG Dip Fashion 04				1				1		3
INGOU Openmat 04		1		4		2				4
PO Canara Bank 03			1			1			2	2
Corporation Bank 03						1	2		1	2
Bank of Maharashtra 03		1						1	2	1
GIC AAO 03			1		1		1		1	3
Mat 03		1								2
CDS 03		3	1	2	1				2	6
PNB 02				1		1	1	1		1
NABARD 02			1			1			1	2

Examinations	Items									
Examinations	*Noun*	*Pronoun*	*Adjective*	*Connector*	*Article*	*Preposition*	*Idioms*	*Miscellaneous wrong word misplaced 1*	*No error*	*Verb tense related 4*
Corporation Bank 02				1				1		3
LIC 02	1	1	1							
Hotel M 02			1			7	1		1	
APF Com 02		1		2		1			1	
Info Tech 02				1	1	1	3	1		3
NDA 02				2	1	1		1	2	
SCRA 02	1		1					1	1	6
Indian Engineer 01	1		1					1	2	5
SSC Com 01				1		1		1		2
	3	8	7	16	4	19	6	11	14	49

Number of examinations 20, Total number of questions 137

Finding :				
	1	Highest Frequency	Verb-tense related	49
	2	Next	Preposition	19
	3	Next	Connector	16

Table Spotting Error: Frequency Analysis – Recent Trends (2009 to 2013)

Examination	*Items*											
	Noun	*Pronoun*	*Degree*	*Adjective*	*Connector Adverb*	*Article*	*Preposition*	*Idioms/ Phrases*	*Wrong Word Misplaced*	*No Error*	*Verb Tense Related*	*Missce-llaneous*
RBI GradeB-2009			1		1		1				1+1	
SCRA-2011		1			1				1		1+1	
Tourism & Travel-2012						1	1	1				1+1
NDA-2012		1				1+1	1+1		1		1+1+ 1+1	
CDS-2011	1	1		1		1	1+1+1		1+1+1	1+1 +1	1	1
IES-2010							1+1+1+1+1		1	1	1+1+1	
SSC ,TR2-2013	1+1				1		1+1+1		1+1+ 1+1 +1	1+1 +1	1+1 +1+1 +1	1

Noun-3, PRONOUN-3, Degree-1, ADJECTIVE-1, CONNECTOR-3, ARTICLE-4, PREPOSITION-15, IDIOMS/PHARESES-1, WRONG WORD MISPLACED-11, NO ERROR-7, VERB TENSE RELATED-17, MISCELLANEOUS-4

PART THREE

FILLING IN PARAGRAPH GAPS

Chapter 9
Cloze Test or Numbered Gaps

Chapter 9 explains the process of solving the questions on **cloze test** or filling the gaps in a paragraph. This test requires the dual skills of vocabulary and comprehension.

Elimination Technique has been suggested for solving these questions and practical illustrations have been provided to help readers gain the required competence. Practice sets fortify and strengthen the capability of the reader.

CHAPTER 9

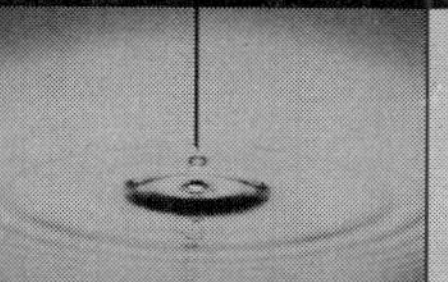

Cloze Test or Numbered Gaps

Concept

Cloze test is an extensive variation of the sentence completion test. Candidates are required to make a choice from multiple alternatives for each word blanked out, not in a sentence but in a passage. Thus this test evaluates the candidate's vocabulary power and his ability to judge the overall meaning of a passage even when some words are missing.

Practical Tip

A passage consists of sentences which are logically related to one another. Therefore, first of all, read the whole passage, get a rough idea of its contents and keep them in your mind as a background. Concentrate on this background to find clues. Use the following tips as well.

1. If you know the answer, immediately tick it. No technique is to be adopted. The whole process will work in a flash.
2. When you are not sure of the answer, make the right choice through the process of elimination.

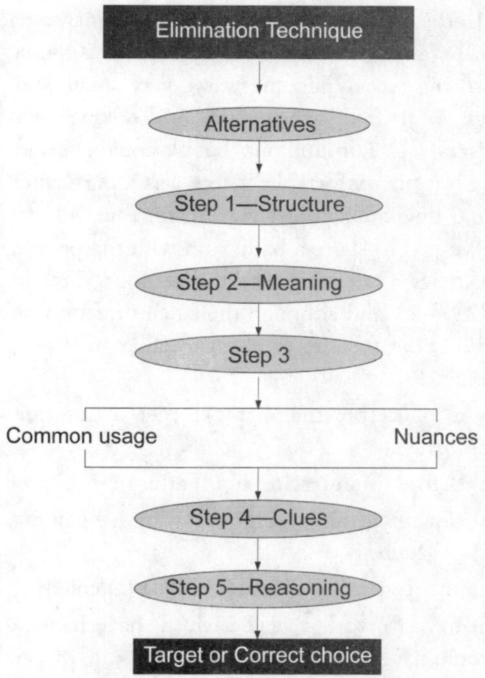

Fig. 9.1 Cloze Test Elimination Technique

Elimination Technique

Step 1 : Judge if any of them does not fit into the structure (eliminate).

Step 2 : Judge if any of them does not fit in with the meaning (eliminate).

Step 3 : Among/between the remaining apply your awareness of the common usage or nuances of words.

Step 4 : Try to find out a clue in the sentence or in a sentence preceding or succeeding it. Sometimes the clue is hidden many sentences away.

Step 5 : If the final choice has not been reached even now, apply the method of reasoning to hit the target.

Cloze Test–1

Fill in each of the numbered blanks in the following passage with the most suitable word out of the alternatives (below the passage) given against each number.

I . .1.. the first flat we lived in ..2.. our marriage very well. I was not ..3.. much, and Radha was ..4.. a student, so our weekly income was l, very small, and we simply ..5.. to find a cheap flat ..6.. Looking over lots of places, we ..7.. found one that we could ..8.. and it was not too uncomfortable. There was a big sitting room and a tiny kitchen, just big ..9.. for one ..10.. to get ..11.. We had to share a bathroom with the people in the next flat. Ours was on the first floor, directly over a ..12.. shop, and although the smell of fruit was quite ..13.., ..14.. of some of the vegetables was not. ..15.. agreeable.

1. (a) recollect (b) remember (c) forget (d) decorate (e) furnish
2. (a) before (b) during (c) in (d) after (e) for
3. (a) obtaining (b) earning (c) paying (d) gaining (e) collecting
4. (a) just (b) hardly (c) firmly (d) fast (e) chiefly
5. (a) have (b) had (c) will have (d) have had (e) would have
6. (a) upon (b) in (c) after (d) about (e) at
7. (a) would (b) have (c) will (d) had (e) could
8. (a) sell (b) rent out (c) give away (d) afford (e) use
9. (a) about (b) adequate (c) efficient (d) afford (e) enough
10. (a) group (b) family (c) personal (d) get-together (e) party
11. (a) about (b) by (c) along (d) down (e) in
12. (a) grocer's (b) mercantile (c) sweetmeats (0) retail (e) green grocer's
13. (a) smelly (b) stinking (c) pleasant (d) dislikeable (e) sad
14. (a) which (b) that (c) who (d) where (e) the
15. (a) quite (b) too much (c) far (d) so as (e) but

HINTS AND EXPLANATIONS

1. *Decorate* and *furnish* are eliminated at Step 1. They do not fit into the structure. The word *lived* makes the past form of the sentence clear. Thus *decorated or furnished* could have been right. *Recollect, remember* and *forget* indicate the past, but *forget* is eliminated at Step 2 as it does not fit with the meaning.

   Recollect and *remember,* both are correct, but *remember* is in common use. And if we go by nuance also, recollect *indicates* calling up some incident and *remember* some object or person. Thus *recollect* is eliminated at Step 3. *Remember* is the right choice.
2. *In* and *during* do not fit in the structure. They are eliminated at Step 1. *For* is eliminated at Step 2 as the spirit of the passage makes the meaning clear. *Before* and *after* pass through Steps 2 and 4. But *before* is eliminated at Step 5. In our society, the couples live together normally after marriage. We can therefore reason it out. *After* is thus the right choice.
3. *Obtaining, gaining* and *collecting* do not make the meaning clear. *Paying* will also not fit with the meaning as it is obvious from the background in the passage. Thus all four are eliminated at Step 2. Thus *earning* is the right choice.
4. *Hardly, firmly, fast and chiefly—all* these adverbs do not fit in the structure of the sentence and thus are eliminated at Step 1. If any doubt persists about any of them, it is eliminated at Step 2. *Just* is thus the right choice. common usage.
5. *Have had* and *would have* are eliminated at Step 1 as they do not fit in the structure. *Will have* and

have are also eliminated at Step 1 because the sentence is in the past tense. Thus, *had* is the right choice.

6. *Upon, in, after* and *at* are eliminated at Step 1 as they are wrongly used prepositions and do not fit in the structure. *About* is the right choice.
7. *Would, will* and *could* do not fit in the structure. *Have* is also structurally wrong as it does not go with the past tense. All four are thus eliminated at Step 1. Had is the right choice.
8. All pass through Step 1. Sell, rent out and give away are eliminated at Step 2. They do not fit with the meaning. Use is eliminated at Step 4. The clue is in the previous part of the sentence 'income was very small'. Thus *afford* is the right choice.
9. *About, adequate. efficient* and *less* do not fit in the structure and thus are eliminated at Step 1. *Enough* is the right choice. It is also confirmed by common usage.
10. *Personal* is eliminated at Step 1. *Get-together* and *party* are eliminated at Step 2 as they do not fit with the meaning. *Group* is eliminated at Step 3 according to common usage. A wife and a husband do not make a group but a family. This family is the right choice.
11. All pass through Step 1. *By, down* and *in* are eliminated at Step 2 as they do not fit with the meaning. *About* is eliminated at Step 3, as *get along* is in common use. *Along* is thus the right choice.
12. All pass through Steps 1, 2 and 3. *Grocer's, mercantile. sweetmeats* and *retail* are eliminated at Step 4 as there is the clue in the words *fruit* and *vegetable.* Thus green grocer's is the right choice.
13. All pass through Step 1. *Smelly, stinking, dislikeable* and *sad* are eliminated at Step 2 as they do not fit in with the meaning. *Pleasant* is thus the right choice.
14. *Which, who, where* and *the* are eliminated at Step 1 as they do not fit into the structure. *That* is thus the right choice.
15. *Far, so as* and *but* are eliminated at Step 1 as they dot not fit in the structure. *Too much* is eliminated at Step 2 as it disturbs the meaning. *Quite* is thus the right choice.

Cloze Test–2

The skin's worst enemy is the sun. If you aviod ..**1**.. you can ..**2**.. to prolong the young and ..**3**.. skin. The sun ..**4**.. deprive the skin of ..**5**.. hastening the appearance of ..**6**.. lines and wrinkles that ..**7**.. is all about. It is ..**8**.. responsible for many skin ..**9**.. like pigmentation, discoloration, freckles and ..**10**.. skin cancer. So, protect the skin with a sunscreen and moisturise it daily.

1. (a) extra exposure to the sun (b) much (c) additional (d) excessive
2. (a) aid (b) help (c) assist (d) make
3. (a) handsomeness of the (b) luxury (c) beauty (d) suppleness
4. (a) can (b) may (c) shall (d) will
5. (a) water (b) dampness (c) wetness (d) moisture
6. (a) these (b) those (c) some (d) certain
7. (a) growing (b) increasing (c) ageing (d) mellowing
8. (a) also (b) besides (c) even (d) possibly
9. (a) itches (b) illness (c) questions (d) problems
10. (a) a certainly (b) even (c) some (d) certain

HINTS AND EXPLANATIONS

1. *Much, additional* and *excessive* are eliminated at Step 1 because they do not fit in the structure. *Extra exposure to the sun* is the right answer.
2. All alternatives pass through Step 1 and 2. *Make* is eliminated at Step 3 as it is not in common use. Now let us check the nuances. *Assist* means there is somebody whom you are assisting. Here, there is none. *Aid* means you are giving something to help others that also does not apply. *Help* is thus the correct choice.
3. *Luxury, beauty* and *suppleness* are eliminated at Step 1 as they do not fit in the structure in the absence of a preposition. *Handsomeness of the* is thus the correct choice.
4. *May* is eliminated at Step 2, because *may* indicates 'permission' or 'possibility'. This is not in tune with the meaning. *Shall* and *will* are eliminated by common usage. 'Will' shows a general sense which is not required here. *Shall* means 'must' when used with a third person. This is not the

meaning required here. *Can* shows capacity and this fits with the meaning. Thus, this is the right choice.

5. All pass through Steps 1 and 2. *Water, dampness* and *wetness* are eliminated at Step 3 as they are not in common usage with the word 'skin'. *Moisture* is thus the correct choice. There is a clue also in; the last sentence in the word 'moisturise.
6. *These* and *those* are eliminated at Steps 1 as they do not fit in the structure. *These* and *those* indicate that there is a noun before which is referred to. There is no such indication earlier. *Some* indicates a vagueness and is thus eliminated at Step 2. *Certain* means 'of a particular kind'. This meaning fits here and thus *certain* is the correct choice.
7. All alternatives pass through Steps 1 and 2. *Growing, increasing* and *mellowing* are eliminated at Step 3. *Growing* shows development. *Increasing* shows rise. *Mellowing* shows ripening of a fruit in common use and *enrichment* in its nuance. All these do not fit with the meaning in the sentence or the passage. Thus *ageing* is the correct choice.
8. *Besides* is eliminated at Step 1, as it does not fit into the structure. *Possibly* shows a certain vagueness. *Even* shows special emphasis. Both of them do not fit with the meaning. *Also* is thus the correct answer.
9. All alternatives pass by Step 1. *Itches, illness* and *questions* do not fit with the meaning and are thus eliminated at Step 2. *Problem* is thus the right choice.
10. *Certain* and *some* do not fit in the structure and thus are eliminated at Step 1. *Certainly* suggests 'surety' and thus does not fit with the meaning. It is eliminated at Step 2. *Even* is thus the correct choice.

Cloze Test–3

The World Bank will take a decision soon on whether to continue supporting the Sardar Sarovar dam on the Narmada, which it had been funding ..1.. it was launched. An internal ..2.. of the Sardar Sarovar project ..3.. by the Bank, following protests ..4.. some environmental groups, is ..5.. completion and its board ..6.. expected to decide in May or ..7.. 1993, whether to continue funding the ..8.. The Bank's Vice-president for ..9.. sustainable development, Ismail Seralgdin ..10.. commissioned the review, will make appropriate recommendations to the Board soon, according to World Bank sources here.

1. (a) as (b) since (c) when
2. (a) assessment (b) opinion (c) examination
3. (a) commissioned (b) launched (c) constituted
4. (a) against (b) of (c) by
5. (a) getting (b) nearing (c) having
6. (a) was (b) is (c) had been
7. (a) April (b) August (c) June
8. (a) effort (b) project (c) people
9. (a) socially (b) economically (c) environmentally
10. (a) whom (b) who (c) whose

HINTS AND EXPLANATIONS

1. *As* and *when* are eliminated at Step 1 because they are incorrect and do not fit into the structure of the sentence. *Since* shows the point of time and it is the right answer.
2. All alternatives pass through Step 1. *Opinion* is eliminated at Step 2 because it does not fit in with the meaning. *Examination* is eliminated at Step 3 because *examination* is not commonly used with a word like project. *Assessment* is thus the right choice.
3. All alternatives pass through Step 1. *Launched* is eliminated at Step 2 because it does not fit in with the meaning. *Constituted* is eliminated at Step 3 because the word is not commonly associated with *assessment.* Thus *commissioned* is the right choice.
4. *Against* and *of* are eliminated at Step 1 as they are grammatically incorrect. *By* is the right choice.
5. *Getting* and *having* are eliminated at Step 1 because they do not fit into the structure. *Nearing* is the right choice. It is commonly used with *completion.*
6. *Was* and *had been* are eliminated at Step 1 because they are not correct and do not fit into the structure. The correct answer is *is.*

7. *June* is the right choice as there is a clue in the word *or.* Normally *or* is followed by the next number or month.
8. All alternatives pass Steps 1 and 2. *Effort* and *people* are eliminated at Step 3 because *effort* and *people* are not funded. A project is funded. Therefore *project* is the correct answer.
9. All alternatives pass Steps 1 and 2. *Socially* and *environmentally* are eliminated at Step 3 because the bank is normally associated with the economic aspect. *Economically,* thus, is the right choice.
10. *Whom* and *whose* are eliminated at Step 1 because they are structurally wrong. *Who* is the right choice.

Cloze Test–4

Countries which do not have a very well developed machine tool industry can never ..**1**.. to be even a first grade ..**2**.. and economic power, much less a global industrial player. This is known from the ..**3**.. of countries like Germany, USA, Japan, Switzerland and so on. When at the end of the Second World War, Japan wanted to become an industrial power, the ..**4**.. step she took was to ..**5**.. a machine tool industry. She decided to be ..**6**.. and not depend on ..**7**.. industrial nations. This was ..**8**.. in the long term rather than going in for the ..**9**.. advantage of importing machine tools. Similarly, India also established a machine tool industry ..**10**.. after independence to foster its fledgling industry.

1. (a) aspire (b) manifest (c) agree (d) prosper (e) pursue
2. (a) political (b) industrial (c) military (d) progressive (e) rich
3. (a) feelings (b) perceptions (c) plans (d) experiences (e) establishment
4. (a) important (b) useful (c) economic (d) wise (e) first
5. (a) developed (b) nurture (c) introduce (d) admit (e) establish
6. (a) revolutionary (b) industrious (c) self-sufficient (d) systematic (e) progressive
7. (a) European (b) developed (c) neighbouring (d) technical (e) foreign
8. (a) planned (b) decided (c) tried (d) beneficial (e) achieved
9. (a) temporary (b) exceptional (c) easy (d) fast (e) financial
10. (a) days (b) months (c) immediately (d) years (e) much

HINTS AND EXPLANATIONS

1. *Manifest, agree, prosper* and *pursue* are all eliminated at Step 2 because they do not match with the meaning. *Aspire* is thus the right choice.
2. All alternatives pass Steps 1 and 2. At Step 3, the term *industrial* becomes a choice because *industrial* and *economic* go together in common usage. There is a clue also in the word *industrial player.*
3. At Step 3, *feelings, perceptions* and *plane* are eliminated because it is common knowledge and also in common usage. *Establishment* is eliminated at Step 2 itself because it does not go with the meaning and we have *experience* as the right answer.
4. All alternatives except *first* do not match with the meaning, this becomes clear when you read the sentence a little carefully. This word gives force and real meaning to the sentence. Thus *first* is the right choice.
5. *Nurture* and *admit* are eliminated at Step 2 because they do not make any meaning. The clue is in the word *first.* We nurture a thing which is already there. *Admit* is out of context. Out of *develop, introduce* and *establish, establish* is the right choice because normally an industry is established. Common usage, and inference confirm this choice.
6. The clue is in the context and also in the neighbouring word *depend.* Thus all alternatives except *self-sufficient* are eliminated at Step 4. Reasoning also confirms this choice.
7. The word *depend* again provides us with a definite clue because one depends on only developed nations. Thus at Step 4, all other alternatives like *European, neighbouring, technical* and *foreign* are eliminated.
8. The context of the passage now gives sufficient clues. *Planned* is eliminated at Step 1 as it does

not fit into the structure. *Achieved* is eliminated at Step 2 because it does not go with the meaning. *Beneficial* is the right choice also because the expression in the long term match with it.

9. *Exceptional, easy, fast* and *financial* are eliminated at Step 2 because the clue is in the word *long term* before and *advantage* after the gap. In common usage also *long term* is matched by *temporary.*

10. *Days* and *months* and also *years* are eliminated because there is no definite information given in the passage. *Much* is contradictory in meaning and thus is eliminated at Step 2. The only choice left is *immediately* and this also matches with the meaning.

Practice Set —1

For generations man has ..1.. against the wilds to create a world where only he ..2.. whether animals and plants survive or are ..3.. out. Earlier we accepted as self-evident that any ..4.. in our environment brought about by science and technology must be improvements ..5.. the world of our ..6.. However many people all over the world have begun to feel that ..7.. are going too far, and that we should try to ..8.. some of the world's original life before we find it ..9.. too late. The same sciences which had led us away from nature are now ..10.. the miracle of creation.

1. (a) faced (b) stood (c) struggled (d) challenged

2. (a) decides (b) thinks (c) advises (d) observes

3. (a) taken (b) wiped (c) put (d) thrown

4. (a) differences (b) increments (c) changes (d) replacements

5. (a) in (b) at (c) over (d) for

6. (a) aborigines (b) ancients (c) successors (d) ancestors

7. (a) ourselves (b) we (c) us (d) some

8. (a) demolish (b) cherish (c) save (d) renovate

9. (a) occurs (b) sounds (c) seems (d) gets

10. (a) unfolding (b) discussing (c) arguing (d) narrating

Practice Set —2

It is neither the size nor the length of life which makes man ..1.. The growth of mind and the intellect is ..2.. in proportion to the growth of the human body. The man may ..3.. physically the stature of a giant, yet he may remain ..4.. a dwarf. The true worth of man ..5.. upon his action, deed and thought. Man is not like a tree. An oak tree ..6.. to a huge size and lives for hundreds of years, only to ..7.. to the ground, withered, dry an leafless ..8.. It is not in ..9.. things that ..10.. is sought.

1. (a) human (b) polite (c) better (d) humble

2. (a) roughly (b) usually (c) ever (d) never

3. (a) earn (b) attain (c) keep (d) grow

4. (a) morally (b) spiritually (c) socially (d) intellectually

5. (a) depends (b) lies (c) revolves (d) gathers

6. (a) lifts (b) grows (c) manages (d) raises

7. (a) decay (b) dwindle (c) disappear (d) fall

8. (a) log (b) wood (c) pole (d) chip

9. (a) big (b) small (c) broad (d) lengthy

10. (a) interest (b) value (c) curiosity (d) perfection

Practice Set —3

The population of the country poses a ..1.. economic situation, for we are not able to ..2.. it by our own agriculture produce. Besides ..3..all development efforts, the problem brings ..4.. to the community, to the family and the individual. To plan when population growth is ..5.. is like building a house where the ground is constantly ..6.. An argument is put ..7.. that our country is overpopulated. The vast potent resources of the country still lie ..8.. It is indeed a pity that our vast resources ..9.. unused. If we are able to ..10.. our productive forces, even double the present population can be ..11.. Our population problem does not lie ..12.. in the increase in the number of people. The real ..13.. and the menace to the ..14.. of us all, lies in the effect of this rapidly increasing population on our ..15.. to provide essentials of life to everyone.

1. (a) satisfactory (b) hopeful (c) grim (d) foul
2. (a) finance (b) flourish (c) support (d) maintain
3. (a) rejecting (b) dismissing (c) boosting (d) neutralising
4. (a) pain (b) difficulty (c) distress (d) relief
5. (a) increased (b) encouraged (c) checked (d) unchecked
6. (a) flat (b) fertile (c) futile (d) flooded
7. (a) down (b) up (c) through (d) forward
8. (a) tapped (b) untapped (c) uncontrolled (d) dormant
9. (a) appear (b) stay (c) lie (d) go
10. (a) mould (b) bridle (c) stem (d) harness
11. (a) supported (b) enhanced (c) encouraged (d) tolerated
12. (a) generally (b) widely (c) broadly (d) merely
13. (a) point (b) idea (c) meaning (d) threat
14. (a) life (b) welfare (c) future (d) career
15. (a) will (b) inability (c) ability (d) intention

Practice Set —4

Scalping each other was one of the ..1.. pastimes of the American Indians ..2.. of the colonial settlers of the ..3.. discovered world for four centuries ..4.. the end of the 19th ..5.. To the white man, arriving ..6.. hordes from the European countries ..7.. red-skinned man, who had migrated ..8.. Asia more than 10 centuries earlier ..9.. a barrier to settlement and ..10.. wealth. To the Indian, the white man promised only the end of a free way of life, a total humiliation, so they killed each other.

1. (a) liked (b) favourite (c) enjoyable (d) practical
2. (a) so (b) while (c) because (d) and
3. (a) freshly (b) lately (c) newly (d) recently
4. (a) up (b) on (c) till (d) until
5. (a) millennium (b) annum (c) century (d) decade
6. (a) over (b) with (c) on (d) in
7. (a) such (b) the (c) that (d) any
8. (a) out (b) off (c) away (d) from
9. (a) was (b) were (c) is (d) are
10. (a) possible (b) potential (c) probable (d) certain

Practice Set —5

Fundamentally, all human ..1.. possess combinations of fixed inherited traits. All men possess the ..2.. highly developed nervous system, backbones, erect posture, hair, etc. Therefore ..3.. among men arise only in ..4.. changes of this ..5.. pattern. Racial ..6.. represent one of the finest distinctions and are based on certain ..7.. differences. Two races may be ..8.. in hair colour and in eye colour but ..9.. in stature while two others may be ..10.. in stature but differ in colour of eyes and hair.

1. (a) animal (b) beings (c) mind (d) society
2. (a) large (b) different (c) same (d) natural
3. (a) sameness (b) naturalness (c) artifical (d) variations

4. (a) no (b) large
(c) fundamental (d) minor
5. (a) fluctuating (b) basic
(c) mad (d) picturesque
6. (a) differences (b) clashes
(c) hatred (d) tolerance
7. (a) clearcut (b) minor
(c) unnoticeable (d) massive
8. (a) alike (b) different
(c) mismatched (d) beautiful
9. (a) alike (b) tall
(c) same (d) different
10. (a) similar (b) short
(c) uncouth (d) different

Practice Set —6

In all compositions ..1.. is the most ..2.. virtue. You should write in a simple and ..3.. manner. The words chosen should be ..4.. in meaning. Try not to use ..5.. words merely because they are ..6.. Do not allow poetic images or ..7.. to spoil the grace of good style. It is no longer ..8.. to stuff your composition with too many ..9.. or proverbs especially if their relevance is ..10..

1. (a) complexity (b) flourish
(c) simplicity (d) reserve
2. (a) hidden (b) described
(c) depicted (d) admired
3. (a) straightforward (b) showy
(c) ornate (d) decorative
4. (a) haphazard (b) quick
(c) discriminating (d) clear
5. (a) difficult (b) short
(c) appropriate (d) small
6. (a) familiar (b) literary
(c) distant (d) admired
7. (a) pictures (b) stories
(c) similes (d) examples
8. (a) disliked (b) uncommon
(c) difficult (d) fashionable
9. (a) philosophies (b) writers
(c) quotations (d) systems
10. (a) good (b) observed
(c) clear (d) doubtful

Practice Set —7

In 1893, Lokmanya Tilak converted the Ganapati festival into a national celebration. He campaigned ..1.. the ..2.. celebration of this public festival throughout Maharashtra. It was ..3.. this festival that he could ..4.. public ..5.. for the nationalist movement. The desired ..6.. of this festival was further ..7.. by the Shivaji festival. It was inaugurated in honour of Chhatrapati Shivaji, the greatest Maratha King, in the ..8.. of several thousand people. In the ..9.. the Marathas were ..10.. and this helped a lot in mounting an attack on the British rule.

1. (a) with (b) withstanding
(c) against (d) for
2. (a) early (b) wide
(c) sudden (d) slow
3. (a) indeed (b) exactly
(c) through (d) before
4. (a) enhance (b) demand
(c) control (d) mobilise
5. (a) support (b) grievances
(c) places (d) festival
6. (a) decoration (b) publicity
(c) importance (d) impact
7. (a) decided (b) reinforced
(c) displayed (d) manifested
8. (a) protest (b) service
(c) presence (d) honour
9. (a) fight (b) beginning
(c) meantime (d) activity
10. (a) glorified (b) forbidden
(c) absent (d) neglected

Practice Set —8

The Congress ..1.. issued on the eve of the ..2.. elections contains an open endorsement of the Dunkel Draft. Stress has been ..3.. allaying two specific apprehensions. The Dunkel Draft, the manifesto says, poses no ..4.. to food subsidies and the subsidy-based public ..5.. system. The GATT treaty, it is explained, would allow ..6.. to the extent of 10% of the market price. Second, there should ..7.. be no fear on account of the Dunkel stipulation of allowing ..8.. of farm products up to three per cent of its domestic output. Imports of such a piffling order, according to the manifesto, could ..9.. no threat to the domestic price ..10..

1. (a) manifesto (b) paper (c) draft (d) souvenir
2. (a) past (b) recent (c) immediate (d) old
3. (a) put on (b) laid on (c) give (d) placed on
4. (a) threat (b) danger (c) problem (d) situation
5. (a) dealing (b) working (c) distribution (d) relation
6. (a) concession (b) allowance (c) subsidy (d) aid
7. (a) too (b) even (c) also (d) exactly
8. (a) imports (b) exports (c) sell (d) purchase
9. (a) make (b) pose (c) create (d) affect
10. (a) system (b) line (c) structure (d) pattern

Practice Set —9

Operation Flood was ..1.. with the primary objective of ..2.. rural milk producers with urban milk consumers, by ..3.. viable producer cooperativesin the milk sheds, and thus ..4.. rural milk producers to earn higher income from milk. The programme ..5.. some 72 lakh members in nearly 61,000 village societies ..6.. over diverse ecologies in 174 milk sheds. The cooperatives procure an average of 90 lakh litres of milk a day to ..7.. the ever growing urban demand for fresh milk from the country.

1. (a) visualised (b) created (c) launched (d) devoted
2. (a) joining (b) linking (c) bringing (d) identifying
3. (a) exposing (b) creating (c) generating (d) providing
4. (a) offering (b) enabling (c) activating (d) justifying
5. (a) covers (b) rotates (c) motivates (d) follows
6. (a) distributed (b) assembled (c) spread (d) situated
7. (a) control (b) meet (c) satisfy (d) attend

Practice Set —10

Essentially I am interested in ..1.. world, in this ..2.., not in some other ..3.. or a future life. Whether there is such a ..4.. as a soul, or whether there is a survival after ..5.. or not, I do not know and important as these ..6.. are, they do not trouble me in ..7.. The environment in which I have ..8.. upholds the soul and a future the karma theory of ..9.. and effect and reincarnation for ..10..

1. (a) this (b) that (c) real (d) imaginary
2. (a) life (b) reality (c) existence (d) truth
3. (a) reality (b) world (c) life (d) plane
4. (a) fact (b) thing (c) reality (d) idea
5. (a) life (b) existence (c) death (d) reality
6. (a) problems (b) situations (c) questions (d) queries
7. (a) the least (b) the most (c) not at all (d) actually
8. (a) reared (b) grown (c) increased (d) thrived
9. (a) cause (b) question (c) problem (d) reason
10. (a) permitted (b) granted (c) allowed (d) sure

Practice Set —11

The ..1.. of a survey by the National Institute of ..2.. Health give ..3.. for ..4.. According to the survey about 14 million people in India are affected by ..5.. mental ..6.. at any point of time. In the case of the mentally ill, it is ..7.. difficult to ..8.. them, let alone ..9.. them. The most ..10.. are those in the ..11.. areas, for whatever ..12.. for the mentally sick exist are concentrated around major urban centres.

1. (a) verdicts (b) decisions
(c) judgements (d) measures
(e) findings
2. (a) spiritual (b) pyshichal
(c) social (d) physical
(e) mental
3. (a) food (b) cause
(c) purpose (d) support
(e) reinforcement
4. (a) alarm (b) discontent
(c) fear (d) dissatisfaction
(e) vexation
5. (a) dangerous (b) strong
(c) serious (d) fatal
(e) important
6. (a) disorders (b) perturbation
(c) dislocation (d) confusion
(e) involvement
7. (a) seldom (b) occasionally
(c) very (d) hardly
(e) never
8. (a) cure (b) recognise
(c) identify (d) select
(e) rehabilitate
9. (a) facilitate (b) guide
(c) cure (d) advise
(e) treat
10. (a) indifferent (b) neglected
(c) careless (d) abandoned
(e) serious
11. (a) urban (b) rural
(c) forest (d) suburban
(e) metropolitan
12. (a) facilities (b) advantages
(c) avenues (d) remedies
(e) solicitations

Practice Set —12

We can appreciate the importance of Chemistry if we understand what chemistry is. It is an experimental science which has the tasks of ..1.. the materials out of which the things in the universe are made. Analyses have ..2.. things to be composed of elements aggregated in different ..3.. Millions of ..4.. which are used in our daily life are prepared with only a few dozen elements. Even the ..5..vmolecule does not contain more than four or five types of elements. Both the giant and the micro molecules are ..6.. important. Water which is composed of only two types of elements, i.e., hydrogen and oxygen, is one of the ..7.. of life. Proteins, the compounds of four elements, play a ..8.. role in cell formation. Vitamins, hormones, etc., are all chemical compounds and are ..9.. in laboratories. Dyes, plastics, fertilisers, drugs, synthetic fibres, etc., are all ..10.. substances. Therefore, it would be appropriate to say that chemistry is an important subject and it should be studied by all.

1. (a) listing (b) investigating
(c) inventing (d) collecting
2. (a) revealed (b) allowed
(c) facilitated (d) assumed
3. (a) shapes (b) manners
(c) styles (d) proportions
4. (a) products (b) compounds
(c) substances (d) items
5. (a) biggest (b) heaviest
(c) longest (d) darkest
6. (a) proportionally (b) critically
(c) equally (d) rarely
7. (a) requirements (b) blessings
(c) essentials (d) components
8. (a) major (b) positive
(c) reasonable (d) suitable
9. (a) collected (b) found
(c) synthesised (d) used
10. (a) physical (b) light
(c) imported (d) chemical

ANSWER KEY

Set 1	Set 2	Set 3	Set 4	Set 5
1. (c)	1. (a)	1. (c)	1. (b)	1. (b)
2. (a)	2. (d)	2. (c)	2. (c)	2. (c)
3. (b)	3. (b)	3. (d)	3. (c)	3. (d)
4. (c)	4. (d)	4. (c)	4. (c)	4. (d)
5. (d)	5. (a)	5. (d)	5. (c)	5. (b)
6. (c)	6. (b)	6. (d)	6. (d)	6. (a)
7. (b)	7. (d)	7. (d)	7. (b)	7. (b)
8. (c)	8. (a)	8. (b)	8. (d)	8. (a)
9. (d)	9. (a)	9. (c)	9. (a)	9. (d)
10. (a)	10. (d)	10. (d)	10. (b)	10. (a)
		11. (a)		
		12. (d)		
		13. (d)		
		14. (c)		
		15. (c)		

Set 6	Set 7	Set 8	Set 9	Set 10
1. (c)	1. (d)	1. (a)	1. (c)	1. (a)
2. (d)	2. (b)	2. (b)	2. (b)	2. (a)
3. (a)	3. (c)	3. (b)	3. (b)	3. (b)
4. (d)	4. (d)	4. (a)	4. (b)	4. (b)
5. (a)	5. (a)	5. (c)	5. (a)	5. (c)
6. (b)	6. (d)	6. (c)	6. (c)	6. (c)
7. (c)	7. (b)	7. (c)	7. (b)	7. (a)
8. (d)	8. (c)	8. (a)		8. (b)
9. (c)	9. (b)	9. (b)		9. (a)
10. (d)	10. (d)	10. (c)		10. (b)

Set 11	Set 12
1. (e)	1. (b)
2. (e)	2. (a)
3. (b)	3. (d)
4. (a)	4. (a)
5. (c)	5. (a)
6. (a)	6. (c)
7. (c)	7. (c)
8. (c)	8. (a)
9. (c)	9. (c)
10. (e)	10. (d)
11. (b)	
12. (a)	

Additional Practice Sets

Set–I

Directions (Qs 1 to 3)

In the following passage there are blanks, each of which has been numbered. These numbers are printed below the passage and against each, five words are suggested, one of which fits the blank appropriately. Find out the appropriate word in each case.

As the country embarks on planning **..(1)..** the 12th Plan (2012-17) period, a key question mark **..(2)..** hangs over the process is on the energy requirements, Growth is energy hungry, and the aspirations of growing at 9-10% will **..(3)..** huge demands on the energy resources of the country. In this energy jigsaw, renewable energy will **..(4)..** like never before in the 12th Plan and **..(5)..** By the rule of the thumb, India will **..(6)..** about 100 gigawatts (Gw)-100,000 megawatts— of capacity addition in the next five years. Encouraging trends on energy efficiency and sustained **..(7)..** by some parts of the government—the Bureau of Energy Efficiency in particular needs to be complimented for this—have led to substantially lesser energy intensity of economic growth. However, even the tempered demand numbers are **..(8)..** to be below 80Gw. As against this need the coal supply from domestic sources is unlikely to support more than 25Gw equivalent capacity. Imported coal can add some more, but at a much **..(9)..** cost. Gas-based electricity generation is unlikely to contribute anything substantial in view of the unprecedented gas supply challenges. Nuclear will be **..(10)..** in the foreseeable future. Between imported coal, gas, large hydro and nuclear, no more than 15-20Gw equivalent can be **..(11)..** to be added in the five-year time block.

..(12).. ..(13).. this, capacity addition in the renewable energy based power generation has touched about 3Gw a year. In the coming five years, the overall capacity addition in the electricity grid **..(14)..** renewable energy is likely to range between 20Gw and 25Gw. Additionally, over and above the grid-based capacity, off-grid electricity applications are reaching remote places and **..(15)..** lives where grid-based electricity supply has miserably failed.

1. (a) against (b) for (c) onwards (d) at (e) on

2. (a) that (b) inside (c) always (d) who (e) where

3. (a) forward (b) subject (c) place (d) demand (e) replace

4. (a) pass (b) publish (c) feature (d) find (e) light

5. (a) likewise (b) publicity (c) next (d) after (e) earlier

6. (a) waste (b) require (c) highlight (d) generate (e) consumed

7. (a) structures (b) efforts (c) projections (d) practices (e) developmental

8. (a) sure (b) unsure (c) unexpected (d) unlikely (e) likely

9. (a) nominal (b) excelled (c) higher (d) lower (e) expected

10. (a) energy (b) demand (c) desire (d) hope (e) dispair

11. (a) certain (b) linked (c) remarked (d) expected (e) sure

12. (a) When (b) But
(c) However (d) If
(e) As

13. (a) through (b) project
(c) versus (d) against
(e) capacity

14. (a) lightning (b) making
(c) touching (d) saving
(e) generating

15. (a) lightning (b) making
(c) touching (d) saving
(e) generating

Set–2

Directions—(Q. 16-25)

In the following passage there are blanks each of which has been numbered. These numbers are printed below the passage and against each five words are suggested one of which fits the blank appropriately. Find out the appropriate word in each case.

I had ..**(16)**.. to become a multipurpose manager. I took three steps to accomplish this. First, I took very ..**(17)**.. part in professional associations. I ..**(18)**.. the National President of the Indian Society for Training and Development-one of the ..**(19)**.. organizations for HR professionals. This helped me to grow professionally. My communication skills ..**(20)**.. It also taught me ..**(21)**.. to conduct meetings in an effective manner. My job ..**(22)**.. me to different parts of the country and I ..**(23)**.. believe that ..**(24)**.. provided me with an education. I also wrote a lot. Newspaper editors often approached me with ..**(25)**.. to write articles for their publications.

16. (a) achieved (b) aim
(c) try (d) dreamed
(e) wanted

17. (a) selected (b) active
(c) interesting (d) often
(e) joint

18. (a) elected (b) voted
(c) became (d) applied
(e) decided

19. (a) respected (b) status
(c) impressed (d) aged
(e) common

20. (a) lacked (b) grown
(c) learnt (d) improved
(e) earned

21. (a) that (b) why
(c) how (d) never
(e) anyhow

22. (a) saw (b) showed
(c) posted (d) discovered
(e) took

23. (a) quiet (b) firmly
(c) strong (d) first
(e) not

24. (a) traveling (b) journey
(c) visit (d) migrating
(e) shift

25. (a) wish (b) offer
(c) appointments (d) requests
(e) commands

Set–3

Directions—(Q. 26—35)

In the following passage there are blanks each of which has been numbered. These numbers are printed below the passage and against each five words are suggested, one of which fills the blank appropriately. Find out the appropriate word in each case.

Delinking of jobs from degrees is one of the ..**(26)**.. features of our education ..**(27)**.. There has been a ..**(28)**.. fall in ..**(29)**.. in the academic field in recent years. There is a ..**(30)**.. of degree holders in the country, as a result, university degrees have ..**(31)**.. their value and charm while the number of students in colleges and universities of the country has been **..(32)..** rising. Consequently thousands of graduates and post graduates come out of these institutions and stand in queues waiting to get some **..(33)..** jobs **..(34)..** in the country. Moreover, these degree holders do not have any technical or vocational knowledge needed for a particular job. As a result, the number of educated unemployed has been rising **..(35)..** It has created a very serious problem.

26. (a) minor (b) trivial (c) unachievable (d) irrelevant (e) salient

27. (a) process (b) policy (c) development (d) (e) procedures

28. (a) expected (b) sheer (c) rough (d) steep (e) gentle

29. (a) assessment (b) evaluation (c) competence (d) fees (e) value

30. (a) flood (b) class (c) party (d) mob (e) rabble

31. (a) mislaid (b) lost (c) increase (d) found (e) establish

32. (a) slowly (b) hastily (c) deeply (d) waiting (e) out

33. (a) suitable (b) remain (c) study (d) live (e) place

34. (a) frequency (b) occurrence (c) event (d) chance (e) blocking

35. (a) fever (b) outshine (c) lean (d) dwarfed (e) horribly

Set–4

Directions—(Q. 36-45)

In the following passage, there are blanks, each of which has been numbered. These numbers are printed below the passage and against each, five words are suggested, one of which fits the blank appropriately. Find out the appropriate word in each case.

Jamshedji Tata is **..(36)..** to be the path-finder of modem industrial builders. He is known as the grandfather of the Indian industry for his acumen and enthusiasm. Nobody else could have **..(37)..** of the new industries started by Jamshedji at that time when industrial **..(38)..** and revolution was yet to come to India. Jamshedji's father Nasarvanji Tata used to trade in jute with China and Britain. He started **..(39)..** from India. Jamshedji started a cloth mill in Nagpur more than hundred years ago. At that time almost all the **..(40)..** used to come from Lancashire in England. What Jamshedji **..(41)..** was praiseworthy.

Jamshedji **..(42)..** very well that an industrial revolution can only be brought in the country by setting up iron and steel industry. **..(43)..** he did not live to see the industry he had in mind, he had done all **..44..** work. In fact, he laid the ground work for it He had planned the entire steel city now known as Jamshedpur, complete with streets, roads, schools, parks, play grounds, temples, mosques, churches, etc. His **..(45)..** was fulfilled by his sons, Sir Dorabji Tata and Sir Rattan Tata, when they started the Tata iron and Steel Factory in 1907 just after three years of his death.

36. (a) rewarded (b) agreed (c) empowered (d) determined (e) considered

37. (a) absolved (b) thought (c) ventured (d) set (e) planned

38. (a) imports (b) acts (c) machinery (d) awakening (e) factories

39. (a) export (b) industries
(c) import (d) trade
(e) dispatch

40. (a) goods (b) imports
(c) cloth (d) machines
(e) industries

41. (a) did (b) dreamt
(c) agreed (d) told
(e) meant

42. (a) felt (b) advocated
(c) planned (d) thought
(e) knew

43. (a) because (b) although
(c) surprisingly (d) luckily
(e) even

44. (a) insignificant (b) complete
(c) trivial (d) preliminary
(e) external

45. (a) need (b) task
(c) dream (d) industry
(e) sentiment

Set–5

Directions—(Q. 46-53)

In the following passage there are blanks, each of which has been numbered. These numbers are printed below me passage and against each, five words are suggested, one of which fits the blank appropriately. Find out the appropriate word in each case.

What this approach lacks is the essential interaction with **..(46)..** and with other humans. Indeed in many environmental activities the **..(47)..** takes place. A classic example of this is making of a herbarium or even worse, an insect **..(48)..** so common in both formal and non-formal education in India. A child is **..(49)..** encouraged to pluck leaves and **..(50)..** and run after butterflies with a net and is **..(51)..** of a large group of children similarly working a **..(52)..** of nature within it. Such a child is not likely to develop any strong **..(53)..** of respect for nature, or for the individual 'specimens' pressed in the **..(54)..** file or trapped in a jar. It is worse when the activity is also competitive, i.e., who **..(55)..** the maximum.

46. (a) habit (b) tradition
(c) practice (d) custom
(e) nature

47. (a) antonym (b) against
(c) energy (d) opposite
(e) opponent

48. (a) gathering (b) compilation
(c) collection (d) assembly
(e) bulk

49. (a) oft (b) often
(c) frequently (d) mostly
(e) many

50. (a) flowers (b) petals
(c) buds (d) blossoms
(e) delight

51. (a) division (b) segment
(c) particle (d) portion
(e) part

52. (a) piece (b) thatch
(c) plot (d) patch
(e) spot

53. (a) thinking (b) experiencing
(c) feeling (d) knowing
(e) viewing

54. (a) sapling (b) plant
(c) creeper (d) nursery
(e) tree

55. (a) collects (b) meets
(c) piles (d) gathers
(e) assembles

Set–6

Directions (Q. 56-57)

In the following passage there are blanks, each of which has been numbered.

These numbers are printed below the passage and against each, five words are suggested, one

of which fits the blank appropriately. Find out the appropriate word in each case.

In July 2008, one of the most inspiring leaders of our times, will **..(56)..** his ninetieth birthday. Nelson Mandela retired from politics in 1999, but he has remained **..(57)..**, continuing his work through the Nelson Mandela Foundation. The foundation has launched an Aids awareness campaign, 76664, named **..(58)..** Mandela's prison number. He has also set up a scholarship programme whose **..(59)..** was to promote leadership among young Africans.

During the 1990s, **..(60)..** I worked with Mr. Mandela on his autobiography "Long Walk to Freedom", **..(61)..** his leadership first hand. During his election campaign we were on board a plane discussing his book. Twenty minutes **..(62)..** landing the engine failed. Many began to panic. The only thing that **..(63)..** them was looking at Mandela, who was reading his paper as if he was a passenger on a morning train to work. The plane landed safely and when we got into the car taking us to the hotel he **..(64)..** to me, "I was terrified on the plane!" As a leader he realised he was a model for others and this gave him the strength to **..(65)..** over his own fear.

56. (a) tribute (b) remember (c) honour (d) celebrate (e) rejoice

57. (a) resigned (b) active (c) influenced (d) participant (e) reserved

58. (a) by (b) with (c) after (d) as (e) thereafter

59. (a) wish (b) pursuit (c) result (d) plot (e) aim

60. (a) when (b) that (c) period (d) later (e) alongside

61. (a) felt (b) acquainted (c) experienced (d) underwent (e) learned

62. (a) before (b) sooner (c) close (d) prior (e) advance

63. (a) calmed (b) soothing (c) composed (d) restraint (e) discipline

64. (a) speaks (b) confided (c) confidentially (d) entrusted (e) assured

65. (a) success (b) overcame (c) dominate (d) victory (e) triumph

Set–7

Directions for Questions – 66 to 75

In the following passage, there are blanks, each of which has been numbered. These numbers are printed below the passage and against each, four words are suggested, one of which fits the blank appropriately. Find out the appropriate word in each case.

First aid experts stress that **..(66)..** what to do for an **..(67)..** victim until a doctor or other trained person gets to the accident scene can **..(68)..** a life, especially in cases of stoppage of breathing, severe bleeding, and shock.

People with special **..(69)..** problems, such as diabetes, cardiovascular disease, epilepsy, or allergy, are **..(70)..** to wear some sort of emblem identifying the problem, as a safeguard against administration of medication that might be injurious or even **..(71)..** When emergencies do occur, **..(72)..** first aid within the first few minutes often **..(73)..** life or death. **..(74)..** administering of first aid **..(75)..** medical professionals to provide better care.

66. (a) before (b) attempting (c) regarding (d) knowing (e) about

67. (a) injured (b) inquiring (c) efficient (d) important (e) accident

68. (a) harm (b) comfort (c) take (d) soothe (e) save

69. (a) mental (b) ethical
(c) medical (d) accident
(e) moral

70. (a) prohibited (b) invited
(c) compelled (d) allowed
(e) urged

71. (a) appropriate (b) dangerous
(c) beneficial (d) fatal
(e) remedial

72. (a) expecting (b) providing
(c) avoiding (d) ignoring
(e) neglecting

73. (a) determines (b) offers
(c) vanishes (d) reflects
(e) begs

74. (a) Hasty (b) Careless
(c) Proper (d) Probable
(e) Reasonably

75. (a) resists (b) instigates
(c) hinders (d) prevents
(e) enables

Set–8

Directions for Questions 76 to 85

In the following passage, there are blanks, each of which has been numbered. These numbers are printed below the passage and against each, four words are suggested, one of which fits the blank appropriately. Find out the appropriate word in each case.

Tea prices in the domestic **..(76)..** continue to rule high in the **..(77)..** year despite theexpectation of a **..(78)..** production as compared to the previous year. According to a preliminary assessment **..(79)..** on the weather **..(80)..** in recent months, tea output in the next year may reach 800 tons as **..(81)..** 780 tons last year. During the past three months tea prices have shown an. **..(82)..** Unlike last year, when tea prices were dramatically low, this year prices seem to have **..(83)..** at rather high level. In the subsequent four months, the **..(84)..** average price showed a downtrend, but in September the price has **..(85)..** hardened to a considerable extent.

76. (a) Market (b) Area
(c) Sector (d) Profit
(e) Production

77. (a) Last (b) First
(c) Current (d) Second
(e) Earlier

78. (a) Lower (b) Large
(c) Higher (d) Maximum
(e) Reasonable

79. (a) Shared (b) Based
(c) Carried (d) Strategy
(e) Conducted

80. (a) Pattern (b) Forecast
(c) Condition (d) Outbreak
(e) Out bursts

81. (a) To (b) Per
(c) Above (d) Against
(e) Compared

82. (a) Upgrade (b) Uptrend
(c) Increased (d) Increment
(e) incline

83. (a) Stabilised (b) Surfaced
(c) Increased (d) Moderated
(e) Synchronised

84. (a) Annual (b) weekly
(c) daily (d) Quarterly
(e) Monthly

85. (a) Now (b) Then
(c) Since (d) from
(e) Again

ANSWER KEY

1. (b)	2. (a)	3. (c)	4. (c)	5. (b)
6. (d)	7. (b)	8. (e)	9. (c)	10. (a)
11. (d)	12. (b)	13. (b)	14. (c)	15. (c)

16. (e)	17. (b)	18. (c)	19. (a)	20. (d)
21. (c)	22. (e)	23. (b)	24. (a)	25. (d)
26. (e)	27. (b)	28. (d)	29. (c)	30. (a)
31. (b)	32. (b)	33. (a)	34. (d)	35. (e)
36. (e)	37. (b)	38. (d)	39. (a)	40. (c)
41. (a)	42. (e)	43. (b)	44. (d)	45. (c)
46. (e)	47. (d)	48. (c)	49. (b)	50. (a)
51. (e)	52. (d)	53. (c)	54. (b)	55. (a)
56. (d)	57. (b)	58. (c)	59. (e)	60. (a)
61. (c)	62. (d)	63. (a)	64. (b)	65. (e)
66. (d)	67. (e)	68. (e)	69. (c)	70. (e)
71. (d)	72. (b)	73. (a)	74. (c)	75. (e)
76. (a)	77. (c)	78. (c)	79. (b)	80. (a)
81. (d)	82. (b)	83. (a)	84. (e)	85. (e)

Part Four

Sentence Skills

This part has four chapters—Sentence Completion, Sentence Fillers, Sentence Reconstruction and Sentence Improvement. Two interesting ways of solving questions are described in these chapters—The Key Elimination (KE) Method (for the Sentence Completion part) and the Stem Filler Matching (SFM) technique (for the Sentence Filler part). For sentence reconstruction several helpful techniques have been given. Sentence Improvement is an interesting variation of spotting errors.

CHAPTER 10

SENTENCE COMPLETION

Introduction

Sentence completion is one of the most important tests designed to assess the vocabulary skills of candidates. In a sentence, one or two blanks are left out to be filled with one of the alternatives given below it. Let us examine a few such sentences.

EXAMPLES

One Sentence One Blank

Although he was a hardened criminal, his one __________ feature was his love.

(a) saving (b) redeeming
(c) recovering (d) acquiring

The answer is (b).

One Sentence Two Blanks

Disarmament and development in our time are __________ interrelated but __________ development will depend on a change in the world's political thinking.

(a) essentially, true
(b) naturally, final
(c) closely, real
(d) inevitably, substantial

The answer is (c).

Two Sentences Two Blanks

1. The entire class was invited to __________ the model of the proposed new city.
2. There is a lovely __________ of the town from the window.

(a) look (b) impression
(c) sight (d) view

The answer is (d).

Now, let us analyse the process of finding the correct answer. If you know the answer, you can make a flash response and tick the choice. No technique is required at all. If you do not know the answer, you may use the key words and elimination method.

KE (Key elimination) Method

K stands for key; *E* stands for elimination. Every sentence must have an idea. A sentence is not merely a group of words but a meaningful group of words. So there is an idea, a message behind every sentence.

Example Ram is an honest man.

Here the idea or message is the honesty of Ram. The message may be expressed or is generally expressed through a word or words. This we may call key word/ words. In this sentence the key word is *honest.*

Example The Director pointed out in favour of the Manager that the profitability of the plant had __________ since he took over.

(a) arisen (b) declined
(c) developed (d) increased

Here the message or idea is profitability of the plant. The key words reflecting the idea are profitability and favour. Keeping profitability and favour in mind, we can very easily eliminate *arisen, declined* and developed. Only *increased* remains uneliminated. This is the answer.

At times, you can find the answer by locating the key words.

Past is to future as yesterday is to __________.

(a) today
(b) tomorrow
(c) day after tomorrow
(d) day before yesterday

The answer is (b), 'tomorrow'. The key word is 'yesterday' for which an opposite has to be found out.

Sometimes you can find the answer by the process of elimination.

A __________ of ships was kept ready to scour the sea in case of an emergency.

(a) group (b) pack
(c) battalion (d) fleet

Now we can find out the answer by eliminating different alternatives.

(a) *Group* can be eliminated because 'group' is used for human beings or, at least, for living beings.
(b) *Pack* is used normally for playing materials. A pack of cards is a popular expression.
(c) *Battalion* is normally used for a group of soldiers.

Thus the alternatives (a), (b) and (c) are eliminated. The only alternative left is (d), fleet, which is the right answer.

Thus we see that sometimes we find the answer by locating the key words and sometimes through the process of elimination. But in most cases, we can find out thc answer by combining both. However, we may use some clues for locating key words as well as for eliminating different alternatives.

The 'KE Method' can be illustrated in the figure below.

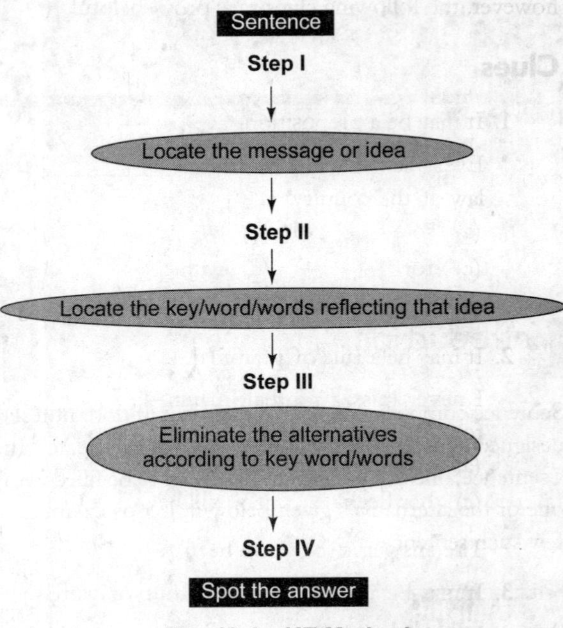

Fig. 10.1 KE Method

Clues for Key Words

Key words are words which assist you to get at the idea being expressed in the sentence. In the first example, the key words are 'hardened criminal'. Thus the missing word in this context must be a word that gives the opposite idea. Thus *'recovering'* and *'acquiring'* are eliminated because they do not give the opposite idea of the key words. 'Saving' and 'redeeming' have an opposite implication, but 'saving' has a general connotation and thus it may be rejected. 'Redeeming' implies a contrast against a bad trait. Thus 'redeeming' is the correct choice.

In the second example, 'disarmament' and 'development' are key words. These two words imply man-made actions. The words 'naturally' and 'inevitable' do not agree with the key words as natural or inevitable interrelation cannot exist between man-made actions. 'Essential' is also eliminated as the essential relationship between two things cannot be influenced by time. It is eternal. However, there can exist a close relationship between one thing and another in a particular situation or time. Thus (c) is the right choice.

It depends on your common sense and intelligence to improvise and locate clues for a particular sentence; however, the following clues may prove helpful.

Clues

1. It may be a preposition.

Every sensible citizen abides __________ the law of the country.

(a) to (b) by
(c) for (d) with

The answer is (b), 'by'.

2. It may be a rule of grammar.

I never miss a football match. I __________ fond of it since my childhood.

(a) am (b) have been
(c) has been (d) will be

The answer is (b), 'have been'.

3. It may be a substitute for a group of words.

His wife died five years ago; since then he has been living as a __________.

(a) divorcee (b) widower
(c) misogynist (d) celibate

The answer is (b), 'widower', because the word for 'a man whose wife is dead' is 'widower'.

4. It may be an idiom or pharse.

The judge decided to resign when he was __________ for promotion to Chief Justice.

(a) passed by (b) passed over
(c) passed off (d) passed out

The answer is (b) because the idiom with the meaning that is required here is 'passed over'.

5. It may be an opposite word.

Most of the issues discussed here in the meeting were trivial and only a few were __________.

(a) interesting (b) practical
(c) significant (d) irrelevant

The answer is (c), 'significant'; it is the opposite word.

6. It may be a word denoting a group.

Questions will be answered by a __________ of experts.

(a) staff (b) panel
(c) bunch (d) band

The answer is (b), 'panel' because the word denoting a group of experts is 'panel'.

7. It may require an idea of the nuance or usage of a particular word.

1. According to the weather __________ it is going to be cloudy today.

(a) announcement (b) indication
(c) predication (d) forecast

The alternatives here have similar meaning, but they have different nuances. 'Announcement' is used for proclaiming something in common usage. 'Indication' denotes pointing out something. 'Predication' is normally used for a prophecy or statement for the future. For indicating the weather, 'forecast' is appropriate.

2. The villagers __________ the death of their leader by keeping all the shops closed.

(a) consoled (b) avenged
(c) mourned (d) protested

Here the answer is (c), 'mourned' because the word in use for expressing sorrow over the death of someone is 'mourn'. This is a matter of usage.

8. It may require a simple inference.

I had not expected to meet him. It was quite an __________ meeting.

(a) organised (b) intentional
(c) accidental (d) undesirable

The answer is (c), 'accidental'. The key words here are 'not expected' and thus it can be easily inferred that 'accidental' is the right choice. There is a logical relationship between the two.

Other Clues for Elimination

Similarly, there are certain helping clues for elimination. It has five stages:

Stage **1.** Structure

Stage **2.** Meaning

Stage **3.** Usage/nuances

Stage **4.** Clues

Stage **5.** Reasoning

(For details, refer to the Elimination Technique in Chapter 12: 'Cloze Test'.)

EXAMPLES

1. While on a routine flight, the aircraft was hit by a missile and __________ into flames.

(a) shot (b) burst

(c) caught (d) blew

(e) fired

Here the answer is (b), 'burst' because all other words are not in keeping with 'into' and thus they are eliminated at the first stage-structure.

2. Authority __________ when it is not supported by the moral purity of its users.

(a) empowers (b) crumbles

(c) prevails (d) waits

The answer is (b), 'crumbles', because other alternatives are eliminated at Stage 2—meaning. 'Empower' is opposite in meaning, 'prevails' is also opposite in meaning and 'waits' is not in accord with the meaning. Thus the only choice left is 'crumbles'.

3. He did not register a __________ to the proposal.

(a) dissent (b) disfavour

(c) divergence (d) deviation

The answer is (a), 'dissent', because other alternatives may have similar meanings, but 'dissent' is the word in use for showing agreement to an idea or a proposal. So other alternatives are eliminated at Stage 3.

Let us take some more examples to illustrate our point.

1. No sooner had he entered the room __________ the light went out and everyone started talking loudly.

(a) but (b) than

(c) if (d) and

The answer is (b). Here the rule of grammar operates.

2. When I saw him through the window __________.

(a) I have run out to open the door

(b) I ran out to open the door

(c) I am running out to open the door

(d) I should run out to open the door

The answer is (b). Here the rule of tense operates.

3. I congratulate you __________ your success.

(a) on (b) for

(c) at (d) in

The answer is (a), 'on'. It is a rule of preposition.

4. I prefer seeing the film __________ reading.

(a) than (b) to

(c) over (d) as

The answer is (b), 'to'. It is a rule of preposition.

5. The festival is always of a very high order because there are a large number of__________ before any performance.

(a) practices (b) exercise

(c) rehearsals (d) repetitions

Here the answer is (c), 'rehearsals'. Here the point to remember is common usage. For preparations done beforehand for performances in dance, drama and theatre the word in common usage is 'rehearsal'.

6. I read 'Treasure Island' because it was __________ by my friend who said it was very exciting.

(a) recommended (b) exhorted

(c) motivated (d) commended

Here the answer is (a), 'recommended'. The word commonly used in such a context is 'recommended'.

7. His English was roughly ________ with my French, so communication was rather difficult.
(a) in accordance with
(b) at par
(c) in time
(d) in tune

Here the answer is (b), 'at par'. The correct phrase with the required meaning is 'at par'.

8. I could not ________ what he wanted to say.
(a) make up (b) make out
(c) make in (d) make away

Here the correct phrase is 'make out' and thus the answer is (b).

9. A committee has been set up to ________ on the problem of terrorism in this region.
(a) investigate (b) inquire
(c) research (d) report

Here the answer can be either 'investigate' or 'report'. Since the connecting word is 'on', the choice will be report.

10. We can't eat this food; it is ________.
(a) rotten (b) old
(c) bad (d) rancid

Here the answer is (a), 'rotten', because this word has the required nuance of meaning.

11. Keats and Shelley were poets of the same period; they were ________.
(a) contemporary (b) colleague
(c) associate (d) co-writers

Here the word 'contemporary' stands for the expression of the same period and thus (a) is the answer.

12. Ramesh has been nominated as the person to settle the dispute between the two warring parties; he is the ________.
(a) judge (b) advocate
(c) arbitrator (d) barrister

Here the answer is (c), 'arbitrator', because this is the substitute word.

13. He has been winning the election, but this time his popularity is on the ________; he may not win this time.
(a) rise (b) wane
(c) ascendance (d) increasing

Here the answer is (b), 'wane' as an antonym is required.

14. Do not ________ him; he has done no harm to any of you.
(a) accuse (b) admire
(c) discuss (d) refer

Here the answer is (a), 'accuse', as an antonym is required.

Practice Set —1

1. It was the help he got from his friends which ________ him through the tragedy.
(a) supported (b) helped
(c) parked (d) boosted

2. Anil got the company car for a ________ price as he was the seniormost employee in the company.
(a) discounted (b) nominal
(c) fixed (d) reduced

3. His ________ of the topic was so good that students had few doubts to raise at the end.
(a) exposition (b) picturisation
(c) clarity (d) exposure

4. Beauty is to ugliness as adversity is to ________.
(a) happiness (b) prosperity
(c) misery (d) cowardice

5. All of us should abide ________ the laws of our country.
(a) on (b) to
(c) by (d) in

6. Everyone in this universe is accountable to God ________ his actions.
(a) for (b) about
(c) of (d) against

7. I never miss a cricket match. I ________ fond of cricket since childhood.
(a) have been (b) has been
(c) will be (d) am

8. He ordered his servant ________.
(a) if he could bring a glass of water
(b) that bring a glass of water
(c) to bring a glass of water
(d) that he should bring a glass of water

9. Though Bindu is poor, ________ she is honest.
(a) still (b) nevertheless
(c) but (d) yet

10. A determined effort will be needed to restrict the country's ________ social services.
(a) profligate (b) profiteering
(c) renegade (d) variegated
(e) expensive

11. I am not concerned ________ him ________ that business.
(a) for; with (b) with; in
(c) with; for (d) by; in

12. He deals ________ foreign goods only, but our firm deals ________ several leading merchants who trade ________ a variety ________ goods.
(a) in, in, with, of
(b) with, with, with, of
(c) with, in, of, with
(d) in, with, in, of

13. The controversy is likely to create ________ between the two communities.
(a) amity (b) bitterness
(c) doubt (d) revenge

14. She is much too ________ to have anything to do with that obnoxious affair.
(a) happy (b) hasty
(c) noble (d) proud

15. His ________ in his family's position is great but he does not boast about it.
(a) deceit (b) presumption
(c) pride (d) status

16. My finger is still ________ where I caught it in the door yesterday.
(a) bruised (b) injured
(c) sore (d) wounded

17. Non-violence is the law of saints as violence is the law of the ________.
(a) brute (b) coward
(c) haughty (d) ignorant

18. We felt as if the ground were ________ beneath our feet.
(a) bursting (b) sinking
(c) slipping (d) smashing

19. The task seemed impossible but somehow he ________ very skilfully in the end.
(a) pulled it off (b) pulled it away
(c) pulled it out (d) pulled it up

20. The enemy paid a large sum as ________.
(a) compensation (b) punishment
(c) redress (d) amends
(e) restitution

21. The unruly behaviour of the soldiers ________ their commander.
(a) incensed (b) aggrieved
(c) impeached (d) tempered
(e) clashed

22. Jayanth was so good at mathematics that his friends considered him to be a ________.
(a) profligate (b) prodigy
(c) prodigal (d) primeval
(e) protocular

23. When Raju heard the news of his selection to the college team he felt ________.
(a) effervescent (b) enamoured
(c) elated (d) embittered
(e) exasperated

24. A son who is unable to look his father in the face is ________.
(a) timid (b) guilty
(c) arrogant (d) ashamed

25. He said that there was no going back because his decision was ________.

(a) peremptory (b) premeditated
(c) parsimonious (d) palatable

26. Progress in government, science, art, literature, philosophy and religion__________ great civilisations from mere groups of communities.
(a) extol (b) describe
(c) distinguish (d) relinquish

27. Since there was adequate grazing area for the herds, the land was __________ populated.
(a) disproportionately(b) sparsely
(c) inadequately (d) rustically

28. The new owners of the paper changed the __________ completely.
(a) outlay (b) layout
(c) outlet (d) outlook

29. This legend has been __________ from father to son.
(a) handed in (b) handed out
(c) handed over (d) handed down

30. Many young men were __________ at street corners for the coffee bar to open.
(a) hanging about (b) hanging on
(c) hanging together(d) hanging back
(e) hanging out

31. Whenever he refers to his favourites he is voluble, but when he talks of his adversaries he is __________.
(a) aggressive (b) bitter
(c) rough (d) miserly
(e) reticent

32. If a man keeps his fingers crossed, he __________.
(a) hopes for the best
(b) suspects everybody
(c) demonstrates peevishness
(d) welcomes every danger
(e) prays for good health

33. Although I had pledged not to tell anyone of the previous evening's trauma, the compulsive urge to unburden myself became __________.
(a) overwhelming
(b) irresistible
(c) impassive
(d) preponderous
(e) indomitable

34. The accused was released on pending hearing of his case.
(a) bale (b) bail
(c) bond (d) deposit

35. I decided to sell a piece of land when I was offered a more __________ price.
(a) exact (b) correct
(c) true (d) realistic

36. You will have to catch the morning flight, so you __________ better get ready.
(a) may (b) had
(c) should (d) would

37. His persuasive tone was able to tackle the boy whom other professors had found.
(a) peripatetic (b) dissolute
(c) tenacious (d) squeamish
(e) obdurate

38. Through a __________ circumstance, they unexpectedly found themselves on the same bus with Uncle Morris.
(a) fortuitous (b) elusive
(c) referential (d) lambent
(e) friable

39. We had a wonderful view of the bay through the __________.
(a) zenith (b) nadir
(c) vicinity (d) proximity
(e) window

40. Lalita failed in the examination because none of her answers was __________ to the questions asked.
(a) referential (b) revealing
(c) pertinent (d) allusive
(e) impeccable

41. The __________ man treated everyone in a __________ manner.
(a) superficial, thorough
(b) defiant, belligerent

(c) supercilious, depreciatory
(d) corrupt, ubiquitous
(e) suspicious, ingenuous

42. We never believed that he would resort to ________ in order to achieve his end; we always regarded him as an honest man.
(a) subterfuge (b) logic
(c) diplomacy (d) charm
(e) cunning

43. His monotonous voice acted like ________ and his audience was soon asleep.
(a) a sedative (b) an anaesthetic
(c) an emetic (d) a purgative
(e) a cathartic

44. In the ________ areas of the rail-road terminal thousands of travellers lingered while waiting for their train.
(a) commodious (b) accomodious
(c) capricious (d) extensive
(e) capacious

45. A legislation was passed to punish brokers who ________ their clients funds.
(a) devastate (b) devour
(c) embezzle (d) defalcate
(e) dawdled

46. Modern architecture has discarded the ________ trimming on buildings and emphasises simplicity of line.
(a) gaudy (b) gaunt
(c) flabbergasting (d) flamboyant
(e) flagrant

47. In the twentieth century, physicists have made their greatest discoveries about the characteristics of ________ objects like the atom and its parts.
(a) infinitesimal (b) infinite
(c) microscopic (d) kaleidoscopic
(e) intangible

48. His moral decadence was marked by his ________ from the ways of integrity and honesty.
(a) declivity (b) obsession
(c) opprobrium (d) departure

Practice Set —2

1. Even when Mohan's reputation was in ________ almost everyone was willing to admit that he had genius.
(a) peregrination
(b) accumulation
(c) eclipse
(d) rebuttal
(e) failure

2. Patriotism, like so many other objects of this imperfect world, is a ________ web of good and evil.
(a) complicated
(b) intricate
(c) entrapped
(d) entangled
(e) tangled

3. The Indian princes and rulers seldom thought in terms of the country as a whole and ________ their time and energy in ________ warfare.
(a) exhausted, common
(b) dissipated mutual
(c) depreciated, expensive
(d) desiccated, isolationist
(e) wasted, reciprocal

4. In his attempt to ________ the condition of poor people in the slums, he found that he needed the aid of wealthy benefactors.
(a) delineate
(b) assay
(c) evaluate
(d) ameliorate
(e) extricate

5. You should ________ this paragraph in order to make the essay more ________.
(a) enlarge, poignant
(b) revise, abstruse
(c) delete; succinct
(d) excise, expansive
(e) expunge; witty

6. He __________ sometimes force himself to work on till late in the night only to find himself unable to do anything the next day.
(a) could (b) used to
(c) would (d) would be
(e) should

7. They have some difficulty __________ all the employees, especially the smaller ones, to confirm __________ the adopted scale of wages.
(a) to get, with
(b) getting, to
(c) in getting, upon
(d) to getting, over
(e) to be getting, up to

8. Fate smiled __________ him in all his ventures.
(a) at (b) with
(c) on (d) above
(e) over

9. The event came __________ as he had predicted it.
(a) by (b) about
(c) off (d) up
(e) on

10. So many servants attended __________ him during his illness.
(a) at (b) upon
(c) on (d) with
(e) about

11. He congratulated his friend __________ the latter's success.
(a) about (b) for
(c) on (d) against
(e) with

12. __________ the event of his resigning his job, his family would starve.
(a) at (b) on
(c) within (d) in

13. In the world of today, material values take precedence __________ spiritual values.
(a) at (b) on
(c) over (d) about

14. His answer was such __________ I expected him to give.
(a) that (b) which
(c) as (d) like which
(e) who

15. Idleness squanders what __________ in a previous generation has won.
(a) laziness (b) indolence
(c) resourcefulness (d) industry
(e) work

16. That charming girl was the __________ of all eyes.
(a) target (b) aim
(c) cynosure (d) doggerel
(e) ambition

17. Any political leader who allows nepotism to flourish should be subject, to __________.
(a) autopsy (b) stringency
(c) stricture (d) punishment
(e) condemnation

18. His attitude to his boss was __________ and caused a good deal of repulsion.
(a) refulgent (b) arrogant
(c) hybrid (d) sycophantic
(e) aggressive

19. His __________ way of life seemed inconsistent with his professions of virtue.
(a) equable (b) tremulous
(c) squeamish (d) compromising
(e) dissolute

20. The influence of the environment on man is revealed by an __________ study.
(a) anthropological (b) ecological
(c) epigraphic (d) numismatic
(e) ecumenical

21. She had a terrible night caused by an __________ during her sleep.
(a) incubus (b) debility
(c) obsession (d) delusion
(e) hypochondria

22. The appropriate word used for marriage between people of different races is __________.

(a) scurrility
(b) miscegenation
(c) reverberation (d) embolism
(e) non sequitur

23. India, for the present, is deeply __________ in economic difficulties, but the Government has taken a pledge to set everything right within five years.
(a) saturated (b) engrossed
(c) swamped (d) vexed
(e) ruined

24. Knowledge is like a deep well fed by __________ springs, and your mind is the little bucket that you drop in it.
(a) immortal (b) inexhaustible
(c) eternal (d) perennial
(e) sterling

25. True health and true success go together for they are inseparably __________ in the thought realm.
(a) tied up (b) bound up
(c) interwined (d) interrelated
(e) interspersed

26. I do not think you will gain anything by insulting and __________ the man you do not agree with.
(a) defaming (b) depicting
(c) charging (d) revamping
(e) enervating

27. The Indian __________ have discovered a way to boost the yield per acre of different __________ of wheat.
(a) agronomists; varieties
(b) economists, kinds
(c) anthropologists, sorts
(d) phrenologists, layers
(e) agroanalysts, vistas

28. The opposition parties allege that prices of essential commodities are __________ like a runaway balloon.
(a) flying (b) reviving
(c) leaping (d) soaring
(e) shooting

29. Success in great ventures calls for __________ concentration and strong personal.
(a) sterling, attachment
(b) standing, participation
(c) continued, apathy
(d) unflagging, involvement
(e) hectic, interest

30. The admiration some leaders earn is __________ by their __________ instinct for hitting the frontlines in newspapers.
(a) developed, uncanny
(b) generated, feeble
(c) engendered, unerring
(d) evolved, aggressive
(e) concended; provocative

31. With the realisation, we have found ourselves left with __________ moral values and little ethical __________.
(a) extreme, judgement
(b) fundamental, scruples
(c) incidental, standards
(d) obsolete, direction
(e) stereotyped, perspective

32. Diplomacy is the best means of __________ peace which a society of sovereign nations has to offer, but, especially under the conditions of __________ world politics and of contemporary war, it is not good enough.
(a) maintaining, today's
(b) presenting, contemporary
(c) retaining, present
(d) promoting, modem
(e) evolving, self-centred

33. For nations conscious of the __________ of modem war, peace must be the goal of their foreign policies.
(a) perils (b) incidence
(c) prudence (d) redundancies
(e) potentialities

34. Nothing is so __________ to a nation as an extreme of self-partiality, and the total want of __________ of what others will naturally hope or fear.

(a) repugnant, sense
(b) delusionary, methodly
(c) fatal, consideration
(d) unethical, discretion
(e) detrimental, concern

35. Charles Lamb's prose is richly __________ with literary ornaments like similes, metaphors, alliterations, transferred epithets, etc.
(a) embalmed (b) saturated
(c) embellished (d) embroidered
(e) embroiled

36. These were reduced to skeletons for they had long been __________ for food.
(a) impinging (b) snarling
(c) craving (d) longing
(e) famishing

37. Even more than beauty, youth attracts me and with __________ appeal.
(a) an ineluctable
(b) an irresistible
(c) an incomprehensible
(d) a delectable
(e) a sententious

38. It was through the Second World War that Russia __________ herself increased __________ in power and wealth and prestige.
(a) saw, abundantly
(b) noticed, gullibly
(c) witnessed, prodigiously

39. Sometimes it is necessary for an author to know what is going on in the minds of his characters. This is called __________.
(a) omnipresence
(b) ominiscience
(c) omnipotence
(d) truculence
(e) introversion

40. The speaker painted a __________ picture of hunger in parts of India.
(a) chimerical (b) passionate
(c) parisimonious (d) poignant

41. Some parents make their commands so __________ that they antagonise their children.
(a) perfunctory (b) peremptory
(c) acrimonious (d) spasmodic
(e) sporadic

42. Discontented wives, dejected lovers, frustrated politicians, all these tend to be __________.
(a) specious (b) abstemious
(c) euphemistic (d) persiflagus
(e) querulous

44. __________ is a person who dabbles in art and letters.
(a) dilettante (e) connoisseur
(c) philistine (d) chauvinist
(e) epicurean

45. The assassination of the Archduke was followed by __________ throughout the whole European continent.
(a) repercussions (b) concatenations
(c) reprisals (d) consternations
(e) enervations

46. A great literary or artistic work is known as a __________.
(a) pot-pourri (b) par excellence
(c) bete noire (d) pecadillo
(e) magnum opus

47. The person who is looking for sympathy talks.
(a) glibly (b) didactically
(c) ominously (d) plaintively
(e) disparagingly

48. As the market becomes __________ competitive, some companies will make larger and larger profits.
(a) well (b) good
(c) more (d) fully
(e) mainly

49. The government should provide attractive tax __________ to create the market of quality goods.
(a) revenues (b) structures
(c) resources (d) incentives
(e) controls

50. The salaries and perks of the employees were not in __________ with their status in this industry.
(a) value (b) conformity
(c) accordance (d) capacity
(e) possession

51. She is so __________ that she easily catches cold.
(a) sensible (b) sincere
(c) sensitive (d) sober

52. The accused __________ having made any statement.
(a) refused (b) denied
(c) rejected (d) declaimed

53. The scientist made a __________ discovery for which he was honoured.
(a) sentimental (b) sensational
(c) sensuous (d) sensual

54. The industrial workers __________ a fair __________ for their work.
(a) request, price (b) sought, salary
(c) demanded, wage(d) asked, pay

55. __________ diseases spread like wild __________.
(a) contagious, flames
(b) contagious, fire
(c) fatal, wind
(d) minor, breeze

56. We decided to take the shortest __________ to our __________.
(a) route, destination(b) root, house
(c) route, residence(d) distance, place

57. It is our __________ to __________ the elders.
(a) object, defy
(b) duty, respect
(c) aim, degrade
(d) hope, disappoint

58. He __________ his fault and was __________.
(a) agreed, excused
(b) refused, freed
(c) denied, sentenced
(d) confessed, pardoned

59. No sooner did he me __________ he tried to run away.
(a) notice, when (b) see, than
(c) watch, that (d) observe, soon

60. I __________ him because of his __________.
(a) love, impertinence
(b) hate, rudeness
(c) admire, hypocrisy
(d) detest, generosity

61. The security forces fired at the __________ who was armed to the __________.
(a) dacoit, teeth (b) criminal, toe
(c) thief, head (d) culprit, nail

62. During the __________ many buildings were __________ to the ground.
(a) riots collapsed
(b) disturbances, brought
(c) fire, razed
(d) floods, razed

63. Weather __________, I shall __________ the office.
(a) allowing, reach
(b) permitting, attend
(c) granting, manage
(d) favourable, visit

64. But for his __________ I would not have __________.
(a) advice, lost
(b) suggestion, won
(c) assistance, failed
(d) help, succeeded

65. Not to __________ of milk, even __________ was not there.
(a) talk, bread (b) mention, rice
(c) speak, water (d) discuss, tea

66. If I __________ a doctor, I would __________ you free.
(a) am, see (b) were, treat
(c) was, examine (d) be, advise

67. You will __________ in business if you get him out of your __________.
(a) prosper, presence
(b) succeed, way

(c) fail, path

(d) lose, sight

68. Many tourists to India visit the beautiful ___________ of Kashmir ___________ in spring and summer.

(a) scencery, generally

(b) town, frequently

(c) lakes, rarely

(d) valley, especially

69. Only ___________ people are ___________ after death.

(a) brave, forgotten

(b) vicious, admired

(c) virtual, known

(d) virtuous, remembered

70. Prices keep on going ___________ these days, and never move ___________.

(a) up, downward

(b) up, underneath

(c) high, low

(d) above, below

Practice Set —3

1. Today Wegener's theory is____; however, he died an outsider treated with ____ by the scientific establishment.

(a) unsupported - approval

(b) dismissed - contempt

(c) unaccepted - approbation

(d) unchallenged - disdain

(e) unrivalled - reverence

2. The revolution in art has not lost its steam; it _____on as fiercely as ever.

(a) trudges

(b) meanders

(c) edges

(d) ambles

(e) rages

3. Each occupation has its own____; bankers, lawyers and computer professionals, for example, all use among themselves language which outsiders have difficulty following.

(a) merits

(b) disadvantages

(c) rewards

(d) jargon

(e) problems

4. ____by nature, Jones spoke very little even to his own family members.

(a) garrulous

(b) equivocal

(c) taciturn

(c) stagnant

(d) pellucid

(e) rancid

5. After the accident, the nerves to her arm were damaged and so the muscles ____ through disuse.

(a) atrophied

(b) contracted

(c) elongated

(d) invigorated

(e) dwindled

6. Some critics maintain that Tennyson's poetry is uneven, ranging from the ____ to the ____.

(a) sublime - elevated

(b) trite - inspired

(c) vacuous - inane

(d) succinct - laconic

(e) sonorous - voluble

7. After grafting there is a ____ of lymphocytes in the lymph glands; the newly produced lymphocytes then move in to attack the foreign tissue.

(a) diminution

(b) proliferation

(c) obliteration

(d) paucity

(e) attraction

8. One ____ the new scheme is that it might actually ____ just those applicants that it was intended to encourage.

(a) highlight of - stimulate

(b) feature of - attract

(c) problem with - induce
(d) attraction of - intimidate
(e) drawback of - daunt

9. Corruption is ____ in our society; the integrity of even senior officials is____.
(a) growing - unquestioned
(b) endangered - disputed
(c) pervasive – intact
(d) tractable
(e) stoic

10. The intellectual flexibility inherent in a multicultural nation has been____in classrooms where emphasis on British-American literature has not reflected the cultural ____ of our country.
(a) eradicated - unanimity
(b) encouraged - aspirations
(c) stifled - diversity
(d) thwarted - uniformity
(e) inculcated - divide

11. The conclusion of his argument, while____, is far from____.
(a) stimulating - interesting
(b) worthwhile - valueless
(c) esoteric - obscure
(d) germane - relevant
(e) abstruse - incomprehensible

12. In the Middle Ages, the ____ of the great cathedrals did not enter into the architects' plans; almost invariably a cathedral was positioned haphazardly in ____ surroundings.
(a) situation - incongruous
(b) location - apt
(c) ambience - salubrious
(d) durability - convenient
(e) majesty – grandiose

13. He was treated like a ____ and cast out from his community.
(a) ascetic
(b) prodigy
(c) prodigal
(d) pariah
(e) tyro

14. The teacher accused me of ____ because my essay was so similar to that of another student.
(a) procrastination
(b) plagiarism
(c) Celerity
(d) confusion
(e) decorum

15. We live in a ____ age; everyone thinks that maximizing pleasure is the point of life
(a) ubiquitous
(b) propitious
(c) sporadic
(d) corrupt
(e) hedonistic

16. Thankfully the disease has gone into____; it may not recur for many years.
(a) treatment
(b) sequestration
(c) quarantine
(d) remission
(e) oblivion

17. People from all over the world are sent by their doctors to breathe the pure, ____ air in this mountain region.
(a) invigorating
(b) soporific
(c) debilitating
(d) insalubrious
(e) aromatic

18. As were many colonial administrators, Gregory was ____ in his knowledge of the grammar of the local language, though his accent was____.
(a) deficient - poor
(b) competent - adequate
(c) faultless - awful
(d) well-versed - effective
(e) erratic - eccentric

19. Though Adam Bede is presented to us by the author as ____ fiction, there are none of the life-like meanderings of the story of Amos Barton.
(a) realistic
(b) romantic

(c) imaginative
(d) educational
(e) entertaining

20. There is a general ____ in the United States that our ethics are declining and that our moral standards are____.
(a) feeling - normalizing
(b) idea - futile
(c) optimism - improving
(d) complaint - deteriorating
(e) outlook - escalating

21. Homo sapiens, the proud splitter of the atom, inventor of the electronic computer, ____of the genetic code may be humbled by a lowly ____ of the sewers and soils the microbe.
(a) designer - inhabitant
(b) discoverer - rodent
(c) writer - organism
(d) decipherer - denizen
(e) author - purifier

22. After centuries of obscurity, this philosopher's thesis is enjoying a surprising____.
(a) dismissal
(b) remission
(c) decimation
(d) longevity
(e) renaissance

23. The threat of war, far from____, lay heavily in the air, and the villagers, while ____ going about their normal activities, were unable to shake off the feeling of impending catastrophe.
(a) receding - ostensibly
(b) diminishing - contentedly
(c) increasing - apparently
(d) escalating - joyfully
(e) subsiding - felicitously

24. Although alarmed by the____, Professor Symes had no reason to doubt the ____ of his student's results, for this student was nothing if not reliable.
(a) conclusions - folly
(b) deductions - impudence
(c) implications - veracity
(d) errors - truth
(e) inferences – invalidity

25. Although I was_____ of his plans, I encouraged him, because there was no one else who was willing to help.
(1) sceptical
(2) remorseful
(3) fearful
(4) excited

26. You have no business to___ pain on a weak and poor person.
(1) inflict
(2) put
(3) direct
(4) force

27. Her uncle died in a car accident. He was quite rich. She suddenly, ___ all her uncle's money.
(1) succeeded
(2) caught
(3) gave
(4) inherited

28. There was a major accident. The plane crashed. The pilot ____did not see the tower.
(1) likely
(2) probably
(3) scarcely
(4) hurriedly

29. The car we were travelling in _____ a mile from home.
(1) broke off
(2) broke down
(3) broke into
(4) broke up

30. What are you ____ in the kitchen cupboard ?
(1) looking in
(2) looking on
(3) looking to
(4) looking for

ANSWER KEY

Set 1

1. (b)	25. (a)
2. (b)	26. (c)
3. (a)	27. (b)
4. (b)	28. (b)
5. (c)	29. (d)
6. (a)	30. (a)
7. (a)	31. (e)
8. (c)	32. (a)
9. (d)	33. (b)
10. (e)	34. (b)
11. (b)	35. (d)
12. (d)	36. (c)
13. (b)	37. (e)
14. (c)	38. (a)
15. (d)	39. (e)
16. (a)	40. (c)
17. (a)	41. (b)
18. (c)	42. (a)
19. (c)	43. (a)
20. (a)	44. (a)
21. (a)	45. (c)
22. (b)	46. (a)
23. (c)	47. (c)
24. (a)	48. (d)

Set 2

1. (c)	25. (c)	49. (b)
2. (e)	26. (a)	50. (b)
3. (e)	27. (a)	51. (c)
4. (d)	28. (d)	52. (b)
5. (c)	29. (d)	53. (b)
6. (c)	30. (a)	54. (c)
7. (b)	31. (a)	55. (b)
8. (c)	32. (a)	56. (c)
9. (b)	33. (e)	57. (b)
10. (c)	34. (c)	58. (d)
11. (c)	35. (c)	59. (b)
12. (d)	36. (e)	60. (b)
13. (c)	37. (b)	61. (b)
14. (c)	38. (c)	62. (c)
15. (d)	39. (b)	63. (b)
16. (c)	40. (d)	64. (d)
17. (e)	41. (b)	65. (c)
18. (d)	42. (e)	66. (b)
19. (e)	43. (b)	67. (b)
20. (b)	44. (a)	68. (d)
21. (c)	45. (a)	69. (d)
22. (e)	46. (e)	70. (a)
23. (c)	47. (d)	
24. (d)	48. (c)	

Set 3

1. (d)	16. (d)
2. (e)	17. (a)
3. (d)	18. (c)
4. (c)	19. (a)
5. (d)	20. (d)
6. (a)	21. (d)
7. (b)	22. (e)
8. (e)	23. (a)
9. (b)	24. (c)
10. (c)	25. (a)
11. (e)	26. (a)
12. (a)	27. (d)
13. (d)	28. (b)
14. (b)	29. (b)
15. (e)	30. (d)

Appendix

Sentence Completion: Questions from Various Competitive Examinations with Frequency Analysis

Set I

1. He is too __________ to be deceived easily.
(a) strong (b) modem
(c) kind (d) honest_
(e) intelligent

2. Ravi's behaviour is worthy of __________ by all the youngsters.
(a) trail (b) emulation
(c) following (d) exploration
(e) experiment

3. The speaker did not properly use the time as he went on __________ on one point alone.
(a) dilating (b) devoting
(c) deliberation (d) diluting
(e) distributing

4. The principal and staff have made __________ efforts to enable the students to attend college on the days of the bus strike.
(a) integrated (b) deliberate
(c) concerted (d) systematic

5. It was __________ that a mind so pure and searching could miss the truth.
(a) likely (b) unlikely
(c) possible (d) scarcely

6. The __________ is working on wood.
(a) artifact (b) artistic
(c) artist (d) artisan

7. If an indelible ink is used, this will not be __________.
(a) observed (b) obligated
(c) obliterated (d) obviated

8. He __________ that he could speak languages
(a) challenged
(b) boasted
(c) submitted
(d) suggested

9. It is indeed __________ that 40 years after independence, we have failed to __________ a suitable education or examination system.
(a) bad, produce
(b) improper, create
(c) sad, evolve
(d) objectionable, present

10. The boy you met yesterday is in class. __________.
(a) ninth
(b) the ninth
(c) nine
(d) the nine

11. The children were disappointed because they had hoped __________ with us.
(a) to have gone
(b) to go
(c) would have gone.

12. He is the friend __________ I trust most.
(a) him (b) whom
(c) which (d) who

13. The meeting was presided __________ by the Prime Minister.
(a) on (b) upon
(c) up (d) over

14. He __________ his camera on the railway.
(a) laid (b) lay
(c) lain

15. The doctor tried both pencillin and sulphamilamide; the pencillin proved to be the __________ effective drug.
(a) very
(b) more
(c) most

Set 2

1. The soldiers were instructed to ________ restraint and handle the situation peacefully.
(a) exercise (b) control
(c) prevent (d) enforce
(e) remain

2. My friend took his first pay to the bank to ________ it in his account.
(a) deposit (b) deficit
(c) debit (d) demote

3. Family planning is essential for curbing the rapid ________ in population.
(a) spread (b) increase
(c) spurt (d) augment

4. The ties that bind a family together are ________ that they can hardly withstand any strain.
(a) tenacious (b) twisted
(c) tenuous (d) tentative

5. The stenographer is very efficient. He is ________ to his firm.
(a) a credit (b) a blessing
(c) an asset (d) a boon

6. The young man lost his way in the forest and found that he had become a/an ________ to the dacoits.
(a) enemy (b) adversary
(c) decoy (d) quarry

7. He sold property because he was under a lot of ________.
(a) account (b) debt
(c) loan (d) credit

8. He was an ________ who was fond of weird pets.
(a) ambitious (b) amiable
(c) eccentric (d) emotional

9. He bought new shoes last month but they are already ________ out.
(a) given (b) gone
(c) knocked (d) worn

10. He knew everything better than anybody else, and it was an affront to his ________ vanity that you should disagree with him.
(a) overwrought (b) overwhelming
(c) overweening (d) overstrung

11. The Government is confident that the standard of living will begin to ________ again soon.
(a) revive (b) lift
(c) flourish (d) rise

12. The communalists represent the ________ of everything noble we have inherited from our culture and history.
(a) antagonism (b) immorality
(c) antiodote (d) antithesis

13. The bureaucrat was ________ for his role in the scam.
(a) reinstated (b) criticised
(c) indicted (d) indited

14. The transfer of territories could not take place because one state ________ the findings of the Commission.
(a) objected (b) questioned
(c) rejected (d) disputed

15. The mounting pressure was so overwhelming that he ultimately ________ to her wish.
(a) agreed in (b) cowed in
(c) gave in (d) yielded in

Set 3

1. Joseph introduced me ________ his mother as the best batsman.
(a) to (b) by
(c) with (d) of

2. She ________ in the crowd because of her height and flaming red hair.
(a) stood by (b) stood off
(c) stood up (d) stood out

3. History records seventeen incursions of Sultan Mahmood ________ India.
(a) against (b) into
(c) upon (d) on

4. He is being considered ________ senior managerial position.
(a) of (b) to
(c) for (d) towards
(e) by

5. It should be the aim of every educated Indian to see that as ________ as possible people become literate.
(a) few (b) most
(c) many (d) much

6. He ________ for their company since 1972.
(a) is working (b) had worked
(c) worked
(d) had been working

7. Washing machines ________ popular in India in the last ten years or so.
(a) became (b) are become
(c) have become (d) are becoming

8. He succeeded in getting possession ________ his land after a long court case.
(a) for (b) to
(c) of (d) with
(e) against

9. Prabha's ________ in athletics yielded rich ________ as she got a scholarship.
(a) performance, money
(b) defeat, results
(c) behaviour, appreciation
(d) excellence, dividends
(e) failure, disappointment

10. In a changing and ________ unstructured business environment, creativity and innovation are being ________ demanded of executives.
(a) excessively, rapidly
(b) highly, extremely
(c) increasingly, moderately
(d) progressively, increasingly

11. In ________ of international matters, there is always an element of risk in ________ one might do.
(a) view, whichever
(b) many, doing
(c) defence, wrong
(d) case, whatever
(e) spite, whatever

12. Moreover, a fact-finding mission ________ by BSN to India in January this year strongly recommended that the French group should do it alone, and not hand over to ________ an Indian partner.
(a) constituted, authority
(b) organised, papers
(c) dispatched, control
(d) sponsored, power

13. Many women in the developing countries experience a cycle of poor health that ________ before they are born and persists through adulthood passing from generation to generation.
(a) derives (b) establishes
(c) begins (d) originates

14. He didn't have the ________ idea of the villagers' problems.
(a) smallest (b) finest
(c) faintest (d) feeblest

15. Everyone should ________ himself against illness since medical care has now become expensive.
(a) vaccinate
(b) insure
(c) brace
(d) ensure
(e) inoculate

Set 4

1. These essays are intellectually ________ and represent various levels of complexity.
(a) revealing
(b) modern
(c) superior
(d) demanding
(e) persistent

2. His interest in the study of human behaviour is indeed very ________.
(a) strong (b) large
(c) broad (d) vast
(e) deep

3. I will be leaving for Delhi tonight and ________ to return by this weekend.
(a) waiting (b) plan
(c) going (d) likely
(e) making

4. You need ________ shoes for walking in the hills.
(a) good (b) comfortable
(c) satisfactory (d) sturdy

5. Authority ________ when it is not supported by the moral purity of its user.
(a) waits (b) crumbles
(c) empowers (d) prevails

6. Though they did not speak to each other much, there was a ________ understanding between them.
(a) placid (b) contractual
(c) tacit (d) verbal

7. Walking at three O'clock, I heard the ________ of thunder.
(a) clank (b) crackle
(c) rumble (d) ripple

8. If something is beyond the ________ of human knowldege man can know nothing about it.
(a) edge (b) view
(c) end (d) boundary

9. He ________ in wearing the old fashioned coat in spite of his wife's disapproval.
(a) resists (b) desists
(c) persists (d) insists

10. The Education Minister emphasised the need to discover and ________ each student's ________ talents.
(a) enlarge, dormant
(b) belittle, concealed
(c) suppress, potential
(d) flourish, hidden
(e) develop, intrinsic

11. He is usually ________, but today he appears rather ________.
(a) strict, unwell (b) tense, restless
(c) quiet, calm
(d) happy, humorous
(e) calm, disturbed

12. He is so ________ that everyone is always ________ to help him in his work.
(a) helpful, reluctant
(b) aloof, cooperative
(c) admant, enthusiastic
(d) miserly, ignorant
(e) magnanimous, eager

13. ________ is a criminal ________ in England and covers cases where offensive descriptions of Christianity are published.
(a) Nepotism, act
(b) Sacrilege, violence
(c) Blasphemy, offence
(d) Obscenity, deviation
(e) Impiety, transgression

14. Priya is not ________ for this kind of a job.
(a) cut in (b) cut up
(c) cut through (d) cut out

15. The lawyer was threatened ________ dire consequences.
(a) from (b) by
(c) with (d) of

Set 5

1. It was very difficult to dig as the ground was very ________.
(a) thin (b) soft
(c) rigid (d) hardest
(e) hard

2. Would you ________ giving your book to me?
(a) desires (b) mind
(c) call (d) observe
(e) thought

3. His ________ speech has seriously ________ the young minds.
(a) audacious, delighted

(b) maiden, flattered
(c) humorous, damaged
(d) irresponsible, misled
(e) eccentric, questioned.

4. On ________ of the enquiry, if it is found that the ________ are true, the enquiry officer will report the matter to the higher authority.
(a) demand, finding
(b) completion, allegations
(c) instituting, charges
(d) withdrawal, inferences
(e) establishment, results

5. Shoppers used to surly clerks behind retail counters elsewhere in China are in for a ________.
(a) gift
(b) shock
(c) treat
(d) None of the above

6. This was a dangerous method of ________ popular support.
(a) securing (b) soliciting
(c) extracting (d) expecting

7. The commandos took a long time to ________ the resistance of the rebels.
(a) cut down (b) pull down
(c) tone down (d) break down

8. The priest addressed the ________ for more than an hour and was listened to with rapt attention.
(a) staff
(b) audience
(c) congregation
(d) crew

9. Workers in earlier days were ________ because of which the industries a lot.
(a) honest, lost
(b) rich, flourished
(c) autocrats, developed
(d) inefficient, suffered
(e) idle, prospered

10. If you do not ________, all your monthly expenses would ________ your income.
(a) spend, gain
(b) save, outwit
(c) economise, exceed
(d) think, swallow
(e) realise, enhance.

11. After the present tax holiday period ________ the power cost to users may become ________.
(a) starts, unreasonable
(b) sets, perishable
(c) ends, less
(d) enhances, negligible
(e) ends, intolerable

12. A good teacher-student relationship helps create a ________ and peaceful atmosphere where there is no room for any ________ of educational activity.
(a) harmonious, interruption
(b) congenial, development
(c) quiet, confusion
(d) cordial, education
(e) delightful, exaggeration

13. Whom would you prefer ________ the two of us?
(a) among
(b) of
(c) between
(d) to
(e) in

14. The cashier ________ the money and signed a receipt for it.
(a) collects (b) accepts
(c) receives (d) measured
(e) counted

15. No sooner does he arrive than everyone ________ up in his honour.
(a) stood (b) stands
(c) stand (d) got
(e) bowed

ANSWER KEY

Set 1	Set 2	Set 3	Set 4	Set 5
1. (e)	1. (a)	1. (a)	1. (a)	1. (e)
2. (b)	2. (a)	2. (b)	2. (e)	2. (b)
3. (a)	3. (b)	3. (b)	3. (b)	3. (d)
4. (c)	4. (c)	4. (c)	4. (b)	4. (b)
5. (b)	5. (c)	5. (c)	5. (b)	5. (c)
6. (d)	6. (d)	6. (d)	6. (c)	6. (b)
7. (c)	7. (b)	7. (c)	7. (c)	7. (d)
8. (b)	8. (c)	8. (c)	8. (d)	8. (c)
9. (c)	9. (d)	9. (d)	9. (c)	9. (d)
10. (c)	10. (c)	10. (d)	10. (e)	10. (c)
11. (b)	11. (d)	11. (d)	11. (e)	11. (c)
12. (b)	12. (d)	12. (c)	12. (e)	12. (a)
13. (d)	13. (c)	13. (d)	13. (c)	13. (c)
14. (a)	14. (d)	14. (c)	14. (d)	14. (e)
15. (b)	15. (c)	15. (b)	15. (c)	15. (b)

Table Sentence Completion: Frequency Analysis (Examination covered from 2009 to 2012)

Examination / Year	*Noun*	*Verb*	*Adjective*	*Adverb*	*Preposition*	*Misscellaneous*
RBI GradeB-2009	1	1+1+1+1				
LIC AAO-2011	1	1	1+1+1			
IES-2011	1	1+1+1+1	1+1+1+1	1		
New India INSURENCE-2011	1	1	1+1			
MBA Rural Mangment		1+1+1+1				
SSC TR1-2012		1+1	1	1+1		

Noun-4, Verb-16, Adjective-10, Adverb-3, Prepositon-0, Miscellaneous-0

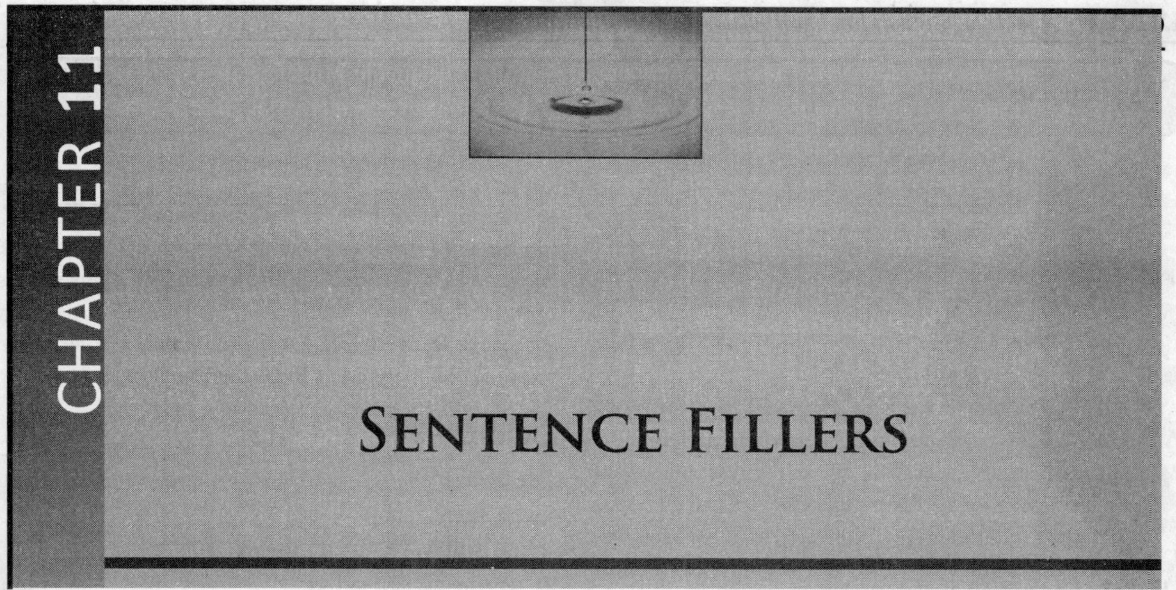

SENTENCE FILLERS

Stem Filling or Sentence Filler is sentence completion with a variance. In a simple sentence completion, you fill the blank with one of the words given as choices to you. In this format, part of a sentence is given which needs to be completed with one of the various sentence parts provided to you as alternatives. The apparent difference is that now we have a group of words in place of a single word. This requires an understanding of the spirit of the stem part of the sentence and the filler part is to be matched with it both in terms of structure and meaning.

We can find a structural clue or a semantic clue or both in the stem part and match the stem with the alternatives one after another. Only one choice will match; the rest will be wrong.

We may present it as Stem Filler Matching (SFM) Technique.

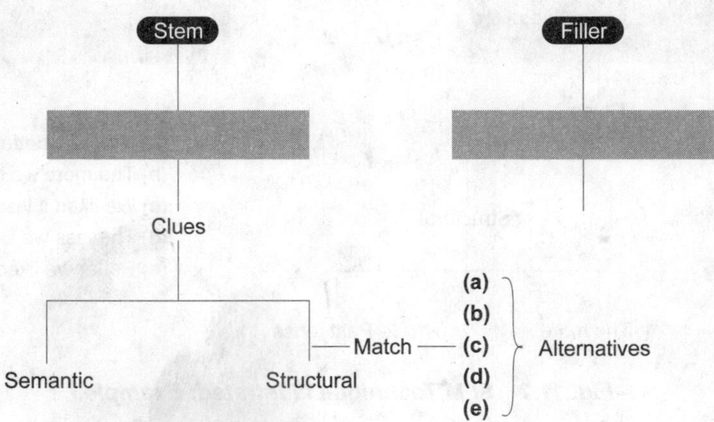

Fig. 11.1 Stem Filler Matching Technique

SFM Technique

Example 1

The more we looked at the piece of modern art, ________.

(a) it looked better (b) the more we like it
(c) we liked it less (d) the less we liked it
(e) better we liked it

In the stem part we have structural clue 'the more' and it is a past tense sentence. The structural demand is that the filler part also must have an expression like 'the more' (the + a word). Taking this clue, we can eliminate alternatives (a), (c) and (e). Now alternative (b) has 'the more' and the alternative (d) has the 'the less'. These two are correct, but (b) is further eliminated because the filler is in the present tense and the stem is in the past tense. (d) is the correct answer because it is in the past tense. We can illustrate it by a chart.

Example 2

He is so lazy that he ________

(a) always extends help to others to complete their work.
(b) dislikes to postpone the work that he undertakes to do.
(c) can seldom complete his work on time.
(d) can't delay the schedule of completing the work.
(e) can't depend on others for getting his work done.

(Bank PO, 1995.)

In the stem part we have **a semantic clue 'lazy'**. On the basis of this we can match with the alternatives. Alternative (a) is opposite in meaning; alternative (b) is opposite in meaning; alternative (c) is opposite in meaning; alternative (e) is irrelevant; only (c) matches in terms of meaning and therefore it is the correct answer.

Example 3

The doctor warns him that unless he gives up smoking ________

(a) will he be able to recover.
(b) he will not suffer.
(c) his health will soon be recovered.
(d) he will not recover.

In the stem part we have two clues:

1. **unless—structural**
2. **smoking—semantic**

'Unless' here demands a 'not' in the filler part. Thus alternatives (a) and (c) are wrong. Alternatives (b) and (d) are structurally right, but according to 'smoking' the expression 'not suffer' is wrong, but 'not recover' is right. Thus only (d) matches. Here we have matched on the basis of two clues, one structural, one semantic.

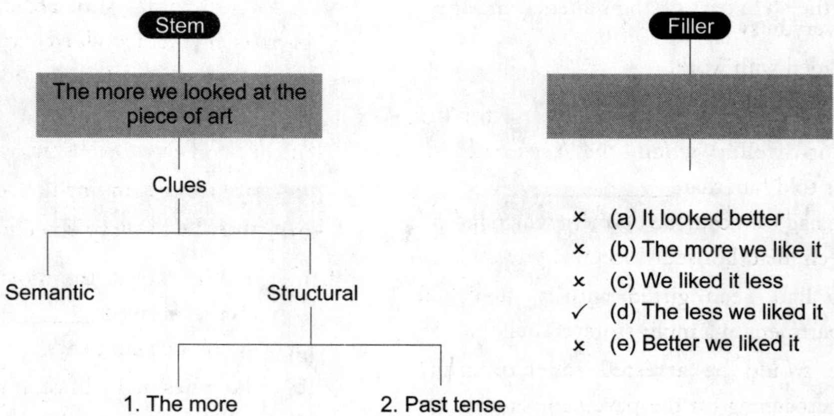

Fig. 11.2 SFM Technique Illustrated: Example I

Practice Set —1

1. Despite his best efforts to conceal his anger __________

(a) we could detect that he was very happy.

(b) he failed to give us an impression of his agony.

(c) he succeeded in camouflaging his emotions.

(d) he could succeed in doing it easily.

(e) people came to know that he was annoyed.

2. Even though it is a very large house, __________

(a) there is a lot of space available in it for children.

(b) there is hardly any space available for children.

(c) there is no dearth of space for children.

(d) the servants take a long time to clean it.

(e) the municipal taxes on it are very heavy.

3. Practically, very little work could be completed in the last week as it was __________

(a) full of working days.

(b) a very hectic week.

(c) full of holidays.

(d) a very busy week.

(e) loaded with work.

4. It was an extremely pleasant surprise for the hutment-dweller when the Government officials told him that __________

(a) he had to vacate the hutment which he had been unauthorisedly occupying.

(b) he had been gifted with a furnished apartment in a multi-storeyed building.

(c) he would be arrested for wrongfully encroaching on the pavement outside his dwelling.

(d) they would not accede to his request.

(e) they had received the orders from the court to take possession of all his belongings.

5. Although he is reputed for making very candid statements, __________

(a) his today's speech was not fairly audible.

(b) his promises had always been realistic.

(c) his speech was very interesting.

(d) people follow whatever he instructs them.

(e) his todays's statements were very ambiguous.

6. I felt somewhat more relaxed __________

(a) but tense as compared to earlier.

(b) and tense as compared to earlier.

(c) as there was already no tension at all.

(d) and tension-free as compared to earlier.

(e) because the worry had already captured my mind.

7. With great efforts his son succeeded in convincing him not to donate his entire wealth to an orphanage __________

(a) and lead the life of a wealthy merchant.

(b) but to a home for the forsaken children.

(c) and make an orphan of himself.

(d) as the orphanage needed a lot of donations.

(e) as the orphanage had been set up by him.

8. In Asian countries, stiff tariffs and other import barriers, plus undervalued currencies __________

(a) make imported goods prohibitively expensive.

(b) do not encourage smuggling.

(c) make the economy noncompetitive.

(d) give rise to sharp economic inequalities.

9. In the third world, the most over-militarised countries tend to be __________

(a) the oil rich countries.

(b) the ones who have traditionally had a military past.

(c) neighbours scared of each other.
(d) the ones economically interdependent.

10. It is neither the acquistion of knowledge nor the use of knowledge that distinguishes the outstanding performer, but rather the cognitive skills that are ______________
(a) inborn and unalterable.
(b) learnt with great determination and effort.
(c) inherited and are passed on from one generation to another.
(d) developed and exercised in the process of acquiring and using knowledge.

11. The value of a work of art is seldom precisely measurable in terms of ______________
(a) aesthetic harmony.
(b) goods produced, or manhours saved or an increase in the GNP.
(c) the abstract sense of harmony the work exudes.
(d) the labour invested in it.

12. Where there is no order, human beings attempt to impose it ______________.
(a) that proves the point that humans everywhere are orderly beings.
(b) that's why we do not have anarchy anywhere.
(c) disorder is alien to human nature.
(d) we look at the welter of stars in the night sky and see bears, dippers, crabs and scorpions.

13. Until recently psychologists believed certain mistreatment and poverty bred these kinds-to-adult criminals, and that they were psychotics. But ______________
(a) now it is proved that they are not necessarily psychotic.
(b) this point appears to be illogical.
(c) the environment factors, it is now proved, do not have any significant effect on man's ability to adjust socially.
(d) according to a bold new theory of the criminal mind, some kids just choose to be criminals, just as the others opt to be lawyers, teachers, or musicians.

14. Some kids bully their friends and shun the love showered on them. Eventually, they ______________
(a) grow up to be good law-abiding citizens.
(b) become disgusted with their way of life and take a turn for the better.
(c) grow up to be poets and artists of great merit.
(d) grow up to rob, rape and kill.

15. Somewhat further in the future lies the auspicious possibility of creating geothermal wells where none naturally exists. This could be accomplished by ______________
(a) harnessing thermal energy from the seas and storing it in these wells in unlimited quantity.
(b) building atomic reactors underground which use the earth's heat for fuel.
(c) splitting underground rocks heated naturally by volcanic activity deep in the earth and then pumping in water to produce steam.
(d) altering climatic conditions which would make it possible to have these wells in any part of the world.

16. Sucrose polyester pours like vegetable oil and spreads like margarine. You can eat it to your heart's delight, because ______________
(a) it has maximum fat.
(b) it doesn't contain calories.
(c) it is artificially produced.
(d) it is not toxic.

17. It is a shame to say it, but apparently mankind thrives on conflict ______________
(a) a nation is never so ălert and alive as when it is a nation at war.
(b) actually, life originated in conflict.

(c) peace is an interval between two wars.

(d) wars in many subtle ways have contributed to the betterment of human life.

18. Public opinion is notoriously fickle. Cold fusion came into spotlight for a week or two, ________

(a) and now is being discussed with rare intensity all over the world.

(b) but could not hold public attention for long.

(c) and then held the stage for over a month feebly.

(d) only to be pushed offstage when the arguments became too complicated.

19. For centuries, society had made the mentally ill pay a heavy price for their affliction. Their bizzare behaviour has long aroused ________

(a) sympathy and understanding for the mentally unsound.

(b) a strange mixture of care and anxiety about their condition.

(c) the cruel hostility of the ignorant.

(d) a strong feeling of antipathy in the minds of the sane.

20. He always stammers in public meetings, but his today's speech ________

(a) was fairly audible to everyone present in the hall.

(b) was not received satisfactorily.

(c) was not liked by the audience.

(d) could not be understood properly.

(e) was surprisingly fluent.

21. He tames animals because he ________

(a) is fond of them.

(b) hates them.

(c) wants to set them free.

(d) is afraid of them.

(e) seldom loves them.

22. He has no money now ________

(a) although he was very poor once.

(b) as he has given up all his wealth.

(c) becuase he was very rich once.

(d) because the had received huge donations once.

(e) because he always spends money with utmost care.

23. In order to raise the company's profit, the employees ________

(a) demanded two additional increments.

(b) decided to go on paid holidays.

(c) requested the management to implement new welfare schemes.

(d) offered to work overtime without any compensation.

(e) decided to raise the cost of raw material.

24. Although the details of dreams tend to be highly individual, varying from person to person, their overall themes and patterns are ________

(a) of a bewildering variety.

(b) too difficult to comprehend.

(c) too simplistic to require any scientific explanations.

(d) remarkably consistent.

25. A seed cast by the wind, fallen from its parent or planted by man, sinks into the earth and germinates ________

(a) as rain waters send it deep down the earth.

(b) when air and water seep through its outer coat.

(c) into a plant and then produces seeds of its own.

(d) into a hundred thousand plants producing their own seeds.

Additional Set

Based on Questions and Trends in Very Recent Examinations

Practice Set —2

Directions 1-5

Which of the phrase (a), (b), (c) and (d) given below each statement should be placed in the blank space provided so as to make a meaningful and grammatically correct sentence? If none of the sentences is appropriate, mark (e) i.e. 'None of these' as the answer.

1. Refuting the rationale behind frequent agitations for formation of separate states, a recent report______.
   (a) proved that such agitations result in loss of governmental property
   (b) indicated that the formation of small states does not necessarily improve the economy
   (c) suggested that only large scale agitations have been effective in bringing out desired change in the past
   (d) recommended dividing large states into smaller ones to improve governance
   (e) None of these

2. Overlooking the fact that water scarcity intensifies during summer ____.
   (a) the government issued guidelines to all builders to limit their consumption to acceptable limits
   (b) provision for rainwater harvesting has been made to aid irrigation in drought prone areas
   (c) the water table did not improve even after receiving normal monsoon in the current year
   (d) many residential areas continue to use swimming pools, wasting large quantities of water
   (e) None of these

3. He has lost most of his life's earning in the stock market but________.
   (a) he still seems to be leading his life luxuriously and extravagantly
   (b) he could not save enough to repay his enormous' debts
   (c) stock market is not a safe option; to invest money unless done with caution
   (d) experts have been suggesting to avoid investments in stock market because of its unpredictable natures
   (e) None of these

4. Achieving equality for women is not only a laudable goal, ______.
   (a) political reforms are also neglected preventing women from entering legislatures and positions of power
   (b) the problem is also deep rooted in the society and supported by it
   (c) their empowerment is purposefully hampered by people with vested interests in all sections of the society
   (d) it is also equally difficult to achieve and maintain for a long term
   (e) None of these.

5. ______ or else they would not keep electing him year after year.
   (a) The party leader gave a strong message to the mayor fact improving his political style
   (b) Owing to numerous scandals against the mayor, he was total to resign from the post immediately
   (c) The mayor threatened the residents against filing a complaint against him

(d) The residents must really be impressed with the political style of their mayor

(e) None of these

Directions 6-10

In each question below two sentences or parts of sentences are given with two blank spaces (___), (___) between them. From among the three parts / sentences denoted by (A), (B) and (C) given below each, find out which two can fill up the blanks in proper sequence (i.e., the order in which these are given in the answer options) to make the sentence / group of sentences meaningfully complete.

6. Four years ago, I had major surgery. (_____) (_____). I was too ill.

(A) It left me disabled.

(B) My attempts to go back to work could not succeed.

(C) I had fully recovered except for some minor weakness.

(a) (B) and (A) only

(b) (C) and (A) only

(c) (B) and (C) only

(d) (A) and (B) only

(e) (A) and (C) only

7. Based on scientific research, scientists conclude that (_____) (_____), they will live even more than a hundred years.

(A) keep themselves active all through.

(B) exercise more, ensure proper vitamin intake.

(C) human species, if regulate their diet.

(a) only (A) and (B)

(b) only (A) and (C)

(c) only (C) and (A)

(d) only (C) and (B)

(e) Either C and (A) and (C) and (B)

8. Central Government's plans to (_____) (_____), despite the fact that the opposition parties united front had mobilized support of general public at the outskirts of Mumbai.

(A) defy the curfew imposed to prevent the proposed rally from protesting against the hike in petrol prices.

(B) exercise more, ensure proper vitamin intake.

(C) human species, if regulate their diet.

(a) only (A) and (B)

(b) only (A) and (C)

(c) only (C) and (A)

(d) only (C) and (B)

(e) Either (B) and (c) or (A) and (C)

9. The economic gloom was exacerbated yesterday by Greek Prime Minister's surprise announcement (_____) (_____), and vote might put the torturously conceived package in jeopardy.

(A) that was struck last week.

(B) that he would recommend the Parliament to strike down the obnoxious deal.

(C) that his country would hold a referendum on the European debt deal.

(a) (C) and (A) only

(b) (B) and (A) only

(c) (A) and (C) only

(d) Either (C) and (A) or (B) and (A)

10. The world's most powerful nations were warned (_____) (_____), and trigger mass social unrest.

(A) that could cost millions of jobs around the globe.

(B) that international economy was on the brink of a deep new economic crisis.

(C) that his country would hold a referendum on the European debt deal.

(a) (C) and (A) only
(b) (B) and (A) only
(c) (A) and (C) only
(d) Either (C) and (A) or (B) and (A)

Directions (Qs. 11 to 15)

Which of the phrases (a), (b), (c) and (d) given below each statement should be placed in the blank space provided so as to make a meaningful and grammatically correct sentence ? If none of the sentences is appropriate, mark (e) as the answer.

11. Although information technology has entered the homes, offices and hearts of many citizens of India, _______
(a) India provides the highest number of IT experts to the world every year
(b) ninny people in rural areas still remain ignorant of its immense benefits
(c) government has done its best by funding research in this Held appropriately
(d) the face of communication in the years to come would change completely from the bygone years
(e) None of these

12. While the environment friendly-Nuclear energy could make a large addition to the energy resources, ______
(a) experts have a lot of expectations from this cleaner method or producing energy
(b) the government is determined to extract maximum out or this technology in the near future
(c) international lobby has been pressurizing the developing nations to shift their energy production from coal to nuclear power.
(d) the problem of locating adequate numbers of Uranium reserves to run the reactors is yet to be sorted out
(e) None of these

13. _______, experts proposed the idea of a common school system.
(a) Overlooking the fundamental right of quality education of every child in India
(b) Since the curricular requirements of a rural child is different from an urban child
(c) Based on the fact that difference in the quality of schools acts as a ground for discrimination
(d) Since a large percentage of Indian children are getting free education
(e) None of these

14. _______, the soil today is nowhere as rich in native minerals as it used to be some centuries ago.
(a) As there is a growing consent among farmers regarding limiting the use of chemical fertilizers
(b) As the chemical inputs in agriculture improved the yield many folds
(c) Owing to the uninhibited use of chemical inputs in agriculture
(d) Awareness among farmers regarding the side effects of chemical farming grew when
(e) None of these

15. As allegations of crores of rupees changing hands to permit illegal mining began to fly thick and fast, _______.
(a) government ordered an enquiry which exposed a nexus between mine operators and bureaucrats
(b) it caused great damage to the surrounding ecosystem and the environment in general
(c) the officials have been irresponsible in failing to bring it to the notice of the court in time
(d) the powerful mining lobby has bribed the officials to obtain permit for mining on

ecological sensitive land
(e) None of these

Directions to Questions 16-20

Each question below has two blanks, each blank indicating that something has been omitted. Choose the set of words for each blank that best fits the meaning of the sentence as a whole.

16. Drawing attention to the pitfalls of ______ solely on Uranium as a fuel for nuclear reactors, Indian scientists warned that Uranium will not last for long and thus research on Thorium as its ______ must be revived.
(a) using, substitute
(b) believing, replacement
(c) depending, reserve
(d) reckoning, option
(e) relying, alternative

17. In an effort to provide ______ for higher education to all, most of the universities have been providing education without adequate infrastructure, thus churning out ______ graduates every year.
(a) chances, fresh
(b) platform, capable
(c) opportunities, unemployable
(d) prospects, eligible 2-3
(e) policy, incompetent

18. The move to allow dumping of mercury ______ an outcry from residents to the area who____ that high levels of mercury will affect their health and destroy ecologically sensitive forest area.
(a) resulted, insist
(b) provoked, fear
(c) incited, determined
(d) activated, accept
(e) angered believe

19. ______has been taken against some wholesale drug dealers for dealing in surgical Items without a valid license and, maintaining a stock of ____ drugs.
(a) Note, overwhelming
(b) Step, impressive
(c) Execution, outdated
(d) Action, expired
(e) Lawsuit, invalid

20. Even as the _____ elsewhere in the world are struggling, to come out of recession, Indian consumers are splurging on consumer goods and to _____ this growth, companies are investing heavily in various sectors.
(a) economies, meet
(b) countries, inhibit
(c) governments, measure
(d) nations, inflict
(e) companies, counter

ANSWER KEY

Set 1

1. (e)
2. (b)
3. (c)
4. (b)
5. (e)
6. (a)
7. (c)
8. (d)
9. (c)
10. (a)
11. (a)
12. (a)
13. (d)
14. (d)
15. (a)
16. (a)
17. (a)
18. (b)
19. (b)
20. (e)
21. (a)
22. (b)
23. (d)
24. (d)
25. (c)

Set 2

1. (d)	2. (d)	3. (a)	4. (d)	5. (d)
6. (d)	7. (e)	8. (c)	9. (a)	10. (b)
11. (b)	12. (d)	13. (c)	14. (c)	15. (a)
16. (c)	17. (d)	18. (a)	19. (e)	20. (d)

CHAPTER 12

SENTENCE RECONSTRUCTION

Introduction

One of the interesting and difficult units of objective test in English is sentence arrangement. In this test, you have to rearrange parts of a sentence into a meaningful sentence or sentences into a meaningful paragraph. This requires a sound knowledge of grammar, a command over the structure of sentences, an over-all sense of composition, and an ability to form a logical sequence of ideas behind sentences. This art can be gradually mastered by reading good books and newspapers, and constant practice. You must read books very carefully giving full attention to the structures of the sentences. Gradually you will begin to feel that there are internal rules that bind a sentence. This will help you discern clues for arranging parts of sentence correctly.

EXAMPLES

This question appears in a variety of different forms in various competitive examinations. Some common types are discussed in this chapter.

I. One Sentence in Parts

Lakhs of students

P. on an all India basis

Q. from all over India

R. which are held

S. appear in the examination.

by different recruiting organisations.

(a) PQSR (b) SRQP

(c) QSRP (d) QSPR

(Combined Defence Services Exam.)

This type of a question may be solved by Subject-Verb-Object-Qualifiers Location. S + V + O + Q $\neq$ L)

Let us look at the above example:

1. Lakhs of students	—	subject
2. from all over India	—	qualifier of the subject (Q)
3. appear in the examination	—	verb (S)
4. which are held	—	qualifier of the verb (R)
5. on an all India basis	—	qualifier of *which are held* (P)
6. by different the last part organisations		

Thus the sequence is QSRP: S + Q + V + Q + Q + Q.

Let us analyse the following sentence in the graph below:

Ram who is the son of Shyam reads hurriedly the book which has been written by Premchand.

The correct sentence, therefore, is: 'Lakhs of students from all over India appear in the examinations which are held on an all-India basis by different recruiting organisations'.

Look at the structure of a sentence. The basic form is like this:

Here, the subject, the verb and the object, all three have qualifiers.

Now it is clear from the chart that, in a sentence, there can appear a subject, a verb, an object and qualifiers as well. You have to locate and identify each qualifier and attach it to its subject.

The steps may be summarised as follows:

1. subject of the sentence;
2. qualifiers of the subject, if any;
3. verb;
4. qualifiers of the verb, if any;
5. object; and
6. qualifiers of the object, if any.

This may be described as the **Subject – Verb – Object + Qualifiers Location Technique.**

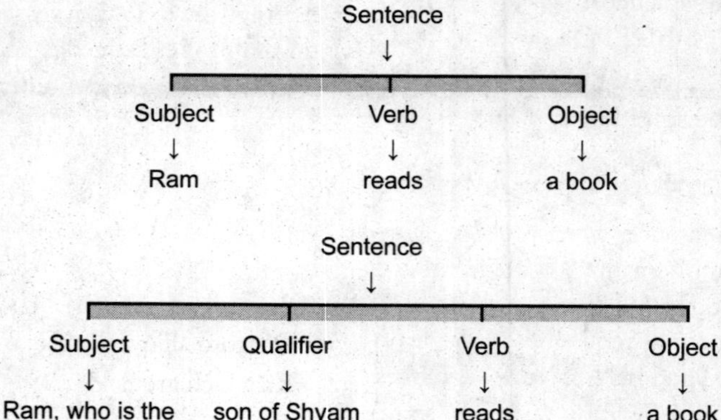

Here, *who is the son of Shyam*, is the qualifier of *Ram*, the subject.

Or

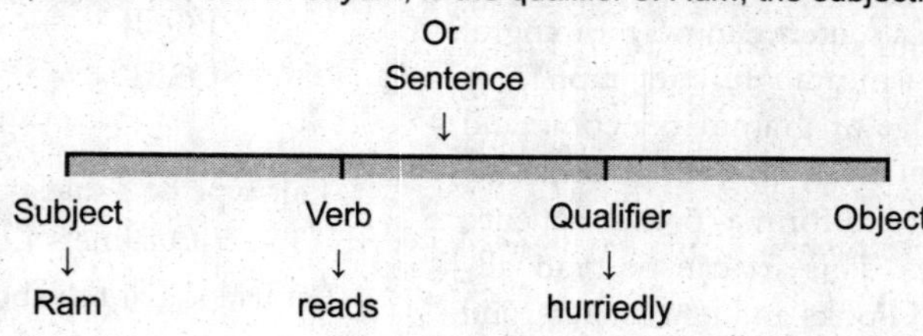

Here, *hurriedly* is the qualifier of *reads*, the verb.

Or

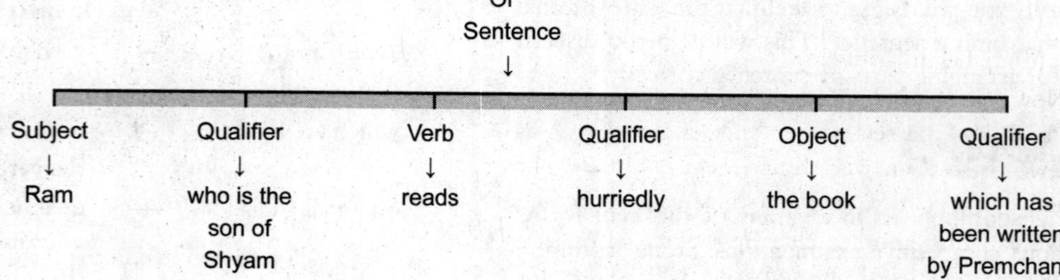

2. Sentences with the First and the Last Part Given

In the passage below the first and the last sentences are numbered 1 and 6. The rest four sentences are numbered as PQRS and they are not in correct sequence. Rearrange them.

1. India's message has always been of love and peace.

P. Our Budha was the light of Asia.

Q. It has been a source of light and wisdom to the rest of the world.

R. Ashoka moved by the horrors of Kalinga war gave the message of non-violence.

S. The greatest apostle of non-violence in recent years was Gandhi.

6. He shook the foundation of the British rule in India through non-violence.

(a) PSQR (b) RPQS
(c) SRQP (d) QPRS

Such questions can be solved by applying.

Idea to Sentence Stepping (ITSS) Method

A paragraph consists of sentences which are connected to one another logically and semantically. Thus, first of all, read every sentence carefully, discern the meaning of the passage, then form a sequence at the level of idea (the meaning). Then arrange the sentences accordingly. You can do this by improvising on some clues. Clues can be found out on the basis of your general knowledge, your sense of language and your ability to correlate ideas and structures.

In the above example, we can find many clues. The first sentence is given. It is about India. Now look at the alternatives. The second sentence must follow the first at the level of meaning and also at the level of structure.

(a) P. begins with *our*

(b) Q. begins with *it*

(c) R. begins with *Ashoka*

(d) S. begins with *the*

Now *it* is the only pronoun that can be used for India and thus the second sentence should be Q. In other words, our answer should begin with Q. The alternative (b) begins with Q and thus this is the choice.

We can find another clue by looking at the last sentence. It tells us about someone who shook the foundation of the British rule in India through non-violence. All of us know that Mahatma Gandhi was the man who did it. Thus S is the sentence that must come before the last sentence. In other words, our correct choice must end with S. The alternative (b) ends with S.

We can find another clue to decide which is the correct answer between (a) and (c). The sense of time gives us a clue. There are references to Buddha, Ashoka and Gandhi. Keeping their periods in mind. We can arrange sentences by putting the sentence with Ashoka just before the sentence that mentions Gandhi. Thus S must be preceded by R. Thus the correct alternative is D because S is preceded by R in this arrangement.

3. Several Sentences Without Any Definite Beginning or End

Rearrange the following six sentences, A, B, C, D, E and F, in the proper sequence so as to form a meaningful paragraph and then answer the questions given below.

A. Miss Sullivan arrived at the Keller home when Helen was seven.

B. The deaf and blind Helen learned to communicate verbally.

C. But, eventually, Miss Sullivan's effort was rewarded.

D. Before Helen Keller was two years old, she lost her sight and her hearing.

E. Miss Sullivan worked closely with Helen, her new student.

F. At times, the teacher became frustrated.

(P.O. Examination, BSRB, Delhi, Lucknow, Baroda, 1992)

1. Which sentence should come last?
   A. B. C.
   D. E. F.
2. Which sentence should come first?
   A. B. C.
   D. E. F.
3. Which sentence should come second?
   A. B. C.
   D. E. F.
4. Which sentence should come third?
   A. B. C.
   D. E. F.
5. Which sentence should come fourth?
   A. B. C.
   D. E. F.

6. Which sentence should come fifth?

A. B. C.
D. E. F.

Method The same method of arranging the paragraph first at the level of idea and then at the level of sentences should be followed. Since the first and the last sentences are not given, the first step is to locate the beginning sentence.

First, find some clues. For instance, in this paragraph, we may find a clue in the reference to time. The paragraph is about Helen and Miss Sullivan. The first thing that happened in relation to time was the fact that Helen lost her sight before she was two years old. Miss Sullivan arrived when Helen was seven. The other incidents took place later. Thus, it is logical that the first sentence should be D—the sentence telling us that Helen lost her sight before she was two years old. After that we can arrange other sentences according to the time sequence. The sequence is D A E F C B. All questions may be answered now.

1. B 2. D 3. A
4. E 5. F 6. C

Time-Saver Clue Qualifier Elimination (CQE) Technique

In addition to the above devices we may also try a time-saver technique. This technique will be directly applicable to type one and type two and will also be helpful in type three of sentence arrangement. In type three question, five or six sentences are given in a disorderly sequence. In most cases the first and the last sentences are specified and the remaining four are to be arranged. Four answer sets are provided as the alternative choice to the candidates. Only one choice is correct which the candidates have to spot out.

First of all, we shall find some clues in the set. About clues we shall discuss later. On the basis of the clue we shall locate a *qualifier*. We shall define *qualifier* as a sentence that tells us something about the following sentence. That following sentence is the *qualified* sentence. The qualifier will be placed by the side of the qualified. It is just possible that there may be two qualifiers of the same sentence. In that case we have to decide the preference on the basis of sequence.

Now there are three possibilities

Possibility (1) Our qualifier may be qualifying the first sentence. In this case our answer choice begin with the Qualifier.

EXAMPLE

1. It is regrettable that there is widespread corruption in the country at all levels.

P. So there is hardly anything that the government can do about it now.

Q. And there are graft and other malpractices too.

R. The impression that corruption is a universal phenomenon persists and the people do not cooperate in checking this evil.

S. Recently several offenders were brought to book, but they were not given deterrent punishment.

6. This is indeed a tragedy of great magnitude.

Answer:(a) QSRP (b) SQRP
(c) RSQP (d) PQSR

Q is the qualifier of (1) because and connects itself to widespread corruption of sentence number (1). Thus our answer should begin with Q. Of the four choices (a), (b), (c), (d) only (a) begins with Q. Therefore (a) is the answer.

2. Duryodhana was a wicked prince.

P. One day Bhima made Duryodhana fall from a tree from which Duryodhana was stealing fruits.

Q. He did not like that Pandavas should be loved and respected by the people of Hastinapur.

R. Duryodhana specially hated Bhima.

S. Among the Pandavas, Bhima was extraordinarily strong and powerful.

6. This enraged Duryodhana so much that he began to think of removing Bhima from his way.

Answers: (a) PSQR (b) QPRS
(c) QSRP (d) PSRQ

Here Q is the qualifier of sentence (1) because *he* is the pronoun used for Duryodhana. So our answer will begin with Q. But both choices (b) and (c) begin with Q. Therefore we have to decide by sequence and then (c) will be the correct answer.

Possibility (2) Our qualifier may qualify any sentence other than the first and the last. In this case we have to spot out the answer where the qualifier by the side of the qualified.

3. Love for the country is a necessity.
   P. But it should in no way exceed the limits and take the shape of jingoism.
   Q. Similarly nationalism has to be sacrificed at the altar of internationalism.
   R. There is no reason why the nations of the world cannot treat one another as belonging to one family of nations.
   S. Provincialism has to be sacrificed in the interest of the nation as a whole.
   6. God created the globe, but man drew lines on it to demarcate countries and sow the seeds of hatred and enmity on it.

Answers: (a) QRSP (b) PSQR (c) RQPS (d) SPRQ

Q is the qualifier of S because similarly connects the word *nationalism* to *provincialism.* Thus our answer should show SQ together. Among the four choices only (b) has SQ together. Therefore (b) is the answer:

Possibility (3) The last sentence may be a qualifier in some cases. In that situation our answer should end with the qualified sentence.

4. Once King Shantanu met a young and beautiful fisher girl.
   P. He went to the fisherman and asked him for her hand in marriage.
   Q. The king was extremely sad and returned to his palace.
   R. He fell in love with the fisher girl.
   S. The fisherman agreed to it on the condition that the son of his daughter should be the heir to the throne of Hastinapur.
   6. Devavrata, the king's son, asked him the reason of his sadness.

Answers: (a) PQRS (b) RPSQ (c) QSPR (d) PSQR

Here, sentence number 6 is the qualifier of Q because words *sadness* and *sad* are connected. Thus our answer will end with Q. Among the four choices only (b) ends with Q. Therefore (b) is the answer.

Whenever we have more than one choice we have to depend on our sense of sequence. We can now illustrate our technique with a figure:

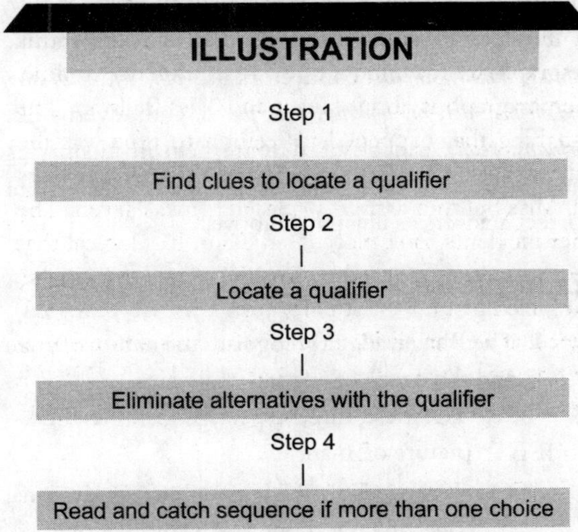

Fig. 12.1 Time-saver CQE Technique

1. Just as some men like to play football or tennis, so some men like to climb mountains.
   P. This is often very difficult to do, for mountains are not just big hills.
   Q. Paths are usually very steep, and some mountain-sides are straight up and down so that it may take many hours to climb as little as one hundred feet.
   R. There is always the danger that you may fall off and be killed or injured.
   S. Men talk about conquering a mountain and the wonderful feeling it is to reach the top of a mountain after climbing for hours and, may be, even for days.
   6. You look down and see the whole country below you.

Answers: (a) PQRS (b) QPSR (c) RQPS (d) SRQP

This is a clue that makes P as the qualifier of sentence number 1.

Thus our answer should begin with P. Among the answer choices only (a) begins with P. Therefore (a) is the correct answer.

Now another important point is how to locate clues. Clues can be located or improvised with the help of grammatical rules. However, pronouns, like *he, she, it, this, that, these, those,* article *a* and *the,* definers like *actually, finally, another* connectors like *but, yet, both, also, and neither nor, or, however, nevertheless,* and adverbs like *formally, really,* can be of definite help in identifying the qualifiers on the basis of which we may select our correct answers as illustrated above.

Example (A)

1. The Bhagavadgita recognises the nature of man and the needs of man.

P. All these three aspects constitute the nature of man.

Q. It shows how the human being is a rational one, an ethical one and a spiritual one.

R. More than all, it must be a spiritual experience.

S. Nothing can give him fulfilment unless it satisfies his reason, his ethical conscience.

6. A man who does not harmonise them, is not truly human.

Answers: (a) PSRQ (b) RSPQ (c) QPSR (d) PSQR

It is the pronoun which acts as the clue and helps us to locate the qualifier and through that the correct answer. It is a neutre gender pronoun and thus it will come for *the Bhagavadgita.* Thus our answer will begin with Q. Only answer choice (c) begins with Q. Thus (c) is the answer.

Example (B)

S_1. Gandhis' first political fast was made soon after his return from Africa.

P. He did not fast against the mill owners, but in order to strengthen the determination of strikers.

Q. He had also received help from this man's sister.

R. This was when the poor labourers of the cotton mills of Ahmedabad were on strike.

S. He was a friend of the largest mill owner.

S_6. Gandhi had made the strikers promise to remain on strike until the owners agreed to accept the decision of an arbitrator.

Answers: (a) PQSR (b) QSRP (c) RPQS (d) SRPQ

This is the pronoun that stands for Gandhi's *fast.* Thus Q is the qualifier of S_1. Our answer begins with Q. Thus (c) is the answer.

Example (C)

1. While talking to a group, one should feel self-confident and courageous.

P. Nor is it a gift bestowed by providence and on only a few.

Q. One should also learn how to think calmly and clearly.

R. It is like the ability to play golf.

S. It is not as difficult as most men imagine.

6. Any man can develop his capacity if he has the desire to do so.

Answers: (a) SQPR (b) QSPR (c) QRS (d) RSQP

Here the clue is *nor* because *nor* will come after the sentence which contains *not.* Thus through this clue we can locate that P is the qualifier of S. Thus P will come after S. Only in choice (b). P comes after S. Thus (b) is the answer.

Example (D)

S_1. Our own country is a little world in itself with an infinite variety and places for us to discover.

P. I wish I had more time, so that I could visit the odd nooks and comers of India.

Q. I have travelled a great deal in this country and I have grown in years.

R. And yet I have not seen many parts of the country we love so much and seek to serve.

S. I would like to go there in the company of bright young children whose minds are opening out with wonder and curiosity as they make new discoveries.

S_6. I should like to go with them, not so much to the great cities of India as to the mountains and the forests and the great rivers and the old monuments, all of which tell us something of India's story.

Answers: (a) QRPS (b) PQSR
(c) RPQS (d) SPQR

And yet is the clue that helps us locate the qualifier R which qualifies the sentence 1 and thus it helps us find the correct answer. Our answer should begin with R. Only (c) begins with R. (c) is the answer.

Example (E)

1. Religion has been used
P. Both as a weapon of isolation
Q. To dull awareness
R. About real problems
S. And as morphia
6. Like education, health and employment

Answers: (a) PQRS (b) PSQR
(c) QPSR (d) RPQS

Here *and* is the clue which connects itself with both and thus helps us find the qualifier and also the correct answer. Here the answer is (b).

Example (F)

1. As a dramatist Rabindranath was not what might be called a success.
P. His dramas were moulded more on the lines of the traditional Indian village dramas than the dramas of the modem world.
Q. His plays were more a catalogue of ideas than a vehicle of the expression of action.
R. Actually drama has always been the life of the Indian people, as it deals with legends of gods and goddesses.
S. Although in his short stories and novels he was able to create living and well-defined characters, he did not seem to be able to do so in his dramas.
6. Therefore drama forms the essential part of the traditional Indian culture.

Answers: (a) SRQP (b) QPSR
(c) QSPR (d) RSQP

Here *actually* is the clue; it helps us conclude that our answer will close with R. Since there are two choices ending with R the sense of sequence helps us find the correct answer (d).

Example (G)

1. American private lives may seem shallow.
P. Students would walk away with books they had not paid for.
Q. A Chinese journalist commented on a curious institution: the library.
R. Their public morality, however impressed visitors.
S. But in general they returned them.
6. This would not happen in China, he said.

Answers: (a) PSQR (b) QPSR
(c) RQPS (d) RPSQ

Here *however* may work as a clue. The sentence R qualifies sentence 1. because *however* reverses the word *shallow.* Thus the answer will begin with R. There are two choices with R. The sense of sequence helps us locate (c) as the correct answer.

We can have a large number of illustrations with such words. Now students can develop the knack of locating clues this will help them identify a qualifier which, in turn, will help them spot the correct answer.

Practice Set —1

Produce the correct sentence.

1. P. to dispose of the waste matter
Q. the modernisation would reduce
R. provide better sanitary facilities
S. manual labour considerably and would also
(a) QSRP (b) SRPQ
(c) RPQS (d) PQSR

2. P. supported by soft term loans
Q. to supply imported equipment worth Rs 8 crore
R. the Hungarian Government has offered
S. with a very low rate of interest
(a) SRQP (b) PSRQ
(c) RQPS (d) QPSR

3. P. environmental and psychological stress and strain
Q. he said that
R. the development of positive attitudes to cope with
S. what the world needed today was
(a) PQSR (b) RPQS
(c) QSRP (d) SRPQ

4. P. expresses itself in many diverse art forms
Q. ancient in origin
R. the essence of the spirit of Bulgaria
S. of great creativity
(a) PQRS (b) RQPS
(c) QPSR (d) PSRQ

5. P. will normally be granted
Q. candidates should note
R. that no request for
S. change of centre
(a) PSQR (b) SPQR
(c) QRSP (d) RSPQ

6. P. accidents are still bound to happen
Q. occasionally
R. though
S. despite everyone's best efforts
(a) SPRQ (b) RSPQ
(c) SRPQ (d) PQRS

7. P. through the long, hot summer
Q. if you plan to train hard
R. continually
S. you will need to acclimatise yourself
(a) QPRS (b) SRPQ
(c) QRSP (d) PQRS

8. P. it becomes difficult
Q. satisfying our desire
R. but once we set about
S. if not impossible to restrain them
(a) RQPS (b) RQSP
(c) QRPS (d) PQRS

9. P. four degrees below normal
Q. icy winds lashed Srinagar
R. with minimum temperature registering
S. which was already in the grip of a gruelling cold wave conditions
(a) QSRP (b) SRPQ
(c) RPQS (d) PQSR

10. P. when a chemical substance
Q. the food poisoning occurred
R. in the food preparations
S. was mistaken for salt and used
(a) RQPS (b) SRQP
(c) QPSR (d) PSRQ

11. Ashoka was successful
P. by the cruelty and horrors of war
Q. but he was so disgusted
R. in his military operations
S. and alone among conquerors,
T. that he renounced it
(a) RSQP (b) SQPR
(c) QPRS (d) PSQR

12. There are people
P. to be able to say
Q. not because they enjoy the book,
R. who read a book
S. but because they want
T. that they have read it
(a) PSQR (b) SQPR
(c) RSPQ (d) RQSP

13. She had understood
P. so she withdrew herself from the ordinary people,
Q. like a curse to her father's house,
R. that God had sent her,
S. from her earliest childhood
T. and tried to live apart
(a) SRQP (b) PRQS
(c) QSPR (d) SPQR

14. People read and recite the Ramayana
P. which refers to those high ideals of human conduct
Q. with great devotion,
R. that aspect of its greatness
S. but they mostly fail to appreciate
T. that this great epic places before us
(a) RSPQ (b) SRQP
(c) QSRP (d) PRQS

15. As his hunting skill increased,
P. till at last it was as impossible for him
Q. so did his love for the hunt,
R. as it is for the opium eater
S. to pass a day without it
T. to forego his daily portion
(a) RSQP (b) PSQR
(c) QPSR (d) PQRS

16. What usually happens
P. and then choose the gifts
Q. organise a collection
R. is that two or three persons
S. and find a suitable occasion
T. for presenting them
(a) PQRS (b) RQPS
(c) SRQP (d) QRPS

17. Economic domination
P. anger and
Q. a different language
R. of persons speaking
S. often causes
T. a sense of revolt
(a) PSRQ (b) QRPS
(c) RQSP (d) SPQR

18. What the country needs
P. and change tactics
Q. who would encourage players
R. are coaches and officials
S. to read the game as it progresses
T. accordingly
(a) RQPS (b) SPRQ
(c) QSPR (d) RQSP

19. Though Indian sportsmen
P. who accompanied them
Q. the large number of
R. did not set many records in the Seoul Asiad
S. officials and politicians
T. did set a record of sorts
(a) RQSP (b) SPRQ
(c) PQSR (d) QSRP

20. Public sector companies
P. and scale of operations
Q. take a peculiar pride
R. without talking
S. in the size of their investment
T. of their profitability
(a) SQRP (b) PRQS
(c) QSPR (d) SPRQ

21. P. Rama who studied
Q. in the same school and
R. paid the fees of his friend
S. who was rich
(a) PQSR (b) QRPS
(c) QSRP (d) PRSQ

22. I shall go
P. my work here
Q. to Calcutta
R. I have finished
S. after
(a) PQSR (b) QRPS
(c) QSRP (d) PRSQ

23. I saw
P. a dead bull
Q. while walking across
R. the street
S. yesterday
(a) PQRS (b) QPRS
(c) QRPS (d) SPQR

24. The social worker devoted
P. to the upliftment
Q. of the people
R. his entire life
S. of his village
(a) QRSP (b) PQRS
(c) SRQP (d) RPQS

25. P. The doctor prescribed
Q. some antibiotics
R. having examined the patient
S. for over an hour
(a) RSPQ (b) SRPQ
(c) QPRS (d) RPQS

26. P. I decided to call on him
Q. at the earliest opportunity
R. having heard of the palmist
S. before I came into town
(a) RSPQ (b) PQRS
(c) SQPR (d) QPRS

27. Copra is good
P. because it contains
Q. and it is nourishing
R. when it has been dried
S. to eat, both fresh and
6. so much oil
(a) PSRQ (b) QPSR
(c) RQPS (d) SRQP

28. The men
P. in cutting out the white kernel of the nut
Q. are very skilful
R. who split open the ripe nuts
S. with their sharp
6. knives
(a) SQPR (b) PRSQ
(c) RQPS (d) QPRS

29. The coconut tree, therefore,
P. in the lives of the people of Kerala
Q. plays a very important part
R. where coconuts
S. and of other coastal lands in Southern Asia
6. grow well
(a) QPSR (b) PSRQ
(c) SRQP (d) RQPS

30. The areca palm has
P. egg-shaped nuts
Q. that hang in thick bunches
R. which produces yellow
S. a perfectly straight slender trunk
6. under the leaves
(a) PSRQ (b) QPSR
(c) RQPS (d) SRPQ

Practice Set —2

Directions: The first and last sentences or parts of the sentences given below are in correct order, arrange PQRS in the correct sequence.

1. O. The settlement between the Government of Assam and the leaders of Bodoland movement
P. public property and socio-economic destabilisation
Q. a six-year old campaign that has cost the state
R. rather heavily in terms of human lives
S. augurs well for the fulfillment of
T. the legitimate aspirations of an articulate group of tribals
(a) PQRS (b) PRQS
(c) QRPS (d) QRSP

2. O. The Bodoland accord is a pragmatic piece
P. following the realisation that confrontation
Q. of compromise
R. in which both the Government and the Bodo leaders
S. have made major concessions
T. was hurting both parties
(a) QPRS (b) QRSP
(c) QRPS (d) RQSP

3. O. Considering that the signs
P. in the approach of ABSO and BPAC
Q. of realism
R. the settlement has been rather late in coming
S. were indeed discernible much earlier
T. thanks to the protracted nature of the negotiations
(a) QPRS (b) QRPS
(c) QPSR (d) PQSR

4. O. The Union Government's plans
P. the BJP had made it clear even on the very day the Government announced that the proposed rally would not be allowed
Q. at a minimal cost
R. to prevent the BJP rally have worked
S. considering the circumstances
T. that it would defy the ban come what may
(a) PQRS (b) PRQS
(c) PSRQ (d) RQSP

5. O. The election results in both Meghalaya and Nagaland
P. to give a decisive verdict
Q. for the fourth time in a row

R. appear to conform to past patterns
S. the people of Meghalaya have failed
T. in favour of any single party of political formation.
(a) RQSP (b) RSQP
(c) RQPS (d) RSPQ

6. O. On one hand we are proud of being Indians,
P. on the other hand we behave as if we were still at the dawn of our civilisation
Q. murders of our own brothers and sisters is not the way to please Ram or Rahim,
R. the citizens of the land where Buddha and Gandhi taught
S. the principle of love and non-violence,
T. nor does it fetch us any prosperity.
(a) PQRS (b) QRSP
(c) RSQP (d) RSPQ

7. O. The Finance Minister announced
P. which now has
Q. the floating of new bond scheme
R. along with public sector bonds,
S. to raise resources for the banking sector
T. to meet new capital adequacy norms.
(a) PQRS (b) QPRS
(c) RQSP (d) RPSQ

8. O. So far, the Government was reluctant
P. to move towards full convertibility
Q. because a high rate of inflation creates expectations
R. of a depreciation of the exchange rate
S. which is required to offset the higher costs
T. as a result of increase in prices.
(a) PQRS (b) QRSP
(c) RSPQ (d) SPQR

9. O. On the basis of experiments with rats
P. health experts here say that
Q. exercise more and consume vitamins,
R. they will live up to 100 years or more
S. if humans eat less,
T. and be vigorous in their eighties and nineties.
(a) PQSR (b) PSQR
(c) PSRQ (d) SPQR

10. O. The way the proprietors of these bogus agencies flatter
P. today their board appears at one corner of a street
Q. by guaranteeing jobs for them
R. and receive money from the public
S. is simply charming and marvellous
T. and in a week's time the same board can be seen at the farther end of another street and so on.
(a) RQSP (b) RSQP
(c) RPQS (d) PQRS

11. O. The release of atomic energy is the greatest achievement which science has yet attained
P. but the first invention to which their discoveries were applied was a bomb
Q. the atom was split by physicists whose minds were set on the search for knowledge
R. it was more deadly than any other weapon invented so far
S. it is with dread that scientists regard the first use to which their greatest discovery was put
T. however, they are gratified by the numerous applications of atomic energy for peaceful and constructive population
(a) PQRS (b) SQPR
(c) QPRS (d) RSQP

12. O. The problem of food is intimately connected with population.
P. wages will seldom rise in proportion to the rising prices.
Q. the market is governed by demand and supply.
R. without enough food. such people lack health, strength of efficiency.
S. if too many people demand goods to go round, prices will rise and poor classes will starve.
T. they fall an easy prey to all sorts of diseases.

(a) QSPR (b) PQRS
(c) RPSQ (d) SQRP

13. O. India is mostly the land of villages.
P. India was very backward before independence.
Q. But after independence India has made tremendous progress.
R. Most of the people live in villages.
S. Agriculture is the main occupation of these people.
T. Today India exports many industrial goods all over the world.
(a) SRQP (b) RSPQ
(c) PRQS (d) QPRS

14. O. In theory, India is an example of a perfect democracy.
P. the vast majority of people are illiterate and ignorant.
Q. but, in practice, the working of democracy does not provide much cause for satisfaction.
R. general elections have no doubt been held, at regular interval.
S. but the very first condition of a properly educated electorate is lacking in this country.
T. it is said that the greatest of all dangers of democracy is that it may turn out to be the rule of ignorance.
(a) PQRS (b) RPSQ
(c) SRQP (d) QRSP

15. O. The newspaper is a great power in the modern world.
P. In the busy world of today the editorial thinks for those who have no time to sit down and ponder over various problems.
R. The editorial generally deals with a burning topic of public importance.
S. It moulds the people's opinion and also adds to their vocabulary.
T. The various types of articles deal with a variety of topics.
(a) PQRS (b) SRQP
(c) RPQS (d) QRSP

16. O. The United Nations has a General Assembly comprising most of the countries of the world.
P. The second organ of the UN is the Security Council.
Q. It is more or less a debating society.
R. This has eleven members of which six are temporary and five permanent.
S. The most effective organ of the UN is the Security Council.
T. However, it suffers from certain handicaps.
(a) PQRS (b) QPRS
(c) SPQR (d) QSPR

17. O. The world government is the only answer to the threat of the Third World War.
P. The emergence of world government presupposes a surrender of sovereignty by all nations of the world.
Q. A world government, if it is to prevent wars, must be all powerful.
R. But a world government seems to be a mere dream under the present circumstances.
S. Such a surrender is not even remotely possible under the present situation.
T. Even if such a surrender does take place, it may not last.
(a) QRPS (b) PQRS
(c) RPSQ (d) PSQR

18. O. The great Rodin lay, old and infirm, on a sickbed outside Paris.
P. He muttered that he wanted to see his wife.
Q. "She is right beside you," they said- Rose Beuret, his faithful mistress and housekeeper for 50 years.
R. 'Not her, the other one.'
S. 'No, no' he said fretfully.
T. The 'other one'—Camille Claudel, was at that moment 400 miles away, in a madhouse near Avignon.

(a) PQSR (b) QPSR
(c) SRQP (d) RQPS

19. O. Camille, however, was not content to be a muse.
P. She wanted an independent career.
Q. And there were fundamental differences of character.
R. They are less bombastic, more contained, more intimate.
S. She was never a servile copyist of Rodin—her works all have her own personal stamp.
T. Rodin at bottom remained a man of the people, simple of taste, coarse of grain.
(a) PSRQ (b) SRQP
(c) RQPS (d) QPSR

20. O. 'As a matter of fact', said the boy modestly, 'I'm a spaceman.'
P. 'You can't see it from here.'
Q. 'From another planet.'
R. 'I'm a spaceman', he said again.
S. George and Cathy stared at the boy.
T. Cathy gasped, and George gave a shout of laughter.
(a) PSRQ (b) QPSR
(c) RQPS (d) SRQP

21. O. Suddenly it began to climb swiftly, and the next I knew it was speeding eastward again till it became a speck in the blue morning.
P. I didn't know what force they could command, but I was certain it would be sufficient.
Q. My enemies had located me, and the next thing would be a cordon round me.
R. That made me do some savage thinking.
S. The aeroplane had seen my bicycle, and would conclude that I would try to escape by the road.
T. In that case there might be a chance on the moors to the right or left.
(a) RQPS (b) QPSR
(c) PSRQ (d) SRQP

22. O. His penance grew harder, he abjured even fruit.
P. Then the water, too, that the girl offered him in leaf-cups lay untouched.
Q. Birds pecked at them as they lay rotting at his feet.
R. She gathered wild blossoms and laid them humbly before him.
S. The girl mused in sorrow: 'Is there nothing left for me to do?'
T. The ascetic took no notice.
(a) RQPS (b) SRQP
(c) QPSR (d) PSRQ

23. O. The chief source of power in industrial undertakings is electricity.
P. Electricity from water also presupposes enormous river valley projects involving huge expenditure.
Q. In contrast, electricity from atomic power stations will result in a tremendous saving of expenditure.
S. But the production of electricity needs huge quantities of coal.
T. The installation of atomic plants will help in meeting the shortage of these resources.
(a) PQRS (b) SPQR
(c) RSPQ (d) QRSP

24. O. It would be foolish to deny that the countryside has many attractions to offer.
P. One soon gets tired of looking at the same old scenes and creatures day in and day out.
Q. But there is another side to the picture.
R. The honesty and frankness of the country folk, too, is a refreshing change from the dishonesty and selfishness we find in so many urban people.

S. There is the lovely scenery; the interesting and varied wildlife; the long rambles through woods and fields; and the clean, healthy air.

T. The loveliness and monotony in the country soon begin to make themselves felt and we long for the familiar side-walks and street corners.

(a) SRQP (b) PQRS
(c) SPQR (d) QSRP

25. O. Human experience tends to show that the more we mix with a man, the more we come to dislike him.

P. When acquaintance with him ripens into intimacy, we are likely to become very keenly aware of his defects and imperfections.

Q. In the beginning, we may feel greatly attracted by someone because of certain qualities that we find in him.

R. But, on closer acquaintance, we begin to perceive his faults and shortcomings.

S. Nobody is free from faults and weaknesses.

T. But while a man makes a show of his strong points and his good qualities, he generally tries to conceal or cover his faults and defects.

(a) SQRP (b) PSQR
(c) QRPS (d) RPSQ

26. O. A welfare state in the attainment of its objective must avoid coercion or violence.

P. But communism attains its ends through compulsion, coercion and even bloodshed.

Q. Communism implies the loss of freedom of expression and action and introduces a regimentation of life.

R. These are all serious disadvantages which perhaps outweigh the economic gains.

S. Communism aims at the welfare state, and perhaps the complete form of the welfare state in most respects.

T. A true welfare state can develop only by following the path of peace and democracy.

(a) QRSP (b) RSPQ
(c) SPQR (d) PQSR

27. O. It is wrong to think that city life is altogether unhealthy.

P. Cities are planned in such a way as to provide open space with parks and open grounds for the benefit of the dwellers.

Q. Perhaps it was so at one time, but nowadays with proper roads, pavements and drainage system, sickness is kept at bay.

R. Even when sickness does strike, there are doctors and hospitals at hand.

S. This is not the case in the countryside where people frequently suffer and sometimes die for want of medical facilities.

T. Life in the countryside is all right as a break from the feverish pace of city life; but the city has far more to offer one who wishes to lead a full, exciting and satisfying life.

(a) SRQP (b) RQPS
(c) QPRS (d) PRSQ

28. O. It was late at night that I found myself in an emergency.

P. It was a blessing for all of us that Dr Naveen had set up a practice in our town.

Q. It was a pleasant surprise to discover that my bicycle was fit for riding after all.

R. My wife was about to de.\iver her first child and Dr Naveen was the only qualified doctor.

S. Before he arrived we had to go all the way to Kolar to get a doctor if there was an emergency.

T. I hurriedly put on my clothes and cycled off to fetch the obsetrician.

(a) PRSQ (b) RPSQ
(c) SQPR (d) QSRP

Practice Set—3

Rearrange the following sentences into a meaningful sequence and then answer the questions given below.

1. (a) They brought gifts to the babe in the manger.

(b) Being wise, their gifts were, no doubt, wise ones.

(c) The Magi were wise men.

(d) They invented the art of giving Christmas presents.

(e) They were wonderfully wise men.

1. Which sentence should come last?

(a) (b) (c) (d) (e)

2. Which sentence should come first?

(a) (b) (c) (d) (e)

3. Which sentence should come second?

(a) (b) (c) (d) (e)

4. Which sentence should come third?

(a) (b) (c) (d) (e)

5. Which sentence should come fourth?

(a) (b) (c) (d) (e)

2. (a) He was a great heavy fellow from the Middle West.

(b) He was on a flying visit to New York to fetch his wife.

(c) Mrs Ramsay was a very pretty little thing.

(d) Ramsay was in the American Consular service.

(e) He was on his way back to resume his post.

1. Which sentence should come first?

(a) (b) (c) (d) (e)

2. Which sentence should come last?

(a) (b) (c) (d) (e)

3. Which sentence should come second?

(a) (b) (c) (d) (e)

4. Which sentence should come third?

(a) (b) (c) (d) (e)

5. Which sentence should come fourth?

(a) (b) (c) (d) (e)

3. (a) The spark of nobility hidden in him emerges at this last moment.

(b) It emerges in a most unexpected manner.

(c) Then, he appears to the reader in a wholly unexpected light.

(d) Mr Know-all is a ridiculous person.

(e) He is subject to all kinds of petty vices.

1. Which sentence should come last?

(a) (b) (c) (d) (e)

2. Which sentence should come first?

(a) (b) (c) (d) (e)

3. Which sentence should come second?

(a) (b) (c) (d) (e)

4. Which sentence should come third?

(a) (b) (c) (d) (e)

5. Which sentence should come fourth?

(a) (b) (c) (d) (e)

4. (a) Doctors rearrange them.

(b) People make jokes about their unflattering characteristics.

(c) Boxers flatten them.

(d) Worst of all when it comes to smell no one really understands them.

(e) Noses have it pretty hard.

1. Which sentence should come last?

(a) (b) (c) (d) (e)

2. Which sentence should come first?

(a) (b) (c) (d) (e)

3. Which sentence should come second?

(a) (b) (c) (d) (e)

4. Which sentence should come third?

(a) (b) (c) (d) (e)

5. Which sentence should come fourth?

(a) (b) (c) (d) (e)

5. (a) This is the fundamental concept of a filter.

(b) The action of a light filter is to stop light of certain colours

(c) A light, appears coloured by the colour which it absorbs.

(d) It should be kept in mind whenever a filter is so used.

(e) That is, rays of some colours are allowed to pass through freely, while others are partially or wholly absorbed.

1. Which sentence should come last?
(a) (b) (c) (d) (e)
2. Which sentence should come first?
(a) (b) (c) (d) (e)
3. Which sentence should come second?
(a) (b) (c) (d) (e)
4. Which sentence should come third?
(a) (b) (c) (d) (e)
5. Which sentence should come fourth?
(a) (b) (c) (d) (e)

6. (a) The more fundamental and far-reaching a scientific theory, the more speculative it is likely to be.
(b) But speculaton is its very life-blood.
(c) A mature science tries to arrange facts in significant patterns to see the relationship between unrelated aspects of the universe.
(d) Idle speculation has no place in science.
(e) It is erroneous to believe that science is only concerned with pure facts.

1. Which sentence should come last?
(a) (b) (c) (d) (e)
2. Which sentence should come first?
(a) (b) (c) (d) (e)
3. Which sentence should come fourth?
(a) (b) (c) (d) (e)
4. Which sentence should come third?
(a) (b) (c) (d) (e)
5. Which sentence should come second?
(a) (b) (c) (d) (e)

7. (a) But this time a curious philosophy has emerged.
(b) But it seems a regulatory solution has been farther away.
(c) It says that the more we know about a problem, the more uncertainty is introduced and the more it needs to be studied.
(d) The recent debates on acid rain have pitted the environmentalists head to head against industry.
(e) As a result, we know more about acid rain and its effect than ever before.

1. Which sentence should come last?
(a) (b) (c) (d) (e)
2. Which sentence should come first?
(a) (b) (c) (d) (e)
3. Which sentence should come second?
(a) (b) (c) (d) (e)
4. Which sentence should come third?
(a) (b) (c) (d) (e)
5. Which sentence should come fourth?
(a) (b) (c) (d) (e)

8. (a) Seconds later, the glaring object swept past and he thought he had outmanouvred it.
(b) While flying over enemy territory, Jones received the warning of an oncoming missile.
(c) He was proved wrong when he saw the vertical tail fins on fire.
(d) Without wasting time, he slammed the throttles forward and made the plane roll into a high speed turn.
(e) Hardly had he responded to the message when he actually saw whatever the fighter pilot dreaded most.

1. Which sentence should come fourth in the paragraph?
(a) (a) (b) (b)
(c) (c) (d) (d)
(e) (e)
2. Which sentence should come third in the paragraph?
(a) (a) (b) (b)
(c) (c) (d) (d)
(e) (e)
3. Which sentence should come second in the paragraph?
(a) (a) (b) (b)
(c) (c) (d) (d)
(e) (e)

4. Which sentence should come last in the paragraph?
   (a) (a) (b) (b)
   (c) (b) (d) (d)
   (e) (e)
5. Which sentence should come first in the paragraph?
   (a) (a) (b) (b)
   (c) (c) (d) (d)
   (e) (e)

9. (a) But by then it was too late to correct things.
   (b) It is impossible to steer such a large project to success without planning.
   (c) He had to stand by and watch helplessly.
   (d) The whole scheme was destined to fail from the beginning.
   (e) Bhasker started realising this only towards the end.

1. Which sentence should come second in the paragraph?
   (a) (a) (b) (b)
   (c) (c) (d) (d)
   (e) (e)
2. Which sentence should come fourth in the paragraph?
   (a) (a) (b) (b)
   (c) (c) (d) (d)
   (e) (e)
3. Which sentence should come first in the paragraph?
   (a) (a) (b) (b)
   (c) (c) (d) (d)
   (e) (e)
4. Which sentence should come last in the paragraph?
   (a) (a) (b) (b)
   (c) (c) (d) (d)
   (e) (e)
5. Which sentence should come third in the paragraph?
   (a) (a) (b) (b)
   (c) (c) (d) (d)
   (e) (e)

10. (a) The director has to translate this scenario into film language.
   (b) The novelist works in the written word.
   (c) The film director works in pictures, in visual movement.
   (d) The pictures may be supported by speech, sound and colour.
   (e) But primarily the film is a pictorial art. So that when we reduce the elements of film making, we find that the essential item of the film maker is celluloid.

1. Which sentence should come second in the paragraph?
   (a) (a) (b) (b)
   (c) (c) (d) (d)
   (e) (e)
2. Which sentence should come fourth in the paragraph?
   (a) (a) (b) (b)
   (c) (c) (d) (d)
   (e) (e)
3. Which sentence should come first in the paragraph?
   (a) (a) (b) (b)
   (c) (c) (d) (d)
   (e) (e)
4. Which sentence should come last in the paragraph?
   (a) (a) (b) (b)
   (c) (c) (d) (d)
   (e) (e)
5. Which sentence should come third in the paragraph?
   (a) (a) (b) (b)
   (c) (c) (d) (d)
   (e) (e)

ANSWER KEY

Set 1	Set 2	Set 3	
1. (a)	1. (c)	1-1. (b)	6-1. (c)
2. (c)	2. (b)	2. (c)	2. (d)
3. (c)	3. (c)	3. (e)	3. (e)
4. (b)	4. (d)	4. (a)	4. (a)
5. (c)	5. (a)	5. (d)	5. (b)
6. (a)	6. (d)		
7. (b)	7. (c)	2-1. (d)	7-1. (b)
8. (b)	8. (a)	2. (c)	2. (d)
9. (a)	9. (b)	3. (a)	3. (a)
10. (d)	10. (a)	4. (e)	4. (c)
11. (b)	11. (a)	5. (b)	5. (e)
12. (d)	12. (a)		
13. (a)	13. (b)	3-1. (c)	8-1. (a)
14. (c)	14. (d)	2. (d)	2. (d)
15. (c)	15. (c)	3. (e)	3. (e)
16. (b)	16. (b)	4. (a)	4. (c)
17. (d)	17. (a)	5. (b)	5. (b)
18. (a)	18. (a)		
19. (a)	19. (a)	4-1. (d)	9-1. (b)
20. (c)	20. (d)	2. (e)	2. (a)
21. (a)	21. (b)	3. (c)	3. (d)
22. (c)	22. (c)	4. (a)	4. (c)
23. (c)	23. (b)	5. (b)	5. (e)
24. (d)	24. (a)		
25. (a)	25. (c)	5-1. (d)	10-1. (b)
26. (a)	26. (c)	2. (b)	2. (d)
27. (d)	27. (c)	3. (e)	3. (a)
28. (c)	28. (b)	4. (c)	4. (e)
29. (a)		5. (a)	5. (c)
30. (d)			

Appendix

Questions from Examination Papers

Set–I

1. When you
P. which one is closest in meaning
Q. read the four sentences in your text book and decide
R. to the statement you have heard
S. hear a statement
(a) SRPQ (b) SQPR
(c) SPQR (d) QPSR
(CDS)

2. There is a fashion now-a-days
P. as an evil
Q. who is born with a silver spoon
R. to bewail poverty
S. and to pity the youngman
6. in his mouth
(a) PSRQ (b) RPSQ
(c) RSQP (d) SPRQ
(SSC)

3. A typical Prakash Padukone day
P. or even a game of tennis
Q. starts off
R. on some days
S. with an early morning
(a) QSPR (b) SQRP
(c) RPSQ (d) RSQP
(NDA)

4. When I reached my office
P. to get home early
Q. I phoned my mother
R. that I wouldn't be able
S. to tell her
6. as I had promised.
(a) PQRS (b) QSRP
(c) RPQS (d) SQPR
(Stenographer's Exam.)

5. When he
P. did not know
Q. he was nervous and
R. heard the hue and cry at midnight
S. What to do
(a) PQRS (b) QSPR
(c) RQPS (d) SQPR
(Railways)

6. The claim is not
P. of any kind
Q. but
R. that it is without morality
S. that science is actively anti-moral
(a) PSQR (b) RPSQ
(c) RQSP (d) SQRP
(SCRA)

7. At the end of the assignment
P. the field worker
Q. submitted his papers
R. for the work done by him
S. and also bills
6. to the office superintendent
(a) PQSR (b) QPRS
(c) QSRP (d) RSQP
(B.E.d.)

8. If evil consisted
P. men would be drawn to virtue
Q. but, alas! how many know their duty
R. merely in ignorance
S. as soon as it was explained to them
6. and yet do not do it
(a) RPQS (b) RPSQ
(c) RSPQ (d) SPRQ
(CBI)

9. I enclose
P. and the postage
Q. a postal order
R. the price of the books
S. which will cover
(a) QPSR (b) QSPR
(c) QSRP (d) RPSQ
(SCRA)

10. Though the government claims
P. it has failed to arrest
Q. the rate of inflation is down
R. or the decrease
S. the rise in prices
6. in the per capita income
(a) PQRS (b) PQSR
(c) PSQR (d) QPSR
(Asstt. Grade)

11. If all the nations
P. for the common good of mankind
Q. then they will never fight with each other
R. work together
S. and agree to obey these laws,
6. and there will be no war
(a) PRQS (b) RPSQ
(c) RQPS (d) SQRP
(SSC)

12. No part of this publication may be
P. without the written permission
Q. reproduced, stored in or transmitted
R. of the copyright owner and
S. in any form or by any means
6. the publisher of this book
(a) PQRS (b) QSPR
(c) RPSQ (d) SRQP
(Stenographers' Exam.)

13. Padukone's retirement
P. as is obvious
Q. his concern for the game
R. has not diminished
S. when he talks of the Badminton Association of India
(a) PQRS (b) PSQR
(c) RPQS (d) RQPS
(NDA, 1995.)

14. He had started the book thinking
P. he had decided to
Q. that it would be an interesting work,
R. but by the time
S. he reached the middle,
6. throw it into the bin.
(a) PSQR (b) QRSP
(c) RSPQ (d) SPRQ
(Stenographers' Exam.)

15. The main purpose
P. how much
Q. is to find out
R. of this test
S. of English
6. he knows
(a) PQSR (b) PRQS
(c) RQPS (d) SPQR
(Central Excise)

16. Some achievements
P. have made
Q. happier and more comfortable
R. of science
S. human life
(a) PQRS (b) QRSP
(c) RPSQ (d) RSPQ
(SCRA, 1994.)

17. Almost every country in the world
P. that it is of the chosen people
Q. it has some special dispensation from Providence
R. and that others are somewhat
S. believes that '
6. inferior creatures
(a) RPQS (b) RQPS
(c) SQPR (d) SQRP
(CHl)

18. They would gather information
P. and then report the findings
Q. of the lands
R. through which they travelled
S. about the wealth and military strength
6. to the king

(a) *PQSR* (b) *PSQR*
(c) *QRSP* (d) *SQRP*

(SSC)

19. The man whom I hit on the head
P. says that when he meets me
Q. on my way back home from school
R. on the road
S. he will beat me
6. till I cry for mercy.
(a) PSRQ (b) QPRS
(c) RPSQ (d) RQSP

(Stenographers' Exam.)

20. The two men who were following
P. and who were separated from the tigress by the rock,
Q. when they saw me stop
R. a few yards behind me
S. stood still
6. and turn my head.
(a) PSQR
(b) QSPR
(c) RPSQ
(d) SQRP

(Asstt. Grade)

ANSWER KEY

1. (b)	8. (b)	15. (c)
2. (b)	9. (c)	16. (c)
3. (a)	10. (d)	17. (c)
4. (b)	11. (b)	18. (d)
5. (c)	12. (b)	19. (b)
6. (d)	13. (d)	20. (c)
7. (a)	14. (b)	

SET 2

1. S_1. The Hound of Baskervilles was feared by the people of the area.
S_6. The Hound of Baskervilles remains an unsolved mystery.
P. Some people spoke of seeing a huge, shadowy form of a hound at midnight on the moor.
Q. But they spoke of it in tones of horror.
R. Nobody had actually seen the hound.
S. This shadowy form did not reveal any details about the animal.
(a) PQRS (b) PSRQ
(c) SPQR (d) SPRQ

(CDS)

2. S. Man has existed for about a million years.
P. Science, as a dominant factor determining the beliefs of educated men, has existed for about 300 years; as a source of economic technique, for about 150 years.
Q. When we consider how recently it has risen to power, we find ourselves forced to believe that we are at the very beginning of its work in transforming human life.
R. In this brief period it has proved itself an incredibly powerful revolutionary force.
S. He has possessed writing for about 6,000 years, agriculture somewhat longer, but perhaps not much longer.
S_6. What its future effects will be is a matter of conjecture, but possibly a study of its effects hitherto may make the conjecture a little less hazardous.
(a) PQSR (b) PRSQ
(c) RQPS (d) SPRQ

(Railways)

3. S_1. He tried the door.
P. The room was neat and clean.
Q. Then he stepped into the room.
R. He waited for a minute or two.
S. It opened easily and he peeped in.
S_6. He was careful not to touch anything.
(a) PQRS (b) QSPR
(c) RPQS (d) SPRQ

(I Tax & Central Excise)

4. S_1. Jawaharlal Nehru was born November 14.
P. He loved children.
Q. On this day, children take part in many activities.
R. Sports, music, drama and debates are arranged in schools.
S. That is why his birthday is celebratd as Children's Day.
S_6. Exhibitions of photographs of Pandit Nehru showing his lifetime are also arranged in some schools.
(a) PQRS (b) PSQR
(c) QPSR (d) SPQR

(B. Ed. Exam.)

5. S_1. Smoke oozed up between the planks.
P. Passengers were told to be ready to quit the ship.
Q. The rising gale fanned the smouldering fire.
R. Every one now knew there was a fire on board.
S. Flames broke out here and there.
S_6. Most people bore the shock bravely.
(a) QPSR (b) QSRP
(c) RSPQ (d) SRQP

(Asstt. Grade)

6. S_1. Most of the perishable foods are shipped by refrigerator ships.
S_6. Ripe bananas are poor travellers and even one ripe banana at the start of the trip can spoil a whole shipload of fruit.
P. They are placed in the refrigerated hold of the ship.
Q. Some foods, such as bananas, are shipped before they get ripe.
R. As the green bananas are loaded, a man watches closely the signs of yellow on them.
S. The cool temperatures keep the bananas from getting ripe during the trip.
(a) PQRS (b) PSQR
(c) QPSR (d) SRPQ

(SSC.)

7. S_1. There was once a Persian king called Shahryar who had a beautiful wife.
P. When the King discovered this he killed her.
Q. He gave orders that he was to be provided with a new wife every day.
R. He loved her very much, but she was a wicked woman.
S. He decided that all women were wicked and that he would punish them.
S_6. After one day's marriage he would cut off her head and marry again.
(a) PQRS (b) QSPR
(c) RPSQ (d) SPRQ

(CBI)

8. S_1. The commonest form of forgetfulness, I suppose, occurs in the matter of posting letters.
S_6. Weary of holding it in my hand, I. then put it for safety into one of my pockets and forget all about it.
P. So common is it that I am always reluctant to trust a departing visitor to post an important letter.
Q. As for myself, anyone who asks me to post a letter is a poor judge of character.
R. Even if I carry the letter in my hand I am always past the first pillar box before I remember that I ought to have posted it.
S. So little I rely on his memory that I put him on his oath before handing the letter to him.
(a) PRQS (b) PSQR
(c) QSPR (d) RQSP

(SCRA)

9. S_1 We must learn to depend on ourselves and not to look to others for help everytime we are in trouble.
S_1 A country's freedom can be preserved only by her own strength and self-reliance.
P. We should not forget that those who lean too much on others tend to become weak and helpless.
Q. Certainly we want to make friends with the rest of the world.
R. We welcome help and cooperation from every quarter, but we must depend

primarily on our own resources.

S. We also seek the goodwill and cooperation of all those who reside in this country, whatever their race or nationality.

(a) PQRS (b) QPRS
(c) QSRP (d) SRQP

(IES)

10. S_1. It was early 1943 and the war in the East was going disastrously.

P. How this unlikely bunch of middle-aged civilians accomplished their missions makes fascinating reading.

Q. To stop the sinkings a spy ring had to be broken, a German ship assaulted, and a secret radio transmitter silenced.

R. U-boats were torpedoing Allied ships in the Indian ocean faster than they could be replaced.

S. And the only people who could do the job were a handful of British businessmen in Calcutta-all men not called out for active service.

S_6 *Boarding Party,* James Leasor's latest bestseller is a record of this tale of heroics tinged with irony and humour.

(a) PRSQ (b) QSRP
(c) RQSP (d) SQPR

(NDA)

11. S_1. Growing up means not only getting larger, but also using our senses and our brains to become more aware of the things around us.

P. Not only does he have a memory but he is able to think and reason.

Q. In this, man differs from all other animals.

R. Before we spray our roadside plants or turn sewage into our rivers, we should pause to think what the results of our actions are likely to be.

S. That is to say, he is able to plan what he is going to do in the light of his experience before he does it.

S_6 In other words, we must develop and use our ability to reason, because the destruction or the preservation of the places in which we live depends on us.

(a) QPSR (b) QRSP
(c) SPQR (d) SPRQ

(CDS)

12. S_1 We talk about democracy, but when it comes to any particular thing, we prefer a man belonging to our caste and community.

P. We must be in a position to respect a man as a man.

Q. It means our democracy is a phoney kind of democracy.

R. We must extend opportunities of development to those who deserve them.

S. Our weakness for our own caste and community should not influence our decision.

S_6 Favouritism and nepotism have been responsible for much discontent in our country.

(a) PQRS (b) QPRS
(c) RPQS (d) SRPQ

(Bank PO)

ANSWER KEY

1. (a)	5. (d)	9. (a)
2. (d)	6. (a)	10. (c)
3. (d)	7. (c)	11. (a)
4. (b)	8. (b)	12. (b)

Set–3

1. (A) Would you steal a software program out of a retail shop?

(B) The industry on its part has formed an organisation to specially gather information, educate and drag the software pirates to courts.

(C) But more than the legality, there is always a different way of looking at piracy and that is in terms of morality.

(D) The Government on the other hand has initiated National Enforcement Committees.

(E) As far as the issue of tackling piracy is concerned, both the industry and the Government have already started initiating action.

1. Which of the following should be the third sentence?
   (a) E (b) A
   (c) B (d) D
   (e) C
2. Which of the following should be the first sentence?
   (a) B (b) C
   (c) A (d) E
   (e) D
3. Which of the following should be the second sentence?
   (a) A (b) D
   (c) C (d) E
   (e) B
4. Which of the following should be the last sentence?
   (a) C (b) B
   (c) E (d) A
   (e) D
5. Which of the fallowing should be the fourth sentence?
   (a) D. (b) B
   (c) C (d) A
   (e) E

(BSRB)

2. (A) She decided to go to school and meet the Principal.

(B) Suddenly she realised that she had no money with her.

(C) By the time she reached there, he had left the office.

(D) Therefore, she dedicd to go to the office of Ravi's father and get the money.

(E) Sudha wanted her son Ravi to get admission in a convent school.

1. Which sentence should come fourth in the paragraph?
   (a) A (b) B
   (c) C (d) D
   (e) E
2. Which sentence should come second in the paragraph?
   (a) A (b) B
   (c) C (d) D
   (e) E
3. Which sentence should come third in the paragraph?
   (a) A (b) B
   (c) C (d) D
   (e) E
4. Which sentence should come first in the paragraph?
   (a) A (b) B
   (c) C (d) D
   (e) E
5. Which sentence should come last in the paragraph?
   (a) A (b) B
   (c) C (d) D
   (e) E

(BSRB)

3. (A) But, we all helped in the first few days.

(B) Chandrapur is considered as a rural area.

(C) Pradeep was transferred to this office recently.

(D) Initially he was not getting adjusted to the city life.

(E) Now, Pradeep is very proud of his colleagues.

(F) Before that he was working in Chandrapur branch of our office.

1. Which sentence should come first in the paragraph?
   (a) A (b) C
   (c) D (d) E
   (e) F
2. Which sentence should come second in the paragraph?
   (a) A (b) C
   (c) D (d) E
   (e) F

3. Which sentence should come last in the paragraph?
   (a) A (b) C
   (c) D (d) E
   (e) F
4. Which sentence should come third in the paragraph?
   (a) A (b) C
   (c) D (d) E
   (e) F

(SBI, PO)

4. (a) The following represents a condensed statement of what we think we now know about the relationship between education and employment.
(B) Although the linkage between education and employment are complex and, in the past, often analysed with simplistic notions of casuality, recent research results have yielded new insights about the nature of these linkages.
(c) In the interests of brevity, the argument is put forward as a series of major propositions and derivative strategies relating to the education-employment nexus.
(D) Intensive research efforts are currently being supported throughout the developing world both by national governments and international donor agencies in the hope of improving understanding of the nature and causes of rising unemployment.
(e) The massive problems of widespread and chronic unemployment in less developed nations will remain among the most serious challenges to development policy during the next several decades.

1. Which of the following would be the third sentence?
   (a) A (b) B
   (c) C (d) D
   (e) E
2. Which of the following would be the first sentence?
   (a) A (b) B
   (c) C (d) D
   (e) E
3. Which of the following would be the fifth sentence?
   (a) A (b) B
   (c) C (d) D
   (e) E

4.Which of the following would be the second sentence?
   (a) A (b) B
   (c) C (d) D
   (e) E

(LIC)

5. (A) A taxi was summoned and Satish was taken to Lifeline Hospital.
(B) While hurrying home from school, Satish was hit by a car.
(C) Since they did not succeed, they decided to take him to a hospital.
(D) When Satish opened his eyes, he found himself surrounded by doctors and nurses.
(E) Some people rushed towards him and tried to bring him to his senses.
(F) He was thrown a couple of feet away and lost consciousness.

1. Which sentence should come last (i.e., sixth) in the paragraph?
   (a) B (b) C
   (c) A (d) D
   (e) E
2. Which sentence should come first in the paragraph?
   (a) D (b) F
   (c) B (d) E
   (e) C
3. Which sentence should come second in the paragraph?
   (a) E (b) A
   (c) D (d) C
   (e) F
4. Which sentence should come third in the paragraph?
   (a) F (b) B
   (c) E (d) A
   (e) D
5. Which sentence should come fourth in the paragraph?
   (a) C (b) E
   (c) F (d) B
   (e) A

ANSWER KEY

1-1. (d)	2-1. (d)	3-1. (b)	4-1. (b)	5-1. (d)
2. (d)	2. (a)	2. (e)	2. (a)	2. (c)
3. (e)	3. (b)	3. (b)	3. (e)	3. (e)
4. (d)	4. (e)	4. (a)	4. (d)	4. (c)
5. (c)	5. (c)			5. (a)

CHAPTER 13

SENTENCE IMPROVEMENT

Sentence improvement is a variation upon spotting error. In a spotting error question you are asked to locate the error and tick the answer. Here, you are asked to evaluate the highlighted part of the sentence and improve it by making it correct if its incorrect, or appropriate, if it is inappropriate or a better sentence by changing it with a choice if it can be done so. This is therefore a more complex exercise. The error or inappropriateness may be in any part of speech, or in tense verb form, or sentence pattern, or in the use of an idiom or a phrase or proverb.

In fact, the improvement can be done by correcting the error or making the meaning clear. We can illustrate it with this figure:

Look at the italicised part of each sentence. Below each sentence are given possible substitutions for the italicised part. If one of them — ***a, b*** or ***c*** makes the sentence correct, or is better than the italicised part or makes the meaning clear indicate your response against the corresponding ***a, b*** or ***c***. If none of the substitutions improves the sentence, indicate d as your answer.

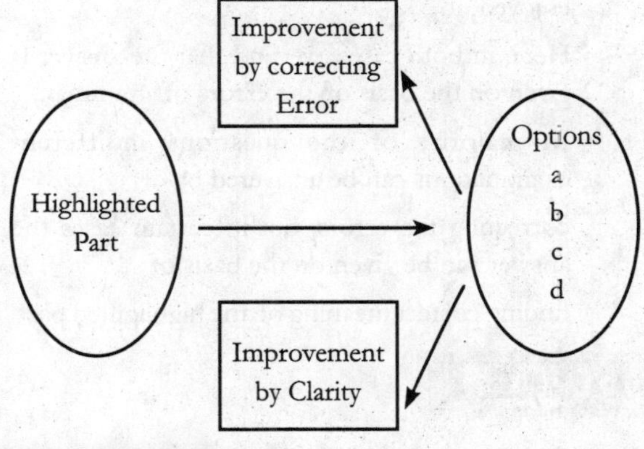

EXAMPLES

1. They **are waiting** for her since morning.
   (a) have been waiting
   (b) were waiting
   (c) wait
   (d) No improvement

Here in this sentence, the error is in the tense form. The correct answer is (a), "have been waiting" because the sentence shows a continuous sense requiring the present perfect continuous tense form.

2. **If you would have seen** the movie, you would have enjoyed it. *(Bank PO exam)*
   (a) had you been seen
   (b) if you have had seen
   (c) had you seen
   (d) No correction required

The answer is (c), 'had you seen'. The error here lies in the tense sequence. According to the rules of grammar, when there are two actions of past probability, one dependent on the other, the sequence should be as follows; past perfect + future perfect.

Had + past participle + would + have + past participle

1 2 3 4 5

Thus the correct form of the sentence in this example will be:

Had you seen the movie, you would have enjoyed it.

Here, in both cases, we find that the answer is given on the basis of the errors of grammar.

In majority of the questions indifferent examinations can be answered by

correcting the errors, but in certain cases the answer can be given on the basis of

finding correct meaning of the highlighted part.

EXAMPLE

My neighbour was caught stealing, he now has to face the music. *(United India Assurance Company, AAO, 2011)*
(1) ask for forgiveness
(2) come face to face with the police
(3) attempt to protect himself
(4) suffer the consequences of his action
(5) hear the song

Here the answer is 4, 'suffer the consequences of his action'. This is the meaning of this phrase.

Illustrations

CDS, 2012

Directions (for the following 14 items):

Look at the underlined part of each sentence. Below each sentence, three possible situations for the underlined part are given. If one of them (a), (b) or (c) is better than the underlined part, indicate your response on the Answer Sheet against the corresponding letter (a), (b) or (c). If none of these substitutions improves the sentence, indicate (d) as your response on the Answer Sheet. Thus a "No Improvement" response will be signified by the letter (d).

1. More than one person **was killed** in the accident.
   (a) were killed
   (b) are killed
   (c) have been killed
   (d) No improvement
2. Not a word **they spoke** to the unfortunate wife about it.
   (a) did they speak
   (b) they will speak
   (c) they had spoken
   (d) No improvement
3. The poor villagers **have waited** in bitter cold for more than four hours now.
   (a) have been waiting
   (b) had waited
   (c) has been waiting
   (d) No improvement
4. If he **had** time he will call you.
   (a) would have
   (b) would have had
   (c) has
   (d) No improvement
5. **All, but her**, had made an attempt.
   (a) All, but she,
   (b) All but her

(c) All, but her

(d) No improvement

6. I am used to **hard work.**

(a) work hard

(b) work hardly

(c) hard working

(d) No improvement

7. Twenty kilometres **are not a great distance** in these days of fast moving vehicles.

(a) is not a great distance

(b) is no distance

(c) aren't a great distance

(d) No improvement

8. They were working **as usually.**

(a) usual

(b) as usual

(c) usually

(d) No improvement

9. He is unlikely to come to the party. But **if he comes** I would talk to him.

(a) if he would come

(b) if he is to come

(c) if he will come

(d) No improvement

10. The passengers **have formed** queue at the booking-counter much before a train arrives.

(a) formed

(b) have been forming

(c) form

(d) No improvement

11. You must complete this work **up to Sunday.**

(a) within Sunday

(b) by Sunday

(c) until Sunday

(d) No improvement

12. If it will rain, the match will be abandoned.

(a) If it rains

(b) If it would rain

(c) If it rained

(d) No improvement

13. How long do you think Mr. Kamal **knew** John?

(a) will know

(b) knows

(c) has known

(d) No improvement

14. I have still to meet a person who is perfectly satisfied with his job.

(a) am still to meet

(b) am yet to meet

(c) might still meet

(d) No improvement

EXPLANATORY COMMENTS

1. Answer is d, no improvement. It is a question of subject-verb agreement. More than one is treated as a singular subject.
2. Answer is a, 'did they speak'. This is the correct form of tense.
3. Answer is a 'have been writing'. This is the correct form of tense. The continuous sense has to be expressed here.
4. Answer is c, 'has'. 'Has' is appropriate here to make correct tense form.
5. Answer is a, 'All but she'. The error here is in the use of pronoun. She can be the subject in the active voice.
6. Answer is a, 'work hard'. This will be the correct expression.
7. Answer is a, 'is not a great distance'. Twenty kilometers makes a singular subject as it is one unit.
8. Answer is a, 'usual'. As usual will be the correct form.
9. Answer is d, no improvement.
10. Answer is c, 'form'. Here the present times verb form is required. It is a present indefinite terms form.
11. Answer is b, 'by Sunday'. By Sunday will be the correct expression.
12. Answer is a, 'if it rains'. This will make the sentence grammatically correct. In both clauses future tense should not be used. The first part has to be in simple present form.

13. Answer is c, 'has known'. This is the correct tense form.

14. Answer is a 'am still to meet'. This is the correct expression.

IBPS Specialist Officer in Public Sector Bank Commown Written Examination, 2012

1. By initiating the fight with Sakshi in office, Kajal had killed the goose that lays the golden egg.
 (a) By initiating the fight with Sakshi in office, Kajal had left her speechless.
 (b) Kajal had ruined her chances of success by picking a fight with Sakshi in office.
 (c) Kajal had exacted her revenge by picking a fight with Sakshi in office.
 (d) Kajal had hurt Sakshi by picking a fight with her in office.
 (e) By initiating the fight with Sakshi in office, Kajal had missed getting the golden egg.

2. I let the chips fall where they may and do not worry too much about what I want to do next.
 (a) I take calculated risks.
 (b) I let others do what they want and do not interfere.
 (c) I am clumsy.
 (d) I do not try to control my destiny.
 (e) I prefer chaos to calm.

3. After trying hard to convince Narendra to change his ways, Raman realised that a leopard cannot change its spots.
 (a) Raman realised that Narendra would never change his ways.
 (b) Raman realised that Narendra was helpless.
 (c) Raman realised that he was not good at convincing others.
 (d) Raman realised, that Narendta would change his ways soon.
 (e) Raman realised that someone else was forcing Narendra to act in a certain way.

4. Before starting work on our new project, our mentor told us to not count our chicken before they hatched.
 (a) Our mentor warned us against being over-confident about achieving success.
 (b) Our mentor asked us to meticulously count the chicken first and then the eggs.
 (c) Our mentor warned us against being over-enthusiastic in implementing the project.
 (d) Our mentor warned us about all the challenges that lay ahead of us.
 (e) Our mentor informed us about the prizes that we would get on succeeding.

EXPLANATORY COMMENTS

1. Answer is (b). The appropriate and clear meaning of the sentence needs this expression Kajal had revised her chances of success by picking a fight with Sakshi in office. The sentence gets improved and the meaning because clear.
2. Answer is (d). The sentence means that 'I do not try to control my destines'.
3. Answer is (a), 'Raman realised that Narendra would never change his way'. This is the clear meaning of the sentence.
4. Answer is (c), 'Our monitor warned us against being over-enthusiastic in implementing the projct'. This is the clear meaning of the sentence.

 All above sentences are examples where the subjected options make the meaning of the sentences clean and thus they improve the expressions.

IBPS Common Written Examination, 2011

Directions (1 – 4): Which of the phrases (a), (b), (c) and (d) given below each statement should replace the phrase printed in bold in the sentence to make it grammatically correct ? If the sentence is correct as it is given and 'No correction is required,' mark (e) as the answer.

1. A twenty-first century economy **cannot be held** hostage by power cuts nor travel on nineteenth century roads.
 (a) cannot be hold
 (b) can either be held

(c) can neither be held
(d) can either be hold
(e) No correction required

2. The company's philosophy is to make sure that the employees are happy, have the ability to be intellectually stimulated and **contributes towards their growth.**
(a) contribute to their growth
(b) contribute towards its growth
(c) contributes towards its growing
(d) contribute to its growing
(e) No correction required

3. **Even though many companies are** now penetrating rural India, it would help to give India a real chance of witnessing a double digit GDP growth.
(a) Despite many companies are
(b) As many company is
(c) Besides many companies are
(d) Since many companies are
(e) No correction required

4. Today, governments are introducing more and more technology into their system to address the needs of citizens at a pace **fast than that of** manual operations.
(a) faster than that of
(b) more fast than that of
(c) as fast as
(d) fastest than that of
(e) No correction required

ANSWER & EXPLANATIONS

1. Answer is (c), 'can neither be held'. Neither is followed by nor.
2. Answer is (b). 'contribute towards its growth'. The verb contribute will be used for the subject the employees' which is plural. Its will be the pronoun for three company.
3. Answer is (d) 'Since many companies are'. 'Even though' is contradictory there. The appropriate connector will be since.
4. Answer is a, 'faster than that of'. Here faster will be used for comparative degree. 'That of' is correct for 'pace' which is singular. Degree and pronoun errors are to be corrected here.

Practice Set —1

Direction: Which of the words/phrases, (a), (b), (c) and (d), should replace the words/phrases given in italics in each of the following sentences so as to make them most effective and meaningfully correct. If the sentence is correct and needs no change, mark (d) or (e) as your answer.

1. I love the man so well that I wish *he should overlive me.*
(a) may overlive me
(b) ought to overlive me
(c) might overlive me
(d) try to overlive me
(e) No correction needed

2. Can this machine be adapted *in* farm work.
(a) by
(b) into
(c) for
(d) to
(e) No correction needed

3. When the Prime Minister said this, we know whom he *was eluding to.*
(a) referring
(b) alluding
(c) hinting
(d) suggesting
(e) No correction needed

4. The weather was not good; it was *a bit* pleasant.
(a) a little
(b) to some extent
(c) fairly
(d) rather
(e) No correction needed

5. He *lives* in a remote colony since August 1989.
(a) is living
(b) has been living

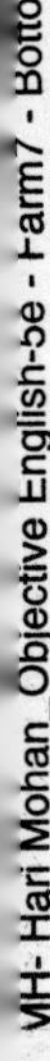

(c) has lived
(d) continues to live
(e) No correction needed

6. When we reached the site of the crash, we saw only three *alive* men in the wreck.
(a) living (b) lively
(c) live (d) breathing
(e) No correction needed

7. Hardly had she entered the police station *then* all officers stood up.
(a) than (b) when
(c) before (d) since
(e) No correction needed

8. Do *how* I say.
(a) which (b) that
(c) as (d) like
(e) No correction needed

9. Stop taking drugs lest *you are caught.*
(a) might be caught
(b) will be caught
(c) may be caught
(d) would be caught

10. Though a hero, he acted *a coward.*
(a) with cowardice
(b) as coward
(c) cowardly
(d) as like a coward
(e) No correction

11. They were all astonished *at* his failure in the examination.
(a) for (b) on
(c) in (d) from
(e) No correction

12. Due to bad weather the number of ships crossing the channel last week *is very* small.
(a) are being (b) are
(c) were (d) was
(e) None

13. She is worried about his health and *also me.*
(a) also is me (b) so am I
(c) so come too (d) me also are
(e) None

14. Roads are wet, it *must had* rained last night.
(a) must have been (b) might had
(c) would have been (d) must have
(e) None

15. She is *tallest* of all the girls.
(a) the tallest (b) taller
(c) the taller (d) a taller
(e) None

16. It will depend now on *they* coming on time.
(a) their coming (b) them coming
(c) theirs coming (d) they come
(e) None

17. He has studied French *since four* years.
(a) since four years ago
(b) from four years ago
(c) from four years
(d) for four years
(e) None

18. He *had not ought to do* it.
(a) has not ought to do
(b) ought not had done
(c) ought not has done
(d) ought not have done
(e) None

19. He decided to *quickly* leave the house.
(a) quickly to leave the house
(b) quickly leave house
(c) leave the house quickly
(d) leave quickly the house
(e) None

20. The bag is *so heavy* that I can hardly carry it.
(a) as (b) too
(c) much (d) more
(e) None

21. Most willingly Rama agreed *to go* to Madras and remain there for a month.
(a) go to (b) on going to
(c) to going to (d) to going
(e) None

22. I felt that the music was *sweetly* and *soothingly.*
(a) sweetly but soothingly
(b) sweet and soothing

(c) sweetly and soothing
(d) sweet but soothing
(e) None

23. He did not know the answer and I *did not neither.*
(a) and neither did I
(b) and either did I
(c) and neither have I
(d) and either did have
(e) None

24. He spent much time and energy over it and lost a large sum *in the bargain.*
(a) will bargain (b) for bargain
(c) off the bargain (d) into bargain
(e) None

25. It is *all and one* to me whether he lives in Mumbai or Kolkata
(a) all but one
(b) all one
(c) one and the same
(d) all or one
(e) No correction

26. At an early age *he had made his mark* as a chemist.
(a) made his mark
(b) makes his mark
(c) has made his mark
(d) has been making his mark
(e) No correction

27. He is not *in the good books* of his master.
(a) in the better book
(b) in the good book
(c) in the best book
(d) into the good books
(e) No correction

28. He has been working *off and on* for several years to compile a dictionary.
(a) regularly (b) constantly
(c) on and off (d) on or off
(e) No correction

29. On the day of the match, everyone hoped *about* fine weather.
(a) of
(b) at
(c) for
(d) No improvement

30. Although her parents warned her *of* what would happen, she continued to disobey them.
(a) off
(b) on
(c) to
(d) No improvement

31. In his lecture, he dealt *about* the causes of the Gulf War.
(a) with
(b) on
(c) for
(d) No improvement

32. When new coins were issued, the old ones were *called out.*
(a) in
(b) up
(c) off
(d) No improvement

33. But for the two incomes, we would be *hard out.*
(a) help up
(b) hard on
(c) hard up
(d) No improvement

34. History is a *little more* than the register of the crimes, follies and misfortunes of mankind.
(a) little less
(b) very little more
(c) little more
(d) No improvement

35. The centre forward was constantly being cheered and applauded because *he had made many goals.*
(a) he had secured many goals
(b) he made many goals
(c) he had scored many goals
(d) No improvement

36. Our neighbours are extremely noisy but *even more are they quarrelsome.*
(a) they are even more quarrelsome
(b) more even are they quarrelsome

(c) more are they quarrelsome
(d) No improvement

37. I prefer *to ride than to walk.*
(a) ride to walk
(b) riding than walking
(c) riding to walking
(d) No improvement

38. Would you mind *help* me with these questions?
(a) helping
(b) to help
(c) of helping
(d) No improvement

39. Is the coffee *so cool for you to drink?*
(a) too cool that you can drink
(b) cool enough for you to drink
(c) enough cool to drink
(d) No improvement

40. While walking across the road *a bus knocked him down.*
(a) a bus knocked him
(b) he was by a bus knocked
(c) he was knocked down by a bus
(d) No improvement

41. We had to stop for diesel because we had *hardly much* left.
(a) some
(b) more
(c) any
(d) No improvement

42. If you had arrived earlier, you *would have found* me in the bus.
(a) will find
(b) have found
(c) found
(d) No improvement

43. The robber *entered into* the old man's room very quietly.
(a) entered in
(b) entered inside
(c) entered
(d) No improvement

44. Unless he *does not leave* this house, I will not say anything.
(a) had left (b) left
(c) did not leave (d) leaves
(e) None

45. As the summer vacation approaches, the number of tourists *are increasing by leaps and bounds.*
(a) has increased by leaps and bounds
(b) increases by leaps and bounds
(c) are increasing by leaps and bounds
(d) increased by leaps and bounds
(e) None

46. It is *one and quarter hours* since Harish went away.
(a) one and quarter
(b) one and quarter hour
(c) one hours and quarter
(d) one hour and a quarter
(e) No correction

47. Where politics fails, economics *may sometime succeed.*
(a) may sometimes succeeds
(b) may sometime succeeds
(c) sometimes succeed
(d) sometimes succeeds
(e) No correction

48. In which newspapers *the advertisement appeared*?
(a) did the advertisement appear
(b) did the advertisement was appeared
(c) the advertisement was appeared
(d) the advertisement appear
(e) No correction

49. The teacher asked "why you are late?"
(a) why you were late
(b) why late you are
(c) why are you late
(d) No correction

50. He killed the enemy *by his sword.*
(a) with his sword
(b) by sword
(c) by a sword
(d) No correction

51. He told us the story *in a nutshell.*
(a) in the nutshell
(b) putting in a nut
(c) in nutshell
(d) No correction

52. She *is having a lot of* money.
(a) has lot of (b) has a lot of
(c) is having lot of (d) No correction

53. He shouted *that he might attract attention.*
(a) to attract attention
(b) for attracting attention
(c) that he may attract attention
(d) No correction

54. You can mix it *with some sugar* and eat it.
(a) in some sugar
(b) into some sugar
(c) any sugar
(d) No correction

55. I don't want to disturb you, please *get with your work.*
(a) get up with (b) get over with
(c) get on with (d) No correction

56. There is plenty of time to catch the train.
(a) to get (b) to reach
(c) to hold (d) No correction

57. Hundreds of people were killed *by* earthquake.
(a) in (b) from
(c) of (d) No correction

58. He *insisted on* he was innocent.
(a) insisted on that (b) insisted that
(c) insists that (d) No correction

59. John, who *studies* medicine at present, hopes to go abroad after graduation.
(a) is studying (b) will study
(c) studied (d) No correction

60. Students *are attending* spoken English classes since 6th February.
(a) were attending
(b) have been attending
(c) have attended
(d) No correction

61. Ramesh went to the nearest shop *to getting* presents for his son.
(a) to get (b) for to get
(c) for getting (d) No correction

62. They *have still not responded* to our proposal.
(a) have not still responded
(b) still have not responded
(c) not have still responded
(d) No correction

63. I cannot remember where *I did leave* my black shirt.
(a) did I leave
(b) I left
(c) left I
(d) No correction

64. Would you please tell me *when the next train comes.*
(a) when does the next train come
(b) when comes the next train
(c) when the next train does come
(d) No correction

65. In this *deteriorate* condition, you should call in a good doctor.
(a) deteriorating (b) deterioration
(c) to deteriorated (d) No correction

66. It is important that he *should have been arriving* here in time.
(a) could arrive
(b) arrive
(c) could have arrived
(d) No correction

67. One should be careful to check the grease and oil in *our* car every day.
(a) one's
(b) his
(c) their
(d) No correction

68. I want to see the film as it *is being directed* by Satyajit Ray.
(a) has been directed by
(b) was directed by
(c) had directed by
(d) No correction

69. To lock up a man and *let him doing nothing* is a cruel punishment.
(a) let him do nothing
(b) letting him do nothing
(c) to let him do nothing
(d) No correction

70. At last we realised *what was* truth.
(a) what was the truth
(b) what the truth was
(c) the truth was
(d) No correction

71. Only three-fourths of the work *are complete.*
(a) is complete (b) has completed
(c) have completed
(d) No correction

72. More than one person *has found* it correct.
(a) have found (b) were found
(c) is found (d) No correction

73. In summer, days are *more warmer* than nights.
(a) more warm (b) warmer
(c) warmest (d) No correction

74. It is better to say *too little* than too much.
(a) little (b) only little
(c) very little (d) No correction

75. A large number of houses *has come up* around Kolkata.
(a) is coming up (b) are coming up
(c) had come up (d) No correction

76. The rules of chess require that one *made* only one move at a time.
(a) makes (b) make
(c) will make (d) None

77. In a few minutes time, when the clock strikes six, I *would be waiting* here three-quarters of an hour.
(a) shall be waiting
(b) shall have been waiting
(c) will have waited
(d) None

78. He enjoys *to tell stories* to children.
(a) telling stories
(b) how to tell stories
(c) to narrate stories
(d) None

79. 'Arms and the Man' *have been written* by George Bernard Shaw.
(a) are written
(b) are being written
(c) has been written
(d) None

80. By temperament *the French* are reserved, so they prefer to live in solitude.
(a) French people (b) French
(c) some French (d) None

81. Do take an umbrella *lest you do not* get wet.
(a) lest you should
(b) lest you should not
(c) lest you might not
(d) None

82. The person *who* they are referring to is a good friend.
(a) whom (b) which
(c) that (d) None

83. The short essay should not *exceed more than* two hundred pages.
(a) exceed (b) exceed than
(c) more exceed (d) None

84. My copy is *as good or* better than yours.
(a) as good as
(b) as good and better
(c) as good as or
(d) None

85. I could not help *to laugh at* the joke.
(a) help laughing at(b) laugh at
(c) to laughing at (d) None

86. *What to talk of* standing first, he could not even pass at the examination.
(a) not to talk of (b) but to talk of
(c) let to talk of (d) None

87. *If I was you* I would not sign the document.
(a) If I have been you(b) If I were you
(c) Was I you (d) None

88. The candidates will be interviewed *between 10 a.m. to 11 a.m.*

(a) between 10 a.m. and 11 a.m.
(b) between 11 a.m. from 12 a.m.
(c) between 11 a.m. for 12 a.m.
(d) None

89. *Since we are living* in Bombay, we are unwilling to move to another city.
(a) since we have been living
(b) being that we are living
(c) since we were living
(d) None

90. If I **were** you, I would do it at once.
(a) was
(b) am
(c) would be
(d) No improvement

91. They set a strong guard, lest anyone *could* escape.
(a) would
(b) might
(c) should
(d) No improvement

92. The matter called *up* an explanation of his conduct.
(a) out
(b) in
(c) for
(d) No improvement

93. The accused *refused* having murdered anybody.
(a) disagreed
(b) denied
(c) declaimed
(d) No improvement

94. We need honest workers, not people of *redoubtable* integrity.
(a) doubting
(b) doubtful
(c) doubtless
(d) No improvement

95. By the time *he arrived,* everybody had gone home.
(a) when he arrived
(b) at which he arrived
(c) by which he arrived
(d) No improvement

96. There is no *alternate,* so we must leave now.
(a) altering
(b) alternative
(c) alternation
(d) No improvement

97. I cannot *listen what* she is saying.
(a) hear what
(b) listen for what
(c) listen to that
(d) No improvement

98. He is still in vigorous health although he is on the *right* side of sixty.
(a) wrong
(b) left
(c) negative
(d) No improvement

99. We are sorry to hear *regarding* your father's death.
(a) of
(b) over
(c) for
(d) No improvement

100. Babu asked his friend, "*Where you went yesterday*?"
(a) "Where did you go yesterday?"
(b) "Where you had gone yesterday?"
(c) "Where you did go yesterday?"
(d) No improvement

101. He *lay* on the grass enjoying the sunshine.
(a) laid
(b) lied
(c) led
(d) No improvement

102. Some passengers were *flown* to Paris on the last trip.
(a) fled
(b) flied
(c) flew
(d) No improvement

103. Fifty miles *are* a long distance to walk.
(a) is
(b) become
(c) be
(d) No improvement

104. After the vote was taken the meeting *broke.*
(a) broke down
(b) broke up
(c) broke out
(d) No improvement

105. The speaker asked the audience to bear *upon* him for a few minutes more.
(a) on
(b) with
(c) for
(d) No improvement

106. Many people find it difficult to make *both hands meet.*
(a) both accounts
(b) both hand to mouth
(c) both ends meet
(d) No improvement

107. All their efforts *were direct to* promote harmony among various groups of people.
(a) were directing to
(b) were directed at
(c) have directed for
(d) were directed to
(e) No correction

108. *What did happen* there in the first place in a matter of our concern.
(a) what happen
(b) what would have happened
(c) what happened
(d) what should have happened
(e) no correction

109. The speaker highlighted the contribution of women *for bringing about* social, changes.
(a) for bringing in
(b) in bringing of
(c) for the brought over
(d) in bringing about
(e) no correction

110. Such inequalities *can be fonded* enshrined in the constitution of other countries also.
(a) could have been founded
(b) can be found
(c) could be found
(d) could have found
(e) no correction

111. The local authorities *were never bothering* to care about the unfortunate happenings.
(a) Were never bothered to
(b) never bothered to
(c) never were bothering to
(d) Was never bothering to
(e) no correction

112. India's out look on he world is *composing of* these various element,
(a) is composed of
(b) is composed by
(c) is composing with
(d) has been composing at
(e) no correction

113. How religious intolerance can blight social peace and harming can be gauged from events *take place around* the globe.
(a) taken place over
(b) taking place around
(c) took place around
(d) taken place in
(e) no correction

114. This exploitation of the helpless tribal *needs be condemnated.*
(a) need to be condemned
(b) needs condemnation
(c) needs to be condemned
(d) need to condemnation
(e) no correction

115. The fact-finding team *which had been to* the area found villagers giving information to police,
(a) which had been for
(b) that led to
(c) which led to
(d) that has been to
(e) no correction

116. The faster he completes the work given to him *the largest will be* his profit,
(a) the larger will be
(b) the largest would be
(c) the larger would be
(d) the largest shall be
(e) no correction

117. The custom of *many centuries ago origin* is slowly disappearing.
(a) With many centuries of origin.
(b) Which originated many centuries ago
(c) Originating for many centuries
(d) Which was originated ago many centuries
(e) No correction

118. If *you would have seen* the movie, you would have enjoyed it.
(a) Had you been seen
(b) if you have had seen
(c) had you seen
(d) If you would seen
(e) No correction

119. Just *in hour's time,* he could complete the work to my satisfaction,
(a) In an hour's time
(b) In the time of an hour
(c) In the duration of one hour
(d) in an hour
(e) No correction

120. The young hikers went *as Far as they* finally get lost in the valley,
(a) Too far that
(b) very far there for
(c) so far as that
(d) So far that
(e) No correction

121. *Not only did he criticise* the party's policies but also the leader's personal matters.
(a) He did not criticise
(b) neither did he criticise
(c) he not only criticise
(d) He criticised not only
(e) No correction

122. Despite his old age, his moments were as spirited as *a young man.*
(a) A young man's
(b) if a young man's
(c) those of a young man
(d) Of a young man's
(e) No correction

123. It is essential *to throughout clean* the machine after each use.
(a) To clean through
(b) to through clean
(c) to thoroughly cleaning
(d) To through cleaning
(e) No correction

124. If you get confused while performing the act, just *don't stop to try.*
(a) Continue your tries
(b) keep on trying
(c) not give up trying
(d) Keep your try on
(e) No correction

125. The indecisive man *was readily persuaded* to change his mind origin.
(a) Could readily persuaded
(b) was persuaded
(c) was ready persuaded
(d) Was ready to persuade
(e) No correction

126. He said that he would *rather starve to stealing* to get what he needed.
(a) Rather starve than steal
(b) rather starving to stealing
(c) Starve to rather steal
(d) starve to rather stealing
(e) No correction

127. Mahesh and his servant *looks after* our garden in our prolonged absence,
(a) Look over
(b) look after
(c) are looking at
(d) Has looked after
(e) No correction

128. People are *timing* very soon in an activity, which they don't like,
(a) Tried
(b) tiring
(c) tired
(d) trying
(e) No correction

129. He *has been writing* a long letter for the last four hours,
(a) Has written
(b) was written
(c) had been written
(d) is writing
(e) No correction

130. We *might have been* visited your shop if your had told us to do so.
(a) May have been
(b) would have been
(c) Will have
(d) would have
(e) No correction

131. He asked me *that how I got* time to write all these poems,
(a) That how did I get
(b) would have been
(c) Will have
(d) would have
(e) No correction

132. *As soon as,* walked into the building, I could here the sound of a celebration in progress.
(a) No sooner had
(b) sooner than
(c) hardly
(d) no correction

133. I *was very interesting* in the lessons.
(a) Was very interesting
(b) am having interest
(c) was having interest
(d) no correction

134. It is difficult *to cope with* the affairs of the sick mills,
(a) To meet with
(b) to face with
(c) to cope with
(d) no correction

135. The teacher *saw though the game* and punished him
(a) Saw into the game
(b) saw at game
(c) saw the game
(d) no correction

136. This is the *least expensive* of the two cars.
(a) Least expensive
(b) the less expensive
(c) the lesser expensive
(d) no correction

137. *Scarcely had he left* when his father arrived,
(a) He had no sooner left
(b) had he left scarcely
(c) he had left scarcely
(d) no correction

138. The train *left* before I reached the station.
(a) Will leave
(b) leaves
(c) had left
(d) no improvement

139. In a few minutes time, when the clock Sticks six *I shall be waiting* for her three quarters of an hour.
(a) I would have been waiting
(b) 1 would have waited
(c) I shall have waited
(d) no improvement

140. Ramesh told Kamla that he *may visited* Churabanpur.
(a) may visit
(b) has visit
(c) had visiting
(d) would be visit.

ANSWER KEY

1. (e)	2. (c)	3. (a)	4. (c)	5. (b)
6. (a)	7. (b)	8. (c)	9. (a)	10. (c)
11. (e)	12. (d)	13. (b)	14. (d)	15. (a)
16. (a)	17. (d)	18. (d)	19. (c)	20. (e)
21. (b)	22. (b)	23. (a)	24. (b)	25. (c)
26. (a)	27. (b)	28. (c)	29. (a)	30. (d)
31. (a)	32. (c)	33. (c)	34. (c)	35. (c)
36. (a)	37. (b)	38. (a)	39. (b)	40. (c)
41. (c)	42. (d)	43. (c)	44. (d)	45. (b)
46. (d)	47. (d)	48. (a)	49. (c)	50. (a)
51. (d)	52. (b)	53. (a)	54. (d)	55. (c)
56. (d)	57. (a)	58. (b)	59. (a)	60. (b)
61. (a)	62. (a)	63. (a)	64. (a)	65. (a)
66. (a)	67. (a)	68. (a)	69. (a)	70. (b)
71. (a)	72. (d)	73. (b)	74. (a)	75. (b)
76. (a)	77. (c)	78. (a)	79. (c)	80. (d)
81. (a)	82. (a)	83. (a)	84. (a)	85. (a)
86. (a)	87. (b)	88. (a)	89. (a)	90. (d)
91. (c)	92. (c)	93. (b)	94. (b)	95. (d)
96. (b)	97. (a)	98. (a)	99. (a)	100. (a)
101. (b)	102. (d)	103. (a)	104. (b)	105. (b)
106. (c)	107. (d)	108. (e)	109. (e)	110. (c)
111. (b)	112. (b)	113. (b)	114. (c)	115. (d)
116. (a)	117. (b)	118. (c)	119. (a)	120. (d)
121. (d)	122. (c)	123. (a)	124. (b)	125. (e)
126. (a)	127. (b)	128. (c)	129. (e)	130. (d)
131. (a)	132. (a)	133. (c)	134. (c)	135. (c)
136. (b)	137. (d)	138. (c)	139. (b)	140. (a)

Appendix

SENTENCE IMPROVEMENT: QUESTIONS FROM VARIOUS COMPETITIVE EXAMINATIONS WITH FREQUENCY ANALYSIS

Set I

1. He has said so out of affection, do not take *it to heart*

(a) in heart (c) by the heart
(b) it in the heart (d) No improvement

2. Sumit *would have been looked* smart in traditional clothes.

(a) was looked
(b) would be looked
(c) had looking
(d) would have looked
(e) No correction required.

(Bank PO)

3. I am sorry, but *I don't believe* what you say.

(a) I will not believe
(b) I am not believing
(c) I will not be believing
(d) No improvement.

(NDA)

4. Let's buy a new sari with the annual bonus, *can we?*

(a) can't we (c) shall we
(b) don't we (d) No improvement

(IES)

5. The *need* of the hour was some fast action on the part of the leaders.

(a) needed
(b) needing
(c) needs
(d) No correction required

(Income Tax)

6. The teacher asked the intruder *who was he and why was he* occupying his chair.

(a) who he was and why he was
(b) who he was and why was he
(c) did he return home than
(d) No improvement

(CBI)

7. No sooner *he had returned home than* explain his mother felt happy.

(a) he had returned home than
(b) had he returned home when
(c) did he return home than
(d) No improvement

(Section Officers)

8. He stayed back so that it *can look* as if he was unaware of the entire incident.

(a) may look
(c) will look
(b) would look
(d) No improvement

(SCRA)

9. In the modern world it is difficult *to live through* one's ideals.

(a) to live up to (c) to live for
(b) to live by (d) No improvement

(IES)

10. In accordance *to* your instructions, we have remitted the amount in the bank.

(a) by
(c) for
(b) with
(d) No improvement

(Section Officers)

11. Young men and women should get *habituated* to reading and writing about current affairs.

(CDS)

(a) prepared
(c) used
(b) trained
(d) No improvement

12. He has cooked that meal so often he can do it with his *eyes closed.*
(a) mind blank
(c) hands full
(b) eyes covered
(d) No improvement

(NDA)

13. Because of his mastery in this field, his suggestions *are wide accepted.*
(a) are widely accepted
(b) are side accentance
(c) have widely accepted
(d) have been wide accepted
(e) No correction required

(Bank PO)

14. I waited for half an hour for my friend, but the train didn't *turn in.*
(a) turn about
(b) turn around
(c) turn up
(d) No improvement

(SCRA)

15. None of the guests *were introduced* to the bride.

(1ES)

(a) introduced
(b) was introduced
(c) have been introduced
(d) No improvement

Set 2

1. All the allegations *levelled against* him were found to be baseless.
(a) levelled for
(d) levelling with
(b) eye with
(e) No correction is
(c) eye against required

(SBIPO)

2. He *did many mischiefs.*
(a) made many a mischiefs
(b) made much mischief
(c) committed many mischiefs
(d) No improvement

(UDC)

3. I *would gladly accompany* your sister if you had asked him.
(a) would have gladly accompanied
(b) was to have gladly accompanied
(c) will gladly accompany
(d) No improvement

(CDS)

4. Is there any *place* for me to sit?
(a) space
(c) area
(b) room
(d) No improvement

(CBI)

5. I am used to *hard work.*
(a) hard working
(c) work hardly
(b) work hard
(d) No improvement

(1ES)

6. Try to be diplomatic when you refuse any invitation, *so far not* to cause bad feelings.
(a) as far not
(c) if as far not
(b) so as not
(d) since then not

(Bank PO)

7. Old habits *die hardly.*
(a) die much hardly
(c) die too hard
(b) die hard
(d) No improvement

(NDA)

8. One of the men gave first aid to Hitesh *who is injured* in a road accident.
(a) who had injured
(b) who was injured

(c) which was injured
(d) as he was to injure
(e) No correction required

(Bank PO)

9. The members of his family are coming *in* this train.
(a) with (c) on
(b) by (d) No improvement

(Railways)

10. Never has the inadequacy of police been in *clearer* focus than in the communal violence that flared up recently.
(a) higher (c) better
(b) stronger (d) sharper

(Translators Exam.)

11. She *cut a sad figure* in her first performance on the stage.
(a) made a sorry figure
(c) cut a sorry figure
(b) cut a sorry face
(d) No improvement

(CDS)

12. His trousers are *three sizes large.*
(a) three sizes too
(c) three sizes over
(b) three size
(d) No improvement

(Asstt. Grade)

13. There is a shortage of well qualified teachers of most subjects, *specially of* English and economics.
(a) especially of
(c) in special of
(b) especially in
(d) No improvement

(UDC)

14. Not till he got home *he did realise* that he had lost his keys in the theatre.
(a) did he realise
(b) he did not realise
(c) he realised
(d) No improvement

(Railways)

15. I complimented him *for* his success in the examination.
(a) with (c) in
(b) on (d) No improvement

(SCRA)

Set 3

1. What *are* needed are not large houses but small cottages.
(a) were (c) is
(b) was (d) No improvement

(NDA)

2. She could not help *but laugh*
(a) laughing (c) laugh
(b) but laughing (d) No improvement

(CDS)

3. The various practices and norms for bank's transactions *are laid down* by the Reserve Bank of India.
(a) are laid up
(b) are led down
(c) are lead up
(d) have been lay down
(e) No improvement

(Bank PO)

4. The matter must be considered *in* every point of view.
(a) with (c) at
(b) from (d) No improvement

(UDC)

5. On seeing the lion she felt *too much* afraid.
(a) very much
(c) much
(b) excessively
(d) No improvement

(CBI)

6. They have stopped *from constructing* new buildings.
(a) to construct
(c) constructing
(b) at constructing
(d) No improvement

(Asstt. Grade)

7. Five years ago today, I *am sitting* in a small Japanese car, driving across Poland towards Berlin.
   (a) was sitting
   (b) have been sitting
   (c) sat
   (d) No improvement
   (CDS)

8. Many believed that girls who *received* western education would make slaves of their husbands.
   (a) could receive (c) have received
   (b) had received (d) No improvement
   (CDS)

9. She *gave* most of her time to music.
   (a) devoted (c) lent
   (b) spent (d) No improvement
   (UDC)

10. When I was fourteen, I *sat* the entrance examination for senior secondary school.
   (a) sat for (c) sat at
   (b) sat in (d) No improvement
   (CDS)

11. You ought not to *have gone* there, but you did.
   (a) be going (c) go
   (b) have been (d) No improvement
   (NDA)

12. *Being worked for* the whole day, you should have taken some rest and started the work tomorrow.
   (a) after having work
   (b) having worked for
   (c) working for
   (d) after being worked for
   (e) No correction required
   (Bank PO)

13. Your results depend not only on how much you have studied *but how long* you have read.
   (a) but also how long
   (b) but also on how long
   (c) but also on how much long
   (d) No improvement
   (CBI)

14. I am looking forward *to see* you soon.
   (a) looking forward towards seeing
   (b) looking forward for seeing
   (c) looking forward to seeing
   (d) No improvement
   (Asstt. Grade)

15. It was quite clear that the runner *could be able* to improve upon his own record.
   (a) will be able
   (c) would be able
   (b) should be able
   (d) No improvement
   (NDA)

Set 4

1. He doesn't hesitate to do whatever his brother *does*.
   (a) will do (d) would done
   (b) would do (e) No improvement
   (c) shall do
   (BSRB)

2. The problems of translation *are still remain.*
   (a) are remain (c) will still remain
   (b) will remained (d) No improvement
   (NDA)

3. One should exercise *their* right to vote.
   (a) his (c) one's
   (b) our (d) No improvement
   (NDA)

4. Can you tell me *why did you not speak* the truth?
   (a) why did not you speak
   (b) that why did you not speak
   (c) why you did not speak
   (d) why did you not spoke
   (e) No improvement
   (BSRB)

5. If the pain *is returning*, you would better take another pill.
   (a) has returned
   (c) returned
   (b) should return
   (d) no improvement
   (Asstt. Grade)

6. The greatest thing in style is to have a *use* of metaphor.
(a) command (c) need
(b) knowledge (d) No improvement
(Asstt. Grade)

7. Nothing but books and magazines *pleases* her.
(a) were pleasing (c) are pleasing
(b) please (d) No improvement
(NDA)

8. Why *did you not spoken* to me earlier?
(a) did you not spoke
(b) you did not speak
(c) did you not speak
(d) were you not spoken
(e) No improvement
(BSRB)

9. *Any able bodied man is* eligible for the job.
(a) any able-bodied men are
(b) each able-bodied man is
(c) any able-bodied men have been
(d) No improvement
(NDA)

10. The fast train *came a halt to before* crossing the bridge.
(a) came before to a halt
(b) came to a halt before
(c) came before a halt to
(d) No improvement
(BSRB)

11. May I know *who did accompany you* to the bus station?
(a) whom did accompany you
(b) whom you accompanying
(c) whom did you accompany
(d) who accompanied you
(e) No improvement
(BSRB)

12. *On basis this information* the Deputy Collector took strong action.
(a) on basis of (c) on the basis of
(b) on the basis (d) No improvement
(NDA)

13. The record for the biggest tiger hunt has not been *met* since 1911 when Lord Hardinge, then Viceroy of India, shot a tiger that measured eleven feet six and three-fourth inches.
(a) bettered (c) broken
(b) improved (d) No improvement
(Asstt. Grade)

14. Poor Tom *laid* in the shade of a tree before he could walk further.
(a) lied (c) lay
(b) lain (d) No improvement
(NDA)

15. I can always *count on him* in times of difficulty.
(a) count at him (d) count with him
(b) count on he (e) No correction required
(c) count him on
(BSRB)

Set 5

1. He is a singer of repute, but his *yesterday's performance was* quite disappointing.
(a) performances for yesterday were
(b) yesterday performance was
(c) yesterday performances were
(d) performances about yesterday were
(e) No correction required
(Bank PO, Mumbai)

2. The courts *are actively to safeguard* the interests and rights of the poor.
(a) are actively to safeguarding
(b) have been actively safeguarding
(c) have to active in safeguarding
(d) are actively in safeguarding
(e) No correction required
(Bank PO, Mumbai)

3. I gave my niece *a children's very colourfully illustrated encyclopaedia.*
(a) a very colourfully illustrated children's encyclopaedia
(b) a child's very colourfully-illustrated encyclopaedia
(c) an Illustrated Child's Very Colourful encyclopedia
(d) No improvement
(CDS)

4. He asked me where *was my book.*
(a) my book was (c) is my book
(b) my book is (d) No improvement
(CDS)

5. *Had I realised* how close I was to the edge of the valley, I would not have carried the bags there.
(a) had I been realised
(b) if I would have realised
(c) when I realised
(d) had I had realised
(e) no corrections required
(Bank PO, Hyderabad)

6. She cooks, washes dishes, does her homework and *then relaxing.*
(a) relaxing then (b) then relaxes
(b) then is relaxing (d) No corrections required
(c) relaxing is then
(Bank PO, Hyderabad)

7. The chemist *hadn't hardly any of those* kind of medicines.
(a) had hardly any of those kinds
(b) had hardly not any of those kinds
(c) had scarcely any of those kind
(d) had hardly any of those kind
(e) No corrections required
(Bank PO, Hyderabad)

8. Because of his ill health, the doctor has advised him *not to refrain from* smoking.
(a) to not refrain from
(b) to resort to
(c) to refrain from
(d) to be refrained from
(e) No correction required
(Bank PO, Mumbai)

9. The cheeta can run faster than the gazelle; it is *the speediest* of the two.
(a) the most speedier(c) the speedier
(b) more speedy (d) No improvement
(NDA)

10. Often one *is hearing* reports of explosions in the provinces.
(a) was hearing (c) has been heard
(b) hears (d) No improvement
(NDA)

11. It is better to *love and lose* than not to have loved at all.
(a) be loved and lost
(b) have loved and lost
(c) have been loved and lost
(d) No improvement
(CDS)

12. They have not spoken to each other *since* they quarrelled.
(a) because
(b) for
(c) ever since
(d) No improvement
(CDS)

13. The easiest *of the thing* to do is to ask the address from the postman.
(a) of the things to do
(b) among the things to do
(c) of the thing to be done
(d) of all the things done
(e) No correction required
(BSRB, Patna)

14. Hardly *does the sun rise* when the stars disappeared.
(a) have the sun rose
(b) had the sun risen
(c) did the sun rose
(d) the sun rose
(e) No correction required
(BSRB, Patna)

15. Ramesh is *as tall if not*, taller than Mahesh.
(a) not as tall but
(b) not so tall but as
(c) as if not
(d) as tall as, if not
(e) No correction required
(BSRB, Patna)

ANSWER KEY

Set 1	Set 2	Set 3	Set 4	Set 5
1. (d)	1. (e)	1. (d)	1. (e)	1. (e)
2. (d)	2. (c)	2. (a)	2. (c)	2. (b)
3. (d)	3. (a)	3. (e)	3. (c)	3. (a)
4. (a)	4. (b)	4. (b)	4. (a)	4. (a)
5. (d)	5. (b)	5. (a)	5. (a)	5. (e)
6. (a)	6. (b)	6. (c)	6. (a)	6. (d)
7. (c)	7. (b)	7. (a)	7. (b)	7. (a)
8. (b)	8. (b)	8. (b)	8. (c)	8. (c)
9. (b)	9. (b)	9. (a)	9. (b)	9. (c)
10. (b)	10. (d)	10. (c)	10. (b)	10. (b)
11. (c)	11. (c)	11. (d)	11. (c)	11. (b)
12. (b)	12. (b)	12. (b)	12. (c)	12. (c)
13. (a)	13. (a)	13. (b)	13. (c)	13. (a)
14. (c)	14. (a)	14. (c)	14. (a)	14. (b)
15. (b)	15. (b)	15. (d)	15. (e)	15. (d)

PART FIVE

BUILDING VOCABULARY

Vocabulary is a very important aspect of the language process.

Chapters 14 and 15 describe the ways of building a strong vocabulary and how to solve related questions which are set in different formats. Once you develop a powerful vocabulary, you can tackle any question on vocabulary with a little imagination and inference.

Chapters 16 and 17 deal with the new pattern of vocabulary questions asked in various banks and other UPSC-conducted examinations in the recent years. Two new techniques have been described in these chapters to make the whole process simple and lucid.

Chapter 18 covers various types of complex synonyms foreign expressions, group terms, words denoting sound, offsprings of birds and animals, places to live in, idiomatic use of names of animals, specific words for certain places, etc. Chapters 19 and 20 deal with one word substitution and spelling.

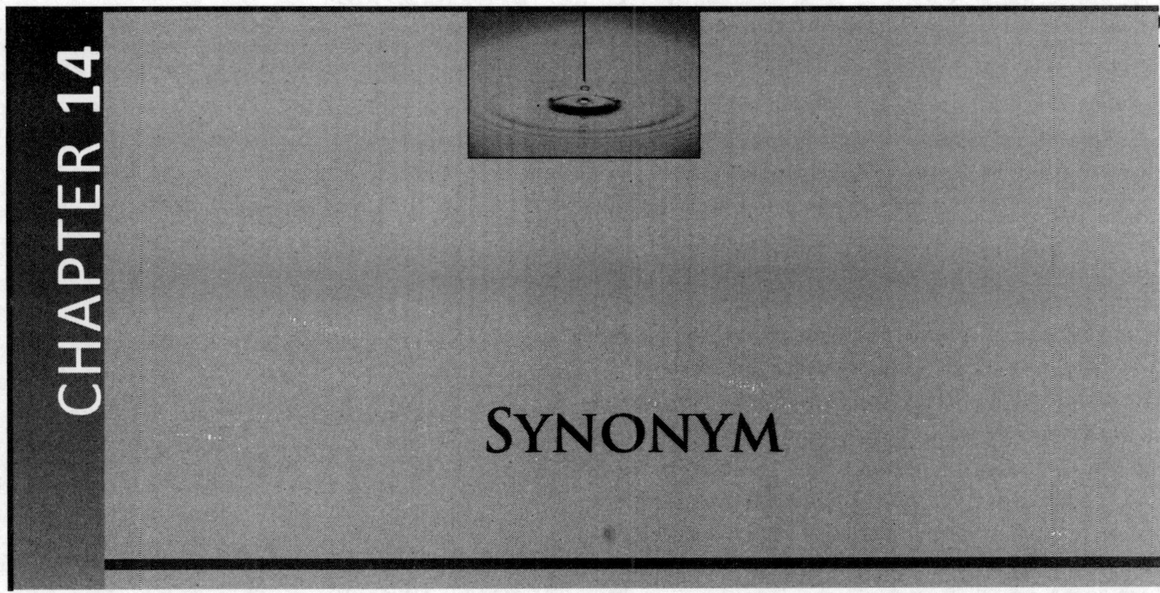

CHAPTER 14

SYNONYM

Vocabulary

Relevance of Vocabulary

Words constitute the *elan vital* of language. A speech or a written passage, however short or large, is essentially a group of sentences and a sentence, in its turn, is a group of words. A rich stock of words thus becomes quite logically an essential prerequisite of language ability development. All competitive examinations take a direct test of vocabulary under items like Synonym, Antonym, Sentence Completion and Cloze Test. Besides, Comprehension and Sentence Arrangement require indirectly a competent understanding of words, their meaning, nuances and usage.

How to Build a Powerful Vocabulary

Learning is difficult, forgetting easy. It is a real challenge: how to learn words and not forget them? We can devise several methods in accordance with our habits, living conditions and time availability. However, the basic factor that remains germane in every case is repetition or recalling of words at short intervals, so that they are etched deep in our memory. It is advisable to learn words from newspapers, speeches, magazines and good books because through sentences you can have an idea of their use and variations rather than simple denotations. Words change their nuances according to the context. For example, we can phrase out two sentences from the word *expose*.

1. Several leaders have been exposed for their involvement in scams.
2. If you go to a good institute you will expose yourself to a better academic atmosphere.

While in the first sentence it has a negative nuance, in the second it has a positive connotation. Thus both memorisation of words and understanding of their nuances and usage are necessary to develop a rich treasure of vocabulary.

We may adopt the following methods.

1. Card System Make cards of a manageable size. Learn 15 new words everyday from newspapers and magazines and write them on the card along with their meanings. Gradually, cards will pile up. Keep them on your reading table. Spare five minutes everyday anytime during the day. Shuffle them, give a look at the top card and revise the words. Next time another card will be on the top. Thus you will go on adding and revising. More and more words will become your possession.

2. Calendar System Just select a good old calendar with as many pages as possible. Hang it on the wall of your reading room from the reverse side. Write fifty good selected words on each page. Look at the page everyday anytime during the day whenever you feel free. Change the page after a week. Looking at the same page for a week means deepening your acquaintance with the same set of words several times. This way, you will be revising a lot of words without strain. Words will etch themselves deep into your memory.

3. Word Profile Making a word profile may work as a powerful and enduring technique to master words. Make a separate profile of every important word on a separate card. Write its meaning, its synonyms, its antonyms, its other parts of speech, its usage and its differences from other synonyms. We may use some private symbols for our understanding.

P: *Positive* A word which should always be preferably used in a good sense is a P word.

Example Alacrity, aplomb, benign.

N: *Negative* A word which should always be preferably used in a negative sense is a N word.

Example Cahoots (in collaboration). We cannot say 'in cahoots with and honest person', but we can say 'in cahoots with a dishonest person'.

NT: *Neutral* A word which can be used in both senses according to the need of the context.

Example Catalyst. Tyranny acts as a catalyst *for* terrorism. A challenge acts as a catalyst for a brave man to show his worth.

C: *Concrete* There are certain words which have a definite shape and size, a physical entity. Such a word is a C word.

Example Lamp. A lamp is a concrete thing.

A: *Abstract* There are certain words which have an abstract form. They exist only on the level of idea. Such a word is an A word.

Example Kindness, hiatus, aplomb.

O: *Open* There are certain words which can be used in both concrete and abstract senses. Such a word is an O word.

Example Fetter. Fetter means a chain of iron. The prisoner is in fetters. Fetter also means some kind of bondage. India is in fetters of poverty and unemployment.

Fan. A fan in the concrete sense means a device to give air. In the abstract sense it means to enhance. For example, It is a new fan, Suppression fans protest.

S: *Specific* There are certain words which have a specific meaning. Such a word is a S word.

Example Ablution. It means cleaning of body or a part of a body before doing a ritual.

Franchise. It means the right to vote.

L: *Living* There are certain words which can be used only for living things.

Example Gregarious. Man is gregarious. Such a word is a L word.

NL: *Not living* There are certain words which can be used only for non-living things.

Example Cogent. We can say that it is a cogent argument. We cannot say that Ramesh is a cogent man.

U: *Universal* There are certain words which can be used for both living and non-living.

Example Excellent. Mr. Sinha is an excellent man. It is an excellent idea or proposal. Both sentences are correct. Such a word is a U word.

These are our personally developed symbols. We can make symbols according to our choice. The idea is to catalogue more and more usage of words. In the above manner we can make profiles of words. Words which are learnt in such details will remain in memory for ever or at least for a long time.

Model I

Fantastic

Part of speech	:	Adjective
Other parts of Speech	:	Fantastically (Adverb)
Synonyms	:	Excellent, large, wonderful, strange, unlikely, unbelievable.
Antonyms	:	Common, ordinary, small, familiar.

Usage : 1. Something very good and exciting. This painting is fantastic.
2. A very large amount of something. This business has brought me a fantastic profit.
3. Strange. This bird is fantastic because its colour is unusual.
4. Unbelievable. This story is too fantastic to believe.

Symbols : NT. It has both positive and negative nuances.
: O. It can be used in both concrete and abstract senses.
: U. It can be used both for human beings and non-living things.

Synonym

A synonym is a word which has the same, or nearly the same meaning which another word has. Let us look at some such words.

1. Choose the word nearest in meaning to the given word.

Fragile:

(a) strong (b) grave
(c) weak (d) showy

The answer is (c), *weak,* as this is similar in meaning to *fragile.*

Esoteric:

(a) fair (b) popular
(c) alluring (d) private

The answer is (d), *private.* This is not exactly equivalent to *esoteric* but it is nearest in meaning among the alternatives.

The test can be given directly, as shown above, or even through a sentence.

2. The italicised word or phrase is followed by four words marked (a), (b), (c) and (d). Choose the one which is the nearest in meaning to the given word.

He used to *regale* us with anecdotes.

(a) flatter (b) bore
(c) fix (d) entertain

The answer is (d), *entertain.* It is the nearest in meaning among the alternatives.

He is believed to be a very *industrious* worker.

(a) successful (b) sensible
(c) punctual (d) diligent

There answer is (d), diligent; it is similar in meaning.

Clues or Tips

1. When the test is made through a sentence, try to find the key word and then use the technique of elimination.

He had the *nerve* to suggest that I was cheating.

(a) strength (b) capacity
(c) audacity (d) courage

The key word here is *cheating* and the sense therefore is negative. Now *strength, capacity* and *courage*—all these have a positive nuance. Thus they have to be eliminated. *Audacity* is therefore the right answer.

Suppose we have been given this sentence:

He had the *nerve* to face the robbers all alone.

(a) strength (b) capacity
(c) audacity (d) courage

Here the key word is *face* and the sense is positive. Thus *courage,* becomes the right choice. The same word *nerve* has different nuances in different contexts. Thus one should try to locate the sense behind the italicised word.

2. If the test is made directly, try to use the same form of word and tense.

Wane:

(a) decline (b) tired
(c) dead (d) shine

Now *wane* is used here as a verb. *Tired* and *dead* are not in the verb form but in the adjective form and thus they can be eliminated. The correct answer is *decline* which is also a verb here.

Baptise:

(a) christen
(b) holy
(c) dehumanise
(d) something that had been ostracised.

The word *baptise* is in the present tense; it is a verb and it is in the active voice. *Holy* is an adjective. Something *that had been ostracised* is in the past tense. Thus, both these alternatives are eliminated. The answer is *christen* as *dehumanise* is an antonym.

3. One of the frequent tricks used by the examiner is to include an antonym in choices given as answers for a synonym's question.
Hence be careful whether you are looking for an antonym or a synonym

Benediction:

(a) rise (b) blessing
(c) curse (d) prayer

The alternative (c), curse, is an antonym here. One should be alert in such a case.

Practice Set —1

Against each key word are given some suggested meanings. Choose the word or phrase which is nearest in meaning to the key word.

1. Lethargy
(a) serenity (b) listlessness
(c) impassivity (d) laxity

2. Prognosis
(a) scheme (b) forecast
(c) preface (d) identification

3. Emaciated
(a) very tall (b) very sleepy
(c) very thin (d) very aged

4. Contract
(a) tract (b) expand
(c) give (d) abridge

5. Inedible
(a) unfit for human consumption
(b) polluted
(c) vitiated
(d) eatable

6. Docile
(a) vague (b) gentle
(c) stupid (d) stubborn

7. Hybrid
(a) crossbred (b) pedigreed
(c) hackneyed (d) unusual

8. Latent
(a) concealed (b) apparent
(c) lethargic (d) prompt

9. Erotic
(a) wandering
(b) given to mistakes
(c) difficult
(d) amorous

10. Aromatic
(a) crippled (b) fragrant
(c) sentimental (d) stinking

11. Nostalgic
(a) indolent (b) diseased
(c) homesick (d) soothing

12. Sadistic
(a) smart
(b) malicious
(c) given to deriving pleasure from inflicting pain on others
(d) depressed

13. Enigmatic
(a) displeased (b) puzzling
(c) learned (d) short-sighted

14. Sporadic
(a) epidemic (b) whirling
(c) occasional (d) stagnant

15. Compendium
(a) summary (b) index
(c) reference (d) glossary

Practice Set —2

1. Histrionic
(a) hypersensitive
(b) overdramatic
(c) historically important
(d) inactive

2. Fiasco
(a) festival (b) failure
(c) ridiculous plan (d) misfortune

3. Amoral
(a) loving (b) immoral
(c) uninvolved (d) highly ethical

4. Virile
(a) athletic (b) pompous
(c) manly (d) boastful

5. Ameliorate
(a) to appease
(b) to make excuses
(c) to humiliate
(d) to improve

6. Consummation
(a) act of devouring
(b) act of forgiveness
(c) failure
(d) ultimate completion

7. Duplicity
(a) innocence (b) cleverness
(c) double-dealing (d) repetition

8. Homage
(a) excessive humility
(b) show respect and reverence
(c) poverty
(d) insincere flattery

9. Licentious
(a) generous (b) gay
(c) hungry (d) immoral

10. Ostentatious
(a) wealthy (b) talkative
(c) showy (d) noisy

11. Paramount
(a) above others in rank of authority
(b) famous
(c) wide and extensive
(d) very important

12. Arbiter
(a) very bitter
(b) a priest
(c) one appointed by two parties to settle a dispute
(d) a despot

13. Didactic
(a) blunt
(b) in poetic metre
(c) direct
(d) of the nature of teaching

14. Emulate
(a) imitate (b) deny
(c) question (d) discuss

15. Resume
(a) a new start
(b) judgment based on insufficient evidence
(c) summary
(d) long withdrawn account

Practice Set —3

1. Tour de force
(a) long journey (b) feat of skill
(c) spectacle (d) show of force

2. Largesse
(a) extravagant (b) bribe
(c) liberal (d) great size

3. Melange
(a) mixture of medley
(b) household
(c) optical illusion
(d) desert

4. Debonair
(a) superficial
(b) pleasant and gracious
(c) in high style
(d) flighty

5. Pensive
(a) habitually tardy
(b) confident
(c) given to quiet reflection
(d) affectionate

6. Coup
(a) sudden overthrow of a government
(b) small enclosure
(c) accident
(d) clever reply

7. Baton
(a) cargo
(b) cane
(c) stick used in conducting an orchestra

8. Composure
(a) assumed attitude (b) liberty
(c) restlessness (d) tranquility

9. Implicate
(a) to insult (b) doubt
(c) involve (d) make clear

10. Concert
(a) agreement
(b) beauty
(c) power
(d) musical performance

11. Mitigate
(a) to heal
(b) soften
(c) pardon
(d) send on a mission

12. Buoyant
(a) child-like (b) brisk
(c) sturdy (d) light-hearted

13. Unalloyed
(a) not connected
(b) calm
(c) absolutely pure and complete
(d) inferior

14. Flagging
(a) becoming afraid (b) hesitation
(c) growing weak (d) limping

15. Rectify
(a) to command (b) destroy
(c) correct (d) to build

Practice Set —4

1. Incitement
(a) stir up (b) calm
(c) stimulate (d) noise

2. Devoid
(a) stupid (b) lacking
(c) evasive (d) hopeless

3. Resolved
(a) summarised (b) dispelled
(c) strengthened (d) tangled

4. Privy
(a) dishonest (b) cautious
(c) secretive (d) quiet

5. Pilfer
(a) to gossip (b) steal
(c) trifle (d) loiter

6. Hallowed
(a) old (b) decayed
(c) sacred (d) mellowed

7. Bridle
(a) to bow (b) insult
(c) show anger (d) criticise

8. Slothful
(a) fat (b) stubborn
(c) lazy (d) ignorant

9. Shift
(a) to manage (b) move
(c) slide (d) drag one's feet

10. Lest
(a) unless
(b) but

(c) fear
(d) anything but that

11. Cite
(a) to memorise
(b) see clearly
(c) point out with a finger
(d) quote

12. Satellite
(a) sparkling
(b) rules
(c) a servile attendant
(d) gem

13. Respite
(a) reform (b) fatigue
(c) ill will (d) short break

14. Incite
(a) to cut off
(b) arouse or stir up
(c) perceive the inner nature of a thing
(d) commence

15. Parasite
(a) disease
(b) a loss of motion
(c) one that clings
(d) exterminator

Practice Set —5

1. Apposite
(a) appropriate
(b) highly unpleasant
(c) foolish
(d) painful

2. Bald
(a) broad (b) rash
(c) unadorned (d) insulting

3. Glean
(a) to gather bit by bit
(b) speak
(c) to discover
(d) to polish

4. Barge
(a) to thrust forward (b) to brag
(c) to swell (d) to oppose

5. Drab
(a) dull or colourless
(b) tired
(c) discouraged
(d) shabby

6. Irk
(a) to scold
(b) to make a wry face
(c) to urge
(d) to annoy

7. Wield
(a) to throw
(b) to use with full effect
(c) to grasp
(d) to cut

8. Wreak
(a) to twist
(b) to emit an unpleasant odour
(c) to inflict
(d) to sweat

9. Cryptic
(a) a puzzle (b) silence
(c) precise (d) vault

10. Elude
(a) to evade
(b) to omit or leave out
(c) to make mention of
(d) to deceive

11. Embroil
(a) to anger
(b) to bring to boiling point
(c) to encompass
(d) to involve in dissension or strife

12. Compound
(a) to emphasise (b) to confuse
(c) to put together (d) to compress

13. Beguile
(a) to charm (b) to become shy
(c) to flatter (d) to smile at

14. Submerge
(a) to walk on (b) to sink
(c) to appear
(d) to join together

15. Placate
(a) to flatten out (b) to pacify
(c) to annoy (d) to make sure

Practice Set —6

1. Augury
(a) dispute (b) altar
(c) place of refuge (d) omen

2. Ecstasy
(a) exhausted (b) strong
(c) joy (d) greed
(e) rival

3. Effusion
(a) shocking (b) exclamation
(c) compensation (d) threatening
(e) pouring forth

4. Elated
(a) debased (b) respectful
(c) dropping
(d) extremely happy
(e) charitable

5. Emancipate
(a) set free (b) exist
(c) correct morally (d) restrain
(e) make a solemn declaration

6. Enigma
(a) reply (b) puzzling
(c) praise (d) lowest point
(e) sharp

7. Estranged
(a) difficult (b) heavy
(c) mild (d) witty
(e) separated

8. Eulogistic
(a) prank (b) wanderer
(c) well-settled (d) practical
(e) praising

9. Exhort
(a) urge
(b) to give examples
(c) waste
(d) prevent
(e) condemn

10. Carcass
(a) mind (b) association
(c) soul (d) dead body

11. Contingency
(a) autonomous (b) independence
(c) originality (d) conditionality

12. Disparage
(a) command (b) exalt
(c) undervalue (d) shallow

13. Gluttony
(a) satisfaction (b) beatitude
(c) sadness (d) greedy

14. Ingenuous
(a) sly (b) honest
(c) wily (d) prepare

15. Kindred
(a) foreigners (b) similar
(c) disconnection (d) enemy

Practice Set —7

1. Ravish
(a) accumulate (b) preserve
(c) uphold (d) misuse

2. Meddle
(a) disregard (b) interfere
(c) overlook (d) free

3. Repugnance
(a) affection (b) disinclination
(c) like (d) approve

4. Skip
(a) overlook (b) introduce
(c) insert (d) notice

5. Unfold
(a) stunt (b) compress
(c) restrict (d) elaborate

6. Accolade
(a) balcony (b) outer garments
(c) drink (d) honour
(e) fruit

7. Abjure
(a) discuss (b) renounce
(c) run off secretly (d) perjure
(e) project

8. Abortive
(a) unsuccessful (b) consuming
(c) financing (d) familiar
(e) fruitful

9. Acumen
(a) ferocity (b) brilliance
(c) swiftness (d) greed
(e) keenness

10. Admonition
(a) weapon (b) preamble
(c) warning (d) alarm
(e) hysteria

11. Baleful
(a) doubtful (b) virtual
(c) deadly (d) headless
(e) virtuous

12. Banal
(a) philosophical (b) original
(c) dramatic (d) headless
(e) commonplace

13. Baneful
(a) generous (b) kindly
(c) ruinous (d) severity
(e) superfluous

14. Boroque
(a) polished (b) constant
(c) transformed (d) highly ornate
(e) aglow

15. Beguile
(a) irritable (b) loudly offensive
(c) cheat (d) unfavourable
(e) spacious

Practice Set —8

1. Bellicose
(a) war-like (b) naval
(c) amusing (d) piecemeal
(e) errant

2. Benign
(a) tenfold (b) peaceful
(c) gentle (d) wavering
(e) favourable

3. Boisterous
(a) conflicting (b) vociferous
(c) testimonial (d) grateful
(e) adolescent

4. Bountiful
(a) pretty (b) generous
(c) shameful (d) spiritual
(e) rude

5. Brazen
(a) shameless (b) quick
(c) modest (d) pleasant
(e) melodramatic

6. Bucolic
(a) citified (b) rustic
(c) sick (d) intoxicated
(e) healthy

7. Cache
(a) lock (b) hiding place
(c) tide (d) automobile
(e) grappling hook

8. Cacophony
(a) discordant
(b) dance
(c) applause
(d) type of telephone
(e) rooster

9. Candid
(a) vague (b) secretive
(c) experienced (d) anxious
(e) frank

10. Cohesion
(a) independence
(b) sticking together
(c) shift
(d) climbing

11. Fictitious
(a) false (b) fraud
(c) foul (d) flattering

12. Ghastly
(a) useless (b) unholy
(c) horrible (d) mean

13. Obscene
(a) dirty (b) unhealthy
(c) indecent (d) unwanted

14. Dexterity
(a) efficiency (b) zest
(c) tempo (d) skill

15. Gall
(a) bitterness (b) poison
(c) sour (d) taste

Practice Set —9

1. Haughty
(a) tall (b) proud
(c) straightforward (d) careless
(e) casual

2. Breach
(a) break (b) slander
(c) uncertain (d) restrict
(e) rift

3. Cajole
(a) scold (b) intimidate
(c) threaten (d) persuade
(e) craze

4. Open
(a) confused (b) sordid
(c) frank (d) upright
(e) loose

5. Desolate
(a) deserted (b) gloomy
(c) hard (d) fiery
(e) cheerful

6. Perilous
(a) inane (b) useless
(c) risky (d) frivolous
(e) shaky

7. Give in
(a) yield (b) refuse
(c) deny (d) refute
(e) find

8. Give up
(a) start (b) give
(c) receive (d) distribute
(e) stop doing

9. Reiterate
(a) frustrate (b) illustrate
(c) repeat (d) deny
(e) receipt

10. Remorse
(a) boisterous (b) vehement
(c) voluble (d) reliant
(e) repentance

11. Rejoice
(a) rejoin (b) rebuild
(c) rename (d) delight
(e) lighten

12. Discontented
(a) dislike (b) disinfection
(c) dissatisfied (d) disenchanted
(e) dismembered

13. Starve
(a) float (b) be naked
(c) be hungry (d) be naughty
(e) crawl

14. Obscure
(a) famous (b) well known
(c) rampant (d) unknown
(e) prevalent

15. Rash
(a) rush (b) hurry
(c) unthoughtful (d) meditated
(e) rootless

Practice Set —10

1. Handful
(a) few, little (b) useless
(c) useful (d) powerless

2. Rigid
(a) sticky (b) voluminous
(c) hard (d) bent
(e) solid

3. Refund
(a) deduct (b) receive
(c) distribute (d) give
(e) reimburse

4. Careless
(a) spotless (b) faceless
(c) negligent (d) vigilant
(e) arrogant

5. Nymph
(a) clinch (b) flinch
(c) airy (d) fairy
(e) cheery

6. Shortage
(a) paucity (b) niggardly
(c) wastage (d) hostage
(e) foliage

7. Infamous
(a) populous (b) prosperous
(c) notorious (d) deciduous
(e) spurious

8. Ideal
(a) useless
(b) model to be followed
(c) thorough
(d) civilised
(e) forming an idea

9. Ingenious
(a) misleading
(b) false
(c) clever at inventing
(d) intoxicated
(e) alarm

10. Immune
(a) exempt (b) statutory
(c) hostile (d) disturbing
(e) misfortune

11. Incentive
(a) objective (b) goad
(c) stimulation (d) beginning
(e) simulation

12. Incessant
(a) irritated (b) overflowing
(c) extreme (d) co-operative
(e) continue

13. Impetuous
(a) rash (b) violent
(c) pleasing (d) freezing
(e) resourceful

14. Incompatible
(a) capable (b) reasonable
(c) faulty (d) indifferent
(e) contradictory

15. Inconsequential
(a) disorderly (b) insignifiant
(c) subsequent (d) insufficient
(e) preceding

Practice Set —11

1. Acronym
(a) poem of sorrow
(b) similar meaning
(c) word formed from an abbreviation
(d) pen name used by an author

2. Antiquated
(a) existing since old times
(b) without a name
(c) obsolete
(d) coming before its time

3. Arcane
(a) common place
(b) old fashioned
(c) modern
(d) secret

4. Bowdlerize
(a) to take out words that might be considered improper
(b) give firmness to
(c) use unnecessary strength
(d) cut into two or more separate parts

5. Catharsis
(a) sudden happening
(b) outlet for strong emotions
(c) anti-climax
(d) informal discussion

6. Deterrent
(a) cleansing substance
(b) defence
(c) restraint of action
(d) warning

7. Extinct
(a) dull
(b) wonderful
(c) no longer in existence
(d) still in existence

8. Coeval
(a) of the same age
(b) duplicate
(c) counterfeit
(d) corresponding

9. Damp squib
(a) insignificant happening
(b) an old technique
(c) unsuccessful attempt
(d) short, shrill cry

10. Prowess
(a) understanding (b) keenness
(c) eagerness (d) bravery

11. Bigamy
(a) biblical reference
(b) having two wives or husbands living
(c) fruit of a thorny shrub
(d) ambiguity

12. Braggadocio
(a) bribery
(b) empty boasting
(c) misadventure
(d) sad plight

13. Credence
(a) assurance (b) belief
(c) credit (d) preference

14. Slake
(a) rub (b) sharpen
(c) quench (d) erase

15. Attrition
(a) attraction (b) suffering
(c) decline (d) friction

Practice Set —12

1. Bovine
(a) an expert (b) like an ox
(c) meat extract (d) dim-witted

2. Appellation
(a) ghost
(b) a nickname or title
(c) ultimate solution
(d) beginning

3. Credence
(a) religion or personal
(b) reliance on the truth of something
(c) gullible
(d) simplicity

4. Baffle
(a) to disconcert (b) tease
(c) strike (d) send away

5. Amalgamate
(a) to unite (b) gather
(c) astonish greatly (d) frustrate

6. Acumen
(a) bitterness
(b) quickness of insight
(c) abundance
(d) deficit

7. Apathy
(a) anger
(b) lack of confidence
(c) odd behaviour
(d) indifference

8. Divulge
(a) to strip (b) conceal
(c) explore (d) reveal

9. Avocation
(a) the pleading of a legal cause
(b) contradiction
(c) a main occupation
(d) a side interest

10. Fastidious
(a) overfed
(b) overconfidence
(c) finicky
(d) overaspiring

11. Incredulous
(a) superstitious (b) unreliable
(c) unimaginative (d) skeptical

12. Culinary
(a) creative
(b) to do with cookery
(c) delicious
(d) fragrant

13. Facade
(a) hilly view
(b) exact copy
(c) aspect
(d) front of a building

14. Nascent
(a) initial (b) unpleasant
(c) latest (d) crude

15. Sonorous
(a) sleepy (b) loud
(c) bright (d) heavy

Practice Set —13

1. Presage
(a) to foretell (b) assume
(c) make ready (d) consider

2. Subjugate
(a) to capitulate (b) conquer
(c) cause to wither (d) confuse

3. Yammer
(a) strike
(b) lament/grumble
(c) whimper
(d) shiver

4. Embroil
(a) to get involved in hostilities
(b) arouse bitter feelings
(c) weaken
(d) include

5. Exacerbate
(a) to aggravate (b) bring out
(c) throw up (d) wear away

6. Hypothetical
(a) methodical
(b) based on supposition
(c) double faced
(d) to do with superstition

7. Incidence
(a) stubbornness
(b) the range of occurrence
(c) anecdotes
(d) conclusion

8. Gargoyle
(a) stone spout (b) golden eagle
(c) garish (d) vile

9. Interim
(a) interval (b) timely
(c) internal (d) temporary

10. Helm
(a) edge (b) head
(c) handle (d) corner

11. Incision
(a) event (b) indecisiveness
(c) dispute (d) cut

12. Malaise
(a) sickness (b) curse
(c) spite (d) stagnation

13. Precipitous
(a) exact (b) very steep
(c) uncertain (d) absurd

14. Propriety
(a) right (b) nearness
(c) decorum (d) estate

15. Soporific
(a) impressive (b) soothing
(c) merry (d) lethargic

Practice Set —14

1. Upheaval
(a) outcome (b) slow change
(c) upward turn (d) radical change

2. Patron
(a) person of noble birth
(b) venerable old man
(c) capable person
(d) one who gives encouragement to others

3. Scavenger
(a) worthless person
(b) a bird that lives on decaying flesh
(c) kind of beetle
(d) one who mocks

4. Myriad
(a) bright
(b) imaginary
(c) very great number
(d) variety

5. Obliterate
(a) to blot out (b) slow down
(c) block up (d) decline

6. Malediction
(a) a curse against someone
(b) farewell words
(c) omen
(d) a closing prayer

7. Notoriety
(a) public shame
(b) unpleasant experience
(c) wrong option
(d) unfavourably known

8. Lachrymose
(a) impious (b) moist
(c) mournful (d) unimpressive

9. Fusillade
(a) confusion
(b) unwarranted aggression
(c) excitement
(d) sustained outburst of criticism

10. Reminiscent
(a) deserving to be remembered
(b) remembrance
(c) reminding one of
(d) revival

11. Sonorous
(a) sleepy (b) loud
(c) bring (d) heavy

12. Trumpery
(a) treasure
(b) trick
(c) rubbish
(d) useless argument

13. Expertise
(a) experience
(b) skill
(c) smartness
(d) art of expressing

14. Genesis
(a) beginning (b) style
(c) movement (d) relevant

15. Humane
(a) human species (b) kind-hearted
(c) destitute (d) humorous

Practice Set —15

1. Compulsion
(a) joy
(b) being compelled
(c) danger
(d) the state of excitement

2. Cynosure
(a) repel
(b) threat
(c) centre of attraction
(d) rejoice

3. Dissolute
(a) immoral (b) honest
(c) repulsive (d) distant

4. Doleful
(a) mournful (b) bright
(c) jovial (d) colourful

5. Festal
(a) noisy (b) merry
(c) sad (d) serious

6. Hustings
(a) voice (b) craze
(c) election campaigns(d) celebration

7. Lurid
(a) shocking (b) bright
(c) abundant (d) happy

8. Mottle
(a) spoil (b) mark with spots
(c) erase (d) colour

9. Outre
(a) eccentric (b) traditional
(c) real (d) fair

10. Mural
(a) writing
(b) music
(c) a painting on wall
(d) ancient

11. Pastel
(a) Light shades or colours
(b) attempt
(c) dark shade
(d) conflict

12. Rookie
(a) an old man (b) a new recruit
(c) a fighter (d) a wrestler

13. Sentient
(a) capable of feelings
(b) dry
(c) dull
(d) dirty

14. Swan/song
(a) the first work of a man
(b) the last work of a man
(c) a poem
(d) a piece of music

15. Smear
(a) mark (b) avoid
(c) quarrel (d) encourage

Practice Set —16

1. Perspicacious
(a) clear (b) hazy
(c) shrewd (d) bad

2. Proscribe
(a) allow (b) prescribe
(c) banish (d) advance

3. Obfuscation
(a) confusing others(b) prone
(c) to darken (d) infer

4. Prone
(a) thrown forward(b) disease
(c) supine (d) inactive

5. Intrepid
(a) ugly (b) fearless
(c) selfish (d) coward

6. Vernal
(a) luxuriant (b) springlike
(c) scale (d) dirty

7. Gluttony
(a) happiness (b) contentment
(c) satisfaction (d) greed

8. Incensed
(a) incited (b) affected
(c) encouraged (d) inspired

9. Sozzled
(a) cultured (b) drunk
(c) moderate (d) burning

10. Vituperate
(a) encourage (b) appraise
(c) abuse (d) appreciate

11. Compunction
(a) regret (b) appreciate
(c) wonder (d) anger

12. Obstreperous
(a) cheerful (b) noisy
(c) calm (d) obstinate

13. Ostracise
(a) welcome (b) include
(c) expedite (d) cut off

14. Deplete
(a) take away (b) fill
(c) make greater (d) to exhaust

15. Osmosis
(a) gradual acceptance
(b) slow recovery
(c) abrupt ending
(d) crowded

Practice Set —17

1. Fiasco
(a) strength (b) success
(c) failure (d) hope

2. Viaduct
(a) railroad (b) bridge
(c) pipe (d) leave

3. Spew
(a) throw in water
(b) split
(c) to come forth in a flush
(d) take up liquids

4. Repugnance
(a) disinclination (b) affection
(c) like (d) approve

5. Alacrity
(a) eagerness (b) hesitatingly
(c) unwillingly (d) with suspicion

6. Vendetta
(a) threat (b) mortal
(c) friendship (d) feud

7. Whim
(a) desire
(b) unnatural behaviour
(c) clumsy
(d) fancy

8. Penchant
(a) disability (b) like
(c) eagerness (d) dislike

9. Anathema
(a) something strongly detested
(b) accepted
(c) difficult to collect
(d) constant

10. Cavil
(a) munch (b) quibble
(c) amuse (d) appreciate

11. Estrange
(a) endanger
(b) to become puzzling
(c) miscalculate
(d) alienate

12. Hansom
(a) man's clock
(b) Elaborate serving dish

(c) gardening tool
(d) two-wheeled carriage

13. Mottled
(a) dirty
(b) pock-marked
(c) full of holes
(d) having splotches of colour

14. Parry
(a) cut away bit by bit
(b) pierce
(c) to reject
(d) ward off

15. Troglodytic
(a) cadaverous
(b) ominous
(c) unbridled
(d) resembling a caveman

ANSWER KEY

Set 1	Set 2	Set 3	Set 4	Set 5
1. (d)	1. (b)	1. (b)	1. (a)	1. (a)
2. (d)	2. (b)	2. (c)	2. (b)	2. (c)
3. (c)	3. (c)	3. (a)	3. (a)	3. (a)
4. (d)	4. (c)	4. (b)	4. (c).	4. (d)
5. (a)	5. (d)	5. (c)	5. (b)	5. (a)
6. (b)	6. (d)	6. (a)	6. (c)	6. (d)
7. (a)	7. (c)	7. (c)	7. (c)	7. (b)
8. (a)	8. (b)	8. (d)	8. (c)	8. (c)
9. (d)	9. (d)	9. (c)	9. (b)	9. (c)
10. (b)	10. (c)	10. (a)	10. (a)	10. (a)
11. (c)	11. (a)	11. (a)	11. (d)	11. (d)
12. (c)	12. (c)	12. (d)	12. (c)	12. (c)
13. (b)	13. (d)	13. (c)	13. (d)	13. (a)
14. (c)	14. (a)	14. (c)	14. (b)	14. (b)
15. (d)	15. (a)	15. (c)	15. (c)	15. (b)

Set 6	Set 7	Set 8	Set 9	Set 10
1. (d)	1. (d)	1. (a)	1. (b)	1. (a)
2. (c)	2. (b)	2. (c)	2. (a)	2. (c)
3. (e)	3. (b)	3. (b)	3. (d)	3. (e)
4. (d)	4. (a)	4. (b)	4. (c)	4. (c)
5. (a)	5. (d)	5. (a)	5. (a)	5. (d)
6. (b)	6. (d)	6. (b)	6. (c)	6. (a)
7. (e)	7. (b)	7. (b)	7. (a)	7. (c)
8. (e)	8. (a)	8. (a)	8. (e)	8. (b)
9. (a)	9. (b)	9. (e)	9. (c)	9. (c)
10. (d)	10. (c)	10. (b)	10. (e)	10. (a)
11. (d)	11. (c)	11. (a)	11. (d)	11. (c)
12. (c)	12. (e)	12. (c)	12. (c)	12. (e)
13. (d)	13. (c)	13. (c)	13. (c)	13. (a)
14. (b)	14. (d)	14. (d)	14. (d)	14. (e)
15. (b)	15. (c)	15. (a)	15. (c)	15. (b)

Set 11	Set 12	Set 13	Set 14	Set 15
1. (c)	1. (b)	1. (a)	1. (d)	1. (b)
2. (c)	2. (a)	2. (b)	2. (d)	2. (c)
3. (d)	3. (b)	3. (b)	3. (a)	3. (a)
4. (a)	4. (a)	4. (a)	4. (d).	4. (a)
5. (b)	5. (a)	5. (a)	5. (a)	5. (b)
6. (c)	6. (b)	6. (b)	6. (c)	6. (c)
7. (c)	7. (d)	7. (b)	7. (d)	7. (a)
8. (a)	8. (d)	8. (a)	8. (c)	8. (b)
9. (c)	9. (c)	9. (d)	9. (d)	9. (a)
10. (d)	10. (c)	10. (b)	10. (b)	10. (c)
11. (b)	11. (d)	11. (d)	11. (a)	11. (a)
12. (b)	12. (b)	12. (a)	12. (c)	12. (b)
13. (c)	13. (d)	13. (b)	13. (b)	13. (a)
14. (c)	14. (a)	14. (c)	14. (a)	14. (b)
15. (c)	15. (a)	15. (b)	15. (b)	15. (a)

Set 16	Set 17
1. (c)	1. (c)
2. (c)	2. (b)
3. (a)	3. (c)
4. (a)	4. (a)
5. (b)	5. (a)
6. (b)	6. (d)
7. (d)	7. (d)
8. (a)	8. (b)
9. (b)	9. (a)
10. (c)	10. (b)
11. (a)	11. (d)
12. (b)	12. (d)
13. (d)	13. (d)
14. (d)	14. (d)
15. (a)	15. (d)

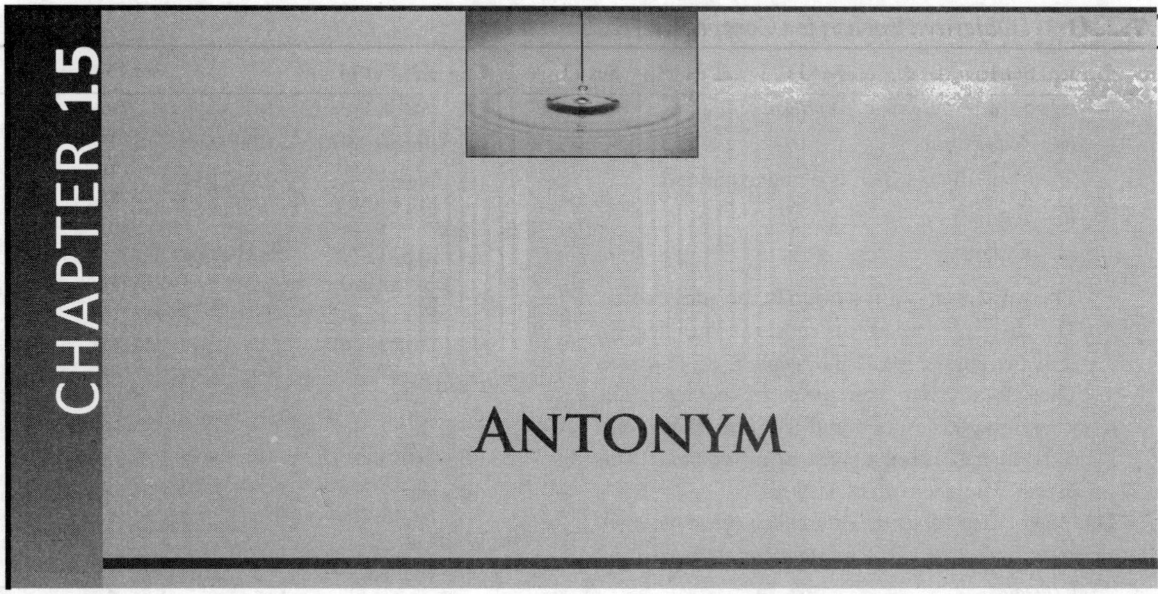

Antonym

An antonym is a word which has the opposite, or nearly the opposite meaning of the given word.

EXAMPLES

A. Choose the word *opposite* in meaning to the given word.

1. Profane
   (a) beautiful (b) sacred
   (c) glorious (d) insane
   The answer is (b), sacred.
   The test can be given directly as shown above or at times through a sentence.

B. Choose the word *opposite* in meaning to the word in italics in the given sentence.

1. He led an ascetic life but his wife had her ________________ ways.
   (a) self-indulgent (b) austere
   (c) artificial (d) pompous
   The answer is (a), *self-indulgent*.
2. There is something *repulsive* about the way he handles people.
   (a) attractive (b) smooth
   (c) reflective (d) distinctive
   The answer is (a), *attractive*.

Clues or Tips

A. Note that the given word and the answer must belong to the same parts of speech.

Pragmatic:
(a) angry (b) quixotic
(c) colourful (d) pungent

Here the choice (c), *colourful,* is a noun while the word *pragmatic* is an adjective and thus this alternative may be rejected. *The correct answer is (b), quixotic.*

B. Note that the given word and the answer must belong to the same tense form.

Perceived:
(a) ignored (b) created
(c) apprehend (d) conceive

Here the alternatives *apprehend* and *conceive* are in the present tense and thus they can be rejected. *Ignored* gives an opposite meaning and it is also in the past tense as the word *perceived* is. Thus it is the correct answer.

C. Make sure that the given word and the answer are in the same voice. *Contraction:*

(a) reduction
(b) something which is being expanded
(c) increase
(d) expansive

The word *contraction* is a noun in the active voice. The alternative *reduction* is similar in meaning. (b) is in the passive voice. *Expansive* is an adjective. Thus all these *three* alternatives are incorrect. The word *increase* is a noun and is in the active voice and matches with the given word *contraction.* This is, therefore, the correct answer.

D. A favourite trick of the examiner is mix a synonym in the alternatives to confuse the examinee. *Venerate:*

(a) respect (b) condemn
(c) inculcate (d) initiate
(e) severe

The alternative (a), *respect,* is a synonym. One needs to be alert in such cases. The correct answer is (b) *condemn.*

Practice Set —1

Pick out the word opposite or nearly so in the meaning of the given words.

1. Accepted
(a) followed (b) noted
(c) provided (d) considered
(e) rejected

2. Anger
(a) party (b) happiness
(c) approval (d) love
(e) joy

3. Loved
(a) refused (b) defamed
(c) distracted (d) averted
(e) hated

4. Obey
(a) attract (b) disobey
(c) repel (d) diffuse
(e) None

5. Outwit
(a) laugh (b) victory
(c) defeat (d) win
(e) None

6. Come
(a) play (b) fast
(c) go (d) got
(e) None

7. Hard
(a) soft (b) smooth
(c) delicate (d) easy
(e) less

8. Wealthy
(a) wicked (b) famous
(c) ill (d) poor
(e) harmful

9. Dull
(a) pale (b) wise
(c) shining (d) colourful
(e) foolish

10. Alleviation
(a) lessening (b) magnification
(c) intensify (d) aggravation
(e) exaggeration

11. Receded
(a) bloomed (b) advanced
(c) increased (d) diminished
(e) rebuilt

12. Transparent
(a) translucent (b) vague
(c) blind (d) opaque

13. Extrovert
(a) boaster (b) mixer
(c) introvert (d) social

14. Virtuous
(a) vicious (b) vulgar
(c) miserly (d) insincere

15. Urban
(a) rustic (b) rural
(c) civil (d) domestic

Practice Set —2

1. Genuine
(a) rotten (b) bogus
(c) unsound (d) impure

2. Militant
(a) religious (b) spiritual
(c) combative (d) pacifist

3. Unruly
(a) curious (b) obedient
(c) intelligent (d) indifferent

4. Ruthless
(a) militant (b) might
(c) majestic (d) merciful

5. Erudite
(a) ignorant (b) unknown
(c) illiterate (d) unfamiliar

6. Churlish
(a) young (b) cultured
(c) cowardly (d) accommodating

7. Latent
(a) hidden (b) forbidding
(c) obvious (d) artificial

8. Antipathy
(a) indifference (b) willingness
(c) fondness (d) liking

9. Deviate
(a) obliviate (b) break
(c) locate (d) follow
(e) concentrate

10. Vividly
(a) unintentionally (b) unimpressively
(c) unscrupulously (d) unwillingly
(e) unpopular

11. Releases
(a) liberates (b) closes
(c) confines (d) provides
(e) strengthens

12. Morose
(a) healthy (b) gloomy
(c) haggard (d) cheerful

13. Inspired
(a) overwhelmed (b) dispirited
(c) disillusioned (d) sceptical

14. Cynical
(a) mature (b) eccentric
(c) naive (d) crazy

15. Malevolent
(a) kindly (b) vacuous
(c) ambivalent (d) primitive

Practice Set —3

1. Autonomous
(a) magnanimous (b) ambiguous
(c) exiguous (d) dependent
(e) operational

2. Baffle
(a) make way (b) thwart
(c) confuse (d) check
(e) substitute

3. Blithe
(a) joyless
(b) gay in disposition
(c) light-hearted
(d) generosity
(e) cheerfulness

4. Brazen
(a) bold
(b) made of brass
(c) made of copper
(d) insolent
(e) shy

5. Churlish
(a) boorish (b) coarse
(c) courteous (d) niggardly
(e) modest

6. Extravagant
(a) developing (b) wonderful
(c) disappearing (d) economical
(e) real

7. Desultory
(a) disconnected (b) lacking order

(c) pertinent (d) random
(e) frequent

8. Debonair
(a) awkward (b) windy
(c) balmy (d) sportive
(e) stomy

9. Ecstasy
(a) rapture (b) beatitude
(c) exaltation (d) oily
(e) misery

10. Embellish
(a) garnish (b) disfigure
(c) adorn (d) disarm
(e) perish

11. Euphoria
(a) strident (b) lethargy
(c) literary (d) significant
(e) musical

12. Exhilarate
(a) gladden (b) invigorate
(c) shabbily (d) inspiring
(e) depress

13. Exhume
(a) decipher (b) dig
(c) integrate (d) admit
(e) enter

14. Exalt
(a) ennoble (b) glorify
(c) extol (d) depreciate
(e) simplify

15. Extrinsic
(a) reputable (b) inherent
(c) swift (d) ambitious
(e) cursory

Practice Set —4

1. Eulogistic
(a) pretty (b) critical
(c) brief (d) stern
(e) free

2. Inevitable
(a) unavoidable (b) eatable
(c) half-baked (d) uncertain
(e) mutilated

3. Facsimile
(a) reproduction (b) sincere
(c) original (d) fact-finding
(e) engineered

4. Fervent
(a) fiery (b) arbour
(c) poisonous (d) apathetic
(e) original

5. Fiasco
(a) cameo (b) mansion
(c) pollution (d) success
(e) gamble

6. Fluster
(a) upset (b) disconcert
(c) arrange (d) disobey
(e) acclaim

7. Abundant
(a) fertile (b) infertile
(c) prolific (d) transparent
(e) harsh

8. Felicitous
(a) effeminate (b) canine
(c) sensuous (d) notorious
(e) inappropriate

9. Glossy
(a) sleek (b) ventilating
(c) dull (d) obscene
(e) dedicated

10. Hybrid
(a) mongrel (b) purebred
(c) composite (d) familiar
(e) ignorant

11. Hypothesis
(a) fact (b) theory
(c) conclusive (d) suppressed
(e) conjecture

12. Ingenuity
(a) skilfulness (b) cunning
(c) sentimental (d) certain
(e) dullness

13. Isolation
(a) seclusion (b) segregation
(c) association (d) hardihood
(e) hardness

14. Invincible
(a) invulnerable (b) visible
(c) wanton (d) ancient
(e) conquerable

15. Malign
(a) disparage (b) slander
(c) praise (d) purify
(e) repress

Practice Set —5

1. Instil
(a) extract (b) eradicate
(c) express (d) expand

2. Esoteric
(a) external (b) familiar
(c) native (d) pleasant

3. Ponderous
(a) simple (b) thoughtless
(c) empty (d) light

4. Nominal
(a) huge (b) clear
(c) real (d) solid

5. Parallelism
(a) obliquity (b) contrast
(c) disparity (d) divergence

6. Antiquity
(a) common (b) recent
(c) innovation (d) youthfulness

7. Swear
(a) support (b) reject
(c) deny (d) praise

8. Transparent
(a) translucent (b) vague
(c) blind (d) opaque

9. Extrovert
(a) boaster (b) mixer
(c) introvert (d) social

10. Virtuous
(a) vicious (b) vulgar
(c) miserly (d) domestic

11. Sophisticated
(a) rustic (b) rural
(c) civil (d) domestic

12. Genuine
(a) rotten (b) bogus
(c) unsound (d) impure

13. Exonerate
(a) reject (b) contract
(c) accuse (d) admit

14. Husbandry
(a) mistersshood (b) subordination
(c) discipline (d) wastefulness

15. Laudatory
(a) cheerless (b) defamatory
(c) quiet (d) inadmirable

16. Neophyte
(a) old (b) experienced
(c) orthodox (d) tasteless

17. Bestial
(a) least acceptable (b) unanimated
(c) heavenly (d) noble

18. Compliant
(a) defective (b) adamant
(c) elementary (d) appreciative

19. Quell
(a) praise (b) recommend
(c) incite (d) contract

20. Avidity
(a) over-active (b) carelessness
(c) greedy (d) stupidity

21. Bawdy
(a) decent (b) indecent
(c) dirty (d) inflexible

Practice Set —6

1. Odious
(a) familiar (b) pleasant
(c) insignificant (d) cacophony

2. Serene
(a) impure (b) agitated
(c) showy (d) complicated

3. Immaculate
(a) up-to-date (b) significant
(c) untidy (d) expressive

4. Expurgate
(a) stain (b) admit
(c) entertain (d) renew

5. Turgid
(a) clean (b) smooth
(c) bright (d) detailed

6. Laudation
(a) reduction (b) passive
(c) criticism (d) simplification

7. Reprimand
(a) encourage (b) recommend
(c) release (d) praise

8. Gullible
(a) unreliable
(b) uncompanionable
(c) rigid
(d) distrustful

9. Rectitude
(a) firmness (b) deception
(c) smoothness (d) atheism
(e) anarchy

10. Clemency
(a) corporal (b) compromise
(c) transformation (d) sensibility
(e) intolerance

11. Dogmatic
(a) peremptory (b) spellbound
(c) simple (d) unscrupulous
(e) uncertain

12. Progress
(a) reversion (b) advance
(c) movement (d) silence
(e) conformity

13. Taciturnity
(a) reciprocity (b) endorsement
(c) talkative (d) flamboyance
(e) transparency

14. Synchronised
(a) noisy (b) discordant
(c) consequent (d) following
(e) adorned

15. Urbanity
(a) rustic (b) crudeness
(c) cruelty (d) sociability
(e) affability

Practice Set —7

1. Incarcerate
(a) mobilise (b) impersonate
(c) treat (d) liberate
(e) impress

2. Malefactor
(a) assistant (b) supervisor
(c) performer (d) benefactor
(e) malingerer

3. Laceration
(a) insensitivity (b) armour
(c) preoccupation (d) palpitation
(e) healing

4. Annularity
(a) smooth (b) revival
(c) cancellation (d) stubborn
(e) vertical

5. Pretentious
(a) transparent (b) humble
(c) clear (d) obvious

6. Considerable
(a) inadequate (b) inattentive
(c) usual (d) common

7. Deserter
(a) sympathiser (b) favourite
(c) flatterer (d) loyalist

8. Inflexible
(a) soft (b) tender
(c) yielding (d) obedient

9. Inquisitive
(a) uninterested (b) dull
(c) indolent (d) careful

10. Gratify
(a) defeat (b) distress
(c) frustrate (d) discourage

11. Wane
(a) widen (b) fatten
(c) prosper (d) swell

12. Shrill
(a) weak (b) muffled
(c) inaudible (d) blunt

13. Wavering
(a) straight (b) tight
(c) strong (d) poor

14. Fabulous
(a) literary (b) commonplace
(c) real (d) poor

15. Erratic
(a) free (b) punctual
(c) right (d) reliable

Practice Set —8

1. Endow
(a) rob (b) snatch
(c) divest (d) dispossess

2. Polemic
(a) friendship (b) agreement
(c) amity (d) cooperation

3. Mundane
(a) excellent (b) superior
(c) heavenly (d) extraordinary

4. Furtive
(a) open (b) obvious
(c) unambiguous (d) straight

5. Objective
(a) personal (b) familiar
(c) deleted (d) intimate

6. Extant
(a) destroyed (b) extinguished
(c) forgotten (d) unheeded

7. Ephermeral
(a) spiritual (b) ethical
(c) permanent (d) stable

8. Strident
(a) musical (b) pleasant
(c) melodious (d) stable

9. Fecund
(a) hard (b) unpolughed
(c) solid (d) barren

10. Outstrip
(a) cooperate (b) compete
(c) follow (d) cover

11. Corpulence
(a) slender (b) cheerful
(c) guilt (d) poverty

12. Mitigate
(a) expedite (b) worsen
(c) slacken (d) repair

13. Dilettante
(a) stupid (b) rapid
(c) tidy (d) professional

14. Languid
(a) cheerful (b) progressive
(c) vigorous (d) fashionable

15. Dastard
(a) open (b) brave
(c) concise (d) innocent

Practice Set —9

1. Impeccable
(a) reasonable (b) practical
(c) repulsive (d) faulty

2. Morose
(a) harmless (b) decent
(c) cheerful (d) unusual

3. Clarity
(a) reserve (b) confusion
(c) candour (d) exaggeration

4. Bridge
(a) release (b) open
(c) bind (d) divide

5. Auspicious
(a) condemn (b) conspicuous
(c) unfavourable (d) spicy

6. Frugal
(a) charitable (b) extravagant
(c) generous (d) gaudy

7. Laudable
(a) commendable (b) negligible
(c) admirable (d) praiseworthy
(e) blameful

8. Stagnant
(a) effervescence (b) mobile
(c) progress (d) inertia
(e) flamboyance

9. Deleterious
(a) fatal (b) nourishing
(c) vital (d) injurious
(e) benevolent

10. Pernicious
(a) innocuous (b) healthy
(c) hygienic (d) fine
(e) excellent

11. Predicament
(a) firmness (b) confidence
(c) fantasy (d) certainty
(e) ease

12. Relinquish
(a) keep (b) possess
(c) claim (d) persist
(e) stick to

13. Retrogressive
(a) progressive (b) advancing
(c) furthering (d) forwarding
(e) improving

14. Vivacious
(a) languid (b) open
(c) strong (d) bright

15. Voluntary
(a) involuntary (b) instinctive
(c) compelled (d) coercive
(e) forced

Practice Set —10

1. Brilliant
(a) shining (b) dull
(c) flat (d) apparent

2. Labyrinthine
(a) clear (b) opaque
(c) obscure (d) straight

3. Tyro
(a) virtuoso (b) new
(c) learner (d) good-looking

4. Onrush
(a) flow (b) obstruction
(c) force (d) blocked

5. Flamboyant
(a) excited (b) quiet
(c) angry (d) multi-coloured

6. Demented
(a) enraged (b) calm
(c) angry (d) original

7. Insolent
(a) proud (b) humble
(c) ashamed (d) ignorant

8. Copious
(a) plentiful (b) little
(c) accommodative (d) abundant

9. Nostalgic
(a) wistful (b) airy
(c) forgetful (d) ambitious

10. Heterogeneous
(a) homogeneous (b) similar
(c) different (d) colourful

11. Inhibit
(a) refrain (b) discard
(c) activate (d) surrender

12. Wholesome
(a) robust (b) rough
(c) weak (d) complete

13. Arduous
(a) rugged (b) fragile
(c) robust (d) hard

14. Melancholy
(a) sad (b) laborious
(c) cheerful (d) blue

15. Candid
(a) silent (b) frank
(c) close (d) taciturn

Practice Set —11

1. Analogous
(a) dissimilar (b) showy
(c) haughty (d) senile

2. Devious
(a) indirect (b) direct
(c) random (d) abnormal

3. Candid
(a) anxious (b) vague
(c) secretive (d) shallow

4. Turbulence
(a) hostility (b) noisy
(c) impropriety (d) calmness

5. Antediluvian
(a) isolated (b) celebration
(c) ancient (d) modern

6. Chimerical
(a) economical (b) unnatural
(c) realistic (d) wonderful

7. Arduous
(a) difficult (b) easy
(c) gluttony (d) exertion

8. Dank
(a) dry (b) gutters
(c) wet (d) babbling

9. Vanguard
(a) rear (b) front
(c) regiment (d) echelon

10. Dastard
(a) warmth (b) hero
(c) idol (d) presence

11. Austerity
(a) extreme (b) harsh
(c) lenience (d) ascetic

12. Cozen
(a) prate (b) vilify
(c) cheat (d) treat honestly

13. Debonair
(a) balmy (b) awkward
(c) good-looking (d) windy

14. Blanch
(a) bleach (b) enlighten
(c) darken (d) analyse

15. Audacious
(a) accountable (b) vulnerable
(c) extremely daring (d) cowardly

Practice Set —12

1. Husbandry
(a) wastefulness (b) friction
(c) cowardice (d) hard labour

2. Fantastic
(a) good (b) unique
(c) real (d) imaginary

3. Anathematise
(a) locate (b) radiate
(c) deceive (d) bless

4. Antithesis
(a) similarity (b) quite
(c) different (d) regular

5. Deferential
(a) disorganised (b) disrespectful
(c) distinguishable (d) respectful

6. Exhume
(a) exit (b) inter
(c) admit (d) decipher

7. Ulterior
(a) tipped (b) sparkling
(c) stated (d) rampaging

8. Craven
(a) greedy (b) generous
(c) coward (d) brave

9. Euphonious
(a) strident (b) significant
(c) lethargic (d) distasteful

10. Gaucherie
(a) tact (b) culminate
(c) dwindle (d) quiet

11. Grandiose
(a) clumsy (b) simple
(c) proud (d) heavy

12. Hibernal
(a) spring-like (b) seasonal
(c) regular (d) attitude

13. Peer
(a) equivalent (b) equal
(c) certain (d) unequal

14. Gnome
(a) gloom (b) casual
(c) small (d) giant

15. Moot
(a) strict (b) difficult
(c) not disputable (d) disputable

Practice Set —13

1. Callous
(a) hardened (b) soft
(c) sensitive (d) compact

2. Haggard
(a) plump (b) vast
(c) maidenly (d) shrewd

3. Capacious
(a) confining (b) ferocious
(c) militant (d) extrovert

4. Laconic
(a) wicked (b) verbose
(c) milky (d) fragrance

5. Capricious
(a) insured (b) photographic
(c) satisfied (d) steadfast

6. Kith
(a) relative (b) son
(c) strangers (d) outfit

7. Hegira
(a) oasis (b) return
(c) calm (d) noise

8. Carte blanche
(a) restriction (b) investment
(c) order (d) importance

9. Lackadaisical
(a) intelligent (b) dull
(c) ambitious (d) monthly

10. Chaffing
(a) capitalisitc (b) happily
(c) sneering (d) serious

11. Objurgation
(a) rebuke (b) elegy
(c) hate (d) praise

12. Nefarious
(a) lacking (b) emperious
(c) benign (d) neglected

13. Neophyte
(a) veteran (b) novice
(c) unknown (d) newly born

14. Noisome
(a) clean (b) fragrant
(c) sleepy (d) dirty

15. Fantastic
(a) illusion (b) real
(c) wonderful (d) economical

Practice Set —14

1. Obloquy
(a) hate (b) praise
(c) circle (d) cure

2. Churlish
(a) naughty (b) coarse
(c) courteous (d) modest

3. Puissant
(a) healthy (b) indifferent
(c) weak (d) strong

4. Dainty
(a) coarse (b) graceful
(c) delectable (d) obedient

5. Gasconade
(a) modesty (b) seizure
(c) cleanliness (d) illusive

6. Probity
(a) cleanliness (b) corruption
(c) regret (d) upswing

7. Defile
(a) ride (b) purify
(c) assemble (d) order

8. Prim
(a) formal (b) prior
(c) informal (d) private

9. Pulchritude
(a) masculinity (b) female
(c) notoriety (d) ugliness

10. Scurrilous
(a) decent (b) savage
(c) descent (d) volatile

11. Sacerdotal
(a) frank (b) layman
(c) region (d) religious minded

12. Demure
(a) sedate (b) close
(c) indecorous (d) open

13. Rubicund
(a) wanted (b) dangerous
(c) indicative (d) pallid

14. Rueful
(a) impertinent (b). hated
(c) colourless (d) permitted

15. Derogatory
(a) conferred (b) praising
(c) immediate (d) roguish

ANSWER KEY

Set 1	Set 2	Set 3	Set 4	Set 5
1. (e)	1. (b)	1. (d)	1. (b)	1. (a)
2. (d)	2. (d)	2. (a)	2. (d)	2. (b)
3. (e)	3. (b)	3. (a)	3. (c)	3. (a)
4. (b)	4. (d)	4. (e)	4. (d)	4. (a)
5. (c)	5. (a)	5. (c)	5. (d)	5. (d)
6. (c)	6. (b)	6. (d)	6. (c)	6. (b)
7. (a)	7. (c)	7. (c)	7. (b)	7. (c)
8. (d)	8. (c)	8. (a)	8. (e)	8. (d)
9. (c)	9. (d)	9. (e)	9. (c)	9. (c)
10. (d)	10. (b)	10. (b)	10. (b)	10. (a)
11. (b)	11. (c)	11. (b)	11. (a)	11. (a)
12. (d)	12. (d)	12. (e)	12. (e)	12. (b)
13. (c)	13. (b)	13. (e)	13. (c)	13. (c)
14. (a)	14. (a)	14. (d)	14. (e)	14. (a)
15. (b)	15. (a)	15. (b)	13. (c)	15. (b)
				16. (a)
				17. (d)
				18. (b)
				19. (c)
				20. (b)
				21. (a)

Set 6	Set 7	Set 8	Set 9	Set 10
1. (b)	1. (d)	1. (d)	1. (d)	1. (b)
2. (b)	2. (d)	2. (b)	2. (c)	2. (d)
3. (c)	3. (e)	3. (c)	3. (b)	3. (a)
4. (b)	4. (e)	4. (d)	4. (d)	4. (b)
5. (a)	5. (b)	5. (a)	5. (c)	5. (b)
6. (c)	6. (a)	6. (a)	6. (b)	6. (b)
7. (a)	7. (d)	7. (c)	7. (e)	7. (b)
8. (c)	8. (c)	8. (b)	8. (b)	8. (b)
9. (b)	9. (a)	9. (d)	9. (b)	9. (b)
10. (e)	10. (c)	10. (c)	10. (b)	10. (a)
11. (d)	11. (c)	11. (a)	11. (c)	11. (c)
12. (a)	12. (b)	12. (b)	12. (e)	12. (c)
13. (a)	13. (a)	13. (a)	13. (a)	13. (b)
14. (b)	14. (d)	14. (a)	14. (a)	14. (c)
15. (a)	15. (c)	15. (b)	15. (a)	15. (d)

Set 11	Set 12	Set 13	Set 14
1. (a)	1. (a)	1. (b)	1. (b)
2. (b)	2. (c)	2. (a)	2. (c)
3. (c)	3. (d)	3. (a)	3. (c)
4. (d)	4. (a)	4. (b)	4. (a)
5. (d)	5. (b)	5. (d)	5. (a)
6. (c)	6. (b)	6. (c)	6. (b)
7. (b)	7. (c)	7. (b)	7. (b)
8. (a)	8. (d)	8. (a)	8. (c)
9. (a)	9. (a)	9. (c)	9. (d)
10. (b)	10. (a)	10. (d)	10. (a)
11. (c)	11. (b)	11. (d)	11. (b)
12. (d)	12. (c)	12. (c)	12. (c)
13. (b)	13. (d)	13. (a)	13. (d)
14. (c)	14. (d)	14. (b)	14. (a)
15. (d)	15. (c)	15. (b)	15. (b)

CHAPTER 16

VOCABULARY TEST: TYPE-I

There are immense possibilities for variation in vocabulary test. Different banking recruitment bodies as well as other organisations have introduced new patterns of test. One of the latest trends in this context is a two-way test of the similar or opposite meaning. Here test of four words will be given, out of which two words would be of nearly the same or opposite meaning. Candidates are required to find those two words and select the number of the correct word combination as their answer.

Example (Corporation Bank PO Exam, 2002).

(A) Enthralling (B) Respecting
(C) Projecting (D) Alluring

(1) A-B (2) B-C
(3) C-D (4) A-D
(5) B-D

You have to find out the correct answer which may be any of the above 5 choices. The answer may be synonym or antonym.

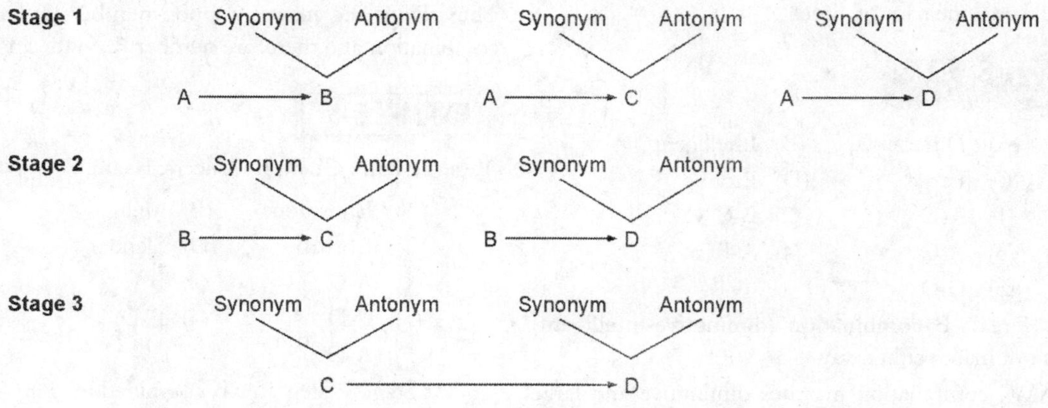

Fig. 16.1 Two Way Synonym Antonym Matching Technique

This test appears to be more difficult and puzzling than the simple synonym or antonym test which was the trend of the past. You can solve this question by the following method.

Therefore C-D combination is the automatic answer.

Illustrations

First of all, match A with B and see if it is a synonym or antonym and eliminate this combination. Similarly, repeat the matching process for A-C combination and then to A-D combination. Wherever you find a combination having a similar or opposite meaningfully them with the answer choices given and choose the answer, whichever is required.

EXAMPLE–1

(A) Perfunctory (B) Deep
(C) Wanton
(D) Compassionate
(1) A-C (2) A-B
(3) B-D (4) C-D
(5) B-C

Here we begin with A-B combination, and it is evident that these two words are antonyms. Thus we stop at the first step of Stage I itself and we shall now locate the number in answer choices. Option number (2) has this combination and thus (2) is the answer.

Remember that you should not try with the options; just try with words, the answer will be automatically found in the options. If you start trying with options, it will cousume a lot of time.

EXAMPLE–2

(A) Diminutive (B) Intelligent
(C) Large (D) Prolific
(1) A-D (2) B-C
(3) A-C (4) A-B
(5) C-D

Here A-B combination (diminutive-intelligent) does not match either way.

A-C combination matches diminutive and large as antonyms.

Thus choice number (3) (A-C) is the answer. Therefore, we could stop here at step 2 of Stage I.

EXAMPLE–3

(P.N.B. Specialist Officers Examination, April 2003).

(A) Serene (B) Jealous
(C) Identical (D) Calm
(1) A-B (2) A-C
(3) A-D (4) B-C
(5) B-D

Here the answer could be arrived at step 3 of Stage I. A-B combination and A-C combination do not match either way. A-D combination matches because serene and calm are good synonyms.

Thus the answer is (3) which has A-D combination.

EXAMPLE–4

(Reserve Bank of India Grade B Exam, 2002).

(A) Endemonia (B) Extole
(C) Eulogise (D) Enhemerise
(1) A-B (2) B-C
(3) B-D (4) A-D
(5) C-D

Here, A-B, A-C and A-D combinations do not match and therefore the answer could not be arrived at Stage I.

At Stage II, step I goes for B-C combination and we find that Extole and Eulogise are synonyms. Thus this is the answer. Option number (2) has B-C combination and therefore number (2) is the answer.

EXAMPLE–5

(Reserve Bank Grade B Officers, Exam, 2002).

(A) Enormous (B) Malign
(C) Absorb (D) Slander
(1) A-C (2) B-C
(3) C-D (4) B-D
(5) A-D

At Stage I, step 1 A-B combination, step 2, A-C combination and step 3 A-D combination do not match.

At Stage II, step 1 B-C combination also does not match.

At step 2, in B-D combination we find that malign and slander are synonyms. Thus, this combination is the answer. Therefore choice no. (4) with B-D combination is the correct answer.

EXAMPLE–6

(P.N.B. Specialist Officers Examination, April 2003).

(A) Prosper (B) Intense
(C) Seldom (D) Frequent
(1) A-D (2) B-C
(3) B-D (4) C-D
(5) A-C

Here it is evident that at Stage I, **(a)** step 1, A-B combination; **(b)** step 2, A-C combination; and **(c)** step 3, A-D combination would not match.

At Stage II, B-C combination and B-D combination also would not match.

Therefore, the answer is automatically the C-D combination. We find that 'seldom' and 'frequent' are good antonyms. Thus option number (4) with C-D combination is the correct answer.

Practice Set

1. (A) Ameliorate (B) Intensity
(C) Celestial (D) Fustian
(1) A-B (2) B-C
(3) C-D (4) A-D
(5) B-D

2. (A) Amnesty (B) Baneful
(C) Chary (D) Remission
(1) A-B (2) B-C
(3) C-D (4) A-D
(5) B-D

3. (A) Banter (B) Adjure
(C) Implore (D) Avarice
(1) A-B (2) B-C
(3) C-D (4) B-D
(5) A-D

4. (A) Verdant (B) Gregarious
(C) Amiable (D) Gruesome
(1) A-B (2) B-C
(3) C-D (4) B-D
(5) A-D

5. (A) Demeanour (B) Modest
(C) Humane (D) Compassionate
(1) A-B (2) B-C
(3) C-D (4) A-D
(5) B-D

6. (A) Erudite (B) Scholarly
(C) Docile (D) Extravagant
(1) A-B (2) B-C
(3) C-D (4) A-D
(5) B-D

7. (A) Hideous (B) Amusing
(C) Terrific (D) Weak
(1) A-B (2) B-C
(3) C-D (4) A-C
(5) B-D

8. (A) Gluttonous (B) Gracious
(C) Sumptuous (D) Voracious
(1) A-B (2) B-C
(3) C-D (4) A-C
(5) A-D

9. (A) Futile (B) Frugal
(C) Economical (D) Whimsical
(1) A-B (2) B-C
(3) C-D (4) A-D
(5) B-D

10. (A) Precarious (B) Intolerable
(C) Deceitful (D) Insidious
(1) A-B (2) B-C
(3) C-D (4) A-D
(5) B-D

11. (A) Rescind (B) Modify
(C) Revoke (D) Pulverise
(1) A-B (2) B-C
(3) A-D (4) B-D
(5) A-C

12. (A) Admonish (B) Pervade
(C) Pollute (D) Censure
(1) A-B (2) B-C
(3) A-D (4) B-D
(5) C-D

13. (A) Relatives (B) Accountrements
(C) Companions (D) Belongings
(1) A-B (2) B-D
(3) C-D (4) A-C
(5) B-C

14. (A) Vindictive (B) Strategic
(C) Triumphant (D) Revengeful
(1) A-B (2) A-C
(3) B-C (4) A-D
(5) B-D

15. (A) Flimsy (B) Erudite
(C) Boisterous (D) Foolish
(1) A-B (2) B-C
(3) A-D (4) B-D
(5) A-C

16. (A) Discovery (B) Excellence
(C) Paradigm (D) Model
(1) A-B (2) A-C
(3) B-C (4) B-D
(5) C-D

17. (A) Brilliant (B) Honorary
(C) Clandestine (D) Secret
(1) A-B (2) A-C
(3) A-D (4) B-C
(5) C-D

18. (A) Bland (B) Affable
(C) Tasteless (D) Unlawful
(1) A-B (2) A-C
(3) A-D (4) B-C
(5) B-D

19. (A) Tense (B) Phenomenal
(C) Scarce (D) Extraordinary
(1) A-B (2) A-C
(3) B-C (4) B-D
(5) C-D

20. (A) Disincline (B) Expiate
(C) Atone (D) Enfeeble
(1) A-B (2) A-C
(3) B-C (4) B-D
(5) C-D

21. (A) Sagacious (B) Recalcitrant
(C) Quixotic (D) Wise
(1) A-B (2) A-C
(3) B-C (4) B-D
(5) A-D

22. (A) Preposterous (B) Profligate
(C) Promiscuous (D) Wanton
(1) A-B (2) A-D
(3) B-D (4) C-D
(5) A-C

23. (A) Gleam (B) Gainsay
(C) Contradict (D) Seize
(1) A-B (2) A-C
(3) B-C (4) B-D
(5) C-D

24. (A) Eloquent (B) Articulate
(C) Dogmatic (D) Dominant
(1) A-B (2) A-C
(3) B-C (4) B-D
(5) C-D

25. (A) Somnolent (B) Blithe
(C) Penurious (D) Cheerful
(1) A-D (2) B-D
(3) C-D (4) B-C
(5) A-C

26. (A) Luminous (B) Commodious
(C) Egregious (D) Resplendent
(1) A-C (2) A-D
(3) B-C (4) B-D
(5) C-D

27. (A) Naive (B) Infirm
(C) Clever (D) Frail
(1) A-B (2) A-D
(3) B-C (4) B-D
(5) A-C

28. (A) Insipid (B) Ersatz
(C) Immitation (D) Glaze
(1) A-B (2) B-C
(3) C-D (4) A-D
(5) A-C

29. (A) Consummate (B) Scintillating
(C) Pernicious (D) Perfect
(1) A-B (2) A-C
(3) B-C (4) B-D
(5) A-D

30. (A) Diffident (B) Sardonic
(C) Sagacious (D) Ironical
(1) A-B (2) A-C
(3) B-C (4) A-D
(5) B-D

31. (A) Figurative (B) Flaccid
(C) Fiendish (D) Diabolical
(1) A-B (2) A-C
(3) B-D (4) C-D
(5) A-D

32. (A) Hamstring (B) Humiliate
(C) Inculcate (D) Faciliate
(1) A-B (2) B-D
(3) B-C (4) A-D
(5) C-D

33. (A) Antagonist (B) Connoisseur
(C) Protagonist (D) A lover of art
(1) A-B (2) B-C
(3) B-D (4) A-D
(5) C-D

34. (A) Brazen (B) Boisterous
(C) Choleric (D) Shameless
(1) A-B (2) A-C
(3) B-C (4) B-D
(5) A-D

35. (A) Vivacious (B) Virtuoso
(C) Adroit (D) Belicose
(1) A-B (2) A-C
(3) B-C (4) B-D
(5) A-D

36. (A) Jet (B) Chill
(C) Relax (D) Contrive
(1) A-B (2) A-C
(3) B-C (4) C-D
(5) A-D

37. (A) Vociferous (B) Flamboyant
(C) Prismatic (D) Irrevocable
(1) A-B (2) C-D
(3) B-C (4) A-D
(5) A-C

38. (A) Consummate (B) Fantastic
(C) Perfect (D) Benevolent
(1) A-B (2) B-C
(3) C-D (4) A-D
(5) A-C

39. (A) Haunter (B) Dereliction
(C) Arrogance (D) Stupidity
(1) A-B (2) A-C
(3) B-C (4) A-D
(5) C-D

40. (A) Maudlin (B) Sloth
(C) Sentimental (D) Romantic
(1) A-B (2) A-D
(3) A-C (4) B-C
(5) B-D

41. (A) Tenancious (B) Tedious
(C) Fragile (D) Sordid
(1) A-B (2) B-C
(3) B-D (4) A-C
(5) A-D

42. (A) Sanguine (B) Scandalous
(C) Shoddy (D) Despondent
(1) A-B (2) B-C
(3) C-D (4) A-C
(5) A-D

43. (A) Frugal (B) Morose
(C) Extravagant (D) Insolent
(1) A-B (2) B-C
(3) B-D (4) C-D
(5) A-C

44. (A) Chimerical (B) Candid
(C) Iconoclast (D) Fanciful
(1) A-B (2) B-C
(3) A-D (4) A-C
(5) C-D

45. (A) Loguacious (B) Taciturn
(C) Indifferent (D) Negligent
(1) A-B (2) B-C
(3) C-D (4) B-D
(5) C-D

46. (A) Eulogistic (B) Ingenuous
(C) Enigmatic (D) Appreciative
(1) A-B (2) A-C
(3) A-D (4) B-C
(5) C-D

47. (A) Brazen (B) Bucolic
(C) Incessant (D) Overflowing
(1) A-B (2) B-C
(3) A-C (4) C-D
(5) B-D

48. (A) Fussilade (B) Trumpery
(C) Criticism (D) Malidiction
(1) A-B (2) B-C
(3) C-D (4) A-C
(5) A-D

49. (A) Rubicand (B) Pallid
(C) Griandiose (D) Capricious
(1) A-B (2) A-C
(3) A-B (4) C-D
(5) B-D

50. (A) Lackadaisical (B) Haggard
(C) Laconic (D) Verbose
(1) A-B (2) A-C
(3) B-C (4) B-D
(5) C-D

ANSWER KEY

1. (1)	2. (4)	3. (2)	4. (3)	5. (3)
6. (1)	7. (2)	8. (5)	9. (2)	10. (3)
11. (5)	12. (3)	13. (2)	14. (4)	15. (4)
16. (5)	17. (5)	18. (2)	19. (4)	20. (3)
21. (5)	22. (4)	23. (3)	24. (1)	25. (2)
26. (4)	27. (5)	28. (2)	29. (5)	30. (5)
31. (4)	32. (4)	33. (3)	34. (5)	35. (3)
36. (3)	37. (3)	38. (5)	39. (2)	40. (3)
41. (4)	42. (2)	43. (5)	44. (3)	45. (3)
46. (3)	47. (4)	48. (4)	49. (1)	50. (5)

CHAPTER 17

Vocabulary Test: Type-II

Location-Elimination-Selection (LES) Technique

This is also a variation of the vocabulary test. In this type of test two lists are given, List I and List II. List I contains four words and List II contains six meanings. You have to locate the correct meanings of all these four words eliminating the two extra meanings or expressions. Thereafter, you have to select the correct answer from the four choices provided: A, B, C, D. All these four choices have sets of numbers. The correct choice contains all four correct meanings of the four different words.

This type of test has been introduced by UPSC for Assistant Provident Fund Commissioners Examination and it is now being followed by other recuiting Boards.

Apparently this is a difficult test. In fact, it requires a knowledge of all four words, their meaning and usage given in the list. The simple logic is that you should develop a good vocabulary, and this could be done only by extensive reading,careful listening to good speeches and by giving full attention to the usage of words in various contexts. Above all, drilling exercises must be done regularly to sharpen your recalling and memorising abilities.

However, we can solve this problem through a location, elimination and selection technique.

You can move from the word list to the meaning list or even *vice-versa*; sometimes meanings can strike and give you some idea to locate the corresponding word.

In a majority of cases, the answer can be found at Stage 2 or 3. Thus we can locate the correct answer choice without knowing the exact meaning of all four words. But, as good can-didates, you should build up a strong vocabulary and develop a command over usage of words.

Stage I

↓

(Select the easiest word in list I and locate its meaning in list II and get its number)

↓

Stage 2

↓

(Find the located number in the answer table)

↓

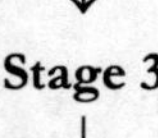

Stage 3

↓

(With the help of the located number eliminate wrong choices and select the correct answer).

↓

Stage 4

↓

(Select the next easy/known word and locate its answer if there are two or three answer choices).

↓

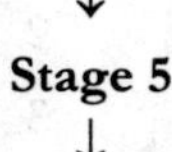

Stage 5

↓

(Select still another word and repeat the same process till you find the answer)

Illustration-1

List I	*List II*
A. Delusion	1. Friendly
B. Cordial	2. A feeling of annoyance
C. Brutal	3. Fancy
D. Chagrin	4. Something that is savage
	5. Cogent
	6. Something that is not pious

	A	B	C	D
(a)	1	2	3	4
(b)	3	4	6	5
(c)	3	1	4	2
(d)	4	3	6	2

Let us begin with Stage I. The easiest word is the word that we know exactly. Here in List I, the most common word known is *cordial.* In List II, the word *friendly* is the synonym of *cordial.* Thus we know now that the answer for B is 1. Now we have four answer choices (a), (b), (c), and (d). Here, only option (C) has the B-1 answer combination, and therefore the correct answer is (c).

The answer has been found at Stage 2.

Illustration-2

List I	*List II*
A. Meticulous	1. Fanciful
B. Moribund	2. Coming to an end
C. Adamant	3. Careful about detail
D. Whimsical	4. Inflexible
	5. In a miserable state
	6. Something written

	A	B	C	D
(a)	3	3	1	5
(b)	3	5	4	6
(c)	2	4	3	1
(d)	3	2	4	1

Here let us begin with Stage I. The easiest word in List I is *meticulous.* Its synonym in List II is no. 3. Now, the answer choices (c) and (a) have no. 3 as answer to A. So we eliminate choices (b) and (d). At Stage 3, we find next word (B), *adamant* which has a synonym inflexible at no. 4 in list II. Now we find that both (a) and (c) choices have no.4 as answer to B. Thus we are not able to find the final answer. Then we move to the third word *whimsical* (c). The similar word in list 2 is *fanciful* at no. 1. Both these words have some amount freedom of mind. With this clue we can locate them as synonyms.

Now we find that answer (a) has no. 2 as answer to C which is wrong. Answer choice (c) has 1 for C and thus choice no. (c) is the correct answer.

Practice Set

1.

List I	*List II*
A. Construe	1. Hard and boring work
B. Dissipate	2. Coercion
C. Duress	3. To scatter away
D. Diligent	4. Realistic
	5. Showing perseverence
	6. To interpret

	A	B	C	D
(a)	1	4	5	3
(b)	6	3	2	5
(c)	3	2	4	6
(d)	6	3	1	4

2.

List I	*List II*
A. Facile	1. Implied
B. Hilarious	2. A political group
C. Implicit	3. Characterised by merriment
D. Junta	4. Humiliating
	5. Requiring little effort
	6. Courageous

	A	B	C	D
(a)	5	6	1	4
(b)	2	3	3	6
(c)	4	2	3	1
(d)	5	3	1	2

3.

List I	*List II*
A. Condescend	1. Showing great happiness
B. Beatific	2. To come down to equal terms with inferiors
C. Blasphemy	3. Something that terrifies everybody
D. Buffoon	4. To show contempt for sacred things
	5. Reward
	6. A clown

	A	B	C	D
(a)	1	2	4	6
(b)	2	1	4	6
(c)	3	2	4	5
(d)	1	3	5	2

4.

List I	*List II*
A. Cataclysm	1. To find fault
B. Conscript	2. Not shaken by fear
C. Dauntless	3. A violent upheaval
D. Carp	4. Summon for army service
	5. Surrender
	6. Divine

	A	B	C	D
(a)	5	3	2	4
(b)	1	2	4	5
(c)	3	4	2	1
(d)	2	6	3	4

5. ***List I*** ***List II***

A. Ignominy — 1. Advisor
B. Inscrutable — 2. A pattern of changing scenes
C. Kaleidoscope — 3. Hatred
D. Mentor — 4. That cannot be understood
5. Public disgrace
6. To pacify

	A	B	C	D
(a)	5	4	2	1
(b)	4	6	3	2
(c)	4	3	6	5
(d)	3	2	5	4

6. ***List I*** ***List II***

A. Maudlin — 1. Faithfulness
B. Panacea — 2. A remedy for all evils
C. Obselete — 3. Reality
D. Fidelity — 4. Dangerous
5. Excessively sentimental
6. Out dated

	A	B	C	D
(a)	2	4	6	3
(b)	1	3	2	4
(c)	5	2	6	1
(d)	5	3	2	4

7. ***List I*** ***List II***

A. Furore — 1. Costly
B. Grotesque — 2. To steal
C. Precious — 3. Great rage
D. Purloin — 4. Warmful
5. Ugly
6. Something fascinating

	A	B	C	D
(a)	1	2	3	4
(b)	3	5	1	2
(c)	2	4	6	3
(d)	3	2	1	4

8. ***List I*** ***List II***

A. Braggadocio — 1. Something that delights
B. Celestial — 2. Hard to please
C. Diatribe — 3. Heavenly
D. Fastidious — 4. A political rally
5. Empty boasting
6. A malicious speech

	A	B	C	D
(a)	1	3	4	6
(b)	2	5	6	3
(c)	5	3	4	2
(d)	5	3	6	1

9. ***List I*** ***List II***

A. Fatalism — 1. Highly sacred
B. Grandiose — 2. Averse to work
C. Indolent — 3. A concept that all things are preditermined
D. Maestro — 4. Meaningless
5. Grand
6. A great composer

	A	B	C	D
(a)	1	3	4	6
(b)	3	5	2	6
(c)	4	6	2	1
(d)	3	4	2	5

10. ***List I*** / ***List II***

A. Inundate
B. Gainsay
C. Atone
D. Baffle

1. To follow the model of
2. Deny
3. To make amends for
4. Confuse
5. To overflow
6. Engross

	A	B	C	D
(a)	5	2	6	5
(b)	4	3	3	2
(c)	5	2	3	4
(d)	5	1	4	3

11. ***List I*** / ***List II***

A. Enervate
B. Engender
C. Engulf
D. Enunciate

1. Enfeeble
2. Produce
3. To confuse
4. To pronounce clearly
5. Deter
6. Swallow up

	A	B	C	D
(a)	1	2	4	6
(b)	2	4	3	5
(c)	5	4	2	3
(d)	1	5	4	3

12. ***List I*** / ***List II***

A. False
B. Despotic
C. Convincing
D. Sordid

1. Filthy
2. Something that is credible
3. Artificial
4. Humane
5. Dictatorial
6. Something which is not relevant to the context

	A	B	C	D
(a)	2	3	1	5
(b)	3	5	2	4
(c)	2	4	3	1
(d)	3	2	4	1

13. ***List I*** / ***List II***

A. Fabulous
B. Arbitrary
C. Commensurate
D. Delactable

1. Out of fashion
2. Great
3. Despotic
4. Something that delightful
5. Depressed
6. Suitable

	A	B	C	D
(a)	2	3	6	4
(b)	1	3	2	4
(c)	5	6	5	3
(d)	4	4	2	6

14. ***List I*** / ***List II***

A. Delusion
B. Cordial
C. Brutal
D. Chagrin

1. Friendly
2. A feeling of annoyance
3. Fancy
4. Something that is savage
5. Cogent
6. Impious

	A	B	C	D
(a)	1	2	3	4
(b)	3	4	6	5
(c)	3	1	4	2
(d)	4	3	6	2

15. ***List I*** / ***List II***

A. Candour
B. Garrulous
C. Sinister

1. Reasonable
2. One who talks much
3. Dangerous

D. Doughty — 4. Fearless
5. A work of art
6. Frankness

	A	B	C	D
(a)	2	3	1	5
(b)	6	2	3	4
(c)	2	6	3	4
(d)	6	1	2	5

16. *List I* — *List II*

A. Cantankerous — 1. One who is prone to quarrel
B. Capacious — 2. One who loves mankind
C. Genteel — 3. One who is very polite
D. Philanthropic — 4. Pliable or very accomodating
5. Innocent
6. Admirable

	A	B	C	D
(a)	1	4	3	2
(b)	2	3	5	6
(c)	4	2	1	3
(d)	2	3	4	1

17. *List I* — *List II*

A. Jet — 1. Relax
B. Chill — 2. Leave in a hurry
C. Evanescent — 3. Quiet
D. Placid — 4. Something that disturbs everybody
5. A place of worship
6. Temporary

	A	B	C	D
(a)	4	2	1	3
(b)	4	3	2	1
(c)	2	1	6	3
(d)	6	5	3	2

18. *List I* — *List II*

A. Blithe — 1. Cheerful
B. Desultory — 2. Something which is not in order
C. Ecstasy — 3. A rare sense of joy
D. Ruthless — 4. Something or someone that does a thing mercilessly
5. Very emotional
6. Highly impressive

	A	B	C	D
(a)	4	3	6	2
(b)	1	2	3	4
(c)	3	5	1	4
(d)	6	2	3	1

19. *List I* — *List II*

A. Melange — 1. Sad
B. Debonair — 2. One who lives in high style
C. Pensive — 3. Very important
D. Paramount — 4. Interesting
5. Mixture
6. One who is very liberal

	A	B	C	D
(a)	4	3	1	6
(b)	2	3	1	5
(c)	4	3	5	2
(d)	5	2	1	3

20. *List I* — *List II*

A. Histrionic — 1. Something

	that happens at intervals
B. Homage	2. Very pleasant
C. Erotic	3. Overdramatic
D. Sporadic	4. To show respect
	5. Puzzling
	6. Amorous

	A	B	C	D
(a)	3	4	6	1
(b)	2	3	5	4
(c)	6	3	2	1
(d)	1	2	3	4

21.

List I	***List II***
A. Hallowed	1. Hidden
B. Parasite	2. Appropriate
C. Apposite	3. One who clings to another
D. Unalloyed	4. Something that attracts all
	5. Absolutely pure
	6. Sacred

	A	B	C	D
(a)	2	3	6	1
(b)	4	3	2	6
(c)	5	4	3	2
(d)	6	3	1	5

22.

List I	***List II***
A. Baffle	1. Highly enjoyable
B. Presage	2. To foretell
C. Facade	3. Front of a building
D. Lachrymose	4. To disconcert
	5. Mournful
	6. Destructive

	A	B	C	D
(a)	2	6	4	3
(b)	3	2	1	5
(c)	4	2	3	5
(d)	3	2	5	4

23.

List I	***List II***
A. Extrovert	1. One who is free and open
B. Extravagant	2. A new person in a field
C. Neophyte	3. A insidious thing
D. Militant	4. One who is polite
	5. One who is aggressive
	6. One who spends lavishly

	A	B	C	D
(a)	2	4	6	3
(b)	1	2	4	5
(c)	1	6	2	3
(d)	2	6	2	1

24.

List I	***List II***
A. Hypnotic	1. Very amusing
B. Hilarious	2. A great person in a field
C. Wizard	3. Something that attracts forcefully
D. Hamstring	4. Open
	5. To obstruct
	6. Original

	A	B	C	D
(a)	4	1	3	2
(b)	3	1	2	5
(c)	3	4	6	5
(d)	2	1	3	4

ANSWER KEY

1. (b)	2. (d)	3. (b)	4. (c)	5. (a)
6. (c)	7. (b)	8. (d)	9. (b)	10. (c)
11. (a)	12. (b)	13. (a)	14. (c)	15. (b)
16. (a)	17. (c)	18. (b)	19. (d)	20. (a)
21. (d)	22. (c)	23. (c)	24. (b)	

CHAPTER 18

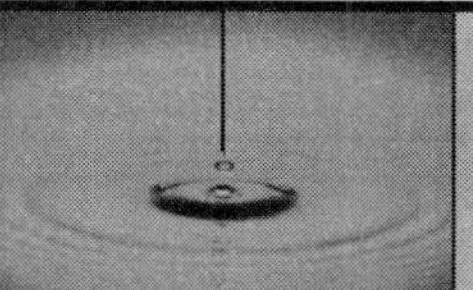

VOCABULARY (MISCELLANEOUS)

Introduction

Vocabulary tests constitute the lion's share of the objective English syllabi of the various competitive examinations. Synonyms, antonyms, idioms and substitution directly test vocabulary, but the sentence completion, the cloze test and the sentence arrangement demand a precise knowledge of the shades and nuances of words, their proper usage and a wide variety of vocabulary including important foreign expressions. Let us examine a few questions in sentence completion.

1. Mahatma Gandhi was very simple and innocent; his behaviour was ____________.

   (a) childish (b) child-like

   (c) proud (d) humble

   Here the answer is (b), *child-like,* because *childish* has a negative connotation. The knowledge of complex synonyms also helps in locating answers.

2. Pakistanis are the ____________ behind terrorism in India.

   (a) agent provocateurs

   (b) annus mirabills

   (c) dramatis personae

   (d) ex-officio

   Here the answer is (a), *agent provocateurs.* The knowledge of foreign expressions comes to our aid in locating the correct choice.

3. It is one of the biggest churches of the world; we find a good ____________ of worshippers on every Sunday.

   (a) cluster (b) chain

   (c) class (d) congregation

   Here the answer is (d), *congregation,* because this is the specific group term for worshippers.

Keeping this important point in mind, this unit offers a selective list of miscellaneous vocabulary.

Complex Synonyms

1. Accident; incident; mishap

   Accident is something that happens by chance; it can be both negative or positive, but it is usually associated with something negative.

   The *accident* that took place yesterday proved fatal for the car driver.

   By *accident* of birth, he was very rich.

   An *incident* is an occurrence, it is normally used in a neutral sense.

Little *incidents* also play an important role in life.

Mishap refers to an unfortunate accident, but it is less serious than an accident.

Yesterday he injured his leg; it was the second *mishap* in this week for him.

2. Anxious; eager

Anxious persons are willing to do something but there is also some element of anxiety.

I am *anxiously* awaiting my son's examination result.

Eagerness shows one's keenness to do something.

I am *eager* to take up a new project.

3. Bear; endure

To bear means to put up with something painful.

A soldier is expected to *bear* the pain of any wounds of war.

Endure implies a quality to bear patiently for a long stretch of time.

A brave man *endures* misfortunes with smiles.

4. Careful; cautious

A *careful* person is one who tries to do a thing in a right manner.

He is a *careful* officer.

A *cautious* man is he who is always anxious that he should not make any mistake.

A *cautious* man is often nervous.

5. Deep; profound

Deep can be used with both concrete and abstract things.

I have *deep* feelings for my mother.

Look at this well; it is very *deep.*

Profound is used in a metaphorical sense.

He is a man of *profound* knowledge.

6. Increase; grow

Increase means a sudden growth.

The price of essential items have *increased* this year.

Growth means a steady development.

A healthy child *grows* into a young man.

7. Oppose; resist

Oppose means to act against.

I *oppose* the idea proposed by the chairman.

Resist means to oppose in defense. It also means to refuse to give in.

We must *resist* the tyranny of wicked people.

8. Practical; practicable

Both mean realistic, but while *practical* can be used for both man and things, *practicable* can be used only for things.

A *practical* man succeeds in life.

The project of running a car by gas is now *practicable.*

9. Suspect; doubt

Suspect means that something exists or is to happen.

The Government *suspects* trouble on the eve of elections.

Doubt means to be uncertain.

I *doubt* if he is telling the truth.

10. Advice; advise

Advice is used as a noun.

He has given me a good piece of *advice.*

Advise is used as a verb.

I *advise* my students to read the texts carefully.

11. Street; road

A *street* is a road with buildings on the sides.

Every town has many *streets.*

A *road* is a way leading from one place to another.

The *road* goes to Bodh Gaya.

12. Wounded; injured

Wounded implies severe injuries got during a battle or a war.

Many officers and soldiers were *wounded* in the 1962 war.

Injured stands for physical hurt in accidents etc.

Ram was *injured* in an accident and his leg got fractured.

13. Child-like; childish

Child-like implies simplicity and innocence.

Gandhiji had *child-like* qualities.

Childish has a derogatory implication.

His behaviour is so *childish* that no one likes him.

14. Womanly; womanish

Womanly is used in a good sense.

She is a beautiful woman; her figure is *womanly.*

Womanish is used in a bad sense.

It is a *womanish* quality to be unnecessarily jealous and critical.

15. Steal; rob

Steal is used for things taken away by thieves.

The thief has *stolen* his bag.

Rob is used for persons or places from whom or where the things have been taken.

The bandits *robbed* the bank manager.

16. Refuse; deny

To refuse means not to take what is offered.

He refused to work for this small pay.

To deny implies that a statement is false.

He *denied* that this has been done by him.

17. Press; persuade

To *press* means to put undue pressure on someone or something.

Sometimes students *press* the principal to suspend the classes.

Persuade implies a sense of request.

We must *persuade* our elders to maintain their health.

18. Bonus; dividend

Bonus is a sum paid out of surplus profit.

The company pays a *bonus* to its employees every year.

Dividend is a share of any sum of money, especially profit of a joint stock company to be divided among the share holders.

It is a very common habit nowadays to earn through *dividends.*

19. Gentle; genteel

Gentle means cultured or a man of good manners.

He is a *gentle* man.

Genteel means belonging to a good family.

He belongs to a *genteel* family.

20. Famous; notorious

Famous is used in a positive sense for well-known persons or things.

Keats is *a famous* poet.

Notorious is used in a negative sense.

He is a *notorious* criminal.

21. Able; capable

Able: capacity or power to do something physically, mentally. *Capable:* having the power, ability or inclination.

Dilip Kumar was *able* to act as a tragic hero even when he was young.

Indians are *capable* of withstanding great suffering and pain.

22. Adapt; adopt

Adapt: to adjust to a new situation or thing

Adopt: to accept

We must *adapt* to the new circumstances.

I am at a loss to decide which motion to *adopt.*

23. Beside; besides

Beside: by the side of

Besides: in addition to

We sat *beside* the fireplace.

Besides Rita, Juhi also came to the party.

24. Canon; cannon

Canon: a practice that has become binding through long usage

Cannon: guns used in war

It is an offence to break the *canons* of society.

We heard the loud noise of a *cannon* from a distance.

25. Coalition; collision, collusion

Coalition: union of political parties for a special purpose

Collision: accident

Collusion: a secret arrangement

The *coalition* government at the Centre will not last long. Some forty people died in a train *collision.*

The dacoits raided the village in *collusion* with the chowkidar.

26. Cool; cold

Cool: denotes absence of warmth.

Cold: is opposite to *warm.*

The shade of a banyan tree is rather *cool.*

It is *cold* outside.

27. Artisan; artisian

Artisan: one who practises handicrafts.

Artisian: a kind of well

Rajasthan is known for its *artisans.*

Artisian wells are found in Australia.

28. Brake; break

Brake: device to stop a moving vehicle

Break: to communicate

Good *brakes* have been developed now.

I enjoy *breaking* good news to people.

29. Cereal; serial

Cereal: grains

Serial: forming a series

Rice and wheat are the major *cereals* of India.

Now we can watch many educative *serials* on the TV.

30. Continual; continuous

Continual: with little gaps

Continuous: without any break

It has been raining *continuously* for the last four hours.

The speech was *continually* interrupted by the angry audience.

31. Defer; differ

Defer: put off temporarily

Differ: disagree

I had to *defer* my plan to launch my project because of the scarcity of funds.

I *differ* with you on this issue.

32. Flair; flare

Flair: gift

Flare: spread

He has a *flair* for music.

The fire *flared* up.

33. Historic; historical

Historic: famous in history

Historical: based on history

The Taj Mahal is *historic*

"A Tale of Two Cities" is a *historical* novel by Dickens.

34. Literal; literary

Literal: actual meaning

Literary: educated or concerned with literature

Let us first learn the *literal* meaning of these words.

Jawaharlal wrote in a *literary* language.

35. Lovable; lovely

Lovable: worthy of love

Lovely: beautiful

Ram is a *lovable* character.

The rose is a *lovely* flower.

Foreign Expressions

1. *Ad hoc* (workable, temporary)
An *ad hoc* committee has been set up to work until the regular committee is formed.

2. *Ad antiquo* (from ancient times)
Indians have been God-fearing *ad antiquo.*

3. *Ad infinitum* (for ever)
It appears that the practice of idol worship will continue in India *ad infinitum.*

4. *Ad interim* (in between)
The Government is trying to rehabilitate those victims who were uprooted by flood but it should also give some aid *ad interim.*

5. *Alma mater* (the institution where one is educated)—Everybody has great admiration for his *alma mater.*

6. *Alumni* (old students of an institution) We are the *alumni* of LS College.

7. *Alpha and omega* (from beginning to end)
The *alpha and omega* of a patriot's life is the preservation of the freedom of his country.

8. *Alter ego* (a very close friend)
Nehru was the *alter ego* of Mahatma Gandhi.

9. *Ad verbum* (word for word) A true student tries to translate the ideas of his teacher *ad verbum.*

10. *Annus mirabilis (a* year of wonderful events)
1993 was an *annus mirabilis* in Indian history.

11. *Agent provocateurs (culprits* in disguise)
Pakistanis are the *agent provocateurs* behind terrorism in India.

12. *Bonafide* (genuine)
He is a *bonafide* candidate for his post.

13. *Coup d'etat* (to change a government by rebellion)
These days *coup d'etat* is a common phenomenon among Asian countries.

14. *Carte blanche* (full freedom) Indian people give a *carte blanche* to the Government it elects for shaping the country.

15. *Charge d'affairs* (one who acts as an ambassador) Mr A was the *charge d' affairs* in Ceylon.

16. *De jure* (legally) Ram is the heir of this kingdom *de jure.*

17. *De facto* (really) America rules *de facto* over a big part of the world.

18. *De novo* (afresh) Forget the past and start your life *de novo.*

19. *Dramatis personae* (characters in a drama) Acquaint yourself with the *dramatis personae* to understand a drama properly.

20. *En bloc* (in a body) All the teachers went on a strike *en bloc.*

21. *El dorado* (a country of gold) India was an *el dorado* the British.

22. *En route* (in way) I met my old friend *en route* to the station.

23. *Ex officio* (by virtue of your post) The Pro- Vice-Chancellor is a member of the syndicate *ex officio.*

24. *Ex parte* (one-sided) If one party does not turn up in the court, at times the judge gives his judgement *ex parte.*

25. *Fait accompli* (a work surely done) Now the Human Rights Commission is *a fait accompli* and nobody can undo it.

26. *Ipso facto* (really) The prime minister is *ipso facto* the ruler of this country.

27. *In camera* (confidentially, secretly) The interview was held *in camera.*

28. *Laissez faire* (the state of being as it is) Indian economy has come out of its *laissez faire* condition.

29. *Lingua franca* (the language of the masses) Hindi is the *lingua franca* of India.

30. *Locus standi* (a right to participate in a process) Unless I have a *locus standi,* I cannot give my opinion in this matter.

31. *Mala fide* (with a bad intention) The *mala fide* of the criminals is at times not proved and thus they are left free.

32. *Magnum opus* (the best work) 'War and Peace' is the *magnum opus* of Tolstoy.

33. *Modus operandi* (the mode of working) The police tries to assess the *modus operandi* of a criminal first.

34. *Par excellence* (superb) Ravi Shankar is a musician *par excellence.*

35. *Per capita* (of one individual) The *per capita* income of an Indian is far less than that of an American.

36. *Prima facie* (at the appearance). A *prima facie* can be made against him.

37. *Sub judice* (in consideration by a court). The case of teachers' promotion is *sub judice.*

38. *Summun bonum* of (of high goals) Service to humanity was the *Summun bonum* of Gandhi's life.

39. *Tabula rasa* (clean slate) A villager's mind is a *tabula rasa* in the beginning.

40. *Ultra vires* (not valid; not within powers) The recent orders of the Government have been declared *ultra vires* by the court.

41. *Viva-voce* (oral examination) A *viva-voce* is held before awarding PhD degree to a candidate.

42. *Tete-e-tete* (informal talk) He had a *tete-e-tete* with Sita.

43. *Sine die* (for an idenfinite period) Because of students' strike, the college was closed *sine die.*

44. *Sine qua non* (necessary condition) Hard labour is the *sine qua non* for success.

45. *Raison d'etre* (real purpose) It is difficult to understand the *raison d' etre* of terrorists in India.

46. *Sang froid* (remaining in the face of danger) A strong man can bear with bad news with *sang froid.*

Group Terms

1. An *army* of soldiers
2. An *assembly* of people
3. A *ball* of cotton or wool
4. A *band* of singers
5. A *bevy* of girls
6. A *board* of trustees or directors
7. A *bunch* of grapes, plantains, keys
8. A *bundle* of sticks, hay
9. A *caravan* of merchants, pilgrims, travellers
10. A *century* of years
11. A *chain* of mountains
12. A *choir* of singers
13. A *class* of students, persons
14. A *cloud* of locusts
15. A *clump* or *grove* of trees
16. A *cluster* of stars, grapes, islands
17. A *code* of laws
18. A *collection* of stamps, coins
19. A *company* of soldiers, merchants
20. A *congregation* of worshippers
21. A *consignment* of goods
22. A *constellation* of stars
23. A *course* of lectures
24. A *crew* of sailors
25. A *crowd* of people
26. A *drove* of cattle
27. A *faggot* of sticks
28. A *fleet* of ships
29. A *flock* of birds, sheep
30. A *gang* of robbers, thieves, prisoners, workmen
31. A *garland* of flowers
32. A *group* of persons, islands
33. A *heap* of stones, ruins
34. A *herd* of cattle, deer, goats
35. A *hive* of bees
36. A *litter* of pigs, pups
37. A *multitude* of people
38. A *mob* of rioters
39. A *pack* of hounds, playing-cards
40. A *pair* of shoes
41. A *peal* of bells
42. A *regiment* of soldiers
43. A *series* of lectures
44. A *sheaf* of arrows
45. A *shower* of rain, arrows
46. A *stock* of hay
47. A *stock* of goods
48. A *string* of camels
49. A *suite* of clothes
50. A *suite* of rooms
51. A *swarm* of flies, bees, ants
52. A *team* of players, oxen, horses
53. A *train* of wagons, followers
54. A *crowd* of people
55. A *throng* of people
56. A *troop* of scouts, horsemen
57. A *tribe* of natives
58. A *tuft* of grass, hair
59. A *volley* of shots, bullets, stones, arrows, abuse
60. A *yoke* of oxen
61. A *wreath* of flowers.

Words Denoting Sounds

1.	Apes	:	gibber
2.	Asses	:	bray
3.	Bears	:	growl
4.	Bees	:	hum, drone, buzz
5.	Birds	:	sing, warble, chirp, twitter
6.	Bulls	:	bellow
7.	Cattle	:	low
8.	Calves	:	bleat
9.	Camels	:	grunt
10.	Cats	:	mew, purr
11.	Cocks	:	crow
12.	Crows	:	caw
13.	Cows	:	low
14.	Dogs	:	bark, yelp

15. Goats/sheep : whine, bleat
16. Doves : coo
17. Ducks : quack
18. Elephants : trumpet
19. Eagles : scream
20. Vultures : scream
21. Wolves : yell, howl
22. Flies : buzz
23. Frogs : croak
24. Geese : cackle
25. Crickets : chirp
26. Hens : cluck
27. Horses : neigh, snort
28. Hyenas : laugh
29. Jackals : howl
30. Lions : roar
31. Mice : squeak
32. Monkeys : chatter
33. Nightingales : warble
34. Owls : hoot
35. Pigeons : coo
36. Pigs : grunt
37. Puppies : yelp
38. Serpents : hiss
39. Sheep : bleat
40. Squirrels : squeak
41. Tigers : roar
42. Turkeys : gobble

Sounds

1. Beating of drums
2. Blowing of bugles or trumpets
3. Banging of doors
4. Clatter of weapons or hoofs
5. Clank of chains or steel
6. Chattering of teeth
7. Clapping of hands
8. Flapping of wings
9. Jingling of coins
10. Lisping of babies
11. Moaning of people in agony
12. Mutter of old or discontented persons
13. Rattling of wheels
14. Ringing of bells
15. Roaring of lions, guns
16. Rustling of leaves
17. Thud of falling things.
18. Thundering of clouds
19. Tinkling of bells
20. Whistling of engines
21. Whining of a sickly child
22. Creaking of shoes, doors
23. Rippling of water
24. Blare of trumpets

Offsprings of Birds and Animals

1. Bear, fox, lion, tiger and wolf : cub
2. Cat : kitten
3. Cow : calf
4. Deer : fawn
5. Dog : puppy
6. Duck : duckling
7. Fish : minnow
8. Frog : tadpole
9. Goat : kid
10. Goose : gosling
11. Hare : leveret
12. Horse : colt, filly or foal
13. Hen : chicken
14. Peacock : peachicken
15. Sheep : lamb
16. Swan : signet
17. Elephant : foal
18. Camel : foal

Idiomatic Use of The Names of Animals

1.	A dog, hound, cur, puppy	: a nasty man
2.	A duck	: a simple man
3.	A fox	: a cunning fellow
4.	A goose	: a fool
5.	A gull	: to be easily befooled
6.	A lamb	: innocent man
7.	A monkey	: one who imitates
8.	A parrot	: one who crams
9.	A pig	: a glutton
10.	A phoenix	: a noble man
11.	A scorpion	: a flatterer
12.	A viper	: a wicked man
13.	A vixen	: a corrupt woman
14.	A wolf in the sheep's clothing	: a dangerous man who does not seem to be so

Places to Live In

1.	Convict	: prison
2.	King	: palace
3.	Lunatic	: asylum
4.	Monk	: monastery
5.	Nun	: convent
6.	Soldier	: barracks
7.	Bee	: hive
8.	Bird	: nest
9.	Cow	: shed
10.	Dog	: kennel
11.	Fowl	: coop
12.	Horse	: stable
13.	Lion	: den
14.	Mouse	: hole
15.	Owl	: barn or tree
16.	Pigeon	: dove-cote
17.	Rabbit	: burrow
18.	Sheep	: pen
19.	Spider	: web
20.	Tiger	: lair

Specific Words for Certain Places

1. Wine is made in a *brewery.*
2. Bread is made in a *bakery.*
3. Films are made in a *studio.*
4. Goods are made in a *factory.*
5. Leather is made in a *tannery.*
6. Coins are made in a *mint.*
7. Ships are made in a *dockyard.*
8. Aeroplanes are kept in an *aerodrome.*
9. Bees are kept in an *apiary.*
10. Birds are kept in a *cage.*
11. Birds and animals are kept in a *zoo.*
12. Clothes are kept in a *wardrobe.*
13. Fishes are kept in an *aquarium.*
14. Curios are kept in a *museum.*
15. Luggage at a railway station is kept in a *cloak room.*
16. Motor cars are kept in a *garage.*
17. Weapons are kept in an *arsenal.*

CHAPTER 19

ONE-WORD SUBSTITUTION

Introduction

Substitution is also a variant of vocabulary test. In this test, you are required to use one word for a sentence or a part of a sentence. There are certain specific words that stand for a group of words or indicate a place, a situation or state of mind.

EXAMPLES

1. I was sure that he would *bear a hand in* my new enterprise.
   (a) interfere (b) join
   (c) assist (d) rejoice
   Here the answer is (c), assist. Assist stands for the group of words, bear a hand.

2. I cleared off all my debts with the *large money paid to me* on retirement.
   (a) golden handshake
   (b) gold mine
   (c) lion's
   (d) windfall
   The answer is (a), golden handshake. This expression stands for the underlined words.

3. That which makes it difficult to recognise the presence or real nature of somebody or something.
   (a) cover (b) camouflage
   (c) pretence (d) mask
   Here the answer is (b), camaouflage, because this word stands for the whole sentence.

4. A place where animals are kept.
   (a) zoo (b) aviary
   (c) museum (d) sanctuary
   Here the answer is (a), zoo because a place where the animals are kept is known as a zoo.

5. A place where gambling is practised.
   (a) hotel (b) casino
   (c) restaurant (d) theatre
   The answer is (b), casino

6. A house where an Eskimo lives.
   (a) dower (b) igloo
   (c) mint (d) hamlet
   Here the answer is (b), igloo

7. One who is unable to pay one's debt.
   (a) bankrupt (b) borrower
   (c) loanee (d) obliged

The answer is (a), bankrupt, because this word indicates the economic situation of the man concerned.

8. The plants and vegetation of a region.
   (a) fauna (b) flora
   (c) landscape (d) climate
   The answer is (b), flora, as this word indicates the vegetation of the concerned area.

9. The period between two reigns.
   (a) interregnum (b) gap
   (c) anachronism (d) stasis
   The answer is (a), interregnum, because this word indicates the political situation of a country.

10. One who hates mankind.
    (a) misanthrope (b) philanthropist
    (c) lover (d) hater
    The answer is (a), misanthrope, because this word indicates the mentioned state of mind

11. One who believes in God.
    (a) atheist (b) theist
    (c) moral (d) immoral
    The answer is (b), theist.

12. A man who hates marriage.
    (a) polyandrist (b) bigot
    (c) misogamist (d) widower
    The answer is (c), misogamist.

In fact, substitution plays a great role in achieving brevity of speech and writing. In this age of jet-set competition, one has to communicate effectively in minimum time and space. Thus this art helps you adjust to the contemporary situation. You can master it by the usual process of learning it and committing it to memory by constant use and rigorous practice. A command in the art of substitution will help you immensely in sentence completion as well.

Some Substitutes

1. One who looks at the bright side of things: optimist
2. One who looks at the dark side of things: pessimist
3. One who does not believe in God: atheist
4. One who believes in God: theist
5. One who knows everything: omniscient
6. One who is present everywhere: omnipresent
7. One who is all powerful: omnipotent
8. One who cannot read and write: illiterate
9. One who acts against religion: heretic
10. One who offers one's services: volunteer
11. One who is unable to payoff one's debt: bankrupt
12. One who loves mankind: philanthropist
13. Love for mankind: philanthropy
14. One who hates mankind: misanthrope
15. One who is out to destroy the government: anarchist
16. One who eats human flesh: cannibal
17. One who lives on flesh: carnivorous
18. One who lives at the same time: contemporary
19. One who is more than a hundred years old: centenerian
20. One who is eighty years old: octogenarian
21. One for whom the world is a home: cosmopolitan
22. One who is indifferent to pain and pleasure: stoic
23. One who champions the cause of women: feminist
24. One who is given to pleasures of the flesh: epicure
25. One that lives on others: parasite
26. One who is sympathetic to mankind: humanitarian
27. One who walks on foot: pedestrian
28. One who studies things of the past: antiquarian
29. One who is gifted with

several talents: versatile

30. One who does not drink wine: teetotaller

31. One who is new to a profession: novice

32. One who is a habitual drunkard: sot; toper

33. One who settles in another country: immigrant

34. One who knows many languages: polygot

35. One who carves in stones: sculptor

36. One who cuts precious stones: lapidist (lapidary)

37. One who deals in cattle: drover

38. One who cures eye diseases: oculist

39. One who sells sweets and pastries: confectioner

40. One who collects postage stamps: philatelist

41. One who mends shoes: cobbler

42. One who loads and unloads ships: stevedore

43. One who compiles a dictionary: lexicographer

44. One who walks in one's sleep: somnambulist

45. One who talks in one's sleep: somniloquist

46. One who has an irresistible tendency to steal: kleptomaniac

47. One who breaks images or church omaments: iconoclast

48. One who retires from society to live a solitary life: recluse

49. One who has special skill in judging art, music, etc.: connoisseur

50. One who is devoted to the pleasures of eating and drinking: epicure

51. One who is given to the sensual pleasures of body: voluptuary

52. One who pretends to be what he is not: hypocrite

53. One who imitates the voice and gestures of another: Mimic

54. A professional rider in horse races: jockey

55. A place with gambling tables: Casino

56. A number of sheep: flock

57. A number of sailors working on a ship: crew

58. A collection of flags: bunting

59. A number of ships: fleet

60. A cluster of houses in a village: hamlet

61. A number of stars grouped together: constellation

62. The house of an Eskimo: igloo

63. The house of an Arab: dowar

64. A factory for manufacturing beer: brewery

65. A place for the collection of dried plants: herbarium

66. A building for lodging of soldiers: barrack

67. A place where money is coined: mint

68. A place where orphans are housed: orphanage

69. An institution for reforming young offenders: reformatory

70. A place for improving one's health: resort

71. A case in which the sword is kept: sheath

72. A substance that destroys germs: antiseptic

73. A medicine which produces insensitivity: anaesthetic

74. A medicine to counteract poison: antidote

75. An instrument for listening to the activities of the heart and lungs: stethoscope

76. Free from infection: immune
77. A cure for all diseases: panacea
78. A place where dead bodies are kept mortuary: mortuary
79. A place where dead bodies are interred: cemetery
80. A place where dead bodies are kept for identification: morgue
81. An examination of a dead body: postmortem
82. Occurring after death: posthumous
83. An inscription on a tomb: epitaph
84. The dead body of an animal: carcass
85. The science of colours: chromatics
86. The science of the structure of human body: anatomy
87. The art of effective speaking: elocution
88. The study of mankind: anthropology
89. The study of the human mind: psychology
90. The study of physical life: biology
91. The study of plants: botany
92. The study of animals: zoology
93. The study of rocks and soils: geology
94. The study of birds: ornithology
95. The study of mountains: oralogy
96. The study of languages: philology
97. The study of stars: astronomy
98. The study of the origin and history of words: etymology
99. The study of ancient writing: paleography
100. The art of beautiful handwriting: calligraphy
101. The art of preserving skin: taxidermy
102. Government by the nobility: aristocracy
103. Government by a few: oligarchy
104. Government by departments of state: bureaucracy
105. Government of, for and by the people: democracy
106. The right of self-government: autonomy
107. The period between two reigns: interregnum
108. A council of clergymen: synod
109. The ceremony at which a man becomes a priest: ordination
110. Violating religious things: sacrilege
111. One intolerantly devoted to a particular creed: bigot
112. A man who has more than one wife at a time: polygamist
113. A woman who has more than one husband at a time: polyandrist
114. A hater of women: misogynist
115. One who is vowed to unmarried life: celibate
116. A man whose wife is dead: widower
117. A woman whose husband is dead: widow
118. Engaged to be married: betrothed
119. An instrument for recording the revolutions of the earth: gyroscope
120. An instrument for measuring electric current: ammeter
121. Smuggled goods: contraband
122. The act of spying: espionage
123. A knife fixed on the end of a gun: bayonet
124. Soldiers on horses: cavalry
125. Soldiers on foot: infantry
126. A book of accounts showing debit and credit: ledger
127. A book containing information on all the branches of knowledge: encyclopedia
128. A record of one's life autobio-

written by oneself: graphy

129. A record of one's life written by somebody else: biography

130. A speech by the dramatist at the beginning of a play: prologue

131. A speech by the dramatist at the end of the play: epilogue

132. A poem of mourning: elegy

133. A hollow space in a wall for a statue: niche

134. Unable to pay off one's debt: insolvent

135. Language that has been very much used: hackneyed

136. Correct spelling: orthography

137. A place where ancient works are kept: musuem

138. A very private room: sanctum sanctorum

139. A place where mad men are kept: lunatic asylum

140. A war of religion: crusade

141. A lover of books: bibliophile

142. Animals that live in water: acquatic

143. A written declaration made on an oath: affidavit

144. A bunch of flowers: bouquet

145. A child born of unlawful marriage: bastard

146. A game or battle where no party wins: draw

147. A person's first speech: maiden speech

148. Killing a man: homicide

149. Killing one's king: regicide

150. Killing one's mother: matricide

151. Killing one's father: patricide

152. Killing one's brother: fratricide

153. Killing oneself: suicide

154. Animals that suckle their young: mammals

155. A speech made without preparation: extempore

156. A decision on which all agree: unanimous

157. A writer who steals ideas from another: plagiarist

158. One that lives on others: parasite

159. A medicine that loosens the bowels: laxative

160. A speech made to oneself: soliloquy

161. The place where clothes are kept: wardrobe

162. A person's last utterance: swan song

163. Asking everyone for an opinion: referendum

164. Separation from other people to avoid infection: quarantine

165. An imaginary ideal: utopia

166. A thing kept in memory of an event: souvenir

167. That which can be heard: audible

168. That which cannot be heard: inaudible

169. That which can be read: legible

170. That which cannot be read: illegible

171. Liable to catch fire easily: inflammable

172. That which can be eaten: edible

173. That which can be carried: portable

174. Incapable of being corrected: incorrigible

175. Commonplace remarks: platitudes

176. Belief of God in Nature: pantheism

177. The green colouring matter in the leaves of plants: chlorophyll

178. The animals of a certain region: fauna

179. The plants and vegetation of a region: flora

180. Incapable of being burnt: incombustible

181. An instrument for seeing

distant things: telescope

182. A disease that ends in death: fatal

183. A person suffering from nervous breakdown: neurotic

184. A book or paper written by hand: manuscript

185. Government which honours all religions: secular

186. A word no longer in use: obsolete

187. An instrument for detecting earthquakes: seismograph

188. An instrument for measuring gases: manometer

189. The property left to someone by a will: legacy

190. Promise given by a prisoner not to escape: parole

191. An exaggerated statement: hyperbole

192. A nation that goes to war: belligerent

193. A person who lives in a foreign country: hyperbole

194. Too much official formality: red tapism

195. One extremely fond of one's wife: uxorious

196. A list of things to be discussed at a meeting: agenda

197. Unduly attached to one's own opinions: opinionated

198. Very exact or scrupulous in the observance of forms, of etiquette, ceremony or behaviour: punctilious

199. One who is completely self-satisfied: complacent

200. Simple and easily deceived: gullible

201. One who has delusions of one's grandeur: megaloma niac

202. The most capable part of a group, town or place: elite

203. One who flaunts newly acquired wealth: parvenu

204. The intelligent and educated group or class of a society or country: intelligentsia

205. Weariness of and sadness for life and world: weltschmerz

206. Boredom and frustration in life: ennui

207. Shy, timid, unwilling to face a situation: diffident

208. One who looks at everything from a personal point of view: egocentric

209. One who is chivalrous, idealistic and unpractical: quixotic

210. One who is grave and gloomy: saturnine

211. One who gets pleasure in others trouble and pain: sadistic

212. The act of enjoying or having an experience indirectly: vicariously

213. The tendency to postpone things for future: procrasti- nation

214. To relax in a countryside far away from the humdrum of town: recupeate

215. To spend life without purpose and initiative: vegetate

216. One who is interested in the welfare of other people: altruist

217. One who believes in keeping things as they are: conservative

218. A girl who flirts egregiously : coquette

219. A woman who lures men to destory them: Circe

220. A tall, strong, masculine kind of woman: amazon

221. A loud-mouthed turbulent kind of woman: virago

222. A traitor who can sell out even his friend: Judas

223. A person with vulgar taste: vulgarian

224. A person who flaunts learning all the time: pedant

225. Understanding without the interference of feelings: empathy

226. An embarrassing mistake: a faux pas

227. A medley or heterogeneous mixture of great variety: potpourri

228. A slang of the underworld: argot

229. A language of a region having its own usage: dialect

230. A language of a special group: patois

231. The ascribing of human motivation, characteristics or behaviour to inanimate objects, animal or natural anthropomor-phenomena: phism

232. A payment not legally binding but for which some moral obligation is felt: ex gratia

233. One who gives directions from behind the scene on a stage: prompter

234. A washing or cleansing of the body especially in a religious ceremony: Ablution

235. Something perfectly neat and tidy: immaculate

236. A legal defence by which an accused person tries to show that he was somewhere else when the crime was committed: alibi

237. The money that a court ask a man to pay to his divorced or legally separated wife: alimony

238. A treatise on one subject: monograph

239. A speech uttered by one person: monologue

240. Mental derangement confined to one idea: monomania

241. An airplane with one pair of wings: monoplane

242. Exclusive possession or control of anyone thing: monopoly

243. The group, especially in the arts, regarded as being the most experimental: avant-garde

244. Words or action showing deliberate contempt for sacred things: blashphemy

245. An official bulletin: communique

246. An agreement entered between two or more parties: convenant

247. A passage with only one end: cul-de-sac

248. Something very brightly colourful: flamboyant

249. The art of painting on a plaster surface: fresco

250. A record or table showing the descent of a person or a family: genealogy

251. A connoisseur of food and drink: gourmet

252. A person or thing that goes before and announes the coming of something: harbinger

253. A persistent anxiety about one's health, usually involving imagined symptoms of illness: hypochondria

254. An odd, atypical or eccentric trait: idiosyncrasy

255. Not planned ahead of time: impromptu

256. To compensate a person, etc., for loss or damage: lindemnify

257. Originating or occurring naturally in the place or country where found: indigenous

258. A time between periods or events: interim

259. A plan for or the route to be followed on a journey: itinerary

260. A group of persons who band together for some secret purpose, especially for political intrigue: junta

261. A short journey for pleasure: jaunt

262. A swiftly changing scene or pattern: kaleidoscope

263. A lightly constructed open booth generally used as a newsstand: kiosk

264. That cannot be pacified: implacable

265. A written attack using humour to provoke contempt: lampoon

266. A false written statement to damage a person's repute: libel

267. A phrase or sentence that is comical or nonsensical because the speaker used a wrong word that sounded something like a right word: malapropism

268. An instruction from an electorate to its representative: mandate

269. A full-size model of a complete or partial human figure: mannequin

270. Personal reminiscences in a narrative form: memoir

271. The manner of operating or proceeding: modus operandi

272. A long wandering journey: odyssey

273. An authoritative decree or law of the government: ordinance

274. A person having authority to inquire into grievances of citizens against public authorities: ombudsman

275. A speech or writing praising a person or a thing: panegyric

276. A lover, specially one who unlawfully takes the position of a wife or a husband: paramour

277. An expression of the popular will concerning some important questions given by a direct vote of the people: plebiscite

278. The presentation to the people of a proposed bill for decision by vote: referendum

279. A portrait of a person with only the outline of the profile: silhouette

280. Causing or tending to cause sleep: soporific

281. Retired on account of age, usually with pension: superannuated

282. A substitute: surrogate

283. A close watch kept over someone: surveillance

284. Existing only in name: titular

285. A short literary description marked by delicacy: vignette

286. A place where a monk lives: monastery

Practice Set

Direction: Out of the given alternatives, choose the one which can be substituted for the given words or sentence.

1. One who believes in God.
(a) agnostic (b) theist
(c) devotee (d) secularist

2. One whose wife is dead.
(a) widower (b) widow
(c) divorcee (d) celibate

3. A place good for the sick.
(a) resort (b) sanitorium
(c) hospital (d) asylum

4. Government by one man.
(a) anarchy (b) monarchy
(c) autocracy (d) democracy

5. One who walks in one's sleep.
(a) dreamer (b) somnambulist
(c) neomatic (d) ignorant

6. A person suffering from nervous breakdown.
(a) eccentric (b) neurotic
(c) lunatic (d) mongrel

7. A book or paper written in hand.
(a) handwritten (b) manuscript
(c) edition (d) draft

8. The practice of having more than one wife at a time.
(a) polygamy (b) monogamy
(c) polyandry (d) digamy

9. One who abstains totally from alcoholic drinks.
(a) recluse (b) teetotaler
(c) sceptic (d) stoic

10. A cluster of houses in a village.
(a) mohalla (b) hamlet
(c) colony (d) sector

11. A place where money is coined.
(a) mint (b) press
(c) treasury (d) bank

12. A professional rider in horse races.
(a) rider (b) horse courser
(c) jockey (d) coach

13. The house of an Eskimo.
(a) hamlet (b) dowar
(c) igloo (d) hut

14. One who collects postage stamps.
(a) philatelist (b) stamp collector
(c) vendor (d) lexicographer

15. One who is an expert in judging art, music, etc.
(a) expert (b) connoisseur
(c) musician (d) artist

16. One who hates mankind.
(a) philanthropist (b) misanthrope
(c) hater (d) rebel

17. The art of beautiful handwriting.
(a) paleography (b) calligraphy
(c) draftsman (d) painter

18. The story of a man written by himself.
(a) biography (b) autobiography
(c) life history (d) history

19. The history of a man written by others.
(a) biography (b) autobiography
(c) history (d) manuscript

20. The plants and vegetation of a certain region.
(a) fauna (b) flora
(c) forest (d) vegetation

21. That which catches fire quickly.
(a) incombustible (b) inflammable
(c) invincible (d) inaudible

22. That which cannot be heard.
(a) inaudible (b) audible
(c) unheard (d) ineffaceable

23. Unable to pay one's debt.
(a) beggar (b) insolvent
(c) poor (d) borrower

24. Born of unmarried parents.
(a) legitimate (b) illegitimate
(c) orphan (d) adopted

25. An instrument for measuring the force of the wind.
(a) manometer (b) micrometer
(c) telescope (d) anemometer

26. A book containing information of all branches of knowledge.
(a) refresher (b) compendium
(c) encyclopedia (d) ledger

27. A poem of mourning.
(a) elegy (b) sonnet
(c) lyric (d) epic

28. A game in which no one wins.
(a) abandoned (b) drawn
(c) postponed (d) obsolete

29. Too much official formality.
(a) delayed (b) officiousness
(c) formality (d) red tapism

30. A speech made without preparation.
(a) prepared (b) debate
(c) extempore (d) elocution

31. One who is hundred years old.
(a) octogenarian (b) septagenarian
(c) centenarian (d) old

32. A person's first speech.
(a) maiden (b) extempore
(c) opener (d) preface

33. A decision on which all are agreed.
(a) anonymous (b) unanimous
(c) obsolete (d) confession

34. One for whom the whole world is one's home.
(a) cosmopolitan (b) humanitarian
(c) international (d) tourist

35. A job without salary.
(a) free service (b) honorary
(c) voluntary (d) amateur

36. A cure for all diseases.
(a) panacea (b) cure
(c) antibiotic (d) remedy

37. One who knows many languages.
(a) linguist (b) polyglot
(c) stylist (d) debator

38. A place where animals are kept.
(a) zoo (b) aviary
(c) museum (d) sanitorium

39. That which can be carried.
(a) portable (b) edible
(c) potable (d) bearable

40. A writer who steals ideas from others.
(a) plagiarist (b) copier
(c) editor (d) translator

41. Examination of a dead body.
(a) postmortem (b) surgery
(c) operation (d) tanning

42. A speech made to oneself.
(a) dialogue (b) speech
(c) soliloquy (d) intercourse

43. A commonplace remark.
(a) platitude (b) remark
(c) statement (d) epigram

44. That which cannot be perished.
(a) impregnable (b) incorrigible
(c) imperishable (d) invincible

45. The study of birds
(a) ornithology (b) philology
(c) orology (d) geology

46. An insect with many legs is called
(a) centipede (b) mammal
(c) herbivorous (d) vertebrate

47. A disease which ends in death.
(a) fatal (b) cancer
(c) lifesucking (d) deadly

48. Government in which all religions are honoured.
(a) fanatic (b) secular
(c) catholic (d) progressive

49. One who lives among strangers.
(a) recluse (b) alien
(c) stoic (d) rustic

50. A word no longer in use.
(a) extant (b) obsolete
(c) out-dated (d) nervous

51. A person who is more interested in himself rather than anything that is going on around him.
(a) introvert (b) extrovert
(c) eccentric (d) prophet

52. A person who gets help or advice from a lawyer or any professional man.
(a) despot (b) barrister
(c) client (d) party

53. A sneering person who always finds faults.
(a) cupid (b) kleptomaniac
(c) cynic (d) crone

54. A place for keeping bees.
(a) aviary (b) apiary
(c) cage (d) nest

55. A long journey, especially by sea.
(a) flight (b) voyage
(c) odyssey (d) safari

56. A short walk for pleasure or exercise.
(a) stroll (b) gallop
(c) jog (d) promenade

57. A place where government or public records are kept.
(a) *attuic* (b) museum
(c) cellar (d) archive

58. A person who kills somebody especially for political reasons.
(a) criminal (b) assassin
(c) murderer (d) hangman

59. A person who opposes another.
(a) soldier (b) fighter
(c) antagonist (d) prophet

60. A person carrying a message from one place to another.
(a) postman (b) messenger
(c) peon (d) bearer

61. A person who does not want to see the realities of life and tries to escape.

(a) escapist (b) hovel
(c) plunderer (d) scavenger

62. A person who is very selective, disgusted easily, and is hard to please.
(a) misanthrope (b) fastidious
(c) selector (d) ambiguous

63. A person who can be cheated easily.
(a) credulous (b) faithful
(c) client (d) egoist

64. A plant or animal living on another.
(a) parasite (b) hydra
(c) creeper (d) bush

65. A sweet music.
(a) lullaby (b) melody
(c) folk song (d) duet

66. A place where everything is perfect.
(a) heaven (b) platoon
(c) cosmos (d) utopia

67. A figure with more than four angles or sides.
(a) polygon (b) octagon
(c) parallelogram (d) pentagon

68. Something that cannot be harmed.
(a) strong (b) harmless
(c) inviolate (d) affected

69. An artificial pond or tank for keeping fish or aquatic plants.
(a) aquarium (b) reservoir
(c) squad (d) pool

70. Decision that cannot be taken back.
(a) irrevocable (b) rigid
(c) order (d) brief

71. Fear of crowds.
(a) oclophobia (b) hydrophobia
(c) xenophobia (d) whoopee

72. Physical features of an area.
(a) geography (b) sociology
(c) contour (d) topography

73. Release of a prisoner from jail on certain terms and conditions.
(a) parole (b) parley
(c) pardon (d) acquit

74. Scientific study of fungi.
(a) mycology (b) botany
(c) physiology (d) zoology

75. A thing kept in the memory of a person.
(a) memento (b) epitaph
(c) elegy (d) gift

76. Words inscribed on a tomb.
(a) epitaph (b) memento
(c) lyric (d) honour

77. The place where clothes are washed.
(a) laundry (b) mortuary
(c) kit (d) wardrobe

78. A funeral bell.
(a) knell (b) replica
(c) windfall (d) call

79. A speech given at the opening of a cer-emony.
(a) inaugural (b) prelude
(c) welcome (d) thanks

80. A person who is pure and clean.
(a) immaculate (b) neat
(c) clean (d) irrevocable

81. A person who has just started learning.
(a) novice (b) foreman
(c) supervisor (d) apprentice

82. A person who is filled with excessive enthusiasm.
(a) extrovert (b) fanatic
(c) fastidious (d) introvert

83. A person who is appointed by two parties to solve a dispute.
(a) judge (b) arbitrator
(c) advocate (d) barrister

84. A person who wishes to throw over all establishments.
(a) anarchist (b) hooligan
(c) criminal (d) rebel

85. A person claiming to be superior in culture and intellect to others.
(a) highbrow (b) elite
(c) aristocrat (d) intellectual

86. A person who is bad in spelling.
(a) cacographist (b) linguist
(c) calligraphist (d) pedant

87. A person leaving his native country to settle in another.
(a) immigrant (b) emigrant
(c) traveller (d) nomad

88. A person coming to a foreign land to settle there.
(a) immigrant (b) emigrant
(c) visitor (d) tourist

89. A person living in the same time as another
(a) comrade (b) colleague
(c) contemporary (d) pedant

90. A person who speaks for another.
(a) reporter (b) spokesman
(c) alien (d) supporter

91. A person working in the same place with another.
(a) colleague (b) contemporary
(c) assistant (d) comrade

92. A person having the same name as another.
(a) namesake (b) absconder
(c) colleague (d) nickname

93. A person who is always dissatisfied.
(a) heresy (b) malcontent
(c) felon (d) surrogate

94. A person who enters without any invitation.
(a) thief (b) burglar
(c) vandal (d) intruder

95. A person who has beautiful handwriting.
(a) calligraphist (b) writer
(c) artist (d) painter

96. A person who is talkative.
(a) garrulous
(b) speaker
(c) orator
(d) laxative

97. A person who is ready to believe things.
(a) credulous
(b) faithful
(c) client
(d) egoist

98. One who cuts precious stones.
(a) lapidist (b) philatelist
(c) oculist (d) drover

99. A number of ships.
(a) fleet (b) galaxy
(c) constellation (d) group

100. Something that cannot be taken away.
(a) inalienable (b) edible
(c) legible (d) natural

ANSWER KEY

1. (b)	21. (b)	41. (a)	61. (a)	81. (d)
2. (a)	22. (a)	42. (c)	62. (b)	82. (a)
3. (a)	23. (b)	43. (a)	63. (a)	83. (b)
4. (c)	24. (b)	44. (c)	64. (a)	84. (a)
5. (b)	25. (d)	45. (a)	65. (b)	85. (a)
6. (b)	26. (c)	46. (a)	66. (d)	86. (a)
7. (b)	27. (a)	47. (a)	67. (a)	87. (b)
8. (a)	28. (b)	48. (b)	68. (c)	88. (a)
9. (b)	29. (d)	49. (b)	69. (a)	89. (c)
10. (b)	30. (c)	50. (b)	70. (a)	90. (b)
11. (a)	31. (c)	51. (a)	71. (a)	91. (a)
12. (c)	32. (a)	52. (c)	72. (d)	92. (a)
13. (c)	33. (b)	53. (c)	73. (a)	93. (b)
14. (a)	34. (a)	54. (b)	74. (a)	94. (d)
15. (b)	35. (b)	55. (b)	75. (a)	95. (a)
16. (b)	36. (a)	56. (a)	76. (a)	96. (a)
17. (b)	37. (b)	57. (d)	77. (a)	97. (a)
18. (b)	38. (a)	58. (b)	78. (a)	98. (a)
19. (a)	39. (a)	59. (c)	79. (a).	99. (a)
20. (b)	40. (a)	60. (b)	80. (a)	100. (a)

Appendix

Questions from Examination Papers

1. He does *unpaid work* for the Red Cross.
(a) honorific (b) honest
(c) honorary (d) honourable
(CDS)

2. The officer was *not willing to take a definite stand* on that point.
(a) vague (b) evasive
(c) ambiguous (d) complex
(RBI)

3. A *careful preservation and protection* of wildlife is the need of the hour.
(a) embarkment (b) promotion
(c) conservation (d) management
(e) enhancement
(Bank PO)

4. Rajesh was a *hater of learning and knowledge.*
(a) misogynist (b) misologist
(c) misanthropist (d) bibliophile
(MBA)

5. One who travels from place to place.
(a) itinerant (b) mendicant
(c) journeyman (d) tramp
(CBI)

6. A short walk for pleasure or exercise.
(a) jog (b) stroll
(c) gallop (d) promenade
(Income Tax)

7. That which cannot be understood.
(a) illegible (b) unintelligible
(c) unknown (d) undecipherable.
(Section Officers' Exam.)

8. To move along with quick, short twisting actions.
(a) swagger (b) stumble
(c) wriggle (d) crawl
(Transmission Executives)

9. One who can use either of his hands with ease.
(a) amateur (b) expert
(c) ambidextrous (d) gluttonous
(Railways)

10. One who promotes the idea of absence of government of any kind, when every man should be a law unto himself.
(a) anarchist (b) belligerent
(c) iconoclast (d) agnostic
(Asstt. grade)

11. Thing that can be felt or touched.
(a) pandemic (b) palpable
(c) paltry (d) panchromatic
(BSRB)

12. One who thinks that human nature is essentially evil.
(a) agnostic (b) misogynist
(c) cynic (d) sceptic
(Translator's Exam.)

13. A style in which a writer makes a display of his knowledge.
(a) pedantic (b) ornate
(c) verbose (d) pompous
(Central Excise)

14. To present opposing arguments or evidence.
(a) rebut (b) criticise
(c) rebuff (d) reprimand
(Bank PO)

15. Parts of a country behind the coast or a river's bank.
(a) swamps (b) archipelago
(c) hinterland (d) isthmus
(UDC)

16. One who loves books.
(a) bibliphoebe (b) bibliographer
(c) bibliophile (d) bibliophagist
(CBI)

17. A low area storm with high winds rotating about a centre of low atmospheric pressure.
(a) cyclone (b) tornado
(c) typhoon (d) hurricane
(Asstt. Grade)

18. Be the embodiment or perfect example of
(a) signify (b) characterise
(c) personify (d) masquerade
(Bank PO)

19. Constant effort to achieve something.
(a) perseverance (b) attempt
(c) enthusiasm (d) vigour
(SBI PO)

20. One who deserts his religion.
(a) deserter (b) turn-coat
(c) fanatic (d) apostate
(Railways)

21. Custom of having many wives.
(a) monogamy (b) bigamy
(c) polygamy (d) matrimony
(MBA)

22. Person who believes that God is everything and everything is God.
(a) agonostic (b) theist
(c) pantheist (d) pantechnicon
(BSRB)

23. Opposed to great or sudden change.
(a) static (b) revolutionary
(c) conservative (d) evolutionary
(SBI PO)

24. Relationship by blood or birth.
(a) parentage
(b) affiliation
(c) consanguinity
(d) nepotism
(Translator's Exam.)

25. Belief or opinion contrary to what is generally accepted.
(a) unbelief (b) superstition
(c) non-conformity (d) heresy
(Central Excise)

ANSWER KEY

1. (c)	6. (d)	11. (b)	16. (c)	21. (c)
2. (c)	7. (b)	12. (c)	17. (b)	22. (c)
3. (c)	8. (c)	13. (a)	18. (b)	23. (c)
4. (b)	9. (c)	14. (a)	19. (a)	24. (c)
5. (d)	10. (a)	15. (c)	20. (d)	25. (d)

Spelling test is often a part of the English language section in examination papers. As a matter of fact, spelling of words is very difficult to master for native speakers and language learners alike. As English developed from several different language families, and because it so easily absorbs new words from other languages even today, the English language has many different ways to spell the same sound and many different ways to pronounce the same spelling. But improving your English spelling is not impossible with some patience, you will see a noticeable improvement in your spelling by using some techniques that good spellers use. We can make use of the common spelling rules that may help the learners.

Rule 1: Word endings

- No English word ends in 'v' except spiv. Use 've' instead.
- No English word ends in 'j'. Use 'ge' or 'dge' instead.
- No English word ends in 'i'. Use 'y' instead. Exceptions: macaroni, spaghetti, vermicelli (Italian) and taxi (short for taxicab).
- The word endings 'dge', 'tch', may only be used after a short vowel e.g. badge, hedge, lodge, fetch, Dutch, catch. Exceptions to this rule are: much, such, rich, which.
- We double 'l', 'f', 's' and 'z', after a single vowel at the end of a short word.e.g. call, tell, toss, miss, stiff, stuff, fizz, jazz. Exceptions to this spelling rule: us, bus, gas, if, of, this, yes, plus, nil, pal.

Two-syllable words that end with 's'.

Many words that end with 's' have the stress on the first syllable, e.g, crisis, bonus, crocus, circus, litmus and fungus .... These follow the rule the use only one's' at the end of the word.

If the stress is on the final syllable of a disyllabic word, the final's' 'is' doubled, e.g. address, redress, discuss, unless, dismiss, undress, remiss, amiss, recall, rebuff. Also, the letters're', 'dis' and 'un' in the examples above are prefixes, and the rule when adding these prefixes is to keep the base word the same and just add the prefix.

Two-syllable words that end with 'l'.

With regard to final 'l', and final 'f', the rule concerning prefixes applies, e.g. refill, recall, rebuff.

In words where there is no prefix, the question of where the stress lies does not apply. 'Fulfil' and 'until' have the stress on the final syllable and many words, e.g. pistol, petrol, petal, metal, lintel, lentil and pencil have the stress on the first syllable.

The letters 'ck' are used at the end of one-syllable base words that have a single short vowel, e.g, sack, stick, clock.

Use only a single letter 'c' at the end of words like picnic, cubic, metric and arithmetic.

Rule 2: Making Plurals

- Regular plurals are made by adding 's', e.g., dogs, horses, monkeys, cliffs.
- To form plurals of words with a hissing ending, add 'es'. Use **suffix** 'es' after s, x, z, sh, ch, ss in words like bonuses, boxes, fizzes, wishes, churches and misses.
- To make nouns ending in a single 'f' plural change the 'f' to 'v' before adding 'es' to form the plural, e.g., loaf, loaves; wolf, wolves, shelf, shelves. Exceptions to this rule are: dwarfs, roofs, chiefs.
- Words ending in an 'o' preceded by a consonant usually end in suffix 'es' to form the plural, e.g., potato-es, volcano-es, torpedo-es. Some exceptions are: pianos, solos, Eskimos.

Rule 3: Adding suffixes

- Short words ending in both a single vowel and a single consonant always double the last consonant before adding a suffix (ending) beginning with a vowel, e.g., hop, hopped, hopping; flat, flatter, flatten; win, winner, winning; bit, bitty, bitten . We sometimes refer to these base words as 1,1,1 words because they have one vowel, one consonant after the vowel, and one syllable. Examples of vowel suffixes are: ed, es, ing, en, y, al, able and ible.
- **Do not** double the final consonant when the base word has two vowels or two final consonants, e.g., leaf, leafy; shout, shouting; fool, foolish; self, selfish; mend, mending.
- Drop the final 'e' from a root word before adding a suffix beginning with a vowel, but keep it before a consonant suffix. e.g., love, loving, lovely; taste, tasting, tasty; ride, bubble, bubbling, bubbly: drive, driving, driver; rattle, rattled, rattling.
- 'Ful' is a suffix added onto the end of a root (or base) word. It has only one 'l', e.g., hopeful, useful, cheerful. Because this suffix begins with a consonant, just add it to the base (root) word, without changing the root word. Notice that we keep the silent e in 'hopeful' and 'useful' above.
- Other consonant suffixes follow the same rule as above. They include 'ment', 'ly', ty, 'ness', 'less'. They are used to make words like 'statement', 'lonely', 'cruelty', 'lateness' and 'homeless'. Remember to keep the final 'e' of thee base word in word spellings like this.
- If a word ends in a consonant plus 'y', change the 'y' to 'i' before adding any suffix except 'ing'. e.g. lady, ladies; party, parties; 'heavy', 'heavier', 'heaviest'; 'marry', 'married'; 'funny', 'funnily'; but there are some exceptions, e.g. 'cry', 'crying'; 'hurry', 'hurrying'.
- If a base word ends with the letters 'oy', 'ay', or 'ey', do not change the final 'y' to 'i' when adding any vowel suffix, e.g. annoying, played, displayed, surveyed, boyish. Exceptions to this are the words 'said', 'paid' and 'laid'.

Rule 4: Adding prefixes

- The letters 'al' are a prefix followed by another syllable in words like 'also', 'already', 'always', 'although'. Although the word 'all' has two lls, the prefix 'al' has only one 'l'.
- Other prefixes are: re, pre, de, in, im, un, en, under, over, dis, and mis, as in rethink, preset, deactivate, incapable, impossible, undecided, enslave, underachieve, overcook, discontinue and so on.

Rule 5: Using 'soft' c and 'soft' g

- When 'c' is followed by 'e', 'i', or 'y', it says 's'. Otherwise it says 'k', e.g., city, centre, ceiling, circle, cycle, receive, access.
- When 'g' is followed by 'e', 'i', or 'y' it says 'j'. Otherwise it says 'g' as in gold, e.g., gentle, giant, gymnastic, gyroscope.Exceptions: get, begin, girl, give, gear, gees

Rule 6 : for using 'w' and 'qu'

- When 'w' or 'qu' comes before 'a' it often says (wo) or (kwa) as in wash, want, wander, wallet, quarrel and quads.
- When 'w' comes before 'or' it often says (wer) as in worm, word, work, worth, worship. Exceptions include worry, worried, wore, worn.
- When 'w' or 'qu' come before 'ar', it often says (wor) or (quor) as in war, ward, warden, quarter, quart.
- The sound (kw) is written as 'qu'. It never stands by itself. The letter u is a "silent" partner. It is not a "sounded vowel" when used after the letter q.

Rule 7: Using 'i' and 'e' together to make one sound

- 'i' comes before 'e' when it is pronounced 'ee', except when it follows 'c', e.g. brief, field, priest, receive, deceive, ceiling.
- 'e' comes before 'i' when sounded like (ay) as in neighbour and weigh.

The letters i and e are sometimes used together and sounded as separate vowels, e.g. in diet, quiet and client.

Rule 8 : Using 'ti', 'ci' or 'si' to make the sound (sh)

- 'ti', 'ci', 'si', are three spellings most frequently used to say 'sh' at the beginning of all syllables except the first, e.g., nation, patient, torrential, infectious, spacious, ancient, optician, financial, tension, session, admission, pension, division.

Rule 9 : Doubling 'l' and 't' in multi-syllabic words before suffixes

- In words ending in a single 'l' after a single vowel, double the 'l' before adding a suffix regardless of accent, e.g., cancelled, levelling, travelled, signalling, metallic.
- If a word of more than one syllable ends in a 't', preceded by a single vowel, and has the accent (stress) on the last syllable, double the final consonant, e.g., permit, permitted; admit, admitted; regret, regretted; but do not double the final t in words like visit, visited; benefit, benefited because the stress is on the first syllable of the root or base word.

Another important point to keep in mind is to watch some easily confusable words.

English words have identical or similar pronunciations but different spellings. Using the wrong word of a homophone pair is one of the most common spelling pitfalls for all writers. Learn to check these types of commonly misspelled words carefully during your revision.

accept/except	discreet/discrete
oral/aural	adverse/averse
elude/allude	palette/palate
affect/effect	eminent/imminent
populace/populous	altar/alter
ensure/insure	precede/proceed
boarder/border	elicit/illicit
prescribe/proscribe	broach/brooch
hanger/hangar	principle/principal
callous/callus	illusion/allusion
right/write/rite	casual/causal
incidents/incidence	stationary/stationery
censor/censure	isle/aisle
tenet/tenant	cite/site/sight
its/it's	there/their/they're
climactic/climatic	led/lead
tortuous/torturous	compliment/complement
liquor/liqueur	waver/waiver
conscience/conscious	lose/loose
whose/who's	desert/dessert
naval/navel	your/you're

Some Commonly Misspelled Words

Accelerate
Accessible
Accessory
Accommodate
Acknowledge
Acquaint
Acquire
Across
Aficionado
Aggressive
Amphitheatre
Anecdote
Anomaly
Apparent
Arctic
Asphalt
Auxiliary
Indispensable
Inedible
Innocuous
Inoculate
Intercede
Invigorate
Iridescent
Irresistible
Laboratory
Leisure
Liaison
Manoeuvre / maneuver
Mayonnaise
Medieval
Mediterranean
Memento
Millennium
Minuscule
Miscellaneous
Mischievous
Misspell
non sequitur
Noticeable
Nuptial
Occasion
Occurrence
Offered
Ophthalmology
Pageant
Parallel
Parliament

Fiery
Fluorescent
Fluoride
Foresee
fulfill / fulfil
Government
Grammar
Grievous
Guarantee
Handiwork
Handkerchief
Harass
Heinous
Hemorrhage
Hygiene
Hypocrisy
Idiosyncrasy
Remuneration
Rendezvous
Renowned
Repertoire
Restaurateur
Rhyme
Rhythm
Sacrilegious
Seize
Seizure
Separate
Sergeant
Silhouette
Smorgasbord
Solely
Soliloquy
Sophomore
Subtle
Supersede
Susceptible
Synonymous
Tariff
Tenterhook
Threshold
Tortuous
Tragedy
Ukrainian
Vaccinate
Vacillate
Vague
Weird

Pastime
Pejorative
Penultimate
Perennial
Perseverance
Persuade
Phenomenon
Pneumonia
Portuguese
Pre-eminent
Prerogative
Privilege
Pronunciation
Proverbial
Pursue
Quandary
ReceiveBachelor
Berserk
Besiege
Bizarre
bookkeeper / bookkeeping
Caffeine
Camaraderie
Caribbean
Category
Collaborate
Committee
Concede
Consensus
Corollary
Curriculum
Deceive
de rigueur
Desiccate
Dilapidated
Diphtheria
Diphthong
Dissension
Duly
Dysfunction
Ecstasy
Embarrass
Exaggerate
Excerpt
Exhilarate
Experiential
February

Practice Set—1

Directions: From the following group of words, choose the misspelt word.

1. (a) Interdependent (b) Squalor (c) Permanent (d) Unrivalled
2. (a) Broccoli (b) Imperceptable (c) Communicable (d) Tantalise
3. (a) Bedouin (b) Tyranise (c) Expeditious (d) Pernickety
4. (a) Pasteurize (b) Relinquish (c) Sedition (d) Zelot
5. (a) Dependency (b) Embankment (c) Erodes (d) Illuminant
6. (a) Resplendant (b) Evanescence (c) Asininity (d) Imbecile
7. (a) Paroxym (b) Zealotism (c) Schizophrenia (d) Crochetiness
8. (a) Renaissence (b) Unravelling (c) Bibliophile (d) Canvass
9. (a) Riposte (b) Surreptitious (c) Notoriety (d) Resucitate
10. (a) Camouflage (b) Exagerating (c) Apocryphal (d) Perseverance
11. (a) Vaeilate (b) Vaccilate (c) Vacrelate (d) Vacillate
12. (a) Telbou (b) Tableau (c) Tablo (d) Teblo
13. (a) Semblence (b) Samblance (c) Semblance (d) Samblence
14. (a) axtemout (b) Tantamount (c) Tentamonious (d) Tentemount
15. (a) Sanctimonious (b) Sanktimioious (c) Sanctimonius (d) Senctimonious
16. (a) Reminisent (b) Riminescent (c) Rimnescent (d) Reminiscent
17. (a) Penchromatic (b) Pennchromatick (c) Penchrimatic (d) Panchromatic
18. (a) Recalcitrant (b) Recallcitrant (c) Ricalcetrant (d) Recalcittrant
19. (a) Expartiate (b) Expatriat (c) Expetriate (d) Expettriat
20. (a) Pedagog (b) Pedagogue (c) Pedagoge (d) Pedegogue
21. (a) Fascism (b) Facism (c) Facsism (d) Fasiom
22. (a) Idiosyncrasy (b) Idiosyneracy (c) Ideosincracy (d) Idosyncraso
23. (a) Pankromatic (b) Panchromatic (c) Pechromatic (d) Panchrometic
24. (a) Flabergast (b) Flebergast (c) Flbbergast (d) Flabbergast
25. (a) Jeopardise (b) Jeoppardise (c) Jeoparddiz (d) Jeoppardise
26. (a) Fourboding (b) Frerbboding (c) Foreboding (d) Forebodding
27. (a) Mustache (b) Moustash (c) Mostache (d) Moustache
28. (a) Etiquate (b) Etiquette (c) Etiquete (d) Etiquatte
29. (a) Acquiesee (b) Acqisce (c) Acquice (d) Acquiesce
30. (a) Cantenkorous (b) Cantancrous (c) Cantankerous (d) Contankrous

Practice Set—2

Directions: The following words are spelt wrong; however, the addition of a letter to each will make it correct. Identify the missing letter.

1. Ocurrence
2. Accomodinc
3. Desicant
4. Deliquent
5. Excekncе
6. Coquete
7. Simultaneus
8. Continualy
9 Potasuim
10 Odipus
11 Ameba
12 Vacum
13 Physionomy
14 Pitutary
15 Plebisite
16 Crokery
17. Aborigin

18. Chlorophyl
19. Hamorrhage
20. Epitom
21. Subpena
22. Zorostrian
23. Transferee
24. Odorus
25. Entreprenur
26. Hygene
27. Buffonery
28. Marriagable
29. Ocasion
30. Polytecnic
31. Sesqucentenary
32. Fasinated

Practice Set —3

Choose the correct option.

1. We requested the hotel to ________(conform/confirm) our reservation by telegram.
2. The __________(lone/lore) of bears includes many fascinating stories about their habits.
3. Anne Frank wrote in her________(diary/dairy), her experience of war.
4. The accountant was ________(loathe/loath) to accept a job in a new territory.
5. Good health is largely______(dependent/dependant) on proper nourishment.
6. The ________(later/latter) works of Beethoven are the composer's best.
7. Primitive people________(deify/defy) the sun.
8. Ram was________(ingenuous/ingenious) at solving difficult crossword puzzles in The Hindu.
9. She invented a ________(device/devise) that automatically closes windows when it rains.
10. Our Bermuda vacation was a perfect________(idle/ idyll) .
11. There's nothing to beat a little______(doze/douse) after lunch for that sense of well-being.
12. The thief was sent to ________(jail/ joal) for 6 months for his part in the robbery.
13. The Chief minister's remarks did nothing but ________(elicit/ illiciit) a food of letters.
14. The students showed a________(flagrant/fragrant) abuse of the headmaster's authority.
15. The__________(illusive/elusive) state of tranquillity soon erupted into war by the bombing of Pearl Harbour.

ANSWER KEY

Practice Set 1

1. (a)	2. (b)	3. (b)	4. (d)	5. (c)	6. (a)
7. (a)	8. (a)	9. (d)	10. (b)	11. (d)	12. (a)
13. (c)	14. (a)	15. (c)	16. (c)	17. (b)	18. (c)
19. (b)	20. (a)	21. (c)	22. (c)	23. (b)	24. (c)
25. (a)	26. (c)	27. (c)	28. (a)	29. (c)	30. (b)

Practice Set 2

1. Occurrence	2. Accommodation	3. Desiccant	4. Delinquent	5. Excellence
6. Coquette	7. Simultaneous	8. Continually	9. Potassium	10. Oedipus
11. Amoeba	12. Vacuum	13. Physiognomy	14. Pituitary	15. Plebiscite
16. Crockery	17. Aborigine	18. Chlorophyll	19. Haemorrhage	20. Epitome
21. Subpoena	22. Zoroastrian	23. Transferred	24. Odorous	25. Entrepreneur
26. Hygiene	27. Buffoonery	28. Marriageable	29. Occasion	30. Polytechnic
31. Sesquicentenary	32. Fascinated.			

Practice Set 3

1. confirm	2. lore	3. diary	4. loath	5. dependant
6. latter	7. deify	8. ingenious	9. device	10. idyll
11. doze	12. jail	13. elicit	14. flagrant	15. elusive

PART SIX

OTHER IMPORTANT TOPICS

This part deals with some topics which have not been covered in any other part of the book, but are important from the point of view of some examinations. Voice and Narration are important components of the test in the SSC examinations. Questions on Voice are at times asked in other exams also. Knowledge of prepositions helps in solving questions on sentence errors, sentence improvement and sentence completion. Idioms and Phrases are often a major component of banking and management examinations. Analogy combines logic and language and is often tested in management tests.

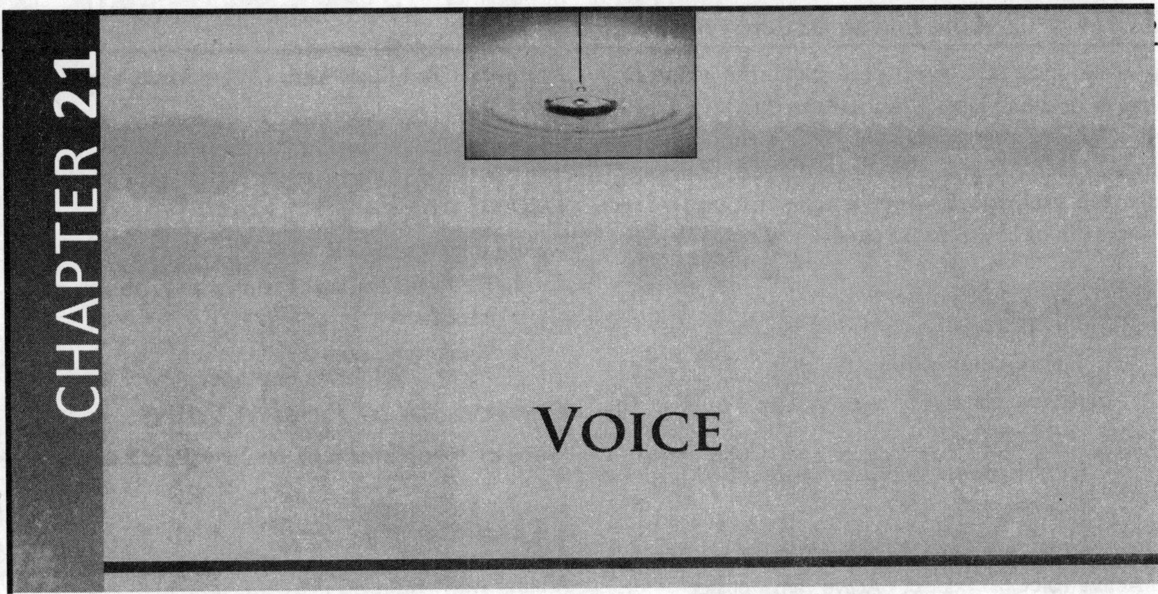

VOICE

Introduction

In grammar, voice is a feature of verb. It tells whether the subject of verb acts or is acted upon. English has two voice: *active* and *passive*.

A verb is in the active voice when its subject is the doer, of the action. For example, the verb is in active voice in the sentence *Hari reads a book* because the subject; *Hari* performs the action; *reads*.

A verb is in *passive* voice when its subject receives the action. For example, in the sentence *The book was read by Hari.* The subject, *book*, receives the action, *was read*.

Let us study the two voices in detail.

Active Voice

A verb is in Active Voice when its form shows that the subject does something.

In sentences written in Active Voice, the subject performs the action expressed in the verb; i.e. the subject *acts*.

EXAMPLES

1. The **dog** *bit* the boy.
2. **Pooja** *will present* her research at the conference.
3. **Scientists** *have conducted* experiments to test the hypothesis.

In each example the subject of the sentence performs the action expressed in the verb.

Construction of the Active Voice

The normal pattern is of a sentence in active voice is:

(S + V) or (S + V + O)

where S = Subject, V = Verb and O = Object

Let us study this pattern in the following examples:

EXAMPLES

1. The dog	bit	the boy
Subject	*Verb*	*Object*
2. Pooja	will present at the conference	the research
Subject	*Verb*	*Object*
3. Scientists	have conducted	experiments to test the hypothesis.
Subject	*Verb*	*Object*

Passive Voice

In sentences written in Passive Voice, the subject receives the action expressed in the verb; i.e. the subject is acted upon. The agent performing the action may appear in the phrase *by the...*, or the phrase or may be omitted. The passive contains some form of the verb *be*: such as *is, was, were, or been*, plus the part participle of the verb. Only *transitive verbs* or verbs that take a direct object can be charged into passive voice.

EXAMPLES

1. The **boy** *was bitten* by the dog.
2. **Research** *will be presented* by Pooja at the conference.
3. **Experiments** *have been conducted* to test the hypothesis.

Note: agent performing action has been omitted.

Active voice: Subject + Active verb + object

Passive voice: Subject + passive verb + 'by' + agent

Construction of the Passive Voice

The structure of the Passive Voice is as follows:

{Subject + Auxiliary Verb (*be*) + Main Verb (*past participle*)}

Look at the examples given in the table below.

Use of the Passive Voice

We use the Passive Voice when:

1. We want to make the active object more important
2. We do not know the active subject.

Conversion to Passive Voice

(Subject + finite form of *to be* + Past Participle)

EXAMPLES

A letter was written.

When rewriting active sentences in Passive Voice, note the following:

1. The object of the active sentence becomes the subject to the passive sentence.
2. The finite form of the verb is changed *to be* + *past participle*
3. The subject of the active sentence becomes the object of the passive sentence (or is dropped).

Table 10.1

Subject	*Auxiliary Verb (to be)*		*Main Verb (past participle)*	*Agent*
water	is		drunk	by everyone.
Hundred people	are		employed	by this company.
I	am		paid	in Euros.
We	are	not	paid	in Dollars
Are	they		paid	in yen?

Table 10.2

	Subject	*Verb*
Give importance to active object (President Kennedy)	President Kennedy	was killed
Active subject unknown	My wallet	has been stolen.

Comparison of Active and Passive Voices

1. Passive sentence with one object.

Table 10.3

Tense	*Voice*	*Subject*	*Verb*	*Object*
Simple Present	Active	Rita	writes	a letter
	Passive	A letter	is written	by Rita
Simple Past	Active	Rita	wrote	a letter
	Passive	A letter	was written	by Rita
Present Perfect	Active	Rita	has written	a letter
	Passive	A letter	has been written	by Rita
Future I	Active	Rita	will write	a letter
	Passive	A letter	will be written	by Rita
Present Progressive	Active	Rita	is writing	a letter
	Passive	A letter	is being written	by Rita
Past Progressive	Active	Rita	was writing	a letter
	Passive	A letter	was being written	by Rita
Past Perfect	Active	Rita	had written	a letter
	Passive	A letter	had been written	by Rita
Future II	Active	Rita	will have written	a letter
	Passive	A letter	will have been written	by Rita
Conditional I	Active	Rita	would write	a letter
	Passive	A letter	would be written	by Rita
Conditional II	Active	Rita	would have written	a letter
	Passive	A letter	would have been written	by Rita

Passive Sentences with Two Objects

Rewriting an active sentence with two objects in passive voice means that one of the two objects becomes the subject, the other one remains an object. Which object to transform into a subject depends on what you want to focus upon in the sentence.

Table 10.4

Voice	*Subject*	*Verb*	*Object 1*	*Object 2*
Active	Rita	wrote	a letter	to me
Passive	A letter	was written	to me	by Rita
Passive	I	was written	a letter	by Rita

Note: As you can see in the examples, adding *by Rita* does not appear to add to the meaning of the sentence as the fact that *a letter was written to me* is the focus of the sentence. Since the agent here is not the focus it can be dropped.

Usage

Most critics agree that for effective writing a writer must as a rule prefer the active voice and avoid passive voice. However, there are certain situation where passive voice may make for more effective writing then active voice.

Passive voice has to do with how important is the identity of the actor in relation to the recipient of the action. When the actor is focus of subject matter active voice should be used. But when the result or the recipient in a sentence is the focus of the Sentence passive voice should be used.

EXAMPLES

- The ballots have been counted.
- Sometimes our efforts are not fully appreciated.

Syntactical Changes in the Active-Passive Conversion Process

Present Indefinite Tense

Active Voice

Subject	*Verb*	*Object*
I	love	my children
Subject	Very	Object

Passive Voice

Subject + helping verb (is/am/are) + past participle + by + object

My children are loved by me
Subject Helping Verb + Past Participle by + Object

Present Continuous Tense

Active Voice

Subject + helping verb (is/am/are) + verb + ing + object

Children are helping the poor
Subject Helping Verb + Verb + ing Object

Passive Voice

Subject + helping verb (is/am/are) + being + third form of verb + by + object

The poor are being helped by children
Subject Helping Verb + Present Progressive by + Object

EXAMPLES

Active Voice

They are not holding a meeting
Subject Verb Present Progressive Object

Passive Voice

A meeting is not being held by them
Subject Helping Verb + Present Progressive by+ Object

Active Voice

Chikky is writing a letter
Subject Helping Verb + Verb + ing Object

Passive Voice

A letter is being written by Chikky.
Subject Helping Verb Present Progressive

Present Perfect Tense

Active Voice

Subject + helping verb (has/have) + Past Participle + object

Monu has invited all his friends
Subject Present Perfect Object

Passive Voice

Subject + helping verb (has/have + been) + Past Participle + by + object

All his friends have been invited by Monu
Subject Present Perfect Progressive by + Object

OTHER EXAMPLES

Active Voice

You have borrowed my book.

Passive Voice

My book has been borrowed by you

Active Voice

I have lost my watch

Passive Voice

My watch has been lost by me

Past Indefinite Tense

Active Voice

Subject + Past tense + object

They elected him president

Subject Past tense Object

Passive Voice

Subject + helping verb (was/were) + Past Participle + by + object

He was elected president by them.

Subject Helping Verb Past Participle by + Object

OTHER EXAMPLES

Active Voice

They kept us waiting

Subject Simple Past Object

Passive Voice

We were kept waiting by them

Subject Helping Verb Past Progressive by + Object

Active Voice

He bought a watch yesterday

Subject Simple Past Object

Passive Voice

A watch was bought by him yesterday

Subject Helping Verb Past Participle by + Object

Past Continuous Tense

Active Voice

Subject + helping verb (was/were) + verb + ing + object

The horses were drawing a cart.

Subject Helping Verb + Verb + ing Object

Passive Voice

Subject + helping verb (was/were + being) + Past Participle + by + object

A cart was being drawn by the horses.

Subject Helping Verb Past Progressive by + Object

OTHER EXAMPLES

Active Voice

The players were making a noise.

Passive Voice

Anoise was being made by the player.

Past Perfect Tense

Active Voice

Subject + helping verb (had) + Past Perfect

Rani had never seen it before.

Subject Helping + Verb Past Participle Object

Passive Voice

Subject + helping verb (had been) + Past Perfect

It had never been seen by Rani before

Subject Helping Verb Past Perfect Object

OTHER EXAMPLES

Active Voice

By eighteen years of age, Dilip had taken the degree.

Passive Voice

By eighteen years of age, the degree had been taken by Dilip.

Future Indefinite Tense

Passive Voice

Subject + helping verb (shall/will) + verb + object

(i) He will write a letter
Subject Helping Verb Verb Object

(ii) We shall teach him
Subject Helping Verb Verb Object

Passive Voice

Subject + helping verb (shall/will+be) + by + object

(i) A letter will be written by him
Subject Helping Verb Past Participle by Object

(ii) He will be taught by us
Subject Helping Verb Past Participle by + Object

Future Perfect Tense

Active Voice

Subject + helping verb (will have/shall have) + Past Participle + Object

(i) They will have planted trees.
Subject Helping Verb Past Participle Object

(ii) The teacher will have called the roll
Subject Helping Verb Past Participle Object

Passive Voice

Subject + helping verb (will have/shall have + been) + Past Participle + by + object

(i) Trees will have been planted by them
Subject Helping Verb Past Participle by + Object

(ii) The roll will have been called by the teacher.
Subject Helping Verb Past Participle by + Object

Other Types of Sentences

There are few verbs which take two objects, a Direct Object and an Indirect Object.

For such sentences, there are two forms of Passive Voice sentences.

1. Verb with two Objects

EXAMPLES

(Active Voice) I gave *him five rupees.*
(Passive Voice) Five rupees were given to him by me.
He was given five rupees by me.

(Active Voice) She has told *me the truth.*
(Passive Voice) I was told the truth by her.
The truth was told to me by her.

(Active Voice) They lent *me their car.*
(Passive Voice) I was lent a car by them.
A car was lent to me by them.

(Active Voice) The government has sent *him a message.*
(Passive Voice) He was sent a message by the government.
A message was sent to him by the government.

2. Imperative Sentence (Commands and Requests)

There is a special formula for changing an imperative sentence into Passive Voice.

(Active Voice) Please open the door.
(Passive Voice) Let the door be opened by you.

Hence the sentence in Active Voice has been changed into a sentence in Passive Voice. "Let" is used to convert the Active Voice sentence into a Passive Voice sentence.

EXAMPLES

(Active Voice) Do not mistake me.
(Passive Voice) *Let* me not be mistaken.
(Active Voice) Cut your nails.
(Passive Voice) *Let* your nails be cut.
(Active Voice) Do not ignore my suggestions.
(Passive Voice) *Let* not my suggestions be ignored.

3. With Modal Verbs

The verbs *can*, *could*, *may*, *might*, and *must* are known as Modal Verbs, as per the following.

OTHER EXAMPLES

(Active Voice) You can take the book.
(Passive Voice) The book can be taken by you.
(Active Voice) Everybody must obey the rules.
(Passive Voice) The rules must be obeyed by everybody.
(Active Voice) They might have studied their lessons
(Passive Voice) Their lessons might have been studied by them.
(Active Voice) He may not accept this plan.
(Passive Voice) This lesson may not be accepted by him.

4. Phrasal Verbs

Some verbs, with certain meaning, are always used with prepositions. In such situations, the prepositions should not be omitted in the sentences.

EXAMPLES

(Active Voice) We are *looking at* the game.
(Passive Voice) The game is being *looked at* by us.
(Active Voice) The fire-brigade *put out* the fire.
(Passive Voice) The fire was *put out by* the fire-brigade.
(Active Voice) The government will *set up* a factory.
(Passive Voice) A factory will be *set up* by the government.

5. With Clauses

In some sentences, instead of a word or a phrase, a clause may be the object of a verb. In such cases there are two ways of changing the sentence into Passive Voice.

A. By making the clause itself as the subject in the Passive Voice

(Active Voice) I hope *that he will realize his mistake.*
(Passive Voice) *That his mistake will be realized* is hoped by us.
(Active Voice) I expected *that they would take up the matter.*
(Passive Voice) *That the matter would be taken up* by them was expected by me.

B. By substituting the clause with pronoun it.

EXAMPLES

(Active Voice) The Romans expected *that they would conquer Carthage.*
(Passive Voice) *It was expected by the Romans* that Carthage would be conquered by them.
(Active Voice) We have learned *that you have secured the first rank.*
(Passive Voice) *It has been learned by us* that the first rank has been secured by you.

MORE EXAMPLES

(Active Voice) The grandmother was telling *her grandchildren an interesting story.*
(Passive Voice) *An interesting story* was being told by the grandmother to her grandchildren.
Her grandchildren were being told an interesting story be their grandmother.
(Active Voice) The postman brought *you a parcel.*
(Passive Voice) *A parcel was brought* to you by a postman.
You were brought a parcel by the postman.
(Active Voice) I have taught *the class the first lesson.*
(Passive Voice) *The first lesson was taught* by me to the class.
The class was taught the first lesson by me.
(Active Voice) The waiter *brought us the menu card.*
(Passive Voice) *The menu card was brought* to us by the waiter.
We were brought the menu card by the waiter.

(Active Voice) They are offering *you another chance.*

(Passive Voice) *You are being offered* another chance by them.

Another chance is being offered to you by them.

(Active Voice) He had told *me a lie.*

(Passive Voice) *I had been told* a lie by him.

A lie had been told to me by him.

(Active Voice) I gave her *your message.*

(Passive Voice) *She was given* your message by me.

Your message was given to her by me.

(Active Voice) Who taught *you Sanskrit?*

(Passive Voice) *Sanskrit was taught* to you by whom?

You were taught Sanskrit by whom?

(Active Voice) Sign *these documents.*

(Passive Voice) *Let these documents* be signed.

CHAPTER 22

PREPOSITIONS

A preposition is a word *which shows the relationship between two objects indicating their position,* such as:

The book is on the table.

On shows the relationship between the book and the table.

Some of the important prepositions are listed below.

Prepositions Showing Time

1. At, in

'At' is used with a definite point of time in mind.

I go to my Department at 7.30. a.m. everyday.

He will come at Holi.

'In' is generally used to denote a specific time, period, month, year.

I play chess in the evening.

I shall come in the next month.

Exception: 'At' is used with noon.

He comes at noon for lunch.

2. On, by

'On' is used with days and dates.

He was born on the 9th of July.

I teach Wordsworth on every Monday.

'By' refers to the latest time by which an action will be over.

The meeting will break by 4 p.m.

3. For, since

'For' denotes a period of time and is used with the perfect continuous tense.

I have been working in Magadh University for the last 27 years.

'Since' shows the point of time. It also indicates continuity.

India has been independent since 1947.

4. From

'From' refers to the starting point of an action.

He is joining the new firm from the 1st of May.

Prepositions Showing Position

1. At, in

'At' refers to an exact point.
He lives at Anugrahapuri.

'In' refers to a big area.
He lives in Bihar.

2. Between, among

'Between' is used to distinguish two persons and things.
The property was divided between Ram and Shyam.

'Among' is used for more than two persons or things.
The food was distributed among the ten boys in the family.

3. Amongst

'Amongst' is also used with more than two persons or things but is always used before a vowel.
Divide the oranges amongst us.

4. Above, below

'Above' is used for higher than.
The aeroplane was flying high in the sky, in fact, above the clouds.

'Below' is used for lower than.
His output is below ours.

5. Under, over

'Under' is used for vertically below.
We sit under the tree when we have no class.

'Over' indicates something vertically above.
There is a separate room over the garage.

6. Beneath

'Beneath' shows a lower position.
The ground was soiled beneath her.

Prepositions Showing Direction

1. *To* is used to indicate movement from one place to another.
The children go *to* the school every morning.

2. *Towards* points out a particular direction.
The Lion ran *towards* the hunter.

3. *Into* indicates a movement inside something.
The thief entered *into* the room.

4. *At* indicates aim.
The hunter aimed *at* the bird.

5. *For* denotes direction.
I shall start *for* Patna today.

6. *Off* refers to separation.
He was thrown *off* from the car during the accident.

7. *From* refers to a point of departure.
We feel unhappy when we depart *from* our parents.

8. *Against* shows pressure.
I rested my arms *against* the wall.

9. *Along* shows the same line.
I walked *along* the shore.

10. *Across* means from one side.
I ran *across* the road.

11. B*efore* denotes face-to-face.
I was standing *before* my wife.

12. *Behind* means at the back of someone or something.
My daughter stood *behind* me.

13. *Beside* means by the side of.
The security guard sits beside the officer.

14. *After* refers to a sequence.
The child came running *after* the mother.

A Stock of Prepositions

(Some Important Prepositions)

A

1. abound *with*
2. absolve *from* (blame)
3. abstain *from*
4. according *to*
5. accordance *with*
6. accuse *of*
7. accustomed *to*
8. acquaint *with*
9. acquit *of*
10. admit *to* (hospital, place, class, etc.)
11. averse *to*
12. affiliate *to*/ *with*
13. afflict *with*
14. afraid *of*
15. agree *to*/ *on*
16. aim *at*
17. allegation *about*
18. alude *to*
19. alternate *with*
20. alternative *to*
21. appear *for* (examination)/ *at*
22. angry *with*
23. apply *to* (body)
24. appreciation *of*
25. apprise *of*
26. approximate *to*
27. arraign *against*
28. arrest *in*
29. arrive *at*/ *in*
30. ashamed *of*
31. aspire *to*/ *after*/ *at*
32. associate *with*
33. assure *of*
34. attribute *to*
35. averse *from*/ *to*

B

1. begin *on*
2. belief *in*
3. bereft *of*
4. beset *with*
5. beware *of*
6. blink *at*
7. blow down (the roof)/ *off* / *over* (pass off)
8. boast *of*
9. break *off*
10. bungle *over*
11. busy *with*
12. busy *in* (market, store)/ *at* (shop)

C

1. compare *with*/ *to*
2. compatible *with*
3. complain *of*
4. comply *with*
5. compliment *on*
6. compared *of*
7. concur *in*
8. condole *with*
9. conducive *to*
10. confer *on*
11. confirmation *of*
12. confirm *to*
13. congratulate *on*
14. conscious *of*
15. consist *of* (to denote the substance)/in (define the subject)
16. contiguity *with*
17. converge *on*
18. convict *of*
19. co-opt *to*
20. cope *with*
21. correspond *with*
22. cost *of*
23. credit *with*
24. criticism *of*
25. cure *of*

D

1. deal *with* (somebody)/*in (goods)*
2. debar *from*
3. decide *on*
4. deliberate *on*
5. delight *in*
6. denude *of*
7. depart *to of*
8. departure *for*
9. depend *on/upon*
10. deprive *of*
11. derive *from*
12. derogate *from*
13. derogatory *to*
14. desist *from*
15. despair *of*
16. detrimental *to*
17. devoid *of*
18. die *of* (disease)/*from* (other causes)
19. differ *from* (to be different from)/ *with* (to disagree)
20. difficulty *in*
21. different *of*
22. disabuse *of*
23. disagree *with*
24. disgusted *with*
25. discourse *with*
26. dispose *of*
27. dissociate *from*
28. divest *of*
29. divide *into*
30. dressed *in*
31. due *to* (used after a noun, not after a verb)

E

1. effort *in*
2. election *to*
3. embroil *in*
4. :mphasis *on*
5. employ *in*
6. enamoured *of*
7. enreach *on*
8. endow *with*
9. enlarge *on*
10. engage *in*
11. entrust *to*
12. entrust (somebody) *with*
13. essential *to*
14. expostulate *with*
15. extend *to*

F

1. fed up *with*
2. fill *with* (enthusiasm)/*in* (a *form)*
3. fire *at* (when not hit)/on
4. focus *on*
5. forbid *to*
6. fraught *with*
7. fritter *in*
8. full *of*

G

1. give *to*
2. glad *of*
3. grapple *with*
4. good *at*
5. gratitude *for*
6. guilty *of*

H

1. hanker *after*
2. hostility *to* / *in* / *on hand* (in possession of)

I

1. identical *with*
2. impose *on*
3. incur *on*
4. indict *for*
5. indifferent *to*
6. indulge *in*
7. infatuated *with*
8. infect *with*
9. infest *with*
10. information *on*
11. ingratiate (oneself) *with*
12. inquire *into* (matter)/*of* (person)/*about*, *after*

(thing)

13. insensible *to*
14. insist *on*
15. interest *in*
16. intimate *to*
17. intoxicate *with*
18. intrigue *with*
19. intrude *on*
20. invest *with* (power)/*in* (bank)
21. investigation *of*
22. involve *in*

J

1. jealous *of*
2. jeer *at*
3. jump *at*
4. just *to*

K

1. key *of* (the *door*)/*to* (a problem)
2. knock *at*

L

1. lash *at*
2. lay siege *to*
3. leave *for*
4. level *against*
5. live *on*
6. long *for*
7. look *at* / *to*
8. lure *into*

M

1. married *to*
2. meddle *with*
3. meeting *for*
4. motive *in* / *for*

N

1. neglect *of*/ *in*
2. nominated *to*
3. noted *for*

O

1. oblivious *of*
2. operate *on*
3. opinion *on*
4. overcome *with*
5. owing *to* (not after a noun)

P

1. part *from*/ *with*
2. pay a call *on*
3. persevere *in*
4. persist *in*
5. plan *for*
6. plead *for*
7. pleased *with*
8. prefer *to*
9. preference *for*
10. present *with*
11. prevent *from*
12. preventive *for*
13. priority *to*
14. probe *into*
15. prohibit *from*
16. proud *of*
17. provide *with*
18. put *out*/ *off*

R

1. recoil *from*
2. reconcile *to*
3. remand *to*
4. remonstrate *with*
5. repent *of*
6. replete *with*
7. reply *to*
8. research *on*
9. resolve *on* / *to*
10. responsibility *of*

S

1. sail *for*
2. satiate *with*

3. satisfied *with*
4. sentence *to*
5. shoot *at*
6. sick *of*
7. side *with*
8. sparing *of*
9. square *with*
10. stickler *for*
11. stricture *on*
12. subsist *on*
13. subversive *of*
14. succeed *in*
15. sue *for*
16. superior *to*
17. supply *with*
18. sure *of*
19. surprised *at*
20. susceptible *to*
21. suspect *of*
22. sympathise *with*
23. sympathy *for*

T

1. take *up*
2. tamper *with*
3. taste *of/for*
4. tear *off/up*
5. testify *to*
6. thank *for*
7. throw *at*
8. tinker *at*
9. tire *of*
10. trace *to*
11. trample *on*
12. translate *into*
13. try *to*

U

1. unequal *to* (the task)

V

1. vest *with/in*
2. view *with*
3. vote *for* (a candidate)

W

1. wait *for*
2. ways *of*
3. wide *of*
4. wish *for*
5. *witness of*
6. wonder *at*
7. write *in/with*

Words Taking More than One Preposition

A large number of words are always followed by a fixed preposition, for example, insist on; prevent from; fond of. But certain words take several prepositions according to the changing meanings of the word. Here is a select list of such words.

1. Accompany:

A. By (for living being).
The Prime Minister was accompanied by the members of his Cabinet.

B. With (subtle things).
His lecture was accompanied with subtle analysis of concepts.

2. Accountable:

A. To (an authority or a person).
All of us are accountable to God.

B. For (action).
We are accountable to God for our deeds and misdeeds.

3. Angry:

A. At (a thing). Ram is angry at Shyam's bad conduct.

B. With (a person). Ram is angry with Shyam.

C. For (for a cause). He is angry with me for my remark.

4. Annoyed:

A. *With* (a person). He is annoyed with his younger brother.

B. *At* (something). He is annoyed with his friend at his laziness.

5. Answerable:

A. *To* (a person). The servant is answerable to the master.

B. For (something). We are answerable to our parents for our conduct.

6. Appeal:

A. *To* (person). He appealed to the judge for his release from jail.

B. *For* (thing). He appealed for his release from the prison.

7. Arrive:

A. *At* (small place). He arrived at the railway colony.

B. *In* (big place). He arrived in India.

8. Attend:

A. To (duties, lessons, work). I attend to my duties sincerely.

B. *On* (service). Children attend on parents.

9. Authority:

A. *On* (subject). Mr. Suresh is an authority on modern physics.

B. Over (rights). The District Magistrate has authority over the Committee.

10. Blind:

A. *Of* (Physical). He is blind of one eye.

B. *To* (mental). Many parents are blind to the faults of their children.

11. Communicate:

A. *With* (to make correspondence). He communicated with us on that matter.

B. *To* (to convey). He communicated his opinion to me.

12. Compare:

A. *With* (Similar things). Shakespeare is compared with Kalidasa.

B. *To* (dissimilar things). Life is compared to a battle.

13. Compete:

A. *With* (person). I cannot compete with the young man.

B. *For* (a thing). They compete for a prize.

14. Complain:

A. *To* (person). He complained to the Magistrate against Shyam.

B. *Against* (a person). He complained to the Magistrate against Shyam.

C. *About* (a thing). He complained to the Magistrate against Shyam about his misconduct.

15. Confer:

A. *On* (to give). The President conferred the title of Bharat Ratna on him.

B. *With* (a person). I shall confer with him about important topics.

16. Die:

A. *Of* (a disease). He died of cholera.

B. *From (a cause).* He died from overwork.

17. Differ:

A. *With* (person). I differ with you.

B. *From* (things). India differs from Japan.

18. Disqualified:

A. *From (action).* He was disqualified from running the race.

B. *For* (post or thing). He was disqualified for the post of Police Inspector.

19. Entrust:

A. *With* (in case of a person). I cannot entrust him with my money.

B. *To* (in case of thing). I cannot entrust my money to him.

20. Familiar:

A. *With* (person). I am familiar with the Chief Minister.

B. *To* (subject). I am familiar to French Language.

21. Fight:

A. *With* (person). We fought with the English.

B. *For* (thing). We fought with the English for freedom.

22. Grateful:

A. *To* (person). I am grateful to Ram.

B. *For* (thing). I am grateful to Ram for his help.

23. Heir:

A. *Of* (descendant): A son is usually the heir of the father.

B. *For* (thing). He was heir to a big fortune.

24. Indebted:

A. *To* (a person). I am indebted to my friend.

B. *For* (thing). I am indebted to my friend for his help.

25. Indignant:

A. *With* (person). He was indignant with his friends.

B. *A* (thing). The teacher was indignant at his carelessness.

26. Live:

A. *On* (to exist). A man lives on food.

B. *By* (to depend on, to believe in). A terrorist lives by the gun.

27. Part:

A. *From* (persons). He parted from his friends.

B. *With (things)*. He cannot part with his money.

28. Responsible:

A. *To* (person). He was responsible to the boss.

B. *For* (thing). We are responsible to God for our actions.

29. Taste:

A. *Of* (experience). Now you will have a taste of new work.

B. *For* (interest). I have no taste for painting.

30. Tired.

A. *Of* (mental). I am tired of poverty.

B. *With* (physical). I am tired with working for five hours continuously.

Practice Set

Direction: Choose the most appropriate preposition:

1. The peasant refused to grovel ________ the feet of this master.

(a) on (b) about
(c) upon (d) at
(e) by

2. It is dangerous to intrude ________ the enemy's camp.

(a) in (b) into
(c) on (d) through
(e) by

3. President Saddam Hussain has lived ________ th gun all his life.

(a) with (b) for
(c) by (d) on
(e) through

4. The mother was anxious ________ the safety of her son.

(a) at (b) about
(c) for (d) upon
(e) with

5. A good judge never jumps ________ the conclusion.

(a) to (b) at
(c) on (d) for
(e) with

6. He was killed ________ a highway man ________ a dagger.

(a) by; for (b) by; with
(c) in; for (d) with; for

7. My uncle was afflicted ________ a serious illness and was almost confined ________ bed ________ more than two months.

(a) by; on; for (b) by; on; since
(c) with; to; for (d) to; to; since

8. Finding myself short ________ money, I wrote ________ my uncle ________ help.

(a) of; to; for (b) in; to; to
(c) with; to; for (d) to; to; about

9. The boys looked ________ the old kites maker ________ the same indifference as they showed ________ the shoemaker.

(a) to; with; for (b) on; in; to
(c) at; in; to (d) at; with; to

10. It is a long time ________ I saw my friend who lives ________ his parents ________ the neighbouring town.

(a) when; at; of (b) since; with in
(c) when; for; in (d) since; for; of

11. He was advised to abstain ________ all alcoholic drinks.
(a) in (b) at
(c) from (d) by

12. It is not always easy to sympathise ________ an unfortunate man.
(a) with (b) for
(c) by (d) at

13. He had to repent ________ what he had done.
(a) at (b) of
(c) over (d) for

14. Take this medicine and you will get rid ________ the bad cold.
(a) from (b) over
(c) at (d) of

15. My cousin has invested a lot of money ________ farming.
(a) on (b) for
(c) in (d) into

16. Give an example pertinent ________ the case.
(a) with (b) on
(c) for (d) to

17. The candidates were tense ________ expectancy.
(a) with (b) in
(c) on (d) from

18. My voice reverberated ________ the walls of the castle.
(a) with (b) from
(c) in (d) on

19. Are not these slums a disgrace ________ the civic authorities.
(a) for (b) to
(c) towards (d) on

20. She could not dissociate herself ________ what she said earlier.
(a) off (b) with
(c) from (d) of

21. The reward was not commensurate ________ the work done by us.
(a) for (b) on
(c) with (d) order

22. Such remarks are certainly derogatory ________ your reputation.
(a) of (b) for
(c) with (d) to

23. Our tragic experience in the recent past provides an index ________ the state of lawlessness in this region.
(a) of (b) in
(c) at (d) by

24. Pakistan is not enamoured ________ the bomb for its own sake.
(a) with (b) for
(c) of (d) by

25. Very often we do not get what we pine ________.
(a) about (b) for
(c) at (d) on

26. Your conduct smacks ________ recklessness.
(a) of (b) with
(c) from (d) in

27. The customer smashed his fist down ________ the table.
(a) into (b) at
(c) on (d) against

28. He has suffered heavy losses, yet he was rolling ________ wealth.
(a) for (b) with
(c) from (d) in

29. The peasant refused to bow ________ his master.
(a) on (b) about
(c) upon (d) to
(e) by

30. It is dangerous to enter ________ the enemy's camp.
(a) in (b) into
(c) on (d) through
(e) by

31. President Saddam Hussain has been familiar ________ a gun all his life.
(a) with (b) for
(c) by (d) on
(e) through

32. The mother was concerned ________ the safety of her child.
(a) at (b) about
(c) for (d) upon
(e) with

33. A good judge never gropes ________ the conclusion.
(a) to (b) at
(c) on (d) for
(e) with

34. In the morning, I simply take a glance ________ the newspaper headlines.
(a) at (b) on
(c) of (d) through
(e) over

35. He thought that his father was not happy ________ him.
(a) with (b) about
(c) for (d) at
(e) over

36. I was disappointed ________ not finding the doctor in his seat.
(a) on (b) from
(c) at (d) over
(e) in

37. Let this be an example ________ the troublemakers.
(a) for (b) about
(c) against (d) to
(e) with

38. There is no exception ________ this rule.
(a) in (b) to
(c) for (d) about
(e) on

39. Nobody in our group has a genius ________ winning friends and in convincing people.
(a) for (b) in
(c) of (d) at

40. If you are averse ________ recommending my name, you should not hesitate to admit it.
(a) about (b) for
(c) to (d) against

41. I am not obsessed ________ such ideas as you are.
(a) in (b) on
(c) for (d) with

42. Religious leaders should not delve ________ politics.
(a) in (b) with
(c) at (d) into

43. What you say has hardly any bearing ________ the lives of tribals.
(a) about (b) for
(c) on (d) with

44. I am ready to say this ________ her face.
(a) at (b) in
(c) to (d) by
(e) on

45. The insects are a great nuisance ________ us.
(a) with (b) for
(c) to (d) at
(e) upon

46. She was a devoted wife and looked ________ her husband.
(a) after (b) at
(c) for (d) to
(e) upon

47. He dispensed with the services ________ his dishonest clerk.
(a) of (b) by
(c) for (d) to
(e) from

48. India is committed ________ a policy of peaceful existence.
(a) for (b) with
(c) to (d) of
(e) on

49. No one can stop a man from doing a thing if he is really keen ____________ it.
(a) in (b) at
(c) for (d) on
(e) with

50. Sometimes we have to put ____________ with irksome or unpleasant situations.
(a) on (b) in
(c) off (d) up
(e) for

51. I am angry with him ____________ his carelessness.
(a) at (b) in
(c) for (d) of
(e) on

52. The rainfall ____________ India varies ____________ place to place and also from year ____________ year.
(a) over; with; by (b) of; from; after
(c) in; from; to (d) for; with; after
(e) None of these

53. Men have made ships that can sail ____________ the sea and fly ____________ the air.
(a) along; above (b) on; in
(c) over; into (d) upon; through
(e) None of these

54. The shopkeeper deals ____________ grain, but did not deal honestly ____________ me.
(a) in; with (b) with; by
(c) with; to (d) in; by
(e) None of these

55. There was no agreement ____________ the great powers ____________ a treaty to ban nuclear weapons.
(a) between; about (b) among; on
(c) in; for (d) with; about
(e) None of these

56. The problem ____________ housing ____________ India is a complex one.
(a) about; in (b) of; in
(c) in; of (d) for; in
(e) None of these

57. I must hold discussions ____________ you ____________ that matter shortly.
(a) about; in (b) with; on
(c) with; for (d) about; for
(e) None of these

58. ____________ the topmost branch of the tree sat a monkey making faces ____________ us.
(a) on; at (b) on; to
(c) over; to (d) in; for
(e) None of these

59. He is labouring ____________ a misapprehension, but labouring ____________ a cause.
(a) under; for (b) in; towards
(c) by; in (d) with; over
(e) None of these

60. I am annoyed ____________ him ____________ what he has done to me.
(a) by; in (b) with; against
(c) at; for (d) with; for
(e) None of these

61. You must apologise ____________ him ____________ the wrong you have done him.
(a) from; against (b) from; on
(c) to; for (d) to; against
(e) None of these

62. Only the blood-stained road was a witness ____________ his assassination.
(a) of (b) to
(c) at (d) on
(e) for

63. After having tea, he settled himself ____________ his arm chair.
(a) on (b) in
(c) over (d) at
(e) into

64. Minority aspirations cannot forever be kept in check ____________ the gun.
(a) with (b) from
(c) by (d) through
(e) under

65. The Indian magpie indulges ________ a long flight.
(a) in (b) with
(c) on (d) at
(e) over

66. Why were the voters disillusioned ________ the Congress (I) is the question?
(a) at (b) by
(c) in (d) of
(e) with

67. A steady mind triumphs ________ difficulties.
(a) in (b) over
(c) at (d) with

68. I do not agree ________ you on this point.
(a) to (b) with
(c) in (d) at

69. The thunder was accompanied ________ heavy rains.
(a) with (b) by
(c) up (d) through

70. I brought him ________ with great difficulty.
(a) about (b) in
(c) round (d) up

71. He turned ________ the proposal without thinking.
(a) out (b) up
(c) down (d) in

72. The principal called ________ the names of the winners.
(a) on (b) at
(c) out (d) for

73. He resembles ________ his mother.
(a) with (b) in
(c) at (d) none of these

74. We must keep ________ something for the rainy day.
(a) by (b) for
(c) in (d) at

75. The teacher has no control ________ the students.
(a) on (b) over
(c) with (d) at

76. Under this heavy load the bridge will give ________
(a) way (b) in
(c) out (d) away

77. I have been waiting here for him ________ three weeks.
(a) for (b) from
(c) since (d) on

78. They quarrelled with me ________ the division of the booty.
(a) about (b) in
(c) above (d) on

79. Good sleep is necessary ________ good health.
(a) of (b) for
(c) at (d) from

80. I am used ________ such hardships.
(a) to (b) at
(c) for (d) from

81. Rita is married ________ Bobby.
(a) with (b) at
(c) between (d) to

82. Let us travel ________ night, it will be cool then.
(a) at (b) by
(c) in (d) during

83. I was astonished ________ the sad news.
(a) at (b) in
(c) with (d) to

84. We travelled ________ a boat to reach Dhaka.
(a) by (b) on
(c) for (d) about

85. ________ the whole, I like the book very much.
(a) at (b) from
(c) on (d) in

86. The man robbed me __________ my possessions.
(a) of (b) from
(c) with (d) on

87. He was vexed __________ Sohan for his behaviour.
(a) with (b) upon
(c) at (d) to

88. Exercise is beneficial __________ health.
(a) towards (b) for
(c) to (d) in

89. Ramesh's mind was attuned __________ music.
(a) at (b) to
(c) with (d) on

90. Keep clear __________ wicked boys.
(a) of (b) from
(c) out (d) with

91. Ram is confident __________ his success.
(a) of (b) for
(c) about (d) towards

92. Shyam has no control __________ his temper.
(a) over (b) in
(c) at (d) after

93. You must listen __________ the question first.
(a) at (b) to
(c) for (d) over

94. Peter's speech pointed __________ some of our defects.
(a) to (b) towards
(c) on (d) at

95. Your statement is very much similar __________ mine.
(a) to (b) of
(c) about (d) on

96. The soldiers rebelled __________ the king.
(a) at (b) on
(c) with (d) against

97. My relations __________ Preeti are good.
(a) to (b) on
(c) with (d) against

98. Pawan's story is devoid __________ truth.
(a) from (b) to
(c) of (d) through

99. I have a distaste __________ publicity.
(a) for (b) about
(c) against (d) at

100. There is no hindrance __________ his going there.
(a) over (b) to
(c) at (d) on

ANSWER KEY

1. (d)	21. (c)	41. (d)	61. (c)	81. (d)
2. (c)	22. (d)	42. (d)	62. (b)	82. (c)
3. (c)	23. (a)	43. (c)	63. (e)	83. (a)
4. (b)	24. (c)	44. (e)	64. (a)	84. (a)
5. (b)	25. (b)	45. (b)	65. (a)	85. (c)
6. (b)	26. (a)	46. (a)	66. (e)	86. (a)
7. (c)	27. (d)	47. (a)	67. (b)	87. (a)
8. (a)	28. (d)	48. (c)	68. (b)	88. (c)
9. (d)	29. (d)	49. (d)	69. (a)	89. (b)
10. (b)	30. (b)	50. (d)	70. (d)	90. (a)
11. (c)	31. (a)	51. (c)	71. (c)	91. (a)
12. (a)	32. (b)	52. (c)	72. (c)	92. (a)
13. (d)	33. (d)	53. (b)	73. (d)	93. (b)

14. (d)	34. (a)	54. (b)	74. (c)	94. (b)
15. (c)	35. (a)	55. (b)	75. (b)	95. (a)
16. (d)	36. (c)	56. (b)	76. (a)	96. (d)
17. (a)	37. (d)	57. (b)	77. (a)	97. (c)
18. (b)	38. (b)	58. (a)	78. (a)	98. (c)
19. (b)	39. (a)	59. (a)	79. (b)	99. (a)
20. (c)	40. (c)	60. (d)	80. (a)	100. (b)

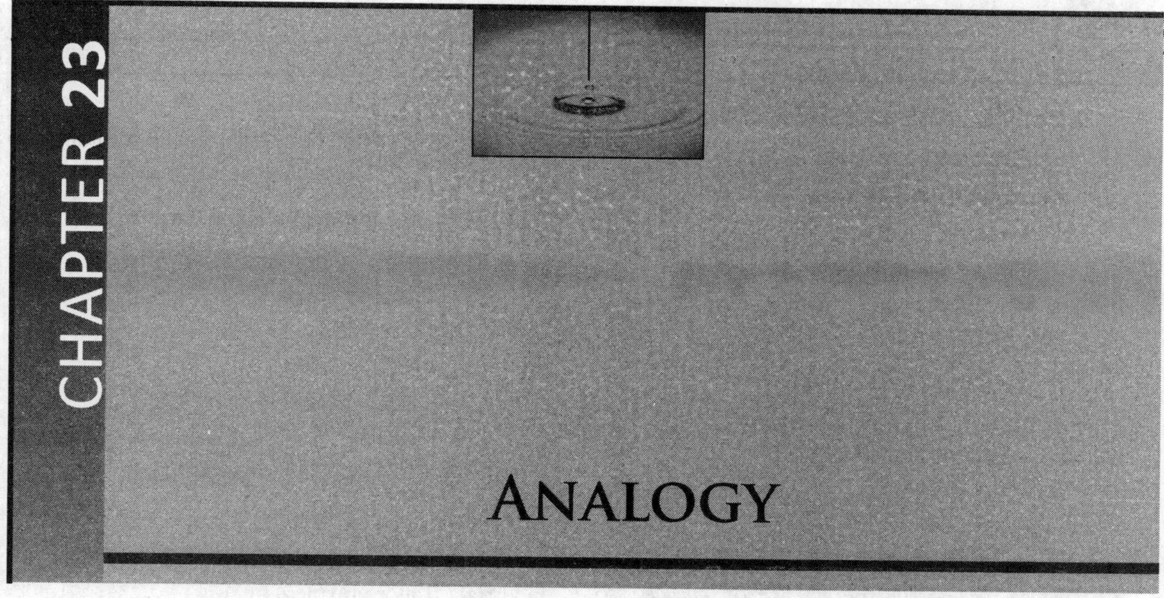

Analogy

Analogy means similarity or resemblance or some kind of relationship between two given things. Analogy test, therefore, intends to evaluate one's ability to comprehend the relationship that exists between two objects, things or figures. There are infinite possibilities in establishing a relationship between two objects. However, for our convenience we can chart out some important kinds of relationships.

1. Cause and effect relationship

Example: *Education : Development*

(a) Man : speech
(b) Nutrition : health
(c) Game : play
(d) Child : growth.

The relationship between development and education is of cause and effect. Education is a cause for development. Among the four choices only (b) *nutrition* is a cause for *health* and thus this is the answer.

2. Part and whole relationship

Example: *House : Room*

(a) Struggle : fight (b) Transport : car
(c) School : college (d) Boy : girl.

Room is a part of house. Similarly car is a part of transport system.

3. Part : Part relationship

Example: *Gill : Fin*

(a) Salad : rice (b) Sea : fish
(c) Kill : bomb (d) Question : team

Just as *gill* and *fin* are two different parts of a fish so *salad* and *rice* are parts of food.

4. Purpose relationship

Example: Glove : *Ball*

(a) Summer : winter(b) Game : study
(c) Stadium : seats (d) Hook : fish

Just as a *glove* helps catch a *ball*, so a *hook* helps catch *a fish*.

5. Action to object relationship

Example: *Break : Piece*

(a) Writer : pen
(b) Bread : bake
(c) Kick : football
(d) Muddy : unclear.

Just as *break* is an action that makes *pieces*, so *kick* is an action that makes the *football* move.

6. Worker and tool relationship

Example: *Sculptor : Chisel*

(a) Pathology : disease
(b) Tailor : needle
(c) Engineer : site
(d) Time : seconds.

Just as a *sculptor* works with a *chisel* so a *tailor* works with a *needle.*

7. Study and topic relationship

Example: *Linguistics : Language*

(a) Gardener : harrow
(b) Hen : chicken
(c) Scale : length
(d) Anthropology : man

Just as *linguistics* is the science of *language,* so *anthropology* is the study of *man's* life.

8. Worker and working place relationship

Example: *Lawyer : Court*

(a) Professor : university
(b) Author : book
(c) Wine : grapes
(d) Volume : litre

Just as a *lawyer* works at a *court* so a *professor* works in a *university.*

9. Worker and product relationship

Example: *Fanner : Crop*

(a) Fabric : yarn
(b) Cat : kitten
(c) Wish : desire
(d) Editor : newspaper

Just as *crops* are the products of a *fanner's* work so a *newspaper* is the product of an *editor's* work.

10. Product and raw material relationship

Example: *Egg: Omellete*

(a) Man : child (b) Spoon : feed
(c) Judge : justice (d) Sack : jute

Just as an *egg* is the raw material for *omelette,* so *jute* is the raw material for a *sack.*

11. Word and synonym relationship

Example: *Abate : Lessen*

(a) Sweet : bitter
(b) Ice : solid
(c) Dog : bitch
(d) Secret : clandestine

Just as *abate* and *lessen* have similar meanings, so *secret* or *clandestine* have similar meanings.

12. Word and antonym relationship

Example: *Confidence : diffidence*

(a) Dastard : coward
(b) Field : farm
(c) House : garbage
(d) Baffle : clarify

Just as *diffidence* is the opposite of *confidence,* so *clarify* is the opposite of *baffle.*

13. Degree relationship

Example: *Wam : Hot*

(a) Tailor : textile
(b) Sun : planet
(c) Horrible : heineous
(d) Fight : war

Just as *hot* is the greater degree of *warm,* so *war* is the greater degree of *fight.*

14. Sequence relationship

Example: *Monday : Tuesday*

(a) Spring : winter
(b) Monday : Sunday
(c) Wednesday : Thursday
(d) Angle : sky

Just as *Tuesday* follows *Monday,* so *Thursday* follows *Wednesday.*

15. Grammatical relationship

Example: *He : his*

(a) I : me (b) He : him
(c) They : these (d) She : her

Just as *he* is third person nominative and *his* is third person possessive case so *she* is third person nominative case and *her* is third person possessive case.

16. Sex relationship

Example: *Lion : lioness.*

(a) Convict : prison(b) Duck : drake
(c) Flag : nation (d) Tiger : leopard

Just as *lioness* is the female of *lion,* so *drake* is the female of *duck*

17. Object and creature symbol relationship

Example: *Flag : nation*

(a) fox : cunning
(b) Soldier : war
(c) Wine : grapes
(d) Cow : herbivorous.

Just as *flag* stands as the symbol of a *nation,* so *fox* stands for *cunningness.* Thus (a) is the answer.

18. Creature and living place relationship

Example: *Bee : hive*

(a) Duck : drake
(b) Warm : tepid
(c) Carcass : corpse
(d) Monk : monastery

Just as a *bee* lives in a *hive.* similarly a *monk* lives in a *monastery.* Thus (d) is the answer.

19. Creature and offspring relationship

Example: *Horse : Colt*

(a) Goat : bleat
(b) Dawn : twilight
(c) Dog : puppy
(d) Actor : stage

Just as *colt* is the young one of *horse* so *puppy* is the young one of *dog.* Thus (c) is the answer.

20. Creature and sound relationship

Example: *Frogs : Croak*

(a) Hare : leveret
(b) Liquor : intoxication
(c) Serpents : hiss
(d) Brake : car

Just as the sound of *frogs* is known by the word *croak.* so the sound of *serpents* is *hiss.* Thus (c) is the answer.

Practice Set —1

Directions: The following questions comprise two words each that have a certain relationship between them. followed by four lettered pair of words. Select the lettered pair that has the same relationship as the original pair of words.

1. Shrub : Prune
(a) Beard : shave (b) Hair : trim
(c) Lawn : mow (d) Wool : shear

2. Creche : Infants
(a) School : pupils
(b) Bedlam : lunatics
(c) Deck : sailors
(d) Cottage : beggar

3. Shield : Soldier
(a) Stethoscope : doctor
(b) Book : author
(c) Advocate : court
(d) Helmet : rider

4. Fox : Cunning
(a) Cat : playful
(b) Horse : runner
(c) Vixen : cute
(d) Ant : industrious

5. Hillock : Mountain
(a) Hare : animal (b) Ant : elephant
(c) Bush : forest (d) Grass : tree

6. Sonnet : Poem
(a) Ballad : stanza (b) Murder : crime
(c) Chapter : book (d) Lie : falsehood

7. Identity : Anonymity
(a) Flaw : perfection
(b) Careless : mistake
(c) Truth : lie
(d) Fear : joy

8. Revolver : Holster
(a) Book : bag (b) Eye : eyelid
(c) School : class (d) String : bead

9. Wrestler : Arena
(a) Cricket : pitch
(b) Ring : finger
(c) Farmer : field
(d) Assistant : Clerk

10. Restaurant : Menu
(a) Library : catalogue
(b) Journal : newspaper

(c) Book : encyclopaedia
(d) College : account

11. Heart : Cardiology
(a) Brain : psychology
(b) History : histology
(c) Civics: polity
(d) Fossils : palaeontology

12. Donkey : trot
(a) Monkey : waddle
(b) Cat : leap
(c) Eagle : stride
(d) Mouse : scamper

13. Infection : Illness
(a) Satisfaction : appetite
(b) Applause : audience
(c) Antidote : disease
(d) Rehearsal : performance

14. Bridge: Cards
(a) Dam : river
(b) Gamble : money
(c) Image : mirror
(d) Fencing : sword

15. Banyan Tree : Proproots
(a) Potato : tuber
(b) Climbers : tendrils
(c) Ginger : stem
(d) Spinach : root

16. Ashes : Fire
(a) Building : debris
(b) Current : bygone
(c) Relics : civilisation
(d) Bottle : stopper
(e) Bullet : barrel

17. Embryo : Child
(a) Fruit : rind (b) Sprout : plant
(c) Seed : fruit (d) Ton : coal
(e) Leaf : chlorophyll

18. Love : Adore
(a) Affection : indifference
(b) Pride : prejudice
(c) Fight : war
(d) Hit : suffer
(e) Legible : eligible

19. Needle : Thread
(a) Leader : follower(b) Prick : sew
(c) Bat : ball (d) Pin : cushion
(e) Nail : hammer

20. Wet: Dry
(a) Worse : worst
(b) Weather : temperature
(c) Scold : praise
(d) Rise : walk
(e) Devil : wrong

Practice Set —2

Directions: In the following sets of analogies one word is missing. Select that word from the words (a), (b), (c), (d) *exhibit* the same analogy as established among the three italicised words:

1. *Bow : Rifle : : Hourglass :*
(a) Clock tower (b) Bullet
(c) Diameter (d) Chronometer

2. *Halcyon : ? : : Placid : Serene*
(a) Calm (b) Irritated
(c) Harmful (d) Peaceful

3. *Errata : ? : : Flaws : Jewels*
(a) Mal1uscripts (b) Books
(c) Literature (d) Prints

4. *Truculent: Agitator : : Pacifier ?*
(a) Powerful (b) Amenable
(c) Subversive (d) Feeble

5. *Inoculation : ? : : Exposure : Toughening*
(a) Immunity (b) Punctuality
(c) Vulnerability (d) Contagious

6. *Breeze : Cyclone : : Drizzle : ?*
(a) Earthquake (b) Storm
(c) Flood (d) Downpour

7. *Oxygen: Burn: : Carbon dioxide : ?*
(a) Isolate (b) Foam
(c) Extinguish (d) Explode

8. *Genuine: Authentic : : Mirage : ?*
(a) Image (b) Transpiration
(c) Reflection (d) Illusion

9. *Drill: Bore : : Sieve : ?*
(a) Thresh (b) Sift
(c) Pry (d) Rinse

10. *Country : President : : State : ?*
(a) Governor (b) Minister
(c) Chief Minister (d) Citizen

11. *Bread : Yeast : : Curd : ?*
(a) Fungi (b) Bacteria
(c) Germs (d) Virus

12. *Chromite : Chromium : : Ilmenite : ?*
(a) Limestone (b) Cobalt
(c) Manganese (d) Titanium

13. *Steel : Rails : Alnico : ?*
(a) Aircraft (b) Machinery
(c) Silverware (d) Magnets

14. *Naphthalene : Coal tar : : Dyes : ?*
(a) Petroleum (b) Oils
(c) Chemicals (d) Carbon

15. *Tree : Forest : : Grass : ?*
(a) Lawn (b) Field
(c) Garden (d) Farm

16. *Conscience : Wrong : : Police : ?*
(a) Thief (b) Law
(c) Discipline (d) Crime

17. *Tehran : Iran : : Beijing : ?*
(a) China (b) Japan
(c) Turkey (d) Malaysia

18. *Porcupine: Rodent : : Mildew : ?*
(a) Fungus (b) Germ
(c) Insect (d) Pathogen

19. *Poodle : Dog : : Homicide : ?*
(a) Duck (b) Donkey
(c) Fowl (d) Deer

20. *Pigeon : Peace : : White Flag : ?*
(a) Friendship (b) Victory
(c) Surrender (d) War

Practice Set —3

1. Cobra is related to Snake in the same way as Leopard is related to . . . ? . . .
(a) Tiger (b) Lion
(c) Cat (d) Zebra

2. Blood is related to Circulation in the same way as Hormone is related to . . . ? . . .
(a) Egestion (b) Control
(c) Co-ordination (d) Digestion

3. Leaf is related to Sap in the same way as Bone is related to . . . ? . . .
(a) Fluid (b) Blood
(c) Marrow (d) Calcium

4. Chlorophyll is related to Chloroplast in the same way as Vulture is related to . . . ? . . .
(a) Flesh (b) Wings
(c) Air (d) Bird

5. Circle is related to Circumference as Square is related to . . . ? . . .
(a) Area (b) Volume
(c) Diagonal (d) Perimeter

6. Grain is related to Granary in the same way as Curios is related to . . . ? . . .
(a) Archives (b) Musium
(c) Library (d) Zoo

7. Formula is related to Constituent in the same way as Equation is related to . . . ? . . .
(a) Numbers (b) Variables
(c) Term (d) Constant

8. Inch is related to Centimetre in the same way as Pint is related to . . . ? . . .
(a) Litre (b) Volume
(c) Gallon (d) Viscosity

9. Crumb is related to Bread in the same way as Morsel is related to . . . ? . . .
(a) Fruit (b) Biscuit
(c) Food (d) Cake

10. Earth is related to Axis in the same way as Wheel is related to . . . ? . . .
(a) Tyre (b) Car
(c) Road (d) Hub

Practice Set —4

1. Hinduism : Christianity : Islam : Religion
   (a) Ear : Nose : Eyesight : Vision
   (b) Plus : Minus : Multiple : Division
   (c) Humid : Hot : Tundra : Region
   (d) Winter : Spring : Summer : Season
2. Orange : Apple : Grape : Fruit
   (a) Window : Door : Apartment : Suite
   (b) Job : Employer : Employment : Recruit
   (c) Description : Analysis : Statement : Report
   (d) Ship : Lead : Basement : Port
3. Kingdom : Slavery : Freedom : Democracy
   (a) Dictatorship : Restrain : Slavery : Liberty
   (b) Press : Slavery : Death : Anarchy
   (c) Bad : Wrong : Worst : Aristocracy
   (d) Evil : Devil : Religion : Theocracy
4. Adjure : Renounce : Alleviate : Relieve
   (a) Abstruse : Obscure : Give : Receive
   (b) Allay : Noisy : Defend : Deceive
   (c) Appease : Soft : Apprehend : Perceive
   (d) Atrocity : Denounce : Aptitude : Believe
5. Tehsil : District : State : Country
   (a) Block : Colony : Zone : City
   (b) Province : District : State : Country
   (c) Madhya Pradesh : Maharashtra : Bombay : Victoria Terminus
   (d) Metropolitan : Megalopolis : Town : City

Practice Set —5

1. PSXM : QRYL : : BFTV : ?
   (a) AESU (b) CEUU
   (c) DHVX (d) CGUW
   (e) AGSW
2. NOPQ : PMRO : : ABCD : ?
   (a) CZEB (b) CDEF
   (c) YZAB (d) CDAB
   (e) YZEF
3. CDE : ZXY : : EDC : ?
   (a) XYZ (b) YXZ
   (c) XZY (d) ZXY
   (e) ZYX
4. AKJ : GNH : : EMD : ?
   (a) CLB (b) CLD
   (c) AKB (d) EMF
   (e) CDB
5. AFHO : GBDJ : : CHFM : ?
   (a) GBLD (b) GBJO
   (c) GPLD (d) GBIM
   (e) IBDE

ANSWER KEY

Set I		Set II		Set III	Set IV	Set V
1. (b)	11. (c)	1. (d)	11. (b)	1. (c)	1. (d)	1. (d)
2. (b)	12. (d)	2. (d)	12. (d)	2. (c)	2. (c)	2. (a)
3. (d)	13. (d)	3. (b)	13. (d)	3. (c)	3. (a)	3. (b)
4. (d)	14. (d)	4. (b)	14. (a)	4. (d)	4. (c)	4. (c)
5. (c)	15. (b)	5. (a)	15. (a)	5. (d)	5. (a)	5. (b)
6. (b)	16. (c)	6. (d)	16. (d)	6. (b)		
7. (a)	17. (c)	7. (c)	17. (a)	7. (c)		
8. (a)	18. (c)	8. (d)	18. (a)	8. (c)		
9. (c)	19. (d)	9. (b)	19. (d)	9. (c)		
10. (a)	20. (c)	10. (a)	20. (c)	10. (d)		

CHAPTER 24

IDIOMS AND PHRASES

Idioms and phrases are recognised through experience. Sometimes ordinary words fail to embody the experience or catch the spirit of the special situation. Idioms and phrases are meant for such situations; they enrich a language. Thus, in order to have a native's command over English, it is necessary to understand idioms. The *Oxford Dictionary of Current Idiomatic English* defines an idiom by calling it as a combination of two or more words which function as a unit of meaning as opposed to non-idiomatic expressions which "are made up of distinct meaningful parts". Thus, often, the unit of meaning is different from what the words actually suggest. For example, the expression 'blue blood' does not mean that blood is blue, but it means 'to belong to a royal family'. Similarly, the 'apple of discord' does not imply any real apple; it means 'a cause of quarrel' or 'Pandora's box' means a cause of several problems and does not imply any real box though it has an association with the box of Pandora. The experience comes out in an idiom in a standardised form.

EXAMPLES

The test is usually set in two forms; either in direct multiple choice or in a sentence form.

A. Direct Multiple Choice

Choose the exact meaning of the idiomatic expressions/ phrase given below.

1. *To get in hot waters*
   (a) to get into trouble
   (b) to enter waters heated by the sun
   (c) to be in a confused state of mind
   (d) to drink hot waters

2. *Between the devil and the deep sea*
   (a) to be in a dilemma
   (b) to be angry in a temper
   (c) to choose correctly
   (d) to live dangerously

B. In Sentence Form

Choose the substitute of the underlined phrase/idiom.

3. For the first week, the apprentice felt *like fish out of water.*
   (a) frustrated (b) homeless
   (c) disappointed (d) uncomfortable

4. The company has been handed over to the new masters *lock, stock and barrel.*

(a) completely (b) financially
(c) administratively (d) partially

Answers: (1) (a) (2) (a) (3) (d) (4) (a).

Students should try to understand the real implication of idioms and phrases and they should learn it by constantly using them in their writing and speech and through continuous practical exercises.

Stock of Phrases

1. *To show white feathers* — to show fear.
2. *A feather in the cap* — a very good achievement.
3. *A good Samaritan* — a really kind man.
4. *To rise like a phoenix* — to start afresh from a low position.
5. *To meet one's waterloo* — to meet one's defeat.
6. *To have cold feet* — to be reluctant.
7. *To raise a dust* — to create confusion.
8. *To bring home the bacon* — to be successful.
9. *To carry the day* — to win after a long effort.
10. *To stick to one's gun* — to maintain one's point against all opposition.
11. *Come cap in hand* — very humble.
12. *Man of Iron* — a man of strong will power.
13. *Man of straw* — insignificant.
14. *Man of letters* — scholar.
15. *To have several irons in the fire* — so many engagements at a time.
16. *At a low key* — at reducing.
17. *At crossroads* — be in confusion because of many choices.
18. *At stake* — in danger.
19. *To die a dog's death* — unheroic death.
20. *To fire on all cylinders* — to exert with all force.
21. *To break the duck* — to begin.
22. *To play ducks and drakes* — to squander money.
23. *A big shot* — important person.
24. *A boon in disguise* — a benefit in loss.
25. *A cry in the wilderness* — An irrelevant effort.
26. *To beat about the bush* — To talk about unimportant things.
27. *To sound a red alert* — to make alert.
28. *Rise from ashes* — to rise high from low.
29. *To put the cat among pigeons* — to be placed in a wrong situation.
30. *Cut the Gordian knot* — to perform a difficult task.
31. *To talk shop* — to talk nonsense.
32. *To turn a deaf ear* — to disregard.
33. *To gain ground* — to become more general.
34. *Through thick and thin* — under all circumstances.
35. *To have finger in the pie* — to do something in an affair.
36. *To have one's heart in the right place* — to be kind.
37. *My hands are full* — I am busy.
38. *To give someone a piece of mind* — to scold.
39. *To kick up a row* — to make great noise and fuss.
40. *To bury the hatchet* — to make peace.
41. *To set the* — to do some

Thames on fire — markable or surprising things.

42. *High and dry* — isolated, stranded.

43. *To be at the end of one's tether* — to have no resources left.

44. *Odds and ends* — various articles.

45. *A hot line* — direct telephone line between heads of states.

46. *To shoot a line one's success.* — to exaggerate about

47. *To read between the lines* — to understand more than the actual words.

48. *To feather one's nest* — to provide money even dishonestly.

49. *To black-ball* — prevent from doing something.

50. *To be in the black (of one's money)* — to be in the credit.

51. *A blue book* — a government report.

52. *To paint the town red* — to celebrate noisily in public places.

53. *To make no bones about something* — to do or say a thing openly if it is unpleasant.

54. *Pull the wool over somebody's eyes* — to deceive.

55. *Nine day's wonder* — short lived achievement

56. *To keep one's fingers crossed* — to remain anxious, wishing good for somebody.

57. *To keep the wolf away from the door* — to keep off poverty from oneself.

58. *A red letter day* — an important day.

59. *To work like a dog* — to work very hard.

60. *To foot the bill* — to make payment.

61. *Bone of contention* — cause of quarrel.

62. *To beggar description* — beyond description.

63. *To play a second fiddle* — to act as a subordinate to do the secondary role.

64. *Cut no ice* — to make no effect.

65. *Under a cloud* — to be in bad book.

66. *Once and for all* — for ever.

67. *Oily tongue* — one who flatters.

68. *Hand in glove* — close friendship.

69. *Hole and corner policy* — improper policy.

70. *Far and wide* — all around.

71. *Far and away* — certainly.

72. *Fair-weather friends* — friends only in good days.

73. *In deed* — really.

74. *Face value* — superficially.

75. *Fancy price* — high price.

76. *Stick one's neck out* — to take risk.

77. *To put a spoke in one's wheel* — to disturb.

78. *Brown study* — in reverie.

79. *Moot point* — controversial point.

80. *To plough a lonely furrow* — to do without anybody's help.

81. *Bring home* — to emphasise.

82. *Make hay while the Sun shines* — to make best use of the favourable opportunities.

83. *Rank and file* — common man.

84. *Talk through one's hat* — talk nonsense.

85. *To lead one by the nose* — to cause to follow blindly.

86. *To explore every avenue* — to try every method.

87. *At the drop of a hat*	—	for no reason at all.
88. *To kick one's heels*	—	to waste time.
89. *To smell something fishy*	—	to feel that there is something wrong.
90. *To get away with*	—	to escape.
91. *All agog*	—	in a state of excitement.
92. *Adam's ale*	—	ordinary water.
93. *One's cup of tea*	—	what one likes and can do well.
94. *In a flutter*	—	in a state of nervous excitement.
95. *A chip of the old block*	—	characteristics of one's ancestors.
96. *A close shave*	—	a lucky escape.
97. *Blow hot and cold*	—	to be inconsistent.
98. *A bull in the china shop*	—	an awkward, tactless or clumsy person.
99. *To have the floor*	—	to make a speech.
100. *A case in point*	—	an illustrative case connected to the subject of discussion.
101. *The cock of the walk*	—	the most dominating person in a group.
102. *A cuckoo in the nest*	—	A child whose parentage is doubtful and may therefore not belong by blood to the family.
103. *Feet of clay*	—	to be weak or cowardly.
104. *A flash in the pan*	—	something which lasts only a short time; an effort or partial success which soon turns to failure; a short-lived outburst of enthusiasm for something.
105. *A mare's nest*	—	a discovery which looks valuable or promising but which turns out to be worthless.
106. *A pig in a poke*	—	an article which was bought without previous inspection and which turns out to be worth much less than what one paid for it.
107. *A skeleton in the cupboard*	—	a past event which is kept secret by a family/ something embarrassing or shameful.
108. *A fair crack of the whip*	—	a period of importance.
109. *To hold something in leash*	—	to restrain
110. *To wrangle over an ass's shadow*	—	to quarrel over trifles
111. *To snap one's fingers*	—	to become contemptuous of.
112. *To stand to one's guns*	—	to preserve when hardships press.
113. *To take people by storm*	—	to captivate them unexpectedly.
114. *To throw up the sponge*	—	to surrender or give up a contest.
115. *To catch somebody on the hop*	—	to catch somebody off guard.
116. *To spill the beans*	—	to reveal secret information.

117. *To bring one's eggs to a bad market* — to fail in one's plans because one goes to the wrong people for help.

118. *To give/get the bird* — to send away.

119. *To throw up one's nose at a thing* — to treat it with contemptuous dislike or disgust.

120. *To split hair* — to indulge in over-refined arguments.

121. *A lady's man* — a lover of women's company.

122. *To draw a bead upon* — to take aim at.

123. *Foam in the mouth* — to be in extreme hatred.

124. *To rip up old soars* — to revive a quarrel which was almost forgotten.

125. *A baker's dozen* — thirteen.

126. *To oil the knocker* — to tip the office-boy.

127. *To cool one's heels* — to be kept waiting for some time.

128. *To play to the gallery* — trying to get appreciation from least intelligent people.

129. *To clinch the issue* — decide.

130. *To turn the comer* — pass the crisis.

131. *To rock the boat* — upset the balance.

132. *Shop-lifter* — a thief in the guise of a customer.

133. *To scream blue murder* — make a great deal of noise and object vehemently.

134. *To run in the same groove* — advance in harmony.

135. *To chew the cuds* — to muse on.

136. *To wear one's heart on one's sleeve* — expose one's innermost feelings to others.

137. *A duck in a thunderstorm* — distressed.

138. *To lead others up the garden* — to deceive others

139. *To keep, the pot boiling* — keep the controversy alive.

140. *To heap coals of fire on one's head* — put one to shame.

141. *To cut both ends* — to argue in support of both sides of the issue.

142. *Midas touch* — ability to succeed in all projects.

143. *Lynch law* — law of mobs.

144. *To come down in the world* — to lose one's social and financial position.

145. *A man of the world* — an experienced man, often with a cosmopolitan background.

146. *All the same* — nevertheless, but, yet.

147. *Cut and dried* — settled, decided.

148. *Fair and square* — in a fair way.

149. *Free and easy* — casual, unworried, unconcerned.

150. *Meek and mild* — gentle and quiet.

151. *Null and void* — invalid, without legal effect.

152. *Rough and ready* — not exact, only approximate.

153. *Short and sweet* — brisk, without delay.

154. *Cloak and dagger* — like a spy.

155. *Hammer and sickle* — the emblem of socialism.

156. *Hammer and tongs* — with all one's strength.

157. *Hole and corner* — secret.

158. *Run-of-the mill* — an average, ordinary, unexciting.

159. *An armchair job* — a regular job which is considered easy and well-paid.

160. *Backstairs gossip* — gossip among servants.

161. *A close fisted man* — a mean or stingy man.

162. *A curtain lecture* — the scolding of a husband by his wife in private.

163. *Elbow room* — room on opportunity to move and act freely.

164. *Forty winks* — short sleep.

165. *French leave* — absence without permission.

166. *The golden handshake* — a large sum of money given to a man of high position when he retires from his employment.

167. *A henpecked husband* — One who is dominated by his wife.

168. *A hot potato* — an issue that is awkward or embarassing to deal with.

169. *An ivory tower* — a place or state of life that is out of touch with people and reality.

170. *A latchkey child* — a child who returns from school etc. to an empty house because both parents are working.

171. *A sleeping partner* — a business partner who provides a share of the capital and therefore owns shares in the business but who does not take an active part in managing it.

172. *A soft spot* — a liking or fondness for something or someone.

173. *Soft soap* — flattery.

174. *The bill of fare* — the menu.

175. *A drug on the market* — goods on the market for which there is no hope.

176. *A storm in the tea-cup* — a lot of excitement and discussion about a trivial matter.

Practice Set

A. Sentence Form

Choose the exact meaning of the idioms/phrases.

1. When I saw him in the morning, he looked like a *duck in a thunderstorm.*
   (a) entrapped
   (b) distressed
   (c) indomitable
   (d) peaceful
   (e) timid

2. Our school is *within a stone's throw* of the railway station.
   (a) very far-off
   (b) with a certain radius
   (c) at a short distance
   (d) within a definite circumference

3. He *burnt his fingers* by interfering in his neighbour's affair.
(a) got himself into trouble
(b) burnt himself
(c) got himself insulted
(d) got rebuked

4. He is *not worth his salt* if he fails at this juncture.
(a) very strange
(b) very proud of himself
(c) quite depressed
(d) quite worthless

5. Mr Gupta, who is one of the trustees of a big charity is suspected of *feathering his own nest.*
(a) being lazy in doing his work
(b) being too generous
(c) neglecting his job
(d) making money unfairly

6. She exhibited remarkable *sang froid* during the crisis.
(a) temper
(b) irritation
(c) composure
(d) anger

7. Mrs Hashmi has been *in the blues* for the last several weeks.
(a) abroad
(b) unwell
(c) depressed
(d) lonely

8. All the political parties are *tarred with the same brush.*
(a) treated, equally
(b) profess the same policies
(c) have the same merits
(d) possess the same defects

9. Let us admit that we could not *heap coals of fire on his head.*
(a) bum him alive
(b) agitate him
(c) make him feel sorry by retuning good for evil
(d) put him to shame

10. Almost everybody *has an eye on the main chance.*
(a) waits for the appropriate time
(b) thinks of outwitting his rival
(c) looks for better prospects
(d) looks after his own welfare

11. For the first week, the apprentice felt *like a fish out of water:*
(a) frustrated
(b) homeless
(c) disappointed
(d) uncomfortable

12. His friends failed to see why he should *ride the high horse* just because he had won an election.
(a) become abnormal
(b) appear arrogant
(c) indulge in dreams
(d) hate others

13. The General Manager of this industry is *a host in himself:*
(a) eats too much
(b) independent of others
(c) capable of doing as much as a number of ordinary persons
(d) very hospitable

14. The cooperation and *esprit de corps* between the soldiers and the officers was directly responsible for their victory.
(a) bravery
(b) loyalty
(c) subordination
(d) unity

15. It is *out of the question* for only one to have a quiet meal with a set of ultras around him.
(a) unthinkable
(b) impossible
(c) unbecoming
(d) indecent

16. The company has been handed over to new masters, *lock, stock and barrel.*
(a) completely
(b) financially

(c) administratively
(d) partially

17. The *study of insects* was a fascinating pursuit for him.
(a) anthropology
(b) zoology
(c) etymology
(d) entomology

18. Believe me, I am *all at sea.*
(a) out of reach
(b) very happy
(c) puzzled
(d) drowning

19. It is evident from the minister's statement that *heads will roll.*
(a) transfers will take place
(b) people will die
(c) dismissals will occur
(d) heads of department will have to repent

20. I saw him *make a wry face.*
(a) abuse
(b) feel sick
(c) cry with pain
(d) show disappointment

21. My father did not know that his brother would *tread on his heels.*
(a) follow closely after
(b) stab him in the back
(c) oppose him immediately
(d) support him blindly

22. He is the sort of man who would do anything *for a consideration.*
(a) out of love
(b) in sympathy with the aggrieved
(c) if he found some merit in it
(d) if he were paid to do it

23. His dealings are all *above board.*
(a) simple
(b) decent
(c) open
(d) friendly

24. He *threw cold water over* the project that the secretary had prepared.
(a) rejected
(b) encouraged
(c) cleared
(d) discouraged

25. There is no need to *rake up* an old quarrel.
(a) forget
(b) revive
(c) start
(d) end

26. My car *broke down* on way to college yesterday.
(a) met with an accident
(b) broke into pieces
(c) stopped due to mechanical failure
(d) dashed against another vehicle

27. The prices are going up by *leaps and bounds.*
(a) irregularly
(b) gradually
(c) rapidly
(d) systematically

28. We *kept our fingers crossed* till the final results were declared.
(a) waited expectantly
(b) kept praying
(c) felt scared
(d) kept hopeful

29. *To fish in* troubled waters
(a) to make the most in a bad situation
(b) to disturb others
(c) to do something silly
(d) to try to find out an impossible object

B. Direct Multiple Choice

Choose the exact meaning of idiomatic expressions/phrases.

30. *Between the devil and the deep sea*
(a) to be in a dilemma
(b) to be in a temper
(c) to choose correctly
(d) to live dangerously

31. *To cut the crackle*
(a) to stop talking and start
(b) to dig a well
(c) to annoy others
(d) to act in a friendly way

32. *To give currency to*
(a) to give someone
(b) to pay much attention to
(c) to carry heavy load to
(d) to offer bribe

33. *To miss the boat*
(a) to miss an opportunity
(b) to feel lonely
(c) to act like a coward
(d) to swim in a river

34. *To have cold feet*
(a) to feel very cold
(b) to pay much attention to
(c) to be reluctant
(d) to pour water on something

35. *Blue blood*
(a) something impossible
(b) an aristocrat
(c) something costly
(d) a funny object

36. *At one's wit's end*
(a) to be very witty
(b) to confuse others
(c) to be completely confused
(d) to minimise expenses

37. *To eat an humble pie*
(a) to eat cheap food
(b) to eat slowly
(c) to swallow one's pride and apologise for doing something wrong
(d) to defy authority

38. A *snake in the grass*
(a) a very poisonous snake
(b) a secret agent
(c) an unrecognisable enemy or danger
(d) not a reliable person

39. *To turn over a new leaf*
(a) to change one's behaviour for the better
(b) to read something attentively
(c) to remain vigilant
(d) to be careful

40. *To hold a candle to*
(a) to be nearly as good as someone in his/her absence
(b) to light up a candle
(c) to find out the true intention
(d) to support someone

41. *Black sheep*
(a) a costly item
(b) a dark shiny object
(c) an unworthy person
(d) a funny man

42. *Oily tongue*
(a) flattery (b) hungry person
(c) strong critic (d) rich food

43. *Lion's share*
(a) no share at all
(b) greater share of a thing
(c) miserly
(d) very small item

44. *Pillar to post*
(a) one place to another
(b) very tiresome journey
(c) main supports of a building
(d) clumsy looking objects

45. *To bury the hatchet*
(a) to dispute over small things
(b) to destroy
(c) to make peace
(d) to repair a costly furniture

46. *At sea*
(a) to travel by boat
(b) to confuse others
(c) perplexed
(d) to incite others

47. *Heart and soul*
(a) very seriously and sincerely
(b) honestly
(c) wearily
(d) very casually

48. *In a nutshell*
(a) cheaply
(b) in a very short form or in a few words
(c) very rapidly
(d) very weakly

49. *Child's play*
(a) a very easy thing
(b) a very cheap thing
(c) funny thing
(d) things that can be done without any cost

50. *Bird's eyeview*
(a) to view something closely
(b) a general view from above
(c) to view suspiciously
(d) to look from a different angle

51. *To scale up*
(a) to measure
(b) to discuss
(c) to divide
(d) to deliver

52. *To clear the air*
(a) to work hard
(b) to wash properly
(c) to remove tension
(d) to create confusion

53. *To chew the cud*
(a) to be very annoyed
(b) to think deeply
(c) to eat humble food
(d) to start doing something new

54. *Out and out*
(a) merely
(b) slightly
(c) to go a faraway place
(d) absolutely

55. *To come in handy*
(a) to be useful
(b) to reach home tired
(c) to stand very close
(d) to come forward to help others

56. *No axe to grind*
(a) to bad situation
(b) to rebuke
(c) to act selflesly
(d) to confuse others

57. *To play foul*
(a) to play rough football
(b) to tackle carelessly
(c) to oppose others
(d) to do something wrong

58. *To see red*
(a) to find fault with
(b) to be very angry
(b) to criticise others
(d) to victimise someone

59. *Not to mince matters*
(a) to speak out frankly
(b) to make matters easy
(c) to be at ease
(d) to be successful in business

60. *To play with*
(a) to be friendly with
(b) to amuse oneself
(c) to win easily
(d) fool

61. *Turn over a new leaf*
(a) hopeful situation
(b) change for the better
(c) promising start followed by failure
(d) expression of anger

62. *Rainy days*
(a) small hours of the morning
(b) critical time in any situation
(c) late hours of the night
(d) unlucky times
(e) peaceful hours in a noisy city

63. *To bell the cat*
(a) to take lead in danger
(b) to tie bell to cat's neck
(c) to be alert of the enemy
(d) to make noise

64. *An axe to grind*
(a) to indulge in evil conspiracies
(b) to catch a fish in disturbed water
(c) to make a personal profit out of a situation
(d) to aggravate the situation

65. *To be in a fix*
(a) to be perplexed
(b) making rounds of something
(c) to attain permanence
(d) to feel happy

66. *To get in hot waters*
(a) to get into trouble
(b) to enter waters heated by the sun
(c) to be so impatient as to take bath with hot water before it gets cool
(d) to be in a confused state of mind

67. *To throw dust into one's eyes*
(a) to put sand into one's eyes
(b) to make blind
(c) to deceive
(d) to point out false things

68. *To fly off the handle*
(a) to break something
(b) to be indifferent
(c) to act foolishly
(d) to get into a rage and lose self-control

69. *The alpha and the omega*
(a) very costly items
(b) assorted items
(c) the beginning and the end
(d) a nice act

70. *To flag a dead horse*
(a) to do a thing in vain
(b) to act in a foolish way
(c) to criticise strongly
(d) try to revive interest in a subject that is out of date

71. *To smell a rat*
(a) bad smell
(b) to misunderstand
(c) to suspect treachery
(d) to see a hidden meaning

72. *Hobson's choice*
(a) first choice
(b) beautiful choice
(c) no choice at all as there is only one thing to choose from
(d) to choose something carefully

73. *A good samaritan*
(a) a genuinely helpful person
(b) an honest politician
(c) a clever person
(d) a priest

74. *Gift of the gab*
(a) lucky
(b) a big surprise
(c) to have a talent for speaking
(d) an honest person

75. *In deep water*
(a) in real trouble
(b) to feel lonely
(c) to act like a coward
(d) to swim in a river

76. *To look blue*
(a) to be annoyed
(b) to look sad
(c) to feel happy
(d) to look sick

77. *To steal a march*
(a) to outshine
(b) to start early
(c) to command an army
(d) to overtake

C. Mixed Questions

78. Never take up *a fool's errand*
(a) to go with a message
(b) one who takes a message

(c) a useless undertaking
(d) an observation

79. The child *pulled a long face* when the sweets were over.
(a) to look disappointed
(b) feel good
(c) retreat
(d) run away

80. In this competition there is complete *fair play.*
(a) honest means
(b) no cheating
(c) good chances
(d) good name

81. To be *fair and square* pays in the long run.
(a) successful
(b) honest means
(c) honest
(d) worthy

82. The poor women do manual labour even when they are *in the family way.*
(a) in a domestic manner
(b) unwell
(c) injured
(d) pregnant

83. He tried *to curry favour* with his employer.
(a) to seek favourable attention
(b) to attract
(c) impartial attitude
(d) to see in a spirit of joy

84. Backbiters have generally *to cut a sorry figure* in the company of friends.
(a) a nominal head
(b) to fight to a finish
(c) to be ridiculed
(d) to struggle

85. I have *burnt my fingers* in this speculative deal and am today penniless.
(a) incur loss of property
(b) to get into unexpected trouble
(c) to burn one's finger
(d) to get confused

86. The leader must have *the lion's share* of the booty.
(a) the stronger one
(b) the smaller part
(c) the worthy part
(d) the larger part

87. The project of building *ended in smoke.*
(a) to give no practical result
(b) to fall
(c) to catch fire
(d) ended in the destruction of the building

88. *Flesh and blood* can bear it no longer.
(a) human nature
(b) warning
(c) in life
(d) at the top speed

89. I am just *a small fry* in the office.
(a) peon
(b) a small creature
(c) humorous
(d) person or thing of little importance

90. The number of *globetrotters* has increased after the Second World War.
(a) great persons
(b) foreign countries
(c) travellers around the world
(d) people of importance

91. Never *hit* even the worst enemy *below the belt,* for even a war has some code of morality.
(a) to hit at the wrong position
(b) to fight
(c) to injure
(d) through unfair means
(e) to cheat

92. No one knew what to say, but at last I *broke the ice.*
(a) to crack the ice
(b) to start a conversation
(c) to start quarrelling
(d) to end the hostility

93. The result of the examination *dashed my hopes.*
(a) frustrate
(b) kill someone

(c) failed
(d) bring great happiness

94. He chose the path of religion *of his own accord.*
(a) forcibly
(b) helplessly
(c) half-heartedly
(d) willingly

95. I can never understand him because he has a bad habit of *mincing matters.*
(a) to leave in difficulties
(b) not to speak plainly
(c) returning
(d) to find fault

96. None of this *hanky-panky,* please talk straight.
(a) obsession
(b) diversification
(c) jugglery
(d) indifference

97. He has only some *hazy ideas* about life.
(a) vulgar ideas
(b) masculine ideas
(c) hazardous
(d) confused

98. *Hot head*
(a) the leader
(b) one who is very rash
(c) the fighter
(d) brave person

99. *Have a go*
(a) go on leave
(b) ride for happiness
(c) make an attempt
(d) take a walk

100. *Mince one's words*
(a) change suddenly
(b) pull back
(c) to speak in a hurry
(d) choose them carefully

101. *Frame a person*
(a) make him appear guilty
(b) befool
(c) ask him to sit idle
(d) flatter somebody

102. *A pipe dream*
(a) an impracticable plan
(b) a pleasant dream
(c) a foolish idea
(d) a bad dream

103. *Fall flat*
(a) to fall in love
(b) fail to win appreciation
(c) lose consciousness
(d) lose confidence

104. *Be in the mire*
(a) be in love
(b) be uneasy
(c) be in difficulties
(d) be under debt

105. *Let on*
(a) reveal
(b) quarrel
(c) give
(d) fight

106. *Make up*
(a) get about
(b) leave
(c) reveal
(d) reconcile

107. *To get along*
(a) to manage to
(b) to go with
(c) to leave
(d) work helplessly

108. *Make too much of*
(a) underestimate
(b) exploit
(c) overestimate
(d) ask to do too much

109. *Lay bare*
(a) expose
(b) take off all clothes
(c) destroy
(d) exploit

110. *Stem from*
(a) ruin
(b) originate

(c) induce
(d) kill

111. *In a jiffy*
(a) suddenly
(b) outstanding
(c) in a fix
(d) appropriate

112. *Stir up a hornet's nest*
(a) money laid by
(b) well-mannered people
(c) neighbourhood
(d) create trouble

113. *On the nod*
(a) on
(b) shake one's head
(c) on credit
(d) to fall as keep

114. *To take occasion*
(a) to take advantage of an opportunity
(b) celebrate
(c) to draw a moral attention
(d) organise a ceremony

115. *To oil the knocker*
(a) to eat greasy items
(b) to fill the tank
(c) to get the vehicle greased
(d) to tip the office-boy

116. *A fool's paradise*
(a) paradise of idiots
(b) to live in illusions
(c) to live in the past
(d) to have happy dreams

117. *Take it ill*
(a) to feel otherwise
(b) to feel good
(c) to be offended
(d) suffering from fever

118. *To chew the end*
(a) to cut the end
(b) to think deeply
(c) to be annoyed
(d) start something new

119. *To scale up*
(a) to kill
(b) to measure
(c) to die for
(d) to deepen

120. *Extinct and obsolete*
(a) exhausted
(b) very old
(c) as dead as a dodo
(d) behind time

121. *In a delicate state*
(a) hanging in balance
(b) hanging in fire
(c) looming large
(d) hanging by a hair

122. *At bottom*
(a) at last
(b) in the end
(c) from beneath
(d) inwardly

123. *In abeyance*
(a) in absence
(b) in no time
(c) in a nutshell
(d) in suspension

124. *With might and main*
(a) big blow
(b) hard blow
(c) with full vigour
(d) penetrating

125. *In a jam*
(a) bad
(b) in trouble
(c) hindrance
(d) eatable

126. *To get at*
(a) to reach
(b) to advance
(c) to proceed
(d) to escape

ANSWER KEY

1. (b)
2. (c)
3. (a)
4. (d)
5. (d)
6. (c)
7. (c)
8. (d)
9. (d)
10. (d)
11. (b)
12. (b)
13. (d)
14. (d)
15. (a)
16. (a)
17. (d)
18. (c)
19. (c)
20. (d)
21. (a)
22. (d)
23. (c)
24. (d)
25. (b)
26. (c)
27. (c)
28. (a)
29. (a)
30. (a)
31. (a)
32. (b)
33. (a)
34. (c)
35. (b)
36. (c)
37. (c)
38. (c)
39. (a)
40. (a)
41. (c)
42. (a)
43. (b)
44. (a)
45. (c)
46. (c)
47. (a)
48. (b)
49. (a)
50. (b)
51. (a)
52. (c)
53. (b)
54. (d)
55. (a)
56. (c)
57. (d)
58. (a)
59. (a)
60. (d)
61. (b)
62. (d)
63. (a)
64. (c)
65. (a)
66. (a)
67. (c)
68. (d)
69. (c)
70. (a)
71. (c)
72. (c)
73. (a)
74. (c)
75. (a)
76. (b)
77. (a)
78. (c)
79. (a)
80. (b)
81. (c)
82. (d)
83. (a)
84. (c)
85. (a)
86. (d)
87. (a)
88. (a)
89. (d)
90. (c)
91. (d)
92. (b)
93. (a)
94. (d)
95. (b)
96. (c)
97. (d)
98. (b)
99. (c)
100. (d)
101. (a)
102. (a)
103. (b)
104. (c)
105. (a)
106. (d)
107. (a)
108. (c)
109. (a)
110. (b)
111. (a)
112. (d)
113. (c)
114. (a)
115. (d)
116. (b)
117. (c)
118. (b)
119. (b)
120. (c)
121. (d)
122. (d)
123. (d)
124. (c)
125. (b)
126. (a)

Appendix

Questions from Examination Papers

1. *Will o' the wisp.*
   (a) anything which eludes or deceives
   (b) to act in a childish way
   (c) to act in a foolish way
   (d) to have desires unbacked by efforts
   (GICAAO)

2. *To give/get the bird.*
   (a) to get the awaited
   (b) to have good luck
   (c) to send away
   (d) to get the impossible
   (MBA)

3. *To cast pearls before a swine.*
   (a) to spend recklessly
   (b) to spend a lot of money on the upkeep of domestic hogs
   (c) to waste money over trifles
   (d) to offer to a person a thing which he cannot appreciate
   (CICAAO)

4. *To bring one's eggs to a bad market.*
   (a) to face a humiliating situation
   (b) to bring one's commodities to a market where there is no demand for them
   (c) to show one's talents before an audience which is incapable of appreciating them
   (d) to fail in one's plans because one goes to the wrong people for help
   (SSPO)

5. *To take the bull by the horns.*
   (a) to punish a person severely for his arrogance
   (b) to grapple courageously with a difficulty that lies in our way
   (c) to handle it by fierce attack
   (d) to bypass the legal process and take action according to one's own whims
   (Railways)

6. *To take with a grain of salt.*
   (a) to take with some reservation
   (b) to take with total disbelief
   (c) to take wholeheartedly
   (d) to take seriously
   (Asstt. Grade)

7. *To take the wind out of another's sails.*
   (a) to manoeuvre or to mislead another on the high seas
   (b) to cause harm to another
   (c) to defeat the motives of another
   (d) to anticipate another and to gain advantage over him
   (IES)

8. *Hard-pressed.*
   (a) bewildered (b) insulted
   (c) hard discipline (d) in difficulties
   (LICAAO)

9. *The pros and cons.*
   (a) for and against a thing
   (b) foul and fair
   (c) good and evil
   (d) former and latter
   (Bank PO)

10. *To cool one's heels.*
    (a) to rest for some time
    (b) to give no importance to someone
    (c) to remain in a comfortable position
    (d) to be kept waiting for some time
    (MBA)

11. The boy *turned a deaf ear* to the pleadings of all his well-wishers.

(a) listened carefully
(b) was deadly opposed
(c) posed indifference
(d) did not pay any attention

(Asstt. Grade)

12. Sumit had to look *high and low* before he could find his scooter key.
(a) nowhere (b) always
(c) everywhere (d) somewhere

13. We should *give a wide berth* to bad characters.
(a) keep away from (b) publicly condemn
(c) give publicly to (d) not sympathise with

(Railways)

14. The popularity of the yesteryears' superstar is *on the wane.*
(a) growing more (b) at its peak
(c) growing less (d) at rockbottom

(Section officers')

15. He has *made his mark* in politics.
(a) attained notoriety
(b) ruined his wealth
(c) acquired wealth
(d) distinguished himself

(Stenographers' Exam)

16. At Christmas, even the elderly fathers *paint the town red.*
(a) indulge in rioting
(b) paint the houses red
(c) spill red wine
(d) have a lively time

(Central Excise)

17. Rahul fought *tooth and nail* to save his company.
(a) with weapons
(b) as best as he could
(c) using unfair means
(d) with strength and fury

(Income Tax)

18. At a party, he is always *in high spirits.*
(a) talkative (b) cheerful
(c) drunk (d) uncontrollable

(NDA)

19. She rejected his proposal of marriage *point-blank.*
(a) directly (b) pointedly
(c) abruptly (d) briefly

(Clerks' Grade)

20. We should guard against our *green-eyed* friends.
(a) rich (b) jealous
(c) handsome (d) enthusiastic

(Translators' Exam.)

21. Kamal was left *high and dry* by his friends when he lost all his money.
(a) isolated (b) rejected
(c) wounded (d) depressed

(CBI)

22. A movement for the world unity is *in the offing.*
(a) at the end (b) about to start
(c) on decline (d) in the air

(CDS)

23. In the organised society of today no individual or nation can *plough a lonely furrow.*
(a) remain unaffected
(b) do without the help of others
(c) survive in isolation
(d) remain non-aligned

(Income Tax)

24. Chandu used very ugly words against his kind uncle; he *threw down the gauntlet before him.*
(a) he abused and insulted him
(b) he threw the challenge
(c) he behaved as if he was a very great and important person
(d) he put several conditions for negotiation
(e) he showed his readiness to leave the place

(SBIPO)

25. He always *cuts both ends.*
(a) works for both sides
(b) inflicts injuries on others
(c) argues in support of both sides of the issue
(d) behaves dishonestly
(e) creates discord among friends

(Bank, PO)

ANSWER KEY

1. (a)	2. (a)	3. (d)	4. (c)	5. (b)
6. (a)	7. (c)	8. (d)	9. (a)	10. (d)
11. (d)	12. (c)	13. (a)	14. (c)	15. (d)
16. (a)	17. (b)	18. (b)	19. (b)	20. (b)
21. (a)	22. (b)	23. (c)	24. (b)	25. (c)

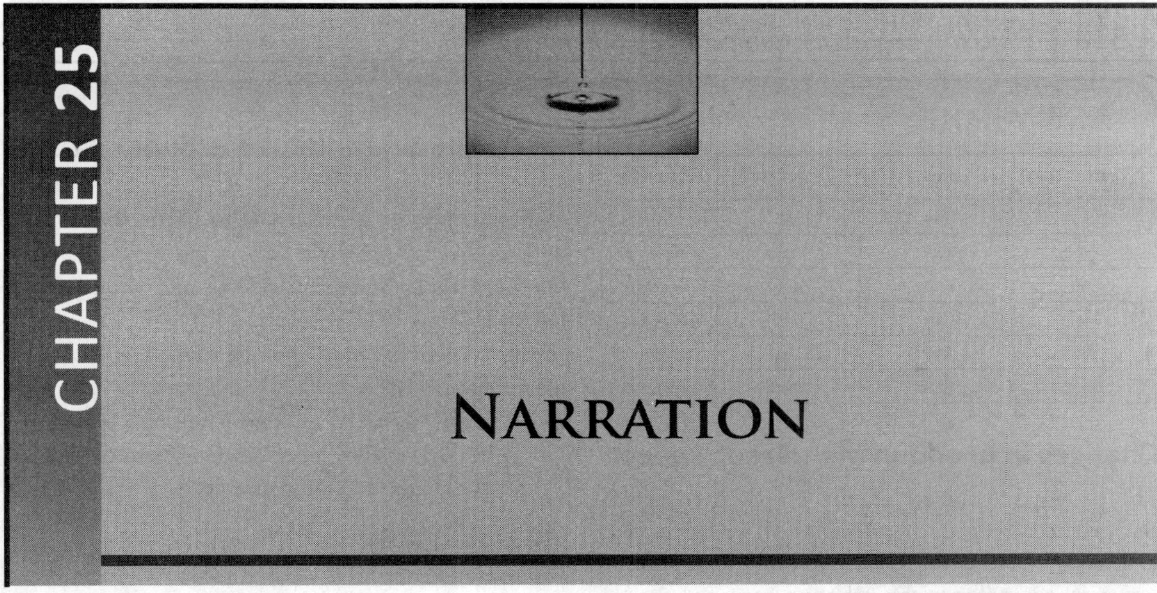

NARRATION

Narration is the art of reporting the words of a speaker. There are two main ways of reporting the words of a speaker.

1. Direct Speech
2. Indirect Speech

Direct Speech

In this form the actual words of the speaker are put in quotes "........".

Example

Rani said," I am very busy now."

In the above example the speaker, i.e,

Rani is known as reporter, 'said' is known as reporting verb and

"I am very busy now" is known as reported speech.

Indirect Speech

In this form the actual words of the speaker are transformed and said/written in simple manner.

Example: Rani said that she was very busy then.

Basic rules to convert a Direct Speech to Indirect Speech

There are five basic things that have to be changed while converting a Direct Speech to an indirect speech

1. To remove the inverted commas from the direct speech and place them with an appropriate conjunction
2. To change the pronoun of reported speech accordingly
3. To change the reporting verb according to the reported speech
4. Change the adverbs of the direct speech

   Direct : Rajnish said to me," I shall go to for the movie today".

Indirect: Rajnish told me that he would go for the movie that day.

In the above example:

Reporting verb **'said to'** is changed into **'told'**.

Inverted commas are replaced by the conjunction that

Reported speechs pronoun **'I'** is changed into **'he'**.

Reported speech's verb **'shall go'** is changed into **'would go'**.

The word **'today'** is changed with the word **'that day'**.

Rules of Change of Pronouns

Nominative	Possessive	Objective	Reflexive
I	My	Me	Myself
We	Our	Us	Ourselves
You	Yours	You	Yourself
He	His	Him	Himself
She	Her	Her	Herself
They	Their	Them	Themselves

Changes in pronoun in Indirect Speech

The pronoun (subject) of the reported speech is changed according to the pronoun of reporting verb or object (person) of reporting verb (first part of sentence). Sometimes the pronoun may not change at all.

1. First person pronoun in reported speech i.e. I, we, me, us, mine, or our, is changed according to the pronoun of reporting verb if pronoun in reporting verb is third person pronoun, i.e., he, she, it, they, him, his, her, them or their.

EXAMPLES

Direct speech: Sonu said, "I live in New Delhi".
Indirect speech: Sonu said that he lived in New Delhi
Direct speech: They said, "We love our country".
Indirect speech: They said that they loved their country.

2. First person pronoun in reported speech, i.e. I, we, me, us, mine, or our, is not changed if the pronoun (subject) of reporting is also first person pronoun i.e., I or we.

EXAMPLES

Direct speech: Gitos said, "I write a blog".
Indirect speech: Gitos said that she wrote a blog.
Direct speech: We said, "we finished our work".
Indirect speech: We said that we had finished our work.

3. Second person pronoun in reported speech i.e. you, yours is changed to the person of object of reporting verb.

EXAMPLES

Direct speech: Aanchal said to Monu, "You are intelligent".
Indirect speech: Aanchal said to Monu that he was intelligent.
Direct speech: Sounjanya said to me, "You are late for the film".
Indirect speech: Sounjanya said to me that I was late for the film.

4. Third person pronoun in reported speech i.e. he, she, it, they, him, his, her, them or their, is not changed in indirect speech.

EXAMPLES

Direct speech: They said, "he will come".
Indirect speech: They said that he would come.
Direct speech: You said, "They are waiting for the bus".
Indirect speech: You said that they were waiting for the bus.

Change in the tense of reported speech

If the first part of sentence (reporting verb part) belongs to past tense the tense of reported speech will change. If the first part of sentence (reporting verb part) belongs to present or future tense, the tense of reported speech will not change.

EXAMPLES

Direct speech: Neelima said, "I am happy".
Indirect Speech: Neelima said that she was happy. (Tense of reported speech changed)
Direct speech: Neelima says, "I am happy".
Indirect Speech: Neelima says that she was happy. (Tense of reported speech didn't change)

Change in tense is made according to rules of indirect speech which are given here.

Tense Change In Indirect Speech

Present simple tense ***into*** past simple
Present continuous tense ***into*** past continuous
Present perfect tense ***into*** pas perfect

Present perfect continuous ***into*** past perfect continuous
Past simple ***into*** past perfect
Past continuous ***into*** past perfect continuous
Past perfect ***into*** past perfect
Future simple, will ***into*** would
Future continuous, will be ***into*** would be
Future perfect, will have ***into*** would have

EXAMPLES

DIRECT SPEECH	INDIRECT SPEECH
PRESENT TENSE	
PRESENT SIMPLE changes into PAST SIMPLE	
Aaryan said, "I read a poem".	Aaryan said that he read a poem.
Mana said, "She goes to school daily".	Mana said that she went to school daily.
They said, "We love our country".	They said that they loved their country
Aditya said, "He does not like computers".	Aditya said that he did not like computers.
PRESENT CONTINUOUS changes into PAST CONTINUOUS	
Vihaan said, "He is listening to the music".	Vihaan said that he was listening to the music.
Aanchal said, "I am washing my dress".	Anchal said that she was washing her dress.
They said, "We are enjoying the film".	They said that they were enjoying the film.
Geetu said, "I am not sleeping".	Geetu said that she was not sleeping.
PRESENT PERFECT changes into PAST PERFECT	
Soujanya said, "He has finished his work".	Soujanya said that he had finished his work.
Vibhat said, "I have started building a new house."	Vibhat said that he had started building a new house.
I said, "She has eaten the meal".	I said that she had eaten the meal.
They said, "We have not gone to Paris.	They said that they had not gone to Paris.
PRESENT PERFECT CONTINUOUS changes into PAST PERFECT CONTINUOUS	
Monu said, "I have been studying since 3 o'clock".	Monu said that he had been studying since 3 O'clock.
Swetali said, "It has been raining for three days."	Swetali said that it had been raining for three days.
I said, "Nehal has been working in this office since 2007".	I said that Nehal had been working in this office since 2007.
PAST TENSE	
PAST SIMPLE changes into PAST PERFECT	
Anish said to me, "You answered correctly".	Anish said to me that I had answered correctly.
Manoj said, "They went to the cinema".	Manoj said that they had gone to the cinema.
Sunil said, "I made a table".	Sunil said that he had made a table.
Anil said, "I didn't buy a car".	Anil said that he had not bought a car.
PAST CONTINUOUS changes into PAST PERFECT CONTINUOUS	
They said, "We were enjoying the show".	They said that they had been enjoying the show.
Mr. Subash said to me, "I was waiting for you".	Mr. Subash said to me that he had been waiting for me.
I said, "It was raining".	I said that it had been raining
Monu said, "I was not laughing".	Monu said that he had not been laughing.

PAST PERFECT changes into PAST PERFECT (Tense does not change.)	
Mrs. Geeta Rani said, "She had visited a doctor friend". Rajnish said, "I had started a business". I said, "Neelima had eaten the meal". They said, "We had not gone to London".	Mrs. Geeta Rani said that she had visited a doctor friend. Rajnish said that he had started a business. I said that Neelima had eaten the meal. They said they had not gone to London.
FUTURE TENSE	
FUTURE SIMPLE TENSE WILL changes into WOULD	
Aaryan said, "I will study the book". Nehal said, "I will buy a computer". They said to me, "We will send you gifts". I said, "I will not take the exam".	Aaryan said that he would study the book. Nehal said that she would buy a computer. They said to me that they would send me gifts. I said that I would not take the exam.
FUTURE CONTINUOUS TENSE WILL BE changes into WOULD BE	
I said to him, "I will be waiting for him". Chiky said," I will be shifting to my new home". Rajnish said, "I will be working hard". Khushi said, "He will not be flying kite".	I said to him that I would be waiting for him. Chiky said that she would be shifting to her new home. Rajnish said that he would be working hard. Khushi said that she would not be flying kites.
FUTURE PERFECT TENSE WILL HAVE changes into WOULD HAVE	
Sonu said, "I will have finished the work". Nehal said, "they will have passed the examination". Aaryan said, "I will have gone".	Sonu said that he would have finished the work. Nehal said that they would have passed the examination. Aaryan said that he would have gone.

Note: The tense of reported speech may not change if reported speech is a universal truth though its reporting verb belongs to past tense.

EXAMPLES

Direct speech: Vihan said, "Mathematics is a science".

Indirect Speech: Vihan said that mathematics is a science.

Direct speech: Sonu said, "Sun rises in the east".

Indirect Speech: Sonu said that sun rises in the east.

(Tense didn't change because reported speech is a universal truth thought its reporting verb belongs to the past tense.)

Questions which can be answered in YES/NO.

To change questions (which can be answered in yes or no) into indirect speech, the words "if" or "whether" are used before the question in indirect speech. Rules for change in tense of question sentences are same as for change in normal tenses in indirect speech but the sentence will not start with the auxiliary verb of the tense. The word "that" is not used between reporting verb and reported speech as a conjunction in indirect speech for question sentence. Question mark is not used in indirect speech.

EXAMPLES

Direct speech: Mrs. Prabha Rani Sinha said to me, "Do you like music?"

Indirect Speech: Mrs. Prabha Rani Sinha asked me if I liked music. (Not, 'did I like music')

Or

Indirect Speech: Mrs. Prabha Rani Sinha asked me whether I liked music.

Direct Speech: Uma Rani Sinha said, "Will he participate in the quiz competition?".

Indirect Speech: Uma Rani Sinha asked me if he would participate in quiz competition.

Direct Speech: I said to him, "Are you feeling well?"

Indirect Speech: I asked him if he was feeling well.

Direct Speech: They said to me, "Did you go to school?"

Indirect Speech: They asked me if I had gone to school.

Direct Speech: Ajay said to me, "Have you taken the breakfast?"

Indirect Speech: Ajay asked me if I had taken the breakfast

Question which cannot be answered in YES/NO.

To change such questions into indirect speech, the words "if' or "whether" is not used. The tense of the question is changed according to the rules for change in normal tenses in indirect speech but sentence will not start with the auxiliary verb of the tense. The word "that" is not used between reporting verb and reported speech as conjunction, in indirect speech for question sentence. Question mark is not used in indirect speech.

EXAMPLES

Direct Speech: Anil said to me, "how are you?"

Indirect Speech: Anil asked me how I was. (Not, 'how was I')

Direct Speech: The teacher said to him, "What is your name?"

Indirect Speech: The teacher asked him what his name was.

Direct Speech: Rani said to him, "Why did you come late?"

Indirect Speech: Rani asked him why he had come late.

Direct Speech: He said, "When will they come?"

Indirect Speech: He asked when they would come.

Direct Speech: Mrs. Abha asked her son, "Why are you eating sweets?"

Indirect Speech: Mrs. Abha asked her son why he was eating sweets.

The model will not change in indirect speech

Direct Speech	Indirect Speech
THESE MODELS DO NOT CHANGE	
Would, could, might, should, ought to	
Would	
They said, "We would apply for a passport". Mr. Vijay said, "I would start a business". Neelima said, "I would appear in the exam".	They said that they would apply for a passport. Mr. Vijay said that he would start a business. Neelima said that she would appear in the exam.
Could	
Vidhi said, "She could play a piano". They said, "We couldn't learn the lesson". Mr. Binod Kumar said, "I could run faster".	Vidhi said that she could play a piano. They said they couldn't learn the lesson. Mr. Binod Kumar said that he could run faster.
Might	
Anish said, "Guest might come". Mrs. Geeta said, "It might rain". Sonu said, "I might meet him".	Anish said that guest might come. Mrs. Geeta said that it might rain. Sonu said that he might meet him.
Should	
Dr. Ramesh said, "I should avail the opportunity". Mrs. Kamala Sinha said, "I should help him". They said, "We should take the exam".	Dr. Ramesh said that he should avail the opportunity. Mrs. Kamala Sinha said that she should help him. They said that they should take the exam.

Direct Speech	Indirect Speech
Ought to	
He said to me, "You ought to wait for him". Prabha said, "I ought to learn the method of study". They said, we ought to attend our classes".	He said to me that I ought to wait for him. Prabha said that she ought to learn the method of study. They said that they ought to attend their classes.

Indirect speech for exclamatory and imperative sentences

Indirect speech of imperative sentence

A sentence which expresses command, request, advice or suggestion is called imperative sentence.

Examples

- Open the door.
- Please help me.
- Learn your lesson.

To change such sentences into indirect speech, the word "ordered" or "requested" or "advised" or "suggested" or "forbade" or "not to do" is added to reporting verb depending upon the nature of the imperative sentence in reported speech.

EXAMPLES

Direct Speech: Anish said to me, "Please help me".

Indirect Speech: Anish **requested** me to help him.

Direct Speech: Shruti said to him, "you should work hard for exam".

Indirect Speech: Shruti **suggested** him to work hard for exam.

Direct Speech: They said to him, "do not tell a lie".

Indirect Speech: They said to him **not to** tell a lie.

Direct Speech: He said, "Open the door".

Indirect Speech: He **ordered** to open the door.

Direct Speech: The teacher said to students, "Do not waste time".

Indirect Speech: The teacher **advised** the students not to waste time.

Direct Speech: He said, "Please give me a glass of water".

Indirect Speech: He **requested** to give him a glass of water.

Direct Speech: Doctor said to me, "Do not smoke".

Indirect Speech: Doctor **advised** me not to smoke.

Direct Speech: The teacher said to him, "Get out".

Indirect Speech: The teacher **ordered** him to get out.

Indirect speech of exclamatory sentences

The sentence which expresses a state of joy, sorrow or wonder is called exclamatory sentence.

For example.

- Hurrah! We won the match.
- Alas! I failed the test.
- Wow! What a nice shirt it is.

To change such sentences, the words "exclaimed with joy" or "exclaimed with sorrow" or "exclaimed with wonder" are added in the reporting verb depending upon the nature of the exclamatory sentence in indirect speech.

EXAMPLES

Direct Speech: He said, "Hurrah! I won a prize".

Indirect Speech: He **exclaimed with joy** that he had won a prize.

Direct Speech: She said, "Alas! I failed in exam".

Indirect Speech: She **exclaimed with sorrow** that she failed in the exam.

Direct Speech: Usha said, "Wow! What a nice shirt it is".

Indirect Speech: Usha **exclaimed with wonder** that it was a nice shirt.

Direct Speech: Jounty said, "Hurrah! I am selected for the job".

Indirect Speech: Jounty **exclaimed with joy** that she was selected for the job.

Direct Speech: Anish said, "Oh no! I missed the train".

Indirect Speech: Anish **exclaimed with sorrow** that he had missed the train.

Direct Speech: They said, "Wow! What a pleasant weather it is".

Indirect Speech: They **exclaimed with wonder** that it was a pleasant weather.

Changes in time and adverbs in indirect speech

Time and adverbs are changed in indirect speech.

EXAMPLES

Direct Speech: He said, "I will buy a book tomorrow".

Indirect Speech: He said that he would buy a book the **next day**.

Direct Speech: She said, "I am happy now".

Indirect Speech: She said that she was happy **then**.

Direct Speech: He said, "I like this book".

Indirect Speech: He said that he liked **that** book.

Common Rules

Today changes to **that day**/the same day .

Tomorrow changes to **the next day/the following day**.

Yesterday changes to **the day before/the previous day.**

Next week/month/year changes to **the following week/month/year.**

Last week/month/year changes to **the previous week/month/year.**

Now/just changes to **then.**

Ago changes to **before.**

Here changes to **there.**

This changes to **that.**

Practice Set —1

Directions to Questions 1 to 45: In the following questions, a sentence has been given in Direct/Indirect speech. Out of the four alternatives suggested, select the one which best expresses the same sentence in Indirect/Direct speech.

1. She said, "Let them play".
(a) She advised that we should be allowed to play.
(b) She advised that you should be allowed to play.
(c) She advised that they would be allowed to play.
(d) She advised that they should be allowed to play.

2. Ramesh said, "Sarla will not dance".
(a) Ramesh said that Sarla will not dance.
(b) Ramesh said that Sarla would not dance.
(c) Ramesh said if Sarla would not dance.
(d) Ramesh said when Sarla would not dance.

3. The professor said, "Alas! he is no more".
(a) The professor exclaimed with sorrow that he was no more.
(b) The professor exclaimed with surprise that he was no more.
(c) The professor exclaimed with sorrow that I was no more.
(d) The professor exclaimed with sorrow that she had been no more.

4. He said to me, "Do you know who is there?"
(a) He asked me if I knew who was there.
(b) He asked me that I knew who was there.
(c) He asked me if he knew who was there.
(d) He asked me if you knew who was there.

5. He said, 'Thanks for reminding me".
(a) He thanked me reminding him.
(b) He thanked me for reminding him.
(c) He thanks me for reminding him.
(d) He thanked me for reminding you.

3. He said, "Hello, what are you doing?"
(a) He greeted and asked me what I was doing.
(b) He greeted and asked me what was I doing.
(c) He greeted and asked me what he was doing.
(d) He greeted and asked him what I was doing.

7. She said, "Congratulations!"
(a) She congratulated me.
(b) She congratulates me.
(c) She congratulated him.
(d) She had congratulated me.

8. She said, "Farewell my dear friends".
(a) She bade farewell for her friends.
(v) She bade farewell her friends.
(c) She bade farewell to her friends.
(d) She bids farewell to her friends.

9. He said to the peon, "Let the visitor have his cap".
(a) He ordered the peon that the visitor might be allowed have my cap.
(b) He ordered the peon that the visitor might be allowed to have his cap.
(c) He requested the peon that the visitor might be allowed to have his cap.
(d) He told to the peon that the visitor might be allowed to have his cap.

10. He says, "Mohan will write a letter".
(a) He says that Mohan will write a letter.
(b) He says that Mohan would write a letter.
(c) He says that Mohan should write a letter.
(d) He says that Mohan will have written a letter.

11. The boy said, "Hurrah! we have won the match".
(a) The boy exclaimed joy that they had won the match.
(b) The boy exclaimed with disgust that they had won the match.
(c) The boy exclaimed with joy that they had won the match.
(d) The boy exclaimed with joy that they have won the match.

12. Sarla said, "Alas! 1 have failed".
(a) Sarla exclaimed for sorrow that she had failed.
(b) Sarla exclaimed with sorrow that she had failed.
(c) Sarla exclaimed by sorrow that she had failed.
(d) Sarla exclaimed with surprise that she had failed.

13. I said to her, "What! you have lost your bridal ring".
(a) I exclaimed with surprise that she had lost her bridal ring.
(b) I exclaimed with sorrow that she had lost her bridal ring.
(c) I exclaimed that she had lost her bridal ring.
(d) I exclaimed with disgust that she had lost her bridal ring.

14. Sumit said, "Father, I want to go abroad after I finish my studies here".
(a) Sumit told his father that he wanted to go abroad after he finished his studies here.
(b) Sumit told his father that I wanted to go abroad after he finished his studies here.
(c) Sumit told his father that you had wanted to go abroad after he finished his studies here.
(d) Sumit told his father that he had wanted to go abroad after he finished his studies here.

15. I said to Sumit, "Why do you want to go abroad? Where actually do you want to go?"
(a) I asked Sumit why he had wanted to go abroad and where he actually wanted to go.
(b) I asked Sumit why he wanted to go abroad and where he actually wanted to go.
(c) I asked Sumit why he wanted to go abroad and where he had actually wanted to go.
(d) I asked Sumit why he wanted to go abroad and where had he actually wanted to go.

16. "Don't go home yet," I told my colleague, "Remember you promised to finish your work before leaving".
(a) I requested my colleague to go home yet and to remember that he promised to finish his work before leaving.
(b) I requested my colleague not to go home yet and to remember that he has promised to finish his work before leaving.
(c) I requested my colleague not to go home yet and to remember that he promised to finish his work before leaving.
(d) I requested my colleague not to go home yet and to remember that he had promised to finish his work before leaving.

17. "Please listen to me, " he answered, "I must go now because my son is very ill".
(a) He asnwered politely listen to him and that he must go then because his son was very ill.

(b) He asnwered politely to listen him and that he must go then because his son was very ill.

(c) He asnwered politely to listen to him and that he must have gone then because his son was very ill.

(d) He asnwered politely to listen to him and that he must go then because his son was very ill.

18. "What a relief to know that the girl has passed!" I exclaimed, "now she can get a job".

(a) I exclaimed with joy that it was a great relief to know that the girl had passed and then she would get a job.

(b) I exclaimed with joy that it is a great relief to know that the girl had passed and then she would get a job.

(c) I exclaimed with joy that it was a great relief to know that the girl had passed and now she would get a job.

(d) I exclaimed with joy that it was a great relief to know that the girl had passed and then she will get a job.

19. The station master said to me, "You are very late, it is one full hour since the train left".

(a) The station master told to me that I was very late and it was one full hour since the train had left.

(b) The station master told me that I was very late and it was one full hour since the train had left.

(c) The station master told me if I was very late and it was one full hour since the train had left.

(d) The station master told me that I am very late and it is one full hour since the train had left.

20. Nitin said to me, "Why don't you come with us? Why do you want to be so unsocial?"

(a) Nitin asked me why I did not come with them. He further asked why he wanted to be so unsocial.

(b) Nitin asked me why he did not come with them. He further asked why I wanted to be so unsocial.

(c) Nitin asked me why I did not come with them. He further asked why I wanted to be so unsocial.

(d) Nitin asked me why you did not come with them. He further asked why I wanted to be so unsocial.

21. The gang leader shouted, "Keep together and run, the police are after us".

(a) The gang leader shouted to his followers keep together and run because the police were after them.

(b) The gang leader shouted to his followers to keep together and run because the police was after them.

(c) The gang leader shouted to his followers to keep together and run because the police were after them.

(d) The gang leader shouted his followers keep together and run because the police were after them.

22. I said to my companions, "Let them not come with us if they don't want to, let's not wait for them any longer".

(a) I told the companions that they need not come with them if they didn't want to, I suggested that they (the companions) should not wait for them any longer.

(b) I told to the companions that they need not come with them if they didn't want to, I suggested that they (the companions) should not wait for them any longer.

(c) I told the companions that they need not come with them if they didn't want to, I suggested if they (the companions) should not wait for them any longer.

(d) I told the companions whether they need not come with them if they didn't want to, I suggested that they (the companions) should not wait for them any longer.

23. ".What a pleasant surprise!" I exclaimed on seeing John in the room, "I never expected to find you here".

(a) I exclaimed after seeing John in the room that it was a veiy pleasant surprise, and I had never expected to find him there.

(b) I exclaimed for seeing John in the room that it was a very pleasant surprise, and I had never expected to find him there.
(c) I exclaimed on seeing John in the room that it was a very pleasant surprise, and I had never expected to find him there.
(d) I exclaimed on seeing John in the room that it is a very pleasant surprise, and I had never expected to find him there.

24. I said to Harish, 'The man who came to meet you asked if we could see his boss tomorrow".
(a) I told Harish that the man who had come to meet him, had asked if we would see his boss tomorrow.
(b) I told Harish that the man who had come to meet him, had asked if we would see his boss the next day.
(c) I told Harish that the man who had come to meet him, had asked we would see his boss the following day.
(d) I told Harish that the man who had come to meet him, has asked if we would see his boss the following day.

25. He said to his secretary, "Why don't you carry out orders exactly? Remember if you don't, you will be punished".
(a) He asked his secretary why he did not carry out orders exactly, he warned him that if he did not carry out orders he would be punished.
(b) He asked his secretary why he did carry out orders exactly, he warned him that if he did not (carry out orders) he would be punished.
(c) He asked his secretary why he did not carry out orders exactly, he had warned him that if he did not (carry out orders) he would be punished.
(d) He asked his secretary why he did not cany out orders exactly, he warned him that if he did not carry out orders he would punish.

26. I said to the boy, "You have no ticket, get out before you are driven out".
(a) I ordered the boy to get out (as he had no ticket) before he is driven out.
(b) I ordered the boy get out (as he had no ticket) before he was driven out.
(c) I ordered the boy to get out (as he had no ticket) before he was driven out.
(d) I ordered the boy to get out (as he has no ticket) before he was drive out.

27. The lecturer paused and said, "Those who are tired of listening to me can go. I shall not mind it".
(a) The lecturer paused and said that those who were tired of listening to him can go and that he would not mind that.
(b) The lecturer paused and said that those who are tired of listening to him could go and that he would not mind that.
(c) The lecturer paused and said that those who were tired of listening to him could go and that he would not mind that.
(d) The lecturer paused that those who were tired of listening to him could go and that he would not mind that.

28. They said, "How very awkward! What shall we say to him?"
(a) They cried out contempt what they would tell him and exclaimed that it was very awkward.
(b) They cried out with contempt what they would tell him, exclaimed that it was very awkward.
(c) They cried out for contempt what they would tell him, exclaimed that it was very awkward.
(d) They cried out with contempt what they would tell him and exclaimed that it was very awkward.

29. Madhur said to his sister, "Before I go to Delhi, I shall meet Sushila".
(a) Madhur told his sister that before he goes to Delhi, he would meet Sushila.
(b) Madhur told his sister that before going to Delhi, he would meet Sushila.
(c) Madhur told his sister if before going to Delhi, he would meet Sushila.
(d) Madhur told his sister and before going to Delhi, he would meet Sushila.

30. Govind said to Mohit, "Do not come here again or you will get a beating".

(a) Govind told Mohit not to come there again or he would get a beating.

(b) Govind told Mohit not to come there again or he will get a beating.

(c) Govind told Mohit not come there again or he would get a beating.

(d) Govind told to Mohit not to come there again or he would get a beating.

31. The traveller enquired of the farmer if he could tell him the way to the nearest inn.

(a) The traveller said to the farmer, "Where is the nearest inn?"

(b) The traveller said to the farmer, "Which is the way to the nearest inn?"

(c) The traveller said to the farmer, "Can you tell me the way to the nearest inn?"

(d) The traveller said to the farmer, "Can you tell me where is the nearest inn?"

32. The spectators said, "Bravo! well played, Ravi".

(a) The spectators called Ravi bravo because he had played well.

(b) The spectators said that Ravi played well and applauded him.

(c) The spectators encouraged Ravi saying that he played well.

(d) The spectators applauded Ravi, saying that he had played well.

33. "If you don't keep quiet I shall shoot you," he said to her in a calm voice.

(a) He warned her to shoot if she didn't keep quiet calmly.

(b) He said calmly that I shall shoot you if you don't be quiet.

(c) He warned her calmly that he would shoot her if she didn't keep quiet.

(d) Calmly he warned her that be quiet or else he will have to shoot her.

34. He says, "Ram is a good player".

(a) He says that Ram is a good player.

(b) He says that Ram will be a good player.

(c) He says that Ram was a good player.

(d) He said that Ram was a good player.

35. Rita says, "Kishore sang a song".

(a) Rita says that Kishore sings a song.

(b) Rita says that Kishore sang a song.

(c) Rita says that Kishore had sang a song.

(d) Rita says that Kishore was sang a song.

36. He said, "Shall I ever forget her?"

(a) He wondered if he would ever forget her.

(b) He wonders if he would ever forget her.

(c) He wondered that he would ever forget her.

(d) He told that he would ever forget her.

37. Kali will say, "Mira will swim in the river".

(a) Kali will say that Mira will swim in the river.

(b) Kali will say that Mira would swim in the river.

(c) Kali says that Mira will swim in the river.

(d) Kali will say Mira will swim in the river.

38. The teacher said to Ram. "Why are you wasting your time?"

(a) The teacher told Ram that why was he wasting his time.

(b) The teacher asked Ram that why was he wasting his time.

(c) The teacher asked Ram why he was wasting his time.

(d) The teacher asked Ram why was he wasting his time.

39. Mohan said to this friend, "Let me go home now".

(a) Mohan requested his friend let him go home then.

(b) Mohan requested his friend that he might be allowed to go home then.

(c) Mohan requested his friend to go home.

(d) Mohan told his friend to go him home.

40. I said to him, "Let us go to the river for swimming".

(a) I proposed him that we should go to the river for swimming.

(b) I asked him that we should go to the river for swimming.

(c) I proposed to him that we should go to the river for swimming.

(d) I requested him to go for swimming.

41. The washerman said, "It has been raining since morning".

(a) The washerman said that it had been raining since morning.

(b) The washerman told that it had been raining since morning.

(c) The washerman said it had been raining since morning.

(d) The washerman said that it was raining since morning.

42. The boys said, 'The teacher did not come".

(a) The boys said that the teacher has not come

(b) The boys said that the teacher had not come.

(c) The boys told that the teacher had not come.

(d) The boys said that the teacher had not coming.

43. The teacher said, "John, why are you always late?"

(a) The teacher asked why he was always late.

(b) The teacher asked John why he was always late.

(c) The teacher asks John why he was always late.

(d) The teacher asked John why he were always late.

44. My sister said to me, "I sent you the book".

(a) My sister told me that she had sent me the book.

(b) My sister told that she had sent me the book.

(c) My sister told me if she had sent me the book.

(d) My sister told me that she sent me the book.

45. He said, "Alas! I am undone".

(a) He exclaimed that he was undone.

(b) He exclaimed for sorrow that he was undone.

(c) He exclaimed with sorrow that he was undone.

(d) He exclaimed with sorrow that he were undone.

ANSWER KEY

1. (d)	11. (c)	21. (c)	31. (c)	41. (a)
2. (b)	12. (b)	22. (a)	32. (d)	42. (b)
3. (a)	13. (a)	23. (c)	33. (c)	43. (b)
4. (a)	14. (a)	24. (b)	34. (a)	44. (a)
5. (b)	15. (b)	25. (a)	35. (b)	45. (c)
6. (a)	16. (c)	26. (c)	36. (a)	
7. (a)	17. (d)	27. (c)	37. (a)	
8. (c)	18. (a)	28. (d)	38. (c)	
9. (b)	19. (b)	29. (b)	39. (b)	
10. (a)	20. (c)	30. (a)	40. (c)	

SECTION B

Practice Test Paper–One

Practice Test Paper–Two

Practice Test Paper–Three

Practice Test Paper–Four

Practice Test Paper–Five

Practice Test Paper–Six

Practice Test Paper–Seven

Practice Test Paper–Eight

Practice Test Paper–Nine

Practice Test Paper–Ten

PRACTICE TEST PAPERS

Practice test papers have been designed to assess the learning level of students preparing for different examinations. These test papers have maintained the same level of difficulty as expected in various examinations. Attempts have been made to approximate the real questions keeping in view the trends of past examination. Additional practice sets have been included keeping in mind the recent trends and difficulty levels.

PAPER 1

PRACTICE TEST PAPER–ONE

Directions for Questions 1 to 11 : Each question consists of sentences, which are divided into four parts, numbered (a) through (d) One part in each sentence is not acceptable in standard written English. Identify that part in each of the sentences which contains the error.

1. (a) Her acceptance of speech
   (b) was well received
   (c) eliciting thunderous applause
   (d) in several points
2. (a) An oppressive solemnity
   (b) and not the festive mood
   (c) one might have expected
   (d) characterised the mood by the gathering
3. (a) All aspiring artists must
   (b) struggle by the conflict
   (c) between faith in their own talent
   (d) and knowledge that, very few are great enough to succeed
4. (a) Despite some bad news,
   (b) Michel's stature was not diminished
   (c) and her fans or critics
   (d) were unanimous in appreciating her work.
5. (a) Jazz is an American art form,
   (b) which was now flourishing in Europe
   (c) through the efforts of expatriates
   (d) in France, Scandinavia and Germany.
6. (a) Character and
   (b) not riches
   (c) win us
   (d) respect.
7. (a) Pickpocketers are
   (b) sometimes spotted
   (c) by policemen
   (d) at bus stops.
8. (a) His both hands
   (b) have been injured
   (c) so he
   (d) cannot work.
9. (a) Several guests noticed Mr. Peter
   (b) fall back
   (c) in his chair
   (d) and gasping for breath.
10. (a) The short story
    (b) should not exceed

(c) more than
(d) two hundred words.

11. (a) Owing to illness
(b) he was unable
(c) to go
(d) for his holiday.

Directions for Questions 12 to 18: These questions consist of a number of sentences which when properly sequenced, form a coherent paragraph. Each sentence is labelled with a letter. Choose the most logical order of sentences from among the four choices lettered (a) through (d).

12. A. The men jumped up and rushed to the river
B. They poured it on the glowing bed of charcoal
C. The water gurgled out and the dying embers hissed and sent up little curls of vapour
D. They quickly came back with pitchers laden with water.
(a) DABC (b) ADCB
(c) CBAD (d) BADC

13. A. A failure to put the right person at the right place could prove expensive for the organisation
B. All managers are decision makers
C. The rightness of a decision largely depends upon whether or not the manager has utilised the right persons in right ways.
D. The effectiveness of managers is largely reflected in their track record in taking the right decisions
(a) DCBA (b) BDCA
(c) ABCD (d) BACD

14. A. I also believe in the possibility as well as the desirability of applying science to problems arising in social science
B. Believing as I do in social science, I can only look with apprehension upon social pseudo-science
C. I am a rationalist, which means that I believe in discussion and argument
D. I may say why I have chosen this particular subject
(a) CDAB (b) DCAB
(c) BCAD (d) DBAC

15. A. The investigation was confined to manufacturing firms in the area
B. Those concerned with mining and quarrying, construction, transport, and trade and commerce, were excluded
C. The number of workers employed by the firms in the area ranged from a dozen to approximately 35,000
D. A long search produced a comprehensive list of 203 manufacturing firms.
(a) ABDC (b) BCDA
(c) DCBA (d) CBDA

16. A. Moreover, private sector competitors claim to be moving from aluminium manufacture to specialised uses of the metal
B. The new concern could probably supply the metal to established companies for use as input,
C. As we all know, there is still shortage of the metal
D. All in all, though, the new plant will not threaten existing manufacturers in a big way
(a) ADCB (b) BCDA
(c) DBCA (d) CDBA

17. A. The causes of success or failure are deep and complex, chance plays a part
B. Motivation and opportunity can be supplied in good part by incentive compensation and decentralisation respectively
C. It is not easy to say why one management is successful and another is not
D. Experience has convinced me, however, that for those who are responsible for a business, motivation and opportunity are very important factors.
(a) CDAB (b) DCAB
(c) CADB (d) ACDB

18. A. The wind at his back also helped him on his course
B. Dark as the night was he found it easy to follow the track
C. Not only that he was confident that there would be few, if any, traces of his passage
D. Thanks to the drought, it was hard and firm and he made good speed
(a) CABD (b) DACB
(c) DBAC (d) BCDA

Directions for Questions 19 to 24: These questions consist of sentences each of which contains one or two idioms. Four possible meanings labelled (a) through (d) are provided below each sentence. Choose the one which best expresses the meaning of the idiom.

19. I would like to see Ramu do his own work for a change instead of always back-seat driving.
(a) driving a car from the back
(b) being critical of work being done by others
(c) offering advice
(d) annoying

20. He proved to be quite a wet blanket at the party for he spoke to no one and morosely sat by himself.
(a) he was crying
(b) discouraged the rest from having fun
(c) he wet the blanket
(d) he had covered himself with a wet blanket

21. The ship was about to weigh anchor when the storm came.
(a) weigh the anchor
(b) leave the docking berth
(c) raise the anchor
(d) drop the anchor

22. Debu had a chequered career since I first knew him as a clerk in the local bank.
(a) had a variety of jobs and experiences
(b) a career which helped him make lots of money
(c) a career where he signed a lot of cheques
(d) did odd jobs

23. Women should be paid the same as men when they do the same job, for surely, what is sauce for gander is sauce for the goose.
(a) both goose and gander should be equally treated
(b) what is thought suitable for a man should also be for a woman
(c) goose and gander eat the same sauce
(d) the principle or equal treatment should be implemented

24. The two women are so jealous that at the drop of a hat they start insulting each other.
(a) on every occasion
(b) for no reason at all
(c) when a hat is dropped
(d) very rarely

Directions for Questions 25 to 39: Each of the questions below contains one or more blank spaces, each blank space indicating an omitted word or phrase. Beneath the sentence are four words or set of words. Choose the word or set of words for each blank space that best fits the meaning of the sentence as a whole.

25. The judge, after ruling that the news report had unjustly .... the reputation of the Physician, ordered the newspaper to .... its libelous statements in print.
(a) injured — retract
(b) sullied — publicise
(c) damaged — disseminate
(d) tarnished — cover up

26. Psychologists agree that human beings have a strong need to.........their time; having too much idle time can be as stressful as having none at all.
(1) compartmentalise
(2) structure
(3) functionalise
(4) remand

27. ....several generations, Alex Haley wrote Roots, a novel explaining both his family history and the history of American bigotry.
(a) Focusing on
(b) Centering around
(c) With an eye on
(d) Living through

28. Although for centuries literature was considered something that would instruct as well as entertain, the modern reader has little patience with .... works and seeks only to be ....

(a) fiction — enlightened
(b) didactic — distracted
(c) voluminous — absorbed
(d) philosophical — entertained

29. To strive, to seek, to find, and .... are the heroic goals of Ulysses in Tennyson's famous poem.

(a) not yielding (b) yet to yield
(c) not to yield (d) yet not yield

30. The most frustrating periods of any diet are the inevitable ...., when weight loss .... if not stops.

(a) moods — accelerates
(b) feasts — halts
(c) meals — ceases
(d) plateaus — slows

31. Since the author's unflattering references to her friends were so .... she was surprised that her .... were recognised.

(a) laudatory — styles
(b) obvious — anecdotes
(c) oblique — allusions
(d) critical — eulogies

32. Gaurav was intent on maintaining his status as first in his class; because even the smallest mistakes infuriated him, he reviewed all his papers .... before submitting them to his teacher.

(a) explicitly
(b) perfunctorily
(c) assiduously
(d) honestly

33. The subtleties of this novel are evident not so much in the character .... as they are in its profoundly .... plot structure.

(a) assessment — eclectic
(b) development — trite
(c) delineation — intricate
(d) portrayal — aesthetic

34. Perhaps because something in us instinctively distrusts such displays of natural fluency, some readers approach John Updike's fiction with ....

(a) bewilderment
(b) suspicion
(c) veneration
(d) recklessness

35. We were amazed that, a man who had been heretofore the most .... of public speakers could, in a single speech electrify an audience and bring them cheering to their feet.

(a) masterful (b) auspicious
(c) pedestrian (d) accomplish;

36. Despite the mixture's .... nature, we found that by lowering the temperature in the laboratory we could dramatically reduce its tendency to vaporise.

(a) volatile (b) resilient
(c) insipid (d) acerbic

37. In one shocking instance of .... research, one of the nation's most influential researchers in the field of genetics reported on experiments that were never carried out and published deliberately .... scientific papers on his nonexistent work.

(a) comprehensive — abstract
(b) theoretical — challenging
(c) fraudulent — deceptive
(d) erroneous — impartial

38. Her novel published to universal acclaim, her literary gifts acknowledged by the chief figures of the Harlem Renaissance, her reputation as yet .... by envious slights, Hurston clearly was at the .... of her career.

(a) undamaged — ebb
(b) untarnished — zenith
(c) unmarred — brink
(d) untainted — extremity

39. New concerns about growing religious tension in Northern India were .... this week after at least fifty people were killed and hundreds injured or arrested in rioting between Hindus and Muslims.

(a) invalidated
(b) restrained
(c) fuelled
(d) lessened

Directions for Questions 40 to 49: Some part of each sentence below are in bold. Four choices numbered (a) through (d) for rephrasing the underlined part follow each sentence. Select the best alternative, following the requirements of standard written English.

40. **Regardless "new modernism" in literature which produces** novels, which often read like the diaries of madmen, most readers still prefer a conventional plot and simple style.
(a) Regardless of the "new modernism" in literature, which produces
(b) Regardless of the "new modernism" literature, which produce
(c) Regardless, the "new modernism" in literature produces
(d) Irregardless of the "new modernism" in literature, which produces

41. A career in the medical profession, **which requires an enormous investment of time and money, do not guarantee success as there is so much competition.**
(a) which requires an enormous investment of time and money, do not guarantee success as there is so much competition
(b) which requires an enormous investment of time and money, does not guarantee success since there is so much competition
(c) requiring an enormous investment of time and money, and cannot guarantee success because there is so much competition
(d) requires that an enormous investment of time and money be .made and success cannot be guaranteed due to competition

42. The more the union stubbornly refused to budge from its original demand for 20% across-the-board salary increase, **the more the company management reiterated its original proposal of a mere 3% raise.**
(a) the more the company management reiterated its original proposal of a mere 3% raise
(b) the company management's original proposal for a mere 3% raise was reiterated all the more
(c) the company management kept on reiterating its original proposal of a mere 3% raise
(d) the more the company management's original proposal of a mere 3% raise was reiterated

43. The president of the resident welfare association tried to convince his neighbours **they should join forces prevent crime in the neighbourhood rather than continuing to be victimised.**
(a) they should join forces to prevent crime in the neighbourhood rather than continuing to be victimised
(b) that they should join forces to prevent crime in the neighbourhood rather than continue to be victimised
(c) about joining forces to prevent crime in the neighbourhood instead of continuing to be victimised
(d) to join forces to prevent crime in the neighbourhood rather than continuing to be victimised

44. Lawyers and doctors **alike both agree something should be done about the rise in medical malpractice cases which are on the increase.**
(a) alike both agree that something should be done about the rise in medical malpractice cases which are on the increase
(b) alike agree that something should be done about the rise in medical malpractice cases
(c) agree that something should be done about the rise in the number of medical malpractices
(d) None of these

45. **The conductor seemed entirely arbitrary the choice of tempo**, because of which each successive movement of the piece seemed to have no connection to what had come before.
(a) The conductor's choice of tempo seemed entirely arbitrary

(b) It seemed the conductor chose tempo entirely arbitrary

(c) The conductor was entirely arbitrary in his choice of tempo

(d) The tempo was chosen entirely by the arbitrary conductor

46. Although the conditions in which she lived suggest that she was miserly, **her contributions to charities show that she is generous.**

(a) her charities showed generous contributions

(b) her generosities made large contributions

(c) her contributions to charities showed that she is not generous

(d) her contributions to charities show that she was generous

47. The governor's intolerance of dissent among his aides was intensified **by loyalty from all.**

(a) by him insisting upon total loyalty from all

(b) by his insistence upon total loyalty from all

(c) by all insisting upon his loyalty

(d) by his insisting upon their g loyalty

48. **Although he was often incomplete in his work,** he was promoted simply because he was with the company longer than anyone else.

(a) Although work was often incomplete

(b) His work was often incomplete although

(c) Although his work was often incomplete

(d) Although he often completed his n work

49. Though the concert had been enjoyable, **it was protracted overly**

(a) it was overly protracted

(b) it overly protracted

(c) it protracted overly

(d) it got protracted overly

50. **All, but here,** had made an attempt.

(a) All, but she,

(b) All, but herself,

(c) All, but her ownself

(d) No improvement required

PAPER 2

PRACTICE TEST PAPER–TWO

Directions 1 to 8: Read the passage carefully and answer the questions given below:

Recent technological advances in manned and unmanned undersea vehicles, along with breakthroughs in satellite technology and computer equipment, have overcome some of the limitations of divers and diving equipments for scientists doing research on the great oceans of the world. Without a vehicle, divers often became sluggish, and their mental concentration was severely limited. Because undersea pressure affects their speech organs, communication among divers has always been difficult or impossible. But today, most oceanographers avoid the use of vulnerable human divers, preferring to reduce the risk to human life and make direct observations by means of instruments that are lowered into the ocean, from samples taken from the water, or from photographs made by orbiting satellites. Direct observations of the ocean floor can be made not only by divers but also by deepdiving submarines in the water and even by the technology of sophisticated aerial photography from vantage points above the surface of the water. Some submarines can dive to depths of more than seven miles and cruise at depths of fifteen thousand feet. In addition, radio-equipped buoys can be operated by remote control in order to transmit information back to land-based laboratories via satellite. Particularly important for ocean study are data about water temperature, currents, and weather. Satellite photographs can show the distribution of sea ice, of slicks, and cloud formations over the ocean. Maps created from satellite pictures can represent the temperature and die colour of the ocean's surface, enabling researchers to study the ocean currents from laboratories on dry land. Furthermore, computers help oceanographers to collect, organize, and analyze data from submarines and satellites. By creating a model of the ocean's movement and characteristics, scientists can predict the patterns and possible effects of the ocean on the environment.

Recently, many oceanographers have been relying more on satellites and computers than on research ships or even submarine vehicles because they can supply a greater range of information more quickly and more effectively. Some of humankind's most serious problems, especially those concerning energy and food, may be solved with the help of observations made possible by this new technology.

1. How is a radio-equipped buoy-operated ?
   (a) By operators inside the vehicle in the part underwater

(b) By operators outside the vehicle on a ship
(c) By operators outside the vehicle on a diving platform
(d) By operators outside the vehicle in a laboratory on shore

2. The word cruise in the given paragraph could best be replaced by
(a) Travel at a constant speed
(b) Function without problems
(c) Stay in communication
(d) Remain still

3. Which of the following are NOT shown in satellite photograph ?
(a) The temperature of the ocean's surface
(b) Cloud formations over the ocean
(c) A model of the ocean's movements
(d) The location of sea ice

4. Undersea vehicles
(a) Are too small for a man to fit inside
(b) Are very slow to respond
(c) Have the same limitations that divers have
(d) Make direct observations of the ocean floor

5. With what topic is the passage primarily concerned ?
(a) Technological advances in oceanography
(b) Communication among divers
(c) Direct observation of the ocean floor
(d) Undersea vehicles

6. The word sluggish in the given paragraph is closest in meaning to
(a) Nervous
(b) Confused
(c) Slow moving
(d) Very weak

7. This passage suggests that the successful exploration of the ocean depends upon
(a) Vehicles as well as divers
(b) Radio that divers use to communicate
(c) Controlling currents and the weather
(d) The limitations of diving equipment

8. Divers have had problems in communicating underwater because
(a) The pressure affected their speech organs
(b) The vehicles they used have not been perfected
(c) They did not pronounce clearly
(d) The water destroyed their speech organs

Directions for Questions 9 to 13: In each of the following questions, out of the given alternatives, choose the one which best expresses the meaning of the given word.

9. CRUCIAL
(a) Savvy (b) Important
(c) Excellent (d) Usual

10. ALUMNUS
(a) Ex-student (b) Saint
(c) Delicate (d) Calm

11. FINERY
(a) Decoration (b) Torture
(c) Extract (d) Imprison

12. SURREPTITIOUS
(a) Submissive (b) Slaughter
(c) Secretly (d) Assassinate

13. FOLIAGE
(a) Tree (b) Plant
(c) Flowers (d) Leaves

Directions for Questions 14 to 18: In the following questions, choose the word opposite in meaning to the given word.

14. DYNAMIC
(a) Sentimental
(b) Intelligent
(c) Unforceful
(d) Carefree

15. INFLORESCENCE
(a) Unflowery
(b) Unintentional
(c) Unique
(d) Unnatural

16. ILLUSTRIOUS
(a) Uneducated (b) Unknown
(c) Unintelligent (d) Uncivilized

17. UNCOUTH
(a) Crude (b) Awkward
(c) Courteous (d) Refined

18. OUTFACE
(a) Submit (b) Stipend
(c) Discount (d) Wages

Directions for Questions 19 to 23 : Pick out the most effective word from the given words to fill in the blanks to make the sentence meaningfully complete.

19. Two buses collided .... each other on the road.
(a) between (b) into
(c) onto (d) with

20. Gandhiji drew the attention of the Indians .... the burning issues.
(a) towards (b) to
(c) into (d) on

21. This test .... no previous knowledge of the subject: any graduate is expected to complete it successfully.
(a) assumes
(b) presupposes
(c) necessitates
(d) concerns

22. A great author adopts a style appropriate .... his subject.
(a) for (b) to
(c) with (d) from

23. The telephone..........several times before I answered it.
(a) was rung (b) would ring
(c) had rung (d) has rung

Directions for Questions 24 to 28: In each of the following questions, find out one word substitute for the sentence given below.

24. A woman of loose moral
(a) Prostitute
(b) Harlot
(c) Concubine
(d) Hostess

25. A person who is obsessed with self
(a) Compulsive (b) Maniac
(c) Narcissist (d) Centroid

26. A name adopted by an author in his writings.
(a) Title
(b) Nomenclature
(c) Nick name
(d) Pseudonym

27. A person who is hopeless
(a) Incorrigible (b) Immodest
(c) Dull (d) Slow

28. A person who collects coins
(a) Philatelist (b) Numismatist
(c) Narcissist (d) Fatalist

Directions for Questions 29 to 33: In each of the following questions, four sentences have been given. Out of the four alternatives suggested select the one which is correct.

29.
(a) He has studied English since five years
(b) He has studied English from five years
(c) He has studied English since the time five years
(d) He has studied English for five years

30.
(a) I didn't understand what he said
(b) I didn't understood what did he
(c) I did not understand what did he say
(d) I did not understood he said

31.
(a) None news is good news
(b) None new is good new
(c) No news is good news
(d) None new is good news

32.
(a) There is not reason to worry
(b) There is no reason to worry
(c) There is doesn't reason to worry
(d) There is does not reason to worry

33.
(a) Very seldom a movie can hold my attention like this one
(b) Very seldom can a movie hold my attention like this one
(c) Very seldom a movie has held my attention like this one
(d) Very seldom a movie has hold my attention like this one

Directions for Questions 34 to 38: In each of the following questions, a word has been written in four different ways out of which only one is correctly spelt. Find the correctly spelt word.

34. (a) Turcuoise
(b) Turcuiose
(c) Turquoise
(d) Turquoisee

35. (a) Scoundrele
(b) Scoundrel
(c) Scoundrale
(d) Scoundral

36. (a) Countenance
(b) Contenance
(c) Coantenance
(d) Centenance

37. (a) Couchatte
(b) Couchette
(c) Couchechette
(d) Couhette

38. (a) Antimacasar
(b) Antimaccasar
(c) Antimecasar
(d) Antimacassar

PAPER 3

PRACTICE TEST PAPER–THREE

Directions for Questions 1-10: Read the following passage carefully and answer the questions given below it. Certain words have been printed in bold to help you locate them while answering some of the questions.

We should recognise the indebtedness of the country to its farm families who toil to safeguard national food security. Loan waiver is the price we have to pay for the neglect of rural India over the past several decades. There has been a gradual decline in investment in key sectors related to agriculture such as infrastructure, marketing, post harvest technology etc. The four crore **farmers** whose debt is to be **relieved** will be eligible for institutional credit for their cultivation expenses during Kharif 2008. The challenge is to prevent them from getting into the debt trap again. For this purpose the Central and various State governments should set up an Indebted Farmers' Support Consortium, comprising scientists, panchayat raj officials and others relevant to assisting farmers to improve the profitability and productivity of their farms in an environmentally sustainable manner. The smaller the farm the greater is the need for marketable surplus to reduce indebtedness.

The Indebted Farmers' Support Consortium should aim to get all the four crore farmers all the benefits of the government schemes such as the Rashtriya Krishi Vikas Yojana, Irrigation Benefit Programme and others. If this is done every farm family released from the debt trap should be able to produce at least an additional half tonne per hectare of food grains. This should help increase food production by about 20 million tonnes by 2008-10. At a time when global and national food stocks are dwindling and prices are rising, this will be a **timely** gain for our national food security. We need to ensure that the outcome of the debt waiver has enhanced tanners' income and production. The prevailing **gap** between potential and actual yields in the crops of rainfed areas such as pulses and oilseeds is over 200 per cent even with the necessary technologies on the shelf. We are now importing without duty large quantities of pulses and oilseeds. If helped, farmers can produce these at a lower cost.

Opportunities for **assured** and remunerative marketing are essential if loan waiver is not to become a recurring event leading to the destruction of the credit system. This is why the Minimum Support Price is necessary for all, not just for a few crops which is the case at present. This is the single most effective step to make loan waivers history. There is another urgent step which needs to be taken. The loan waiver does not cover those who borrow from moneylenders. It will not be possible for the government to scrutinise the veracity of such private deals but steps can be taken such as giving them Smart Cards which will entitle them to essential inputs like seeds and fertilisers. The gram sabha can be entrusted with the task of identifying these farmers so that there is transparency in the process and **elimination** of the chances for falsification and corruption. Fear of occasional misuse should not come in the way of enabling millions of poor farmers who have borrowed from informal sources if we are to achieve the goal of four percent growth in agriculture.

1. What is the likely impact of ensuring farmers benefit from government schemes ?
(A) They can use the credit from these schemes to repay moneylenders.
(B) The government can control the price rise.
(C) Increased agricultural production.
(a) Both (A) and (B)
(b) All (A), (B) and(C)
(c) Only (C)
(d) Both (B) and (C)
(e) None of these

2. Why does the author feel that rural India has been overlooked in the past?
(A) Institutional credit was only made available for Kharif crops.
(B) Drop in investment in central areas related to agriculture.
(C) Records of those eligible for loan waivers have not been maintained over time.
(a) Only (B)
(b) Both (A) and (B)
(c) Only (C)
(d) All (A), (B) and (C)
(e) None of these

3. How can small farmers avoid debt?
(a) They need to acquire additional land holdings.
(b) They need to take advantage of both government schemes as well as credit from moneylenders.
(c) They have to ensure a sufficient amount of their farm produce is sold.
(d) The Government should provide periodic loan waivers.
(e) None of these

4. What is the objective of the Indebted Farmers' Support Consortium?
(a) It is a support group for the families of indebted farmers.
(b) It has to devise new government schemes for farmers.
(c) It has to track farmers eligible for government schemes.
(d) It has to evaluate government schemes and weed out the inefficient ones.
(e) It will assist farmers to improve profitability and productivity.

5. What does the author mean by the phrase 'indebtness of the country to its farm families'?
(a) If farmers are in debt it impacts the entire country
(b) Citizens should be grateful to farmers and their families for the hardships borne by them to cultivate crops and safeguard national food security
(c) India's food production has fallen causing it to be in debt since it has to import food.
(d) The number of farmers' descendants taking up agriculture has fallen.
(e) None of these

6. What is the author's opinion of recurring loan waivers ?
(a) They are beneficial to farmers.
(b) They are detriment to the system of lending.
(c) They will reduce the need for a Minimum Support Price for agricultural products.
(d) Farmers will no longer be in debt to moneylenders.
(e) None of these

Directions for Questions 7 and 8: Choose the word which is most similar in meaning to the word printed in bold as used in the passage.

7. Assured
(a) insured (b) definite
(c) doubted (d) confident
(e) reliance

8. Relieved
(a) exempted (b) backed
(c) supported (d) calmed
(e) substituted

Directions for Questions 9 and 10: Choose the word which is most opposite in meaning to the word printed in bold as used in the passage.

9. Timely
(a) young (b) lately
(c) overdue (d) aged
(e) slowly

10. Elimination
(a) authority (b) forgiveness
(c) attack (d) protection
(e) provision

Directions for Questions 11 to 15: In each question below a sentence with four words printed in bold type is given. These are numbered as (a), (b), (c) and (d) . One of these four words printed in bold may be either wrongly spelt or inappropriate in the context of the sentence. Find out the word, which is wrongly spelt or inappropriate, if any. That word is your answer. If all the words printed in bold are correctly spelt and also appropriate in the context of the sentence, mark (e) i.e. 'All Correct' as your answer.

11. **Usually** (a) / we are **required** (b) / to supply a **tittle** (c) / to the **paragraph.** (d) / All correct (e)

12. The **movement** (a) / he was asked to **recite** (b) a **rhyme,** (c) / he started to do so in his clear **voice.** (d) / All correct (e).

13. The **maintenance** (a) / **expenses** (b) / on such **accounts** (c) / include recovery **charges.** (d) / All correct (e)

14. Under the new exploration **licencing** (a) / **policy,** (b) / companies win exploration blocks in a **competitive** (c) / bidding **process.** (d) / All correct (e).

15. He was **eagrosed** (a) / in his **job** (b) / to the **detriment** (c) / of his **health.** (d) / All correct (e)

Directions for Questions 16 to 20: In each of these questions, two sentences (I) and (II) are given. Each sentence has a blank in it. Five words (a) (b) (c) (d) and (e) are suggested. Out of these, only one fits at both the places in the context of each sentence. That word is the answer.

16. I. It is when he ______ a new method, he faced opposition.
II. The suspect was ______ for the crime.
(a) suggested (b) sentenced
(c) tried (d) found
(e) evolved

17. I. The human ______ has its own healing powers.
II. The elected ______ is responsible for major policy changes.
(a) being (b) body
(c) representative (d) representative
(e) mind

18. I. Even ______ the book doesn't draw from political characters, the possible coincidence is not missing.
II. Our college trip was great ______ it lasted.
(a) while (b) though
(c) until (d) when
(e) if

19. I. Since the sender has not indicated her name, this letter will be classified as ______.
II. Many of the important things that surround you are still the work of ______ minds and hands, about whom we may not know.
(a) known (b) bogus
(c) void (d) anonymous
(e) artistic

20. I. It Is better to keep things on ______ till we get due approval
II. If our conduct is good, we can ______ our head high.
(a) wait (b) keep

(c) watch (d) raise
(e) hold

Directions for Questions 21 to 25: Which of the phrases (a), (b), (c) and (d) given below should replace the phrase given in bold in the following sentence to make the sentence grammatically meaningful and correct. If the sentence is correct as it is and 'No' correction is required', mark (e) as the answer.

21. Two festivals in which I participated recently **brought this home point** to me fairly dramatically.
(a) bring this point
(b) brought this point home
(c) brought home point this
(d) this point brought home
(e) No correction required

22. **As if it had** a rustic look from outside, inside the house was quite modern.
(a) Though it had
(b) As it had
(c) Even when
(d) But for
(e) No correction required

23. I knew it was bad manners, **but I couldn't** help interrupting their conversation.
(a) still I could not
(b) but I had to
(c) facing it I couldn't help
(d) still I was required for
(e) No correction required

24. India does **not always mean** technology, fashion, films or beauty contests.
(a) do not means
(b) do not always means
(c) does it always mean
(d) should not always meant
(e) No correction required

25. I write to **share only those** few every day moments, which my readers can identify with.
(a) those only to share
(b) to share only this
(c) only to share those
(d) only those to share
(e) No correction requited

Directions for Questions 26 to 30: Read each sentence to find out whether there is any grammatical mistake / error in it. The error if any, will be in one part of the sentence. Mark the number of the part with error as your answer. If there is 'no error', mark (e)

26. He contributed a lot (a) / of time and money (b) / by building a hospital (c) / in his village. (d) / No error (e).

27. All our Zonal Office (a) / have received instructions (b) / to process loan applications (c) / within thirty days. (d) / of doing within homework. No error (e)

28. Years of (a) / failure has (b) / sapped him (c) / of his confidence (d) / No error (e).

29. We are already (a) / written to the IT Department (b) / last week seeking permission (c) / to set up our own website. (d) / No error (e).

30. In order to transfer (a) / branch licenses for one (b) / bank to another you (c) / require special approval from RBI. (d) / No error, (e)

Directions for Questions 31 to 40: In the following passage there are blanks, each of which has been numbered. These numbers are printed below the passage and against each, five words are suggested, one of which fits the blank appropriately. Find out the appropriate word in each case.

The idea behind staging the World Cup in South Africa was to change how the world thought about the country.

While to the world, South Africa was (31) as a country of wars (32) famines, South Africans prepared for the (33) by building stadium and airports and (34) their home and cities to visitors. With the (35) of hundreds and thousands of fans (36) only did the world's perception of South Africa (37) as people experienced the hospitality of its (38), but more importantly the African people (39) to believe in themselves and in their country's (40). Now there is hope for South Africa to live up to its potential.

31. (a) thought (b) regard
(c) consider (d) referred
(e) known

32. (a) also (b) resulting
(c) and (d) beside

(e) creating

33. (a) telecast (b) event
(c) issue (d) show
(e) war

34. (a) opening (b) showed
(c) occupying (d) admitting
(e) allowing

35. (a) cost (b) behaviour
(c) population (d) venue
(e) arrival

36. (a) once (b) forever
(c) that (d) not
(e) yet

37. (a) reversed (b) transformed
(c) change (d) exchange
(e) substitute

38. (a) country (b) nation
(c) occasion (d) village
(e) citizens

39. (a) choose (b) began
(c) made (d) start
(e) wanting

40. (a) future (b) nature
(c) friendship (d) competition
(e) freedom

PAPER 4

Practice Test Paper–Four

Directions for Questions 1 to 15: Read the following passage carefully and answer the questions given below it. Certain words/phrases have been printed in bold to help you locate them while answering some of the questions.

It was in the offing. With shortages mounting across the board for water as they are for energy, it was only **inevitable** that the Central government would be stirred into starting a Bureau of Water Efficiency (BWE), much like the Bureau of Energy Efficiency (BEE) that was launched some years ago.

Early reports suggest that the draft norms for various sectors consuming water will be created by the BWE soon. The alarm bells have been ringing for some years now. Water availability per capita in India has fallen from about 5 million litres in the 1950s to 1.3 million litres in 2010 -that's a **staggering** 75 per cent drop in 50 years. Nearly 60 per cent of India's aquifers have slumped to critical levels in just the last-15 years. The rate at which borewells are being plunged in every city with no law to ban such extraction, groundwater tables have depleted alarmingly.

The BEE's efforts in the last seven years have only been **cosmetic**. The bureau has looked at efficiency rating systems for white goods in the domestic sector, and has not paid attention to the massive consumption of energy in metals manufacture, paper, and textiles. These sectors are very intense in both energy and water consumption. But very little attention has been paid to the water and energy used per tonne of steel or cement or aluminium that we buy, and without significant changes in these areas, the overall situation is unlikely to change.

Use of water is inextricably interlinked with energy. One does not exist without the other. The BWE should steer clear of the early mistakes of BEE - of focusing on the "softer targets' in the domestic sector. Nearly 80 per cent of fresh water is used by agriculture, with industry coming a close second. The domestic sector's consumption of fresh water is in single digit. So the BWE's priority should be to look at measures that will gel farmers and industrialists to follow good practices in water use. Water resources have to be made, by law, an indivisible national asset. The protection and withdrawal of this resource, as well as its sustainable development are of general importance and therefore in the public interest. This will mean that individuals and organisations may own land but not water or the other resources that lie below the first 20 metres of the surface of those lands. Drilling of borewells into such 'national assets' will have to be banned, or at the very least they must be regulated. What would be more sensible for the new water bureau to do would be to look at some of the **low-hanging fruits that can be plucked, and pretty quickly**, with laws that can emanate from the Centre, without the risk of either dilution or inaction from state administrations. The other **tactical** approach that the BWE can adopt is to devise a policy that addresses the serious water challenge in industry segments across a swathe of companies: this will be easier than taking on the more disparate domestic sector which hurts the water crisis less than industry. Implementing a law is more feasible when the concentration is dense and identifiable. Industry offers this advantage more than the domestic or the commercial sector of hotels and offices.

As for agriculture, though the country's water requirement is as high as 80 per cent, **the growing of water** within the loop in agriculture de-risks the challenge of any perceived deficit. Rice, wheat, sugarcane are crops that need water-logging, which ensures groundwater restoration. Surface water evaporation doesn't amount to any more than 7-8 per cent and only strengthens precipitation and rainfall.

Agriculture and water need is not quite as much a threat as industry and domestic sectors that account for the rest of the 20 per cent.

The primary challenge in industry and the building sector is that no conscious legal measures have been enacted that stipulate 'growing your own water' with measures that will 'put all water in a loop' in any residential or commercial building. This involves treating all used water to a grade that it can be 'upcyled' for use in flush tanks and for gardens across all our cities with the polluter owning the responsibility for treating and for reuse. The drop in fresh water demand can be **dramatic** with such upcycle, reuse, and recycle of treated water. Water by itself in industry and the domestic sector, is not as much a challenge as pollution of water. Not enough measures exist yet to ensure- that such polluters shift the water back for reuse. If legislation can ensure, that water is treated and reused for specific purposes within industry as well as in the domestic sector, this will make all the difference to the crisis on fresh water.

So is the case in industry, especially in sectors like textiles, aluminium and steel. Agriculture offers us the amusing irony of the educated urbanites dependent on cereals like rice and wheat that consume 4000 litres of Water for every Kilogramme, while the farmer lives on the more nutritious millets that consume less than half the quantity. Sugarcane consumes as much as 12,000 litres of water for a kilo of cane that you buy !

A listing of such correlations of water used by every product that we use in our daily lives will make much better sense than any elaborate rating system from the newly formed BWE. Such sensitizing with concerted awareness campaigns that the new Bureau drives will impact the urban consumer more than all the research findings that experts can present. What is important for us is to understand the life-cycle impact in a way that we see the connect between a product that we use and the resources it utilizes up to the point where we bring the visible connect to destruction of natural resources of our ecosystems.

1. How, according to the author, can the bureau sensitize the urban consumer about careful utilization of water ?

(a) By encouraging them to consume more rice instead of millets daily and thereby reduce the amount of water consumption.

(b) By providing them more insight into the water consumption cycle of the textile, aluminium and steel industries.

(c) By making them aware of the linkages between water consumption for daily activities and the resource utilization and subsequent ecological destruction associated with it.

(d) By publishing research findings of experts in popular media whereby people gain awareness on the impact of water misuse.

(e) By conducting elaborate drives which notify the urban population about the penalties levied on misuse of water resources.

2. Why, according to the-author, is the water consumption for agricultural activities the least risky?

(a) Proportion of water consumed for agricultural activities is much less as compared to that consumed for domestic and industrial purposes.

(b) Most farmers are aware of the popular methods of water conservation and hence do not allow wastage of water.

(c) Water is fairly recycled through groundwater restoration due to water-logging and surface water evaporation.
(d) Farmers in India mostly cultivate crops that require less amount of water.
(e) None of these

3. Which of the following is possibly the most appropriate title for the passage?
(a) Water Challenges in the New Millennium
(b) The Bureau of Water Efficiency Vs the Bureau of Energy Efficiency
(c) Unchecked Urban Consumption of Water
(d) Challenges of the Agricultural Sector and Water Resources
(e) The Route to Conservation of Water Resources.

4. What does **'low-hanging fruits that can be plucked, and pretty quickly'** mean in the context of the passage?
(a) The bureau should employ the cheapest methods possible to effectively control the current situation of improper usage of water resources.
(b) The bureau should target the industrial sector as well as the domestic sector to reduce water wastage.
(c) The bureau should target the agricultural sector only for producing quick results in reducing wastage of water.
(d) The bureau should ensure that all the state officials concerned with the measures are actively involved.
(e) The bureau should start with adopting measures which are simple to execute and produce immediate results in reducing water wastage.

5. Which of the following, according to the author, is/are the indication/s of a water crisis?
(a) Many agrarian areas in the country are facing a drought-like situation.
(b) Almost three-fifth of the naturally available water has been reduced to a very critical level in a relatively short span of time.
(c) There has been a significant drop in the availability of water over the past fifty years
(a) Only (b)
(b) Only (a) and (c)
(c) Only (c)
(d) Only (b) and (c)
(e) All (a), (b) and (c)

6. The author suggests that the Bureau of Water Efficiency devises a strategy or makes laws to meet water challenges in the industrial segments rather than the domestic segments because
(a) The industrial sector is the only one that is in a position to reduce its water consumption by a significant margin.
(b) There is comparatively less serious water misuse in the domestic sector
(c) It would be easy to identify the consumption patterns in the industrial sector because of its density and visibility.
(d) The industrial sector would be capable of paying the fines levied by the Bureau for water misuse whereas the domestic sector would be in no such position.
(e) The industrial sector would be easier to manage in terms of making them understand the importance of water conservation.

7. Which of the following, according to the author, is/are the step/s that the Bureau of Water Efficiency can take to ensure proper utilization of water resources?
(a) Put in place measures that ensure proper water usage.
(b) Concentrate op the water consumption patterns of the domestic sector alone.
(c) Monitor carefully the activity of digging borewells.
(a) Only (a) and (c)
(b) Only (a) and (b)
(c) Only (a)
(d) Only (b) and (c)
(e) All (a), (b) and (c)

8. Which of the following is true about the Bureau of Energy Efficiency, in the context of the passage?

(a) It failed to pay adequate attention to industries like metal, textiles, etc in terms of energy consumption.

(b) It focused on rating systems for efficient use of goods in the domestic sector.

(c) It mostly focused on the energy consumption in the domestic sector.

(a) Only (a) and (c)
(b) Only (a) and (b)
(c) Only (a)
(d) Only (b) and (c)
(e) All (a), (b) and (c)

Directions for Questions 9 to 12: Choose the word/group of words which is most similar in meaning to the word/group of words printed in bold as used in the passage.

9. COSMETIC
(a) enhancive (b) beauty
(c) augmentative (d) superficial
(e) aesthetic

10. STAGGERING
(a) weaving (b) astounding
(c) lurching (d) stumbling
(e) unsteady

11. CONSCIOUS
(a) unknown (b) mindful
(c) self - aware (d) awake
(e) alert

12. DRAMATIC
(a) remarkable (b) moving
(c) theatrical (d) histrionic
(e) staged

Directions for Questions 13 to 15: Choose the word/group of words which is MOST OPPOSITE, in meaning to the word/group of words printed in BOLD as used in the passage.

13. **INTENSE**
(a) smooth (b) serious
(c) low (d) diluted
(e) jovial

14. TACTICAL
(a) unplanned (b) uniform
(c) devious (d) premeditated
(e) deformed

15. INEVITABLE
(a) certain (b) unforeseeable
(c) unavoidable (d) inescapable
(e) predictable

Directions for Questions 16-20: Rearrange the followings even sentences (A), (B), (C), (D), (E), (F) and (G) in the proper sequence to form a meaningful paragraph; then answer the questions given below them.

(A) But seriously, how much would you pay to know what thoughts are swimming around in someone else's head?

(B) In most fictional movies thus, the idea of reading minds - of seeing the private intentions of another, and the possibility of intervening in those plans — has always been highly attractive

(C) Such fantastical questions have long been the bread and butter of fiction.

(D) Today, more than four centuries since the phrase, "A penny for your thoughts ?", was first recorded, inflationary accounting makes that ancient penny worth more than $40.

(E) The going rate for a "thought" - a probe into the thinking of another - was once quite a bargain.

(F) And if you could really know their truthfulness how much more would you pay?

(G) Even with the sliding value of the dollar, this still seems quite a bargain.

16. Which of the following should be the **SECOND** sentence after rearrangement?
(a) F (b) D
(c) C (d) G
(e) A

17. Which of the following should be the **FOURTH** sentence after rearrangement?
(a) A (b) B
(c) G (d) D
(e) F

18. Which of the following should be the **SIXTH**, sentence after rearrangement?
(a) E (b) G
(c) C (d) B
(e) A

19. Which of the following should be the **SEVENTH (Last)** sentence after rearrangement?
(a) A (b) B
(c) F (d) D
(e) e

20. Which of the following should be the **FIRST** sentence after rearrangement?
(a) A (b) B
(c) C (d) D
(e) E

Directions for Questions 21 to 31: In the following passage there are blanks, each of which has been numbered. These numbers are printed below the passage and against each, five wards are suggested, one of which fits the blank appropriately: Find out the appropriate word in each case.

The economics of owning and running a Ration Shop, the familiar name for the outlets in our Public Distribution System (PDS), are such that under normal business terms, the shop-owner could never make a profit. Yet, (21) The government announces that new permits for ration shops will be given out, there is frenzy in the market to grab one of these. (22). The answer is obvious: the business is not for the honest and if one knows the (23), there is a fortune to be made.

What are these tricks of the trade?

Getting fake names into the user list is the most obvious option; the State seems to be 24 a losing battle against this practice, judging by the endless efforts to weed out bogus ration cards.

The next is to get the 'right customers' on the list, not just more customers. These are people who are registered but who do riot have any interest in 25 on their entitlements. In a system where caste and income certificates are for sale, it is not 26 to 'produce' these documents for mutual benefit. Receipts are duly made in their names, and the rations thus 'drawn' are 27 off into the open market. The sale price of an item like rice makes clear the 28 economics - it costs Rs. 8 in a ration shop while in the latter it is Rs. 30 or above. There are also customers who would rather exchange their entitlements for hard cash at the beginning of the month.

As the degradation progresses, the shop keeper, in 29 with the official machinery, manages to withhold effectively the entitlements from even the genuine beneficiaries, and diverts them to the open market. The targeted group is usually not in a position to 30 itself to get its due.

And thus one has all 31 of a good PDS business.

21. (a) whenever (b) quickly
(c) just (d) as soon
(e) time

22. (a) What (b) When
(c) Where (d) Why
(e) How

23. (a) lying. (b) people
(c) sprouting (d) hard work
(e) ropes

24. (a) attempt (b) waging
(c) winning (d) expecting
(e) trying

25. (a) harping (b) discussing
(c) realizing (d) drawing
(e) giving

26. (a) easy (b) must
(c) difficult (d) simple
(e) enough

27. (a) sell (b) borrowed
(c) donated (d) bought
(e) siphoned

28. (a) understood (b) poor
(c) underlying (d) mechanical
(e) unclear

29. (a) meeting (b) collusion
(c) flow (d) show
(e) line

30. (a) ask (b) voiced
(c) assert (d) deliver
(d) willful

31. (a) things (b) ingredients
(c) dictate (d) component
(e) facet

Directions for Questions 32 to 35: Which of the words/phrases (a), (b), (c) and (d) given below each

sentence should replace the word/ phrase printed in bold in the sentence to make it grammatically correct? If the sentence is correct as it is given and no correction is required, mark (e) as the answer.

32. A lot of time we hear from actors that they regret the kind of roles they have been doing all this while, but this actor says he **has never any** regrets,
(a) never has have
(b) have never had
(c) has no
(d) has had
(e) No correction required

33. The actress participated in the event **whole-hearted**, cheered the participants, danced with them and emphasised on the importance of creating awareness for oral care across the country.
(a) whole - heartedly
(b) whole - heart
(c) with whole - heart
(d) wholly - hearted
(e) No correction required

34. **Although** complete treatment of cancer is beyond the reach of the underprivileged but no child should lose his life for want of funds.
(a) Though (b) As
(c) The (d) Since
(e) No correction required

35. Slated to begin this year, the league could provide a **so-needed** boost to hockey in India.
(a) so-needful
(b) much-needy
(c) much-need
(d) much-needed
(e) No correction required

Directions for Questions 36 to 40: Each question below has two blanks, each blank indicating that something has been omitted. Choose the set of words for each blank which best fits the meaning of the sentence as a whole.

36. Much of the ____ that cricket, has is due to the fact it is a ___ sport.
(a) allure, lucrative
(b) criticism, controversial
(c) attraction, unpopular
(d) flak, great
(e) comments, unusual

37. Since foggy weather _____ visibility by several metres, the railways has either partially ____ or diverted some of the trains.
(a) improves, started
(b) impairs, called off
(c) hampers, withdrawn
(d) decrease, stopped
(e) reduces, cancelled

38. The once ____ district is gradually being _____ of its green cover.
(a) remote, eroded
(b) arid, replenished
(c) beautiful, devoid
(d) picturesque, depleted
(e) lush, rob

39. The pilot knew she would be able to see the ____ lights of the city from her cockpit window, but she would not see the fireworks explode to welcome the new year as she would have ____ to cruising altitude.
(a) few, soared
(b) divine, escalate
(c) glistening, jumped
(d) shining, reached
(e) glittering, climbed

40. The New Year has _____ in good news for city hotels as most properties are ____ for the whole month.
(a) brought, deserted
(b) ushered, packed
(c) pushed, full
(d) steered, renovating
(e) escorted, vacant

Directions for Questions 41 to 50: Read each sentence to find out whether there is any grammatical error or idiomatic error in it. The error, if any, will be in one part of the sentence. The number of that part is the answer. If there is no error, the answer is (e) (Ignore errors of punctuation, if any)

41. The bane of Indian hockey today is (a)/ lack of interest by the part of the public (b)/ which in turn is fuelled by the perception that (c)/ it doesn't pay to take up the sport as a career. (d)/ No error (5).

42. Illegal sand mining has become (a) / a boom business fuelled (b)/ by the ever-increasing demand (c)/ of the construction industry. (d)/ No error (5).

43. Much is the inflow of travellers that (a)/ it is tough to book an air ticket (b)/ to Ahmedabad and the international flights (c)/ too are almost over-booked. (d)/ No error (5).

44. Experts believe that a (a)/ gradually decreasing infant mortality rate (b)/. is lead to a proportionate (c)/ decrease in the size of our brains. (d)/ No error (5).

45. In just two months after having (a)/ planted these, most of the plants have (b)/ either dried up and are suffering (c)/ due to lack of maintenance. (d)/ No error (5).

46. In cities people don't (a)/ always have the time to (b)/ catch up with old friends or (c)/ spend times with their family. (d)/ No error (5).

47. The band have been (a)/ performing at many cause-oriented concerts (b)/ to encourage people to come forward and (c)/ lend their support to the noble cause. (d)/ No error (5).

48. As market leaders, (a)/ we have always been at (b)/ the forefront of creating awareness (c)/ between the public. (d)/ No error (5).

49. If the IPL has succeeded in drawing (a)/ an audience across the country, it is because (b)/ cricket has always had a strong foundation (c)/ and a dedicated audience. (d)/ No error (5).

50. In view of the intense cold wave conditions (a)/ prevailing in the state, the government is declared (b)/ holidays in all the schools (c)/ for a period often days. (d)/ No error (5).

PAPER 5

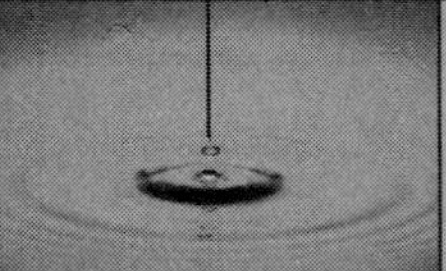

PRACTICE TEST PAPER–FIVE

Directions for Questions 1-5: In each of the following questions, a sentence/passage is given with two blank spaces. Three phrases/sentences are given below, two of which can be placed in blank spaces to make a meaningful sentence/passage. If none of the phrases/sentences is appropriate, mark (e) as the answer.

1. We are______ a great chemical experiment and _____to scientists.

A. living in the midst of

B. some serious consequences are becoming apparent

C. in threat of

(a) A and B

(b) A and C

(c) B and C

(d) C and B

(e) None of these

2. The ensure ___ and thus facilitate economic growth China ___North Korea.

A. destabilisation of a flash point

B. a stable security environment within the region

C. played an active role in facilitating negotiations with

(a) A and B

(b) B and C

(c) C and A

(d) A and C

(e) None of these

3. Indian corporate leaders ____ global giants ____ and market share.

A. had done well standing up

B. as their companies have grown in size

C. have done well standing up to

(a) A and B

(b) B and C

(c) C and B

(d) A and C

(e) None of these

4. Every country has _____ for citizens_____.

A. lay down comprehensive rules

B. laid down comprehensive series of practical rules.

C. for resolving mutual contradictory rights and interests.

(a) A and B (b) B and C
(c) C and A (d) A and C
(e None of these

5. ____that the developed world ___of the world's poor.
   A. It is a myth
   B. already gives plenty of aid
   C. It was a myth
   (a) A and B
   (b) B and C
   (c) C and B
   (d) A and C
   (e) None of these

Directions for Questions 6 to 15: In the following passage there are blanks, each of which has been numbered. These numbers are printed below the passage and against each five words/phrases are suggested, one of which fits the blank appropriately. Find out the appropriate word/ phrase in each case.

Marine life **(6)** along the coast and in the ocean results from harmful fishing practices such as trawling or dynamite fishing; poor land use practices in agricultural, **(7)** development and forestry sectors; and the human activities such as mining and anchoring. Destroyed habitats include sea grasses, marshes, corals and mangroves - all of which are important nurseries for fish and critical for buffering coasts from storm damage. Damaging habitat can lead to increased **(8)** and sedimentation, increased impact from storms, fewer **(9)** grounds and fewer places for animals and plants to live. Destructive fishing, land-based sedimentation, dredging, marine recreation, typhoons and storms, poor agricultural practices, and coastal development and land **(10)** increasingly **(11)** and devastate productive marine habitats. One major ecological impact derives from increased sediment loads in coastal waters from activities such as logging. Sedimentation, which produces turbidity and limits the **(12)** of sunlight **(13)** primary and secondary "producers- thus altering food web dynamics. The smothering of coral reefs by sediment also **(14)** fish and produces ecosystem changes. Chemicals in sediments, such as DDT or heavy metals, may bioaccumulate in marine life as well. Oil spilling is also major problem for the destruction of the **(15)** life.

6. (a) destruction
   (b) construction
   (c) obstruction
   (d) description
   (e) evolution
7. (a) coast
   (b) coastal
   (c) coasting
   (d) bank
   (e) edge
8. (a) igneous
   (b) deposit
   (c) erosion
   (d) metamorphic
   (e) deposition
9. (a) nursing
   (b) hospitablity
   (c) nourishing
   (d) nursery
   (e) helpful
10. (a) reclamation
    (b) accumulate
    (c) accommodation
    (d) deserting
    (e) habitat
11. (a) add
    (b) impair
    (c) sound
    (d) destructive
    (e) construct
12. (a) penetrate
    (b) filter
    (c) obstruction
    (d) passing
    (e) penetration
13. (a) effects
    (b) affects
    (c) endangers
    (d) facilitates
    (e) reduces
14. (a) increases
    (b) negates

(c) reduces
(d) produces
(e) reduced

15. (a) coastal
(b) ocean
(c) marine
(d) land
(e) forest

Directions for Questions 16-20: Rearrange the following six sentences (a) , (b) , (G), (d) , (E) and (F) in the proper sequence to form a meaningful paragraph; then answer the questions given below them.

(a) Development of drought resistance could benefit large numbers of farmers.
(b) Hence the human race has no choice but to adapt to these impacts.
(c) India has to be concerned about climatic changes.
(d) This impact can run into decades and centuries.
(e) Environment day is thus an important occasion to assess the past and our future,
(f) Since there is a possibility of adverse impact on agriculture which could deter growth.

16. Which is the FIFTH sentence of the passage after the rearrangement ?
(a) (F)
(b) (d)
(c) (E)
(d) (a)
(e) (c)

17. Which is the THIRD sentence of the passage ?
(a) (a)
(b) (d)
(c) (b)
(d) (c)
(e) (E)

18. Which is the SECOND sentence of the passage?
(a) (b)
(b) (d)
(c) (F)
(d) (c)
(e) (E)

19. Which is the LAST (SIXTH) sentence of the passage ?
(a) (c)
(b) (b)
(c) (F)
(d) (d)
(e) (E)

20. Which is the FIRST sentence of the passage ?
(a) (a)
(b) (d)
(c) (c)
(d) (b)
(e) (E)

Directions for Questions 21 to 30: Read the following passage carefully and answer the questions given below it. Certain words/phrases are printed in bold to help you to locate them while answering some of the questions.

The outside world has pat answers concerning extremely impoverished countries, especially those in Africa. Everything comes back, again and again, to corruption and misrule. Western officials argue that Africa simply needs to behave itself better, to allow market forces to operate without interference by corrupt rulers. Yet the critics of African governance have it wrong. Politics simply can't explain Africa's **prolonged** economic crisis. The claim that Africa's corruption is the basic source of the problem does not withstand serious scrutiny. During the past decade I witnessed how relatively well-governed countries in Africa, such as Ghana.

Malawi, Mali and Senegal, failed to prosper, whereas societies in Asia perceived to have **extensive** corruption, such as Bangladesh, Indonesia and Pakistan, enjoyed rapid economic growth.

What is the explanation? Every situation of extreme poverty around the world contains some of its own unique causes, which need to be diagnosed as a doctor would a patient. For example, Africa is burdened with malaria like no other part of the world, simply because it is unlucky in providing the perfect conditions for that disease high temperatures, plenty of breeding sites and particular species of malaria-transmitting mosquitoes that prefer to bite humans rather than cattle.

Another **myth** is that the developed world already gives plenty of aid to the world's poor. Former U.S. Secretary of the Treasury, Paul O'Neil expressed a common frustration when he remarked about aid for Africa : "We've spent trillions of dollars on these problems and we have damn near nothing to show for it". O'Neil was no foe of foreign aid. Indeed, he wanted to fix the system so that more U.S. aid could be justified. But he was wrong to believe that vast flows of aid to Africa had been **squandered**. President Bush said in a press conference in April 2004 that as "the greatest power on the face of the earth, we have an obligation to help the spread of freedom. We have an obligation to feed the hungry", Yet how does the U.S. fulfill its **obligation**? U.S. aid to farmers in poor countries to help them grow more food runs at around $200 million per year, far less than $1 per person per year for the hundreds of millions of people living in subsistence farm households. From the world, as a whole, the amount of aid per African per year is really very small, just $30 per sub-Saharan African in 2002. Of that **modest** amount, almost $5 was actually for consultants from the donor countries, more than $3 was for emergency aid, about $4 went for servicing Africa's debts and $ 5 was for debt-relief operations. The rest, about $12, went to Africa. Since the "money down the drain" argument is heard most frequently in the U.S., it's worth looking at the same calculations for U.S. aid alone. In 2002, the U.S. gave $3 per sub-Saharan African. Taking out the parts for U.S. consultants and technical cooperation, food and other emergency aid, administrative costs and debt relief, the aid per African came to grand total of 6 cents.

The U.S. has promised repeatedly over the decades, as a signatory to global agreements like the Monterrey Consensus of 2002, to give a much larger proportion of its annual output, specifically upto 0.7% of GNP, to official development assistance. The U.S. failure to follow through has no political fallout domestically, of course, because not one in a million U.S. citizens even knows of statements like the Monterrey Consensus. But no one should underestimate the salience that it has around the world. Spin as American might about their nation's generosity, the poor countries are fully aware of what the U.S. is not doing.

21. The passage seems to emphasize that the outside world has

(a) correct understanding about the reasonable aid provided by the USA to the poor countries

(b) definite information about what is; happening in under developed countries

(c) stopped extending any financial aid to underdeveloped countries

(d) misconceptions about the aid given !to the poor nations by developed countries

(e) None of these

22. According to the Westerners the solution to eradicate poverty of African nations lies in

(a) corruption

(b) improving their own national behaviour

(c) misrule

(d) prolonged economic crisis

(e) None of these

23. The author has given the example of Bangladesh, Indonesia and Pakistan in support of his argument that

(a) corruption is the major culprit in the way of prosperity

(b) mis-governance hampers the prosperity of nations

(c) despite "rampant corruption, nations may prosper

(d) developed nations arrogantly neglect underdeveloped countries

(e) None of these

24. The author has mentioned Ghana as a country with

(a) reasonably good-governance

(b) corrupt leadership

(c) plenty of natural resources

(d) rapid economic growth

(e) None of these

25. The cases of malaria in Africa are mainly due to

(A) high temperature

(B) climatic conditions conducive for breeding.

(C) malaria carriers' liking for human blood in preference to that of cattle.

(a) None of these

(b) Only B and C

(c) Only A and C
(d) Only A and B
(e) All the three

Directions for Questions 26 to 28: Choose the word/group of words which is most nearly the same in meaning to the word/group of words printed in bold as used in the passage.

26. OBLIGATION
(a) lip sympathy
(b) true empathy
(c) self pity
(d) conditional responsibility
(e) moral binding

27. SQUANDER
(a) use economically
(b) spend wastefully
(c) siphon judiciously
(d) donate generously
(e) None of these

28. MODEST
(a) humble
(b) sufficient
(c) meagre
(d) sober
(e) unpretentious

Directions for Questions 29 and 30: Choose the word/group of words which is most OPPOSITE in meaning of the word given in bold as used in the passage.

29. MYTH
(a) reality
(b) mystery
(c) misery
(d) misconception
(e) exaggeration

30. EXTENSIVE
(a) intensive
(b) abominable
(c) inherent
(d) rampant
(e) negligible

PAPER 6

Practice Test Paper–Six

Directions for Questions 1-15: Read the following passage carefully and answer the questions given below it. Certain words have been printed in bold to help you locate them while answering some of the questions.

Thinking of what education might look like in the next decade, one quickly realizes that the trends in technology are leaving a large number of our students behind. Today is an age of exponential, change. New and ever-improving technologies are popping up every day and in every corner of society.

Educating the best and the brightest in this brave new world will take a new and improved educational **paradigm.** Allowing our educational tools to age in the corner of the classroom will be the mistake that may cost us our future. Throwing away masses of children to **inequitable** access will ensure that we **languish** at the bottom of the global pool of employable workers for decades to come.

Technology will shape the way we educate students in the next decade. A user is not simply a person who uses. For the student, being a user should involve using the latest technology in a free and **autonomous** manner. This new-found freedom will allow the student to become an active participant in his/her education instead of a passive passenger. In our current technological society, being a user also means being tracked. Tracking a student means having the ability to target education towards weaknesses and strengths. The ability to accurately customize curricula to the individual has been the holy grail of educational philosophy for many years. This golden age of technological development may soon enable this dream to become a reality.

Current educational curricula and individual assessment is **arbitrary** at best. Accurately assessing a student can only be achieved by using modern tracking and database technologies, imagine a world where every child has a tablet computer with ready access to the internet. Further, imagine that every student can access all the knowledge of humankind freely at any moment in time. Continue to imagine a world where a misspelled word brings up a spelling challenge application instead of an auto correction. Try to contemplate what, it would mean for a teacher to have a database of every misspelled word, every misunderstood concept or every missed, equation for each of their students. Try to envision a teacher with the ability to customize the experience of the individual "user" with minimal effort. Imagine the curriculum being automatically targeted to the user through an intuitive educational platform that knows all strengths and each unique weakness. In the last few hundred years, most individuals would consider an education as something you receive. You often hear the question asked "Where did you receive your education?" As we proceed through the next decade, education will slowly move away from reception and toward being custom designed for the individual user. New technology will not only allow us to receive an education, but also develop an education. The question we might ask in ten years, "How did you develop your education?" The question of where will still be important, but the how of the matter will be the focus that defines the individual.

To make this a reality we will need a standardized platform from which to develop a student's unique education. This standardized platform will allow us to tailor a custom curriculum that will be matched to talents, interests and life goals. For the educator, a standardized platform will create a way to assist the student in discovering a true purpose in life through a unique educational experience. The basics of reading, writing and arithmetic will not be taught as much as they will be discovered and used. Learning will become a **reciprocal** experience between the teacher, the student and the machine.

Under a standardized platform, each of these three participants will have a role to play. The teacher will be the facilitator, assisting the development of the curriculum and inspiring the direction the student takes. The student will be the user, gathering resources, skills and knowledge in an efficient and measured sequence. The machine will do the work of data gathering and analysis, which will assist the teacher and student in refining the curriculum. This data gathering work of the machine will also free the teacher from the burden of record-keeping and tedious tasks that currently distract from the real job of teaching and learning.

Under a standardized system, grade level will be far less important. Achievement and progression will be measured by accomplishment and intelligence as a benchmark for success. The question of failure or success will be irrelevant and replaced with a standard and consistent measurement of potential and overall intelligence. Information will no longer be missed but continually rehearsed and monitored for retention by the machine. Tasks such as data tracking, reporting and record keeping are currently accomplished manually. These tasks could easily be **delegated** to an intuitive database. Developing a standard to follow would eliminate these tasks and free the teacher to do their main job of teaching students.

The next decade may mark the moment in history when all are granted equal access to technology. Access to quality education will only be gained through investment and universal standardization of this technology. If we continue to divert wealth towards fruitless goals and corporate greed, this opportunity will be lost or hopelessly delayed.

1. According to the author, which of the following will be the benefit(s) of introducing a standardized technological platform?
   (A) Potential of a child will take precedence over the grades he/she scores.
   (B) improving the educational syllabus would become easier.
   (C) Teachers would be able to devote more time to teaching,
   (a) Only (C)
   (b) All (A) , (B) and (C)
   (c) Only (B) and (C)
   (d) Only (A) and (B)
   (e) Only (A)

2. Which of the following is/are **true** in the context of the passage?
   (A) In the presence of technology each student would require constant monitoring by other individuals to `maximize learning
   (B) Educational philosophy is based on the belief of tailoring educational syllabus to individual student capability.
   (C) The author visualizes that each student will have access to technology in the future.
   (a) Only (A) and (B)
   (b) Only (B)
   (c) Only (C)
   (d) Only (B) and (C)
   (e) All (A), (B) and(C)

3. Which of the following is possibly the most appropriate title for the passage ?

(a) Technology - A Welcome Relief to Teachers
(b) Revamping the Educational Sector - An Impossible Future
(c) Education - Arbitrary But a Reality
(d) Technology and the Economy
(e) Technology - Reshaping the Future of Education

4. How, according to the author, will the perception towards education change over the next decade ?
(a) Where an individual gets his education will gain increasing importance
(b) Education will be viewed as a prerogative of the elite only
(c) Creativity in an individual will be regarded as needless
(d) The importance of education will decline
(e) None of these

5. What does the author mean by the term "tracking a student" ?
(a) Analyzing the strengths and weaknesses of a student and designing an educational syllabus accordingly
(b) Assessing whether a student is paying due attention to the existing curriculum offered by an institute of learning
(c) Analyzing the positives and negatives of an educational institute and modifying it suitably to cater to industrial requirements
(d) Following a student to the educational institute that he visits frequently in order to estimate the time he spends there
(e) None of these

6. According to the author, why is the current education provided not satisfactory ?
(a) The teachers providing education are not qualified enough to emphasize on quality
(b) Quality of education provided is not uniform across the globe and individual assessment is subjective
(c) The educational sector is fraught with corrupt practices and thus does not produce the desired result
(d) The education system is not guided by technology and hence the pace of learning is slow
(e) There are too many schools in the country which cannot be monitored effectively

7. What is the author's vision regarding the integration of technology with education ?
(A) A substantial database consisting of each student's learning curve would be readily available.
(B) An error would activate a software which would encourage learning rather than auto-correcting.
(C) Experimentation in academics would be encouraged.
(a) Only (C)
(b) Only (A) and (B)
(c) All (A), (B) and (C)
(d) Only (A) and (C)
(e) None of these

8. How has the author defined the term 'user' ?
(a) One who invests in the latest technology even when it is beyond his/her means
(b) One who uses available technology to the maximum and for the longest period
(c) One who freely and actively participates in acquiring skills and knowledge in a systematic manner
(d) Anyone who invests in technology as per his/her requirement and wherewithal
(e) None of these

Directions for Questions 9-12 : Choose the word which is most similar in meaning to the word printed in bold as used in the passage.

9. RECIPROCAL
(a) interactive
(b) unresponsive
(c) reverse
(d) regular
(e) inverse

10. PARADIGM
(a) change
(b) shift

(c) future
(d) model
(e) diagnosis

11. AUTONOMOUS
(a) single
(b) independent
(c) governed
(d) forceful
(e) insufficient

12. DELEGATED
(a) taxed
(b) demoted
(c) input
(d) authorized
(e) assigned

Directions for Questions 13-15 : Choose the word which is most opposite in meaning to the word printed in bold as used in the passage.

13. INEQUITABLE
(a) abundant
(b) complete
(c) unequal
(d) fair
(e) sufficient

14. LANGUISH
(a) ripen
(b) hasten
(c) flourish
(d) weaken
(e) climb

15. ARBITRARY
(a) objective
(b) deliberate
(c) random
(d) transparent
(e) lawful

Directions for Questions 16-20 : Which of the phrases (a) , (b) , (c) and (d) giver. below each sentence should replace the phrase given in bold in the following sentence to make the sentence grammatically meaningful and correct If the sentence is correct as it is and 'No correction is required', mark (e) as the answer.

16. After enjoying one of the biggest successes of Indian cinema, the actor **is pulled the brakes** on his career.
(a) has putting brake
(b) has pulled the brakes
(c) is braking
(d) is put brakes
(e) No correction required

17. Many of our tinsel town beauties **will hit the panic button** if they didn't have at least one movie in hand.
(a) would hit panicky buttons
(b) would hit the panic button
(c) will be hitting panic buttons
(d) have hit panicky button
(e) No correction required

18. **Alarm to** declining marriage figures and increasing divorce rates, the government has come up with a novel way to tackle the issue.
(a) Alarmingly on
(b) Alarming as
(c) Alarms with
(d) Alarmed by
(e) No correction required

19. The two sisters **dropped in to** watch the film with none other than their father.
(a) dropping in for
(b) dropped by as
(c) drop on to
(d) dropped in for
(e) No correction required

20. The researchers found that children with lung disease **are at increase risk** for developing a second type of pneumonia.
(a) were at increased risk
(b) is increasingly risking
(c) is increased risky
(d) are increasingly risky
(e) No correction required

Directions for Questions 21-25 : Each question below has two blanks, each blank indicating that something has been omitted. Choose the set of words for each blank which best fits the meaning of the sentence as a whole.

21. What goes into making a marriage can only be ___ by trial and error and couples are best left to ___ out what works.
(a) discovered, translate
(b) regulated, find
(c) learnt, figure
(d) seen, thrash
(e) experienced, judge

22. The producer is known to ___ with new stars and fresh talent, and though there have been a few hits and misses, this filmmaker totally ____ for the new breed.
(a) try, demands
(b) experiment, vouches
(c) sign, goes
(d) produce, promises
(e) work, supports

23. The Government stated that it had the ____ right to use as much force as was necessary to regain control of areas ____ by terrorists.
(a) free, marked
(b) practical, left
(c) fundamental infest
(d) basic, undertaken
(e) legitimate, dominated

24. Obesity and alcohol ____ together to ____ the risk of liver disease in both men and women.
(a) act, increase
(b) result, aggravate
(c) taken, arrest
(d) put, heighten
(e) mix, lower

25. There were screams, chills and thrills ____ at the discotheque the other night as the director along with the producers hosted a party to ____ the success of their latest horror flick.
(a) combined, downplay
(b) alike, mourn
(c) experiences, mark
(d) galore, celebrate
(e) risen, generate

Directions for Questions 26-30 : Rearrange the following six sentences (a) , (b) , (c) , (d) , (E) and (F) in the proper sequence to form a meaningful paragraph; then answer the questions given below them.

(A) However, many people may not be aware of the numerous other areas where it has been applied.
(B) Today, even, those who have little knowledge about the production of virtual reality are now most likely aware of its use in video games.
(C) Similarly, medical students have substituted a cadaver for a fiberglass mould of a body and a headset when training to perform surgery.
(D) Virtual reality was an unfamiliar concept to many people till the early 90's.
(E) Introducing virtual reality to the real world, thus, has already proven to be beneficial for every industry it encounters.
(F) For example, astronaut trainees have recently used virtual reality to simulate a trip to space.

26. Which of the following should be the **FOURTH** sentence after rearrangement ?
(a) E (b) F
(c) A (d) D
(f) B

27. Which of the following should be the **FIRST** sentence after rearrangement ?
(a) A (b) B
(c) C (d) D
(e) E

28. Which of the following should be the **LAST (SIXTH)** sentence after rearrangement ?
(a) A (b) B
(c) C (d) D
(e) E

29. Which of the following should be the **SECOND** sentence after rearrangement ?
(a) B (b) C
(c) D (d) E
(e) F

30. Which of the following should be the **FIFTH** sentence after rearrangement ?
(a) A (b) B
(c) C (d) D

(e) E

Directions for Questions 31-40 : Read each sentence to find out whether there is any grammatical error in it. The error if any will be in one part of the sentence, the number of that part will be the answer. If there is no error, the answer is (e) i.e. 'No error'. (Ignore the errors of punctuation, if any.)

31. Human babies whose mothers (a) / have had the flu while pregnant may (b) / have a greater risk of developing (c) / schizophrenia lately in life. (d) No error (e)

32. Six women achievers, who continue (a) / to inspire the younger lot, were honoured (b) / with their contributions in their chosen fields (c) / on the occasion of women's day. (d) / No error (e)

33. All Indians know that they are (a) / superior in all respects not only to (b) / those unfortunately beings called foreigners, but (c) / also that they are superior to all other Indians. (d) / No error (e)

34. While the handsome actor was busy (a) / belting out one-liners, his (b) / graceful co-star was a (c) / complete imagery of woman power. (d) / No error (e)

35. He is one of the first film producers (a) / to actually take the much needed step (b) / against stare putting up information about (c) / under production films on social networking websites. (d) / No error (e)

36. It was an evening of (a) / fun and frolic as the city's glitterati (b) / and high-profile businessmen made sure (c) / that they didn't miss the show (d) / No error (e)

37. Results founding that boys not only (a) / play more than girls, but (b) / they start earlier, an outcome that (c) / could be clearly related to a cultural influence (d) / No error (e)

38. Videogames may not (a) / necessarily adversely affect (b) / the academic results in children (c) / contrary to most parents' perception (d) / No error (e)

39. Celebrities showed their childlike side (a) / yesterday, as most of them turn up wearing (b) / cartoon T-shirts for the screening of (c) / the latest animated film in town (d) / No error (e)

40. The study focusing exclusively to (a) / critically ill children found that children with chronic ill-nesses (b) / especially respiratory illnesses, are most likely (c) / to develop influenza the requires critical care (d) / No error (e)

Directions for Questions 41 to 50: In the following passage there are blanks, each of which has been numbered. These numbers are printed below the passage and against each, five words are suggested one of which fits the blanks appropriately. Find out the appropriate word in each case.

Prior to independence the healthcare sector in India was in a (41), with a large number of deaths and rampant spread of infectious diseases. After independence the Government of India laid (42) on primary healthcare and India has put in sustained efforts to better the healthcare system (43) the country. The government initiative was not enough to meet the demands of a growing population be it in primary, secondary or tertiary healthcare. Alternate sources of finance were critical for the sustainability of the health sector.

Till about 20 years ago, private sector ventures in the healthcare sector (44) of only solo practitioners, small hospitals and nursing homes. The quality of service provided was excellent especially in the hospitals run by charitable trusts and religious foundations. In 1980's realizing that the government on its own would not be able to (45) health care, the government allowed the entry of private sector to reduce the (46) between supply and demand for healthcare. The establishment of the private sector has resulted in the (47) of opportunities in terms of medical equipment, information technology in health services, BPO, telemedicine and medical tourism.

Large companies and (48) individuals have now started five star hospitals which dominate the space for the high, end market. The private sector has made (49) progress, but on the flip side it is also responsible for increasing (50) in the healthcare sector. The private sector should be more socially relevant and effort must be made to make private sector accessible to the weaker sections of society.

41. (a) shambles (b) failure
    (c) demand (d) prosperity
    (e) ruined

42. (a) bricks (b) emphasize
(c) request (d) stress
(e) important
43. (a) through (b) across
(c) sharing (d) with
(e) on
44. (a) made (b) comprise
(c) consisted (d) is
(e) contained
45. (a) cater (b) provide
(c) manage (d) survive
(e) give
46. (a) gap (b) position
(c) distance (d) length
(e) thought
47. (a) reduction (b) sea
(c) cropping (d) disabling
(e) emergence
48. (a) needy (b) destitute
(c) bigger (d) affluent
(e) much
49. (a) slowly (b) improve
(c) many (d) improvised
(e) tremendous
50. (a) speed (b) pace
(c) inequality (d) uniformity
(e) seriousness

PAPER 7

PRACTICE TEST PAPER–SEVEN

Directions for Questions 1 to 5: Which of the words (a) , (b) , (c) or (d) given below each sentence should fill the blank space (.....) or spaces sentence in the to make it complete and correct?

1. He went to the library ..... to find that it was closed.
(a) seldom
(b) never
(c) only
(d) solely

2. The ties that bind us together in common activity are so ..... that they can disappear at any moment.
(a) tentative
(b) tenuous
(c) consistent
(d) restrictive

3. Her reaction to his proposal was ..... she rejected it.
(a) inevitable; vehemently
(b) subtle ; Violently
(c) clever ; abruptly
(d) sympathetic ; angrily

4. His ..... direction misled us we did not know which of the two roads to take.
(a) complicated
(b) ambiguous
(c) narrow
(d) fantastic

5. It would be difficult for one so ..... to believe that all men are equal irrespective of caste, race and religion.
(a) emotional
(b) democratic
(c) tntolerant
(d) liberal

Directions for Questions 6 to 10: In each of the follwing sentences four words or phrases have been made bold. Only one bold part in each sentence is not accepted in standard English. Identify that part and mark a, b, c or d as your answer.

6. **Gaze** for a thing / (a) **that are not** / (b) available **easily** / (c) in the county is a universal **phenomenon**/ (d) .

7. It is foolish to **be expecting**/ (a) one person to be **like another** / (b) person **for**/ (c) **each**

individual is born/ (c) **with his** characteristic traits (d).

8. **The tendency** to believe/ (a) **that**/ (b) man is inherently dishonest is **something that**/ (c) **will decried**/ (d) .

9. **I have not** come across/ (a) **very few people**/ (b) **who**/ (c) **think of thing** beyond/ (d) **their daily** work.

10. He managed **to board**/ (a) **the running** train/ (b) but all his **luggages**/ (c) **was**/ (d) left **on the** station.

Directions for Questions 11 to 15: Select the pair of words which are related in the same way as the capitalised words are related to each other.

11. SCALES: JUSTICE::
    (a) weights: measures
    (b) laws: courts
    (c) torch : liberty
    (d) launch: peace

12. HOBBLE: WALK::
    (a) gallop: run
    (b) stammer: speak
    (c) stumble: fall
    (d) sniff: smell

13. FRAYED: FABRIC::
    (a) watered: lawn
    (b) renovated: building
    (c) thawed: ice
    (d) worn: nerves

14. YOLK: EGG::
    (a) rind.: melon
    (b) nucleus: cell
    (c) stalk: com
    (d) web: spider

15. BAMBOO: SHOOT::
    (a) bean: sprout
    (b) pepper: com
    (c) oak: tree
    (d) holly: sprig

Directions for Questions 16 to 20: For each of the following capitalised words, four words or phrases are given of which only one is synonymous with the given word. Select the synonym.

16. DEFER
    (a) respect
    (b) dislike
    (c) postpone
    (d) disrespect

17. DUBIOUS
    (a) clear
    (b) undoubtedly
    (c) hesitant
    (d) pmproper

18. COARSE
    (a) Impolite
    (b) rough
    (c) polished
    (d) improper

19. PROXIMI1Y
    (a) nearness
    (b) aloofness
    (c) completely
    (d) nearly

20. ABSTAIN
    (a) stay
    (b) tempt
    (c) refrain
    (d) pardon

Directions for Questions 21-25: Fill in the blanks by selecting appropriate alternative.

21. I met him only a week when shown
    (a) back
    (b) past
    (c) ago
    (d) previous

22. Lovely asked me, when shown
    (a) why are you angry
    (b) why I am angry
    (c) why I was angry.
    (d) why was I angry?

23. Even after repeated warnings. he to office on time.
    (a) never come
    (b) never comes

(c) is never coming
(d) have never come

24. He lold his wife that when shown from Germany.
(a) he will like to visit France
(b) he was liking to visit France
(c) he would like to visit France
(d) he is liking to visit France

25. Some people can even wilh murder.
(a) get on
(b) get out
(c) get off
(d) get away

Directions for Questions 26-30: Choose the correct antonym from the choices for each of the following capitalised words:

26. INDIFFERENT
(a) curious
(b) alike
(c) varied
(d) uniform

27. DISCREET
(a) wise
(b) prudent
(c) diplomatic
(d) careless

28. OBSOLETE
(a) free
(b) current
(c) ancient
(d) cultured

29. RATIONAL
(a) sound
(b) judicious
(c) insane
(d) sensible

30. SCEPTICAL
(a) doubtful
(b) convinced
(c) questioning
(d) cynic

PAPER 8

PRACTICE TEST PAPER–EIGHT

Directions for Questions 1 to 15 : Read the following passage carefully and answer the questions given below it. Certain words/phrases have been printed in bold to help you locate them while answering some of the question.

Health insurance policies were first introduced in 1986 at a time when the Indian insurance industry was nationalised. The policies on offer were **complicated** to read and offered limited cover. There were no third party administrators operating in India, and there was no direct settlement of claims between health insurer and hospital There were therefore issues concerning claims servicing, which involved an Insured following cumbersome procedures to get claims **authenticated** and paid. The business was not profitable for the nationalised insurers, and not popular with the public at large.

The original 'Mediclaim Policy', **however**, developed and in many cases has provided the base model for the health care insurance policies that were introduced immediately after liberalisation of the general insurance sector at the turn of the Millennium.

Health insurance, however, saw no specialist players until relatively recently, This is because there was a general expectation that, the insurance industry regulator, the IRDA would set a smaller capitalisation requirement for health insurers and/or amend the rules for foreign equity ownership in Indian Insurers in recognition of the fact that health insurance loss ratios were not good, and therefore finding an Indian partner to invest 76% in a health insurer would be a difficult task. The IRDA did not, however, relax either the capitalisation requirements or foreign investments caps. Initially, therefore, the health insurance market did not grow as quickly as may have been expected.

Growth in policyholder numbers, more effective third party administration and an **effective** network of hospitals is expected to see the numbers improve. Other changes have been effected to encourage growth in this sector. Life insurers have been allowed to sell health insurance. Initially, life insurers were only allowed to sell certain types of health covers as a supplement to a life policy. However, the IRDA has allowed life insurers to sell pure health insurance products **subject to** product specific approvals. The standard mediclaim policy has undergone several revisions and modifications. In recent years, private health insurers have been offering fresh products with increased covers and sums insured. Private hospital rates are still low compared to the rates charged in more developed countries, but high when compared to average Indian earnings. It is no longer uncommon for Indian employees to now expect that health care will be part of an employment package. With the opening up of the market to private competition, the claims process has become much less cumbersome. Support for a health insurance market has also come from some less obvious sources. Indian states have started relying on insurance policies to meet some of their legal obligations to provide health care to their citizens. The central government has also proposed the introduction of free health care insurance for the poor. This plan is meant to cover every poor family for INR 30,000 per annum. The central government will pay 75% of the premium, leaving the remaining 25% to be covered by state governments. The IRDA has also encouraged Micro-insurance as a means of extending the availability of health insurance to areas of the market that, geographically and economically, may not have been at the forefront of Insurers' business plans.

At the same time as the market grows, the IRDA is stepping in to create a more consumer friendly playing field, particularly as regards the treatment of senior citizens; the operation of the preexisting diseases exclusion, and the reluctance of insurers to renew policies where the claims experience has been bad.

Senior citizens had been complaining about the **reluctance** of Insurers to issue policies to them, and the inclusion of **disadvantageous** terms when policies were offered—such as **hefty** increases in premium rates, added exclusions and conditions, etc. In May 2007, the IRDA set up a Committee on Health Insurance for Senior Citizens to make recommendations. The Committee reported in November 2007 and made the following main recommendations: Senior Citizens should have some assurance that their policies will be renewed; the Industry should adopt standard terms and conditions, such as for the definition of pre-existing diseases. The Committee also said that policy wordings should be simpler for the lay person to follow, suggesting that uniform terminology be used by all Insurers to lessen confusion in the public mind.

1. Which of the following is/are the reason/s because of which the health insurance industry has witnessed growth ?

(A) The format of the policy has been improvised since its inception.

(B) Organisations provide health insurance cover to their employee as part of the remuneration process.

(C) The process of settlement of claims has become less troublesome as compared to the time when it was first introduced.

(a) Only (B)
(b) Only (A) and (C)
(c) Only (C)
(d) Only (B) and (C)
(e) All (A), (B) and (C)

2. What step has the Central Government taken in terms of insurance for the poor ?

(a) The poor will have access to free health care insurance, the payment of premium for which will be shouldered by the central and state government in the ratio of 3 : 1 respectively
(b) The poor people belonging to a particular region will get group health care insurance cover of INR 30,000 per annum.
(c) The poor will be insured for a sum of INR 45,000 per annum.
(d) The government has devised special health care insurance policies for the poor wherein no premium needs to be paid either by the individual or the government
(e) None of these

3. Which of the following is/are the reason/s that health insurance policies were not popular in the beginning.

(A) The process for settlement of claims was lengthy and tiresome.

(B) The clauses in the policy were very difficult to understand.

(C) There were no direct claim settlements with the hospitals.

(a) Only (B)
(b) Only (A) and (C)
(c) Only (C)
(d) Only (B) and (C)
(e) All (A) , (B) and (C)

4. Which of the following, is/are true in the context of the passage

(A) Private hospital fees can be easily afforded by the general public now as their earnings are significantly higher.

(B) More people are now buying insurance policies as compared to almost two decades ago.

(C) Insurance agencies initially allowed to independently sell life insurance policies only can also sell health insurance policies independently now.

(a) Only (B)
(b) Only (A) and (C)
(c) Only (C)
(d) Only (B) and (C)
(e) All (A), (B) and (C)

5. Which of the following is possibly the most appropriate title for the passage ?

(a) The Indian Health Insurance Industry—The Gradual Change
(d) IRDA and its Functioning
(c) Health Insurance Vs. Life Insurance
(d) Challenges Faced by the IRDA
(e) The Downfall of the Health Insurance Industry in India

6. What was the plight of senior citizens with respect to buying insurance cover prior to IRDA intervention ?

(A) Insurance agencies were unwilling to sell policies to them

(B) Clauses disadvantageous to senior citizens were included in the policies.

(C) They had to pay higher premiums.

(a) Only (A) and (C)
(b) Only (A) and (B)
(c) Only (B) and (C)
(d) Only (B) and (C)
(e) All (A), (B) and (C)

7. Which of the following are the commendations of the Committee on Health Insurance for Senior Citizens ?

(A) Standardise wordings in the policy so as to avoid any misinterpretation.

(B) Simplify language of the policy so that the common man can understand.

(C) Policies of senior citizens may not be renewed.

(a) Only (A) and (C)
(b) Only (A) and (B)
(c) Only (A)
(d) Only (B) and (C)
(e) All (A), (B) and (C)

8. Which of the following is not true in the context of the passage ?

(a) The general public now has a greater choice in selection of health insurance products since its inception
(b) The number of private players in the insurance industry has gone up since 1986
(c) The IRDA's plan of 'micro-insurance' is for people who can easily afford insurance cover
(d) The business of insurance was initially not very profitable.
(e) All are true

Directions for Questions 9 to 12 : Choose the word/ group of words which is most similar in meaning to the word/group of words printed in bold as used in the passage.

9. EFFECTED

(a) hampered
(b) brought about
(c) concerned
(d) troubled
(e) asked for

10. SUBJECT TO

(a) conditional on
(b) matter for
(c) issue to
(d) topic of
(e) question on

11. AUTHENTICATED

(a) falsified
(b) real
(c) verified
(d) genuine
(e) faked

12. COMPLICATED
    (a) knotty
    (b) invisible
    (c) gibberish
    (d) complex
    (e) dense

Directions for Questions 13 to 15 : Choose the word/group of words which is most opposite in meaning to the word/group of words printed in bold as used in the passage.

13. HEFTY
    (a) thin (b) uniform
    (c) small (d) bulky
    (e) fragile

14. RELUCTANCE
    (a) intensity (b) unwillingness
    (c) fanaticism (d) keenness
    (e) devotion

15. DISADVANTAGEOUS
    (a) detrimental
    (b) beneficial
    (c) healthy
    (d) monetary
    (e) healing

Directions for Questions 16 to 25 : Read each sentence to find out whether there is any grammatical error in it. The error if any, will be in one part of the sentence. The number of that part is the answer. If there is no error, the answer is (e) i.e. "No error"

(Ignore errors of punctuation, it any.)

16. The power of the mind (a) / over the body (b) / has became a very significant subject (c) / of research in recent years, (d) / No error (e)

17. She, was held to guilt (a) / practising witchcraft and misdemeanours (b) / such as cutting her hair short (c) / and dressing up like a man (d) / No error (e)

18. Researchers at the University of Nottingham (a) / have discovered that (b) / putting tobacco outside of sight in shops (c) / can change the attitude of young people towards smoking. (d) / No error (e)

19. The young sales manager (a) / is about to resign (b) / despite of his success (c) / in the organization (d) / No error (e)

20. More and more people (a) / are using different colour schemes (b) / in their homes (c) / that reflecting their personalities (d) / No error (e)

21. Because art is so subjective, (a) / no form of art (b) / can be most effective (c) / than the other (d) / No error (e)

22. A 2007 study of Hurricane Katrina survivors (a) / found that those whom scored high (b) / on two measures of creativity—originality and flexibility (c) / coped with the crisis better (d) / No error (e)

23. Ken Follett has made a career (a) / out of keeping readers at (b) / the edge of their seat (c) / engrossed in his suspense thrillers (d) / No error (e)

24. In the moment, (a) / there is no conclusive evidence (b) / that the virus can spread (c) / from one human to another. (d) / No error (e)

25. The newspaper reported a moving story (a) / how one woman channelled (b) / her own bitterness into good by making (c) a commitment to help other people's kids. (d) No error (e)

Directions for Questions 26-30 : Each question below has two blanks, each blank indicating that something has been omitted. Choose the set of words for each blank which best fits the meaning of the sentence/s as a whole.

26. In his latest book, the author gives a real ____ into the sufferings of individuals who have experienced the loss of a loved one ____ to a physical illness.
    (a) testimony, owning
    (b) account, attribute
    (c) praise, following
    (d) insight, owing
    (e) knowledge, new

27. Everybody has had the flu at some point of time, with its ____ symptoms, aches, chills, fatigue and cough. So why is the "bird flu" ______ so many headlines ?

(a) familiar, making
(b) knowing, hitting
(c) same, targeting
(d) similar, cause
(e) drastic, topping

28. Bollywood actors may have set the stage on fire _______ the rock stars from the Indian music industry_______ the house down during the gala night.
(a) as, bring (b) yet, sang
(c) for, took (d) and, had
(e) but, brought

29. In his latest book and documentary, the world renowned author explains that if we continue to_______ what we are doing to our planet, we risk the very future of our civilisation.
(a) do, appreciating
(b) ignore, destroying
(c) secure, losing
(d) establish, maintenance
(e) probe, questioning

30. Although carbon dioxide levels are _______ all over the world, the _______ are most obvious at the North and South Poles.
(a) booming, explosion
(b) exploding, scene
(c) rising, effects
(d) firing, consequences
(e) spilling, disaster

Directions for Questions 31 to 35 : In each of the following sentences, an idiomatic expression or a proverb is highlighted. Select the alternative which best describes its use in the sentence.

31. At an early age my colleague **made his mark** as a chemist
(a) was destined to be
(b) secured good marks
(c) distinguished himself
(d) created a vacancy
(e) got inducted

32. The thief was caught **red-handed.**
(a) in the very act of committing the theft
(b) on red tape
(c) after being given a warning
(d) with blood on his hands
(e) in an attempt to escape

33. He decided to **jump the gun** and apply for the job before it was advertised in the press.
(a) play safe
(b) fake his credentials
(c) use influence
(d) call for a personal meeting
(e) be over hasty

34. My neighbour was caught stealing, lie now has to **face the music.**
(a) ask for forgiveness
(b) come face to face with the police
(c) attempt to protect himself
(d) suffer the consequences of his actions
(e) hear the song

35. Rs. 60 for a kilo of onions ? That's **daylight robbery.**
(a) robbing during the day
(b) robbing people on the basis of their income
(c) unfair overcharging
(d) cheating people with regards to the quality of food
(e) extracting more from the rich

Directions for Questions 36 to 40: Rearrange the following six sentences/group of sentences (A), (B), (C), (D), (E) and (F) in the proper sequence to form a meaningful paragraph; then answer the questions given below them.

(A) "It makes me happy that people are beginning to change their views on the environment and make changes in their lifestyle", he said after receipt of the award.
(B) For him, vindication would be when we stop polluting the earth and turn the corner, the exciting news however, is that there are a lot of good changes underway.
(C) As part of his campaigns, he turned a lecture on global warming and climate change into a well known documentary titled 'An Inconvenient-Truth, by which he encouraged millions of

people worldwide to make earth-friendly changes in their lives.

(D) Though many people are doing their part by being sensitive to the environment, Al Gore expressed a serious concern of the world being still at risk due to global warming.

(E) Al Gore, former Vice President of America, is well known for his campaigns on climate change.

(F) Because of this documentary and his tireless efforts to educate the world about global warming he was awarded the Nobel Peace Prize on Climate Change in 2007

36. Which of the following will be the FIRST sentence after rearrangement ?

(a) E
(b) B
(c) C
(d) D
(e) A

37. Which of the following will be the SECOND sentence after rearrangement ?

(a) D
(b) B
(c) C
(d) F
(e) A

38. Which of the following will be the THIRD sentence after rearrangement ?

(a) D
(b) F
(c) B
(d) C
(e) A

39. Which of the following will be the FIFTH sentence after rearrangement ?

(a) A
(b) B
(c) C
(d) D
(e) F

40. Which of the following will be the SIXTH (LAST) sentence after rearrangement ?

(a) D
(b) B
(c) C
(d) F
(e) E

Directions for Questions 41-50 : In the following passage there are blanks, each of which has been numbered. These numbers are printed below the passage and against each, five words/phrases are suggested, one of which fits the blank appropriately. Find out the appropriate word/phrase in each case.

The insurance industry is …(41)… myriad challenges arising from intense competition, rising regulatory compliance and growing payouts …(42)… to fraud and natural disasters.

It is ...(43)... that competitive pressure will make offshoring of information technology (IT) and business processes a growing imperative in the insurance industry. ...(44)... to mainstream banking and financial services, where the early adoption of automation and IT helped facilitate outsourcing, first in IT service and later in BPO, the insurance industry has lagged ...(45)… This is one reason why insurance companies have beep more conservative in their attitude to "business process outsourcing", and ...(46)... to offshoring.

With expected cost savings of 30% to 40%, and other ...(47)… such as focussing on core competencies and …(48)... to skilled labour, it is ...(49)… that the insurance offshoring industry as …(50)... for significant growth in the next three to four years.

41. (a) looking (b) pressing
(c) watching (d) facing
(e) focusing

42. (a) reason (b) due
(c) owed (d) lent
(e) made

43. (a) featured (b) proof
(c) wanted (d) thought
(e) expected

44. (a) Compared (b) Similar
(c) Unlike (d) Balanced
(e) Alike

45. (a) in (b) back
(c) up (d) behind
(e) slow

46. (a) especially (b) important (c) precise (d) main (e) regularly

47. (a) benefit (b) advantages (c) measure (d) losses (e) detriments

48. (a) excess (b) open (c) availability (d) gain (e) access

49. (a) deem (b) rimed (c) believed (d) idea (e) doubted

50. (a) available (b) assured (c) poised (d) gear (e) concentrated

PAPER 9

PRACTICE TEST PAPER–NINE

Directions: The passage below is followed by questions on its content. Answer the questions on the basis of what is stated or implied in the passage.

Not long ago there was a discussion in which the panelists talked about the 'future of religion'. Towards the end of this half-hour programme it became obvious that the discussants were not going to be able to agree on the 'future of religion—whether indeed it has a future. Quite properly, one panelist suggested that since apparently the word did not mean the same thing to the various participants, perhaps each member of the panel should state how he was using the term. But at this stage, all their time had been used up, and the thing they should have done at the outset was never even to have begun. Another illustration of the complexity of the manifestations of 'religions' and resulting vagueness of meaning of the term is provided by the story of the graduate student in one of our great universities. He 'earned' an M. Phil degree by cataloguing in his thesis the various definitions of religion that appear in literature stopping when he had culled fifty definitions. A cynic might point out that if this had been a doctoral dissertation, the student could have gone on with the research and collected one hundred definitions.

One might surmise that a major conclusion to result from an adequate discussion of the' future of religion would be this: if one employs a narrow and rigid definition, then religion in its organised and insitution-alised forms may have little future; but if one recognises that religion is a dynamic thing capable of flexibility, it may have a future as bright as that of the human race—indeed, it might even help light the way to this uncertain world of tomorrow.

The *New Century Dictionary* defines religion as the 'recognition' on the part of man of a controlling, superhuman power 'entitled to reverence and worship'. If this 'superhuman power' is not limited to a personalised entity, but is broad enough to include the more abstractly conceived realities such as the universal lawfulness of nature of the pantheists and the 'infinite eternal energy' of Herbert Spencer, there is no difficulty in accepting the *New Century Dictionary* definition.

The importance of the problem of definition in determining the character of one's conclusions was brought out in an interesting manner when the *Life* magazine in an article on the Huxley brothers described Julian Huxley as 'an atheist' and 'a materialist, denying the need for religion or God'. Commenting on the article, Dr Charles Francis Potter, founder of the First

Humanist Society of New York, accused the writer of a *non sequitul:* Dr Potter agreed that Julian Huxley does deny the need for God, but stated that the assertion that Dr Huxley therefore denies the need for religion is evidently based on the false assumption that one must believe in God to have a religion.

1. The title that best suits the passage is
   (a) Religion and Man
   (b) The Future of Religion
   (c) Religion as a Dynamic Force
   (d) A Comprehensive Definition of Religion.
2. The panelists wanted to discuss:
   (a) What is meant by religion?
   (b) What is the future of religion?
   (c) Whether religion had a future?
   (d) How could religion have a future?
3. What does the author mean by the complexity of the manifestations of religions?
   (a) The multiplicity of religious sects
   (b) Varieties of religious experiences
   (c) Innumerable interpretations of the term 'religion'
   (d) Conflicting views about religion
4. Why did the student stop when he had culled fifty definitions of religion?
   (a) For his purpose, this number was enough
   (b) There were no more definitions to be found by him in the literature that he had studied
   (c) He was afraid that more definitions would make his thesis vague
   (d) Brevity is an essential characteristic in any thesis
5. It can be inferred from this passage that the author is
   (a) orthodox by nature
   (b) a believer in non-theistic religion
   (c) an atheist
   (d) a cynic
6. In the definition given by the *New Century Dictionary,* the phrase 'superhuman power' means
   (a) God
   (b) God as everybody believes Him to be
   (c) A universal power based on eternal laws
   (d) A great power that is beyond understanding and exacts reverence and worship.
7. Which of the following statements is untrue?
   (a) Julian Huxley was a materialist
   (b) A materialist may be an atheist
   (c) An atheist has no need for religion
   (d) Humanism is not against religion.
8. To accuse a writer of a *non sequitur* is to say:
   (a) His conclusion does not logically follow from the given statements
   (b) He is biased
   (c) He has no knowledge of the subject on which he is commenting
   (d) He is narrowminded.

Directions: Each of the questions below consists of a word in capital letters, followed by four lettered words or phrases. Choose the word or phrase that is most nearly similar in meaning to the given words.

9. Conceive
   (a) to imagine (b) admit
   (c) prepare (d) calculate
10. Rote
    (a) rotten thing
    (b) a list of persons
    (c) mechanical repetition
    (d) small disc
11. Delve
    (a) defer
    (b) to make a careful search for infonnation
    (c) for a way
    (d) postpone
12. Spore
    (a) sore opening
    (b) tiny opening
    (c) feelings
    (d) minute reproductive organism
13. Impromptu
    (a) powerless (b) improper
    (c) important (d) offhand
14. Mayhem
    (a) majesty (b) havoc
    (c) defeat (d) king

Directiosn: Choose the word opposite in meaning to the given words.

15. Clandestine
(a) dim (b) clear
(c) open (d) congested

16 **Onerous**
(a) light (b) tough
(c) heavy (d) dark

17. Lackadaisical
(a) dull (b) sensible
(c) hopeful (d) enthusiastic

18. Turgid
(a) fair (b) rough
(c) tall (d) smooth

19. Laudation
(a) passiveness (b) reduction
(c) simplification (d) praise loudly

20. Reprimand
(a) praise (b) hate
(c) worship (d) remake

Directiosn: Fill in the blanks with an appropriate alternative.

21. Do not enter this area, it is mined and contains animals dangerous to human life. This is ________ .
(a) a warning (b) a suggestion
(c) an order (d) a signal
(e) an advertisement

22. Mohan will have to take ________ the matter with your superior.
(a) away (b) to
(c) in (d) up
(e) down.

23. Drinking is injurious for health. Why don't you give it ________?
(a) away (b) in
(c) up (d) off
(e) out

24. On the eve of the Republic Day, many leaders ________ the nation on television.
(a) talk (b) address
(c) lecture (d) advise
(e) welcome

25. Your sister is good in the class but mine is .
(a) best (b) top
(c) better (d) fine
(e) well

Directions: Find out the error which is in one part of the sentence. If there is no error, the answer is E.

26. None of the London paintings/took more/than few days/to complete./No error
(a) (b) (c) (d) (e)

27. If Shyamla had/worked hard she/will have got the job/she desired./No error
(a) (b) (c) (d) (e)

28. A writer as considerable as Golding/invites specialised/investigation as well as general/biography and criticism./No error
(a) (b) (c) (d) (e)

29. Political education in real sense/should develop people/who will be committed to/bring social change./No error
(a) (b) (c) (d) (e)

30. Considering the/gravity of the problems/an early reply/has expected./No error
(a) (b) (c) (d) (e)

Directiosn: Give a substitute for the following sentences.

31. The story of a man written by another
(a) biography (b) autobiography
(c) story (d) life-story

32. One filled with excessive and mistaken enthusiasm in a cause
(a) pedant (b) patriot
(c) fanatic (d) martyr

33. List of the points of business to be transacted at a meeting
(a) minutes (b) agenda
(c) excerpts (d) proceedings

34. Regard for others as a principle of action
(a) altruism (b) philanthropy
(c) nepotism (d) cynicism

35. Study of mankind
(a) pathology (b) philology
(c) physiology (d) anthropology

Directiosn: In the following passage, there are blanks, each of which has been numbered. These numbers are printed below the passage and, against each, five words are suggested, one of which fits the blank appropriately. Find out the appropriate words.

Belief systems are the framework upon which cultures and societies function. It is the bond that ..36.. civilisations together, and it is the small voice ..37.. each of us that urges us to be ..38.. to what we have been taught. We cannot ..39.. our spiritual teachings from our learning, nor can we separate our beliefs about who and what we are ..40.. our values and our behaviours. We ask that educational systems ..41.. our right to religious freedom and our right to live in harmony. Tribal beliefs vary, as does the ..42.. to which a tribe embraces ..43.. traditional cultural beliefs ..44.. tribal group has distinct and unique beliefs that are basic to that tribe's culture. Most tribes cling to the old teachings because they know that once gone, it means the ..45.. of their culture.

36. (a) compels (b) holds
(c) makes (d) breaks
(e) completes

37. (a) outside (b) around
(c) about (d) inside
(e) near

38. (a) true (b) habitual
(c) accurate (d) graceful
(e) upright

39. (a) see (b) separate
(c) upset (d) distinguish
(e) search

40. (a) near (b) on
(c) from (d) about
(e) across

41. (a) recognise (b) destroy
(c) diminish (d) reach
(e) infer

42. (a) capacity (b) nearness
(c) practice (d) extant
(e) principle

43. (a) for (b) their
(c) itself (d) about
(e) its

44. (a) many (b) all
(c) one (d) several
(e) each

45. (a) mark (b) regeneration
(c) death (d) tradition
(e) mistake

PAPER 10

PRACTICE TEST PAPER–TEN

Directions for Questions 1 to 15: Read the following passage carefully and answer the questions given below it. Certain words/expressions are given in bold in the passage to help you locate them while answering some of the questions:

A few weeks ago I ran into an old friend who is currently one of the mandarins deciding India's economic and financial policies. He asked "And so, how is IIT doing?" As one can only indulge in friendly banter at such gatherings, I responded with 'Not so well actually. Your market-friendly policies have forced us to raise the fee, so we have 50% fewer Ph.D. applicants this year'. Not batting an eyelid, he shot back: "Obviously. Your Ph.D. students don't have any market value." Taken aback, I shifted to a more serious tone and tried to start a discussion on the need for research in these globalised times. But he had already walked away. The last word on the imperatives of the 'market' had been spoken.

Actually, this view of higher education should not have surprised me. Worthies who look at everything as consumer products classify higher education as a 'non-merit' good. Non-merit goods are those where only the individual benefits from acquiring them and not the society as a whole. Multilateral agencies like The World Bank have too been pushing countries like India to stop subsidies to higher education.

When Ron Brown, former US commerce secretary visited India, a public meeting was organized at IIT Delhi. At that meeting I asked him: "I understand that since the 19th century all the way up to the 1970s, most land grant and State universities in the US virtually provided free education to State citizens. Was that good for the economy, or should they have charged high fees in the early 20th century? "He replied," it was great for the economy. It was one of the best things that the US government did at that particular time in American history-building institutions of higher education which were accessible to the masses of the people. I think it is one of the reasons why our economy grew and prospered, one of the ways in which the US was able to close some of its social gaps. So people who lived in rural areas would have the same kind of access to higher education as people living in other parts of the country. It was one of the reasons for making America strong."

Our policy-makers seem unaware that their mentors in the US did not follow policies at home which they now prescribe for other countries. Ron Brown's remarks summarise the importance policymakers in the US place on higher education as a vehicle for upward mobility for the poorer sectors of their population. Even today, a majority of Americans study in State-run institutions. Some of these institutions, like Berkeley and the Universities of Michigan, Illinois, Ohio, Wisconsin and Taxas are among the best in the world. The annual tuition charged from State residents (about $5000 a year) is about a month's salary paid to a lecturer. Even this fee is waived for most students. In addition, students receive stipends for books, food and hostel charges. The basic principle is that no student who gets admission to a university should have to depend on parental support if it is not available.

Ron Brown's remarks went unnoticed in India. Every other day some luminary or the other opines that universities and technical education institutions should increase their charges and that such education should not be subsidised. Most editorials echo these sentiments. Eminent industrialists pontificate that we should run educational institutions like business houses. Visiting experts from the Bank and the IMF, in their newly emerging concern for the poor, advise us to divert funds from higher education to primary education.

1. The author of the passage seems to be a /an
- (a) official working in economic affairs department
- (b) financial advisor to government or a bureaucrat in finance department
- (c) social activist devoted to illiteracy eradication programme
- (d) educationist in IIT or some such Educational Institution
- (e) industrialist employing highly qualified technocrats

2. What was the net tangible impact of raising fees on the higher level of technological research?
- (a) The number of prospective researchers was reduced to almost a half
- (b) The market value of Ph.D. students was almost lost
- (c) Research studies attained a higher market value
- (d) Research became more and more relevant to market demands
- (e) In the current globalised times, the need for research was less than ever

3. According to the author, the US policy-makers consider education as a
- (a) hindrance in the way to economic growth and prosperity
- (b) means for achieving upward mobility for the poor
- (c) wastage of resources and a totally futile exercise
- (d) matter of concern only for the parents of the students
- (e) None of these

4. Who among the following support the view that higher education should be free to everyone aspiring for it?
- (A) Editors and Journalists
- (B) Industrialists
- (C) Visiting Experts from Banks and IMF
- (a) A only
- (b) B only
- (c) C only
- (d) All the three
- (e) None of these

5. Which of the following makes the policy-makers classify education as "non-merit" commodity?
- (a) The tendency of people to seek any individual benefits
- (b) The attitude of giving unreasonably more weightage to society
- (c) The tendency of viewing everything as mere consumer product
- (d) Undue pressure from International Agencies like the World Bank, etc.
- (e) None of these

6. What was Ron Brown's reaction to the author's question on free education provided by US universities to their citizens? Ron Brown
- (a) criticised the US government for their action
- (b) appreciated the author but remained non-committed
- (c) ignored the fact and gave an ambiguous reaction

(d) mentioned that the author's information was not correct
(e) None of these

7. The basic principle adopted by the renowned State-run universities in the US is that the students___
(a) must pay the lecturer's salary from their own resources
(b) should earn while they learn and pay higher education fees
(c) must seek the necessary help from their parents on whom they depend
(d) need not be required to depend upon their parents for acquiring higher education
(e) None of these

8. What was the outcome of US strategy of imparting free university education to US citizens?
(a) Education was easily accessible to the vast majority
(b) US citizens found it unaffordable and expensive
(c) US Economy suffered due to such a lop-sided decision
(d) US government could not plug the loopholes in their economic policies
(e) None of these

9. Multilateral agencies like The World Bank have been___
(a) pressurising India and other countries to stop substantial higher education
(b) insisting on discontinuance of subsidies to higher education
(c) analysing the possibilities of increasing subsidies to higher learning
(d) emphasising on the need of lowering fees for higher education
(e) forcing countries like India to strengthen only industrial development

Directions for Questions 10 to 12: Which of the following is MOST NEARLY THE SAME in meaning as the word printed in bold as used in the passage?

10. UNWARE
(a) Famous (b) Ignorant
(c) Familiar (d) Unworthy
(e) Negligent

11. WAIVED
(a) Moved (b) Charged
(c) Condoned (d) Overlooked
(e) Paid

12. MASSES
(a) Institutions (b) Groups
(c) Students (d) Officers
(e) Parents

Directions for Questions 13 to 15: Which of the following is MOST OPPOSITE in meaning of the word printed in bold as used in the passage?

13. GLOBALISED
(a) Universalised (b) Liberalised
(c) Earthly (d) Prospering
(e) Decentralised

14. PROSPERED
(a) Declined (b) Progressed
(c) Improved (d) Decomposed
(e) Enlightened

15. CONCERN
(a) Worry (b) Anxiety
(c) Sympathy (d) Indifference
(e) Nullification

Directions for Questions 16 to 20: Rearrange the following six sentences (A); (B), (C), (D), (E) and (F) in the proper sequence to form a meaningful paragraph; then answer the questions given below them.

(A) For other wishes, it enlists the help of those who make or own what the child desires.
(B) It grants some wishes with its own funds depending upon the availability of funds.
(C) I was deeply moved when I learnt about the activity of "Make-a-Wish Foundation".
(D) From parents, friends, or hospital attendants, the foundation learns about the child's wish for anything from a special toy to a visit to Disneyland.
(E) I am sure you also now must have been moved by the noble act of the foundation.
(F) It grants the wishes of children who are terminally ill.

16. Which of the following should be the **FOURTH** sentence after rearrangement?
(a) F (b) E
(c) D (d) C
(e) B

17. Which of the following should be the **SIXTH (LAST)** sentence after rearrangement?
(a) F (b) E
(c) D (d) C
(e) B

18. Which of the following should be the **SECOND** sentence after rearrangement?
(a) F (b) E
(c) D (d) C
(e) B

19. Which of the following should be the **THIRD** sentence after rearrangement?
(a) F (b) E
(c) D (d) C
(e) B

20. Which of the following should be the **FIRST** sentence after rearrangement?
(a) F (b) E
(c) D (d) C
(e) B

Directions for Questions 21 to 30: Read each sentence to find out whether there is any grammatical mistake/ error in it. The error if any, will be in one part of the sentence. Mark the number of that part with error as your answer. If there is no error, mark(e).

21. People are worried (a) more because of the frequency (b) of occurrence of the crime rather (c) than the magnitude of each one. (d) No error. (e)

22. The quality of construction (a) of our building was (b) highly appreciable by (c) most of the visitors. (d) No error. (e)

23. The discrete enquiry revealed (a) that his involvement in (b) the fraud cases have been (c) more than what was first guessed. (d) No error. (e)

24. I know nothing (a) about chess because (b) my games teacher also (c) was not knowing nothing about it. (d) No error. (e)

25. Due to uncertainty (a) capital market conditions, (b) there has been tremendous (c) growth in bank deposits. (d) No error. (e)

26. Her sympathetic nature (a) and ability of motivation of people (b) make her the best (c) of all the supervisors. (d) No error. (e)

27. To lose weight, (a) cut down on (b) what you eat (c) and exercise regularly. (d) No error. (e)

28. The limitations and constrains with which (a) we have been managing our work (b) have been duly realized (c) by our superiors. (d) No error. (e)

29. How could one, (a) who had all along (b) been a criminal, (c) be granted privileges? (d) No error. (e)

30. The child complaint that (a) he was denied his (b) father's love due to (c) his step-mother's intervention. (d) No error. (e)

Directions for Questions 31 to 40: Which of the phrases (a), (b), (c) and (d) given below should replace the phrase given in bold in the following sentence to make the sentence grammatically meaningful and correct. If the sentence is correct as it is and no correction is required, mark (e), as the answer.

31. The increased time **devoting to watch** television is one of the important cases of the decline in reading ability.
(a) devoted for the watch
(b) devoted to watching
(c) devoted for the watch of the
(d) devoted to keep watch
(e) No correction required

32. Walking has **distinctly advantageous** over driving as you see many things while walking that you often miss while driving.
(a) have advantages distinctly
(b) is distinctly advantages
(c) has distinct advantages
(d) is distinct in advantageous
(e) No correction required

33. He turned down our proposal which we **had prepared** by so much dedication.
(a) had prepared with

(b) have prepared by
(c) were prepared with
(d) have been preparing for
(e) No correction required

34. Although family TV serials **do vary**, they have certain common elements.
(a) do not vary (b) seldom vary
(c) rarely vary (d) are varying
(e) No correction required

35. We have profound **faith and hopes** for the future.
(a) faith for also hopes for
(b) faith in and hopes for
(c) faith and hopes for
(d) faith about and hopes in
(e) No correction required

36. They can't decide **who should they blame** for inefficiency.
(a) who they should blame for
(b) whom should they be blamed for
(c) whom should they blame on
(d) whom should they blame for
(e) No correction required

37. Because our foreign policy is **not well defined**, it creates confusion among the people of other countries.
(a) is not defining well
(b) has not well-defined
(c) was not well defined
(d) has been not defining well
(e) No correction required

38. Guests must register at the front desk; otherwise, they **don't obtain** a key.
(a) will not obtain a
(b) don't obtained a
(c) cannot obtain a
(d) can obtain not a
(e) No correction required

39. Emission controls were created to eliminate or at **least reduction** in air pollution.
(a) at least to reduce
(b) to reduce in the least
(c) for reducing in the
(d) to at least reduction in
(e) No correction required

40. Because certain scientific theories are **contradicting with people's** religious beliefs, they are reluctant to accept them.
(a) contracting to
(b) contracting with
(c) conflicting for
(d) contrary to
(e) No correction required

Directions for Questions 41 to 50: In the following passage, there are blanks, each of which has been numbered. These numbers are printed below the passage and against each, four words are suggested, one of which fits the blank appropriately. Find out the appropriate word in each case.

First aid experts stress that (41) what to do for an (42) victim until a doctor or other trained person gets to the accident scene can (43) a life, especially in cases of stoppage of breathing, severe bleeding, and shock.

People with special (44) problems, such as diabetes, cardiovascular disease, epilepsy, or allergy, are (45) to wear some sort of emblem identifying the problem, as a safeguard against administration of medication that might be injurious or even (46). When emergencies do occur, (47) first aid within the first few minutes often (48) life or death. (49) administering of first aid (50) medical professionals to provide better care.

41. (a) before (b) attempting
(c) regarding (d) knowing
(e) about

42. (a) injured (b) inquiring
(c) efficient (d) important
(e) accident

43. (a) harm (b) comfort
(c) take (d) soothe
(e) save

44. (a) mental (b) ethical
(c) medical (d) accident
(e) moral

45. (a) prohibited (b) invited
(c) compelled (d) allowed
(e) urged

46. (a) appropriate (b) dangerous
(c) beneficial (d) fatal
(e) remedial

47. (a) expecting (b) providing
(c) avoiding (d) ignoring
(e) neglecting

48. (a) determines (b) offers
(c) vanishes (d) reflects
(e) begs

49. (a) Hasty (b) Careless
(c) Proper (d) Probable
(e) Reasonably

50. (a) resists (b) instigates
(c) hinders (d) prevents
(e) enables

ANSWER KEY

Practice Test Paper–One

1. (a)	11. (d)	21. (b)	31. (d)	41. (a)
2. (d)	12. (d)	22. (c)	32. (c)	42. (b)
3. (b)	13. (b)	23. (a)	33. (c)	43. (a)
4. (c)	14. (b)	24. (d)	34. (c)	44. (b)
5. (b)	15. (b)	25. (b)	35. (b)	45. (b)
6. (c)	16. (c)	26. (a)	36. (c)	46. (c)
7. (a)	17. (d)	27. (a)	37. (a)	47. (d)
8. (a)	18. (c)	28. (b)	38. (c)	48. (d)
9. (d)	19. (d)	29. (d)	39. (b)	49. (c)
10. (c)	20. (c)	30. (c)	40. (c)	50. (a)

Practice Test Paper–Two

1. (d)	11. (a)	21. (d)	31. (c)
2. (a)	12. (c)	22. (a)	32. (b)
3. (a)	13. (d)	23. (c)	33. (c)
4. (d)	14. (c)	24. (b)	34. (c)
5. (a)	15. (a)	25. (c)	35. (b)
6. (c)	16. (b)	26. (d)	36. (a)
7. (a)	17. (d)	27. (a)	37. (b)
8. (a)	18. (a)	28. (b)	38. (d)
9. (b)	19. (d)	29. (d)	
10. (a)	20. (a)	30. (a)	

Practice Test Paper–Three

1. (d)	11. (c)	21. (b)	31. (e)
2. (a)	12. (a)	22. (a)	32. (c)
3. (c)	13. (b)	23. (e)	33. (b)
4. (e)	14. (b)	24. (e)	34. (a)
5. (b)	15. (a)	25. (c)	35. (e)
6. (b)	16. (c)	26. (c)	36. (d)
7. (b)	17. (b)	27. (a)	37. (c)
8. (a)	18. (b)	28. (b)	38. (e)
9. (c)	19. (d)	29. (a)	39. (b)
10. (e)	20. (e)	30. (b)	40. (a)

Practice Test Paper–Four

1. (c)	11. (b)	21. (a)	31. (b)	41. (b)
2. (c)	12. (a)	22. (d)	32. (c)	42. (b)
3. (e)	13. (c)	23. (e)	33. (a)	43. (a)
4. (e)	14. (a)	24. (b)	34. (e)	44. (c)
5. (d)	15. (b)	25. (a)	35. (d)	45. (c)
6. (b)	16. (b)	26. (c)	36. (a)	46. (d)
7. (a)	17. (a)	27. (e)	37. (e)	47. (a)
8. (b)	18. (c)	28. (c)	38. (d)	48. (d)
9. (d)	19. (b)	29. (b)	39. (e)	49. (e)
10. (b)	20. (e)	30. (c)	40. (b)	50. (b)

Practice Test Paper–Five

1. (a)	11. (b)	21. (d)
2. (b)	12. (e)	22. (b)
3. (c)	13. (b)	23. (c)
4. (b)	14. (c)	24. (a)
5. (a)	15. (c)	25. (e)
6. (a)	16. (d)	26. (e)
7. (b)	17. (b)	27. (b)
8. (c)	18. (c)	28. (a)
9. (d)	19. (e)	29. (a)
10. (a)	20. (c)	30. (e)

Practice Test Paper–Six

1. (b)	11. (b)	21. (c)	31. (d)	41. (a)
2. (d)	12. (e)	22. (b)	32. (c)	42. (d)
3. (e)	13. (d)	23. (e)	33. (c)	43. (b)
4. (e)	14. (c)	24. (a)	34. (e)	44. (c)
5. (a)	15. (e)	25. (d)	35. (a)	45. (b)
6. (d)	16. (b)	26. (b)	36. (e)	46. (a)
7. (c)	17. (a)	27. (d)	37. (a)	47. (b)
8. (c)	18. (d)	28. (e)	38. (c)	48. (d)
9. (a)	19. (e)	29. (a)	39. (b)	49. (e)
10. (d)	20. (a)	30. (c)	40. (a)	50. (c)

Practice Test Paper–Seven

1. (c)	11. (a)	21. (a)
2. (b)	12. (b)	22. (c)
3. (c)	13. (c)	23. (b)
4. (b)	14. (b)	24. (c)
5. (c)	15. (d)	25. (d)
6. (b)	16. (c)	26. (a)
7. (a)	17. (d)	27. (d)
8. (d)	18. (b)	28. (c)
9. (b)	19. (a)	29. (b)
10. (c)	20. (c)	30. (b)

Practice Test Paper–Eight

1. (e)	11. (c)	21. (c)	31. (c)	41. (d)
2. (a)	12. (d)	22. (b)	32. (a)	42. (b)
3. (e)	13. (c)	23. (b)	33. (e)	43. (e)
4. (d)	14. (d)	24. (a)	34. (d)	44. (a)
5. (a)	15. (b)	25. (c)	35. (c)	45. (d)
6. (e)	16. (a)	26. (d)	36. (a)	46. (a)
7. (b)	17. (a)	27. (a)	37. (c)	47. (b)
8. (c)	18. (c)	28. (e)	38. (b)	48. (e)
9. (b)	19. (c)	29. (b)	39. (d)	49. (c)
10. (a)	20. (d)	30. (e)	40. (b)	50. (c)

Practice Test Paper–Nine

1. (d)	11. (b)	21. (a)	31. (a)	41. (a)
2. (c)	12. (d)	22. (d)	32. (c)	42. (c)
3. (c)	13. (d)	23. (c)	33. (b)	43. (e)
4. (a)	14. (b)	24. (b)	34. (a)	44. (e)
5. (b)	15. (c)	25. (c)	35. (d)	45. (c)
6. (c)	16. (a)	26. (c)	36. (b)	
7. (c)	17. (d)	27. (c)	37. (d)	
8. (a)	18. (d)	28. (a)	38. (a)	
9. (a)	19. (b)	29. (d)	39. (b)	
10. (c)	20. (a)	30. (d)	40. (c)	

Practice Test Paper–Ten

1. (d)	11. (c)	21. (d)	31. (b)	41. (a)
2. (a)	12. (b)	22. (c)	32. (c)	42. (e)
3. (b)	13. (e)	23. (c)	33. (a)	43. (e)
4. (e)	14. (a)	24. (d)	34. (b)	44. (c)
5. (d)	15. (d)	25. (b)	35. (b)	45. (e)
6. (e)	16. (e)	26. (b)	36. (d)	46. (d)
7. (d)	17. (b)	27. (b)	37. (e)	47. (b)
8. (a)	18. (a)	28. (e)	38. (a)	48. (a)
9. (b)	19. (c)	29. (b)	39. (a)	49. (c)
10. (b)	20. (d)	30. (a)	40. (d)	50. (c)

SECTION C

Part 1
Examinations Conducted by Banks

Part 2
Insurance Sector Examinations

Part 3
Defence Services Examinations

Part 4
Management Admission Tests

Part 5
Miscellaneous Examinations Conducted by UPSC, SSC and other Organisations

Previous Years' Question Papers

This section has questions taken from the English section of various competitive examinations along with their answer key and detailed explanatory notes, wherever required. The purpose is to give the candidates a real feel of the actual examination, and also provide them with an understanding of the general trend across the examinations. This section has been divided into five parts: (a) Bank examinations; (b) Insurance examinations; (c) Defence examinations; (D) Management admission tests; and (e) Miscellaneous examinations (which include various examinations conducted by UPSC and SSC).

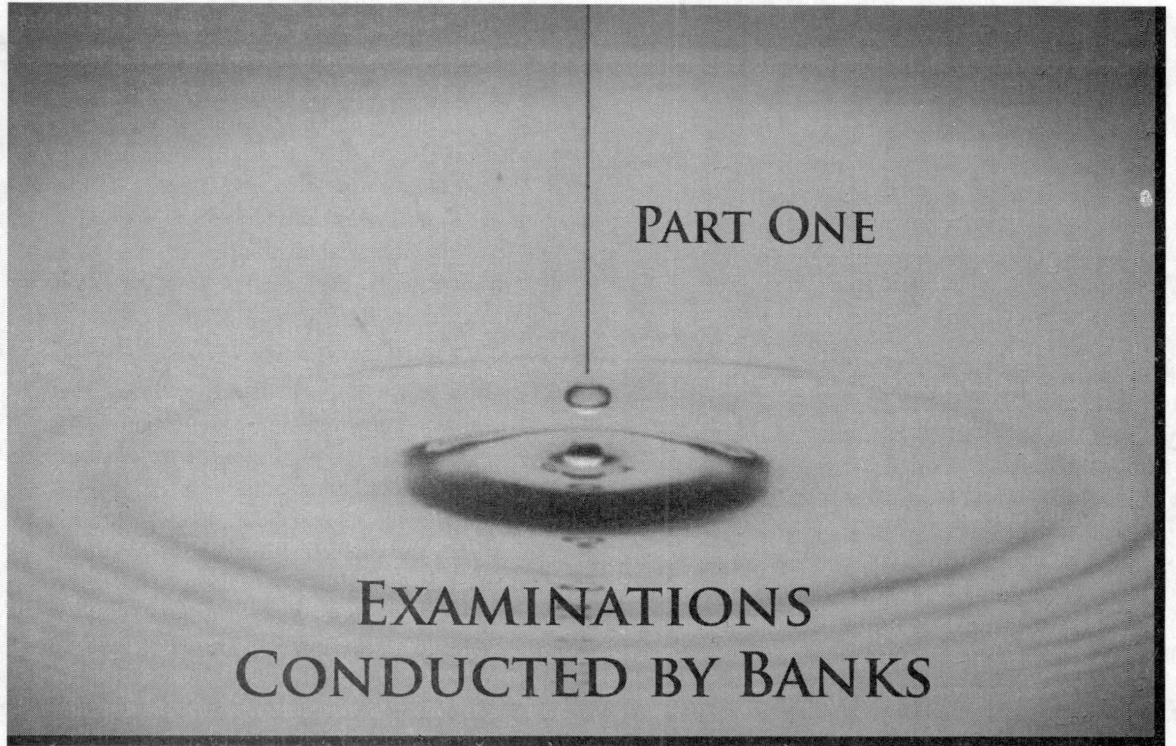

Banking is one of the most fascinating and rewarding sectors in the country. It assures secure, satisfying and highly remunerative career prospects. Openings in banks are available at various levels, from bank clerical to Probationary Officers (PO).

In 1978, Banking Services Recruitment Boards (BSRBs) were established to have a uniform standard and eligibility criteria for recruitment of personnel to Nationalised Banks. There were 15 BSRBs covering one or more states and they were assigned to recruit both officers and clerks. However, Central Recruitment Board of the State Bank of India undertook recruitment of officers for the State Bank group on the all-India level separately.

After dissolution of BSRB's, banks are now advertising directly for their vacancies. Now IBPS conducts and rates the written examination (comprising objective and descriptive parts) on behalf of banks. The banks usually prefer to have for interviews anything from three to four times the number of vacancies advertised, and then make the final selection.

Now the current situation is like this. RBI conducts examination for Grade B officers and Assistant Grade. SBI conducts examination for Bank PO, Bank Assistant and Bank PO for Associate Banks of SBI and Assistant Grade of Associate Banks of India. IBPS conducts CWE, Common Written Examination for PO, MT and Specialist officers and Assistant Grade for nationalised Banks of India.

Institute of Banking Personnel Selection

Institute of Banking Personnel Selection (IBPS)is an autonomous agency in India, which started its operation in 1975 as Personnel Selection Services (PSS). In 1984, IBPS became an independent entity at the behest of Reserve Bank of India (RBI) and Public Sector Banks. IBPS is envisioned as self-governed acadeiric and research oriented Institute, with a mission of enhancing human-resource development through personnel assessment. In 2011, IBPS announced a common written examination (C WE) for the selection Officers and Clerks in Indian banks. IBPS CWE is now mandatory for anyone who seeks an empbyment in 20 public sector and Regional Rural banks) IBPS periodically accepts the exam applications from the candidates at their websfte www.ibps.in (http://www.ibps.in), and the exams are organized at various locations m the country efther in online or offline mode.

List of Banks that Accept CWE

- Allahabad Bank
- AndhraBank
- Bank of Baroda
- Bank of India
- Bank of Maharashtra
- Canara Bank
- Central Bank of India
- Corporation Bank
- Dona Bank
- Indian Bank
- Indian Overseas Bank
- Oriental Bank of Commerce
- Punjab National Bank
- Punjab & Sind Bank
- Syndicate Bank
- Union Bank of India
- United Bank of India
- UCOBank
- Vijaya Bank
- IDBIBank
- HCGC (Export Credit Guarantee Corporation)(Joined Recently)

English in its objective format still forms a major segment of the test format. There was very little variation in the question units. Such variations have been taking place from earlier times. However, the basic objectives are the same. All questions set in different examinations of different banks during the last three to four years can all be solved by developing and fortifying the skills in comprehension, language skill, and vocabulary.You need to keep the following points in mind at the time of your preparation.

- Read the book carefully, understand all basic units like comprehension, spotting error, sentence improvement, sentence completion, cloze test, synonym, antonym, sentence arrangement, and the accessory units like sentence fillers, preposition, voice, substitution, idioms and phrases, miscellaneous vocabulary, and analogy which have been dealt with in details in the book and go through individual exercises unitwise so that you have a command over all these units.
- Any variation can be easily solved by you.
- The model test papers fortify your preparation and give you swiftness and surety in solving questions.
- Finally the previous years' questions give you further chances to strengthen yourself and acquaint you with exact trends of the examinations you are going to appear at.

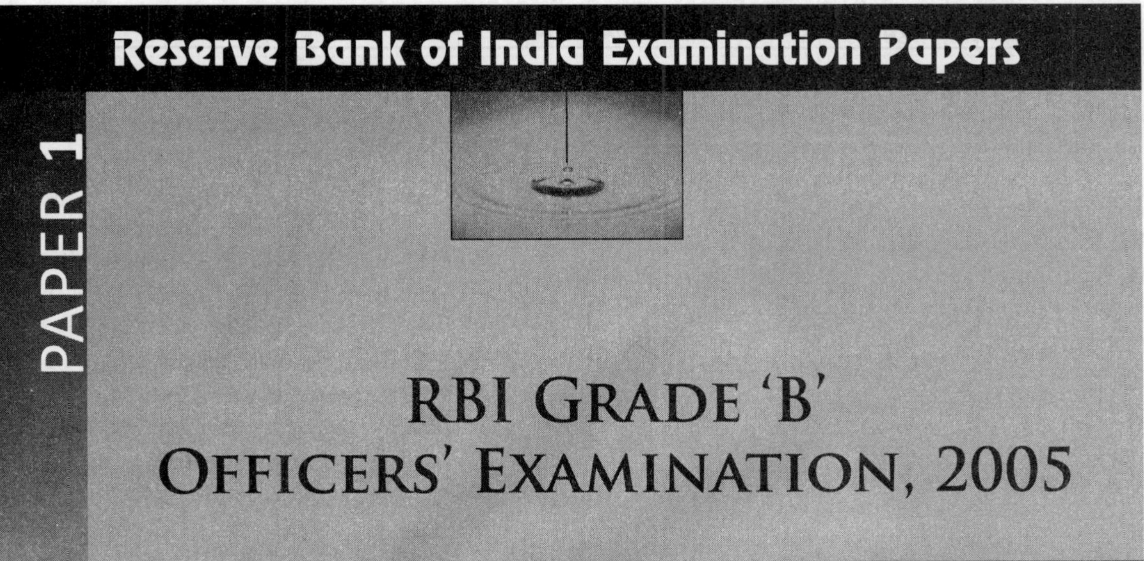

RBI Grade 'B' Officers' Examination, 2005

Directions for Q. 1 to 15

Read the following passage carefully and answer the questions given below it. Certain words/ phrases have been printed in bold to help you to locate them while answering some of the questions.

The structure and operations of banks have undergone a rapid transformation in recent years. Consequent upon the revolution in information technology and the associated increase in competition financial intermediaries have become increasingly global in geographical coverage and universal in the financial operations, encompassing a wide range of activities including banking, securities markets activities and insurance. In the face of widespread concerns about declining profitability of banks, the Basel capital adequacy norms were enacted.

Although the Basel norms helped to arrest the erosion of banks' capital ratios, concerns were raised regarding the mere applicability of baseline capital ratios in the changed environment of operation. The blurring of both functional as well as national divisions among the financial intermediaries, and the speed and complexity of adjustment, made it difficult for regulators to keep up with the growing pace change. In particular the rule of 'one-size-fits-all' aspect of the capital adequacy ratio was the subject of intense debate. Recent banking crisis only emphasized the point that baseline capital adequacy norms wee not adequate to hedge against failures. In response to the same, the Basel Committee on Banks' Supervision came out with the new Consultative Paper on Capital Adequacy. It invited suggestions from the policymakers, academia and other institutes all over the world. After taking into consideration manifold suggestions of the various organisations, the second Consultative Paper on Capital Adequacy was released.

The Accord rests on three pillars; the first pillar of minimum capital requirement, the second pillar of supervisory review process and the third pillar of market discipline. The first pillar sets out the minimum capital requirements. The new framework maintains both the current definition of capital and the minimum requirement of 8% of capital to risk-weighted assets. The revised Accord will be extended on a consolidational basis to holding companies of banking groups. The Accord stresses upon the improvement in measurement of risks. The credit risk measurement methods have been made more elaborate than those in the existing Accord. The new framework also emphasises the measurement of operational risk. For measuring credit risk, two options have been proposed. The first is the standardised approach and the second is the internal rating based approach. Under the standardized approach, the existing approach for credit risk remains conceptually the same, but the risk-weights have been enlarged to encompass exposures to a broad category of borrowers with reference to the rating provided by rating agencies.

1. What necessitated the creation of Basel capital adequacy norms?
(a) To study the profitability pattern in the banks.
(b) The banks wanted its capital reserve ratios to be kept above 8%.
(c) Regulatory body of the banks wanted to have uniform policy.
(d) Corporate buyers compelled the lending institutions to do so.
(e) None of these

2. Which of the following factors are responsible for rapid transformation in banks in recent years?
(a) The forces of privatisation and international players have compelled the banks to do so.
(b) Control from regulators has become meaningless for the banks to survive.
(c) Sudden upsurge in economy.
(d) The competition has increased and information technology has undergone a sea change.
(e) None of these

3. According to the passage activities encompassed by banks are:
(a) insurance, housing finance and low cost funds.
(b) market discipline, profit maximization and priority sector banking.
(c) securities markets, insurance and banking.
(d) geographical coverage, universalization and transformation.
(e) None of these

4. The main features of the standardised approach are:
(a) the credit risk management should encompass large corporate borrowers.
(b) the borrowers should not have more than 8% risk weighted assets.
(c) banks capital reserve ratios should be strictly maintained.
(d) the risk weights should take into consideration the rating of rating agencies.
(e) None of these.

5. The consultative paper of Basel Committee was a result of:
(a) three pillar accord of academic institutes.
(b) contribution from international policy makers, academicians and institutions.
(c) failure of structures and operations of banks in the world.
(d) erosion of banks' fixed assets owing to global competition.
(e) None of these

6. How did Basel norms help the Bank?
(a) It changed the environment of operations.
(b) The decline in capital ratios was arrested.
(c) The banks could successfully keep market discipline.
(d) It did not erode the quality of risk measurement.
(e) None of these

7. Emphasis on operational risk measurement was the main feature of:
(a) theory of three pillars risk management.
(b) first consultative paper on capital adequacy.
(c) second consultative paper on capital adequacy.
(d) Basel capital adequacy norms.
(e) None of these

8. Which of the following difficulties was faced by regulators on prescription of Basel norms?

(a) The regulators could not keep up with growing pace of change.
(b) There was no provision for risk measurement.
(c) The minimum requirement of 8% of capital could not be met.
(d) The supervisory review process could not be carried out.
(e) None of these

9. Which of the following is **NOT** a recommendation of second consultative paper on capital adequacy?
(a) The minimum capital requirement for a bank has been prescribed.
(b) Universal financial operations are permitted within limited geographical coverage.
(c) The supervisory review should be more comprehensive.
(d) The market discipline has to be observed by each bank.
(e) None of these

10. According to passage factor(s) responsible for declining profitability in banks was/were:
(A) cut-throat competition and technology revolution.
(B) globalisation of financial intermediaries.
(C) privatisation of insurance.
(a) Only (A) (b) Only (B)
(c) Both (A) and (B)
(d) Both (B) and (C)
(e) Neither (A) nor (B)

Directions for Q. 11 to 13

Choose the word which is most similar in meaning to the word printed in **bold** as used in the passage.

11. Elaborate
(a) precise (b) discernible
(c) explanatory (d) enumerate
(e) implicit

12. Options
(a) alternatives (b) distracters
(c) answers (d) paths
(e) directions

13. Erosion
(a) loss (b) depletion
(c) assets (d) replenishment
(e) reclamation

Directions for Q. 14 to 15

Choose the word which is most opposite in meaning to the word printed in **bold** as used in the passage.

14. Accord
(a) summit (b) record
(c) disagreement (d) difference
(e) withdrawal

15. Manifold
(a) single (b) alone
(c) lonely (d) isolated
(e) multiple

Directions for Q. 16 to 25

Which of the phrases (a), (b), (c) and (d) given below each sentence should replace the phrase printed in **bold** *italic* in the sentence to make it grammatically correct? If the sentence is correct as it is given and No correction required, mark (e) as the answer.

16. The Governor has a good collection of ***paintings adorning the walls*** of the Raj Bhavan.
(a) painting adoring the walls
(b) painting adorning a walls
(c) paintings sticking the walls
(d) paintings adorn the walls
(e) No correction required

17. The argument against privatisation stems from a fear that the national ***assets were being handed*** to private sector.
(a) assets are being handed over to
(b) assets is being handled by
(c) asset have been handed over to
(d) assets are being handled into
(e) No correction required

18. The principals and teachers ***at the selected English medium*** schools were contacted.
(a) of the selected English medium
(b) at the select English medium
(c) upon the selected English medium
(d) of the selection English medium
(e) No correction required

19. Fast foods can be dangerous as they deprive ***the body of essential*** nutrients.
(a) the body at essential
(b) the body of essentially
(c) the body from essential
(d) the bodies onto essential
(e) No correction required

20. Some people feel that the medium of instruction in all colleges in India ***would be only English.***
(a) should has been only English
(b) will have be only English
(c) should be only English
(d) would be English only
(e) No correction required

21. Besides these norms, ***the data was also analysed*** to form the sub groups.
(a) the data had analysed also
(b) the data were also concluded
(c) the data were also analysed
(d) an data were analysed also
(e) No correction required

22. The children and their specific ***problems needs to be*** identified.
(a) problem need to be
(b) problems needed to be
(c) problems has been
(d) problems need to be
(e) No correction required

23. He does not know that Mount Everest is the ***most highest mountain*** peak.
(a) is a more highest mountain
(b) is the most high mountain
(c) is the higher mountain
(d) is the highest mountain
(e) No correction required

24. The complex nature of the modern industrial civilization and explosion of knowledge ***have made the education process*** very complicated.
(a) has made the education process
(b) have made the educational process
(c) have mede the education processed
(d) have been mede educational process
(e) No correction required

25. Learning is defined as a ***relatively permanently change*** in our potential for performance.
(a) relatively permanent change
(b) relative permanently change
(c) relatively permanent changed
(d) permanently relatively change
(e) No correction required

Directions for Q. 26 to 35

In the following passage there are blanks, each of which has been numbered. These numbers are printed below the passage and against each, five words are suggested, one of which fits the blank appropriately. Find out the appropriate word in each case.

It is a pity that we do not have good books on banking written by Indian authors **(26)** to the steady growth of literature on the subject in other countries especially, the J.K. whose banking laws and **(27)** are very much akin to those of our country. And students studying in our universities and the millions of bank employees appearing or various banking examinations have to depend **(28)** on books written by foreign authors. As these books mainly real with the problems of banking industry of foreign countries the **(29)** of the banking scene in India and the various legal **(30)** and banking procedures remains very weak. To **(31)** the bank employees and the university students no have opted for **(32)** courses in banking with different aspects of theory and practice of banking we should have good and **(33)** textbooks. The book under review, written by experienced and **(34)** banker, on banking law based on reading Indian cases, will be found very useful by students banking as a (35) guide to the principles of banking law.

26. (a) corresponding (b) following
(c) emphasise (d) correcting
(e) paving

27. (a) products (b) notes
(c) initiatives (d) procedures
(e) processes

28. (a) upon (b) still
(c) rarely (d) until
(e) slightly

29. (a) core (b) application
(c) understanding (d) knowledge
(e) purpose

30. (a) aspects (b) experts
(c) books (d) loops
(e) lapses

31. (a) saddle (b) decorate
(c) promote (d) load
(e) equip

32. (a) expensive (b) tough
(c) detailed (d) specialised
(e) optional

33. (a) voluminous (b) many
(c) seasoned (d) shining
(e) authentic

34. (a) qualified (b) rich
(c) merchant (d) desired
(e) consulting

35. (a) powerful (b) ready
(c) comprehensive (d) prescribed
(e) learned

Directions for Q. 36 to 40

Each question below has two blanks, each blank indicating that something has been omitted. Choose the set of words for each blank that best fits the meaning of the sentence as a whole.

36. He knew that a war of liberation ___ great spirit, great sacrifice, ___ and patience.
(a) forced....peace
(b) encouraged....demand
(c) compelled....money
(d) boost....fear
(e) demanded...courage

37. Management has ___ a half forgotten idea; the individual is ___ in directing decisions, skill and services.
(a) constituted....purposive
(b) invented....vulnerable
(c) rediscovered....crucial
(d) developed....objective
(e) devised....subjective

38. You can do franchising if you are ___ to shut your ___ to many things.
(a) willing....eyes
(b) opt....ears
(c) skilled....window
(d) blind....vision
(e) helpless....thoughts

39. The ___ of an organisation depends on several factors, the ___ of leadership is the most important.
(a) effectiveness....quality
(b) delivery....amount
(c) power....paucity
(d) ambience....judgement
(e) strength....gender

40. History is ___ with examples of strong nations ___ the weak ones.
(a) complete....require
(b) organised....advocating
(c) written....asserting
(d) replete....dominating
(e) taught....propagating

PAPER 2

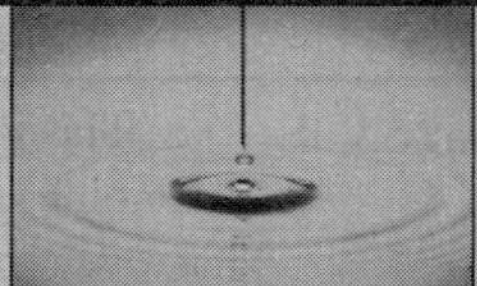

RBI GRADE 'B' OFFICERS' EXAMINATION, 2009

Directions for Q. 1 to 15

Which of the phrases (a), (b), (c) and (d) given below each sentence should replace the phrase printed in **bold** in the given sentence to make it grammatically correct? If the sentence is correct as it is and no correction is required, then mark your answer as (e) :

1. Ultimately he received the honour he deserve.
   (a) Gained the honour he deserve
   (b) Received the honour he deserves
   (c) Received the honour he deserved
   (d) Bags the honour he deserve
   (e) No correction required

2. I am totally opposite in the statement of some of our Managers.
   (a) Totally oppose to the
   (b) Absolutely oppose by the
   (c) Totally opposed to the
   (d) Completely opposed in the
   (e) No correction required

3. Gayatri turned down the job offer to accommodate her friend.
   (a) Job offered in accommodate
   (b) Job offers for accommodate
   (c) Job offer to accommodating
   (d) Job offer in accommodate
   (e) No correction required

4. She was informed that everyone of them are aware of the fact.
   (a) Were aware of (b) Are aware of
   (c) Was aware of (d) Is aware of
   (e) No correction required

5. She has being venturing into areas which she had always avoided in the past.
   (a) Has been venturing into
   (b) Has venturing into
   (c) Would venturing into
   (d) Had venturing into
   (e) No correction required

Directions for Q. 6 to 10

Read each sentence to find out whether there is any grammatical error or idiomatic error in it. The error, if any, will be in one part of the sentence. The number of that part will be your answer. If

there is no error (ignore errors of punctuation, if any), then your answer will be (e).

6. They never thought (a) /that Joshi is (b) /oldest than the other (c) /Professors in the Faculty. (d) /No error (e)

7. Taken into consideration (a) /the advice of his (b) /colleagues he decided (c) /to stay in the Institute. (d) /No error (e)

8. I am likely contact (a) /you sometime in (b) /next week to (c) /discuss with you in detail. (d) /No error (e)

9. The police has making (a) /every effort to provide (b) /best help and (c) /attention to each citizen. (d) /No error (e)

10. He cannot withdraw (a) /all his money (b) /unless he do not (c) /give advance notice. (d) /No error (e)

Directions for Q. 11 to 25

Read the following passage to answer these questions given below it. Certain words / phrases have been printed in bold to help you locate them while answering some of the questions :

The suicide attacks by militant Palestinian groups killing large numbers of Israeli civilians and the harsh Israeli response, have raised the renewed hopes of peace in the region. It is Arafat?s leadership and authority that are being severely tested in the latest phase of the west Asian crisis.

By accusing the Palestinian Authority (PA) of supporting terrorism by groups, Israel hopes to put pressure on Arafat to act. Arafat, on the other hand, has never looked a less powerful force than he does today. If he acts against the militants and elements in his own Fatah movement sympathetic to them, he risks a Palestinian civil conflict. But if he chooses to do nothing, he faces erosion of his authority and all claim to a central role in the peace process. Whatever he does, sections of the Palestinians will hold that he has gone too far and Israel that he has not gone for enough. This is, of course, why Arafat has invariably shrunk from hard decision. He has refrained from curbing the militant groups, explaining his inaction as necessary to maintain Palestinian unity.

The Palestinian leadership's inability to improve economic conditions for its people has been a decisive factor in the erosion of its ability to act. Palestinians in Gaza have targeted the PA as being responsible for their condition. The militant organizations have capitalized on the PA's failure to establish a functioning administrative infrastructure by setting up a parallel welfare system with the help of the millions of dollars. Though the Palestinian security forces claim to have arrested more than 100 militants after the suicide bomb attacks in Israel, the other similar militant groups remain defiant, confident of their popular support and of the certainty that in the ultimate analysis the PA leadership will stop short of decisive action against them.

That the militant groups enjoy popular support in Gaza is hardly surprising. The Gaza Strip today resembles a vast prison camp in which some 1.2 million Palestinians are crammed. Despite the Oslo Accord, 7000 Israeli settlers still remain in 20 percent of the Gaza's area and are protected by heavily armed Israeli forces. With its recent blockade of and extensive incursion into PA controlled territories, the Israeli government has placed the whole civil society in Palestine under siege. Over 450 NGOs, eight universities and numerous other educational, civic, social, developmental and health institutions have had their work impeded and their vital services to the population blocked. An international conference on Israel's treatment of human rights in West Bank and Gaza, attended by signatories to the 1949 Geneva Conventions, that has opened in Switzerland overriding Israeli and American protests, is expected to censor Israel for its treatment of civilians in the Palestinian territories.

Arafat's standing among Palestinians rests on the authority conferred on the PA by the international community to represent and speak for the Palestinians. Even the major militant group has so far never openly challenged Arafat's leadership. Israel's latest vicious attacks directed against the PA and Arafat present the international community with the danger that this precarious balance of power in the Palestinian community may be destroyed. Continuance of the Israeli attacks can only further radicalize and harden the attitudes of ordinary Palestinians. On the other hand, Israeli moves to freeze further expansion of Jewish settlements in the West Bank and Gaza and, as soon as security conditions permit it, ease the economic blockade of Palestinian towns? however remote such measures appear just now alone can restore the authority of the PA and give it a chance to get a grip on Palestinian militancy.

11. Which of the following factors have raised the hope for peace in West Asia?
A. Killings of Israeli civilians
B. Harsh response of Israelites
C. Revocation of Oslo Accord
(a) Only A and C
(b) Only B and C
(c) Both A and B
(d) Either A or B
(e) None of these

12. Which of the following explains the lack of action on the part of Palestinian leader?
(a) He fears the army action against him
(b) This according to him will fasten peace process
(c) He feels that this step will keep Palestinians united
(d) He is seriously worried about the degeneration of his power base
(e) None of these

13. What is ultimate analysis of other similar militant groups?
(a) The PA leadership will only act if a definite forceful action is taken on the PA
(b) The suicidal attacks will only aggravate the situation
(c) The PA leadership should be changed
(d) The action on the Palestinians was justified
(e) None of these

14. Which of the following words is just opposite in meaning to the word impeded as used in the passage?
(a) Hindered
(b) Facilitated
(c) Felicitated
(d) Stopped
(e) Courage

15. What does the word overriding mean as used in the passage?
(a) Notwithstanding
(b) Concurring
(c) Welcoming
(d) Criticizing
(e) None of these

16. Which of the following best describes the meaning of the word challenged as used in the passage?
(a) Questioned
(b) Accepted
(c) Attacked
(d) Scared
(e) None of these

17. Which of the following is the most similar word as accusing as used in the passage?
(a) Abusing
(b) Blaming
(c) Charging
(d) Responding
(e) Praising

18. Which of the following is the expected outcome of International Conference which is in progress in Switzerland?
(a) To revoke 1949 Geneva Convention
(b) Impose censorship on propaganda of PA
(c) To build cordial relations between Conflicting parties
(d) To put a curb on Israel's policies while treating civilians in an alien territory
(e) None of these

19. Which of the following best explains the word vicious as used in the passage?
(a) Dangerous
(b) Fatal
(c) Reoccurring and cyclic
(d) Cyclic but not reoccurring
(e) None of these

20. Which of the following best explains the word remote as used in the passage?
(a) Far away from reality
(b) Distant

(c) Most likely to happen
(d) Control in someone else?s hand
(e) None of these

21. Who according to the passage conferred the authority to PA?
(a) Arafat
(b) Israel
(c) Militant groups
(d) International community
(e) None of these

22. Which of the following can restore the degenerating authority of the PA?
A. Arresting the expansion of Jewish settlements
B. Easening the economic blockade of Palestinian towns
(a) Only A
(b) Only B
(c) Either A or B
(d) Both A and B together
(e) Neither A or B

23. Which of the following is the most opposite in meaning as the word shrunk as used in the passage?
(a) Coming forward
(b) Abdicating
(c) Control
(d) Expand
(e) None of these

24. What may be the affect of continuous Israeli attacks?
(a) It may harness a negative attitude amongst the civil Palestinians
(b) It may destroy militancy from its basic roots
(c) It may revitalize the weakening leadership of the PA
(d) It may enhance militant activities
(e) None of these

25. What dangers are being perceived by the International Community?
(a) Both the nations may get destroyed if war erupts
(b) The PA and Israel will never strike a deal
(c) The attacks against the PA may destroy the balance of power in Palestinians
(d) The militancy may spread in other countries also
(e) None of these

Directions for Q. 26 to 35

In the following passage there are blanks, each of which has been numbered. These numbers are printed below the passage and against each, five words are suggested, one of which fits the blank appropriately. Find out the appropriate word in each case:

Whatever prosperity India enjoyed in the seventeenth century disappeared when the Mughal Empire ???(26) apart. The most immediate cause of this breakdown was the religious intolerance, which led to the open rebellion. It was to ???(27) these revolts that the bigot ruler spent ???(28) years in the field, with immense armies consuming the revenues of the country. There were, however, more deep-seated ???(29) The corruption of officials and the oppression of the masses steadily ???(30) away the empire?s life blood. For sometime, there had been a noticeable deterioration in the character of the ruling class. Wars of succession ???(31) wiped out the leading families, and new blood from central Asia was no ???(32) recruited for the higher governmental posts. Finally, the Mughal Empire was an alien regime. It continues to be so ???(33) Akbar's policy of conciliation was abandoned, and it wore itself out trying to maintain its power ???(34) the ceaseless opposition, only now and then overt but always present, of the (35) citizens.

26. (a) Joined (b) Broke
(c) Dashed (d) Banged
(e) Became

27. (a) Run out (b) Crash
(c) Crush (d) Cajole
(e) Motivate

28. (a) No (b) Hardly
(c) Many (d) Inexpensive
(e) Most

29. (a) Variables (b) Attributes
(c) Characteristics (d) Causes
(e) Affect

30. (a) Drained (b) Gone
(c) Sucked (d) Released
(e) Went

31. (a) Has (b) Have
(c) Was (d) Did
(e) Had

32. (a) Longer (b) Pumped
(c) Far (d) Candidate
(e) Shorter

33. (a) At (b) Into
(c) Over (d) After
(e) Before

34. (a) Far (b) At
(c) Against (d) Favouring
(e) For

35. (a) Discontented (b) Weeping
(c) Ruling (d) Calm
(e) Contented

Directions for Q. 36 to 40

Pick out the most effective word/phrase from the given words to fill in the blanks to make the sentences meaningfully complete:

36. Tiwari?s weill-wishers went to the extreme to_____his business reputation.
(a) Speak (b) Enhance
(c) Cajole (d) Provoke
(e) Advocate

37. A group of junior college boys______the highest peak of the Shivalik range of the Himalayas.
(a) Scaled (b) Walked
(c) Climb up (d) Avoided
(e) Won

38. A special programme to raise the standard of living of the village folks has been______by the Government.
(a) Affixed (b) Stalled
(c) Glued (d) Launched
(e) Propose

39. A herd of elephants______ready to attack the lion.
(a) Were (b) Is
(c) Was (d) Are
(e) Has been

40. It is not possible this year to run this company with so many employees, without increasing the______of deficit.
(a) Loss (b) Altitude
(c) Gain (d) Magnitude
(e) Extend

CHAPTER 3

RBI Grade 'B' Officers' Examination, 2011

Directions for Q. 1 to 8

Read the following passage carefully and answer the questions given below it. Certain words/ phrases are printed in bold to help you to locate them while answering some of the questions.

Food inflation is a significant negative feature of today's economic environment and more so, in respect of our country. It has a tremendous impact on quality of life, as people struggle to maintain nutritional standards that they had previously achieved, or give up some other forms of consumption so as to keep themselves well-fed. For a country that legitimately believed that it had effectively dealt with its vulnerability to food shortages in the form of the Green Revolution of the late 1960s and early 1970s, the current situation comes as a rude reminder that **solutions are rarely permanent.**

To place the current developments in context, it must be pointed out that the world economy is itself facing problems with food prices. Food as a category has been following global trends in commodity prices over the past couple of years. There is a view that this is the outcome of the larger trend towards financialisation of commodities wherein large increases in global liquidity as a response to the 2008 crisis feed directly into higher asset prices, including commodities. Be that as it may, the price dynamics of individual food items suggest that there are also some commodity-specific factors at work, which may either reinforce or counteract the broader trend. Sugar, for example, shows **fluctuations** in response to current supply conditions, while wheat reflects the effect of persistent drought in some major cultivating areas.

India's food inflation is certainly linked to global trends, particularly in relatively heavily traded commodities like sugar and oilseeds, but, given the high degree of self-reliance in many other commodities, domestic factors play a big role, although the drivers of inflation in recent months have been energy prices and demand pressures, as reflected in the non-food manufactured products index, food prices contributed significantly in the first half of 2010 and remain uncomfortably high. Apart from the direct impact on the index, it is also likely to **feed** through into the wider inflationary process through higher wage demands, of which there is some evidence.

It is generally believed that food prices are highly **sensitive** to monsoon performance, but this belief has been tested over the past few years. There is sufficient evidence to suggest that food prices are being driven not by transitory factors, such as rainfall, but by more fundamental forces. Essentially, a long period of relatively rapid growth has taken large numbers of households across a threshold at which they begin to look for nutritional diversification. The predominance of cereals in the typical household diet gives way to greater balance and a consequent increase in the demand for proteins - pulses, milk, meat, fish and eggs, vegetables and fruit. It is no surprise that these items have been the primary causes of food inflation in the recent period.

1. Why, according to the passage, does food inflation affect people's quality of life ?
   (a) It is a fundamental requirement of every individual.
   (b) Generally, people refrain from maintaining their nutritional standards.
   (c) People generally are averse to change their form of consumption.
   (d) People give up some other forms of consumption to keep themselves well-fed.
   (e) None of these

2. Which of the following statements contradicts the general belief that our country has achieved self-sufficiency in respect of food ?
   (a) Food inflation is a significantly negative feature of today's economic environment.
   (b) Our country legitimately believes having mastered food deficiency.
   (c) Green Revolution of the late 1960s and early 70s has helped us conquer dependence on others for food.
   (d) Our vulnerability to food shortages was effectively dealt with by us in the late 1960s and early 70's.
   (e) None of these

3. Which of the following best explains the phrase, **"solutions are rarely permanent"** as used in the passage?
   (A) Our strategies for overcoming the food shortages in a specific period have proved to be futile subsequently.
   (B) The current situation has been a rude reminder of our self-reliance in a specific period in the matter of food.
   (C) The general tendency of people to keep themselves well-fed leads to food inflation.
   (a) A & B only (b) B & C only
   (c) A only (d) C only
   (e) None of these

4. WHat, according to the passage, is **definitely** the root cause of problems with global food prices?
   (a) Shortage of commodities that constitute food items
   (b) Financialisation of commodities
   (c) Food crisis faced globally in 2008
   (d) Increase in global liquidity
   (e) None of these

5. The example of sugar and wheat helps us to conclude that______
   (A) Certain commodity-specific factors help perpetuate a general tendency.
   (B) Certain commodity-specific factors make the trend go in reverse direction.
   (C) The current supply conditions are insensitive to the global trends.
   (a) All the three
   (b) B & C only
   (c) A & C only (d) A & B only
   (e) None of these

6. Which of the following is/are crucial factor(s) responsible for India's food inflation in the recent period ?
   (A) Escalating energy prices and rising demand pressures.
   (B) Changing scenario all over the world that influences food inflation.
   (C) People's inclination to nutritional diversification.
   (a) All the three
   (b) B & C only
   (c) A & C only (d) A & B only
   (e) None of these

7. Which of the following statement(s) is / are definitely TRUE in the context of the passage?
   (A) Past few years' data show that food prices are heavily dependent on monsoon performance.
   (B) Increased food prices have exerted an impact on the index and instigated higher wage demands.

(C) In typical Indian household, consumption of food items with high protein-content is on a higher side.

(a) All the three
(b) A& B only
(c) B & C only
(d) C only
(e) A & C only

8. Which of the following best explains the meaning of the two words **"fluctuations"** and **"sensitive"** taken together in the context of the passage ?

(a) Considerate to establish stability
(b) Vulnerability to changes
(c) High impact of change
(d) Vulnerability leading to chaos
(e) Susceptibility to security

Directions for Q. 9 to 13

Rearrange the following seven sentences (A), (B), (C), (D), (E), (F) and (G) in the proper sequence to form a meaningful paragraph; then answer the questions given below them.

(A) They have to, therefore, necessarily devise strategies for product differentiation and pricing, market segmentation and efficient portfolio management.

(B) There is a great need for the banks to fully exploit these sectors to achieve a win-win situation for both - the farm and non-farm sector units and the banks.

(C) The time has now come to consolidate on the gains of the past decades of nationalized banking.

(D) This means banks will no longer be operating in a "seller's market".

(E) Undoubtedly, an untapped and vibrant market for commercial banking exists in the farm and non-farm sectors of rural economy.

(F) Then, and only then, could it be claimed that the nationalization has, at least to some extent, achieved the purpose of nationalization.

(G) The present era of financial liberalization and globalized banking would entail that banks equip themselves to face the rigours of a highly competitive financial market.

9. Which of the following should be the **SECOND** sentence after rearrangement ?

(a) G (b) F
(c) E (d) D
(e) C

10. Which of the following should be the **THIRD** sentence after rearrangement ?

(a) G (b) F
(c) A (d) D
(e) B

11. Which of the following should be the **FIFTH** sentence after rearrangement ?

(a) G (b) F
(c) E (d) B
(e) D

12. Which of the following should be the **FIRST** sentence after rearrangement ?

(a) G (b) F
(c) E (d) D
(e) C

13. Which of the following should be the **SEVENTH** sentence after rearrangement ?

(a) G (b) F
(c) E (d) C
(e) D

Directions for Q. 14 to 18

In each question below, two sentences or parts of sentences are given with two blank spaces (___) (___) between them. From among the three parts / sentences denoted by (A), (B) and (C) given below each, find out which two can fill up the blanks in proper sequence (i.e. the order in which these are given in the answer options) to make the sentence/ group of sentences meaningfully complete.

14. Four years ago, I had major surgery. (________). (________). I was too ill.

(A) It left me disabled.
(B) My attempts to go back to work could not succeed.

(C) I had fully recovered except for some minor weakness.
(a) (B) and (A) only
(b) (C) and (A) only
(c) (B) and (C) only
(d) (A) and (B) only
(e) (A) and (C) only

15. Based on scientific research, scientists conclude that (________) (________), they will live even more than a hundred years.
(A) keep themselves active all through
(B) exercise more, ensure proper vitamin intake,
(C) human species, if regulate their diet,
(a) Only (A) and (B)
(b) Only (A) and (C)
(c) Only (C) and (A)
(d) Only (C) and (B)
(e) Either C and (A) or (C) and (B)

16. The Central Government's plans to (________) (________) despite the fact that the opposition parties' united front had mobilized support of general public at the outskirts of Mumbai.
(A) defy the curfew imposed to prevent the proposed rally from protesting against the hike in petrol prices
(B) curb the rally called for by the opposition succeeded due to ruling party's announcement to
(C) cancel all the trains entering Mumbai,
(a) (A) and (B) only
(b) (B) and (A) only
(c) (B) and (C) only
(d) (A) and (C) only
(e) Either (B) and (C) or (A) and (C)

17. The economic gloom was exacerbated yesterday by Greek Prime Minister's surprise announcement (________) (________), and vote might put the torturously conceived package in jeopardy.
(A) that was struck last week
(B) that he would recommend the Parliament to strike down the obnoxious deal
(C) that his country would hold a referendum on the European debt deal
(a) (C) and (A) only
(b) (B) and (A) only
(c) (A) and (C) only
(d) Either (C) and (A) or (B) and (A)
(e) None of these

18. The world's most powerful nations were warned (________) (________) and trigger mass social unrest.
(A) that could cost millions of jobs around the globe
(B) that international economy was on the brink of a deep new economic crisis
(C) that the only solution was *** a huge amount of money in the economy
(a) (C) and (A) only
(b) (B) and (A) only
(c) (B) and (C) only
(d) (C) and (B) only
(e) None of these

Directions for Q. 19 to 23

Which of the phrases (a), (b), (c) and (d) given below should replace the phrase given in bold in the following sentence to make the sentence gramatically meaningful an correct. If the sentence is correct as it is and no correction is required, mark (e) as the answer.

19. Innovators create products **which is an outgrowing of what they imagine,** things that help them create a world they would like to live in.
(a) what is an outgrowing of what has been imagined by them
(b) which are an outgrowth of what they imagine
(c) which are outgrowing what they imagine
(d) Which outgrew their imagination
(e) No correction required

20. The product-driven organization has the product as the most important element in everything it does.
(a) does everything to have the product's most important element

(b) does the most important things to have all elements of importance in its products

(c) had the product as the most important element in everything they do

(d) keeps the most important element in every product they do

(e) No correction required

21. He **had always have a full measure of a trait** that is a mark of a successful leader determination.

(a) did always do a full measure of a trait

(b) had always did have a full measure of a trait

(c) had always have a fully measured traits

(d) has always had a full measure of a trait

(e) No correction required

22. Most of the people were dumbfounded and obviously uncomfortable **by the performance that was expected of them.**

(a) with the performance that they were expecting

(b) by the performance that they were expected with

(c) with the performance that was expected of them

(d) at the performance which had expectations of them

(e) No correction required

23. If he considered you **to be a bright, capable and made contribution to** his proposed project, he would listen to your criticizing him.

(a) are bright, capable and had made contribution to

(b) to be bright, capable and making contribution to

(c) to be bright, capable and had been contributed for

(d) would have been bright, capable and contributing with

(e) No correction required

Directions for Q. 24 to 30

In the following passage, there are blanks, each of which has been numbered. These numbers are printed below the passage and against each, five words are suggested, one of which fits the blank appropriately. Kind out the appropriate word in each case.

With fairy lights up in shopping centres and crackers on offer in supermarkets, Britain is already **(24)** up for Christmas. In this tough economic climate, many retailers are hoping the festive season will be a chance for the public to **(25)** their financial difficulties. And, for some companies, the millions of Britons now struggling to make ends meet are an early Christmas present.

As banks stop lending and **(26)** eats away at the pay packets of those lucky enough to still be in work, the past year has seen an **(27)** in high-cost credit lending in the UK. Payday loan companies and hire purchase stores now **(28)** town centres around Britain, offering astronomical interest rates on loans to those who have few other options to (29) their outgoings. Last year, the payday loan sector was worth £1.7bn, a fivefold increase in the past few years. The pace of expansion is **(30)** too. Between April and May this year alone, there was a 58 per cent rise in the number of people applying for a payday loan via money super market. com.

24. (a) paying (b) sweeping (c) fuming (d) gearing (e) giving

25. (a) overcome (b) forget (c) sustain (d) endure (e) minimize

26. (a) interest (b) taxing (c) inflation (d) spending (e) expenditure

27. (a) explosion (b) invasion (c) exploitation (d) epidemic (e) abstination

28. (a) open (b) escalate (c) enshrine (d) cater (e) dominate

29. (a) check (b) reduce (c) liberate (d) cover (e) enhance

30. (a) accelerating (b) sharpening (c) regulating (d) failing (e) evolving

PAPER 4

RBI GRADE 'B' OFFICERS' EXAMINATION, 2012

Directions to Questions 1 to 10

Read the following passage carefully and answer the questions given below it. Certain words/phrases have been printed in bold to help you locate them while answering some of the questions.

Governments have traditionally equated economic progress with steel mills and cement factories. While urban centres thrive and city dwellers get rich, hundreds of millions of farmers remain mired in poverty. However, fears of food shortage, a rethinking of antipoverty priorities and the crushing recession in 2008 are causing a dramatic shift in world economic policy in favour of greater support, for agriculture.

The last time when the world's farmers felt such love was In the 1970s. At that time, as food prices spiked, there was real concern that the world was facing a crisis in which the planet was simply unable to produce enough grain and meat for an expanding population. Government across the developing world and international aid organisations **plowed** investment into agriculture in the early 1970s, while technological breakthroughs, like high-yield strains of important food crops, boosted production. The result was the Green Revolution and food production exploded.

But the Green Revolution became a victim of its own success. Food prices plunged by some 60% by the late 1980s from their peak in the mid-1970s. Policy makers and aid workers turned their attention to the poor's other **pressing** needs, such as health care and education. Farming got **starved** of resources and investment. By 2004, aid directed at agriculture sank to 3.5% and "Agriculture lost its glitter". Also, as consumers in high-growth giants such as China and India became wealthier, they began eating more meat, so grain once used for human consumption got diverted to beef up livestock. By early 2008, panicked buying by importing countries and restrictions **slapped** on grain exports by some big producers helped drive prices upto heights not seen for three decades. Making matters worse, land and resources got reallocated to produce cash crops such as biofuels and the result was the voluminous reserves of grain **evaporated.** Protests broke out across the emerging world and fierce food riots toppled governments.

This spurred global leaders into action. This made them aware that food security is one of the fundamental issues in the world that has to be dealt with in order to maintain administrative and political stability. This also spurred the U.S. which traditionally provisioned food aid from American grain surpluses to help needy nations, to move towards investing in farm sectors around the globe to boost productivity. This move helped countries become more productive for themselves and be in a better position to feed their own people.

Africa, which missed out on the first Green Revolution due to poor policy and limited resources, also witnessed a 'change'. Swayed by the success of East Asia, the primary poverty-fighting method favoured by many policymakers in Africa was to get farmers off their farms and into modern jobs in factors and urban centres. But that strategy proved to be highly insufficient. Income levels in the countryside badly trailed those in cities while the FAO estimated that the number of poor going hungry in 2009 reached an all time high at more than one billion.

In India on the other hand, with only 40% of its farmland irrigated, entire economic boom currently underway is held hostage by the unpredictable monsoon. With much of India's farming areas suffering from drought this year, the government will have a tough time meeting its economic growth targets. In a report, Goldman Sachs predicted that if this year too receives weak rains, it could cause agriculture to contract by 2% this fiscal year, making the government's 7% GDP-growth target **look "a bit rich"**. Another green revolution is the need of the hour and to make it a reality, the global community still has much backbreaking farm work to do.

1. What is the author's main objective in writing the passage ?
(a) Criticising developed countries for not bolstering economic growth in poor nations
(b) Analysing the disadvantages of the Green Revolution
(c) Persuading experts that a strong economy depends on industrialisation and not agriculture
(d) Making a case for the international society to engineer a second Green Revolution
(e) Rationalising the faulty agriculture policies of emerging countries

2. Which of the following is an adverse impact of the Green Revolution ?
(a) Unchecked crop yields resulted in large tracts of land becoming barren
(b) Withdrawal of fiscal impetus from agriculture to other sectors
(c) Farmers began soliciting government subsidies for their produce
(d) Farmers rioted as food prices fell so low that they could not make ends meet
(e) None of these

3. What is the author trying to convey through the phrase "making the government's 7% GDP growth target look "a bit rich" ?
(a) Indian is unlikely to achieve the targeted growth rate
(b) Allocation of funds to agriculture has raised India's chances of having a high GDP
(c) Agricultural growth has artificially inflated India's GDP and such growth is not real
(d) India is likely to have one of the highest GDP growth rates
(e) A large portion of India's GDP is contributed by agriculture

4. Which of the following factors was/were responsible for the neglect of the farming sector after the green revolution ?
(A) Steel and cement sectors generated more revenue for the government as compared to agriculture.
(B) Large scale protests against favouring agriculture at the cost of other important sectors such as education and health care.
(C) Attention of policy makers and aid organisations was diverted from agriculture to other sectors.
(a) None
(b) Only (C)
(c) Only (B) and (C)
(d) Only (A) and (B)
(e) All (A), (B)and(C)

5. What prompted leaders throughout the world to take action to boost the agriculture sector in 2008?
(a) Coercive tactics by the U.S. which restricted food aid to poor nations

(b) The realization of the link between food security and political stability
(c) Awareness that performance in agriculture is necessary in order to achieve the targeted GDP
(d) Reports that high-growth countries like China and India were boosting their agriculture sectors to capture the international markets
(e) Their desire to influence developing nations to slow down their industrial development.

6. What motivated the U.S. to focus on investing in agriculture across the globe ?
(a) To make developing countries become more reliant on U.S. aid
(b) To ensure grain surpluses so that the U.S. had no need to import food
(c) To make those countries more self sufficient to whom it previously provided food
(d) To establish itself in the market before the high-growth giants such as India and China could establish themselves
(e) None of these

Directions to Questions 7 to 8

Choose the word/group of words which is most similar in meaning to the word printed in **bold** as used in the passage,

7. **SLAPPED**
(a) Beaten (b) Imposed
(c) Withdrawn (d) Avoided
(e) Persuaded

8. **PLOWED**
(a) Cultivated (b) Bulldozed
(c) Recovered (d) Instilled
(e) Withdrew

Directions to Questions 9 to 10

Choose the word/phrase which is **most opposite** in meaning to the word printed in **bold** as used in the passage.

9. **PRESSING**
(a) Unpopular (b) Undemanding
(c) Unobtrusive (d) Unsuitable
(e) Unimportant

10. EVAPORATED
(a) Absorbed (b) Accelerated
(c) Grew (d) Plunged
(e) Mismanaged

Directions to Questions 11 to 15

Which of the phrases (a), (b), (c) and (d) given below each statement should be placed in the blank space provided so as to make a meaningful and grammatically correct sentence ? If none of the sentences is appropriate, mark (e) i.e. 'None of these' as the answer.

11. Refuting the rationale behind frequent agitations for formation of separate States, a recent report______.
(a) proved that such agitations result in loss of governmental property
(b) indicated that the formation of small states does not necessarily improve the economy
(c) suggested that only large scale agitations have been effective in bringing out desired change in the past
(d) recommended dividing large States into smaller ones to improve governance
(e) None of these

12. Overlooking the fact that water scarcity intensifies during summer_____.
(a) the government issued guidelines to all builders to limit their consumption to acceptable limits
(b) provision for rainwater harvesting has been made to aid irrigation in drought prone areas
(c) the water table did not improve even after receiving normal monsoon in the current year
(d) Many residential areas continue to use swimming pools, wasting large quantities of water
(e) None of these

13. He has lost most of the life's earning in the stock market but___

(a) he still seems to be leading his life luxuriously and extravagantly

(b) he could not save enough to repay his enormous debts

(c) stock market is not a safe option to invest money unless done with caution

(d) experts have been suggesting to avoid investments in stock market because of its unpredictable nature

(e) None of these

14. Achieving equality for women is not only a laudable goal,_______.

(a) political reforms are also neglected preventing women from entering legislatures and positions of power

(b) the problem is also deep rooted in the society and supported by it

(c) their empowerment is purposefully hampered by people with vested interests in all sections of the society

(d) it is also equally difficult to achieve and maintain for long term

(e) None of these

15. ____or else they would not keep electing him year after year.

(a) The party leader gave a strong message to the mayor for improving his political style

(b) Owing to numerous scandals against the mayor, he was told to resign from the post immediately

(c) The mayor threatened the residents against filing a complaint against him

(d) The residents must really be impressed with the political style of their mayor

(e) None of these

Directions to Questions 16 to 20

Each question below has two blanks, each blank indicating that something has been omitted. Choose the set of words for each blank that best fits the meaning of the sentence as a whole.

16. Drawing attention to the pitfalls of______ solely on Uranium as a fuel for nuclear reactors, Indian scientists warned that Uranium will not last for long and thus research on Thorium as its______must be revived.

(a) using, substitute

(b) believing, replacement

(c) depending, reserve

(d) reckoning, option

(e) relying, alternative

17. In an effort to provide______for higher education to all, most of the universities have been providing education without adequate infrastructure, thus churning out___graduates every year.

(a) chances, fresh

(b) platform, capable

(c) opportunities, unemployable

(d) prospects, eligible

(e) policy, incompetent

18. The move to allow dumping of mercury______ an outcry from residents to the area who____ that high levels of mercury will affect their health and destroy ecologically sensitive forest area.

(a) resulted, insist

(b) provoked, fear

(c) incited, determined

(d) activated, accept

(e) angered believe

19. ______has been taken against some wholesale drug dealers for dealing in surgical items without a valid license and maintaining a stock of_______drugs.

(a) Note, overwhelming

(b) Step, impressive

(c) Execution, outdated

(d) Action, expired

(e) Lawsuit, invalid

20. Even as the________elsewhere in the world are struggling to come out of recession, Indian consumers are splurging on consumer goods and to_______this growth, companies are investing heavily in various sectors.

(a) economies, meet
(b) countries, inhibit
(c) governments, measure
(d) nations, inflict
(e) companies, counter

Directions to Questions 21 to 25

Rearrange the following sentences (A), (B), (C), (D), (E) and (F) to make a meaningful paragraph and then answer the questions which follow:

(A) While these disadvantages of biofuels are serious, they are the only alternate energy source of the future and the sooner we find solutions to these problems the faster we will be able to solve the problems we are now facing with gasoline.

(B) This fuel can also help to stimulate jobs locally since they are also much safer to handle than gasoline and can thus have the potential to turnaround a global economy.

(C) These include dependence on fossil fuels for the machinery required to produce biofuel which ends up polluting as much as the burning of fossil fuels on roads and exorbitant cost of biofuels which makes it very difficult for the common man to switch to this option.

(D) This turnaround can potentially help to bring world peace and end the need to depend on foreign countries for energy requirements.

(E) Biofuels are made from plant sources and since these sources are available in abundance and can be reproduced on a massive scale they form an energy source that is potentially unlimited.

(F) However everything is not as green with the biofuels as it seems as there are numerous disadvantages involved which at times overshadow their positive impact.

21. Which of the following sentences should be the **FIFTH** after rearrangement ?
(a) A (b) B
(c) C (d) E
(e) F

22. Which of the following sentences should be the **THIRD** after rearrangement ?
(a) A (b) B
(c) D (d) D
(e) E

23. Which of the following sentences should be the **FIRST** after rearrangement ?
(a) A (b) B
(c) C (d) D
(e) E

24. Which of the following sentences should be the SIXTH (LAST) after rearrangement ?
(a) A (b) C
(c) D (d) E
(e) F

25. Which of the following sentences should be the SECOND after rearrangement ?
(a) A (b) B
(c) D (d) E
(e) F

Directions to Questions 26 to 30

Which of the phrases (a), (b), (c) and (d) given below each statement should replace the phrase printed in bold in the sentence to make it grammatically correct? If the sentence is correct as it is given and 'No correction is required', mark (e) as the answer.

26. Soon after the Tsunami had killed thousands of people along the coasts of southern India, Parliament passess a bill that proposed to set up an institutional mechanism to respond promptly to natural disasters.
(a) passed a bill that proposed
(b) passes a bill with purpose
(c) pass a bill proposing
(d) passed a bill which propose
(e) No correction required

27. Denial of wages forced scientists and teachers at the agriculture universities throughout the country to go on strike, crippling crucial research that could help the state of agriculture in the country.
(a) from going on strike
(b) which went on strike

(c) on going for a strike
(d) for going to strike
(e) No correction required

28. In an attempt to boost their profits many edible oil producing companies have been engaging themselves in propaganda against commonly used oils and promoting exotic and expensive varieties of oil as more healthier options.
(a) as most healthiest options
(b) as less healthy option
(c) as a healthier option
(d) as much healthiest option
(e) No correction required

29. Thanks to numerous government initiatives, rural masses which was earlier unaware of the luxuries of urban ways of living are now connected to the same lifestyle.
(a) who was earlier unaware
(b) which were earlier aware
(c) who were earlier conversant
(d) who were earlier unaware
(e) No correction required

30. Over the last few months, while most industries are busy in restructuring operations, cutting costs and firing, the Indian pharmaceutical and health care industry was adding manpower and giving salary hikes.
(a) as many industries are
(b) while most industries were
(c) while many industries is
(d) where many industries were
(e) No correction required

ANSWER KEY

RBI Grade 'B' Officers' Examination, 2005

1. (b)	2. (d)	3. (c)	4. (a)	5. (c)
6. (c)	7. (a)	8. (a)	9. (b)	10. (c)
11. (a)	12. (a)	13. (b)	14. (c)	15. (a)
16. (e)	17. (a)	18. (a)	19. (e)	20. (c)
21. (c)	22. (d)	23. (d)	24. (b)	25. (a)
26. (a)	27. (d)	28. (b)	29. (c)	30. (a)
31. (e)	32. (d)	33. (e)	34. (a)	35. (c)
36. (e)	37. (c)	38. (a)	39. (a)	40. (d)

RBI Grade 'B' Officers' Examination, 2009

1. (c)	2. (c)	3. (e)	4. (c)	5. (a)
6. (c)	7. (a)	8. (a)	9. (a)	10. (c)
11. (c)	12. (d)	13. (e)	14. (a)	15. (a)
16. (a)	17. (b)	18. (c)	19. (c)	20. (a)
21. (d)	22. (d)	23. (a)	24. (d)	25. (e)
26. (b)	27. (c)	28. (c)	29. (d)	30. (e)
31. (e)	32. (a)	33. (d)	34. (c)	35. (a)
36. (b)	37. (a)	38. (d)	39. (e)	40. (d)

RBI Officers' Grade 'B' Examination, 2011

1. (d)	2. (a)	3. (a)	4. (b)	5. (a)
6. (a)	7. (c)	8. (b)	9. (a)	10. (d)
11. (c)	12. (e)	13. (b)	14. (d)	15. (e)
16. (c)	17. (a)	18. (b)	19. (b)	20. (b)
21. (d)	22. (c)	23. (b)	24. (d)	25. (b)
26. (c)	27. (a)	28. (e)	29. (d)	30. (a)

RBI Grade 'B' Officers' Examination, 2012

1. (d)	2. (b)	3. (c)	4. (b)	5. (b)
6. (c)	7. (b)	8. (a)	9. (b)	10. (c)
11. (c)	12. (d)	13. (a)	14. (e)	15. (d)
16. (e)	17. (c)	18. (b)	19. (d)	20. (a)
21. (c)	22. (b)	23. (e)	24. (a)	25. (c)
26. (a)	27. (e)	28. (c)	29. (d)	30. (b)

FREQUENCY ANALYSIS

ABBREVIATIONS USED:

Comprehension / **Comp**, Sentence Completion / **SC**, Sentence Filler / **SF**, Cloze Test/ **CT**, Synonyms/ **Syn**, Antonyms/ **Ant**, Idioms and Phrase/ **IP**, Substitution/ **Subt**, Sentence arrangement/ **SA**, Spelling/ **SPL**, Miscellaneous/**Misc**., Total Marks/**TM**, Sentence error/**SE**, Sentence Improvement/ **SI**.

RBI Grade B Officers–2005

	Comp.	SC	SF	CT	Syn	Ant	IP	Subt	SA	SE	SPL	SI	MISC.	TM
	10	5		10	3	2						10		

RBI Officers Grade B–2009

	Comp.	SC	SF	CT	Syn	Ant	IP	Subt	SA	SE	SPL	SI	MISC.	TM
	15	5		10						5		5		

RBI Officers Grade B–2011

	Comp.	SC	SF	CT	Syn	Ant	IP	Subt	SA	SE	SPL	SI	MISC.	TM
	8		5	7					5			5		

RBI Officers Grade B–2012

	Comp.	SC	SF	CT	Syn	Ant	IP	Subt	SA	SE	SPL	SI	MISC.	TM
	6	5	5		2	2			5			5		

TREND ANALYSIS

It we look at the question papers of 2005, 2009, 2011 and 2012, we find that there are variations of items in different years. Comprehension, Sentence Improvement, Cloze test have been set all the years. Other items are synonyms, Antonyms, Sentence Completion, Sentence error, Sentence arrangement, Sentence filler which have been set in one to two years.

All these items are separate chapters of the book which give concept, illustration , tips, techniques and practice sets.

Therefore the student should read the book carefully chapter wise and work at the practice sets given in Section 2 of the book. Finally they should go through the unit on RBI Officers very carefully to understand the trend of variation among units.

The level is above moderate and slightly tough.

A careful study of the book ensures your success.

PAPER 5

STATE BANK OF INDIA PO EXAMINATION, 2005

Directions to Questions 1 to 15

Read the following passage carefully and answer these questions given below it. Certain words/ phrases have been printed in **bold** to help you locate them while answering some of the questions.

As increasing dependence on information systems develops, the need for such systems to be reliable and secure also becomes more essential. As growing numbers of ordinary citizens use computer networks for banking, shopping, etc., network security is potentially a **massive** problem. Over the last few years the need for computer and information system security has become increasingly evident, as web sites are being defaced with greater frequency, more and more denial-of-service attacks are being reported, credit card information is being stolen, there is increased sophistication of hacking tools that are openly available to the public on the Internet, and there is increasing damage being caused by viruses and worms to critical information system resources.

At the organisational level, institutional mechanisms have to be designed in order to review policies, practices, measures, and procedures to review e-security regularly and assess whether these are appropriate to their environment. It would be helpful if organisations share information about threats and vulnerabilities, and implement procedures for rapid and effective cooperation to prevent, detect and respond to security incidents. As new threats and vulnerabilities are continuously discovered there is a strong need for cooperation among organisations and, if necessary, we could also consider cross-border information sharing. We need to understand threats and dangers that we could be **vulnerable** to and the steps that need to be taken to **mitigate** these vulnerabilities. We need to understand success control systems and methodology, telecommunication and network security, and security management practice. We should be well versed in the area of application and systems development security, cryptography, operations security and physical security.

The banking sector is **poised** for more challenges in the near future. Customers of banks can now look forward to a large array of new offerings by banks. From an **era** of mere competition, banks are now cooperating among themselves so that the synergistic benefits are shared among all the players. This would result in the formation of shared payment networks (a few shared

ATM networks have already been commissioned by banks), offering payment services beyond the existing time zones. The Reserve Bank is also facilitating new projects such as the Multi Application Smart Card project which, when implemented, would facilitate transfer of funds using electronic means and in a safe and secure manner across the length and breadth of the country, with reduced dependence on paper currency. The opportunities of e-banking or e-power in general need to be harnessed so that banking is available to all customers in such a manner that they would feel most convenient, and if required, without having to visit a branch of a bank. All these will have to be accompanied with a high level of comfort, which again boils down to the issue of e-security.

One of the biggest advantages accruing to banks in the future would be the benefits that arise from the introduction of Real Time Gross Settlement (RTGS). Funds management by treasuries of banks would be helped greatly by RTGS. With almost 70 banks having joined the RTGS system, more large value funds transfers are taking place through this system. The implementation of Core Banking solutions by banks is closely related to RTGS too. Core Banking will make anywhere banking a reality for customers of each bank, while RTGS bridges the need for inter-bank funds movement. Thus, the days of depositing a cheque for collection and a long wait for its realisation would soon be a thing of the past for those customers who would opt for electronic movement of funds, using the RTGS system, where the settlement would be on an almost **instantaneous** basis. Core Banking is already in vogue in many private sector and foreign banks; while its implementation is at different stages amongst the public sector banks.

IT would also facilitate better and more scientific decision making within banks. Information systems now provide decision makers in banks with a great deal of information which, along with historical data and trend analysis, help in the building up of efficient Management Information Systems, This, in turn, would help in better Asset Liability Management (ALM) which, in today's world of hairline margins, is a key requirement for the success of banks in their operational activities. Another benefit which e-banking could provide for, relates to Customer Relationship Management (CRM). CRM helps in stratification of customers and evaluating customer needs on a holistic basis which could be paving the way for competitive edge for banks and complete customer care for customers of banks.

1. The content of the passage mainly emphasises on
   (a) The threat of competition among banks providing tele-banking services
   (b) The scientific advancements that have facilitated quicker and scientific banking procedures
   (c) Threats to on-line banking and remedies to guard against them
   (d) e-banking and its impact on global economy
   (e) None of these

2. What, according to the passage, is the pre-requisite to lessen the threats of hacking?
   (a) Effective measures to combat vulnerability
   (b) Environment-friendly gadgets to remedy damages
   (c) Detection and timely prevention of the threat
   (d) Effective mechanism to evaluate the e-security
   (e) None of these

3. In what way does IT catalyse better decision-making?
   (A) By providing updated data and trend analysis.
   (B) By providing increasing opportunities of personal contacts.
   (C) By ensuring better asset-liability management.
   (a) A only (b) B only
   (c) C only (d) A and B only
   (e) All the three

4. What is the advantage of RTGS to the customers?
   (a) Anywhere banking
   (b) Instant realisation of cheques
   (c) Easy withdrawal of cash
   (d) Hasslefree depositing of cash-loads
   (e) Availability of transaction facilities at any other bank

5. What, according to the author, should be the ultimate goal(s) of e-banking?

(A) Customers' convenience.
(B) Avoidance of heavy footfall of customers in bank branches.
(C) Protection of customers' interests.
(a) A and B only
(b) B and C only
(c) A and C only
(d) All the three
(e) None of these

6. Why is it obligatory that a system should be perfectly dependable?
(a) To justify escalating dependence on system
(b) To ensure security for the system
(c) To disallow any pilferage whatsoever
(d) To ascertain proper logistic support
(e) None of these

7. Which of the following is/are recommended by the author to ensure security of banking transactions?
(A) Continuous re-examination of policies and procedures.
(B) Ensuring appropriateness of the security measures.
(C) Cooperation among various users to identify and prevent threat.
(a) A and B only
(b) B and C only
(c) A and C only
(d) A and B only
(e) None of these

8. Which of the following statements definitely FALSE in the context of the passage?
(A) Transfer of funds to any part of the country through electronic media is under active consideration.
(B) Cooperation among various competing banks is helpful to all of them in sharing legitimate benefits.
(C) Assessment of customer needs and their clustering in homogeneous groups provides competitive edge to banks.
(a) Only A
(b) Only B and C
(c) Only A and C
(d) All the three
(e) None of these

9. Computer-savvy citizens are also shared to transact on-line due to the following except
(a) Smuggling of vital information regarding credit cards
(b) Availability of hacking tools on the internet
(c) Damage by viruses to critical information
(d) Sophisticated, well-guarded on-line transaction devices
(e) Denial-of-service attacks that put valid customers to inconvenience

Directions to Questions 10 to 12

Choose the word which MOST OPPOSITE in meaning to the word printed in **Bold** as used in the passage.

10. **Instantaneous**
(a) Delayed (b) Quick
(c) Immediate (d) Eventful
(e) Unconventional

11. **Vulnerable**
(a) Susceptible (b) Rigid
(c) Invincible (d) Prone
(e) Weakling

12. **Massive**
(a) Tiny (b) Gigantic
(c) Bulky (d) Insignificant
(e) Actue

Directions to Questions 13 to 15

Choose the word which is most nearly the SAME in meaning as the word printed in **bold** as used in the passage.

13. **Era**
(a) Year (b) Epoch
(c) Span (d) Spirit
(e) Instinct

14. **Poised**
(a) Balanced (b) Adulterated
(c) Stupefied (d) Launched
(e) Ready

15. Mitigate

(a) Investigate (b) Allay
(c) Elevate (d) Invigorate
(e) Amplify

Directions to Questions 16 to 20

In each of the following sentences there are two blank spaces. Below each sentence there are five pairs of words denoted by numbers **(a), (b), (c), (d)** *and* **(e)**. Find out which pair of words can be filled up in the blanks in the sentence in the same sequence to make the sentence grammatically correct and meaningfully complete.

16. Most people are too ________ in their own lives to ________ much about the agonies of others.

(a) absorbed .... care
(b) concerned .... think
(c) indulged .... eradicate
(d) involved .... console
(e) entangling .... worry

17. Doctors and lawyers ________ that advertising will certainly ________ their profession adversely.

(a) trust .... damage
(b) believe .... affect
(c) contemplate .... boost
(d) argue .... effect
(e) plead .... escalate

18. Because the ________ leading to cancellation of flight were murky, the Minister appointed a Commission to ________ and report the matter.

(a) staff members .... undertake
(b) decisions .... decide
(c) facts .... underplay
(d) events .... camouflage
(e) circumstances .... investigate

19. Several plots ________ ________ in various televisions episodes.

(a) Screen .... concurrently
(b) Televised .... consequently
(c) Occur .... repeatedly
(d) Exhibit .... frequently
(e) Demonstrate .... violently

20. By ________ of their athletic activities, a few sportsmen are able to escape the pressures that living in ________ can create.

(a) knowledge .... affluence
(b) way .... prosperity
(c) order .... vicinity
(d) virtue .... poverty
(e) contrast .... adversity

Directions to Questions 21 to 35

Which of the phrases (a), (b), (c) and (d) given below should replace the phrase given in **bold *italics*** in the following sentences to make the sentences grammatically meaningful and correct. If the sentence is correct as it is and no correction is required, mark (e) as the answer.

21. It is now well known that the ***world response to*** the Asian tsunami disaster with an outpouring of generosity.

(a) World responded to
(b) World's response to
(c) World had a response
(d) World responding for
(e) No correction required

22. The most important quality a chief executive candidate ***should have*** a noble character.

(a) Must have a
(b) Should have to be
(c) Should be
(d) Should have is a
(e) No correction required

23. What is needed now is not mere declarations or promises, but actions—actions to fulfill the ***promises already made.***

(a) Promises were, already made
(b) Already made promises
(c) Promises that we make
(d) Promises which already made
(e) No correction required

24. What we ***have done is*** from humanity point of view.
(a) Have been doing was
(b) Had done being
(c) Have done were
(d) Have been doing were
(e) No correction required

25. Despite considerable achievements in other areas, humans still cannot control weather and ***probably never be able*** to do so.
(a) Probably not be able
(b) Perhaps the never have ability
(c) Probably will never be able
(d) Probably never be enabled
(e) No correction required

26. The newly-wed couple was shocked when it was observed that many people who ***had been invited,*** missing.
(a) Were invited
(b) Had been invited were
(c) Had invited were
(d) Had been invited had been
(e) No correction required

27. The people ***should be right to protest,*** it should not be by upsetting the livelihood of others.
(a) Should be righteous in protesting
(b) Should have right to protest
(c) Would be right in protest
(d) Should have been right to protest
(e) No correction required

28. They have made a futile attempt of suppressing the truth ***and suggest falsehood.***
(a) For suggestion of falsehood
(b) After suggesting falsity
(c) And suggesting falsehood
(d) In suggestion of falsehood
(e) No correction required

29. Because his work as a painter ***requires that he use*** products containing strong chemicals, he has developed skin allergy.
(a) Required to use
(b) Requires that he should use
(c) Required that he uses
(d) Requires that he uses
(e) No correction required

30. From time to time, there ***have been reports*** of how children had tried to imitate their favourite hero and landed in trouble.
(a) Has been report
(b) Were reports
(c) Often reported
(d) Had been reported
(e) No correction required

31. We are happy to note that ***the use of emission controls was*** created to reduce air pollution.
(a) Emission controls were
(b) The uses of emission controls were
(c) Emission controls had
(d) Emission controls had to be
(e) No correction required

32. Although he was seen with a drug-peddler, ***he is not necessarily himself a drug-peddler***
(a) It is riot necessary that he be himself a drug-peddler
(b) He is not necessary to be a drug-peddler himself
(c) He was not necessary to be himself a drug-peddler
(d) He is not necessarily a drug-peddler himself
(e) No correction required

33. Optimism coupled with ***faith in and hopes of*** future is the key to progress.
(a) Faithfulness in and hopes of
(b) Faith in and helping of
(c) Faith in and hopes for
(d) Faith and hope of
(e) No correction required

34. We have already identified areas where landslides are possible and **start *evacuation*** of residents to safer locations.
(a) Starting evacuation
(b) Started evacuation

(c) Have started evacuate
(d) Start evacuating
(e) No correction required

35. The law that now stands abolished was a ***flawed and discriminatory peace*** of legislation.
(a) flaw and discrimination of peace of
(b) flawed and discriminating peace for
(c) flawing and discriminating peace of
(d) flawed and discriminatory piece of
(e) No correction required

Directions to Questions 36 to 40

Given below is the first sentence of a paragraph followed by six other disarranged sentences which are denoted by (A), (B), (C), (D), (E) and (F). Rearrange these six sentences to make a meaningful paragraph, keeping the first sentence as the starter of the para and then answer the questions that follow.

Starter: Twenty-five centuries ago when the Greek traveller Herodatus visited the already ancient monument of Egypt, he found that the tourists had gotten there first.

(A) The Egyptians built for eternity.
(B) The 'why' is easy: religious beliefs that sought perpetuation in masses of stones so ponderous they must be measures in tons and acres and that demanded that these material manifestations of faith be not only huge but permanent.
(C) Tourists are still coming to Egypt and are probably still inscribing their names on the old stones.
(D) In the words of Ramses II, who dedicated the magnificent temple of Medinet Habut in the 13th Century B.C., this was to be "a place of the Lord of the Gods, forever".
(E) Their names were scratched on the crumbling ruins in hundreds of ancient languages.
(F) They are probably sharing another experience too—standing in silent and involuntary admiration before the great structures and silently posing those inevitable questions: Why? How?

36. Which of the following should be the **FIFTH** sentence after the starter?
(a) A (b) F
(c) C (d) D
(e) E

37. Which of the following should the **FIRST** sentence after the starter?
(a) A (b) B
(c) F (d) D
(e) E

38. Which of the following should be the **SIXTH (LAST)** sentence after the starter?
(a) A (b) B
(c) C (d) D
(e) E

39. Which of the following should be the **FOURTH** sentence after the starter?
(a) A (b) B
(c) C (d) D
(e) F

40. Which of the following should be the **SECOND** sentence after the starter?
(a) F (b) B
(c) C (d) D
(e) E

Directions to Questions 41 to 50

In the following passage there are blanks, each of which has been numbered. These numbers are printed below the passage and against each, five words are suggested, one of which fits the blank appropriately. Find out the appropriate words without changing the meaning of the passage.

Capital investment is essential for ...**(41)**... of productive capacity and adding new capacity for current and nature industrial growth. The ...**(42)**... of this article is to make an assessment of capital investment in the private corporate sector, which would provide important insights into the business spectations about performance of economy in ...**(43)**..., and the infrastructure and manufacturing sector ...**(44)**.... The method of ...**(45)**... growth in corporate investment should really, be based on the available means of financing an investment project. The talk of the major projects in the private corporate sector is ...**(46)**... by the leading all India term-lending institutions namely the Industrial Development Bank of India (IDBI), the Industrial Finance Carporation of India (IFCI), the Industrial Investment Bank of India (IIBI), ICICI Ltd. (now ICICI Bank) and the Infrastructure Development Finance Company (IDFC). The financial sector reforms in the 1990's have, in effect ...**(47)**... the sources of financing corporate projects; in particular, commercial banks have, in recent years, started ...**(48)**... financial assistance to corporate projects. Since a majority of the private corporate entities, undertaking large projects, ...**(49)**... the term-lending institutions and banks for financing the projects cost, the phasing details of capital expenditure available in the relevant project reports would provide a base for estimating ...**(50)**... growth in capital expenditure.

41. (a) Installations (b) Maintenance
(c) Aggravation (d) Generation
(e) Modernisation

42. (a) Problem (b) Objective
(c) Summary (d) Essence
(e) Moral

43. (a) Abstract (b) Globe
(c) Development (d) General
(e) Details

44. (a) Particular (b) Question
(c) View (d) Future
(e) Industrialisation

45. (a) Reinventing (b) Augmenting
(c) Estimating (d) Amplifying
(e) Checking

46. (a) Financed (b) Encapacitated
(c) Analysed (d) Entrusted
(e) Governed

47. (a) Reduced (b) Enlarged
(c) Deactivated (d) Eurbed
(e) Magnified

48. (a) Arresting (b) Monitoring
(c) Regulating (d) Providing
(e) Withdrawing

49. (a) Mitigate (b) Visit
(c) Explore (d) Finance
(e) Approach

50. (a) Fastidious (b) Sluggish
(c) Likely (d) Complete
(e) Relevant

PAPER 6

STATE BANK OF INDIA PO EXAMINATION, APRIL 2008

Directions to Questions 1 to 10

Read the following passage carefully and answer the questions given after it. Certain words are printed in bold to help you to locate them while answering some of the questions.

There is absolutely no point in complaining that over the years, there has been pressure for increased productivity and higher earnings for workers in industry. There are several ways for increasing employees' earnings. Employee earnings can be increased by raising the selling price of the firm's products and services, reducing profits or costs of raw materials, or augmenting labour productivity. However, increasing employee earnings by means other than increased labour productivity **jeopardises** the firm's competitive strength in the market. Higher prices usually mean fewer customers, reduced profit means less capital investment, and low-cost materials mean poor product quality. But, increasing labour productivity by enhancing skills and motivation creates an almost unlimited resource. The development of economic resources, human as well as non-human, is the product of human effort, and the quality of human effort in large part depends on human motivation.

Enthusing employees with workaholic spirit through traditional authority and financial incentives has become increasingly difficult as employees become economically secure and their dependency on any one particular organisation decreases. According to expectancy theorists, the motivation to work increases when an employee feels his performance is an instrument for obtaining desired rewards. Nevertheless, in many organisations today employees are entitled to organisational rewards just by being employed. Unions, governmental regulations, and the nature of the job itself in some cases prevent management from relating financial rewards to performance. People may be attracted to join and remain in organisations to receive organisational rewards, but being motivated to join an organisation is not the same as being motivated to exert effort in an organisation. The challenge to management is to find and administer alternative forms of incentives which will **induce** employees to improve work performance. Such alternative forms of reinforcement will require increased understanding of motivational theories and programmes.

1. Which of the following statements is true in the context of the passage?
   (a) Development of economic resources is primarily the product of market conditions

(b) Earnings can be increased by lowering the selling price of products.

(c) Employees can be best motivated by providing financial incentives.

(d) All employees should be entitled to organisational rewards just by being employed

(e) None of these

2. Organisations can derive maximum advantages by

(a) Providing financial incentives to employees regardless of performance

(b) Enhancing labour productivity by increasing skills and motivation

(c) Encouraging employees to expend greater physical energy

(d) Inducing employees to improve work performance and control their demands

(e) Strictly adhering to governmental regulations

3. According to the passage, all of the following contribute to an increase in employee earnings, except

(a) Increasing the selling price of the company's products

(b) Reducing profits in favour of employees

(c) Providing incentives and fringe benefits to employees

(d) Enhancing labour productivity

(e) Increased capital investment

4. Employees feel motivated to work when they

(a) Experience good working conditions in the organisation

(b) Decide to produce goods and services as a result of team work

(c) Think of performance as a tool for obtaining rewards

(d) Relate rewards to material prosperity

(e) Are members of the union

5. Choose the word which is most similar in meaning as the word 'induce' as used in the passage.

(a) Appreciate

(b) Stimulate

(c) Exhibit

(d) Inflate

(e) Threaten

6. Which of the following factors, according to the passage, adversely affects the organisation's competitive strength?

(a) Making rewards contingent on performance

(b) Anti-productivity and anti-management activities of labour unions

(c) Motivating employees with traditional authority

(d) Increasing employee earnings regardless of their productivity

(e) None of these

7. Which of the statements is/are not true in the context of the passage?

(A) Human effort is the cause of the development of economic resources.

(B) Management is free to relate financial rewards to performance.

(C) Employees can be easily motivated with traditional authority today.

(a) Both (A) and (B)

(b) Only (C)

(c) Both (A) and (C)

(d) Both (B) and (C)

(e) None of these

8. Which of the following factors determine the quality of human efforts?

(a) Desire and willingness of an individual to excel in whatever he undertakes

(b) Economic resources available with the organisation

(c) The individual's innovativeness

(d) Authoritarian leadership and job security.

(e) None of these

9. In the context of the passage, a company's competitive strength in the market is affected mainly because of

(A) A slump in the international market

(B) Poor inter-departmental coordination

(C) Decreased labour productivity

(a) Only (A) (b) Only (B)

(c) Only (C) (d) Both (B) & (C)

(e) None of these

10. Which of the following words is most opposite in meaning of the word 'jeopardises' as used in the passage?
(a) Safeguards (b) Endangers
(c) Projects (d) Devalues
(e) Decreases

Directions to Questions 11 to 15

One of the four words given in each of these questions may be wrongly spelt. The number of that wrongly spelt word is the answer. If all the four words are correctly spelt, mark (e) i.e. 'All Correct' as the answer.

11. (a) Defamation (b) Arrogant
(c) Solitude (d) Exhorbitant
(e) All Correct

12. (a) Decompose (b) Veteran
(c) Ventursome (d) Definition
(e) All Correct

13. (a) Wastefull (b) Prejudice
(c) Expensive (d) Embarrassing
(e) All Correct

14. (a) Significant (b) Possessive
(c) Impatient (d) Device
(e) All Correct

15. (a) Prosperous (b) Glumy
(c) Dormant (d) Derogatory
(e) All Correct

Directions to Questions 16 to 20

Read each sentence to find out if there is any error in it. The error, if any, will be in one part of the sentence. The number of that part is the answer. If there is no error, the answer is **(e)** i.e. 'No error'. (Ignore the errors of punctuation, if any.)

16. He gave me all the details of when he (a) / had visited all the temples (b) / while he will be going (c) / on official tour. (d) / No error (e).

17. Let's all work (a) / together as like homogenous (b) / group so that (c) / success would be obvious. (d) / No error. (e)

18. The process was so simple (a) / and easy to understand (b) / that it hardly took (c) / five minutes for us to learn it. (d) / No error (e)

19. It is strange that (a) / even after fifteen years of experience (b) / he is still not (c) / able to be performed. (d) / No error (e).

20. What to make people (a) / tense is actually (b) / a mystery, which (c) / is difficult to unfold. (d) / No error (e).

Directions to Questions 21 to 25

Rearrange the following six sentences (A), (B), (C), (D), (E) and (F) in the proper sequence to form a meaningful paragraph; then answer these questions.

(A) The insurance policy has to be deposited with NABARD.
(B) I intend to purchase a tractor and certain other agricultural equipments.
(C) I shall therefore feel obliged if you send your representative to inspect the equipments.
(D) I shall be applying for a loan of Rs. six lakhs from NABARD for that purpose.
(E) On completion, your representative may kindly inform me of the annual insurance premium.
(F) The rules state that the equipments have to be insured against accidents and fire.

21. Which of the following will be the SIXTH (LAST) sentence after rearrangement?
(a) A (b) B
(c) C (d) D
(e) E

22. Which of the following will be the FOURTH sentence after rearrangement?
(a) A (b) B
(c) C (d) D
(e) E

23. Which of the following will be the FIFTH sentence after rearrangement?
(a) A (b) B
(c) C (d) D
(e) E

24. Which of the following will be the SECOND sentence after rearrangement?
(a) A (b) B
(c) C (d) D
(e) E

25. Which of the following will be the FIRST sentence after rearrangement?

(a) A (b) B
(c) C (d) D
(e) E

Directions to Questions 26 to 30

In each of these questions, a sentence with four words printed in **bold** type is given. These are numbered (a), (2, (c) and (d). One of these four words, printed in **bold**, may be either wrongly spelt or inappropriate in the context of the sentence. Find out the word which is wrongly spelt or inappropriate, if any. The number of that word is your answer. If all the words printed in **bold** are correctly spelt and also are appropriate in the context of the sentence, mark (e) i.e. 'All Correct' as your answer.

26. Some people think their life is full of grief (a) / and **miseries** (b) / too **grievous** (c) / to be **born.** (d) / All correct (e).

27. The **opinion** (a) / **expressed** (b) / is based only on our **transactions** (c) / with the party **concerns.** (d) / All Correct (e).

28. I was **surprised** (a) / when I got **confirmation** (b) / of the news that he was the **recipient** (c) / of the **prestigious** (d) / award. All correct (e)

29. The **circomstances** (a) / in which the **claim** (b) / was made are **certainly** (c) / **unbelievable**. (d) / All Correct (e).

30. The **authorities** (a) / always request our **assistance** (b) / whenever they **felt** (c) / they **require** (d) / it. All Correct (e).

Directions to Questions 31 to 35

In each of these questions, a part is printed in **bold**. It may contain an error. If so, find out which of the phrases (a), (b), (c) and (d) given after it should replace the part printed in **bold** in the following sentence to make the sentence grammatically meaningful and correct. If the sentence is correct as it is and 'no correction is required', mark (e) as the answer.

31. When they **start investigating,** several irregularities were detected.

(a) started investigate
(b) started an investigation
(c) start investigation
(d) started off investigation
(e) No correction required

32. You **must be stopped** these undesirable activities immediately.

(a) must have been stopped
(b) may have been stopped
(c) might have been stopped
(d) must stop
(e) No correction required

33. Farmers in our country suffer because of an over dependence on rain and the **threat to natural calamities** like floods.

(a) threat of natural calamities
(b) threat against natural calamities
(c) threatened due to natural calamity
(d) natural calamities threatened
(e) No correction required

34. Automation in agriculture and farm management is considered a boon but in fact, it is not true as **they lid to more unemployment.**

(a) it lids to more employment
(b) they lead to more employment
(c) they lead to more unemployment
(d) it leads to more unemployment
(e) No correction required

35. The agricultural sector **deserves more attention** than the industrial sector in our country.

(a) deserves attention more
(b) deserving more attention
(c) deserve more attention
(d) deserve to be attended more
(e) No correction required

Directions to Questions 36 to 50

In the following passage there are blanks, each of which has been numbered. These numbers are

printed below the passage and against each, five words are suggested, one of which fits the blank appropriately without changing its meaning. Find out the appropriate word in each case.

Many kinds of insects are ... **(36)**... and larger animals learn to ...**(37)**... eating them. It is in the ...**(38)**... of these insects to show a ...**(39)**... flag of some kind. The typical wasp, for example, ...**(40)**... a conspicuous colour pattern of black and yellow ...**(41)**... on its body. This is ...**(42)**... distinctive that it is easy for a ...**(43)**... animal to remember it. After a few unfortunate experiences it quickly learns to ...**(94)**... insects bearing this pattern. Other, unrelated, poisonous insect species may also carry a similar pattern. They become members of what has been called a 'warning club'.

The important point for us, in the present ...**(45)**... is that some harmless species of insects have taken ...**(46)**... of this system by developing colour patterns similar to those of the poisonous members of the 'warning club'. Certain innocuous flies, for instance, ...**(47)**... black and yellow bands on their bodies that mimic the colour patterns of the wasps. By becoming ...**(48)**... members of the 'warning club' they reap the benefits without having to ...**(49)**... any real poison. The killers dare not attack them, even though they would, in reality, make a ...**(50)**... meal.

36.
(a) flying (b) conspicuous
(c) vulnerable (d) big
(e) poisonous

37.
(a) desist (b) adjust
(c) prefer (d) avoid
(e) nurture

38.
(a) habit (b) interest
(c) goodwill (d) welfare
(e) help

39.
(a) dangerous (b) ambiguous
(c) warning (d) coloured
(e) safety

40.
(a) reveal (b) paints
(c) flashes (d) carried
(e) loaded

41.
(a) bands (b) pieces
(c) paint (d) colours
(e) clothes

42.
(a) so (b) extremely
(c) normally (d) too
(e) very

43.
(a) bold (b) prey
(c) chased (d) predatory
(e) hunted

44.
(a) hate (b) love
(c) approach (d) abstain
(e) avoid

45.
(a) text (b) premise
(c) context (d) day
(e) view

46.
(a) profit (b) yield
(c) disadvantage (d) ride
(e) advantage

47.
(a) display (b) indicates
(c) announce (d) wear
(e) bears

48.
(a) unregistered (b) fake
(c) honorary (d) sycophant
(e) original

49.
(a) transport (b) inject
(c) possess (d) earn
(e) load

50.
(a) troublesome
(b) delicious
(c) indigestible
(d) hazardous
(e) cheap

PAPER 7

STATE BANK OF INDIA PO EXAMINATION, MARCH 2010

Directions to Questions 1 to 15

Read the following passages carefully and answer the questions given below after them. Certain words/phrases have been printed in bold to help you locate them while answering some of the questions.

Passage- I

Despite the economic crunch worldwide that saw **pulverisation** of some of the largest banking and finance giants, Indian banking houses have managed to show positive growth this quarter. Some of India's leading national banks have posted a net profit rise of more than 40% over the last quarter amid global **turmoil**. This would come as a big **shot in the arm** for the investors and consumers of these banks even though apprehension is mounting on other banking and broking firms worldwide. One of the main reasons behind the success of these banks this quarter, would be their direct backing by the Government of India. People take solace in their investments in public sector watching the bailout packages being cashed out by governments all over the world to save big business houses.

Other private banks in India have also reported a substantial net profit over the last quarter. Given the international and domestic scenario one cannot put this down as a **mundane** achievement. While others are on a cost cutting spree and firing employees, Indian companies are actually working on boosting staffing in banking and broking sectors. This can be seen as a big boon in the days to come when the current recession eases and the economy gradually comes back on to the fast track. The finance minister has assured Indian public about the sound health of all Indian banks. This could also be evident from the fact that there have been no mergers and takeovers in Indian banking sector in a contrast to world scenario where finance houses are looking for mergers to cut costs on operations. We definitely are not looking to **thrive;** rather we are looking for growth. It is just that the pace of growth is a little slow now as compared to a year or two before. These are hard times to test the hard. The weak in business and career will be weeded out and it is sometimes very beneficial for business in the long run.

1. What, according to the author, is the reason for the success of Indian national banks in this quarter ?

(a) Indian national banks do not have any commitments in troubled foreign markets.

(b) These banks can never face financial crisis because of their sheer size.
(c) These banks are ready to give loans at a very low rate of interest.
(d) The public is ready to invest in these banks because of the knowledge that these banks get strong support from the Government.
(e) None of these

2. What does the phrase 'shot in the arm' as used in the passage mean ?
(a) Shock
(b) Fear
(c) Encouragement
(d) Anxiety
(e) None of these

3. How, according to the author, is the current recession beneficial ?
(a) Worldwide, companies have realised that India is a strong power to reckon with.
(b) India is surging ahead of the other companies throughout the world.
(c) After the recession is over international companies will turn to India for investment.
(d) Recession is bringing down the prices of essential commodities.
(e) None of these

4. What, according to the author, will be a big boon in the days to come ?
(a) The economy coming back on the fast track
(b) The slowing down of the economy
(c) Increased hiring in Indian financial sector in times of economic slowdown
(d) The cost cutting carried out by all the companies
(e) None of these

5. Which of the following statements is definitely true in the context of the passage ?
(A) India has not been affected by the economic slowdown.
(B) Indian Banks are showing growth in this quarter despite the recession.
(C) While banking industry in the West was severely affected by recession in the past, it is now gradually recovering and showing a positive growth.
(a) Only (A)
(b) Only (B)
(c) Only (C)
(d) Only (A) and (B)
(e) Only (B) and (C)

6. Which of the following strengthens the finance minister's statement about the sound health of Indian Banks with respect to the passage ?
(A) There have been no acquisitions and mergers of Indian Banks.
(B) The Indian Banks are recording a positive growth.
(C) Layoffs have been observed worldwide.
(a) Only (A) and (B)
(b) Only (A) and (C)
(c) Only (A)
(d) Only (B)
(e) All (A), (B) and (C)

Directions to Questions 7 to 8

Choose the word/group of words which is most similar in meaning to the word/group of words printed in bold as used in the passage.

7. TURMOIL
(a) danger (b) shock
(c) sadness (d) fear
(e) chaos

8. PULVERISATION
(a) polarisation (b) mashing
(c) debasement (d) fall
(e) crushing

Directions to Questions 9 to 10

Choose the word/group of words which is most opposite in meaning to the word/group of words printed in bold as used in the passage.

9. THRIVE
(a) succeed (b) deteriorate
(c) worry (d) tremble
(e) strive

10. **MUNDANE**
(a) extraordinary (b) regular
(c) severe (d) visionary
(e) routine

Passage-II

Modern bio-technology, especially the creation of genetically modified crops, is often presented as a magic solution or universal panacea for the problems of poverty; inadequate nutrition and even environmental degradation across the world. Conversely, there are people who present the picture of tech generated monsters and major human health hazards being created by science. Many of the technological changes currently in the process of being utilised in agriculture can have unforeseen consequences, and their safety and future viability are far from secure.

The reality, as always, is far more complex than either of these two extremes. Even today the total food production in the world is adequate to feed the hungry of the world; the problem is rather one of unequal distribution, which deprives a large part of the population of even their minimal nutritional requirements. Similarly, farmers, especially in developing countries, face many problems such as lack of infrastructure, poor or unstable market access, **volatile** input and output prices etc. that biotechnology does not address, much less solve.

It is true that transgenic plants can offer a range of benefits which are above and beyond those which emerged from more traditional innovations in cultivation. It is suggested that such new technology offers more effective pest resistance of seeds and crops through genetic control mechanisms, which also reduces the need for pesticide use and leads to improved yield. A basic question, of course, is whether the new GM technology is safe, and whether this is absolutely crucial since the effects may only be known much later. The jury is still very much out on this matter, and the controversy does not appear to be resolved quickly.

The trouble is that most governments in developing countries have relatively low food and beverage regulatory standards, and public systems for monitoring and surveillance of such items are poor or non-existent. This leaves them **open** for entry and even dumping of a range of agricultural products of the new technology, which may not pass regulatory standards in the more developed countries.

11. Which of the following is true in context of the passage ?
(a) Genetically modified crops have been universally recognised as a solution to poverty and environmental degradation.
(b) The only way to improve the deficit in food requirement and food production in the world is by adapting genetically modified crops.
(c) Genetically modified crops produce more yield as compared to yield from the traditional methods.
(d) Taking advantage of absence of regulatory standards, scientists have been dumping new products in the markets without appropriate approval.
(e) None is true

12. Choose the word/group of words which is most similar in meaning to OPEN printed in bold as used in the passage.
(a) Vulnerable (b) Capable
(c) Threatened (d) Uncertain
(e) Weak

13. Choose the word/group of words which is most opposite in meaning to VOLATILE printed in bold as used in the passage.
(a) Never-ending (b) Meager
(c) Valuable (d) Irreversible
(e) Stable

14. The author of the given passage seems to be definitely
(a) Suggesting the use of traditional methods of agriculture as against bio-technology by developing countries owing to their poor regulatory standards
(b) In favour of utilising bio technology as a tool for alleviation of poverty from the world
(c) Urging the policy makers to improve infrastructural facilities so that farmers can maximise the benefits of genetically modified crops

(d) Unconvinced of the long term effects and rationale for immediate requirement of genetically modified products
(e) None of these

15. Why, according to the author, is genetic modification of crops not an answer to the problem of hunger in the world ?

(A) People being highly doubtful of the long term effects of genetically modified crops, do not buy the products grown by such methods.
(B) The problem of hunger in the world is not due to inadequate production of food but due to unequal distribution of it.
(C) Many developing countries have banned genetically modified products as developed countries have been using these countries as dumping grounds for new genetically modified products.

(a) Only A (b) Only B
(c) Both B and C (d) Both A and C
(e) None of these

Directions to Questions 16 to 20

Each question below has two blanks, each blank indicating that something has been omitted. Choose the set of words for each blank that best fits the meaning of the sentence as a whole.

16. A controversial plan to build an immense dam in Brazil's rainforest was stalled when it ______ a formidable bloc of ______ in ecologists and indigenous tribes alike.
(a) resulted, hostilities
(b) gained, supporters
(c) attracted, opponents
(d) lead, protesters
(e) drew, proponents

17. According to a recent survey sales figures of high-end cars have seen an ______ growth in the past year, which shows that Indian consumers have the ______ impact of recession.
(a) unprecedented, negated
(b) unbelievable, suffered
(c) unusual, worsened
(d) insignificant, endured
(e) adequate, proven

18. The National Knowledge Commission has said that India will have to bring ____ in education if it has to emerge as the most ______ work form of the world.
(a) changes, biggest
(b) reforms, talented
(c) alleviation, skilful
(d) quality, brighter
(e) outcomes, demanded.

19. Norway has stolen a march over other developed countries by ____ that it would reduce 40% of in greenhouse gas emissions by 2020 and ______ carbon neutral by 2030.
(a) allowing, turn
(b) posing, grew
(c) estimating, exist
(d) perceiving, arising
(e) declaring, become

20. According to the language experts, children should begin talking in their mother tongue rather than a foreign language which can ______ affect their comprehension abilities leading to serious language based ____ later in their lives.
(a) significantly, abilities
(b) appropriately, achievements
(c) severely, advantages
(d) adversely, problems
(e) positively, issues

Directions to Questions 21 to 25

In each of the following questions four words are given of which two words are most nearly the same or opposite in meaning. Find the two words which are most nearly the same or opposite in meaning and select the number of the correct letter combination as your answer.

21. (A) instigate (B) enquire
(C) construe (D) interpret
(a) A-C (b) A-B
(c) C-D (d) B-D
(e) A-D

22. (A) superficial (B) superfluous
(C) enlightened (D) surplus
(a) A-C (b) A-B
(c) B-C (d) B-D
(e) A-D

23. (A) appalling (B) sinister
(C) perturbed (D) threatening
(a) A-B (b) B-D
(c) A-C (d) A-D
(e) D-C

24. (A) imprison (B) torture
(C) excruciate (D) extract
(a) B-D (b) B-C
(c) A-B (d) C-D
(e) A-C

25. (A) pertinent (B) impolite
(C) irrelevant (D) insecure
(a) A-C (b) B-D
(c) C-D (d) A-D
(e) B-C

Directions to Questions 26 to 30

Rearrange the following sentences (A), (B), (C), (D), (E) and (F) to make a meaningful paragraph and then answer the questions which follow :

(A) According to it, organised retail stores are not wolves at the doors of friendly neighbourhood grocery stores as there is room for expansion of both.

(B) Many have been crying foul over the entry of organised retail stores expressing concern over their impact on small store owners.

(C) The final winner in the competition however, is the common man who gets to choose between the most suitable options and in turn fights with the runaway inflation in prices of essential commodities.

(D) In spite of this potential for expansion, it is doubtless that the small store owners face a decline in profit in initial years if organised retailers set up stores in the vicinity.

(E) But a study conducted over a period of two years goes a long way towards allaying these fears.

(F) This impact, however, wears off once they learn to take on the competition which in turn enhances efficiency all around.

26. Which of the following sentence should be the **FIRST** after rearrangement ?
(a) A (b) B
(c) C (d) D
(e) E

27. Which of the following sentence should be the **THIRD** after rearrangement ?
(a) A (b)
(c) D (d) F
(e) C

28. Which of the following sentence should be the **SIXTH (LAST)** after rearrangement ?
(a) A (b) B
(c) C (d) E
(e) F

29. Which of the following sentence should be the **SECOND** after rearrangement ?
(a) A (b) B
(c) C (d) E
(e) F

30. Which of the following sentence should be the **FIFTH** after rearrangement ?
(a) D (b) B
(c) C (d) E
(e) F

Directions to Questions 31 to 40

In the following passage there are blanks, each of which has been numbered. These numbers are printed below the passage and against each, five words/phrases are suggested, one of which best fits the blank appropriately. Find out the appropriate word/phrase in each case.

Economic growth figures for the first quarter of this financial year seem to support the claim that the worst may be over for the Indian economy. The gradual revival is also an indication that the government's economic stimulus package is **...(31)....** What could, however, upset the positive outlook is the drought which **...(32)...** large parts of the country and its impact on overall growth. Even though the monsoon had picked up **...(33)....** the rains received were grossly **...(34)....** There are clear **...(35)...** that farm output, particularly cereals, will fall drastically. Insufficient rain is bound to shoot up the **...(36)...** of agricultural commodities and that would impact the economy as a whole. The drought would also **...(37)...** a drastic reduction in rural employment and consumption besides inflation in the prices of food articles.

Food prices have been **...(38)...** since the past few months, and lower agricultural production is likely to **...(39)...** the situation. The government has said that food grain from the buffer stocks will be used to keep prices **...(40)...** Subsidised food grain is necessary in these times, but its effectiveness will depend a lot on the distribution system.

31. (a) impractical (b) ambiguous (c) failing (d) working (e) weakening

32. (a) strike (b) affected (c) exposed (d) reverted (e) altered

33. (a) unseasonably (b) unfavourably (c) presently (d) meagerly (e) later

34. (a) inadequate (b) enough (c) missing (d) ample (e) atrocious

35. (a) contradictions (b) advices (c) reasons (d) results (e) indications

36. (a) production (b) requirement (c) prices (d) yield (e) labour

37. (a) trigger (b) lead (c) result (d) contribute (e) dampen

38. (a) improving (b) balanced (c) stable (d) increasing (e) decreasing

39. (a) aggravate (b) amend (c) smoothen (d) improve (e) challenge

40. (a) unprofitable (b) futile (c) maximum (d) growing (e) down

Directions to Questions 41 to 45

Which of the phrases (a) , (b) , (c) and (d) given below each statement should be placed in the blank space provided so as to make a meaningful and grammatically correct sentence ? If none of the sentences is appropriate, mark (e) as the answer.

41. Although information technology has entered the homes, offices and hearts of many citizens of India, ______

(a) India provides the highest number of IT experts to the world every year

(b) Many people in rural areas still remain ignorant of its immense benefits

(c) Government has done its best by funding research in this field appropriately

(d) The face of communication in the years to come would change completely from the bygone years

(e) None of these

42. While the environment-friendly nuclear energy could make a large addition to the energy resources,______

(a) Experts have a lot of expectations from this cleaner method of producing energy

(b) The government is determined to extract maximum out of this technology in the near future

(c) International lobby has been pressurising the developing nations to shift their energy production from coal to nuclear power.

(d) The problem of locating adequate numbers of Uranium reserves to run the reactors is yet to be sorted out

(e) None of these

43. ________, experts proposed the idea of a common school system.

(a) Overlooking the fundamental right of quality education of every child in India
(b) Since the curricular requirements of a rural child is different from an urban child
(c) Based on the fact that difference in the quality of schools acts as a ground for discrimination
(d) Since a large percentage of Indian children are getting free education
(e) None of these

44. ________, the soil today is nowhere as rich in native minerals as it used to be some centuries ago.

(a) As there is a growing consent among farmers regarding limiting the use of chemical fertilizers
(b) As the chemical inputs in agriculture improved the yield many folds
(c) Owing to the uninhibited use of chemical inputs in agriculture
(d) Awareness among farmers regarding the side effects of chemical farming grew when
(e) None of these

45. As allegations of crores of rupees changing hands to permit illegal mining began to fly thick and fast, ________.

(a) Government ordered an enquiry which exposed a nexus between mine operators and bureaucrats
(b) It caused great damage to the surrounding ecosystem and the environment in general
(c) The officials have been irresponsible in failing to bring it to the notice of the court in time
(d) The powerful mining lobby has bribed the officials to obtain permit for mining on ecological sensitive land
(e) None of these.

Directions to Questions 46 to 50

In each of the given sentences select the sentence which would either follow or precede the given sentence in grammatically and conceptually appropriate manner. The instruction is given at the end of every statement.

46. Unfortunately, however, these slum dwellers are looked upon by the society as an appendix causing ills in the urban society.

Which of the following sentence would immediately precede the preceding sentence ?

(a) Health officials have been warning the government against the transmission of contagious diseases from the slum areas other parts of the city
(b) Slum dwellers not only play a significant role in urban economic but also provide cheap labour for everyday work of the cities
(c) A recent report suggested that ** percent of government land was illegally occupied by the slum dwellers
(d) The slum dwellers live in sub human, unhygienic conditions and their tiny shanties and are very often hubs for criminal activity
(e) None of these

47. However, since the begining of the nineties, free market force have been allowed to play for ensuring all round development in Indian markets as well Which of the following sentences would immediately precede the preceding sentence ?

(a) Entry of various market forces increased the competition faced by the indigenous organisations manifold
(b) The severe shortage of hewer technology and products in the late 1980s ended with the entry of foreign players in the Indian market
(c) A major roadblock faced by the foreign investors was the poor infrastructural facilities which was however overtake by the prospects seen in the luge market
(d) India had been following very selective and conservative economic policy during the late 1980s
(e) None of these

48. That was mainly because only two percent of the total farmers could actually comprehend the lengthy procedures to obtain the loan and be benefited from it.

Which of the following sentences would immediately precede the above sentence?

(a) Many moneylenders have been making the most out of this situation and providing loans to the rest of the farmers at inflated prices.

(b) There is thus an urgent need to make the schemes and policy as simple and farmer friendly as possible.

(c) A new loan scheme started by the government a couple of months ago proved to be a huge failure and utterly unpopular among the farmers.

(d) This situation can be improved by providing mediators to carry out and follow-up of the lengthy official procedure for the farmers.

(e) None of these

49. The foreign embassy has now forward a demand to the government that prosecution may be carried out on a foreign land and not in the country to which the terrorists belong.

Which of the following sentences would immediately follow the above sentence?

(a) Army arrested the terrorists responsible for kidnapping four foreign tourists after a daylong operation.

(b) The foreign ministry has offered all possible help to the government for hunting down the terrorists involved in it.

(c) Government has politely declined the request to handover the arrested terrorists for prosecution outside the country.

(d) The arrested terrorists were sentenced to life imprisonment after being prosecuted by a panel of international judges.

(e) None of these

50. This is because most of the institutes for higher learning lack the basic infrastructure, trained staff and equipment necessary for the physically challenged.

Which of the following sentences would immediately precede the above sentence ?

(a) Many physically challenged people have been performing as well as other students perform in their studies.

(b) The percent of illiterate, physically challenged people in rural areas is considerably more than that in the urban areas.

(c) According to a recent survey, only two out of nearly 200 universities in India have adequate number of books in Braille.

(d) Although government has been making many provisions to improve higher education in India, no attention has been paid to the education of the physically challenged students.

(e) None of these

PAPER 8

STATE BANK OF INDIA PO EXAMINATION, 2013

Directions to Questions 1 to 9

Read the following passage carefully and answer the questions given after it. Certain words/ phrases are printed in bold to help you to locate them while answering some of the questions.

The outside world has pat answers concerning extremely impoverished countries, especially those in Africa. Everything comes back, again and again, to corruption and misrule. Western officials argue that Africa simply needs to behave itself better, to allow market forces to operate without interference by corrupt rulers. Yet the critics of African governance have it wrong. Politics simply can't explain Africa's **prolonged** economic crisis. The claim that Africa's corruption is the basic source of the problem does not withstand serious scrutiny. During the past decade I witnessed how relatively well-governed countries in Africa, such as Ghana, Malawi, Mail and Senegal, failed to prosper, whereas societies in Asia perceived to have **extensive** corruption, such as Bangladesh, Indonesia and Pakistan, enjoyed rapid economic growth. What is the explanation ? Every situation of extreme poverty around the world contains some of its own unique cases, which need to be diagnosed as a doctor would a patient. For example, Africa is burdened with malaria like no other part of the world, simply because it is unlucky in providing the perfect conditions for that disease : high temperatures, plenty of breeding sites and particular species of malaria transmitting mosquitoes- that prefer to bite humans rather than cattle.

Another **myth** is that the developed world already gives plenty of aid to the world's poor. Former U.S. Secretary of the Treasury, Paul O'Neil expressed a common frustration when he remarked about aid for Africa : "We've spent trillions of dollars on these problems and we have damn near nothing to show for it". O'Neil was no foe of foreign aid. Indeed, he wanted to fix the system so that more U.S. aid could be justified. But he was wrong to believe that vast flows of aid to Africa had been **squandered**. President Bush said in a press conference in April 2004 that as 'the greatest power on the face of the earth, we have an **obligation** to help the spread of freedom. We have an obligation to feed the hungry". Yet how does the U.S. fulfill its obligation ? U.S. aid to farmers in poor countries to help them grow more food runs at around $ 200 million per year, far less than S1 per person per year for the hundreds of millions of people living in subsistence farm households.

From the world as a whole, the amount of aid per African per year is really very small, just $30 per sub-Saharan African in 2002. Of that **modest** amount, almost $5 were actually for consultants from the donor countries, more than $3 was for emergency aid, about $4 went for servicing Africa's debts and $5 was in debt-relief operations. The rest, about $12, went to Africa. Since the "money down the drain" argument is heard most frequently in the U.S. it's worth looking at the same calculations for U.S. aid alone. In 2002, the U.S. gave $3 per sub Saharan African. Taking out the parts for U.S. consultants and technical co-operation, food and other emergency aid, administrative costs and debt relief, the aid per African came to a grand total of 6 cents. The U.S. has promised repeatedly over the decade, as a signatory to global agreements like the Monterrey Consensus of 2002, to give a much larger proportion of its annual output, specifically up to 0.7% of GNP, with official development assistance. The U.S.'s failure to follow through has no political fallout domestically, of course. Because not one in a million U.S. Citizens even know of statements like the Monterrey Consensus, But no one should underestimate the salience that it has around the world. Spin as an American myth about their nation's generosity, the poor countries are fully aware of what the U.S. is not doing.

1. Which of the following statement is TRUE about U.S. Aid to the Sub-Saharan African countries ?

(a) The U.S. aid meant for of capital African does not reach the incumbent.

(b) The U.S. aid to African countries is more than that for any other developing or underdeveloped nation.

(c) The U.S. aid for farmers in African Countries is $200 m. per year.

(d) The donor country charges $5 per individual as the consultancy charges

(e) U.S. has been contributing more than 0.7% of its GNP for development assistance

2. President Bush's statement in press conference on April 2004 indicates that.....

(a) The aid given by the U.S. to the poor countries is substantially and sufficient

(b) The spread of freedom cannot be achieved through financial aid

(c) Feeding the hungry million outside the U.S. is not possible

(d) The U.S. on its own, assumes the obligation of helping the poor countries

(e) U.S. Has spent trillions of dollars on aid

3. The author has mentioned Ghana as a country with.......

(a) Reasonably good-governance

(b) Corrupt leadership

(c) Plenty of natural resources

(d) Rapid economic growth

(e) None of these

4. The cases of malaria in Africa are mainly due to...........

(A) High temperature

(B) Climatic conditions conducive for breeding

(C) Malaria carriers' liking for human blood in preference to that of cattle.

(a) None of these

(b) Only B & C

(c) Only A & C

(d) Only A & B

(e) All the three

5. The purpose of the author in writing this passage seems to...........

(a) Criticise USA for not providing adequate financial help

(b) Make Africans realise their own problems

(c) Analyse the actual quantum of aid against the perceived one

(d) Highlight how American leaders are power-hungry

(e) None of these

6. The author has given the example of Bangladesh, Indonesia and Pakistan in support of his argument that...........

(a) Corruption is the major culprit in the way of prosperity

(b) Mis-governance hampers the prosperity of nations

(c) Despite rampant corruption, nations may prosper

(d) Developed nations arrogantly neglect underdeveloped countries
(e) None of these

7. The remark of former U.S. Secretary of the Treasury, Paul O'Neil, is according to the author
(a) A statement of fact
(b) Not factually correct
(c) An underestimation of U.S. and
(d) A ruthless remark by an arrogant bureaucrat
(e) None of these

8. The passage seems to emphasise that the outside world has
(a) Correct understanding about the reasonable aid provided by the USA to the poor countries
(b) Definite information about what is happening in underdeveloped countries
(c) Stopped extending any financial aid to underdeveloped countries
(d) Misconceptions about the aid given to the poor nations by developed countries
(e) None of these

9. According to the Westerners the solution to eradicate poverty of African nations lies in
(a) Corruption
(b) Improving their own national behavior
(c) Misrule
(d) Prolonged economic crisis
(e) None of these

Directions to Questions 10 to 12

Which of the following word/group of words is the most OPPOSITE in meaning of the word given in bold as used in the passage.

10. Extensive
(a) Intensive (b) Abominable
(c) Inherent (d) Rampant
(e) Negligible

11. Prolonged
(a) Immediate (b) Shortened
(c) Brevity (d) Short-lived
(e) Narrow

12. Myth
(a) Reality (b) Mystery
(c) Misery (d) Misconception
(e) Exaggeration

Directions to Questions 13 to 15

Which of the following word/group of words is MOST NEARLY THE SAME in meaning as the word printed in bold as used in the passage ?

13. Squander
(a) Use economically
(b) Spend wastefully
(c) Siphon judiciously
(d) Donate generously
(e) Donate with an ulterior motive

14. Modest
(a) Humble (b) Sufficient
(c) Meager (d) Sober
(e) Unpretentious

15. Obligation
(a) Lip sympathy
(b) True empathy
(c) Self pity
(d) Conditional responsibility
(e) Moral binding

Directions to Questions 16 to 25

Read each sentence to find out whether there is any grammatical error in it. The error if any, will be in one part of the sentence. The number of that part is the answer. If there is no error; the answer is (e) i.e. 'No Error'. (Ignore the errors of punctuation, if any.)

16. He was grateful (a) / to me for the help (b) / that I had extended for him (c) / in the hour of his need, (d) / No Error (e)

17. While undergoing a (a) / strenuous workout, (b) / he suffered a massive heart attack (c) / but luckily survived, (d) / No Error (e)

18. Taking care of yourself (a) / cannot be (b) / and should not be considered (c) / as a selfish thing (d) / No Error (e)

19. The smooth and easy (a) / we allow people to navigate (b) / through any device at any place (c) / in the world, the better, (d) / No Error (e)

20. What really agonize them (a) / is the presence of (b) / an unwanted and unscrupulous (c) / member on the panel (d) / No Error (e)

21. People express their expectations (a) / that their leaders should not (b) / resorting to (c) / corrupt practices and nepotism, (d) / No Error (e)

22. Asian culture will, (a) / sooner or later (b) / become an international norm (c) / for the entertainment industry (d) / No Error (e)

23. The business lobby wanted (a) / he to take over (b) / as the new Chairman (c) / of their coveted Board, (d) / No Error (e)

24. He thinks that (a) / a popular magazine would like to (b) / know what are other topics most (c) / no people's minds, (d) / No Error (e)

25. We as the editors of (a) / a popular magazine would like to (b) / know what are other topics most (c) / on people's minds, (d) / No Error (e)

Directions to Questions 26 to 30

Rearrange the following six sentences (A), (B), (C), (D), (E) and (F) in the proper sequence to form a meaningful paragraph, then answer the questions given below them.

(A) It is a general term used to describe over 200 individual diseases.

(B) The abnormal cells grow with-out any control, invade through normal tissue barriers and reproduce indefinitely.

(C) The word "cancer" comes from Latin, meaning a crab.

(D) These characteristics include development within any tissue of a malignant growth.

(E) A tumor was called cancer because of swollen veins around the area resembling a crab's limb.

(F) These disease's progress differently over a period of time and share certain characteristics.

26. Which of the following should be the SECOND sentence after rearrangement ?
(a) A (b) B
(c) C (d) D
(e) E

27. Which of the following should be the THIRD sentence after rearrangement ?
(a) A (b) B
(c) C (d) D
(e) E

28. Which of the following should be the FOURTH sentence after rearrangement ?
(a) A (b) B
(c) C (d) D
(e) E

29. Which of the following should be the FIFTH sentence after rearrangement ?
(a) A (b) B
(c) C (d) D
(e) None of these

30. Which of the following should be the SIXTH (LAST) sentence after rearrangement ?
(a) A (b) B
(c) C (d) D
(e) None of these

Directions to Questions 31 to 35

In each of the following sentences there are two blank spaces. Below each sentence there are five pairs of words denoted by numbers (a), (b), (c), (d) and (e). Find out which pair of words can be filled up in the blanks in the sentence in the same sequence to make the sentence grammatically correct and meaningfully complete.

31. Liberalisation has removed all the legalities......... and.............floodgates to multinational companies.
(a) Hurdles.............Awarded
(b) Barrier............Opened
(c) Obstacles...........Guarded
(d) Manipulation..........Closed
(e) Battles.............Threw

32. The..........on some of the towns has created........ among the residents of the other part of the country.

(a) Attack..............Ambition
(b) Raid..........Awareness
(c) Bombardment.........Panic
(d) Spell...........Satisfaction
(e) Shower............Dampness

33. ....to the popular belief that every astrologer nurtures blind faith in fate, our astrologer believes in
(a) Contrary........Action
(b) According.........Thoughts
(c) Bowing..............Present
(d) Proving............Forecasting
(e) Pointing.............Devotion

34. His...........has yielded him the............fruit.
(a) Fate.........Undesirable
(b) Efforts........Unwanted
(c) Action..........Viable
(d) Perseverance..............Desired
(e) Emphasis.......Expected

35. His...........contribution to the Tsunami relief fund was.............By his staff members.
(a) Meager............Admired
(b) Spontaneous............Nullified
(c) Negligible............Sanctioned
(d) Noteworthy........... Improved
(e) Generous...........Appreciated

Directions to Questions 36 to 40

For each statement there are three different sentences given below it. Pick out the sentence (s) that most appropriately convey (s) the meaning of the statement. The number of that sentence or combination of sentences is the answer.

36. I could not observe his unwillingness while donating to charity.
(A) I observed his willingness to donate to charity.
(B) I failed to detect his reluctance, if there was any, while he was donating to charity.
(C) I noticed his enthusiasm while donating to charity.
(a) Only A
(b) Only B
(c) Only C
(d) Only A and B
(e) Only B and C

37. If you hesitate to participate freely and vigorously, your performance will be adversely affected.
(A) Participate freely and vigorously if you desire to demonstrate your full performance.
(B) Do not participate with reservations if you want your participation to be affected adversely.
(C) Your free and vigorous participation is most likely to affect your performance adversely.
(a) Only A
(b) Only B
(c) Only C
(d) Only A and B
(e) Only B and C

38. Who do you think will be able to handle the work effectively ?
(A) In your opinion, there is none who can handle the work effectively.
(B) Who, in your opinion, can handle the work effectively ?
(C) Can you name the person who, as per your assessment, can handle the work effectively ?
(a) Only A
(b) Only B
(c) Only C
(d) Only A and B
(e) Only B and C

39. How much you speak is less important than how well you speak ?
(A) The quality of your talk is less important than the quantum of your talk.
(B) How well you speak is as important as how much you speak.
(C) The quality of your talk as also the quantum are equally important.
(a) Only A and B
(b) Only B and C

(c) All the three
(d) None
(e) Only A

40. All our efforts were wasted due to the negligence of the clients.
(A) The negligence of the clients was responsible for making our efforts futile.
(B) Our efforts would have been fruitful had there been no negligence on the part of the clients.
(C) The negligence of the clients saved all our efforts from being wasted.
(a) Only A
(b) Only B
(c) Only A and B
(d) Only B and C
(e) All the three

Directions to Questions 41 to 50

In the following passage, there are blanks, each, of which has been numbered. These numbers are printed below the passage and against each, five words are suggested, one of which fits the blank appropriately. Find out the appropriate word in each case

New technology has led directly to **(41)** standards of living yet science tends to follow market forces as well as to **(42)** them. It is not surprising that the rich get richer in a continuing cycle of **(43)** while the poorest are often left behind. A special **(44)** should be made by the powerhouses of world science to address the unmet the challenges of the poor. Ending **(45)** poverty can relieve many of the pressures on the environment. When impoverished households are **(46)**, **(47)** on their farms, for example, they face less pressure to cut down neighboring forests in **(48)** of new farmland. Still, even as extreme poverty ends, we must not fuel prosperity with a lack of **(49)** for industrial pollution and the **(50)** burning of fossil fuels.

41. (a) Visible (b) Declining (c) Improved (d) Amicable (e) Rigorous
42. (a) Fail (b) Claim (c) Market (d) Avoid (e) Lead
43. (a) Wealth (b) Growth (c) Poverty (d) Improvement (e) Economy
44. (a) Effort (b) Care (ANS) (c) Practice (d) Occasion (e) Sanction
45. (a) Marginal (b) Apparent (c) Superficial (d) Extreme (e) Dismal
46. (a) Abnormally (b) Less (c) More (d) Excessively (e) Unreasonably
47. (a) Efficient (b) Meticulous (c) Careful (d) Dependent (e) Productive
48. (a) View (b) Search (c) Expectation (d) Lust (e) Place
49. (a) Attitude (b) Mobility (c) Initiative (d) Concern (e) Ease
50. (a) Unchecked (b) Repeated (c) Periodical (d) Occasional (e) Limited

We will also provide SBI PO previous question papers 2012/2011 in PDF with questions and answers. Stay tuned for latest SBI PO Model question papers and previous question papers for English language, High level reasoning, Quantitative aptitude, Data Interpretation, Analysis, General awareness, computer and marketing sec

PAPER 9

SBI Clerk Written Examination, 2012

Directions to Questions 1 to 15

Read the following passage carefully and answer the questions given below it. Certain words/ phrases have been printed in bold to help you locate them while answering some of the questions.

Sheela and Jairam were a poor old couple. Their only **possession** was one cow. Once, Jairam fell very sick. Soon all their money was used up in buying medicines and they realised that they would have to sell their cow in order to bear the rest of the expenses. Sheela decided to go to the market and sell the cow. She set off, leading the cow by a rope. On the way, she met four young men. They were the local bullies who enjoyed teasing and tormenting old people. When they saw old Sheela with her cow, they decided to play a trick. One of them sneaked up behind her, untied the cow and tied a goat in its place. Sheela had been walking immersed in thought, worried about Jairam. Suddenly she heard a goat bleat behind her. She turned around and was surprised to see that her cow had **vanished**. She was leading a goat to the market. The four bullies came up to her and said, 'There is magic in the air these days. See, it turned your cow into a goat." Poor Sheela walked on with the goat. After a little while, the boys untied the goat and tied a rooster in its place. The rooster crowed and Sheela was surprised again. The goat had turned into a rooster! The four bullies shouted, "Magic in the air, Grandma." She resumed walking with the rooster in tow. After a few minutes the boys crept up again, untied the rooster and tied a log of wood in its place. A few moments later Sheela realised that she was dragging a log of wood with a rope. Again, the bullies shouted, "Magic in the air. Grandma." After a few minutes, the boys untied the log of wood too and ran away with it. When Sheela finally reached the market, she found that she had nothing but a rope in her hand. She came back home **dejected** as she had lost the cow. She told Jairam the whole story. He immediately understood what had happened. "Make chapatti, vegetable and kheer for lunch tomorrow," he said. "Cook for at least four people. I will come home with some guests. As soon as they come you must say, 'I cooked what the rabbit told me. Come, eat your lunch.' Leave everything else to me," Jairam reassured her. The next morning Jairam went and borrowed two identical rabbits from a friend. He left one at home, tied the other one with a string and started walking towards the market with it. On the way he too met the four bullies. 'Hey Grandfather!' they yelled, "Your wife's cow vanished yesterday. Where are you taking this rabbit now?" Jairam sighed sadly and said, "This rabbit is like my son. It obeys everything I say. But now I am sick and we need money, so I am going to sell it in the market." The four bullies were surprised when they heard this. "Does it really understand what you say, Grandfather ?" they asked. Jairam replied, "Of course it does. Here, watch me." Jairam turned towards the rabbit and said, 'Hop home and tell Sheela to make chapattis, vegetable and kheer for four people." Then he untied the string and let the rabbit hop away. He turned towards the four boys and said, "Come home and have lunch with me." When they reached his house his wife welcomed them and said, "I cooked what the rabbit asked me to cook. Come, eat your lunch. She served the chapattis, vegetable and kheer to all of them. The four bullies were stunned when they saw the rabbit sitting in the corner. They told Jairam, "We will buy your rabbit." Jairam pretended to think and said, "It is very precious to me." The four bullies immediately offered him a higher price. Jairam showed some reluctance. The moment he **agreed** to sell the rabbit they paid him the money and left with the rabbit immediately. The four bullies decided to test the rabbit's abilities. They had been blackmailing a landlord for money. So they told the rabbit, "Go and tell the landlord to bring us the money within ten minutes." The rabbit hopped off. They waited for an hour but the landlord did not come with the money. They marched to his house and yelled, "Give us the money and our rabbit." The landlord had been waiting for a chance to teach these bullies a lesson. He ordered his strongest bodyguard to give them a good **thrashing**. Bleeding and bruised they went back to Jairam's house and said, "You fooled us. Return our money at once." Jairam simply smiled and said, The money has disappeared! There is magic in the air."

1. Why did Sheela and Jairam decide to sell the cow ?
   (a) They had spent all their money on Jairam's sickness and needed more money.
   (b) Sheela wanted to buy a rooster and they needed money for that.
   (c) They were fed up of the four bullies and wanted to teach them a lesson
   (d) They wanted to invite the four bullies for lunch and needed money for buying the ingredients.
   (e) They owed money to the landlord.

2. Why was Jairam reluctant to sell the rabbit?
   (a) He only pretended to be reluctant in order to fool the bullies.
   (b) He was found of the little rabbit and did not want to sell it to the bullies.
   (c) He wanted to gift the rabbits to the landlord.
   (d) He knew that the bullies would not take good care of the rabbit.
   (e) He wanted to sell the rabbit in the market and get a better price for it.

3. Which of the following may be an appropriate little to the passage?
   (a) Magic in the air
   (b) Never steal a cow
   (c) The strongest bodyguard
   (d) The smart bullies
   (e) The obedient rabbit

4. What did Sheela do after reaching the market empty handed?
   (a) Determined to earn money, she managed to sell the rope that she was left with.
   (b) She returned home objected and narrated the whole incident to her husband.
   (c) She bought two rabbits and devised a plan to get back at the bullies.
   (d) She want to the landlord and complained about the bullies.
   (e) She want home and cooked lunch for her husband and herself.

5. What did the four bullies tie to Sheela's rope immediately after untying the cow?
   (a) A log of wood
   (b) A rooster
   (c) A rabbit
   (d) A goat
   (e) Not mentioned in the passage

6. Why were the four bullies surprised when they were talking to Jairam?

(a) They knew that Jairam was sick and had not expected to see him.
(b) They had not expected Jairam to invite them for lunch.
(c) They could not believe that the rabbit could understand and obey Jairam.
(d) They knew that Jairam did not own a rabbit and were surprised to see him with one.
(e) They could not believe that Jairam knew the rabbit's language.

7. What did the four bullies see when they reached Jairam's house?
(a) They saw that two rabbits were sitting in the corner.
(b) They saw that Sheela had not prepared any lunch.
(c) They saw the cow they had stolen from Sheela on the previous day.
(d) They saw the log of wood they had tied to Sheela's rope.
(e) They saw that the same rabbit was sitting in the corner.

8. Arrange the following incidents in a chronological order as they occurred in the passage.
(A) Jairam and Sheela needed money.
(B) The four bullies sent the rabbit to the landlord.
(C) Sheela cooked chapattis, vegetable and kheer.
(D) The four bullies tied a log of wood to the rope.
(a) ADBC
(b) ACDB
(c) ADCB
(d) DABC
(e) DACB

9. Which of the following is true according to the passage?
(a) The four boys liked to help old people.
(b) Jairam asked Sheela to cook lunch for attest four people.
(c) The rabbit could understand Jairam.
(d) Jairam could not trick the four boys.
(e) None is true.

10. What did the landlord do when the four bullies went to his house and yelled?
(a)
(b)
(c)
(d)
(e)

Directions to Questions 11 to 13

Choose the word / group of words which is most similar in the meaning to the word / group of words printed in bold as used in the passage.

11. Thrashing
(a) Garbage (b) Beating
(c) Shouting (d) Warning
(e) Rejection

12. Possession
(a) Control (b) Power
(c) Custody (d) Keeping
(e) Belonging

13. Vanished
(a) Gone missing (b) Was found
(c) Was killed (d) Was left behind
(e) Had exchanged

Directions to Questions 14 to 15

Choose the word which is most opposite in meaning to the word printed in bold as used in the passage.

14. Agreed
(a) Decided (b) Arranged
(c) Accepted (d) Declined
(e) Fixed

15. Dejected
(a) Happy (b) Hurried
(c) Crestfallen (d) Slowly
(e) Angrily

Directions to Questions 16 to 20

Each sentence below has two blanks, each blank indicating that something has been omitted. Choose the set of words for each blank which best fits the meaning of the sentence as a whole.

16. The students ____ not reach on time _____ of the transport strike.
(a) can - as (b) could - because
(c) may - account (d) will - despite
(e) should - for

17. They were ____ to vacate that house as ___ as possible.
(a) asked - soon (b) ordered - easy
(c) shown - early (d) told - later
(e) found - fast

18. The teacher ____ the concept by ____ practical examples.
(a) showed - telling (b) gave speaking
(c) liked – citing (d) found - looking
(e) explained - quoting

19. The manager told us ___ Ramesh was very anxious _____ the meeting.
(a) about - in (b) that - before
(c) like - during (d) the - for
(e) said - after

20. She did not tell ___ that she _____ attended the party.
(a) someone - have
(b) no one - has
(c) him - not
(d) her - can
(e) anyone - had

Directions to Questions 21 to 25

Read each sentence to find out whether there is any grammatical error or idiomatic error in it. The error, if any, will be in one part of the sentence. The number of that part is the answer. If there is 'no error' the answer is '5'. (Ignore errors of punctuation if any.)

21. The shepherd counted (a) / his sheep and found (b) / that one of (c) / them is missing (d). No Error (e)

22. The teacher were (a) / impressed by her performance (b) / and asked her to (c) / participate in the competition (d). No Error (e)

23. She asked her (a) /son for help her (b) /find a place to bury (c) / the gold ornaments (d). No Error (e)

24. The painter was (a) / ask to paint a (b) / picture of the king (c) / sitting on his throne (d). No Error (e)

25. The story was (a) / about how an (b) / intelligent man had saving (c) / himself from being robbed (d). No Error (e)

Directions to Questions 26 to 30

Which of the phrases (a), (b), (c) and (d) given below should replace the phrase given in bold in the following sentence to make the sentence grammatically meaningful and correct? If the sentence is correct as it is and no correction is required, mark (e) as the answer.

26. They are **yet to decided** about buying the new furniture.
(a) still decide (b) yet to decision
(c) yet to decide (d) still decided
(e) No correction required

27. Rohan's mother was **feed up** of his laziness.
(a) fed up in (b) fed off
(c) feeds up of (d) fed up of
(e) No correction required

28. She was just looking outside the window when a beautiful bird **caught the eye.**
(a) catch the eye (b) eye catching
(c) caught her eye (d) catch her eyes
(e) No correction required

29. They **sent out** the invitations last evening.
(a) send out (b) sending out
(c) sent at (d) sending in
(e) No correction required

30. He had to **bear the brunt** of his father's mistakes.

(a) bear the burnt (b) bear the bums
(c) bear a brunt (d) bear and burn
(e) No correction required

Directions to Questions 31 to 40

In the following passage there are blanks, each of which has been numbered. These numbers are printed below the passage, against each, five words are suggested, one of which fits the blank appropriately. Find out the appropriate word in each case.

Emperor Akbar was fond of **31** tricky questions to Birbal. One day he asked Birbal what he would **32** if he were given a choice between justice and a gold coin. "The gold coin," said Birbal. Akbar was **33** aback. He had known Birbal for many years and he knew that Birbal was a just person. Then how could he choose the gold coin. "You would prefer a gold coin to justice?" he asked, incredulously. "Yes," said Birbal. The other courtiers were amazed by Birbal's **34** of idiocy. For years they had been trying to discredit Birbal in the emperor's eyes but without success and now the man had gone and **35** it himself. They could not believe their good fortune. "I would have been dismayed if even the lowliest of my servants had said this," continued the emperor. "But coming from you it's shocking— and sad. I did not **36** you were so debased! I never expected this from you. How could you be so shallow?"

"One **37** for what one does not have, Your Majesty!" said Birbal, quietly. "You have **38** to it that in our country justice is available to everybody. So as justice is already available to me and as I'm always **39** of money I said I would choose the gold coin." The emperor laughed. He thought to himself, 'I should have known that Birbal would come up with a witty reply as always'. He was so pleased with Birbal's reply that he gave him **40** one but a thousand gold coins.

31. (a) showing (b) asking (c) naming (d) finding (e) telling

32. (a) look (b) said (c) think (d) choose (e) find

33. (a) pushed (b) fallen (c) pulled (d) sent (e) taken

34. (a) idea (b) display (c) reply (d) place (e) showing

35. (a) speak (b) thought (c) done (d) create (e) told

36. (a) felt (b) said (c) know (d) accept (e) saw

37. (a) asks (b) chooses (c) look (d) find (e) wish

38. (a) sure (b) put (c) shown (d) seen (e) made

39. (a) no (b) rich (c) short (d) poor (e) plenty

40. (a) but (b) not (c) and (d) so (e) only

ANSWER KEY

State Bank of India PO Examination, 2005

1. (b)	2. (d)	3. (a)	4. (e)	5. (c)
6. (b)	7. (b)	8. (c)	9. (d)	10. (a)
11. (c)	12. (a)	13. (b)	14. (e)	15. (b)
16. (a)	17. (b)	18. (e)	19. (c)	20. (d)
21. (a)	22. (d)	23. (e)	24. (a)	25. (c)
26. (b)	27. (b)	28. (c)	29. (b)	30. (e)
31. (a)	32. (d)	33. (c)	34. (b)	35. (d)
36. (d)	37. (e)	38. (a)	39. (b)	40. (c)
41. (b)	42. (b)	43. (d)	44. (a)	45. (b)
46. (a)	47. (b)	48. (d)	49. (e)	50. (c)

State Bank of India PO Examination, April 2008

1. (e)	2. (b)	3. (e)	4. (c)	5. (b)
6. (d)	7. (b)	8. (a)	9. (c)	10. (a)
11. (a)	12. (c)	13. (a)	14. (e)	15. (b)
16. (c)	17. (b)	18. (e)	19. (d)	20. (a)
21. (e)	22. (a)	23. (c)	24. (d)	25. (b)
26. (d)	27. (d)	28. (e)	29. (a)	30. (c)
31. (b)	32. (d)	33. (a)	34. (d)	35. (e)
36. (e)	37. (d)	38. (a)	39. (c)	40. (c)
41. (a)	42. (a)	43. (d)	44. (e)	45. (c)
46. (e)	47. (a)	48. (b)	49. (c)	50. (b)

State Bank of India PO Examination, March 2010

1. (d)	2. (c)	3. (e)	4. (c)	5. (d)
6. (e)	7. (e)	8. (e)	9. (b)	10. (a)
11. (a)	12. (a)	13. (e)	14. (d)	15. (b)
16. (c)	17. (a)	18. (b)	19. (e)	20. (d)
21. (c)	22. (d)	23. (b)	24. (b)	25. (a)
26. (b)	27. (a)	28. (c)	29. (d)	30. (e)
31. (d)	32. (b)	33. (e)	34. (a)	35. (e)
36. (c)	37. (a)	38. (d)	39. (a)	40. (e)
41. (b)	42. (d)	43. (c)	44. (c)	45. (a)
46. (b)	47. (d)	48. (c)	49. (c)	50. (d)

State Bank of India PO Examination, March 2013

1. (e)	2. (d)	3. (a)	4. (e)	5. (e)
6. (c)	7. (b)	8. (e)	9. (d)	10. (e)
11. (d)	12. (a)	13. (b)	14. (a)	15. (e)
16. (e)	17. (d)	18. (b)	19. (a)	20. (d)
21. (c)	22. (d)	23. (b)	24. (b)	25. (c)

26. (e) 27. (b) 28. (d) 29. (a) 30. (e)
31. (b) 32. (c) 33. (a) 34. (b) 35. (e)
36. (b) 37. (a) 38. (e) 39. (b) 40. (c)
41. (c) 42. (e) 43. (d) 44. (b) 45. (d)
46. (c) 47. (d) 48. (b) 49. (d) 50. (b)

State Bank of India, Clerk Written Examination, 2012

1. (a) 2. (a) 3. (a) 4. (b) 5. (d)
6. (d) 7. (d) 8. (a) 9. (b) 10. (d)
11. (b) 12. (d) 13. (a) 14. (d) 15. (c)
16. (b) 17. (a) 18. (e) 19. (b) 20. (e)
21. (e) 22. (a) 23. (b) 24. (b) 25. (c)
26. (c) 27. (d) 28. (e) 29. (e) 30. (b)
31. (b) 32. (d) 33. (c) 34. (c) 35. (e)
36. (c) 37. (b) 38. (a) 39. (c) 40. (b)

FREQUENCY ANALYSIS

ABBREVIATIONS USED

Comprehension / **Comp**, Sentence Completion / **SC**, Sentence Filler / **SF**, Cloze Test/ **CT**, Synonyms/ **Syn**, Antonyms/ **Ant**, Idioms and Phrase/ **IP**, Substitution/ **Subt**, Sentence arrangement/ **SA**, Spelling/ **SPL**, Miscellaneous/**Misc**., Total Marks/**TM**, Sentence error/**SE**, Sentence Improvement/ **SI**.

State Bank of India PO Examination, 2005

	Comp.	SC	SF	CT	Syn	Ant	IP	Subt	SA	SE	SPL	SI	MISC.	TM
	9	5		10	3	3			5			15		50

State Bank of India PO Examination, April 2008

	Comp.	SC	SF	CT	Syn	Ant	IP	Subt	SA	SE	SPL	SI	MISC.	TM
	10			15					5	5	5+5	5		50

State Bank of India PO Examination, March 2010

	Comp.	SC	SF	CT	Syn	Ant	IP	Subt	SA	SE	SPL	SI	MISC.	TM
	6+5	5	5	10	2	2			5				vocs 5/5	10

State Bank of India PO Examination, March 2013

	Comp.	SC	SF	CT	Syn	Ant	IP	Subt	SA	SE	SPL	SI	MISC.	TM
	9			5+10	3	3			5	10			5	50

State Bank of India, Clerk, 2012

	Comp.	SC	SF	CT	Syn	Ant	IP	Subt	SA	SE	SPL	SI	MISC.	TM
	10	5		10	3	2				5		5		40

TREND ANALYSIS

If we look at the question papers of SBI PO 2005, 2008, 2010 and 2013, we find that there is a tendency of variation of items on which questions have been asked. The common items are **comprehension, cloze test** and **sentence arrangment**.

On other items questions have been asked in different years. All these items are covered by the chapters of the book.

There are questions on spelling and sentence fillers also. Thus, it appears that the attitude of the paper setters has been to make some changes from previous years' questions. This is almost similar to the pattern of R B I Examination. The difficulty level is above moderate and slightly tough. The same pattern in expected in forthcoming exams as well. It has been ensured that all these questions types are covered by different units of the book.

IBPS Common Written Examination Papers

PAPER 10

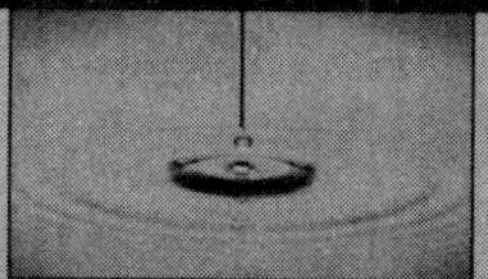

IBPS Common Written Examination for PO, MT and Specialist Officers, 2011

Directions to Questions 1 to 15

Read the following passage carefully and answer the questions given below it. Certain words have been printed in bold to help you locate them while answering some of the questions.

When wealth came into existence, a moral structure was made around money. The Puritan legacy inhibited luxury and self-indulgence. Thoughtful people spread a practical gospel that emphasized hard work, temperance and frugality and the result was quite remarkable.

The world has been affluent since its founding. But it was, by and large, not corrupted by wealth. For centuries, it remained industrious, ambitious and frugal. Over the past 30 years, much of that has been shredded. The social norms and institutions that encouraged frugality and spending what you earn have been undermined. The institutions that encourage debt and living for the moment have been strengthened.. The moral guardians are forever looking for decadence out of movies and reality shows. But the most rampant decadence today is financial decadence, the trampling of decent norms about how to use and harness money.

The deterioration of financial traditions has meant two things. First, it has meant an **explosion** of debt that inhibits social mobility and ruins lives. Second, **the transformation has led to a stark financial polarization**. On one hand, there is what is called an investor class. It has tax-deferred savings plans, as well as an army of financial advisers. On the other hand, there is the lottery class, people with little access to financial planning but plenty of access to payday lenders, credit cards and lottery agents.

The loosening of financial inhibition has meant more options for the well-educated but more temptation and chaos for the most vulnerable. Social norms, the invisible threads that guide behaviour, have deteriorated. Over the past years, people have been more socially conscious about protecting the environment and inhaling tobacco. They have become less socially conscious about money and debt.

The agents of destruction are many and State governments have also played a role. They hawk their lottery products with **aggression**, which some people call a tax on stupidity. Twenty per cent of the world's population consists of frequent players, spending about $60 billion a year. Aside from the financial toll, the moral toll is **comprehensive**. Here is the government, the guardian of order, telling people that they don't have to work to build for the future. They can strike it rich for nothing. Payday lenders have also played a role. They seductively offer fast cash-at **absurd** interest rates - to 15 million people every month. Credit card companies have played a role. Instead of targeting the financially astute, who pay off their debts, they have found that they can make money off the young and vulnerable. Fifty-six per cent of students in their final year of college carry four or more credit cards. The nation's leaders have played a role as they have always had an incentive to shove costs for current promises onto the backs of future generations. It has only now become respectable to do so. The market itself has played a role. Software stalwarts built socially useful products to make their fortune. But what message do the salary packages that their top managers get send across the country when they ignore millions of fellow countrymen who suffer from poverty, malnutrition or hunger? Austerity has become a thing of the past.

The list could go on. But there could be some recommendations. First, raise public consciousness about debt the way the anti-smoking activists did with their campaign. Second, create institutions that encourage **thrift**. Foundations and religious institutions could issue short-term loans to cut into the payday lenders' business. Colleges could reduce credit card advertising on campus. The tax code should tax consumption not income.

But the most important thing is to shift values. The 'wise' made it prestigious to embrace certain middle class virtues. Now it's socially acceptable to undermine those virtues. It is considered normal to play the debt game and imagine that decisions made today will have no consequences in the future.

1. What does the author mean by the phrase **'the transformation has led to a stark financial polarization'** as used in the passage?
   (a) The deterioration of social norms has benefited only the wealthy and the knowledgeable while the vulnerable class of people has fallen into a debt trap
   (b) Since moral inhibitions no longer exist, the debt agents provide loans only to the affluent class thus widening the gap between the rich and the poor
   (c) The debt culture is being utilized as a measure to draw money from the wealthy class by credit card companies
   (d) Both (a) and (b)
   (e) None of these

2. Which of the following is **true** in context of the passage?
   (a) Ever since its existence, money has ruined lives owing to lack of awareness among people regarding its unrestricted usage
   (b) Government has taken many initiatives to control the rampant money lending business to protect vulnerable sections of the society.
   (c) Governments throughout the world have been putting tax on amount of consumption of an individual rather than his/ her income
   (d) Credit card companies are discreet enough to provide credit cards to only those people who guarantee repaying money in the future
   (e) None is true

3. Which of the following can be the most appropriate title for the given passage?
   (a) The debt culture and government initiatives to curtail it
   (b) Breaking social barriers-taking the route of financial indulgence
   (c) Accumulation of debt—a lesson for the future generations
   (d) Effect of 'consumerism' on the world market
   (e) Lack of perseverance for saving money in India

4. Which of the following, according to the author, has/have been responsible for the encouragement of culture of debt in the society lately?
   (A) The changing lifestyle which makes it impossible for a common man to sustain himself without debts and loans.
   (B) Breaking down of moral institutions which supported economic prudence.
   (C) Provision for easy availability of loans to every section of the society regardless of their ability to repay these.
   (a) Only A (b) Only B
   (c) Both A and C (d) Both B and C
   (e) None of these

5. The author of the given passage seems to be definitely ______

(a) suggesting that the agents of debts be banned from the society.
(b) unaware of the benefits associated with the easy availability of loans these days
(c) in favour of bringing back the financial restrictions once imposed by the society
(d) not supportive of campaigns related to anti-tobacco and saving the environment.
(e) None of these

6. Why does the author of the given passage seem to be displeased with the software stalwarts?
(a) They make fortune out of the products which are barely socially useful
(b) They have been drawing colossal salaries and turn a blind eye towards the needs of fellow countrymen
(c) They are directly responsible for the hunger, malnutrition and poverty among their fellow countrymen
(d) They have promoted the culture of debt among various sections of society
(e) None of these

7. Which of the following suggestions have been made by the author in order to check the culture promoting debts?
(a) Putting a ban on the companies providing credit cards indiscriminately.
(b) Taking the help of informal institutions to limit the business of money lending by payday lenders.
(c) Raising public awareness about negative effects of injudicious borrowing of money.
(d) Taking action against governments which have been allowing lottery in their States.
(a) Only A and C
(b) Only D
(c) Only C and D
(d) Only B and C
(e) None of these

8. Which of the following statements would weaken the argument of made by the author in the given paragraph?
(a) A newspaper article reported an improvement in the lifestyle of millions of people after loans were made easy to avail to not only the wealthy but to all sections of society
(b) A man along with his family was forced to live on streets after he lost all of his life's earning to buy lottery tickets
(c) Profit earned from credit card companies has become an essential component in the economy of a growing nation
(d) Last year's recession was mainly due to losses incurred by companies offering loans as a large number of their clients turned out to be defaulters
(e) None of these

9. Which one of the phrases given below the following statement should be placed in the blank space provided so as to make a meaningfully correct sentence in the context of the passage?

__________many State governments have been encouraging people to invest their money in lottery.
(a) Despite the fact that lottery generates substantial revenue
(b) Since it has the potential to ruin lives of millions of people
(c) Instead of educating people against risky financial indulgence
(d) Since only one-fifth of the total world's population invests frequently in lottery
(e) None of these

Directions to Questions 10 to 12

Choose the word/group of words which is most similar in meaning to the word/phrase printed in bold as used in the passage.

10. THRIFT
(a) Compassion (b) Prudence
(c) Pleasure (d) Acceptance
(e) Frugality

11. STRIKE IT
(a) Smash (b) Reveal
(c) Register (d) Assume
(e) Become

12. AGGRESSION
(a) Violence (b) Hostility
(c) Offensively (d) Determination
(e) Belligerence

Directions to Questions 13 to 15

Choose the word/phrase which is most opposite in meaning to the word printed in bold as used in the passage.

13. EXPLOSION
(a) Deflation (b) Split
(c) Reduction (d) Simplification
(e) Alteration

14. ABSURD
(a) Expensive (b) Diplomatic
(c) Consistent (d) Invariable
(e) Reasonable

15. COMPREHENSIVE
(a) Insignificant (b) Massive
(c) Incomplete (d) Abundant
(e) Inappropriate

Directions to Questions 16 to 25

Read each sentence to find out whether there is any grammatical error in it. The error if any will be in one part of the sentence, the number of that part will be the answer. If there is 'No error', mark (e) as the answer. (Ignore errors of punctuation, if any.)

16. Angered over the delay in giving compensation, (a) / factory workers shouted (b)/ slogans against the president (c)/ when he reaches the office. (d) / No error (e)

17. The cascading effect of economic slowdown (a)/ has brought a much unnerving gloom (b) / to the real estate industry last year (c)/ but the industry is looking up this year. (d)/ No error (e)

18. A recycling plant in close proximity to (a)/ the residential area can pose (b)/ serious threats from residents (c)/ by leaving behind persistent pollutants. (d)/ No error (e)

19. The government has the obligation (a)/ to provide basic infrastructure facilities (b)/ to regulating the process of (c)/ urbanization in the country. (d)/ No error (e)

20. Bharatpur is transforming into (a) / India's most fastest growing bird sanctuary (b)/ attracting thousands of rare migratory birds (c) / from Europe and Siberia. (d)/No error (e)

21. Plagued by huge losses, (a)/ full service airlines are struggling (b) to cope with the competition (c)/ from low cost airlines. (d)/ No error (e)

22. Volunteers of an NGO (a)/ interacted with school students (b)/ to spread awareness about (c)/ environment related issues. (d)/ No error (e)

23. The Union health minister said that (a)/ there was an acute shortage of (b)/ health personnel in rural areas (c)/ who needed to be addressed urgently. (d)/ No error (e)

24. Even though most of India's youth (a)/ lives in villages, many people considers (b)/ the ones roaming in dazzling multiplexes (c)/ as their true reflection. (d)/ No error (e)

25. The RBI has proposed to introduce (a)/ polymer notes after taking into considering (b)/ the cost and longevity (c)/ associated with their manufacturing. (d)/ No error (e)

Directions to Questions 26 to 30

Which of the phrases (a), (b), (c) and (d) given below each statement should replace the phrase printed in bold in the sentence to make it grammatically correct? If the sentence is correct as it is given and 'No correction is required,' mark (e) as the answer.

26. A twenty-first century economy **cannot be held** hostage by power cuts nor travel on nineteenth century roads.
(a) cannot be hold
(b) can either be held
(c) can neither be held
(d) can either be hold
(e) No correction required

27. The company's philosophy is to make sure that the employees are happy, have the ability to be intellectually stimulated and **contributes towards their growth.**

(a) contribute to their growth
(b) contribute towards its growth
(c) contributes towards its growing
(d) contribute to its growing
(e) No correction required

28. Even though many companies are now penetrating rural India, it would help to give India a real chance of witnessing a double digit GDP growth.

(a) Despite many companies are
(b) As many company is
(c) Besides many companies are
(d) Since many companies are
(e) No correction required

29. Today, governments are introducing more and more technology into their system to address the needs of citizens at a pace **fast than that of** manual operations.

(a) faster than that of
(b) faster than those for
(c) fast than that for
(d) more than that in
(e) No correction required

30. Making good school education a reality **would require major changes** in existing school system with expansion at both secondary and elementary levels.

(a) should requires major changes
(b) would requires major change
(c) must require some changes
(d) require major changes
(e) No correction required

Directions to Questions 31 to 35

Rearrange the following sentences (A), (B), (C), (D), (E) and (F) to make a meaningful paragraph and then answer the questions which follow:

(A) In fact according to mainstream economists it is inevitable and a necessary evil in any economy.

(B) It is thus important for ever nation to maintain this reserve of labour force to maintain an optimal level of unemployment.

(C) Unemployment is popularly believed to be an index which measures the economic condition of a nation.

(D) This is because it helps avert inflation by providing a reserve army of labour which keeps wages in check.

(E) The problem, however, only emerges when governments indirectly facilitate unemployment in order to curb inflation through various policies and frameworks, depriving a large population of its fundamental rights.

(F) But contrary to popular belief unemployment is not always disadvantageous to the economy of a state.

31. Which of the following sentences should be the **SIXTH (LAST)** after rearrangement?

(a) A (b) B
(c) C (d) E
(e) F

32. Which of the following sentences a/ should be the **FIRST** after rear-fhv rangement?

(a) A (b) B
(c) C (d) D
(e) E

33. Which of the following sentences should be the **FIFTH** after rearrangement?

(a) A (b) B
(c) C (d) E
(e) F

34. Which of the following sentences should be the **SECOND** after rearrangement?

(a) A (b) B
(c) D (d) E
(e) F

35. Which of the following sentences should be the **THIRD** after rearrangement?

(a) A (b) E
(c) D (d) F
(e) C

Directions to Questions 36 to 45

In the following passage there are blanks, each of which has been numbered. These numbers are printed below the passage and against each, five words/phrases are suggested, one of which fits the blank appropriately. Find out the appropriate word/phrase in each case.

The world is going 36 a deep recession. At such a time, one thing we need in abundance is jobs for the semi-skilled and unskilled. This is the only way in which equal 37 of wealth can take place. The healthcare industry is 38 poised to occupy this position. The IT industry hires people from the upper-middle strata and rich families, usually engineers, 39 the healthcare industry hires nurses to the tune of eighty percent of jobs created, from the lower economic strata.

Global healthcare is a $ 4.5 trillion industry, 40 only to the agro industry. Even then healthcare 41 only eight percent of world's population. Policymakers should 42 at healthcare industry as not only an industry which addresses pain but also as one which can 43 the economy. The last century was driven by machines that addressed human toil and it is strongly 44 that this century will be driven by healthcare. This, however, will only happen if policymakers make a conscious effort to 45 the right policies in place soon.

36. (a) past (b) against (c) through (d) across (e) on
37. (a) earning (b) share (c) venture (d) delivery (e) distribution
38. (a) commonly (b) ideally (c) indefinitely (d) preferably (e) invariably
39. (a) whereas (b) unlike (c) besides (d) although (e) despite
40. (a) encouraging (b) second (c) lesser (d) beating (e) greater
41. (a) affords (b) cures (c) visits (d) reaches (e) provides
42. (a) look (b) plan (c) weigh (d) admire (e) consider
43. (a) persuade (b) ascertain (c) influence (d) impede (e) estimate
44. (a) thought (b) credited (c) identified (d) believed (e) supposed
45. (a) derive (b) frame (c) figure (d) consider (e) put

Directions to Questions 46 to 50

Each question below has two blanks, each blank indicating that something been omitted. Choose the set of words for each blank that best fits the meaning of the sentence as a whole.

46. Centre should ______ ministries whose functions ________ with the state ministries to save money, deliver efficiency and avoid duplication of work.
    (a) finish, differ
    (b) establish, contradict
    (c) constitute, matches
    (d) abolish, overlap
    (e) block, vary
47. Many people _____ genetically modified food but the reality that all the food that we eat has been genetically modified naturally by thousands of years of
    (a) praise, manipulation
    (b) grow, mismanagement
    (c) criticize, farming
    (d) avoid, experience
    (e) condemn, abuse
48. Given that only seven percent of the country's labour force is in the organised sector, training

options ______ for the unorganized sectors should also be

(a) available, enhanced
(b) absent, improved
(c) lacking, sustained
(d) existing, restricted
(e) offered, limited

49. Government initiatives and participation of many industrial houses in ______ loans to the villagers have led to the ______ of the farmers.

(a) providing, plight
(b) disbursing, betterment
(c) denying, revitalization
(d) subsidizing, suffering
(e) taking, advancement

50. Indians will ______ one-fourth of total work force in the next five years but India needs to introspect whether its education system is ______ for these demographic dividends.

(a) become, adequate
(b) consist, incompetent
(c) constitute, unequipped
(d) represent, sound
(e) comprise, prepared

PAPER 11

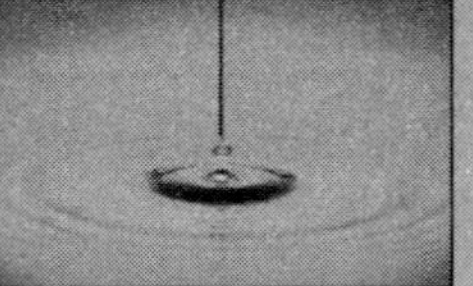

IBPS COMMON WRITTEN EXAMINATION FOR PO, MT

Directions to Questions 1 to 15

Read the following passage carefully and answer the questions given below It. Certain words/phrases have been printed in bold to help you locate them while answering some of the questions.

When times are hard, doomsayers are aplenty. The problem is that if you listen to them too carefully, you tend to overlook the most obvious signs of change. 2011 was a bad year. Can 2012 be any worse? Doomsday forecasts are the easiest to make these days. So let's try a contrarian's forecast instead.

Let's start with the global economy. We have seen a steady flow of good news from the US. The employment situation seems to be improving rapidly and consumer sentiment, reflected in retail expenditures on discretionary items like electronics and clothes, has picked up. If these trends sustain, the US might post better growth numbers for 2012 than the 1.5-1.8 per cent being forecast currently.

Japan is likely to pull out of a recession in 2012 as post-earthquake reconstruction efforts gather momentum and toe fiscal stimulus announced in 2011 begins to pay off. The consensus estimate for growth in Japan is a respectable 2 per cent for 2012.

The 'hard-landing' scenario for China remains and will remain a myth. Growth might decelerate further from the 9 per cent that it expected to clock in 2011 but is unlikely to drop below 8-8.5 per cent in 2012.

Europe is certainly in a spot of trouble. It is perhaps already in recession and for 2012 it is likely to post mildly negative growth. The risk of implosion has dwindled over the last few months — peripheral economies like Greece, Italy and Spain have new governments in place and have made progress towards genuine economic reform.

Even with some of these positive factors in place, we have to accept the fact that global growth in 2012 will be **tepid**. But there is a flipside to this. Softer growth means lower demand for commodities and this is likely to drive a correction in commodity prices. Lower commodity inflation will enable emerging market central banks to reverse their monetary stance. China, for instance, has already reversed its stance and has pared its reserve ratio twice. The RBI also seems poised for a reversal in its rate cycle as headline inflation seems well on its way to its target of 7 per cent for March 2012.

That said, oil might be an exception to the general trend in commodities. Rising geopolitical tensions, particularly the continuing face-off between Iran and the US, might lead to a spurt in prices. It might make sense for our oil companies to hedge this risk instead of buying oil in the spot market.

As inflation fears **abate** and emerging market central banks begin to cut rates, two things could happen. Lower commodity inflation would mean lower interest rates and better credit availability. This could set a floor to growth and slowly reverse the business cycle within these economies. Second, as the fear of untamed, runaway inflation in these economies abates, the global investor's comfort levels with their markets will increase.

Which of the **emerging** markets will outperform and who will get left behind? In an environment in which global growth is likely to be weak, economies like India that have a powerful domestic consumption dynamic should lead; those dependent on exports should, prima facie, fall behind. Specifically for Inda, a fall in the exchange rate could not have come at a better time. It will help Indian exporters gain market share even if global trade remains depressed. More importantly, it could lead to massive import substitution that favours domestic producers.

Let's now focus on India and start with a caveat. It is important not to confuse a short-run cyclical dip with a permanent de-rating of its long-term structural potential. The arithmetic is simple. Our growth rate can be in the range of 7-10 per cent depending on policy action. Ten per cent if we get everything right, 7 per cent if we get it all wrong. Which policies and reforms are critical to taking us to our 10 per cent potential? In judging this, lets again be careful. Lets not go by the laundry list of reforms that FlIs like to wave: increase in foreign equity limits in foreign shareholding, greater voting rights for institutional shareholders in banks, FDI in retail, etc. These can have an impact only at the margin. We need not bend over backwards to appease the FlIs through these reforms - they will invest in our markets when momentum picks up and will be the first to exit when the momentum flags, reforms or not.

The reforms that we need are the ones that can actually raise out sustainable long-term growth rate. These have to come in areas tike better targeting of subsidies, making projects in infrastructure viable so that they draw capital, raising the productivity of agriculture, improving healthcare and education, bringing the parallel economy under the tax net, Implementing fundamental reforms in taxation like GST and the direct tax code and finally easing the myriad rules and regulatios that make doing business in India such a nightmare. A number of these things do not require new legislation and can be done through executive order.

1. Which of the following is **NOT TRUE** according to the passage?
   (a) China's economic growth may decline in the year 2012 as compared to the year 2011
   (b) The European economy is not doing very well
   (c) Greece is on the verge of bringing about economic reforms
   (d) In the year 2012, Japan may post a positive growth and thus pull out of recession
   (e) All are true

2. Which of the following will possibly be a result of softer growth estimated for the year 2012?
   (A) Prices of oil will not increase.
   (B) Credit availability would be lesser.
   (C) Commodity inflation would be lesser.
   (a) Only (B)
   (b) Only (A) and (B)
   (c) Only (A) and (C)
   (d) Only (C)
   (e All (A), (B) and (C)

3. Which of the following can be said about the present status of the US economy?
   (a) There is not much improvement in the economic scenario of the country from the year 2011
   (b) The growth in the economy of the country, in the year 2012, would definitely be lesser than 1.8 percent
   (c) The expenditure on clothes and electronic commodities, by consumers, is lesser than that in the year 2011
   (d) There is a chance that in 2012 the economy would do better than what has been forecast
   (e) The pace of change in the employment scenario of the country is very slow.

4. Which of the following is possibly the most appropriate title for the passage?
   (a) The Economic Disorder
   (b) Indian Economy Versus The European Economy
   (c) Global Trade
   (d) The Current Economic Scenario
   (e) Characteristics Of The Indian Economy

5. According to the author, which of the following would characterise Indian growth scenario in 2012?
   (A) Domestic producers will take a hit because of depressed global trade scenario.
   (B) On account of its high domestic consumption, India will lead
   (C) Indian exporters will have a hard time in gaining market share.
   (a) Only (B)
   (b) Only (A) and (B)
   (c) Only (B) and (C)
   (d) Only (A)
   (e) All (A), (B) and (C)

6. Why does the author not recommend taking up the reforms suggested by FIls?
   (a) These will bring about only minor growth
   (b) The reforms suggested will have no effect on the economy of our country, whereas will benefit the FIls significantly
   (c) The previous such recommendations had backfired
   (d) These reforms will be the sole reason for our country's economic downfall
   (e) The reforms suggested by them are not to be trusted as they will not bring about any positive growth in India

7. Which of the following is **TRUE** as per the scenario presented in the passage?
   (a) The highest growth rate that India can expect is 7 percent
   (b) The fall in the exchange rate will prove beneficial to India
   (c) Increased FDI in retail as suggested by FIls would benefit India tremendously
   (d) The reforms suggested by the author require new legislation in India
   (e) None is true

8. According to the author, which of the following reform/s is/are needed to ensure long term growth in India?
   (A) Improving healthcare and educational facilities.
   (B) Bringing about reforms in taxation.
   (C) Improving agricultural productivity.
   (a) Only (B)
   (b) Only (A) and (B)
   (c) Only (B) and (C)
   (d) Only (A)
   (e) All (A), (B) and (C)

Directions to Questions 9 to 12

Choose the word/group of words which is most similar in meaning to the word/ group of words printed in bold as used in the passage.

9. DRAW
   (a) entice (b) push
   (c) decoy (d) attract
   (e) persuade

10. CLOCK
   (a) watch (b) achieve
   (c) time (d) second
   (e) regulate

11. ABATE
   (a) rise (b) gear
   (c) hurl (d) lessen
   (e) retreat

12. EMERGING
   (a) raising (b) developing
   (c) noticeable (d) conspicuous
   (e) uproaring

Directions to Questions 13 to 15

Choose the word/group of words which is most opposite in meaning to the word/group of words printed in bold as used in the passage.

13. MYRIAD
(a) trivial (b) difficult
(c) few (d) effortless
(e) countless

14. TEPID
(a) moderate (b) high
(c) warm (d) irregular
(e) little

15. MYTH
(a) reality (b) belief
(c) contrast (d) idealism
(e) falsehood

Directions to Questions 16 to 20

Rearrange the following six sentences (A), (B), (C), (D), (E) and (F) in the proper sequence to form a meaningful paragraph; then answer the questions given below them.

(A) If China is the world's factory, India has become the world's outsourcing centre - keeping in line with this image.

(B) But India's future depends crucially on its ability to compete fully in the Creative Economy - not just in tech and software, but across design and entrepreneurship; arts, culture and entertainment; and the knowledge-based professions of medicine, finance and law.

(C) White its creative assets outstrip those of other emerging competitors, India must address several challenges to increase its international competitiveness as the world is in the midst of a sweeping transformation.

(D) This transformation is evident in the fact that the world is moving from an industrial economy to a Creative Economy that generates wealth by harnessing intellectual labour, intangible goods and human creative capabilities.

(E) Its software industry is the world's second-largest, its tech outsourcing accounts for more than half of the $ 300 billion global industry, according to a technology expert.

(F) If the meeting of world leaders at Davos is any indication, India is rapidly becoming an economic 'rock star'.

16. Which of the following should be the **SIXTH (LAST)** sentence after the rearrangement?
(a) A (b) B
(c) C (d) D
(e) E

17. Which of the following should be the **THIRD** sentence after the rearrangement?
(a) A (b) B
(c) C (d) D
(e) E

18. Which of the following should be the **FIFTH** sentence after the rearrangement?
(a) A (b) B
(c) C (d) F
(e) E

19. Which of the following should be the **FIRST** sentence after the rearrangement?
(a) F (b) B
(c) C (d) A
(e) E

20. Which of the following should be the **SECOND** sentence after the rearrangement?
(a) A (b) B
(c) C (d) D
(e) F

Directions to Questions 21 to 25

The following questions consist of a single sentence with one blank only. You are given six words denoted by A, B, C, D, E & F as answer choices and from the six choices you have to pick two correct answers, either of which will make the sentence meaningfully complete.

21. _____ before the clock struck 8 on Saturday night, India Gate was swamped with people wearing black tee-shirts and holding candles.
(A) Minutes (B) Time
(C) Later (D) Quickly
(E) Since (F) Seconds
(a) (B) and (E) (b) (A) and (C)
(c) (A) and (F) (d) (B) and (D)
(e) (C) and (E)

22. The States should take steps to _____ the process of teachers' appointments as the Centre has already sanctioned six lakh posts.
(A) fasten (B) move
(C) hasten (D) speed
(E) early (F) quicken
(a) (D) and (F) (b) (A) and (C)
(c) (C) and(F) (d) (D)and(E)
(e) (B) and (D)

23. A senior citizen's son ____threatened her every day and physically harmed her, forcing her to transfer her property to him.
(A) superficially (B) mistakenly
(C) allegedly (D) miserably
(E) doubtfully (F) purportedly
(a) (C) and(F) (b) (A) and(E)
(c) (C) and (E) (d) (D) and(F)
(e) (A) and(C)

24. Medical teachers said that the management had continued to remain______ to their cause leading to the stretching of their strike.
(A) unmoved (B) lethargic
(C) unconcerned (D) apathetic
(E) Indifferent (F) bored
(a) (B) and (C) (b) (C) and (F)
(c) (A) and (E) (d) (A) and (D)
(e) (D) and(E)

25. The parents had approached the high court to _____ the government order after their children, who passed UKG, were denied admission by a school.
(A) void (B) quash
(C) annul (D) stay
(E) lift (F) post
(a) (A) and (D) (b) (B) and (C)
(c) (C) and (E) (d) (E) and (F)
(e) (C) and(D)

Directions to Questions 26 to 35

Read each sentence to find out whether there is any grammatical error or idiomatic error in it. The error, if any, will be in one part of the sentence. The number of that part is the answer. If there is 'No error', the answer is '(e)'. (Ignore errors of punctuation, if any).

26. The Government has asked individuals (a) / with income of over Rs. 10 lakhs to (b) / electronic file tax returns for the year 2011 -12 (c) / something which was optional till last year (d) / No error (e)

27. The power tariff had already (a) / been increased twice in (b) / the last 15 months and the Electricity Board had also (c) / levied additional monthly charges to consumers (d) / No error / (e)

28. Despite of curfew (a) / in some areas, minor (b)/ communal incidents were reported (c) / from different areas of the walled city (d) / No error (e)

29. This comes (a) / at a time (b) / when fund allocation (c) / is been doubled (d) / No error (e)

30. As the prison will get (a) / an official telephone facility soon, the prisoners (b) / won't have to make calls in discreet manner (c) / through smuggled mobile phones (d) / No error (e)

31. The area was plunged into (a) / darkness mid a wave of (b) / cheering and shouting (c) / slogans like 'Save The Earth' (d) / No error (e)

32. The poll contestants approached (a) / the commission complaining that the hoardings (b) / violated the code of conduct (c) / and influenced public perception (d) / No error (e)

33. The country has (a) / adequate laws but problems (b) / arise when these are not (c) / implemented in letter and spirit (d) / No error / (e)

34. The Management feeds that / the employees of the organisation are (a) /non-productive, and do not want (b) / to work hard (d). No error / (e)

35. As far the issue of land encroachment (a) / in villages is concerned, people will (b)/ have to make a start from their villages by (c) / sensitising and educating the villagers about this issue (d) / No error / (e)

Directions to Questions 36 to 40

Which of the phrases (a), (b), (c) and (d) given below each sentence should replace the word/ phrase printed in bold in the sentence to make it grammatically correct? If the sentence is correct as it is given and no correction is required, mark (e) as the answer.

36. US secretary of state made it clear that time **running out** for diplomacy over Iran's nuclear programme and said that talks aimed at preventing Tehran from acquiring a nuclear weapon would resume in April.
(a) runs out
(b) was running out
(c) ran out
(d) run
(e) No correction required

37. While the war of the generals **rage on,** somewhere in small town India, wonderful things are happening, quietly and minus fanfare.
(a) rage
(b) raging
(c) rages on
(d) raged on
(e) No correction required

38. According to WWF, the small island nation of Samoa was **the first in switch off** its lights for Earth Hour.
(a) first to switch of
(b) the first to switch off
(c) the first of switch off
(d) first in switch of
(e) No correction required

39. The campaign is significant **because not just** the youths are directly appealing to the world but because their efforts challenge the chimera of normalcy in the area.
(a) not just because
(b) just not because
(c) not just
(d) because just
(e) No correction required

40. The doctor's association has threatened to go on indefinite strike **support of** their teachers,
(a) on supporting to
(b) to supporting
(c) for support
(d) in support of
(e) No correction required

Directions to Questions 41 to 50

In the following passage there are blanks, each of which has been numbered. These numbers are printed below the passage and against each, five words/phrases are suggested, one of which fits the blank appropriately. Find out the appropriate word/phrase in each case.

Greenhouse gases are **41** of the story when it conies to global warming. Changes to one part of the climate system can **42** additional changes to the way the planet absorbs or reflects energy. These secondary changes are **43** climate feedbacks, and they could more than double the amount of warming caused by carbon dioxid alone. The primary feedbacks are **44** to snow and ice, water vapour, clouds, and the carbon cycle.

Perhaps the most well **45** feedback comes from melting snow and ice in the Northern Hemisphere. Warming temperatures are already **46** a growing percentage of Arctic sea ice, exposing dark ocean water during then **47** sunlight of summer. Snow cover on land is also **48** in many areas. In the **49** of snow and ice, these areas go from having bright, sunlight-reflecting surfaces that cool the planet to having dark, sunlight-absorbing surfaces that **50** more energy into the Earth system and cause more warming.

41. (a) whole (b) part
(c) material (d) issue
(e) most

42. (a) raise (b) brings
(c) refer (d) stop
(e) cause

43. (a) sensed (b) called
(c) nothing (d) but
(e) term

44. (a) due (b) results
(c) reason (d) those
(e) because

45. (a) done (b) known
(c) ruled (d) bestowed
(e) said

46. (a) mastering (b) sending
(c) melting (d) calming
(e) increasing

47. (a) make-shift (b) ceasing
(c) troubled (d) perpetual
(e) absent

48. (a) dwindling (b) manufactured
(c) descending (d) generating
(e) supplied

49. (a) progress (b) reduced
(c) existence (d) midst
(e) absence

50. (a) repel (b) waft
(c) monitor (d) bring
(e) access

PAPER 12

IBPS Common Written Examination for PO, MT, 2013

Directions to Questions 1 to 10

Read the following passage carefully and answer the questions given below it. Certain words/phrases have been printed in bold to help you locate them while answering some of the questions.

Governments have traditionally equated economic progress with steel mills and cement factories. While urban centres thrive and city dwellers get rich, hundreds of millions of farmers remain mired in poverty. However, fears of food shortage, a rethinking of antipoverty priorities and the crushing recession in 2008 are causing a dramatic shift in world economic policy in favour of greater support for agriculture.

The last time when the world's farmers felt such love was in the 1970s. At that time, as food prices spiked, there was real concern that the world was facing a crisis in which the planet was simply unable to produce enough grain and meat for an expanding population. Government across the developing world and international aid organisations **plowed** investment into agriculture in the early 1970s, while technological breakthroughs, like high-yield strains of important food crops, boosted production. The result was the Green Revolution and food production exploded.

But the Green Revolution became a victim of its own success. Food prices plunged by some 60% by the late 1980s from their peak in the mid-1970s. Policy makers and aid workers turned their attention to the poor's other **pressing** needs, such as health care and education. Farming got **starved** of resources and investment. By 2004, aid directed at agriculture sank to 3.5% and "Agriculture lost its glitter". Also, as consumers in high-growth giants such as China and India became wealthier, they began eating more meat, so grain once used for human consumption got diverted to beef up livestock. By early 2008, panicked buying by importing countries and restrictions **slapped** on grain exports by some big producers helped drive prices upto heights not seen for three decades. Making matters worse, land and resources got reallocated to produce cash crops such as biofuels and the result was the voluminous reserves of grain **evaporated**. Protests broke out across the emerging world and fierce food riots toppled governments.

This spurred global leaders into action. This made them aware that food security is one of the fundamental issues in the world that has to be dealt with in order to maintain administrative and political stability. This also spurred the U.S. which traditionally provisioned food aid from American grain surpluses to help needy nations, to move towards investing in farm sectors around the globe to boost productivity. This move helped countries become more productive for themselves and be in a better position to feed their own people.

Africa, which missed out on the first Green Revolution due to poor policy and limited resources, also witnessed a 'change'. Swayed by the success of East Asia, the primary poverty-fighting method favoured by many policymakers in Africa was to get farmers off their farms and into modern jobs in factories and urban centres. But that strategy proved to be highly insufficient. Income levels in the countryside badly trailed those in cities while the FAO estimated that the number of poor going hungry in 2009 reached an all time high at more than one billion.

In India on the other hand, with only 40% of its farmland irrigated, entire economic boom currently underway is held hostage by the unpredictable monsoon. With much of India's farming areas suffering from drought this year, the government will have a tough time meeting its economic growth targets. In a report, Goldman Sachs predicted that if this year too receives weak rains, it could cause agriculture to contract by 2% this fiscal year, making the government's 7% GDP-growth target look **"a bit rich"**. Another green revolution is the need of the hour and to make it a reality, the global community still has much backbreaking farm work to do.

1. What is the author's main objective in writing the passage?
- (a) Criticising developed countries for not bolstering economic growth in poor nations
- (b) Analysing the disadvantages of the Green Revolution
- (c) Persuading experts that a strong economy depends on industrialisation and not agriculture
- (d) Making a case for the international society to engineer a second Green Revolution
- (e) Rationalising the faulty agriculture policies of emerging countries

2. Which of the following is an adverse impact of the Green Revolution?
- (a) Unchecked crop yields resulted in large tracts of land becoming barren
- (b) Withdrawal of fiscal impetus from agriculture to other sectors
- (c) Farmers began soliciting government subsidies for their produce
- (d) Farmers rioted as food prices fell so low that they could not make ends meet
- (e) None of these

3. What is the author trying to convey through the phrase "making the government's 7% GDP growth target look "a bit rich""?
- (a) Indian is unlikely to achieve the targeted growth rate
- (b) Allocation of funds to agriculture has raised India's chances of having a high GDP
- (c) Agricultural growth has artificially inflated India's GDP and such growth is not real
- (d) India is likely to have one of the highest GDP growth rates
- (e) A large portion of India's GDP is contributed by agriculture

4. Which of the following factors was/were responsible for the neglect of the farming sector after the green revolution?
- (A) Steel and cement sectors generated more revenue for the government as compared to agriculture.
- (B) Large scale protests against favouring agriculture at the cost of other important sectors such as education and health care.
- (C) Attention of policy makers and aid organisations was diverted from agriculture to other sectors.

- (a) None
- (b) Only (C)
- (c) Only (B) and (C)
- (d) Only (A) and (B)
- (e) All (A), (B) and (C)

5. Which of the following had contributed to exorbitant food prices in 2008?
- (A) Hoarding of food stocks by local wholesalers which inadvertently created a food shortage.

(B) Export of foodgrains was reduced by large producers.
(C) Diverting resources from cultivation of foodgrains to that of more profitable crops.

(a) None
(b) Only(C)
(c) Only (B)
(d) All (A), (B) and (C)
(e) Only (B) and (C)

6. Which of the following is true about the state of agriculture in India at present?

(A) Of all the sectors, agriculture needs the highest allocation of funds.
(B) Contribution of agriculture to India's GDP this year would depend greatly upon the monsoon rains.
(C) As India is one of the high-growth countries, it has surplus food reserves to export to other nations.

(a) Only (A) and (C)
(b) Only(C)
(c) Only (B)
(d) Only (B) and (C)
(e) None of these

Directions to Questions 7 to 8

Choose the word/group of words which is most similar in meaning to the word printed in bold as used in the passage.

7. SLAPPED

(a) Beaten (b) Imposed
(c) Withdrawn (d) Avoided
(e) Persuaded

8. PLOWED

(a) Cultivated (b) Bulldozed
(c) Recovered (d) Instilled
(e) Withdrew

Directions to Questions 9 to 10

Choose the word/phrase which is most opposite in meaning to the word printed in bold as used in the passage.

9. PRESSING

(a) Unpopular (b) Undemanding
(c) Unobtrusive (d) Unsuitable
(e) Unimportant

10. EVAPORATED

(a) Absorbed (b) Accelerated
(c) Grew (d) Plunged
(e) Mismanaged.

Directions to Questions 11 to 15

Which of the phrases (a), (b), (c) and (d) given below each statement should be placed in the blank space provided so as to make a meaningful and grammatically correct sentence? If none of the sentences is appropriate, mark (e) i.e. 'None of these' as the answer.

11. Refuting the rationale behind frequent agitations for formation of separate States, a recent report____.

(a) proved that such agitations result in loss of governmental property
(b) indicated that the formation of small states does not necessarily improve the economy
(c) suggested that only large scale agitations have been effective in bringing out desired change in the past
(d) recommended dividing large States into smaller ones to improve governance
(e) None of these

12. Overlooking the fact that water scarcity intensifies during summer____.

(a) the government issued guidelines to all builders to limit their consumption to acceptable limits
(b) provision for rainwater harvesting has been made to aid irrigation in drought prone area.
(c) the water table did not improve even after receiving normal monsoon in the current year
(d) Many residential areas continue to use swimming pools, wasting large quantities of water

(e) None of these

13. He has lost most of the life's earning in the stock market but____.
(a) he still seems to be leading his life luxuriously and extravagantly
(b) he could not save enough to repay his enormous debts
(c) stock market is not a safe option to invest money unless done with caution
(d) experts have been suggesting to avoid investments in stock market because of its unpredictable nature
(e) None of these

14. Achieving equality for women is not only a laudable goal,______
(a) political reforms are also neglected preventing women from entering leglsiatures and positions of power
(b) the problem is also deep rooted in the society and supported by it
(c) their empowerment is purposefully hampered by people with vested interests in all sections of the society
(d) it is also equally difficult to achieve and maintain for long term
(e) None of these

15. ______or else they would not keep electing him year after year.
(a) The party leader gave a strong message to the mayor for improving his political style
(b) Owing to numerous scandals against the mayor, he was told to resign from the post immediately
(c) The mayor threatened the residents against filing a complaint against him
(d) The residents must really be impressed with the political style of their mayor
(e) None of these

Directions to Questions 16 to 25

In the following passage there are blanks, each of which has been numbered. These numbers are printed below the passage and against each, five words/ phrases are suggested, one of which fits the blank appropriately. Find out the appropriate word/phrase in each case.

There is a considerable amount of research about the factors that make a company innovate. So is it possible to create an environment **16** to novation? This is a particularly pertinent **17** for India today. Massive problems in health, education etc. **18** be solved using a conventional approach but **19** creative and innovative solutions that can ensure radical change and **20**. There are several factors in India's **21** Few countries have the rich diversity that India or its large, young population **22**. While these **23** innovation policy interventions certain additional steps are also required. These include **24** investment in research and development by **25** the government and the private sector, easy transfer of technology from the academic world etc. To fulfill its promise of being prosperous and to be at the forefront, India must be innovative.

16. (a) stimuli (b) conducive (c) incentive (d) facilitated (e) impetus

17. (a) objective (b) controversy (c) doubt (d) question (e) inference

18. (a) cannot (b) possibly (c) should (d) never . (e) must

19. (a) necessary (b) apply (c) need (d) consider (e) requires?

20. (a) quantity (b) advantages (c) increase (d) chaos (e) growth

21. (a) challenges (b) praises (c) favour (d) leverage (e) esteem

22. (a) blessed (b) enjoys (c) endows (d) prevails (e) occurs

23. (a) aid (b) jeoparadise (c) promotes (d) endure (e) cater

24. (a) acute (b) utilising
(c) restricting (d) inspiring
(e) increased

25. (a) both (b) besides
(c) combining (d) participating
(e) also

Directions to Questions 26 to 30

Rearrange the following seven sentences (A), (B), (C), (D), (E), (F) and (G) in the proper sequence to; form, a meaningful paragraph; then answer the questions given below them.

(A) They have to, therefore, necessarily devise strategies for product differentiation and pricing, market segmentation and efficient portfolio management.

(B) There is a great need for the banks to fully exploit these sectors to achieve a win-win situation for both- the farm and non-farms sector units and the banks.

(C) The time has now come to consolidate on the gains of the past decades of nationalised banking.

(D) This means banks will no longer be operating in "seller's market".

(E) Undoubtedly, an untapped and vibrant market for commercial banking exists in the farm and non-farm sectors of rural economy,

(F) Then, and only then, could it be claimed that the nationalization has, at least to some extent, achieved the purpose of nationalization.

(G) The present era of financial liberalization and globalized banking would entail that banks equip themselves to face the rigours of a highly competitive financial market.

26. Which of the following should be the **SECOND** sentence after re arrangement?
(a) G (b) F
(c) E (d) D
(e) C

27. Which of the following should be the **THIRD** sentence after rearrangement?
(a) G (b) F
(c) A (d) D
(e) B

28. Which of the following should be the **FIFTH** sentence after rearrangement?
(a) G (b) F
(c) E (d) B
(e) D

29. Which of the following should be the **FIRST** sentence after rearrangement?
(a) G (b) F
(c) E (d) D
(e) C

30. Which of the following should .be the **SEVENTH** sentence after rearrangement
(a) G (b) F
(c) E (d) C
(e) D

Directions to Questions 31 to 35

In each question below, two sentences or parts of sentences are given with two blank space (___) (____) between them. From among the three parts/sentences denoted by (A), (B) and (C) given below each, find out which two can fill up the blanks in proper sequence (i.e. the order in which these are given in the answer options) to make the sentence/group of sentences meaningfully complete.

31. Four years ago, I had major surgery (____)(____). I was too ill.
(A) It left-me disabled,
(B) My attempts to go back to work could not succeed.
(C) I had. fully recovered except for some minor-weakness.
(a) (B) and (A), only
(b) (C) and (A) only
(c) (B) and (C) only
(d) (A) and (B) only
(e) (A) and (C) only

32. Based on scientific research, scientists conclude that (___) (____) they, will live even more, than a hundred years.

(A) keep themselves active all through
(B) exercise more, ensure proper vitamin intake.
(C) human species, if regulate their-diet,
(a) Only (A) and (B)
(b) Only (A) and (C)
(c) Only (C) and (A)
(d) Only (C) and (B)
(e) Either C and (A) or (C) and (B)

33. The Central Government's plans to (____) (____) despite the fact that the opposition parties united front had mobilized support of general public at the outskirts of Mumbai.
(A) defy, the curfew imposed to prevent the proposed rally from protesting against the hike in petrol prices
(B) curb the rally called for by the opposition succeeded due to ruling party's announcement to
(C) cancel all the trains entering Mumbai,
(a) (A) and (B) only
(b) (B) and (A) only
(c) (B) and (C) only
(d) (A) and (C) only
(e) Either (B) and (C) or (A) and (C)

34. The economic gloom was exacerbated yesterday by Greek Prime Minister's surprise announcement (________) (________), and vote might put the torturously conceived package in jeopardy.
(A) that was struck last week
(B) that-he would recommend the Parliament to strike down the obnoxious deal
(C) that his country would hold a referendum on the European debt deal
(a) (C) and (A) only
(b) (B) and (A) only
(c) (A) and (C) only
(d) Either (C) and (A) or (B) and (A)
(e) None of these

35. The world's most powerful nations were warned (___) (___) and trigger mass social unrest.
(A) that could cost millions of jobs around the globe
(B) that international economy was on the brink of a deep new economic crisis
(C) that the only solution was pumping a huge amount of money in the economy
(a) (C) and (A) only
(b) (B) and (A) only
(c) (B) and (C) only
(d) (C) arid (B) only
(e) None of these

Directions to Questions 36 to 40

Which of the phrases (a), (b), (c) and (d) given below should replace the phrase given in bold in the following sentence to make the sentence grammatically meaningful and correct. If the sentence is correct as it is and no correction is required, mark (e) as the answer,

36. Innovators create products **which is an outgrowing of what they imagine,** things that help them create a world they would like to live In.
(a) what is an outgrowing of what has been imagined by them
(b) which are an outgrowth of what they imagine
(c) which are outgrowing what they imagine
(d) which outgrew their imagination
(e) No correction required

37. The product-driven organization **has the product as the most important element in everything it does.**
(a) does everything to have the product's most important element
(b) does the most important things to have all elements of importance in its products
(c) had the product as the most important element in everything they do
(d) keeps the most important element in every product they do
(e) No correction required

38. He **had always have a full measure of a trait that is a mark of a successful leader: determination.**
(a) did always do a full measure of a trait
(b) had always did have a full measure of a trail
(c) had always have a fully measured traits
(d) has always had a full measure of a trait
(e) No correction required

39. Most of the people were dumbfounded and obviously uncomfortable **by the performance that was expected of them.**
(a) with the performance that they were expecting
(b) by the performance that they were expected with
(c) with the performance that was expected of them
(d) at the performance which had expectations of them
(e) No correction required

40. If he considered you **to be a bright, capable and made contribution** to his proposed project, he would listen to your criticizing him,
(a) are bright, capable and had made contribution to
(b) to be bright capable and making contribution to
(c) to be bright, capable and had been contributed for
(d) would have been bright, capable and contributing with
(e) No correction required.

ANSWER KEY

IBPS CWE for PO, MT, 2011

1. (d)	2. (d)	3. (b)	4. (b)	5. (c)
6. (b)	7. (d)	8. (c)	9. (c)	10. (e)
11. (e)	12. (d)	13. (c)	14. (d)	15. (c)
16. (d)	17. (b)	18. (c)	19. (c)	20. (b)
21. (e)	22. (c)	23. (d)	24. (b)	25. (c)
26. (c)	27. (b)	28. (d)	29. (a)	30. (e)
31. (d)	32. (c)	33. (b)	34. (e)	35. (a)
36. (c)	37. (e)	38. (b)	39. (a)	40. (b)
41. (d)	42. (a)	43. (c)	44. (d)	45. (e)
46. (d)	47. (c)	48. (a)	49. (b)	50. (e)

IBPS CWE for PO MT, 2012

1. (e)	2. (c)	3. (d)	4. (d)	5. (a)
6. (a)	7. (e)	8. (e)	9. (b)	10. (e)
11. (d)	12. (b)	13. (c)	14. (a)	15. (a)
16. (d)	17. (c)	18. (a)	19. (d)	20. (b)
21. (c)	22. (a)	23. (c)	24. (b)	25. (a)
26. (e)	27. (e)	28. (a)	29. (d)	30. (a)
31. (b)	32. (c)	33. (a)	34. (e)	35. (a)
36. (b)	37. (c)	38. (b)	39. (a)	40. (d)
41. (d)	42. (e)	43. (b)	44. (a)	45. (b)
46. (c)	47. (e)	48. (a)	49. (e)	50. (d)

IBPS CWE PO MT, 2013

1. (c)	2. (a)	3. (e)	4. (e)	5. (a)
6. (b)	7. (d)	8. (b)	9. (a)	10. (b)
11. (c)	12. (a)	13. (c)	14. (c)	15. (b)

16. (d) 17. (e) 18. (a) 19. (d) 20. (b)
21. (a) 22. (d) 23. (d) 24. (b) 25. (b)
26. (d) 27. (c) 28. (e) 29. (d) 30. (b)
31. (e) 32. (c) 33. (c) 34. (b) 35. (c)
36. (e) 37. (b) 38. (e) 39. (a) 40. (a)
41. (c) 42. (a) 43. (d) 44. (e) 45. (a)
46. (b) 47. (d) 48. (c) 49. (e) 50. (b)

FREQUENCY ANALYSIS

ABBREVIATIONS USED:

Comprehension / **Comp**, Sentence Completion / **SC**, Sentence Filler / **SF**, Cloze Test/ **CT**, Synonyms/ **Syn**, Antonyms/ **Ant**, Idioms and Phrase/ **IP**, Substitution/ **Subt**, Sentence arrangement/ **SA**, Spelling/ **SPL**, Miscellaneous/**Misc.**, Total Marks/**TM**, Sentence error/**SE**, Sentence Improvement/ **SI**.

IBPS Common Written Examination (CWE)–2011

	Comp.	SC	SF	CT	Syn	Ant	IP	Subt	SA	SE	SPL	SI	MISC.	TM
	9	5		10	3	3			5		10	5		

IBPS 2012 CWE for PO/MT

	Comp.	SC	SF	CT	Syn	Ant	IP	Subt	SA	SE	SPL	SI	MISC.	TM
	8	5		10	4	3			5			5		

IBPS CWE PO/MT, 2013

	Comp.	SC	SF	CT	Syn	Ant	IP	Subt	SA	SE	SPL	SI	MISC.	TM
	6	10	5	10	2	2			5			5	5 = SF	

TREND ANALYSIS

If we look at the question papers of CWE 2011, 2012 and 2013, we find that these have a pattern which is maintained throughout. All these years, questions have been set on **comprehension, synonyms, antonyms, sentence completion, sentence improvement, sentence arrangement**. However there has been a trend to give one new item different from the previous year.

In 2011 there was a question on spelling. In 2012 **sentence completion** has been given with a variation.

Therefore, it has to be kept in mind that questions from a new item different from the previous year will be set. But on the whole the pattern is almost fixed.

All units are carefully covered in this book. The level is above moderate and slightly tough.

The Insurance Sector offers lucrative and prestigious job opportunities. The Life Insurance Corporation (LIC) of India and General Insurance Corporation (GIC) are the key players in this field. Recently, private companies have also joined this sector in an aggressive way, giving new opportunities to aspirants.

LIC Officers' Examination

The LIC recruits clerks, development officers and Assistant Administrative Officers (AAOs). There are two channels through which the candidates can seek entry into the Indian insurance companies as AAOs:

- Through Competitive Examination
- Through promotion from Class II and Class III levels.

Anyone recruited as a direct AAO can hope to reach the highest level, according to the individual's performance levels.

GIC Officers' Examination

GIC Officers' Examination is a combined examination conducted for recruiting per the posts of Assistant Administrative Officer (AAOs—Generalist) in the establishments of General Insurance Corporation of India that are mentioned hereunder:

- National Insurance Company Ltd., Kolkata
- The New India Assurance Company Ltd., Mumbai
- The Oriental Fire and General Insurance Company Ltd., New Delhi
- United India Insurance Company Ltd.

The pattern and format of questions in different examinations conducted by LIC and GIC are common. Earlier there used to be emphasis on vocabulary. Gradually the pattern has moved to an almost even distribution of questions on vocabulary, applied grammar and comprehension. There have been little variations. The variations have been made among the basic units themselves.

Thus overall, general preparation will serve the purpose. The level of difficulty is moderate.

LIC AAO Exam Pattern

Life Insurance Corporation of India (LIC) is the largest Insurance Company in India having 2048 branches and

109 Divisional Offices). The details of Exam Pattern are mentioned here.

Online Test

On-line test will be of objective type, multiple choice of two hours duration comprising the following:

Section	Questions	Number of Questions	Marks	Time Hrs.
1	Reasoning Ability	30	90	120 minutes (2 Hours)
2	Numerical Ability	30	90	
3	General Knowledge, Current Affairs	30	60	
4	Computer Knowledge	30	60	
5	English Language with Special emphasis on Grammer, Vocabulary and Comprehension	40	100	
	Total	160	400	

Note: There is negative marking of ¼ marks for each wrong answer.

GIC Officers' Exam Pattern

This exam consists of the following steps in the selection process.

Step-I

Written Exam

This objective type examination consists of four tests, *viz.*

Subject	*No. of Questions*	*Time Allowed*
Test of Reasoning	50	2 hrs.
Test of English Language	50	2 hrs.
Test of Professional Knowledge	50	2 hrs.
Test of General Awareness	50	2 hrs.

Step-2

Group Discussion and Interview

Qualifying candidate will be called for group discussion and interview and the shortlisted candidates from Step-2 will be considered for final selection to the post of GIC's officers.

Test of English Language

This is a test to see how well you know the English language. English Language skills would be tested through questions on grammar, vocabulary, sentence compeetion, synonyms, antonayms, comprehension of a passage, etc.

LIC (AAO) Examination Papers

PAPER 13

LIC AAO EXAMINATION, 2005

Directions to Questions 1 to 15

Which of the phrases (a), (b), (c) and (d) given below should replace the phrase given in bold in the following sentence to make the sentence grammatically meaningful and correct? If the sentence is correct as it is and no correction is required, mark (e) as the answer.

1. **Had you been shown** your driving licence, the **humiliation** event would not have taken place.
   (a) If you had been shown
   (b) Had you showed
   (c) Had you been showing
   (d) Had you shown
   (e) No correction required

2. Don't enter the garden **unless the permission** of the competent authority.
   (a) with the permission
   (b) unless obtain permission
   (c) unless the permit
   (d) without the permission
   (e) No correction required

3. Admission **to any college in** that city is almost impossible, as the seats are reserved only for women.
   (a) in any college of
   (b) of any college into
   (c) for a college of
   (d) with any college in
   (e) No correction required

4. The wounded soldiers **didn't give of a fight** till they succeeded.
   (a) had not given of a fight
   (b) didn't give of a fighting
   (c) had not been given of a fight
   (d) didn't give up a fight
   (e) No correction required

5. Why you are so elated **is not known.**
   (a) was not know
   (b) is not knowing
   (c) was not knowing
   (d) is not knowledgeable
   (e) No correction required

Directions to Questions 6 to 10

Rearrange the following six sentences (A), (B), (C), (D), (E) and (F) in the proper sequence to form a meaningful paragraph; then answer the questions given below them.

(A) E-mail is a convenient way to deliver and request information

(B) Today instantaneous communication is vital.

(C) Voice is often easier than e-mail, but it is not as easy to create and send nor is it possible to send the same message to a large number of people in different places in the world.

(D) It is also a good way to communicate with multiple people at the same time; but e-mail is only one form of communication.

(E) Communication has been an important aspect all through the ages.

(F) The other forms of still faster and easier communication are being explored.

6. Which of the following should be the FOURTH sentence after rearrangement?
(a) A (b) B
(c) C (d) D
(e) E

7. Which of the following should be the FIFTH sentence after rearrangement?
(a) A (b) B
(c) C (d) D
(e) E

8. Which of the following should be the FIRST sentence after rearrangement?
(a) A (b) B
(c) C (d) D
(e) E

9. Which of the following should be the THIRD sentence after rearrangement?
(a) A (b) B
(c) C (d) D
(e) E

10. Which of the following should be the SECOND sentence after rearrangement?
(a) A (b) B
(c) C (d) D
(e) E

Directions to Questions 11 to 15

For each statement there are four different sentences given below it. Pick out the one that most appropriately conveys the meaning of the statement. The number of that sentence is the answer. If none of them conveys the meaning of the statement, the answer is (e) i.e. 'None'.

11. Although it is too late, I shall come.
(a) I shall come if it is too late.
(b) I shall not be able to come if it is too late.
(c) Even though I come, it will be too late.
(d) Whether or not it is too late, I shall come.
(e) None

12. The leader remarked that not all those punished were really innocent.
(a) The leader said that some of those punished were innocent while others were not
(b) The leader remarked that all those punished were not guilty.
(c) The leader remarked that all those punished cannot be necessarily innocent.
(d) The leader remarked that all those who are punished may include really innocent.
(e) None

13. Unlike the labourers who are hardworking, the white-collar employees cannot withstand physical strain.
(a) The labourers do not like to withstand physical strain as the white-collar employees do
(b) The white-collar employees are hardworking but they do not like to undertake physical strain
(c) The labourers can withstand physical strain whereas white-collar employees cannot
(d) Because the labourers are hardworking they can tolerate physical strain
(e) None

14. Should you need an entry pass, you must submit an application for the same.
    (a) Unless you do not submit an application, you will not get any entry pass.
    (b) You should require an entry pass in order to submit an application.
    (c) If you submit an application, you do not need an entry pass.
    (d) If you submit an application, you will get any entry pass.
    (e) None
15. The Manager would like you to help him locate the fault.
    (a) If you help him locate the default, the Manager would like you.
    (b) The Manager desires that you should provide him the necessary assistance to locate the fault.
    (c) The Manager feels that if you do not help him the fault will not be located.
    (d) The Manager expects that the default should be located only with your help
    (e) None

Directions to Questions 16 to 25

Read each sentence to find out whether there is any error in it. The error, if any, will be in one part of the sentence. The number of that part is the answer. If there is no error, the answer is (e). (Ignore errors of punctuation, if any).

16. When the police started (a) to follow his speeding car (b) he brake the signal (c) and drove away. (d) No error. (e)
17. We have not only helped them (a) with money but also (b) with the support of (c) well trained and experienced workers (d) No error. (e)
18. What people think (a) about religious matters (b) assumes importance (c) for a great extent. (d) No error. (e)
19. No sooner did (a) the ship touched the shore (b) than a friend of mine (c) leaped into the water. (d) No error. (e)
20. You can imagine how (a) annoyed I was (b) when I learnt that (c) the match has been postponed. (d) No error. (e)
21. What you (a) said is (b) impertinenting to (c) the occasion. (d) No error. (e)
22. When he hears that news, (a) he was almost (b) in tears and (c) could not utter a word. (d) No error. (e)
23. Since she has (a) been hospitalised, (b) we must wait till (c) she is recovering. (d) No error. (e)
24. Yogesh knew the (a) value of obedient too well (b) not to anticipate some (c) censure of his act. (d) No error. (e)
25. We all are aware (a) that Heramb certainly is (b) one of those who is (c) interested in all kinds of sports. (d) No error. (e)

Directions to Questions 26 to 30

Pick out the most effective word from the given words to fill in the blanks to make the sentence meaningfully complete.

26. We request you to come and enjoy the __________ climate or our small coastal village.
    (a) salubrious (b) memorable
    (c) changing (d) promising
    (e) astonishing
27. Pollution, excessive population, poverty and unemployment are the __________ problems of our country.
    (a) proclaimed (b) situational
    (c) absorbing (d) perpetual
    (e) expressed
28. I have always admired his __________ expertise and humility.
    (a) highest (b) tallest
    (c) declared (d) latent
    (e) profound
29. We have enough __________ to oppose the unjust law.
    (a) promise (b) superiority
    (c) pluck (d) honesty
    (e) mandate

30. Today, as citizens of free India, we ________ both our democracy and our secularism.
(a) postulate (b) cherish
(c) establish (d) achieve
(e) declare

Directions to Questions 31 to 35

In each of the following questions six words are given which are denoted by (A), (B), (C), (D), (E) and (F). By using all the six words, each only once, you have to frame a *meaningful and grammatically correct sentence.* The correct order of words is answer. Choose from the five alternatives the one having the correct order of words and mark the number of that alternative as your answer.

31. (A) Society (B) Followed
(C) Must (D) Of
(E) Be (F) Norms
(a) FDACEB (b) FDABCE
(c) AFDECB (d) BCEDAF
(e) FDCAEB

32. (A) Mould (B) The
(C) Can (D) Opinion
(E) Public (F) Press
(a) EDBFCA (b) BFCAED
(c) BEDFCA (d) FACBED
(e) BFCEAD

33. (A) Crucial (B) Ahead
(C) Democracy (D) Are
(E) Days (F) For
(a) EBDFCA (b) EDABFC
(c) CEDAFB (d) EBDAFC
(e) AEFCDB

34. (A) Being (B) Houses
(C) Here (D) Demolished
(E) Are (F) Dilapidated
(a) CFHAED (b) BAFEDC
(c) FBEADC (d) AFBEDC
(e) BCEDAF

35. (A) Originate (B) Expertise
(C) From (D) Power
(E) Individual's (F) Should
(a) EDFABC (b) FEADCB
(c) BFACED (d) EBFACD
(e) DFACEB

Directions to Questions 36 to 40

In the following passage, there are blanks, each of which has been numbered. These numbers are printed below the passage and against each, five words are suggested, one of which fits the blanks appropriately. Find out the appropriate word in each case.

Conventionalism **(36)** ignorance, superstitions and narrowness of outlook, it **(37)** against the principle of evolution. It is positively harmful. It kills originality and **(38)** mental growth. Society begins to stagnate under its **(39)**. A society which does not modify with the changing times is **(40)** for ever.

36. (a) raises (b) breeds
(c) provides (d) evolves
(e) forwards

37. (a) appeals (b) attacks
(c) directs (d) argues
(e) militates

38. (a) demoralises (b) relegates
(c) neutralises (d) shortens
(e) dangers

39. (a) mandate (b) projection
(c) contribution (d) sway
(e) tenacity

40. (a) doomed (b) devalued
(c) dampened (d) depleted
(e) discouraged

Directions to Questions 41 to 50

Read the following passage carefully and answer the questions given below it. Certain words/expressions are given in **bold** in the passage to help you locate them while answering some of the questions.

Man who is believed to have evolved from apes, is a curious mixture of varied motives. He is not only the subject of needs but is also their creator. He not only **seeks** to satisfy his needs but also caters to his desire for beauty and grace. He is eager to satisfy his passion for more and more knowledge. Although in a general way, the maxim 'necessity is the mother of invention' is true, it is by no means the whole truth. Man is something much greater than an intelligent being using his intellect to make newer inventions from time to time. He has within him a spirit which is ever **exhorting** him to cut down his needs and learn to be happy with what he has. The real purpose underlying this **maxim** lies in its utility in the worldly sense. It tells us to be up and doing, not to be passive in our attitude to life. It asks us not to remain slaves of old habits and ways of life. We must face the new situations with a creative mind. Every new difficulty, every new problem, which confronts us in life can be tackled successfully with the spirit of inventiveness.

41. Which of the following is **NOT** the whole truth, according to the passage?
(a) Man has a desire for beauty and grace
(b) Necessity is the mother of invention
(c) Man desires to cut down his needs and wants
(d) Man learns to be happy with what he has
(e) We should not be passive is our attitude to life

42. What does the maxim mentioned in the passage teaches us?
(a) To be worldly in the strict sense of the term
(b) To be slave or our needs and wants
(c) To endeavour constantly to create new passions and desires
(d) To be active in life and do something to help mankind
(e) To be positive in life and get involved in our work

43. What does the spirit within man tells him to do?
(a) To be a mixture of varied motives
(b) To evaluate the situation intelligently
(c) To cut down his desires and passions
(d) To acquire more and more wealth and comforts
(e) To be philanthropic and Samaritan

44. Which of the following statements is/are **true** in the context of the passage?
(A) Man should be passive in his attitude to life.
(B) Spirit of invectiveness may not stand in good stead in solving every new problem.
(C) Man has a passion for more and more knowledge.
(a) Only A
(b) Only A and B
(c) Only C
(d) Only B and C
(e) All A, B and C

45. Which of the following is **similar** in meaning as word **'maxim'** as used in the passage?
(a) principle (b) direction
(c) value (d) observation
(e) justification

46. Which of the following is **NOT** the characteristic of man, as per the passage?
(a) Man has many needs and motives
(b) Man creates many needs for himself
(c) Man seeks to satisfy his needs
(d) Man desires to have more and more comforts and money
(e) Man has a passion for more and more knowledge

47. Which of the following statements is **NOT TRUE** as per passage?
(a) Spirit of inventiveness will stand man in good stead
(b) Man is the subject of various wants
(c) Man creates new needs because they are sometimes good or beautiful
(d) Man should not remain slave of old habits
(e) Man's inner spirit tells him to be on the lookout for newer and higher wants

48. Choose the word which is **MOST OPPOSITE** in meaning of the word **'seeks'** as used in the passage.
(a) deplored (b) avoids
(c) vanishes (d) approaches
(e) aligns

49. Which of the following is **SIMILAR** in meaning of the word **'exhorting'** as used in the passage?
(a) urging
(b) supporting
(c) demanding
(d) clarifying
(e) proposing

50. According to the passage, man should—
(a) uphold the principles of justice and ethics
(b) give whatever he has to others
(c) follow the traditional style of life and living
(d) use his creativity to face new problems
(e) augment his skills by constant learning

PAPER 14

LIC AAO EXAMINATION, 2008

Directions to Questions 1 to 15

In each of the following sentences there are two blank spaces. Below each sentence there are five pairs of words denoted by numbers (a), (b), (c), (d) and (e). Find out which pair of words can be filled up in the blanks in the sentence in the same sequence to make the sentence grammatically correct and meaningfully complete.

1. Most people are too __________ in their own lives to __________ much about the agonies of others.

(a) absorbed __________ care
(b) concerned __________ think
(c) indulged __________ eradicate
(d) involved __________ console
(e) entangling __________ worry

2. Lawyers and Doctors __________ that advertising will certainly __________ their profession adversely.

(a) trust __________ damage
(b) believe __________ affect
(c) plead __________ escalate
(d) argue __________ effect
(e) contemplate __________ boost

3. Because the __________ leading to cancellation of flight were murky, the Minister appointed a Commission to __________ and report the matter.

(a) staff members __________ undertake
(b) decisions __________ decide
(c) facts __________ underplay
(d) events __________ camouflage
(e) circumstances __________ investigate

4. Several plots __________, __________ in various television episodes.

(a) screen __________ concurrently
(b) televised __________ consequently
(c) about __________ repeatedely
(d) exhibit __________ frequently
(e) demonstrate __________ violently

5. By __________ of their athletic activities, a few sportsmen are able to escape the pressures that living in __________ can create.

(a) knowledge __________ affluence
(b) way __________ prosperity
(c) contrast __________ adversity
(d) virtue __________ poverty
(e) order __________ vicinity

Directions to Questions 6 to 15

Which of the phrases (a), (b), (c) and (d) given below should replace the phrases given in bold in the following sentence to make the sentence grammatically meaningful and correct? If the sentence is correct as it is and no correction is required, mark (e) as the answer.

6. In guest rooms the central portion **is generally reserved** for sofa set.
(a) generally is reserved
(b) is reserved generally
(c) was generally reserved
(d) are generally reserved
(e) No correction required

7. In the production of desert trees, nature seems sometimes to have been **experimenting** with the truly strange.
(a) seem to have been sometimes experimenting
(b) seems sometimes to have been experimented
(c) sometimes seem to be experimented
(d) sometimes seem to have experimented
(e) No correction required

8. In the first round, the participants played in the presence of an accomplice who **was committed deliberate** errors
(a) committed deliberate
(b) was to be committed deliberate
(c) had committed deliberately
(d) committed deliberately
(e) No correction required

9. **What did prevent them from winning** the battle is not known.
(a) What prevented them to win
(b) What prevent them winning
(c) What prevented them from winning
(d) What prevented their winning
(e) No correction required.

10. The scenario was identical to the one that **was to be observed** in the previous tournament.
(a) was observing
(b) had been observing
(c) was observed
(d) was to observe
(e) No correction required

11. The impact of the composite bow on warfare **was equal to the** crossbow of medieval times.
(a) was equal to of the
(b) is equal to the
(c) is equal to that
(d) was to observe
(e) No correction required

12. Culture climate and geography **plays an important part** in the formation of any proverb.
(a) plays an important role
(b) plays a important part
(c) play an important role
(d) play a important part
(e) No correction required

13. This book will be **of particular interested** to those fascinated by the recent philosophy.
(a) of particularly interested
(b) of particular interest
(c) of interested in particular
(d) particularly of interested
(e) No correction required

14. These days developed countries have started **looking down for** underdeveloped countries as it is advantageous for both the parties.
(a) looking after
(b) looking down upon
(c) to look down at
(d) looking for at
(e) No correction required

15. The methods **to adopt for eradication** of poverty should depend upon the magnitude and nature of resources available.
(a) to adopt for eradicating
(b) to be adopted for eradication
(c) to be adopting to eradicate

(d) for adoption of eradicate
(e) No correction required

Directions to Questions 16 to 30

Read the following passage carefully and answer the questions given below it. Certain words/ expressions are given in bold in the passage to help you locate them while answering some of the questions.

Radically changing monsoon patterns, reduction in the winter rice harvest and a quantum increase in respiratory diseases—all part of the environmental doomsday scenario which is reportedly playing out in South Asia. According to a United Nations Environment Programme report, a deadly three-km deep blantant of pollution comprising a fearsome cocktail of ash, acids, aerosols and other particles has enveloped this region. For India, already struggling to cope with a drought, the implications of this are devastating and further crop failure will amount to a life and death question for many Indians. The increase in premature deaths will have adverse social and economic consequences and a rise in **morbidities** will place an unbearable burden on our crumbling health system. And there is no one to blame but ourselves. Both official and corporate India has always been **allergic** to any mention of clean technology. Most mechanical two wheelers roll off the assembly line without proper pollution control systems. Little effort is made R & D on simple technologies, which could make a vital difference to people's lives and the environment.

However, while there is no denying that South Asia must clean up its act, skeptics might questions the timing of the haze report. The Johannesburg meet on Rio +10 is just two weeks away and the stage is set for the usual battle between the developing world and the West, particularly the U.S. President Mr. Bush has adamantly refused to sign any protocol, which would mean a change in American consumption. U.N. environment report will likely find a place in the U.S. arsenal as it points an accusing finger countries like India and China. Yet the U.S. can hardly deny its own **dubious** role in the matter of erasing trading quotas. Richer countries can simply buy up excess credits from poorer countries and continue to pollute. Rather than try to get the better of developing countries, who undoubtedly, have taken up environmental shortcuts in their bid to catch up with the West, the U.S. should take a look at the environment **profligacy**, which is going on within. From opening up virgin territories for oil exploration to relaxing the standards for drinking water, Mr. Bush's policies are not exactly beneficial—not even to Americans. We realise that we are all in this together and that pollution anywhere should be a global concern. Only then there will be more light at the end of the tunnel.

16. Both official and corporate India is allergic to ___
(a) failure of monsoon
(b) poverty and inequality
(c) slowdown in industrial product
(d) mention of clean technology
(e) crop failure

17. Which, according to the passage, is a life and death question to many Indians?
(a) Increase in respiratory diseases
(b) Use of clean technology
(c) Thick blanket of pollution over the region
(d) Failure in crops
(e) Dwindling agricultural yield

18. If the rate of premature deaths increases it will ___
(a) exert added burden on our crumbling economy.
(b) have adverse social and economic consequences.
(c) make positive effect on our efforts to control population
(d) have less job aspirants in the society
(e) have healthy effect on our economy

19. Choose the word which is **SIMILAR** in meaning of the word **'profligacy'** as used in the passage.
(a) wastefulness (b) conservation
(c) upliftment (d) criticalness
(e) denouncement

20. According to the passage, India cannot tolerate any further ___
(a) crop failure
(b) deterioration of health care system

(c) increase in respiratory diseases
(d) proliferation of nuclear devises
(e) social and economic consequences

21. According to the passage, two wheeler industry is not adequately concerned about ________
(a) passenger safety on the roads
(b) life cover insurance of the vehicle owners
(c) pollution control systems in the vehicles
(d) rising cost of the two wheelers
(e) rising cost of the petrol in the country

22. What could be the reason behind timing of the haze report just before the Johannesburg meet, as indicated in the passage?
(a) United Nations is working hand-in-glove with the U.S.
(b) Organisers of the forthcoming meet wanted to teach a lesson to the U.S.
(c) Drawing attentions of the world towards devastating effects of environmental degradation.
(d) U.S. wants to use it as a handle against the developing countries in the forthcoming meet
(e) The meet is a part of political agenda of the U.N.

23. Choose the word which is **SIMILAR** in the meaning of the word **'allergic'** as used in the passage.
(a) liking (b) dispassionate
(c) possessive (d) crumbling
(e) repugnant

24. Which of the following is the indication of environmental degradation in South Asia?
(a) Social and economic inequality
(b) Crumbling health care system
(c) Inadequate pollution control system
(d) Over emphasis on technology
(e) Radically changing monsoon pattern

25. What must we realize, according to the passage?
(a) No country should show superiority over other countries.
(b) U.N. is putting in hard efforts in the direction of pollution control
(c) All countries must join hands in fighting pollution
(d) Nobody should travel through tunnel to avoid health hazards
(e) We all must strive hard to increase agricultural production

26. Which of the following finds place in the United Nations Environment Programme Report
(a) Changing monsoon patterns
(b) Substantial increase in respiratory diseases
(c) A serious cover of pollution over the region.
(d) Reduction in winter rice harvest
(e) None of these

27. Which of the following statements is **NOT TRUE** in the context of the passage?
(a) U.N. environment report blames countries like India and China.
(b) Developing countries have taken environmental shortcuts in their bid to catch up with west.
(c) U.S. is also to be blamed for environmental degradation and pollution.
(d) Indians cannot afford to have any further crop failure
(e) U.S. has tightened safety standards for drinking water.

28. According to the passage, Johannesburg meet is going to witness......
(a) calm and dispassionate thinking on the issue of pollution control.
(b) a blaming game between developed and developing countries
(c) refusal of U.N. to work as arbitrator
(d) U.S. agreeing to look at the issue of lowering its consumption
(e) countries agreeing for higher monetary allocation to R & D.

29. Choose the word which is **MOST OPPOSITE** in meaning of the word **'dubious'** as used in the passage?
(a) unquestionable (b) dissimilar
(c) illegal (d) antisocial
(e) innovative

30. Choose the word which is **MOST OPPOSITE** in meaning of the word **'morbidity'** as used in the passage.
(a) powerfulness (b) healthiness
(c) softness (d) acuteness
(e) purposeful

Directions to Questions 31 to 35

Rearrange the following six sentences (A), (B), (C), (D), (E) and (F) in the proper sequence to form a meaningful paragraph; then answer the questions given below them.

(A) No one knows their names.
(B) with irrigation systems, farmers were able to raise more food with less labour.
(C) The first engineers lived in the Middle East, probably around 3500 B.C.
(D) Today's city, thus, is essentially still a place where specialists live and work.
(E) Thus, an increasing number of people were relieved of agriculture chores and able to gather in cities to practise specialities.
(F) However, they conceived and built the elevated irrigation canal.

31. Which of the following will be the **SIXTH (LAST)** sentence after rearrangement?
(a) A (b) B
(c) C (d) D
(e) E

32. Which of the following will be the **FIRST** sentence after rearrangement?
(a) A (b) B
(c) C (d) D
(e) E

33. Which of the following will be the **FOURTH** sentence after rearrangement?
(a) A (b) B
(c) C (d) D
(e) E

34. Which of the following will be the **FIFTH** sentence after rearrangement?
(a) A (b) B
(c) C (d) D
(e) E

35. Which of the following will be the **SECOND** sentence after rearrangement?
(a) A (b) B
(c) C (d) D
(e) E

Directions to Questions 36 to 45

In the following passage there are blanks, each of which has been numbered. These numbers are printed below the passage and against each, five words are suggested, one of which fits the blank appropriately. Find out the appropriate word in each case.

Studies **(36)** the impact of computer models to support policy-making processes in organizations have **(37)** that client involvement in the model-building process is often a **(38)** for effective model building. One important reason is that the process of model building is frequently more important than the resulting model. Model building itself is largely a **(39)** process about the problem. Most **(40)** about the characteristics of an ill-structured problem are gained during the **(41)** process of designing a computer model, rather than after the model is finished. Another important reason is that most information in an organization **(42)** in the mental models of organizational members. To support policy making in organizations it is this knowledge which needs to be **(43)** and represented in the model. An important topic in client-oriented or **(44)** model building thus becomes the **(45)** of relevant knowledge contained in the mental models of participants.

36. (a) evaluating (b) focussing
(c) projecting (d) advocating
(e) directing

37. (a) devised (b) exhibited
(c) convinced (d) attributed
(e) indicated

38. (a) support (b) valuation
(c) prerequisite (d) material
(e) blueprint

39. (a) valuable (b) durable
(c) tedious (d) learning
(e) critical

40. (a) thinking (b) insights
(c) planning (d) appreciation
(e) opinions

41. (a) elongated (b) concentrated
(c) iterative (d) evolving
(e) consummate

42. (a) resides (b) follows
(c) settles (d) lays
(e) committed

43. (a) extended (b) bisected
(c) subjected (d) captured
(e) attributed

44. (a) revolving (b) interactive
(c) dogmatic (d) accentuated
(e) formative

45. (a) demarcation (b) formation
(c) proliferation (d) association
(e) elicitation

Directions to Questions 46 to 50

In each question below a sentence with four words printed in bold type is given. These are numbered as (a), (b), (c) and (d). One of these boldly printed words may be either wrongly spelt or inappropriate in the context of the sentence. Find out the word which is wrongly spelt or inappropriate, if any. The number of that word is your answer. If all the boldly printed words are correctly spelt and also appropriate in the context of the sentence, mark (e) i.e. 'All Correct' as your answer.

46. The **questionnaire**/(a) reflected various/(b) **phenomena** that are/(c) **sparingly** experienced/(d) All Correct/(e)

47. **Countrary** to popular/(a) belief, ripe fruits are not/(b) **necessaril/**(c) **delicious/**(d) All Correct/(e)

48. The most **ambitious**/(a) **enterprize** undertaken in the/(b) ancient Egypt was of the/(c) construction of pyramid./(d) All Correct/(e)

49. The **astronomical/**(a) calculations were/(b) **admiringly/**(c) **accurate./**(d) All correct/(e)

50. Looking inward from the top of the **ramparts**/(a) the **sentries**/(b) had a marvellous **panerama**/(c) spread before them/(d) All Correct/(e)

PAPER 15

LIC AAO EXAMINATION, 2010

Directions to Questions 1 to 5

In each question, a sentence with two words/group of words printed in bold type are given. One of them or both of them may have a certain error. You have to find out the correct word/group of words from among the four choices given b low each sentence to replace the incorrect words/group of words and make the sentence grammatically correct and meaningful. If the sentence is correct as it is mark (e) i.e.. 'No correction required' as your answer

1. RBI has asked banks **that disclose** the fees and commissions they have earned through the **sell** of life insurance policies.
   (a) disclosure — selling
   (b) disclosed — sell
   (c) to disclose — sale
   (d) can disclose — sales
   (e) No correction required
2. Our Development Officer is very **encourage** and helps me do whatever is **necessity** to achieve my goals.
   (a) encouraging — necessary
   (b) encouraged - necessarily
   (c) encourages — necessary
   (d) encouraging — necessities
   (e) No correction required
3. According to experts, the Indian banking system is **better** that of **every** developed countries.
   (a) very good —any
   (b) best - much
   (c) more better — all
   (d) better than - many
   (e) No correction required
4. People should **be buying** health insurance at a young age and **maintains** it for a lifetime.
   (a) be bought-maintain
   (b) buy - maintain
   (c) have bought - be maintaining
   (d) not buy - will maintain
   (e) No correction required
5. Life Insurance companies have appointed **around** 13 lakhs agents during 2008-09 **despite** the recession.

(a) nearly — because
(b) about — jnspite
(c) approximate — on account
(d) almost — In
(e) No correction required

Directions to Questions 6 to 15

Read the following passage carefully and answer the questions given below it. Certain Words/ phrases are printed in bold to help you locate them while answering some of the questions.

Most of the world's healthcare is financed directly by governments, but private insurance, which now makes up nearly a fifth of the total, looks set for a state-sponsored boom in the hope of solving problems in national systems of healthcare which include inadequate access to care and soaring costs.

In most countries state-financed healthcare is not available to all, so governments want private insurance to be expanded to **cover** everyone. The most prominent effort is underway in America, where about 47 million lack health insurance of any kind. This effort is similar to reforms undertaken over the past decade in the Netherlands and Switzerland. To ensure equitable access, both countries forbid private insurers from discriminating against applicants because they are in poor health or at high risk of falling ill. This practice is known as "lemon dropping".

A tightly regulated expansion of private Insurance-in effect turning health insurance into a utility - can thus expand coverage. This is also likely be true in developing countries, whose public healthcare systems are often hopelessly overstretched and under funded, although because poor countries cannot afford the subsidies and regulatory mechanism of the rich world, coverage is likely to be **confined** to the better off.

The second reason why governments have turned to private insurance is cost **control**. The hope was that by ruthlessly tackling costs and promoting efficiency, market-minded insurers would help rein in runaway health inflation where governments could not. Whatever the role played in a health system, private health insurance has added to total health expenses. It is no coincidence, that the countries with the biggest private health-insurance sectors-America, France, Germany and Switzerland - also have some of the highest healthcare costs per person.

There are several explanations for this because a third party pays the bill, the true cost of health services is rarely made clear to them, nor is the true price of insurance, especially if coverage is provided through an employer. This encourages over-insurance and **over consumption of healthcare.** Another incentive problem also arises from lack of transparent pricing. Studies have shown that the fees for similar procedures vary widely among hospitals in the same area. Because hospitals and doctors both decide on the services patients must have and dictate the price of those services, they often enjoy a powerful informational advantage over insurers. Thus doctors and hospitals have an informational advantage and an incentive to oversupply their services.

6. Why do governments look to private insurers to reduce inflation in the healthcare system?
   (A) Private health insurance companies are professionally managed.
   (B) It is in the interest of the private Insurers to do so
   (C) Their pricing system does not reveal the hidden costs in healthcare.
   (a) Only B
   (b) Only C
   (c) Only B and C
   (d) All A, B & C
   (e) None of these

7. Which of the following is a problem facing healthcare system in developing countries?
   (a) Quality healthcare is available only in private hospitals.
   (b) Constant government interference in the system,
   (c) Healthcare facilities are insufficient and often made available only to the rich.
   (d) Subsidizing healthcare has resulted in many hospitals becoming loss making.
   (e) Profitable hospitals are forced to bail out loss making ones.

8. Which of the following is TRUE about private health insurance?
   (A) According to prevailing laws, private health insurers can cater to only 20 percent of the population.

(B) In western countries private health Insurance is unregulated by the government.

(C) Most governments are now encouraging the participation of private companies in providing healthcare.

(a) Only A and C
(b) Only C
(c) Only A and B
(d) All A, B and C
(e) None of these

9. What does the phrase "over consumption of healthcare' convey in the context of the passage?

(a) People opt for unnecessary medical treatments because they do not have to pay for it.
(b) Healthcare consumes too much of a nation's budget in developed countries.
(c) Government hospitals often recommend unnecessary procedures for patients.
(d) In developing countries, the healthcare system cannot cope with the demands of their population.
(e) None of these

10. Why did the government of Switzerland prohibit the practice of lemon dropping?

(a) To reduce the profits of private health insurers.
(b) To facilitate equitable access to all its citizens.
(c) To prevent discrimination against the poor.
(d) To ensure that America's healthcare system problems do not occur in theirs.
(e) To cut the cost of healthcare per person.

11. What is the author's main objective in writing the passage?

(a) Convincing governments to restrict private sector participation in health care.
(b) Criticizing developing countries for the efforts to reform their health care systems.
(c) Pointing out the advantages of adopting European healthcare reforms in developing countries.
(d) Elaborating the pros and cons of private sector participation in health insurance
(e) Stating that state interference in health insurance is undesirable.

12. What impact has the lack of transparency in pricing had on healthcare costs?

(a) Patients have become key decision 'makers in the treatment process.
(b) Medical personnel do not get uniform incentives.
(c) Insurers and doctors conspire to charge exorbitant fees for treatment.
(d) Well off patients often end up with huge subsidies from hospitals.
(e) Doctors and hospitals have an informational advantage and an incentive to over-supply their services

Directions to Questions 13 to 14

Which of the following is most similar in meaning to the word given in bold as used in the passage?

13. CONFINED

(a) Captured (b) Locked
(c) Detained (d) Limited
(e) Imprisoned

14. COVER

(a) Conceal (b) Hide
(c) Suppress (d) Bury
(e) Include

15. Which of the following is **most opposite** in meaning to the word **CONTROL** given in **bold** as used in the passage?

(a) Permit
(b) Obey
(c) Supremacy
(d) Powerless
(e) Increase

Directions to Questions 16 to 20

Rearrange the following six sentences (A), (B), (C), (D), (E) and (F) in the proper sequence to form a meaningful paragraph; then answer the questions

given below them.

(A) After all India's expected equipment requirement in the next five years will be huge, next only to China's.

(B) Indian cellular equipment manufacturers however were not prepared for this surge in demand.

(C) In the 1990s cellular wireless telecom services in India were liberalized.

(D) To make Indian telecom manufacturers more self-sufficient, concrete steps need to be taken to increase India's R & D efforts in telecom.

(E) This resulted in decrease in tariffs and the volume of cell phone subscribers grew phenomenally.

(F) Their lack of preparedness gave foreign players the opportunity to step in.

16. Which of the following will be the **FIFTH** sentence after rearrangement?
(a) B (b) C
(c) D (d) E
(e) F

17. Which of the following will be the **LAST (SIXTH)** sentence after rearrangement?
(a) A (b) B
(c) C (d) D
(e) E

18. Which of the following will be the **FIRST** sentence after rearrangement?
(a) A
(b) B
(c) C
(d) D
(e) E

19. Which of the following will be the **THIRD** sentence after rearrangement?
(a) A (b) B
(c) D (d) C
(e) E

20. Which of the following will be the **SECOND** sentence after rearrangement?
(a) B (b) C
(c) D (d) E
(e) F

21. RBI is ____ about the fact that many banks are ____ in mutual funds.
(a) concerned, investing
(b) worried, shared
(c) sad, credited
(d) interested, stocking
(e) anxious, lending

22. The high ___ of land in cities is one of the greatest in providing affordable housing.
(a) worth, boost.
(b) quality, decisions
(c) value, prevention
(d) cost, hindrances
(e) price, trouble

23. Today over ____ a million farmer households in India do not have ___ to banks.
(a) less, need
(b) more, opportunity
(c) half, access
(d) extent, contribution
(e) partly, approach

24. Nowadays many general insurance products are ____ through bank____
(a) selling, networking
(b) distributed, branches
(c) disburse, personnel
(d) available, agent
(e) loaned., channel

25. To empower those living in rural areas NGOs are ___ self help groups and ____ youth in vocational subjects.
(a) realising, working
(b) developing, taught
(c) emerging, instructing
(d) creating, learning
(e) forming, training

PAPER 16

LIC AAO EXAMINATION, 2011

Directions to Questions 1 to 5

In each of the following questions, out of the given alternatives, choose the one which best expresses the meaning of the given word.

1. OBSCENE
(a) Objectionable (b) Indecent
(c) Displeasing (d) Condemnable

2. AMPLE
(a) Sufficient (b) Swift
(c) Detail (d) Huge

3. FADE
(a) Suffer (b) Fall
(c) Wither (d) Lose

4. ELUDE
(a) Confuse (b) Dodge
(c) Despair (d) Mislead

5. DOCILE
(a) Stubborn (b) Stupid
(c) Gentle (d) Vague

Directions to Questions 6 to 10

In each of the following questions, choose the word opposite in meaning to the given word

6. MALICE
(a) Honor (b) Ecstasy
(c) Goodwill (d) Happiness

7. EXONERATE
(a) Compel (b) Accuse
(c) Imprison (d) Boldness

8. HAMPER
(a) Open (b) Release
(c) Hold (d) Hasten

9. SELDOM
(a) Rarely (b) Daily
(c) Often (d) Never

10. SUBLIME
(a) strange (b) low
(c) ridiculous (d) mean

Directions to Questions 11 to 15

In each of the following questions, out of the four alternatives choose the one which can be substituted for the given sentences.

11. Murder of brother—
(a) Patricide (b) Homicide
(c) Regicide (d) Fratricide

12. Mania of stealing articles—
(a) Logo-mania (b) Nymphomania
(c) Kleptomania (d) Hypomania

13. A disease which spreads by contacting
(a) Infectious (b) Contagious
(c) Contiguous (d) Epidemic

14. A poem written on the death of someone loved and lost—
(a) Ode (b) Epic
(c) Sonnet (d) Elegy

15. Commencement of words with the same letter—
(a) Rhyme (b) Alliteration
(c) PUN (d) Oxymoron

Directions to Questions 16 to 20

The under note words are followed by four words or phrases out which only one is a Synonym. Choose the correct word.

16. Restive—
(a) Restless (b) Resistant
(c) Retiring (d) Remorseful

17. Phlegmatic—
(a) Calm (b) Cryptic
(c) Practical (d) Dishonest

18. Pertinent—
(a) Relevant (b) Understood
(c) Living (d) Puzzling

19. Petrify-
(a) Turn to stone (b) Refine
(c) Repeat (d) Turn to water

20. Menial-
(a) Intellectual
(b) Servile
(c) Arrogant
(d) Laudatory

Directions to Questions 21 to 25

In each of the sentences below there is a blank to be filled in with appropriate word(s). Four alternatives are given for each question. Choose the correct alternative.

21. The G.M. of the plant, Mr. Tiwari..............me.
(a) accompanied (b) included
(c) organized (d) None of these

22. If I believe I cannot do something, it makes me...........of doing it.
(a) capable (b) incapable
(c) worth (d) worthy

23. It is with utmost.......... that I want to inform you that I am unable to accept your invitation.
(a) regret (b) pain
(c) hesitation (d) confidence

24. Children are too............to be given so much responsibility.
(a) young (b) naive
(c) ignorant (d) inexperienced

25. No weapon ever invented is more...........than hunger.
(a) deadly (b) harmful
(c) destructive (d) violent

Directions to Questions 26 to 30

Passage

From the world of magic, hypnosis is moving into the world of medicine. From hocus-pocus performed by men in black capes, to hypnotherapy practiced by doctors in white coats. The purpose is to help people stop smoking, lose weight, overcome phobias, and control pain in a variety of medical situations, from childbirth to cancer. Research laboratories are currently checking out the success rate of therapy under hypnosis, while medical journals stand by to publish the results. And the important thing is, nobody is laughing. In the 1840's, a British doctor in Calcutta created a controversy by performing over 1000 operations with hypnosis as the only anesthesia. During the World Wars, German and British doctors used hypnosis to treat war neuroses.

26. Hypnosis means—
(a) auto-suggestion
(b) Suggestion made in trance
(c) Anesthesia
(d) Hocus-pocus

27. 'Nobody is laughing' at hypnotherapy now, because they are—
(a) Sad
(b) Angry
(c) Taking it seriously
(d) Annoyed

28. The purpose of hypnotherapy is to—
(a) Cure patients
(b) Make life easier
(c) Carry out research
(d) Check out the success rate

29. German and British doctors used hypnosis as—
(a) Anesthesia was not available
(b) Anesthesia was not needed
(c) It was a substitute for anesthesia
(d) It was fashionable during the war period

30. Treating war neurosis means—
(a) Curing madness
(b) Curing brain fever
(c) Dealing with war problems
(d) Curing war anxiety

Directions to Questions 31 to 40

Groups of four words are given. In each group, one word is wrongly spelt. Find the misspet word and mark your answer in the Answer-Sheet.

31. (a) Prioratise (b) Pictures
(c) Visualize (d) Individualize

32. (a) Mendacious (b) Obnoxcious
(c) Pernicious (d) Ferocious

33. (a) Pennetrate (b) Irritate
(c) Hesitate (d) Perforate

34. (a) Passagway (b) Causeway
(c) Subway (d) Straightway

35. (a) Rapport (b) Support
(c) Repport (d) Purport

36. (a) Stationery (b) Dictionery
(c) revolutionary (d) voluntary

37. (a) Temperature (b) Temperament
(c) Tempastuous (d) Temptation

38. (a) Whether (b) Weathere
(c) Whither (d) Wither

39. (a) Legible (b) Communiceble
(c) Incorrigible (d) Eligible

40. (a) Audacious (b) Auspicious
(c) Capricious (d) Caprisious

Directions to Questions 41 to 50

Four alternatives are given for the Idiom/Phrase Bold in the sentence. Choose the alternative which best expresses the meaning of the Idiom / Phrase and mark it in the Answer-Sheet.

41. Don't worry about the silly row. It was just a **storm in a tea cup**.
(a) Important matter dealt with ease
(b) Hot tea being served
(c) Commotion over a trivial matter
(d) Confusion and chaos

42. The Rajput warriors **set their face** against the invader.
(a) Became enemies
(b) Turned away from
(c) Faced difficulty
(d) Opposed strongly

43. Syria is now **currying favor with** America.
(a) pleasing (b) Favoring
(c) Obliging (d) Ingratiating itself with

44. Our Principal is not a man **to mince matters.**
(a) To confuse issues
(b) To say something mildly
(c) To mix everything together
(d) To be very modest

45. We tend to **take for granted** conveniences of modern life.
(a) To consider
(b) To admit
(c) To accept readily
(d) To care for

46. The prodigal son was left **high and dry** by his friends, when he lost all his money.
(a) Wounded (b) Alone
(c) Depressed (d) Neglected

47. The success of his first novel completely **turned his head.**
(a) Made him vain
(b) Made him look back
(c) Changed him completely
(d) Made him think

48. She **turns up her nose** at this kind of dress.
(a) Despises
(b) Loves
(c) Sees no harm in
(d) Can just tolerate

49. At last the rioters **fell back.**
(a) Fell on the ground
(b) Yielded
(c) Ran back
(d) Turned back

50. The Madagascar Coup attempt **ended in a fiasco.**
(a) had no effect
(b) was an utter failure
(c) resulted in blood-shed
(d) was a disaster

ANSWER KEY

LIC AAO – 2005

1. (d)	2. (d)	3. (e)	4. (d)	5. (e)
6. (d)	7. (c)	8. (e)	9. (a)	10. (b)
11. (e)	12. (a)	13. (c)	14. (d)	15. (e)
16. (c)	17. (e)	18. (d)	19. (b)	20. (d)
21. (c)	22. (a)	23. (d)	24. (b)	25. (c)
26. (a)	27. (d)	28. (e)	29. (e)	30. (b)
31. (a)	32. (b)	33. (e)	34. (c)	35. (e)
36. (b)	37. (e)	38. (c)	39. (d)	40. (a)
41. (b)	42. (a)	43. (c)	44. (c)	45. (d)
46. (b)	47. (b)	48. (b)	49. (a)	50. (d)

LIC AAO – 2008

1. (b)	2. (b)	3. (c)	4. (b)	5. (d)
6. (c)	7. (b)	8. (c)	9. (c)	10. (c)
11. (d)	12. (c)	13. (b)	14. (a)	15. (b)
16. (d)	17. (d)	18. (b)	19. (a)	20. (a)
21. (c)	22. (d)	23. (b)	24. (e)	25. (c)
26. (c)	27. (e)	28. (b)	29. (a)	30. (b)
31. (d)	32. (c)	33. (b)	34. (e)	35. (a)
36. (b)	37. (e)	38. (a)	39. (e)	40. (c)
41. (d)	42. (d)	43. (e)	44. (e)	45. (e)
46. (d)	47. (a)	48. (b)	49. (e)	50. (c)

LIC AAO – 2010

1. (c) 2. (a) 3. (d) 4. (b) 5. (e)
6. (e) 7. (c) 8. (b) 9. (a) 10. (b)
11. (d) 12. (e) 13. (d) 14. (e) 15. (e)
16. (c) 17. (a) 18. (c) 19. (b) 20. (d)
21. (a) 22. (d) 23. (c) 24. (b) 25. (e)

LIC AAO – 2011

1. (b) 2. (a) 3. (c) 4. (b) 5. (c)
6. (c) 7. (b) 8. (a) 9. (c) 10. (b)
11. (d) 12. (c) 13. (b) 14. (d) 15. (b)
16. (a) 17. (a) 18. (a) 19. (a) 20. (b)
21. (a) 22. (b) 23. (a) 24. (a) 25. (a)
26. (b) 27. (c) 28. (a) 29. (a) 30. (d)
31. (a) 32. (b) 33. (a) 34. (a) 35. (c)
36. (b) 37. (c) 38. (b) 39. (b) 40. (c)
41. (c) 42. (d) 43. (d) 44. (a) 45. (c)
46. (d) 47. (a) 48. (a) 49. (d) 50. (b)

FREQUENCY ANALYSIS

ABBREVIATIONS USED:

Comprehension / **Comp**, Sentence Completion / **SC**, Sentence Filler / **SF**, Cloze Test/ **CT**, Synonyms/ **Syn**, Antonyms/ **Ant**, Idioms and Phrase/ **IP**, Substitution/ **Subt**, Sentence arrangement/ **SA**, Spelling/ **SPL**, Miscellaneous/**Misc.**, Total Marks/**TM**, Sentence error/**SE**, Sentence Improvement/ **SI**.

LIC AAO – 2005

	Comp.	SC	SF	CT	Syn	Ant	IP	Subt	SA	SE	SPL	SI	MISC.	TM
	10	5		5					5+5	10		5	5	50

LIC AAO – 2008

	Comp.	SC	SF	CT	Syn	Ant	IP	Subt	SA	SE	SPL	SI	MISC.	TM
	15	5		10					5		5	10		50

LIC AAO – 2010

	Comp.	SC	SF	CT	Syn	Ant	IP	Subt	SA	SE	SPL	SI	MISC.	TM
	15								5			5		25

Life Insurance Corporation of India (LIC) AAO Exam English Questions, 2011

	Comp.	SC	SF	CT	Syn	Ant	IP	Subt	SA	SE	SPL	SI	MISC.	TM
	5	5			5	5	10	5			10		5	50

TREND ANALYSIS

In LIC AAO examination 2005 and 2008, six types of question were asked. These questions were of traditional pattern. There was marginal variation in these two years. In 2011 there was a change in **trend.** **Substitution, idioms** and **phrases** have been added and **spelling** questions have been given importance. In addition to **synonyms** and **antonyms** a question has been given on **vocabulary**, with a variation.

Thus, it is a changing trend; items are being a dded. But there is no cause for concern because all variations are covered by different chapters of the book. The level of question is almost similar to that of the Bank PO examination.

PAPER 17

NEW INDIA ASSURANCE EXAMINATION, 2005

Directions to Questions 1 to 15

Each of the following questions consists of a sequence in which four words or phrases are underlined These are marked as a, b, c, and d. Identify the one that is *not* acceptable in standard written English.

1. For the first time in the history of the person which(a) was recommended(b) by the President to replace(c) a retiring(d) justice of the Supreme Court is a woman.
2. Despite of(a) rain and snow there are(b) always more than(c) fifty thousand people at(d) the Lord's Cricket matches.
3. He was obviously(a) surprised at me refusing(b) his request to involve(c) him(d) in my project.
4. The value of the dollar(a) declines(b) as(c)the rate of inflation raises.(d)
5. The purpose of the(a) United Nations, broad speaking,(b) is(c) to maintain peace and security and to encourage(d) respect for human rights.

Directions to Questions 6 to 10

In the following questions sentences are given with blanks. Choose the most appropriate word to fill in the blank.

6. Though the programme was originally scheduled for seven days, due to heavy monsoons, it was later __________ to four days.
   (a) curtailed (b) ended
   (c) postponed (d) recommended
7. The police have __________ a complaint against four persons and have arrested two of them.
   (a) lodged (b) received
   (c) registered (d) followed
8. The marked difference between the weapons with the police and those possessed by criminals has heightened the sense of __________ even within the police force
   (a) responsibility (b) insecurity
   (c) duty (d) instability

9. People in our office are so __________ that the work never gets done on time.
(a) energetic (b) reflective
(c) lethargic (d) diplomatic

10. To reach the agreement, each side had to __________ by giving up some of its demands.
(a) complement (b) compensate
(c) comply (d) compromise

Directions to Questions 11 to 15

From the given alternatives choose the word which is nearest in meaning to the underlined word.

11. vindictive
(a) triumphant (b) strategic
(c) revengeful (d) demonstrative

12. insipid
(a) witty (b) flat
(c) wily (d) lucid

13. reiterate
(a) further (b) change
(c) publish (d) repeat

14. feign
(a) pretend (b) condemn
(c) condone (d) attend

15. callous
(a) inexperienced (b) unnamed
(c) unfeeling (d) unjust

Directions to Questions 16 to 20

In the following questions choose the word opposite in meaning to the underlined word.

16. counterfeit
(a) standardised (b) original
(c) duplicate (d) discordant

17. morose
(a) gay (b) morone
(c) sullen (d) sick

18. fabricate
(a) restore (b) produce
(c) construct (d) ruin

19. perseverance
(a) persistance (b) resoluteness
(c) reluctance (d) instability

20. hasten
(a) promote (b) hinder
(c) cooperate (d) oppose

Directions to Questions 21 to 25

Fill in the blanks with appropriate words.

21. The examiner made us __________ our identification in order to be admitted to the test centre.
(a) show (b) showing
(c) to show (d) showed

22. Most Americans don't object __________ them by their first names.
(a) That I call (b) to my calling
(c) for calling (d) that I am call

23. The travellers __________ their reservations well in advance if they want to fly during the Christmas holidays.
(a) had better to get
(b) had to get better
(c) had better get
(d) had better got

24. Don't forget to give her the message when you __________ her.
(a) are seeing (b) saw
(c) see (d) would see

25. He has gone to study in __________ European University.
(a) a (b) an
(c) the (d) one

Directions to Questions 26 to 30

Read the following passage carefully and answer the questions given after it.

One of the greatest delusions of modern times is the prevailing belief that we are more civilised than our ancestors. At no other period in the history of mankind has the word 'Civilisation' been so often misused and misunderstood. It is not in the abundance of material goods alone that civilisation lies. Neither does it consist in the advance of scientific knowledge however amazing it may be. The inventions and discoveries of science have undoubtedly brought unheard of blessings and comforts to us. But they are not civilisation. What we have failed to see is that civilisation is a special way of human behaviour, of thought and feeling. The essential quality of civilisation lies in the spirit of man, in his attitude to himself, to his fellowmen and to like as a whole. Looking everywhere around us today, you will find that man has made no progress since the dawn of history, in his attitude towards his fellowmen. On all the highest pillars in the cities of the world, you will find the figure of a conqueror or a general soldier. We know for more about our killers and destroyers than about our saviours and saints. The heroes of the world are the heroes of war.

26. According to the passage what does civilisation consist of?
(a) invention and discoveries
(b) possession of goods
(c) advanced scientific knowledge
(d) man's attitudes and behaviour

27. What have scientific discoveries given to man?
(a) material goods
(b) material comforts
(c) knowledge
(d) civilization

28. What does the word 'delusion' mean?
(a) real truth
(b) wrong belief
(c) correct statement
(d) misplaced interests

29. Why doesn't the author think that we are more civilised than our ancestors?
(a) we possess advanced scientific knowledge
(b) we consider the conquerors as our heroes
(c) we have abundance of material comforts
(d) we respect our saints and saviours

30. The main purpose of the passage is to convey the idea that:
(a) modern man is more advanced in scientific knowledge
(b) we are in more comfortable position than our ancestors
(c) modern man does not possess any different attitudes than his ancestors
(d) we respect our heroes of war, our conquerors.

PAPER 18

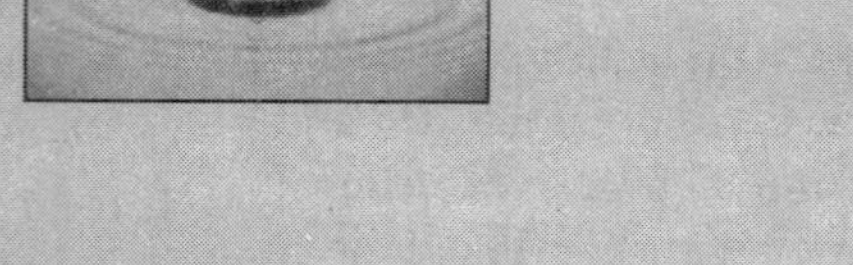

GIC AAO Examination, 2005

Directions to Questions 1 to 5

Fill in the blanks with the most appropriate word/words.

1. Though he was theoretically a friend of peasants, his voting record in the past __________ that impression.

(a) implied (b) created
(c) confirmed (d) belied

2. The child was so spoiled by his parents that he pouted and became __________ when he did not receive all their attention.

(a) discreet (b) suspicious
(c) sullen (d) tranquil

3. We were amazed that a man who had been till now the most __________ of public speakers could, in a single speech, electrify an audience and bring them cheering to their feet.

(a) enthralling (b) accomplished
(c) prosaic (d) masterful

4. We have lost confidence in him because he never __________ the grand promises he had made.

(a) forgot about (b) delivered on
(c) tired of (d) retreated from

5. The fibre optic cables that carry telephone calls cross country are made of glass so __________ that a piece 100 miles thick is clearer than a standard window pane.

(a) transparent (b) fragile
(c) immaculate (d) iridescent

Directions to Questions 6 to 10

Choose the word or phrase which is most nearly similar in meaning to the underlined word in the given sentence.

6. As long as our political leaders <u>emulate</u> the virtues of great leaders of this country, we shall flourish.

(a) rival (b) imitate
(c) demonstrate (d) pursue

7. Your <u>dishevelled</u> appearance will hurt your chances in this interview.

(a) ugly (b) unenthusiastic
(c) untidy (d) unnerved

8. The convict who escaped from the jail was a <u>ruthless</u> murderer.
(a) pitiless (b) dangerous
(c) merciful (d) vile

9. I can recommend him for a position of responsibility for I have found him a very <u>scrupulous</u> young man.
(a) hardworking (b) enthusiastic
(c) conscious (d) conscientious

10. From the doctor's given expressions I could tell he had <u>somber</u> news.
(a) hopeful (b) depressing
(c) fortunate (d) confusing

Directions to Questions 11 to 15

Choose the word *opposite* in meaning to the underlined word.

11. <u>Nebulous</u>
(a) starry (b) clear
(c) porous (d) fundamental

12. <u>Obsession</u>
(a) whim (b) addiction
(c) indifference (d) delusion

13. <u>Corroborate</u>
(a) establish (b) substantiate
(c) confirm (d) contradict

14. <u>Exuberant</u>
(a) apathetic (b) admiring
(c) fervent (d) enchanting

15. <u>Ingenious</u>
(a) unfamiliar (b) inconvenient
(c) unimaginative (d) innovative

Directions to Questions 16 to 20

The following questions consist of fragments of a sentence. The first fragment (1) and the last fragment (6) are in order. The other four are jumbled up and are designated as P, Q, R and S. Find out the correct sequence of these from the given alternatives.

16. No. 1. A report by Goldman Sachs predicts
P. in excess of 5% annually
Q. consistently growing
R. the only economy
S. that India would be
No. 6. till the year 2050.
(a) RPQS (b) SRQP
(c) SQRP (d) PSRQ

17. No. 1. The Andhra Pradesh government
P. has drawn up an ambitious Rs 8.5 crore action plan
Q. silently bearing the brunt of the monkey menace
R. in several parts of the State for years
S. for both control and rehabilitation
No. 6. of the unwanted simians.
(a) QPSR (b) RQPS
(c) PSRQ (d) QRPS

18. No. 1. In the first of its kind of exercise
P. the Indian Institute of Technology, Delhi (IIT-D)
Q. for research and development
R. showcased its potential
S. to members of the corporate world
No. 6. at 12 Tech—an interface between the industry and the institute.
(a) PRQS (b) RQSP
(c) PRSQ (d) SPRQ

19. No.1. Delhi University's top job
P. and the teaching fraternity
Q. is keenly waiting to see
R. falls vacant in May
S. after the present vice chancellor retires
No. 6. who will take over from him.
(a) QPRS (b) RSPQ
(c) RPQS (d) SRPQ

20. No. 1. Air India's fleet acquisition proposal
P. is facing rough weather
Q. over the last minute changes
R. in the tender specifications
S. with Airbus crying foul

No. 6. favouring Boeing.
(a) SQPR (b) PRQS
(c) QRPS (d) PSQR

Directions to Questions 21 to 25

Read the following passage and answer the questions given after it.

At different stages in the educational process different changes are required. In schools, the chief need is for a general change in the attitude towards science, which should be from the beginning an integral part and not a mere addition, often an optional addition, to the curriculum. Science should be taught not merely as a subject, but should come into all subjects. Its importance in history and in modern life should be pointed out and illustrated. The old contrast, often amounting to hostility, between scientific and humane subjects needs to be broken down and replaced by a scientific humanism. At the same time, the teaching of science requires to be humanised. The dry and factual presentation requires to be transformed, not by an appeal to mystical theory, but by emphasising the living and dramatic character of scientific advance itself. Here the teaching of the history of science, not isolated as at present, but in close relation to general history teaching, would serve to correct the existing atmosphere of scientific dogmatism. It would show at the same time how secure are the conquests of science in the control they give over natural processes and how insecure and provisional, however necessary, are the rational interpretations, the theories and hypotheses put forward at each stage. Past history by itself is not enough, the latest development of science should not be excluded because they have not yet passed the test of time. It is absolutely necessary to emphasise the fact that science not only has changed but is continually changing, that it is an activity and not merely a body of facts. Throughout, the social implications of science, the powers that it puts into men's hands, the uses they could make of them and those which they in fact do, should be brought out and made real by a reference to immediate experience of ordinary life.

21. According to the author science should be taught:
(a) as an optional subject
(b) as a special subject
(c) as a part of every subject
(d) as a part of history

22. While teaching science in schools, which of the following should be emphasised?
(a) presentation of facts
(b) appeal to mystical theory
(c) theories and hypotheses
(d) its close relation to life

23. What does the author feel about the "rational interpretations" of science?
(a) They are factual presentations which need to be transformed
(b) They give control over natural processes
(c) They are only provisional as they have not been proved
(d) They have social implications that put power in man's hands

24. The existing atmosphere of scientific dogmatism can be corrected by:
(a) presenting the scientific facts
(b) putting forward hypotheses and theories
(c) teaching the history of science in the context of general history
(d) emphasizing the changing nature of science

25. Science teaching will be most fruitful and purposeful when:
(a) all the scientific facts are presented to students
(b) it is taught in close relationship with humanities
(c) the history of science is taught
(d) the theories and interpretations of science are put forward

Directions to Questions 26 to 30

Each of the following questions consists of sentence in which four words or phrases are underlined. these are marked as (a), (b), (c) and (d). Identify the one that is not acceptable in standard English.

26. As soon as (a) the sun had rose (b) over (c) the mountains, the valley became unbearably hot (d) and stifling.

27. They (a) are both excellent books (b) but this one (c) is best (d)

28. The reason (a) for my prolonged absence (b) from class was (c) because (d) I was ill for three weeks.

29. Whether (a) I were (b) you, I would never (c) permit her to take part in such (4) an exhausting activity.

30. Although the news came (a) as a surprise to all (b) in the room, everyone tried to do their (c) work as though (d) nothing had happened.

PAPER 19

NEW INDIA ASSURANCE AAO EXAMINATION, 2011

Directions for Q. 1 to 4

Choose the word which is opposite in meaning to the given word.

1. Exorbitant
   (a) barbaric (b) famished
   (c) counterfeit (d) moderate
2. Humane
   (a) cruel (b) proud
   (c) cheerful (d) tranquil
3. Obsolete
   (a) heated (b) desolate
   (c) renovated (d) automatic
4. Suppress
   (a) stimulate (b) lengthen
   (c) abandon (d) smother

Directions for Q. 5 to 7

In the following sentences replace the words printed in bold with the appropriate expression from the given alternatives.

5. He is always' **prominent** in a crowd because of his height.
   (a) stands out (b) looks out
   (c) stands up (d) looks up
6. The rebels **offered resistance** for almost a month,
   (a) held over (b) held up
   (c) held out (d) held in
7. He generally **overlooked** the faults of his suboidinates.
   (a) passed out (b) passed by
   (c) passed through (d) passed over

Directions for Q. 8 to 11

Fill in the blanks with the most appropriate words.

8. While a great deal of change and modernisation has taken place in India since 1947, the basic values and family roles have been generally_______
   (a) overturned
   (b) stable
   (c) modified
   (d) appropriate

9. It would be difficult for one so ____to be led to believe that all men are equal and that we must disregard race, colour and creed.

(a) emotional (b) democratic
(c) intolerant (d) obsolete

10. The linguistic ____ of refugee children is reflected in their readiness to adopt the language of their new homeland.

(a) conservatism
(b) inadequacy
(c) adaptability
(d) structure

11. Rent control restrictions on small apartment owners may it unfortunately ____ rather than alleviate the housing problem.

(a) resolve (b) diminish
(c) castigate (d) aggravate

Directions for Q. 12 to 15

In the following questions the word at the top is used in four different ways. Choose the option in which the usage of the word is incorrect or inappropriate.

12. Court

(a) He has been courting Jane for six months.
(b) He has difficulty in courting his feelings into words.
(c) The prisoner was brought to court for trial.
(d) The tennis match will take place on the grass court.

13. Expense

(a) Most children in India are educated at public expense.
(b) We had a good laugh at his expense,
(c) He became a good scholar, but only at the expense of his health.
(d) A man of your expense should do well in life.

14. Demand

(a) The policeman demanded his name and address.
(b) He came to my house and demanded help.
(c) How would you demand than the world is round?
(d) The worker's demands were refused by the employer.

15. Master

(a) She could not master the courage to tell her friend about her loss.
(b) She quickly mastered the an of interviewing people.
(c) The terrorist was a master of disguise.
(d) He is the master of his house.

Directions for Q. 16 to 19

Question below consists of a related pad of words followed by four pairs :J words. Select the pair that best expresses the relationship similar to that original pair.

16. Cobbler : shoes : :

(a) Mechanic, automobile
(b) Carpenter : saw
(c) Painter : easel
(d) Interrogator : question

17. Museum : exhibit : :

(a) Sculptor: statue
(b) Prison : cell
(c) Painting: frame
(d) Theatre : performance

18. Grain : silo : :

(a) Seed : plant
(b) Water: bucket
(c) Druggist : doctor
(d) Furlong: mile

19. Doctor : disease

(a) Moron : imbecility
(b) Paediatrician: senility
(c) Broker : stocks
(d) Psychiatrist: maladjustment

Directions for Q. 20 to 22

Fill in the blanks with appropriate alternative.

20. These weaknesses could______ if you tried hard to improve your standard.

(a) overcome
(b) overcame
(c) be overcome
(d) have been overcome

21. ______the timely help the patient would have died.
(a) Inspite of
(b) Because of
(c) But for
(d) Even after

22. The topic that we were discussing now was first raised by our boss, ________?
(a) wasn't it
(b) isn't it
(c) was it
(d) hasn't it been

Directions for Q. 23 to 26

In the following questions choose the alternative which best expresses the meaning of the given word.

23. Fastidious
(a) doubtful (b) particular
(c) hesitant (d) cautious

24. Emancipate
(a) pass (b) confuse
(c) free (d) imagine

25. Hamper
(a) open (b) hide
(c) notice (d) hinder

26. Despicable
(a) undesirable (b) contemptible
(c) desperate (d) faithless

Directions for Q. 27 to 30

In each of the following sentences four words or phrases have been printed in bold. Define bold part in each sentence is not acceptable in standard English. Pick out that part.

27. If (l)/anyone cares to join (b)/ me in this campaign, either (c)/ now or in future, they (d)/ are most welcome.

28. The government initiated (a)/ various measure (b)/ to raise (c)/ the living standards (d)/of the people.

29. The reason (a) /for my prolonged (b)/absence (c)/from the class was because (d)/I was ill.

30. We admired (a)/his many(b)/attempts bravely (c)/to enter (d)/ the burning building.

PAPER 20

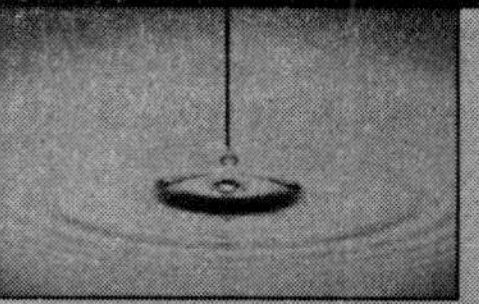

UNITED INDIA INSURANCE AO EXAMINATION, 2013

Directions to Questions 1 to 5

Rearrange the following six sentences (A), (B), (C), (D), (E) and (F) in the proper sequence to form a meaningful paragraph; then answer the questions given below them.

(A) Assuming that all these reasons are true, the fact remains that there is an urgent need to check the accelerated costs and initiate suitable measures.

(B) Some people, attribute it to the increasing greediness among the medicos.

(C) The impact of these measures will be visible only after a considerable passage of time.

(D) Health care costs have been skyrocketing in our country.

(E) The measures include yoga classes with emphasis on physical and mental exercises and also change in food habits.

(F) Certain others feel that it is because of drastic changes in peoples' lifestyle and eating habits.

1. Which of the following would be the **FIRST** statement after rearrangement?

(a) A (b) B
(c) C (d) D
(e) E

2. Which of the following would be the **SECOND** statement after rearrangement?

(a) A (b) B
(c) C (d) D
(e) E

3. Which of the following would be the **FOURTH** statement after rearrangement?

(a) A (b) B
(c) C (d) D

4. Which of the following would be the **FIFTH** statement after rearrangement?

(a) A (b) B
(c) C (d) D
(e) E

5. Which of the following would be the **SIXTH, (LAST)** statement after rearrangement?

(a) A (b) B
(c) C (d) D
(e) E

Directions to Questions 6 to 15

In each of the following sentences there are two blank spaces. Below each sentence there are five pairs of words denoted by numbers (a), (b), (c), (d) and (e). Find out which pair of words can be filled up in the blanks in the sentence in the same sequence to make the sentence grammatically correct and meaningfully complete.

6. To avoid________, there is a need for___ planning of the project.
   (a) cancellation, broad
   (b) problem, deliberate
   (c) pitfalls, systematic
   (d) inconvenience, convenient
   (e) losses, temporary

7. A good management will decide not only the___ for equipment but also its___ for deciding priorities.
   (a) need, urgency
   (b) usefulness, utility
   (c) cost, value
   (d) requirement, necessities
   (e) technology, methodology

8. ________ appears to be a small error in the beginning may turn out to be a ____ in the long run.
   (a) It, disaster
   (b) What, blunder
   (c) That, debacle
   (d) it, slip
   (e) What, incident

9. Being very ____ in nature, he always uses his ____ skills.
   (a) adamant, soft
   (b) polite, basic
   (c) humble, experimental
   (d) pushy, persuasive
   (e) mild, aggressive

10. Demand and supply do not ____ the same relationship as the one that ____ between height and weight.
   (a) possess, has
   (b) incur, is
   (c) defend, volunteers
   (d) bear, borne
   (c) have, exists

11. If the system ____ to yield the desired result, try to ____ the whole procedure in the given sequence.
   (a) entitles, dump
   (b) ignores, reproduce
   (c) fails, reoperate
   (d) imitates, generate
   (e) equips, encompass

12. He is so ____ in his approach that not a single point ever ____his attention.
   (a) meticulous, escapes
   (b) casual, erodes
   (c) fanatic, brings
   (d) deliberate, attracts
   (e) nasty, coincides

13. Generally, ____ students ____ those who are mediocre.
   (a) humble, surmount
   (b) meritorious, surpass
   (c) bright, overestimate
   (d) intelligent, surrender
   (e) studious, respect

14. ____and____should not be tolerated in our country which boasts of 'Ahimsa' as its way of life.
   (a) Politicking, elections
   (b) Dishonour, efficiency
   (c) Lethargy, procrastination
   (d) Nepotism, selfishness
   (e) Hatred, violence

15. He ____ a wrong act because it was ____ for him to do so due to circumstantial forces.
   (a) compelled, necessary
   (b) refused, dangerous
   (c) did, avoidable
   (d) committed, inevitable
   (e) simplified, harmful

Directions to Questions 16 to 25

Read each sentence any to find out whether there is any grammatical error or idiomatic error in it. The error, if any, will be in one part of the sentence. The number of that part is the answer,. If there is no error, the answer is (e). (Ignore, errors of punctuation, if any.)

16. Wheat productions in the region (a)/ will fall drastically (b) unless we do nothing (c)/ to stop climate change. (d)/ No error. (e)

17. The Indian stock market is (a)/ one of the worse (b)/ performing stock markets (c)/ in the recent times. (d)/ No error. (e)

18. With inflation at eleven per cent (a)/ companies need to come up (b)/ with innovative ways to (c)/ get customers to buy its good. (d)/ No error. (e)

19. Private companies which profits (a)/ have grown due to (b)/ the high price of oil (c)/ should offer discounts on cooking gas. (d)/ No error. (e)

20. Having work in (a)/ both public and private sector banks (b)/ Mr. Rao is the ideal choice to (c)/ take over as chairman. (d)/ No error (e)

21. In order to expand, the company (a)/ plans to transform from a (b)/ family based business into (c)/ a professional managed one. (d)/ No error (e)

22. Amit started a small (a)/ construction business two years ago (b) / when the country is (c)/ enjoying a construction boom. (d)/ No error (e)

23. Given the current (a)/ market conditions has (b)/ better for us to invest (c)/ in the infrastructure" sector. (d)/ No error (e)

24. Many athletes have (a)/ taken on yoga (b)/ to develop their concentration (c)/ and reduce stress. (d)/ No error (e)

25. His main aim is (a)/ to create an (b)/ interest in hockey (c)/ among school children. (d)/ No error (e)

Directions to Questions 26 to 35

In the following passage there are blanks, each of which has been numbered. These numbers are printed below the passage and against each five words are suggested, one of which fits the blank appropriately. Find out the appropriate word in each case.

Without doubt there is one thing **26** to all of us-we have all played a game at some time in our lives. Most of us play to relax or have fun, but for many, playing a game or a sport is a way to **27** poverty behind. In fact, in many African countries, playing a sport professionally can **28** the lives of a person's entire family.

For example, in the small town of Bekoji, in Ethiopia **29** than a hundred boys and girls can be seen running at dawn everyday. Each of these youth is **30** and serious and their coach is **31** that one of them will be a world champion. This seems like-an idle **32** but it is virtually a guarantee in this small community **33** mainly farmers. Many of the fastest male and female distance runners in the world hail from this small town. A small handpainted sign which greets visitors outside Bekoji **34** "Welcome to the Village of Athletes". Children here start running at an early age, **35** great distances to fetch water and firewood or to reach school. At the Olympics, runners from this small town are likely to win more medals than those from developed countries. It will give their families a way out of poverty.

26. (a) popular (b) accepted (c) common (d) alike (e) similar

27. (a) leave (b) alleviate (c) forgot (d) prevent (e) reduce

28. (a) shift (b) changes (c) arrange (d) control (e) transform

29. (a) larger (b) further (c) more (d) greater (e) over.

30. (a) performed (b) concentrated
(c) rival (d) focused
(e) playful

31. (a) confident (b) convince
(c) optimist (d) intended
(e) privilege

32. (a) precaution (b) boast
(c) suspicion (d) risk
(e) worship

33. (a) for (b) existing
(c) that (d) comprising
(e) consisting

34. (a) wish (b) warn
(c) inform (d) notices
(e) reads

35. (a) competing (b) covering
(c) driving (d) measuring
(e) following

Directions to Questions 36 to 40

Which of the phrases (a), (b), (c) and (d) given below should replace the phrase given in bold in the following sentences to make the sentence grammatically correct? If the sentence is correct as it is and there is no correction required mark (e) i.e. No correction required' as the answer.

36. The US economy is **present in the face off** a serious recession,
(a) having to face of at present
(b) presently facing up to
(c) presented on the face of
(d) presently facing
(e) No correction required

37. Economists have predicted that the country's economic growth **falls low to** eight per cent this year.
(a) falling as low as
(b) fell to as low as
(c) will fall to as low as
(d) fallen lower than
(e) No correction required

38. In **all likeness** the company will fail to achieve its production targets this year.
(a) With every likeliness
(b) In all likelihood
(c) It is likely for
(d) In every likeness
(e) No correction required

39. We have failed **assessment of** the advantages of outsourcing our IT operations.
(a) in assessment
(b) in not assessing up
(c) to assess
(d) the assessment of
(e) No correction required

40. **One of the key competencies** for managers are ethics and the ability to motivate others.
(a) Among the key competencies
(b) Beside the key competency
(c) Including the key competencies
(d) Within the key competence
(e) No correction required

Directions to Questions 41 to 50

Read the following passage carefully and answer the questions given below it. Certain words/ phrases have been printed in bold to help you locate them while answering some of the questions.

There are various sectors in India that are to be assessed for their strengths, weaknesses, opportunities and threats.

The total population is over 1 billion which will increase to 1.46 billion by 2035 to cross China. The huge population will result in higher unemployment and deterioration of quality. Literacy, in India is yet another factor to be discussed. According to 1991 census, 64.8% of the population was illiterate. The major downtrend of education is due to child labour which has spread all over India and this should be totally eradicated by way of **surveillance** and a good educational system implemented properly by the Government.

Pollution is one more threat to the environment and for the country's prospects. This has been experienced more in urban areas mainly in metropolitan cities. The water pollution by the sewage seepage into the ground water and improper maintenance will lead to various diseases which in turn will affect the next generation. In most of the cities there is no proper sewage disposal. The Government has to take effective steps to control population which, in turn, will minimize the pollution.

Poverty questions the entire strength of India's political view and minimizes the energetic way of approach. The shortfall of rains, enormous floods, unexpected famine, drought, earthquake and the recent tsunami hit the country in a negative way. The proactive approach through effective research and analytical study helps us to determine the effects in advance. Proper allocation of funds is a **prerequisite**. In developed countries like U.S. and Japan precautionary methods are adopted to overcome this, but it has to be improved a lot in our systems.

Increased population is one of the major reasons for poverty and the Government is unable to allocate funds for basic needs to the society. India has nearly 400 million people living below the poverty line and 90% of active population is in informal economy. The children are forced to work due to their poverty and differential caste system. They work in match industry for daily wages, as servants, mechanics, stone breakers, agricultural workers, etc. To prevent child labour, existing laws which favour the Anti Child Labour Act should be implemented by the Government vigorously.

More population results in cheap cost by virtue of the demand supply concept. Most of the foreign countries try to utilize this factor by outsourcing their business in India with a very low capital. According to U.S., India is a "Knowledge pool" with cheap labour. The major advantage is our communication and technical skill which is adaptable to any environment. The cutting edge skill in IT of our professionals helps the outsourcing companies to **commensurate** with the needs of the consumers in a short span. The major competitors for India are China and Philippines and by the way of an effective communication and expert technical ability, Indians are ahead of the race. The major Metropolitan states are targeting the outsourcing field vigorously by giving various amenities to the outsourcing companies like tax concession, allotting land etc., to start their businesses in its cities without any hurdles. Thereby most of the MNCs prefer India as their destinations and capitalize the resources to maximize their assets. Infrastructure is another key factor for an outsourcing company to start a business in a particular city. It includes road, rail, ports, power and water. The increased input in infrastructure in India is very limited where China's record is excellent.

India in earlier days gave more importance to the development of industry and less importance to other departments. But the scenario has quite changed now-a-days by allocating a special budget of funds for security. This is because of the frightening increase in terrorism all around the world especially emerging after the 9/11 terror attack in U.S. In the last ten years, budget towards the development of military forces is higher when compared to others. It shows that the threat from our neighbouring countries is escalating. India has to concentrate more on this security factor to wipe out the problem in the way of cross-border terrorism.

Making India, a developed country in 2020 is not an easy task/India has to keep in check a variety of factors in order to progress rapidly. To quote China as an example is that they demolished an old building to construct a very big port to meet future demands, but India is still waiting for things to happen. The profits gained by India through various sectors are to be spent for the development and welfare of the country. India's vision for a brighter path will come true not only by mere words or speech, but extra effort needed at all levels to overcome the pitfalls.

41. Which of the following, according to the author, is/are a result(s) of increased population in India?

(A) Pollution
(B) Poverty
(C) Unemployment

(a) Only (A)
(b) Only (A) and (B)
(c) Only (B)
(d) Only (A) and (C)
(e) All (A), (B) and (C)

42. Why, according to the author, has the Indian Government allotted more funds to strengthen the military forces?

(a) To improve security in order to counter increasing terrorism

(b) As the security in India over the past ten years was grossly inadequate
(c) As the U.S. too has strengthened its military forces after the 9/11 attack
(d) As the industry is developed enough and is not in need of any more funds
(e) None of these

43. What is the author's main objective in writing this passage?
(a) To exhort the Government to garner support from its neighbouring countries
(b) To suggest to the Government to follow China's example blindly thereby bringing about rapid development
(c) To highlight the plight of the poor
(d) To discuss the problems of child labour and suggest suitable remedies
(e) To bring forth the problems associated with the India's development and to suggest measures to counter. them

44. Why, according to the author, is India one of the favourite destinations for investment by outsourcing companies?
(A) Shorter response time for clients
(B) Better technical skills
(C) Availability of cheap labour
(a) Only (C)
(b) All (A), (B) and (C)
(c) Only (B) and (C)
(d) Only (A) and (B)
(e) Only (A)

45. Which of the following is/are true in the context of the passage?
(A) India leads the way in the amount invested in the development of infrastructure.
(B) Political system in India is not influenced by poverty
(C) Indian population would increase by approximately 50 per cent in the next twenty five years.
(a) Only (A) and (B)
(b) Only (B)
(c) Only (C)
(d) Only (B) and (C)
(e) All (A), (B) and (C)

46. Which of the following is/are the facility(ies) available to MNCs investing in India?
(A) Easy availability of land
(B) Better infrastructure than China.
(C) Tax Concessions
(a) Only (C)
(b) All (A), (B) and (C)
(c) Only (A) and (B)
(d) Only (A) and (C)
(e) None of these

47. Which of the following, according to the author, is a result of poverty in India?
(a) Lack of a robust security system
(b) Child labour and the resulting dearth of educated youth
(c) Floods, famines and other calamities
(d) Rapid increase in population
(e) None of these

48. How, according to the author, can the effects of floods, famines, drought, etc. be minimized?
(a) By limiting pollution thereby reducing the chances of such events taking place
(b) By educating the children about the ill effects of such calamities who in turn will help during the time of need
(c) By following the U.S. system of providing relief to its citizens
(d) By allotting proper funds for research which can predict the outcome of such calamities and thus design relief measures
(e) None of these

Directions to Questions 49 to 50

Choose the word/group of words which is **most similar** in meaning to the word/group of words printed in **bold** as used in the passage

49. **SURVEILLANCE**
(a) spying (b) cameras
(c) security (d) observation
(e) alertness

50. **PREREQUISITE**
(a) result (b) association
(c) necessity (d) factor
(e) mystery

ANSWER KEY

New India Assurance Examination – 2005

1. (a)	2. (a)	3. (b)	4. (d)	5. (b)
6. (a)	7. (c)	8. (b)	9. (c)	10. (d)
11. (c)	12. (b)	13. (d)	14. (a)	15. (c)
16. (b)	17. (a)	18. (d)	19. (c)	20. (b)
21. (a)	22. (b)	23. (c)	24. (c)	25. (a)
26. (d)	27. (a)	28. (b)	29. (b)	30. (c)

GIC AAO Examination – 2005

1. (d)	2. (c)	3. (b)	4. (b)	5. (a)
6. (b)	7. (c)	8. (a)	9. (d)	10. (b)
11. (b)	12. (c)	13. (d)	14. (a)	15. (c)
16. (b)	17. (d)	18. (a)	19. (b)	20. (d)
21. (c)	22. (d)	23. (c)	24. (c)	25. (b)
26. (b)	27. (d)	28. (d)	29. (a)	30. (c)

New India Assurance AAO Examination – 2011

1. (d)	2. (a)	3. (c)	4. (a)	5. (d)
6. (c)	7. (d)	8. (c)	9. (c)	10. (c)
11. (d)	12. (b)	13. (d)	14. (c)	15. (a)
16. (a)	17. (d)	18. (b)	19. (d)	20. (d)
21. (c)	22. (a)	23. (d)	24. (c)	25. (d)
26. (b)	27. (c)	28. (b)	29. (d)	30. (c)

United India Assurance AO Examination – 2013

1. (d)	2. (b)	3. (a)	4. (e)	5. (c)
6. (c)	7. (a)	8. (b)	9. (e)	10. (d)
11. (c)	12. (a)	13. (e)	14. (e)	15. (d)
16. (c)	17. (b)	18. (d)	19. (a)	20. (a)
21. (d)	22. (c)	23. (b)	24. (e)	25. (e)
26. (c)	27. (b)	28. (e)	29. (c)	30. (d)
31. (a)	32. (c)	33. (d)	34. (e)	35. (b)
36. (d)	37. (c)	38. (b)	39. (c)	40. (a)
41. (e)	42. (a)	43. (e)	44. (b)	45. (c)
46. (d)	47. (b)	48. (d)	49. (d)	50. (c)

FREQUENCY ANALYSIS

ABBREVIATIONS USED:

Comprehension / **Comp**, Sentence Completion / **SC**, Sentence Filler / **SF**, Cloze Test/ **CT**, Synonyms/ **Syn**, Antonyms/ **Ant**, Idioms and Phrase/ **IP**, Substitution/ **Subt**, Sentence arrangement/ **SA**, Spelling/ **SPL**, Miscellaneous/**Misc.**, Total Marks/**TM**, Sentence error/**SE**, Sentence Improvement/ **SI**.

New India Assurance Examination – 2005

	Comp.	SC	SF	CT	Syn	Ant	IP	Subt	SA	SE	SPL	SI	MISC.	TM
	5	5+5			5	5				5				30

New India Assurance AAO Exam – 2011

	Comp.	SC	SF	CT	Syn	Ant	IP	Subt	SA	SE	SPL	SI	MISC.	TM
	5	5			5	5			5	5				30

GIC AAO Examination – 2005

	Comp.	SC	SF	CT	Syn	Ant	IP	Subt	SA	SE	SPL	SI	MISC.	TM
		3			3+14	4				4+4			4+4	30

United India Assurance AO – 2013

	Comp.	SC	SF	CT	Syn	Ant	IP	Subt	SA	SE	SPL	SI	MISC.	TM
	10	10		10					10	10		5		50

TREND ANALYSIS

GIC Examinations of 2005 show a simple pattern but there is a change in the year 2011. 'Usage of words' is a variation of the vocabulary test. There is a question on analogy also. So the intention for innovation in the question paper pattern is very clear. In 2013 total marks have been increased, and more units have been a dded, but all the units are covered by the chapters of this book.

The variation should not be a cause of concern among students because it is covered by one or the other unit of the book. The level of questions is almost similar to that of the Bank PO Examination.

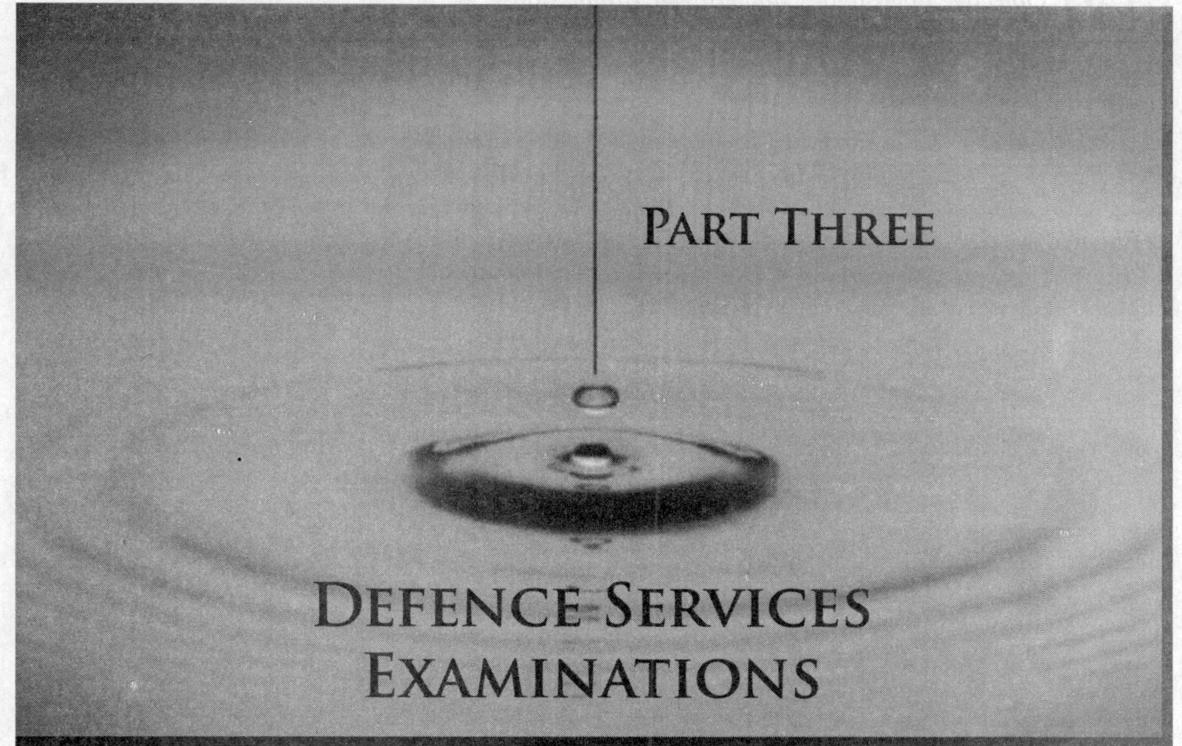

PART THREE

DEFENCE SERVICES EXAMINATIONS

The Indian Defence Services offer esteemed and much prestigious jobs for the Indian Nationals. The Defence jobs of Indian Government demands efficient people with remarkable aptitude, spirit, sense of belonging with the nation and tremendous self-confidence. The jobs offer lucrative benefits and lifestyle to the aspirants.

Following are the different Examinations conducted by the Indian Defence Services:

1. Combined Defence Services (CDS) Exam (UPSC)
2. National Defence Academy (NDA) Exam (UPSC)

Combined Defence Service (CDS) Examination

The Combined Defence Service Exam is conducted by UPSC twice every year for recruitment to officer cadre of the Army, Navy, and Air Force. CDS exam is conducted generally in the months of May and October.

Candidates qualifying at the written test are interviewed by the Service Selection Board and if finally selected, depending upon the choice given by the candidates and their merit list ranking, are sent to one of the following institutes for orientation training:

(a) Indian Military Academy (IMA), Dehradun;
(b) Naval Academy, Goa;
(c) Air Force Academy, Begumpet, Hyderabad and;
(d) Officer's Training Academy (OTA), Chennai.

The test format of English contains 120 questions and almost all basic units are tested. Comprehension passages are short and the level of difficulty is moderate. Questions are spread evenly over comprehension, vocabulary, and applied grammar. There is no tendency to innovate or startle. The pattern is common and has persisted over the years. Overall preparation will ensure success.

National Defence Academy (NDA) Examinations

Recruitment of candidates to Army, Navy, and Air force wings of the NDA is through National

Defence Academy Entrance Exam which is held twice a year, generally in the month of April and September. NDA exam is conducted by the Union Public Service Commission (UPSC). A candidate must be an unmarried male. The course of training is for three years.

English language test forms a part of the examination format. The pattern of the questions has remained same over the years. Questions are usually straightforward and of easy-to-moderate level. Comprehension passages are short and questions are distributed over comprehension, vocabulary, and applied grammar. The pattern will remain hopefully the same. There will be little or no innovation in the test format. Overall preparation will ensure success.

PAPER 21

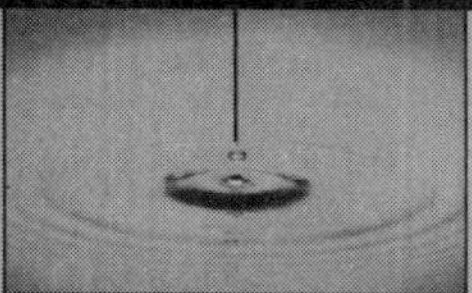

NATIONAL DEFENCE ACADEMY EXAMINATION, APRIL 2004

Fill in the Blanks

Directions to Questions 1 to 16:

Each of the following six sentences has a blank space and four words or groups of words are given after the sentence. Out of these four choices, select the word or group of words which you consider the most appropriate for the blank space and mark your choice on the Answer sheet.

1. To the dismay of all the students, the class monitor was __________ berated by the Principal at a school assembly.
   (a) critically (b) ignominiously
   (c) prudently (d) fortuitously

2. All attempts to revive the fishing industry were __________ failure.
   (a) foredoomed to (b) heading at
   (c) predicted for
   (d) estimated to

3. There are __________ parked outside than yesterday.
   (a) fewer cars
   (b) few cars
   (c) less cars
   (d) a small number of cars

4. The minister had to __________ some awkward questions from reporters.
   (a) fend (b) fend at
   (c) fend out (d) fend off

5. The __________ of evidence was on the side of the plaintiff since all but one of the witnesses testified that his story was correct.
   (a) propensity (b) force
   (c) preponderance (d) brunt

6. Attention to detail is __________ of a fine craftsman.
   (a) hallmark (b) stamp
   (c) seal of authority (d) authenticity

Spotting Errors

Directions to Questions 7 to 11:

(i) In this section a number of sentences are given. The sentences are underlined in three separate parts and each one is labelled (a), (b), and (c). Read each sentence to find out whether there is an error in any underlined part. No sentence has more than one error. When you find an error in any one of the underlined parts (a), (b) or (c), indicate your response on the separate answer sheet at the appropriate space. You may feel that there is no error in a sentence. In that case letter (d) will signify a 'No error' response.

(ii) You are to indicate only one response for each item in your answer sheet. (If you indicate more than one response, your answer will be considered wrong.) Errors may be in grammar, word usage or idioms. There may be a word missing or there may be a word which should be removed.

(iii) You are *not* required to correct the error. You are required only to indicate your response on the answer sheet.

Examples 'P' and 'Q' have been solved for you.

P. The young child(a) singed(b) a very sweet song.(c) No error.(d)

Q. We worked(a) very hard(b) throughout the season.(c) No error.(d)

Explanation:

In item P, the word 'signed' is wrong. The letter under this part is (b); so (b) is the correct answer. Similarly, for item Q, (d) is the correct answer, as the sentence does not contain any error.

7. If it weren't (a) for you, (b) I wouldn't be alive today. (c) No error. (d)
8. He looked like a lion (a) baulked from (b) its prey. (c) No error. (d)
9. Widespread flooding (a) is effecting (b) large areas of the villages. (c) No error. (d)
10. She regards (a) negotiating prices with customers (b) as her special preserve. (c) No error. (d)
11. Often in political campaigns, a point is reached at which (a) the candidates take out their gloves (b) and start slugging with bare fits. (c) No error. (d)

Select ing Word/Phrases

Directions to Questions 12 to 16:

In the following passage at certain points, you are given a choice of *three words/phrases*, underlined and marked (a), (b), and (c). Choose the best word/phrase out of the three and indicate your choice in the relevant column of your Answer Sheet.

Examples 'K' and 'L' have been solved for you.

K. The river has been
(a) rising (b) raising
(c) arising
all night.

L. We built the raft
(a) too strong (b) very strong
(c) strong enough
to hold us.

Explanation:

Out of the list given in 'K', only 'rising' is the correct answer because a river cannot be raised, it rises on its own. So (a) is the correct answer for item 'K'. For item 'L', (c) is the correct answer.

Read the passage carefully before you make your choices.

12. It hasn't worked
(a) by (b) out
(c) off
that way

13. Indeed, the gaps between theory and reality are so numerous that they
(a) raise (b) arise
(c) rise
questions about how much, if at all, the theory will work in the future.

14. Americans projected their own experience onto the rest of the world. If prosperity and material progress had created political cohesion at home—binding together a large and
(a) ethically diverse

(b) ethnically diverse

(c) ethnically wide

15. nation—it could do the same abroad. But this marriage between economics and politics may be losing its power. What seemed to be the ascendancy of American ideas camouflaged new problems and conflicts. The theory may have been

(a) better (b) aptly

(c) much

16. suited to the cold war than its aftermath. The most

(a) conspicuous (b) conscientious

(c) conscious

problem, of course, involves the outbreak of terrorism.

Synonyms

Directions to Questions 17 to 23:

Each of the following seven items consists of a word in capital letters, followed by four words or groups of words. Select the word or group of words that is most *similar* in meaning to the word in capital letters.

17. PROCRASTINATE

(a) Intimidate (b) Humiliate

(c) Predict (d) Postpone

18. ABOMINABLE

(a) Original (b) Detestable

(c) Preferable (d) Complimentary

19. RESCIND

(a) Cancel (b) Enjoy

(c) Praise (d) Receive

20. COLLATERAL

(a) Pathetic (b) Tiresome

(c) Guarantee (d) Magnanimous

21. KNAVE

(a) Novice (b) Dishonest

(c) Futuristic (d) Traditional

22. FINESSE

(a) Skill (b) Softness

(c) Charm (d) Gist

23. ARDOUR

(a) Enthusiasm (b) Candidness

(c) Discipline (d) Fairness

Antonyms

Directions to Questions 24 to 30:

Each of the following *Seven* items consists of a word in capital letters, followed by four words or groups of words. Select the word or group of words that is *furthest* in meaning to the word in capital letters.

24. SAGE

(a) Miser (b) Fool

(c) Traitor (d) Tyrant

25. FLEDGLING

(a) Adversary

(b) Callow

(c) Social outcast

(d) Experienced person

26. PREDILECTION

(a) Predicament (b) Afterthought

(c) Aversion (d) Postponement

27. HIDEBOUND

(a) Strong-willed (b) Open-minded

(c) Well-informed (d) Well-to-do

28. ADULATION

(a) Criticism (b) Purity

(c) Ambiguous (d) Accolades

29. ANIMATED

(a) Penetrating (b) Modern

(c) Dull (d) Similarity

30. ILLUSIVE

(a) Not brilliant (b) Not coherent

(c) Not deceptive (d) Not obvious

Ordering of Sentences

Directions to Questions 31 to 35:

In the following items each passage consists of six sentences. The first sentence (S_1) and the sixth sentence (S_6) are given in the beginning. The middle four sentences in each have been removed and jumbled up. These are labelled P, Q, R and S. You are required to find out the proper sequence of the four sentences and mark accordingly on the answer sheet.

Example 'X' has been solved for you.

X. S_1 : There was a boy named Jack.

S_6 : At last she turned him out of the house.

P : So the mother asked him to find work.

Q : They were very poor.

R : He lived with his mother.

S : But Jack refused to work.

The proper sequence should be:

(a) R Q P S (b) P Q R S
(c) Q P R S (d) R P S Q

Explanation:

The proper sequence in this example is R Q P S which is marked by (a). Therefore, (a) is the correct answer.

31. S_1 : A city tour organised by the airport got our next vote.

S_6 : "We can only grow in height as most of our land is reclaimed from the mud brought from neighbouring countries", said Bernadette.

P : A bumboat ride through the Singapore River gave us a vantage view of the country's prized possession of skyscrapers in the central business district.

Q : The tour is very popular with transit passengers and there are many such buses doing the route.

R : We were greeted into an air-conditioned Volvo bus with a bottle of chilled water.

S : On the drive through the 'colonial heart' of the city, our guide, Bernadette, pointed out the Parliament House, Supreme Court and City Hall to us.

The proper sequence should be:

(a) R S Q P (b) P Q S R
(c) R Q S P (d) P S Q R

32. S_1: But Bhutan is a curious mix of modern and the medieval.

S_6 : His licence plate reads simply "BHUTAN'.

P : It was next to a speed limit sign : 8 km an hour.

Q : Even the king zips through in a navy blue Toyota Land Cruiser.

R : I noticed a rusty sign for the M Kit Kat chocolate bar and realised it was the only advertisement I had seen.

S : Yet in the cities, most middle class people drive brand new Japanese cars.

The proper sequence should be:

(a) S Q R P (b) R P S Q
(c) S P R Q (d) R Q S P

33. S_1: His usually fretful features composed, Javagal Srinath announced his retirement from international cricket.

S_6 : He finished with 236 wickets in 67 Tests and 315 in 229 One-day Internationals.

P : He had spent the early years of his 13-yers career sitting out nine Tests when he was at his quickest, being reminded of everything he was not.

Q : In a classic case of appreciating a good thing when it is gone, the tributes poured in for India's most successful pace bowler after Kapil Dev.

R : Not aggressive enough, not a non-vegetarian, not an all-rounder.

S : Srinath soldiered on, whether wickets were flat or causes lost, as they often were when India toured.

The proper sequence should be:

(a) Q P R S (b) R S Q P
(c) Q S R P (d) R P Q S

34. S_1 : However, the flower industry also has its share of thorns.

S_6 : Also, there are not tax concessions from the government.

P : Most companies have to individually invest in the transport, which is very costly.

Q : Then there are infrastructural bootlenecks—no refrigerated transport or retail chains and warehouses to store the highly perishable commodity.

R : For one, it is extremely fragmented and dominated by small players who don't have the financial muscle to expand the business.

S : Ferns & Petals claims to be the only flower retailer with a multi-city presence in India.

The proper sequence should be:

(a) Q S P R (b) R P Q S
(c) Q P R S (d) R S Q P

35. S_1 : One could well be forgiven for momentarily confusing Spencer Plaza, Chennai, with a Dubai Shopping Mall.

S_6 : Sensing that healthcare plus tourism adds to big opportunities, corporate hospitals, in cooperation with tour operators, are promoting India as a healthcare destination from the Middle East to Far East.

P : Having satiated their shopping instincts, many head back, not to a hotel, but to a hospital, and to ailing relatives.

Q : Arabs pour in and out of trendy showrooms, laden with bags full of branded clothes, footwear and cosmetics.

R : It is a scenario being replicated across India.

S : For these are tourists with a difference, attracted to India for its cutting edge medical expertise more than its charms.

The proper sequence should be:

(a) Q P S R (b) S R Q P
(c) Q R S P (d) S P Q R

Ordering of Words in a Sentence

Directions to Questions 36 to 40:

In the following items some parts of the sentence have been jumbled up. You are required to re-arrange these parts which are labelled P, Q, R and S to produce the correct sentence. Choose the proper sequence and mark in your Answer Sheet accordingly.

Example 'Z' has been solved for you.

Z. It is well known that the effect (P) is very bad (Q) on children (R) of cinema. (S)

The proper sequence should be:

(a) P S R Q (b) S P Q R
(c) S R P Q (d) Q S R P

Explanation:

The proper way of writing the sentence is 'It is well known that the effect of cinema on children is very bad.' This is indicated by the sequence P S R Q and so (a) is the correct answer.

36. Brazil's Guaranis from being Internet savvy(P) are an ancient tribe who live in the country's remote jungles,(Q) excluded them(R) but that has not.(S)

The proper sequence should be:

(a) P S R Q (b) Q R S P
(c) P R S Q (d) Q S R P

37. A game host that could be used at the airport duty-free shops(P) and the winner walked away with(Q) shot out ten witty questions(R) vouchers worth 200 Singapore dollars.(S)

The proper sequence should be:

(a) P S Q R (b) R Q S P
(c) P Q S R (d) R S Q P

38. And while without adequate international support(P) the US military has been forced into remaining in Iraq(Q) the overthrow of Saddam Hussein may have been quick.(R) longer than anticipated.(S)

The proper sequence should be:

(a) R S Q P (b) P Q S R
(c) R Q S P (d) P S Q R

39. The socialist philosophy as it is the market philosophy(P) has been given a decent burial(Q) which is the rage now(R) in political practice.(S)

The proper sequence should be:

(a) Q S P R (b) R P S Q
(c) Q P S R (d) R S P Q

40. It began as an officially sanctioned project, could achieve as a nation(P) but turned into a mass movement and an extraordinary act of faith.(Q) If it got its act together (R) which changed not just the lives of millions but the notions of what India.(S)

The proper sequence should be:

(a) P S R Q (b) Q S R P
(c) P R S Q (d) Q R S P

Comprehension

Directions for Questions 41 to 50:

In this section you have *Three* short passages. After each passage you will find several questions based on the passage. First, read Passage I, and answer the questions based on it. Then go on to the other passages. You are required to select your answers based on the contents of the passage and opinion of the author only.
Examples 'I' and 'J' are solved for you.

Passage

In our approach to life, be it pragmatic or otherwise, a basic fact that confronts us squarely and unmistakably is the desire for peace, security and happiness. Different forms of life at different levels of existence make up the teeming denizens of this earth of ours. And, no matter whether they belong to the higher groups such as human beings or to the lower groups such as animals, all beings primarily seek peace, comfort and security. Life is as dear to a mute creature as it is to a man. Even the lowliest insect strives for protection against dangers that threaten its life. Just as each one of us wants to live and not to die, so do all other creatures.

I. The author's main point is that:
- (a) different forms of life are found on earth
- (b) different levels of existence are possible in nature
- (c) peace and security are the chief goals of all living beings
- (d) even the weakest creature struggles to preserve its life

J. Which one of the following assumptions or steps is essential in developing the author's position?
- (a) All forms of life have a single overriding goal
- (b) The will to survive of a creature is identified with a desire for peace
- (c) All beings are divided into higher and lower groups
- (d) A parallel is drawn between happiness and life, and pain and death.

Explanation:

I. The idea which represents the author's main point is 'peace and security are the chief goals of all living beings', which is response (c). So (c) is the correct answer.

J. The best assumption underlying the passage is 'The will to survive of a creature is identified with a desire for peace', which is response (b). So (b) is the correct answer.

Passage I

I was late bloomer and always envied those people who stood out in high school, because I didn't. I learned early on, though, that it's essential to set yourself apart from the group. Life is one struggle after another to succeed, particularly when you're starting out. If your bio-data is sitting at the bottom of a pile of junk mail, sometimes a distinctive approach will get you noticed, especially if the competition is fierce.

Once, my partner Jerry and I asked the other freelance writers of a TV serial what characters they hated to write for the most. Everybody said the same thing—they disliked writing for the minor characters because they felt that writing for them wouldn't help them get other jobs. Jerry and I decided that we would write scripts for the minor characters because that's what was needed—and we needed to set ourselves apart.

In the first script Jerry and I wrote, a schoolgirl falls in love with a boy in her class. The producers loved the story. And with that one script, Jerry and I were no longer just another comedy-writing team.

41. The author is of the opinion that
- (a) one should be part of the group
- (b) one should be different from others
- (c) it is important to do well in high school
- (d) one should heed to the advice of the seniors

42. The author had been
- (a) into advertising business
- (b) a comedy writer
- (c) a music director
- (d) a newsreader

43. According to the author
   (a) one should be very meticulous in preparing his bio-data
   (b) competition in the job-market is very fierce
   (c) One should follow a conservative approach in preparing his bio-data
   (d) one should try to get noticed by being innovative

44. Jerry and the author wrote scripts for the minor characters
   (a) to realize their creative potential
   (b) to earn more money
   (c) to establish a different image
   (d) because they did not have enough work

Passage II

Wind power has obvious advantages—it is non-polluting, causes no ecological imbalance, requires no throughput fuel and has extremely low gestation period.

After almost a decade of sporadic growth, wind energy finally seems to be stepping out from shadows of alternative technology into the commercial mainstream, worldwide. Even though, India now has an installed base of just over 1,600 MW. This is nothing compared to countries such as Germany, which meets around 20 per cent of its energy requirements from wind energy.

Wind power offers long-term price stability too. Not only are generation costs of such projects low, the capital expenditure is comparable to fossil fuel-based stations. Wind-power plants have low operating and maintenance costs. Long-term economics work out to be quite favourable for the wind-energy. In fact, it is being seen as a solution to sustainable development. By the end of 2001, the installed wind-power was almost 25,000 MW.

45. Which one of the following is correct?
   (a) Wind-power plants take a long time to get commissioned.
   (b) Maintenance cost of wind-power plants is high.
   (c) Wind-power plants lead to violent vibrations.
   (d) Wind-power plants require no fuel.

46. Which one of the following is correct?
   (a) Installation of wind-power plants is resisted by environmentalists.
   (b) Generation cost of wind-power plants is high.
   (c) Installation cost of wind-power plants is much higher than that of fossil fuel-based plants.
   (d) Wind-power is now being commercially harnessed.

47. Which one of the following is correct?
   (a) In Germany, 25,000 MW of electricity is generated by using wind-power.
   (b) Wind-power plants offer no price stability.
   (c) Wind-power is economically viable on long-term basis.
   (d) In America 20% of the power requirements are met through wind-power.

Passage III

A group of prospective jurors was asked by the judge whether any of them felt they had ever been treated unfairly by an officer of the law. "I once got a ticket for running a stop sign", Caroline replied, "even though I definitely came to a complete stop."

"Did you pay the fine?" the judge questioned.

Yes".

If you thought you were innocent", the judge went on, "why didn't you contest it?"

"Your Honour", she replied, "there have been so many times I didn't get a ticket for running a stop sign that I figured this evened things out a little."

48. Which one of the following is correct?
   (a) Caroline was caught travelling without ticket in a local train.
   (b) Caroline was caught while driving at a speed above the speed limit.
   (c) Caroline was driving without a driving license.
   (d) Caroline was fined for jumping the stop signal.

49. Which one of the following is correct?

(a) Caroline made a complaint against the traffic inspector for his high-handedness.

(b) Caroline had to pay a bribe.

(c) Caroline was sent to the jail for her crime.

(d) Caroline decided to pay the fine.

50. Which one of the following is correct?

(a) Caroline had been penalised many times before for driving offences.

(b) Caroline was an officer of the law.

(c) Caroline was a prospective juror.

(d) Caroline was undergoing police training.

PAPER 22

NATIONAL DEFENCE ACADEMY EXAMINATION, 2012

Direction to Questions 1 to 10

(i) In this section, a number of sentences are given. The sentences are underlined in three separate parts and each one is labelled (a), (b) and (c). Read each sentence to find out whether there is an error in any underlined part. No sentence has more than one error. When you find an error in any one of the underlined parts (a), (b) or (c), indicate your response on the Answer Sheet at the appropriate space. You may feel that there is no error in a sentence. In that case, (d) will signify a 'No error' response.

(ii) Errors may be in grammar, word usage or idioms, There may be a word missing or there may be a word which should be removed.

(iii) You are ***not*** required to correct the error. You are required ***only*** to indicate your response on the Answer Sheet.

1. Let us (a) / bring this discussion (b) / to close (c). No error (d)

2. Each of them (a) / have a different version (b) / of the crime (c). / No error (d)

3. I and Gopal (a) / went to the meeting (b) / together (c). / No error (d)

4. Latin is not only hard to write (a) / but also (b) / to read (c). / No error (d)

5. In most villages (a) / the roads are rough; (b) / isn't it? (c) / No error (d)

6. Despite of continuing pain (a) / she worked at her temporary summer job (b) /most of the week (c). / No error (d)

7. As soon the film started (a) / I developed (b) / an irritating headache. (c) / No error (d)

8. He applied for an employment (a)/ in (b) / an office. (c) No error (d)

9. Though we drove fast, the train left, (a) before we could reach (b) / the station. (c) / No error (d)

10. One Indian virtue that has impressed me greatly (a) / and touched me deeply (b) was the Indian people's freedom of rancour. (c) / No error (d)

Direction to Questions 11 to 20

Each of the following items consists of a sentence followed by four words or groups of words. Select the ***synonym*** of the word or words (occurring in the sentence in capital letters) as per the context.

11. The convict's INGENUOUS explanation brought tears in every eye.
(A) Candid (b) Secret
(C) Insincere (d) Consistent

12. The ENORMITY of the population problem is irksome.
(A) Intensity (b) Vastness
(C) Cruelty (d) Fragility

13. EXAGGERATION of facts would always lead to confusion.
(a) Simplification (b) Negation
(c) Emancipation (d) Amplification

14. After his father's death, he became INSOLVENT.
(A) Rich (b) Poor
(C) Bankrupt (d) Nonchalant

15. He INDUCES human beings to want things they don't want.
(a) Influences (b) Dictates
(c) Persuades (d) Appreciates

16. His information is not AUTHENTIC.
(a) Real (b) Reliable
(c) Believable (d) Genuine

17. He is not CUT OUT to be a teacher.
(a) Trained (b) Suited
(c) Selected (d) Guided

18. The Chief Minister REPRIMANDED the officers for their methods of handling the public.
(a) Adulated
(b) Scolded severely
(c) Disapproved of
(d) Suspended

19. Sin is the sole calamity that a wise man should APPREHEND.
(a) Give up (b) Discourage
(c) Comprehend (d) Fear

20. We must be proud of our cultural HERITAGE.
(a) Things we make for ourselves
(b) Things we have lost
(c) Things we have from the past
(d) Things we do for others

Direction to Questions 21 to 30

Each of the following items consists of a sentence followed by four words. Select the ***antonym*** of the word (occurring in the sentence in capital letters) as per the context.

21. The COMPLAINANT was not supportive of providing all facts in the court.
(a) Defendant (b) Advocate
(c) Indulgence (d) Servant

22. Living in a SOLITARY place brings in some kind of satisfaction.
(a) Limited (b) Exotic
(C) Healthy (d) Populous

23. They spent a DISTURBED night after hearing the tragic news.
(a) Restless (b) Sleepless
(c) Mournful (d) Peaceful

24. We have CREATED a beautiful new house from out of the old ruin.
(a) Destroyed (b) Built
(c) Constructed (d) Planned

25. A large number of designer clothes are REVOLTING.
(a) Inviting (b) Beautiful
(c) Fashionable (d) Delightful

26. Though they are twins, they look very DIFFERENT.
(a) Regular (b) Same
(c) Similar (d) Uniform

27. RECESSION is a major cause of unemployment.
(a) Education (b) Inflation
(c) Poverty (d) Computerization

28. He finally CONCEDED that he was involved in smuggling.
(a) Admitted (b) Accepted
(c) Denied (d) Concealed

29. The accused emphatically DENIED the charge in the court.
(a) Accepted (b) Agreed
(c) Asserted (d) Affirmed

30. This cloth is a COARSE of touch.
(a) Delicate (b) Rough
(c) Painful (d) Harsh

Direction to Questions 31 to 40

In the following sentences, parts of the sentences have been jumbled up. You are required to rearrange these parts which are labelled P, Q, R and S to produce the correct sentence. Choose the proper sequence and mark in your Answer Sheet accordingly.

31. even when (P) / are well informed (Q) / people engaged in a conversation (R) / their conversation may be dull (S)
The correct sequence should be
(a) QSPR (b) PRQS
(c) SRQP (d) SQRP

32. a pressure cooker (P) / fits tightly on the top (Q) / consists of a very strong vessel (R) / made of an aluminium alloy with a lid that (S)
The correct sequence should be
(a) PRSQ (b RSPQ
(c) QSPR (d) PQSR

33. is to convince your reader (P) / the aim of an argumentative essay (Q) / you have taken on a subject is right (R) / that the position (S)
The correct sequence should be
(a) SQPR (b) RQSP
(c) PQSR (d) QPSR

34. there is only one way (P) / the world can be (Q) / in which (R) / made safe from the war (S)
The correct sequence should be
(a) RQSP (b) PRQS
(c) PQSR (d) SPRQ

35. the conspiracy (P) / got wind of (Q) / the Government (R) / against the king's life (S)
The correct sequence should be
(a) PQRS (b) RQPS
(c) PSQR (d) SPQR

36. to death penalty is that (P) / in preventing the crime (Q) / the important objection (R) / it has not succeeded (S)
The correct sequence should be
(a) PRSQ (b) PSRQ
(c) RPSQ (d) QSPR

37. choice carefully (P) / when you want to use (Q) / make your (R) / a graphic representation for your data (S)
The correct sequence should be
(a) QRSP (b) SRQP
(C) PRQS (d) QSRP

38. he would like to see some changes (a) but as a junior lecturer (Q) / he does not cut much ice (R) / in the curriculum (S)
The correct sequence should be
(a) PQRS (b) QPSR
(c) QRPS (d) PSQR

39. he simply starves (P) / even when there are good crops (Q) / but if the crops fail (R) he lives from hand to mouth (S)
The correct sequence should be
(a) SQRP (b) PQRS
(c) SRQP (d) SPQR

40. providence had helped me (P)/ to retain my true identity and (Q) / changed the course of my life (R) / in the process (S)
The correct sequence should be
(a) PSQR (b) PQSR
(c) RSQP (d) PRQS

Direction to Questions 41 to 50

Read the following ***three passages*** and answer the items that follow each passage.

Passage–1

Even in the most primitive societies, the great majority of people satisfy a large part of their material needs by exchanging goods and services. Very few people indeed can make for themselves everything they need—all their food, their clothes, their housing, their tools. Ever since men started living in communities, they have been satisfying their needs by means of specialization and exchange; increasingly each individual has concentrated on what he can do best, and has produced more of the special goods or services in which he has concentrated, than he can consume himself. The surplus he has exchanged with other members of the community, acquiring, in exchange the things he needs that others have produced.

41. According to the passage, the great majority of people can satisfy their needs today by
(a) providing things for themselves
(b) exchanging goods and services
(c) concentrating on what they can do best
(d) individual specialization

42. Exchange of goods becomes possible only when
(a) there is no specialization
(b) goods are produced in surplus
(c) primitive societies become modern
(d) individuals make things for themselves

43. Specialization and exchange began when men started
(a) big industries
(b) concentrating on their work
(c) producing things for individual use
(d) living in communities

44. Exchange of goods and services becomes necessary because
(a) man is a social being
(b) reciprocity is the law of life
(c) trade and commerce are means of progress
(d) we cannot produce everything we need ourselves

Passage–2

What interests many people is the possibility of finding an Earth-like planet, and many science fiction stories have been woven around the possibility of there existing a planet somewhere in the universe which is an exact replica of the Earth. There are too many variable quantities for this to be a possibility worth considering. What is possible, if planetary systems are common as they seem to be, is the existence of planets where the conditions are similar to conditions on the Earth and to which our form of life could rapidly adapt. If life had gained a foothold on such a planet, it is possible that life closely paralleling our own planet could have developed.

What sort of conditions is necessary for life as we know it to develop? First of all of course a suitable planetary body is essential. Given this, then two vital conditions must be satisfied. The temperature must be neither too hot nor too cold, since intense heat breaks down organic molecules and severe cold prevents activity from going on. Too much short-wave radiation also upsets living organisms. The other prerequisite is a suitable atmosphere sufficiently dense to give protection from radiation and meteorites and containing oxygen and water vapour in reasonable quantities.

45. This passage suggests that there
(a) cannot be another planet like the Earth
(b) are other planets like the Earth mentioned only in stories
(c) may be other planets like the Earth in this universe
(d) is a planet which is exactly like the Earth

46. The hypothesis about the possibility of planets parallel to the Earth gets its strength from the fact that
(a) the scientists have discovered them
(b) books have been written about them
(c) the planetary system exists
(d) many people have shown interest in it

47. The statement, "If life had gained a foothold on such a planet" means that
(a) if there is life on the planet, it would be like ours
(b) if we go there, we can develop it like this Earth
(c) even if we try, we cannot go and live there
(d) it is impossible for life to develop there

Passage–3

"The doctor's coming in a minute, Inspector", said Miss Smith.

"Yes, thank you for phoning, Miss Smith. It was very kind of you ..... the lady's name is

Mrs. West, you say, ..."

"Yes, that's right."

"And what about Mr. West?"

"Doctor West, Inspector."

"Oh, I see ..... Well, Doctor West, then. Do you know where he is?"

"Not exactly, Inspector. He never told Mrs. West where he was going. You see, they hated each other."

"What do you mean?"

"Well, Doctor West thought that Mrs. West was in love with another man, and everyone knows Doctor West went to see another woman."

48. The conversation appears to be taking place
(a) in a street where an accident has just occurred
(b) in a hotel where Mrs. West suddenly became ill
(c) in Mrs. West's house where the police are enquiring into lady's murder
(d) in Mrs. West's house where a theft has taken place the night before

49. The questions the Inspector asks are
(a) inquisitive
(b) foolish
(c) disturbing
(d) searching

50. "You see, they hated each other." "What do you mean?"

The Inspector seems
(a) to know Doctor West's secret
(b) surprised to get the information
(c) not to have understood Miss Smith
(d) not impressed by Miss Smith's information

ANSWER KEY

NDA Examination, April 2004

1. (b)	2. (a)	3. (a)	4. (d)	5. (b)
6. (a)	7. (b)	8. (b)	9. (b)	10. (d)
11. (a)	12. (b)	13. (a)	14. (b)	15. (a)
16. (a)	17. (d)	18. (b)	19. (a)	20. (c)
21. (b)	22. (a)	23. (a)	24. (b)	25. (d)
26. (c)	27. (b)	28. (a)	29. (c)	30. (c)
31. (a)	32. (c)	33. (a)	34. (d)	35. (a)
36. (d)	37. (b)	38. (c)	39. (a)	40. (d)
41. (b)	42. (b)	43. (d)	44. (c)	45. (d)
46. (d)	47. (c)	48. (d)	49. (d)	50. (c)

NDA Examinations, 2012

1. (c)	2. (b)	3. (a)	4. (d)	5. (c)
6. (a)	7. (a)	8. (a)	9. (a)	10. (c)
11. (a)	12. (b)	13. (d)	14. (c)	15. (a)
16. (b)	17. (b)	18. (b)	19. (d)	20. (c)
21. (a)	22. (d)	23. (d)	24. (a)	25. (a)
26. (b)	27. (c)	28. (a)	29. (a)	30. (a)
31. (b)	32. (a)	33. (d)	34. (b)	35. (c)
36. (c)	37. (d)	38. (d)	39. (b)	40. (b)
41. (b)	42. (c)	43. (d)	44. (d)	45. (c)
46. (b)	47. (a)	48. (a)	49. (d)	50. (b)

Frequency Analysis

ABBREVIATIONS USED

Comprehension / **Comp**, Sentence Completion / **SC**, Sentence Filler / **SF**, Cloze Test/ **CT**, Synonyms/ **Syn**, Antonyms/ **Ant**, Idioms and Phrase/ **IP**, Substitution/ **Subt**, Sentence arrangement/ **SA**, Spelling/ **SPL**, Miscellaneous/**Misc.**, Total Marks/**TM**, Sentence error/**SE**, Sentence Improvement/ **SI**.

NDA Examination, April 2004

	Comp.	SC	SF	CT	Syn	Ant	IP	Subt	SA	SE	SPL	SI	MISC.	TM
	10	6			7	7	5		5+5	5				50

NDA Examinations, 2012

	Comp.	SC	SF	CT	Syn	Ant	IP	Subt	SA	SE	SPL	SI	MISC.	TM
	10				10	10			10	10				50

Trend Analysis

Items covered in 2012 are spotting errors, synonyms, Antonyms, Sentence Ordering and Comprehension.

The trend is simpler than before. The difficulty level in slightly higher. There will not be much innovation. Reading the book carefully ensures grand success.

PAPER 23

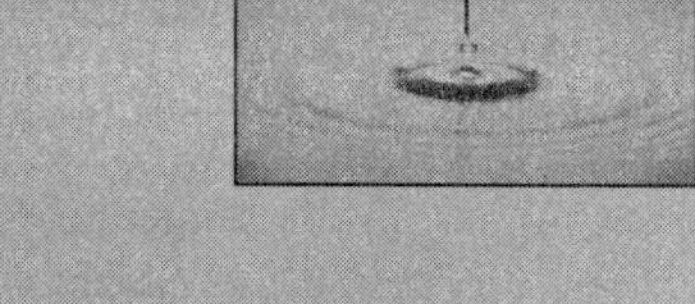

Combined Defence Service Examination, September 2008

Synonyms

Directions for Questions 1 to 18:

Each of these questions consists of a word in capital letters, followed by four words or group of words. Select the word or group of words that is most *similar* in meaning to the word in capital letters.

1. IMPERATIVE
   (a) Negligible (b) Indifferent
   (c) Significant (d) Urgent

2. INTRUDE
   (a) Fault (b) Disagree
   (c) Interrupt (d) Leave

3. RAPPORT
   (a) Love and affection
   (b) Full support
   (c) Harmonious accord
   (d) Sportsmanship

4. SUSTENANCE
   (a) Courage (b) Nourishment
   (c) Health (d) Wisdom

5. VERACITY
   (a) Forcefulness (b) Simplicity
   (c) Truthfulness (d) Humour

6. GUSTO
   (a) Guts (b) Enthusiasm
   (c) Enjoyment (d) Hope

7. INDIGENOUS
   (a) State-of-the-art (b) Indigent
   (c) Native (d) Foreign

8. STARTLED
   (a) Jumped (b) Shocked
   (c) Surprised (d) Offended

9. FACTITIOUS
   (a) Amorous
   (b) Causing dissension
   (c) Controversial
   (d) Artificial

10. DECADENT
(a) Deceased
(b) Disingenuous
(c) Deteriorating
(d) Belonging to the last decade

11. DISPARATE
(a) Different (b) Contrary
(c) Incongruous (d) Unequal

12. PANDEMONIUM
(a) Violence
(b) Quarrel
(c) Wild and noisy disorder
(d) Verbal exchange

13. AFFLICTION
(a) Problem (b) Hardship
(c) Plight (d) Distress

14. EXHORTED
(a) Urged (b) Forced
(c) Persuaded (d) Demanded

15. DISSEMINATE
(a) Develop (b) Popularise
(c) Impart (d) Spread

16. LEGACY
(a) Point (b) Principle
(c) Inheritance (d) Teaching

17. HANDY
(a) Intact (b) Accessible
(c) Supportive (d) Handful

18. INNOCUOUS
(a) Harmless (b) Benevolent
(c) Gentle (d) Non-infectious

Ordering of Words in a Sentence

Directions for Questions 19 to 38:

In these questions, some parts of the sentence have been jumbled up. You are required to rearrange these parts which are labelled P, Q, R and S to produce the correct sentence. Choose the proper sequence.

19. They forget, (P)/ between defeat and victory, (Q)/ that the conditions of warfare have so altered (R)/ that there is not much difference today (S)

Which one of the following is the correct sequence?
(a) SRPQ (b) PQSR
(c) RSQP (d) PRSQ

20. Of all things that distinguish man is his brain (P)/ the most important(Q)/ of the animal kingdom (R)/ from the rest (S)

Which one of the following is the correct sequence?
(a) SRQP (b) QPSR
(c) SRPQ (d) RSQP

21. She introduced me at the party (P)/ I had met (Q)/ to a man(R)/ the previous night (S)

Which one of the following is the correct sequence?
(a) RPQS (b) RQPS
(c) SPRQ (d) PQRS

22. Some men were rarely successful (P)/ but they(Q)/ tried bribing(R)/ their guards(S)

Which one of the following is the correct sequence?
(a) PQRS (b) RQPS
(C) RSQP (D) PQSR

23. Self-taught experts expected to go(P)/ through which (Q)/ the escapers (R)/ prepared maps of the country (S)

Which one of the following is the correct sequence?
(a) PQRS (b) SQRP
(c) SRQP (d) PRQS

24. the nun who was the Principal (P)/ called an assembly (Q)/ of my grand-daughters school (R)/ to announce the result of a fund-raising drive (S)

Which one of the following is the correct sequence?
(a) PQRS (b) PRQS
(c) PQSR (d) PSRQ

25. Whether the plan depends on how it (P)/ suggested will succeed or fail (Q)/ interested in its progress (R)/ will be received by those (S)

Which one of the following is the correct sequence?

(a) SRPQ (b) QPSR
(c) PQRS (d) RSQP

26. This letter is addressed to Mr. Shah (P)/ which is written in Gujarati (Q)/ who is (R)/ my father's best friend (S).

Which one of the following is the correct sequence?

(a) PQRS (b) QPRS
(c) QRSP (d) RSPQ

27. The President a brief vacation at Shimla (P)/ is returning from (Q)/ in order to attend a press conference (R)/ with his wife and children (S)

Which one of the following is the correct sequence?

(a) QSRP (b) QPRS
(c) SQPR (d) RSQP

28. The clothes were sent by mistake (P)/ to my father(Q)/ who was very much surprised (R)/ that I ordered (S)

Which one of the following is the correct sequence?

(a) SQPR (b) PQSR
(c) PQRS (d) SPQR

29. If in their daily lives the people of our country (P)/ and never deceive one another (Q)/ always speak the truth (R)/ then our prestige will be great (S)

Which one of the following is the correct sequence?

(a) PQRS (b) RQPS
(c) SPQR (d) PRQS

30. A tortoise fly in the air (P)/ two geese (Q)/ everyday (R)/ watched (S)

Which one of the following is the correct sequence?

(a) SQPR (b) RSQP
(c) PSQR (d) RPSQ

31. Nobody in the house was kept (P)/ where the key (Q)/ seemed to know (R)/ to the main door (S)

Which one of the following is the correct sequence?

(a) RQPS (b) QPRS
(c) SQPR (d) RQSP

32. the clerk (P)/ was not present (Q)/ in the officer (R)/ whom I wanted to meet (S)

which one of the following is the correct sequence?

(a) PSQR (b) PQRS
(c) PRSQ (d) RPQS

33. the man (P)/ made a complaint (Q)/ at the police station (R)/ whose cycle was stolen (S)

Which one of the following is the correct sequence?

(a) PQRS (b) PRSQ
(c) PSQR (d) RPQS

34. In the middle of (P)/ he stopped (Q)/ his speech (R)/ to take a glass of water (S)

Which one of the following is the correct sequence?

(a) QRSP (b) QRPS
(c) QPRS (d) PQRS

35. after his arrival (P)/ immediately (Q)/ he began to (R)/ quarrel with his wife (S)

Which one of the following is the correct sequence?

(a) QRSP (b) PQRS
(c) QPRS (d) RQSP

36. We met this evening (P)/ on our way home (Q)/ Mr. and Mrs. Gupta (R)/ and asked them if they would be free (S)

Which one of the following is the correct sequence?

(a) QRPS (b) PQRS
(c) RQSP (d) RQPS

37. You can learn and can be quite difficult (P)/ as well as the difficult ones (Q)/ the easy things (R)/ although the easy ones are not so easy (S)

Which one of the following is the correct sequence?

(a) SPRQ (b) PQRS
(c) QSPR (d) RQSP

38. Please equally (P)/ share the prize money (Q)/ that all are satisfied (R)/ among your friends to make sure (S)

Which one of the following is the correct sequence?

(a) QRSP (b) PQSR
(c) QPRS (d) QPSR

Ordering of Sentence

Directions for Questions 39 to 53:

In the following items, each passage consists of six sentences. The first sentence (S_1) and the final sentence (S_6) are given in the beginning. The middle four sentences in each have been removed and jumbled up. There are labelled P, Q, R and S. You are required to find out the proper sequence of the four sentences.

39.

S_1 : It was Saturday.

S_6 : The children had already bought roasted grain and peanuts to get into a picnic mood.

P : A taxi carried us all to, the zoo.

Q : They wanted to he taken out and we decided to take them to the local zoo.

R : My sister's two young children were at our house.

S : We bought the tickets and entered the zoo.

Which one of the following is the correct sequence?

(a) RQSP (b) RPQS
(c) RQPS (d) PRQS

40.

S_1 : The officer rose to his feet, trembling.

S_6 : A half-hour later he returned to camp.

P : He failed to find him there.

Q : Pulling himself together, he ran rapidly away from the cliff to a point a half-mile from its foot.

R : He was disappointed.

S : He expected to find the horseman somewhere there.

Which one of the following is the correct sequence?

(a) RPQS (b) QPSR
(c) QSPR (d) SQPR

41.

S_1 : It was a bitterly cold night and even at the far end of the, bus the wind cut like a knife.

S_6 : I saw trouble brewing.

P : The conductor came in and took the fares.

Q : The younger of the two women was dressed in sealskin, and carried one of those little Pekinese dogs that women like to carry in their laps.

R : The bus stopped, and two women and a man got in together and filled the vacant places.

S : Then his eyes rested with cold malice on the beady-eyed little dog.

Which one of the following is the correct sequence?

(a) RQPS (b) RSQP
(c) RPQS (d) PSRQ

42.

S_1 : Dinner had been served—his daughter laid out the plates.

S_6 : Then, silently she left the table to retire for the night—it was as if she had never been there.

P : She was just a child, only 14—too young, too simple to know to understand.

Q : He sat down gruffly, not saying a word to her.

R : She had already had her meal and was standing by his side, not quite knowing what to do.

S : Bread and cheese—a simple subsistence at the end of a not so simple life.

Which one of the following is the correct sequence?

(a) QPSR (b) RPSQ
(c) QRPS (d) SQPR

43.

S_1 : When my car broke down, I took it to the only mechanic available in our town.

S_6 : They pushed the car down one street and up another and soon we had gone through most of the streets in the town but the car wouldn't start.

P : But it just refused to start.

Q : I went there at the appointed time to collect it.

R : So I sat at the wheel and the mechanic and his helper started to push it.

S : He said it required some minor repairs and asked me to collect it in the evening.

Which one of the following is the correct sequence?

(a) SQPR (b) QSRP
(c) RPQS (d) PQRS

44.

S_1 : Some people prefer country life to city life.

S_6 : For these reasons more and more people are leaving the country to live in the city.

P : Life in the country is quieter, cleaner and less hectic.

Q : The city also offers more privacy since neighbours are too busy to be interfering in the affairs of others.

R : However, the city offers more excitement, a wide variety of activities and a chance to meet more people.

S : Country people live longer and generally seem to be healthier and happier.

Which one of the following is the correct sequence?

(a) PSRQ (b) SRQP
(c) RQPS (d) QPSR

45.

S_1 : The clerk read the statement loudly and clearly.

S_6 : They returned in five minutes.

P : The judge brought down the gavel sharply and roared.

Q : He told the jury to return a lawful verdict.

R : We, the jury, find the defendant not guilty, provided he returns the mule.

S : There is no such verdict in the law; the defendant is either guilty or not guilty.

Which one of the following is the correct sequence?

(a) RPSQ (b) RSPQ
(c) QRPS (d) PSRQ

46.

S_1 : One day I went into the water off the coast of Africa.

S_6 : I hurled at him the rubber fins.

P : I sighted a shark at a short distance from me.

Q : He launched towards me as hard and swift as a missile.

R : I was floating a shallow depth, without making a movement.

S : Every muscle of my body tensed.

Which one of the following is the correct sequence?

(a) PSQR (b) SQRP
(c) RPSQ (d) PQSR

47.

S_1 : There is no reason for the terror which the sight of a snake causes in most people.

S_6 : Being aggressive by nature, they can attack human beings for no reason at all, taking a fisherman or swimmer by surprise in the water, where the man is somewhat helpless.

P : Of the poisonous snakes, only those found in the sea are always dangerous.

Q : They are only too anxious to avoid human beings.

R : Many more people are killed, much more frequently, by motorcycles and cigarettes than by snakes.

S : The majority of snakes are harmless.

Which one of the following is the correct sequence?

(a) SQRP (b) RSQP
(c) RPQS (d) PQRS

48.

S_1 : I had not seen my father for several years.

S_6 : His words sank deep into my heart.

P : I met him late one evening in his flat.

Q : I wrote him a note suggesting a very early meeting.

R : He listened to my story in silence.

S : When he spoke, his voice was soft but without warmth.

Which one of the following is the correct sequence?

(a) QSRP (b) PQRS
(c) QPRS (d) QPSR

49.

S_1 : Gopal worked as a labourer at the building site.

S_6 : He unscrewed the lid and found a valuable collection of old silver in it.

P : But Gopal made a bid and he got the box.

Q : There was no key to it and it seemed useless, but Gopal took it home.

R : Once while returning from his work Gopal stopped at an auction sale.

S : No one seemed to want a rough old box when it was put up for sale.

Which one of the following is the correct sequence?

(a) SPRQ (b) SRPQ
(c) RSPQ (d) RPQS

50.

S_1 : The ancestors of whales, it is said, lived on land, for they still have slight traces of hind-legs.

S_6 : He has flippers on his sides to keep him balanced and layers of fat or oil under the skin which furnish heart and make the huge body light and buoyant.

P : But ages ago, whales changed their home-moving from the land to the sea.

Q : He is shaped like a submarine boat, with a tail turned into a power paddle.

R : The whale is suited to live in water.

S : They are warm-blooded animals, and feed their babies as land mammals do.

Which one of the following is the correct sequence?

(a) PRSQ (b) SPRQ
(c) RQPS (d) QPRS

51.

S_1 : There was a check-post for passing vehicles at a village called Gobindapur, a short distance from where the road to Dhanbad branched off from the Grand Trunk Road.

S_6 : He asked me more than once if I was sure that the man had noted the number down.

P : When I came sufficiently near, he moved back and the barrier was lifted.

Q : I slowed down and found a man coming forward with pencil and book in hand.

R : I told uncle that the man had taken down the number of the car, adding that it was a routine practice.

S : As I approached it, I saw the barrier coming down slowly.

Which one of the following is the correct sequence?

(a) RQPS (b) QRPS
(c) SQPR (d) RSPQ

52.

S_1 : My journey was to last for thirty six hours.

S_6 : In the steel trunk under the seat there was a bag containing two hundred rupees that did not belong to me.

P : Every mile of the country through which the train was running was interesting.

Q : Yet I was not happy.

R : I had the carriage for myself.

S : The train would stop for breakfast, lunch and dinner.

Which one of the following is the correct sequence?

(a) RSPQ (b) SQPR
(c) PQSR (d) RPQS

53.

S_1 : The life of early men had advantages and disadvantages.

S_6 : On the whole, there was friendship and amity within the tribes.

P : Then, they had enough physical exercise which made them healthy and active.

Q : They could roam for months without fear of meeting a stranger.

R : One of the advantages was that they were not overcrowded.

S : They lived in small tribes where everybody knew everybody else.

Which one of the following is the correct sequence?

(a) QSRP (b) RQPS
(c) SPRQ (d) PRQS

Directions for Questions 54 to 58:

You are given four alternative meanings to each idiom/phrase. Choose the most appropriate one.

54. BANK UPON
(a) Accumulate
(b) Consequent upon
(c) Guess
(d) Depend upon

55. UNDER DURESS
(a) With superstition
(b) According to merit
(c) Under compulsion
(d) In good faith

56. THREW DOWN THE GAUNTLET
(a) Challenged (b) Protested
(c) Defeated (d) Surpassed

57. IN THE GUISE OF
(a) In the cloak of (b) In the colour of
(c) In the semblance of
(d)In the pretence of

58. CAUGHT UP WITH
(a) Conversed (b) Tackled
(c) Arrested (d) Overtook

Spotting Errors

Directions for Questions 59 to 76:

(i) In this section a number of sentences are given. The sentences are underlined in three separate parts and each one is labelled (a), (b) and (c). Read each sentence to find out whether there is an error in any underlined part. No sentence has more than one error. When you find an error in any one of the underlined parts (a), (b) or (c), choose that part as your answer. You may feel that there is no error in a sentence, in that case letter (d) will signify a 'No error' response.

(ii) You are to select only one response for each item. (If you indicate more than one response, your answer will be considered wrong.) Errors may be in grammar, word usage or idioms. There may be a word missing or there may be a word which should be removed.

59. During the earthquake (a)/ people listened a strange noise, (b)/ and rushed out of homes (c)/. No error (d)

60. My friend has got an appointment (a)/ in a television company (b)/ some three months ago (c)/. No error (d)

61. When the plane landed, (a)/ he found that (b)/ one of the wings is damaged by a shell. (c) No error. (d)

62. He had no objection (a)/ to forward my application (b)/ to the higher authority (c)/. No error. (d)

63. People shouldn't (a)/ drop litter on pavements, (b)/ should they? (c)/ No error. (d)

64. She could not believe (a)/ that it had all (b)/ happened to her. (c)/ No error. (d)

65. I always like to have (a)/ about four toasts (b)/ for breakfast. (c)/ No error. (d)

66. I was (a)/ baffled with (b) / the instructions he gave me (c)/. No error. (d)

67. Nobody (a)/ in their senses (b)/ would have acted so (c)/. No error. (d)

68. Thousands of people from far and near (a)/ started gathering outside the auditorium (b)/ from early morning to pay their tributes to the departed leader (c)/. No error. (d)

69. He went in the room, (a)/ opened a box (b)/ and took out a gun (c)/. No error. (d)

70. The reason why the plane crashed (a)/ as soon as it took off (b)/ is the failure of one of the engines (c). No error. (d)

71. If you don't start behaving properly, (a)/ I will be forced to (b)/ tell to your supervisor (c)/. No error. (d)

72. Language is a skill activity (a)/ by which fine distinctions of meaning can be made (b)/ for a better understanding of behaviour (c)/. No error. (d)

73. Every man is conditioned by the age in which he lives, (a)/ and if he were to return to another age, (b)/ he would not be happy (c)/. No error. (d)

74. The work of an uneducated farmer (a)/ is far important than (b)/ that of a professor (c)/. No error. (d)

75. The question is often raised (a)/ that whether it is desirable to send Indian students abroad (b)/ since they rarely return (c)/. No error. (d)

76. The watch is a valuable present from my uncle (a)/ and it costed him (b)/ more than two thousand rupees (c)/. No error. (d)

Comprehension

Directions for Questions 77 to 101:

In this Section you have five short passages. After each passage, you will find several questions based on the passage. First, read a passage, and then answer the questions based on it. You are required to select your answers based on the contents of the passage and opinion of the author only.

Passage–I

He dropped off to sleep. The cigarette slipped out of his mouth and burnt a great black hole in his only shirt. The smart of the burn awoke him, and he got up, cursing under his breath, and fumbled in the dark for a needle in order to sew up the hole. Otherwise his wife would see it in the morning and would nag away at him for a couple of hours. But he could not find a needle. He fell asleep again.

77. The cigarette fell out of the man's mouth because
    (a) he fell off his stool
    (b) he was surprised to see that it had made a hole in his shirt
    (c) he fell asleep while smoking
    (d) he fumbled in the dark for a needle

78. The man woke up in the dark because
    (a) the cigarette had burnt his favourite shirt
    (b) the cigarette had burnt his only shirt
    (c) the cigarette had to be lit again
    (d) the cigarette had burnt him

79. The man got up to search for a needle because
    (a) his wife would be very upset
    (b) the cigarette had damaged his only shirt
    (c) he wanted to mend the shirt
    (d) the bum-hole was huge and black

80. The man wanted to sew the hole because
    (a) he wanted to avoid being scolded by his wife
    (b) he had nothing else to do
    (c) he had no other shirt
    (d) he wanted to sleep again

81. Which one of the following statements best sums up the man's reaction to his problem?
    (a) The man is extremely upset to find the shirt burnt and frantically tries to repair the damage
    (b) The hole in the shirt and the wife's anticipated nagging are minor problems, the greater one is that the man cannot find a needle.
    (c) Neither the shirt-hole nor the nagging nor the lack of a needle is of great consequence
    (d) The man is terrified of his wife and dreads her discovering the burnt shirt

Passage–II

It happened one day, about noon, going towards my boat, I was exceedingly surprised with the print of a man's naked foot on the shore, which was very plain to be seen in the sand. I stood like one thunder-struck, or as if I had seen an apparition. I listened, I looked round me, I could hear nothing, nor see anything. I went up the shore, and down the shore, but it was all one, I could see no other impression but that one. I went to it again to see if there were any more, and to observe if it might not be my fancy; but there was no room for that for there was exactly the very print of a foot-toes, heel and every part of a foot.

82. On finding the foot-print on the shore, what did the author do?
(a) Did not pay much attention to it
(b) Observed it with curiosity
(c) Began to investigate its origin
(d) Ran away in fear

83. Which one of the following words best describes the emotion evoked by the foot-print in the author?
(a) Curiosity
(b) Indifference
(c) Fear
(d) Surprise

84. How does the author convince himself that the foot-print is a real one?
(a) By finding the person who made it
(b) By being told about it by a witness
(c) By thinking about it for some time
(d) By examining it carefully and noticing its details

85. Which one of these expressions best brings out the effect of the foot-print on the author?
(a) Seen an apparition
(b) Stood like one thunder-struck
(c) Went up the shore
(d) Looked round himself

86. The passage is full of short simple sentences. Their purpose is to
(a) facilitate easy understanding
(b) give a plain narration
(c) convey breathless excitement
(d) imply the inability of the author to write in a better way.

Passage–III

While I stood drinking in the beauty of this placid scene I became conscious of an alteration. In a moment the sole porter emerged from his midday nap, operated a signal that clanked noisily into position, and then ambled slowly towards me for my return-half-ticket, whilst I remarked that his red amiable face and easy-going gait were in perfect harmony with the tranquil surroundings.

A wisp of smoke on the horizon with a dark snake crawling beneath it announced the approach of the train. As it drew nearer, the deep silence of the place was gradually displaced by a creaking of brakes and a hissing of steam.

Save for myself, no one entered the train and no one alighted. The porter with leisurely expertness, trundled a couple of milk churns on board, the door was slammed, the guard signalled to the driver, and we moved off, leaving the small station once more to its drowsy silence.

87. What does the author suggest by the word 'placid'?
(a) The scene was filled with noise of the train
(b) The place was filled with lively humanity
(c) The place was quite and lonely
(d) The horizon looked smoke laden

88. Who/what does first break the silence in the station?
(a) The train (b) The porter
(c) The passenger (d) Milk churns

89. Who had a midday nap?
(a) The author
(b) The passenger
(c) The Station-master
(d) The porter

90. The central idea of the passage is
(a) Leisure and peace
(b) Hurry and noise
(c) Activity
(d) The porter

91. The meaning of drowsy is
(a) Untidy (b) Sleepy
(c) Freezing (d) Drugged

Passage–IV

Deriving your authority from the government, your position would secure the respect the consideration of everyone, especially in a service where official rank carries so much weight. This would secure to you every attention and comfort on your way and there, together with a complete submission to your orders. I know these things are a matter of indifference to you except so far as they may further the great objects you have in view, but they are of importance in themselves, and of every importance to those who have a right to take an interest in your personal position and comfort.

92. *The great objects* in the passage means
(a) Significant items
(b) Noble goals
(c) Precious merchandise
(d) Objects of praise

93. The writer is asking his reader to accept
(a) great objects
(b) a respected position
(c) an official rank
(d) a significant assignment

94. The person addressed is most likely a
(a) social worker
(b) government servant
(c) commercial agent
(d) foreign dignitary

95. The writer's attitude towards the person addressed is characterised by
(a) Officiousness
(b) Flattery
(c) Humility
(d) Arrogance

96. The above passage most probably is a part of a
(a) Speech
(b) Official communication
(c) Written report
(d) Personal letter

Passage–V

New Year is a time for resolutions. Mentally at least, most of us could compile formidable lists of do's and don'ts. The same old favourites recur year in and year out with monotonous regularity. Past experience has taught us that certain accomplishments are beyond attainment. If we remain inveterate smokers, it is only because we have so often experienced the frustration that results from failure. Most of us fail in our efforts at self-improvement because our schemes are too ambitious and we never have time to carry them out. We also make the fundamental error of announcing our resolutions to everybody so that we look even more foolish when we slip back into our old bad ways.

97. The phrase 'formidable lists of 'do's and don'ts' means that
(a) the bad points of our character are formidable
(b) the list is so long that it is frightening
(c) the things that need to be included is frightening
(d) the realisation that we are so imperfect is frightening

98. The same old favourites recur ... with monotonous regularity' implies that
(a) we went to be so perfect that we includes some items regularly
(b) we have been so regularly doing certain things that they have become monotonous
(c) in spite of repeated failures, we still would like to try one more time
(d) some favourite actions if repeated often could become monotonous

99. The author seems to imply that many are inveterate smokers because
(a) they have not really tried to give up smoking
(b) they know from past experience that they can never succeed in their attempt to give up
(c) they want to forget the frustration of not smoking
(d) they do not have the will power to stop smoking

100. The author says that most of us fail in our attempts at self-improvement because
(a) we set too high goals for ourselves
(b) we do not have the persistence of mind
(c) our nature is such that we cannot become perfect
(d) certain imperfections have become a part and parcel of our lives

101. The author seems to think that others
(a) feel happy when we slip back to our old ways

(b) do not really want us to improve ourselves
(c) are ready to tease and laugh at our attempts
(d) might embarrass us by praising our attempts

Antonyms

Directions for Questions 102 to 120:

Each of these items consists of a word in capital letters, followed by four words or group of words. Select the word or group of words that is *furthest* in meaning to the word in capital letters.

102. PLIABLE
(a) Wilful (b) Stubborn
(c) Firm (d) Opinionated

103. OBSCURE
(a) Filthy (b) Unknown
(c) Untidy (d) Well known

104. HERETICAL
(a) Pious (b) Orthodox
(c) Superstitious (d) Outdated

105. IMPUDENT
(a) Brave (b) Gentle
(c) Polite (d) Boisterous

106. INFERNAL
(a) Paradisiac (b) Majestic
(c) Peaceful (d) Graceful

107. VERDANT
(a) Dry (b) Green
(c) Beautiful (d) Water-logged

108. TEMPORAL
(a) Serious (b) Political
(c) Eternal (d) Divine

109. OSTENTATION
(a) Miserliness (b) Simplicity
(c) Purity (d) Innocence

110. LOFTY
(a) Mean (b) Glorious
(c) Envious (d) Devilish

111. LOQUACIOUS
(a) Flamboyant (b) Silent
(c) Dispirited (d) Dumb

112. DILAPIDATED
(a) Costly
(b) Well-furnished
(c) Broken-down
(d) Renovated

113. ABHORRENCE
(a) Admiration (b) Abomination
(c) Repulsion (d) Acceptance

114. ENIGMATIC
(a) Lethargic (b) Unambiguous
(c) Wrangling (d) Obscure

115. AMENABLE
(a) Obedient (b) Diplomatic
(c) Stubborn (d) Answerable

116. SCRUPULOUS
(a) Lax (b) Shameful
(c) Awful (d) Pitiful

117. EVASIVE
(a) Unreliable (b) Tricky
(c) Straightforward (d) Elusive

118. NADIR
(a) Zenith (b) Climax
(c) Peak (d) The lowest point

119. EXONERATED
(a) Implicated (b) Criticised
(c) Condemned (d) Convicted

120. INSUPERABLE
(a) Predictable (b) Surmountable
(c) Countable (d) Unendurable

PAPER 24

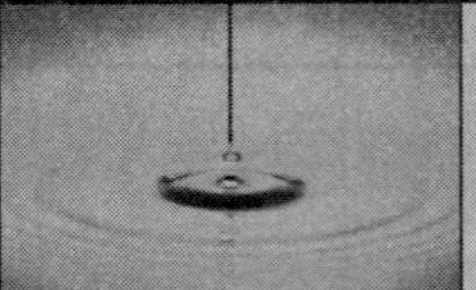

Combined Defence Service Examination, September 2011

Spotting Errors

Directions for Question 1 to 15

Each question in this section has a sentence with three parts labelled (a), (b), (c). Read each sentence to find out whether there is any error in any part and select that part as your answer. If you find no error, your answer should be (d).

1. The composition contained (a)/ even no less (b)/ than twenty mistakes. (c)/ No error (d)
2. He told us (a)/ that (b)/ he has not read the book, (c)/ No error (d)
3. The minister announced (a)/ compensation for (b)/ the victims from the accident, (c)/ No error (d)
4. I should (a)/ have preferred (b)/ to go by myself, (c)/ No error (d)
5. There is (a)/ no place (b)/ in this compartment, (c)/ No error (d)
6. The (a)/ young man (b)/ had no manner, (c)/ No error (d)
7. There are many (a)/ beautiful furnitures (b)/ in the room, (c)/ No error (d)
8. The policeman prevented us from (a)/ entering into (b)/ the hall, (c)/ No error (d)
9. The world (a)/ comprises (b)/ good and bad people, (c)/ No error (d)
10. Would you please order (a)/ for tea and biscuits (b)/ for all of us? (c)/ No error (d)
11. I have paid (a)/ my bill for electricity (b)/ only a week ago. (c)/ No error (d)
12. He has just been appointed (a)/ ambassador to an important country (b)/ for a five-year term, (c)/ No error (d)
13. This is the old man (a)/ whom I said (b)/ had helped me. (c)/ No error (d)
14. The dog pushed (a)/ the door open (b)/ and stole the meat, (c)/ No error (d)
15. The truck driver accused (a)/ the lady for walking (b)/ in the middle of the road, (c)/ No error (d)

Sentence Improvement

Directions for Question : 16 to 32

Look at the underlined part of each sentence. Below each sentence, three possible substitutions for the underlined part are given. If one of them, i.e., (a), (b) or (c) is better than the underlined part, choose that part as your answer. If none of the substitutions improves the sentence, select (d) as your answer. Thus a 'No improvement' response will be signified by the letter (d).

16. If I **were** you, I would do it at once.
(a) was
(b) am
(c) would be
(d) No improvement

17. They set a strong guard, lest anyone could escape.
(a) would
(b) might
(c) should
(d) No improvement

18. The matter called **up** an explanation of his conduct.
(a) out
(b) in
(c) for
(d) No improvement

19. The accused **refused** having murdered anybody.
(a) disagreed
(b) denied
(c) declaimed
(d) No improvement

20. We need honest workers, not people of **redoubtable** integrity.
(a) doubting
(b) doubtful
(c) doubtless
(d) No improvement

21. By the time he **arrived**, everybody had gone home.
(a) when he arrived
(b) at which he arrived
(c) by which he arrived
(d) No improvement

22. There is no **alternate**, so we must leave now.
(a) altering
(b) alternative
(c) alternation
(d) No improvement

23. I cannot **listen what** she is saying.
(a) hear what
(b) listen for what
(c) listen to that
(d) No improvement

24. He is still in vigorous health although he is on the **right** side of sixty.
(a) wrong
(b) left
(c) negative
(d) No improvement

25. We are sorry to hear **regarding** your father's death.
(a) of
(b) over
(c) for
(d) No improvement

26. Babu asked his friend, **"Where you went yesterday?"**
(a) "Where did you go yesterday?"
(b) "Where you had gone yesterday?"
(c) "Where you did go yesterday?"
(d) No improvement

27. He **lay** on the grass enjoying the sunshine.
(a) laid
(b) lied
(c) led
(d) No improvement

28. Some passengers **were flown** to Paris on the last trip.
(a) fled
(b) flied
(c) flew

(d) No improvement

29. Fifty miles **are** a long distance to walk.
(a) is
(b) become
(c) be
(d) No improvement

30. After the vote was taken the meeting broke.
(a) broke down
(b) broke up
(c) broke out
(d) No improvement

31. The speaker asked the audience to bear upon him for a few minutes more.
(a) on
(b) with
(c) for
(d) No improvement

32. Many people find it difficult to make both hands meet.
(a) both accounts
(b) both hand to mouth
(c) both ends meet
(d) No improvement

Synonyms

Directions for Question (33 to 52)

Each Question in this section consists of a word in capital letters followed by four words or groups of words. Select the word or group of words that is most similar in meaning to the word in capital letters.

33. HOSTILITY
(a) Illness
(b) Enmity
(c) Disturbance
(d) Derogatory

34. INDIFFERENT
(a) Dissimilar
(b) Various
(c) Interference
(d) Unconcerned

35. CONDEMN
(a) Censure
(b) Despair
(c) Kill
(d) Hit

36. DEFECT
(a) Loss
(b) Harm
(c) Shortcoming
(d) Delicate

37. JEALOUS
(a) Envious
(b) Unhappy
(c) Regretful
(d) Remorse

38. WEARY
(a) Careless
(b) Shivering
(c) Troubled
(d) Weak

39. PLAUSIBLE
(a) Pleasing to the taste
(b) Seemingly true
(c) Manageable
(d) Cannot be proved

40. CREDITABLE
(a) Able to lend money
(b) Bringing praise
(c) Able to repay a loan
(d) Fit to be believed

41. SALIENT
(a) Most important
(b) Salt-like taste
(c) Pleasing
(d) Satisfactory

42. FRAGILE
(a) Soft
(b) Smooth

(c) Flexible
(d) Easily broken

43. POIGNANT
(a) Bitter
(b) Deep
(c) Very painful
(d) Sharp

44. OUTLOOK
(a) Looking out
(b) Prospect
(c) Outward appearance
(d) Scrutiny

45. FORTITUDE
(a) Fortune
(b) Fortification
(c) Bravery
(d) Breakthrough

46. RETICENT
(a) Sensitive
(b) Secretive
(c) Not feeling well
(d) Not saying much

47. RECIPROCAL
(a) Formal
(b) Favourable
(c) Mutual
(d) Sustainable

48. APPRISE
(a) Inform
(b) Estimate
(c) Admire
(d) Require

49. CONSENSUS
(a) Awareness
(b) General agreement
(c) Careful observation
(d) Praiseworthy

50. UNCEREMONIOUS
(a) Impolite
(b) Informal
(c) Incomplete
(d) Irregular

51. TREASON
(a) Absurdity
(b) Disloyalty (c) Dishonesty
(d) Deception

52. AMIABLE
(a) Popular
(b) Generous
(c) Friendly
(d) Reasonable

Ordering of Sentences

Directions for Question (53 to 60)

In these questions, each passage consists of six sentences. The first and the sixth sentence are given in the beginning as S1 and S6. The middle four sentences in each have been removed and jumbled up. These are labelled P, Q, R and S. You are required to find out the proper sequence of the four sentences and select your answer accordingly.

53.

S1 : I will not be able to see you tomorrow.
S6 : At any rate I'll see you later in the week.
P : There is only a simple laboratory test to be done.
Q : Once I know what the diagnosis is, I can contact the doctor.
R : However, if you like, you can phone me.
S : We will then follow his instructions.

The correct sequence should be
(a) SPRQ (b) RPQS
(c) SRPQ (d) RQSP

54.

S1 : James Watt used the power of steam to drive machines.
S6: The jet engine is relatively more recent.
P : With petrol engines people were able to build motor cars and aeroplanes.
Q : Then, many years later, the petrol engine was invented.

R : These provided quicker means of travelling.

S : His invention was used later by other clever men to give us the railway engine.

The correct sequence should be

(a) SQPR (b) PQRS

(c) PSRQ (d) QSRP

55.

S1 : Stalin sent General Zhukov to assume command in Leningrad.

S6: The battle for Leningrad was the fiercest ever fought.

P : True, the city was prepared for street fighting.

Q : At that time no one knew whether the city could be saved.

R : No one knew the answer.

S : But would the city's defences hold?

The correct sequence should be

(a) RSQP (b) QSPR

(c) QPSR (d) RQPS

56.

S1: Bacteria in the mouth can cause bad odour and painful tooth decay.

S6: Toothpaste advertisements are truthful when they advise us to brush regularly.

P : Children's eating habits leave them prone to tooth decay.

Q : They grow in food particles left between teeth.

R : They often eat sweets and other items between meals.

S : Therefore, regular brushing after every meal eaten at home is essential.

The correct sequence should be

(a) PQSR (b) QPRS

(c) RSPQ (d) QRPS

57.

S1: The Five-Year Plans are meant for the nation's economic development.

S 6: The most important is, certainly, failure on the family-planning front.

P : What are the reasons for it?

Q : One way of measuring a nation's development is by finding out how much progress there has been in the fight against poverty.

R : The reasons are many.

S : In India, every Five-Year Plan ends with more people coming under the poverty line. The correct sequence should be

(a) RPQS (b) QSPR

(c) PRSQ (d) SQRP

58.

S1 : Man's growth from barbarism to civilization is supposed to be the theme of history.

S6: In many ways, therefore, man has not made very great progress.

P : Strong countries attack and oppress weaker ones.

Q : But it is difficult to believe this ideal has been reached.

R : There is ample evidence of barbarism even today.

S : Individuals too exploit their fellows. The correct sequence should be

(a) QRPS (b) RQSP

(c) QRSP (d) RPSQ

59.

S1: The lion used to be very widely distributed in Africa and Asia.

S6: No hunting is permitted in such reserved areas.

P : There are special forest zones set aside for wildlife in various countries.

Q : Indiscriminate killing by hunters has been the cause of this drastic fall in their numbers.

R : Today they are a relatively rare species.

S : If the species survives at all, it will be only in national parks. The correct sequence should be

(a) QSPR (b) RSPQ

(c) SRPQ (d) RQSP

60.

S1 : Though the Finance Minister claims that: prices have become stable, facts do not support his stand.

S6 : This proves that the government is not properly informed.

P : What is worse, in some places it is not available even at the exorbitant price.

Q : Now it is above 10 rupees.

R : Sugar is a glaring example.

S : A month back its open-market price was 7 rupees per kg. The correct sequence should be

(a) PRQS (b) SRQP
(c) PSRQ (d) RSQP

Comprehension

Directions for (Question 61 to 85)

In this section, you nave six short passages. Each passage is followed by questions based on the passage. First, read the passage and answer the questions based on the passage. You are required to select your answers from the given options.

Passage–I

Cozette could have been a pretty child, but she was thin and pale and her eyes were stained with weeping. She was dressed in her thin torn cotton dress and she shivered all the time. Here and there on her body were blue marks from the beatings that her mistress had given her. Her naked legs were red and rough. When she spoke, her voice trembled. Everything about the child, her looks, her behaviour, her speech, her silence, every small gesture she made, showed a terrible fear. She was so afraid that, even though she was wet through, she dared not go near the fire to warm herself, but sat shivering in a corner of the room.

61. Cozette could not be a pretty child because
(a) she was pale and emaciated
(b) she was weeping
(c) she was scantily dressed
(d) she was trembling with fear

62. Cozette's voice trembled because
(a) she was feeling cold
(b) she was frightened
(c) there was no fire near her
(d) she was wearing a thin, cotton dress

63. Cozette's terrible fear is conveyed most vividly by the description of
(a) her constant shivering
(b) her tear-stained eyes
(c) her trembling voice
(d) her inability to go near the fire

64. The cause of Cozette's fear is explained by
(a) her pale appearance
(b) her torn dress
(c) the blue marks on her body
(d) her speech

Passage-II

Discussions on drug addiction should also be concerned with the vast majority of people who are not addicts. Their homes and lives are insecure because our narcotics laws drive such people to crime. The drug addict is almost never dangerous when he is under the influence of drugs. What makes him dangerous is the desperate need for money to buy the next dose. Drugs are available only in an illegal black market. The costs are stupendous, and this is what drives the addict to steal, rob and even kill.

65. According to the author, discussions of drug addiction are generally concerned with
(a) addicts
(b) non-addicts
(c) criminals
(d) black marketers

66. Addicts take to criminal acts because
(a) drugs make them lose self-control
(b) the habit of robbing and stealing is hard to break
(c) they need large sums of money to buy drugs
(d) law is powerless against them

67. The author seems to criticise the narcotics laws for
(a) being too lenient
(b) being too complicated
(c) being ineffective
(d) driving addicts to crime

68. The word 'stupendous' in the passage means
(a) very high
(b) foolish
(c) shocking
(d) illegal

69. With reference to the passage, consider the following statements :
1. Addiction to drugs is a criminal act.
2. Drug addicts cannot be rehabilitated.

Which of the statements given above is/are correct?
(a) 1 only
(b) 2 only
(c) Both 1 and 2
(d) Neither 1 nor 2

Passage-III

Even in the most primitive societies the great majority of people satisfy a large part of their material needs by exchanging goods and services. Very few people indeed can make for themselves everything they need—all their food, their clothes, their housing, their tools. Ever since men started living in communities, they have been satisfying their needs by means of specialisation and exchange; increasingly each individual has concentrated on what he can do best, and has produced more of the special goods or services in which he has concentrated, than he can consume himself. The surplus he has exchanged with other members of the community, acquiring, in exchange the things he needs that others have produced.

70. Very few people can satisfy their needs today by
(a) providing things for themselves
(b) exchanging goods and services
(c) concentrating on what they can do best
(d) individual specialisation

71. Exchange of goods becomes possible only when
(a) there is no specialisation
(b) the goods are produced in surplus
(c) primitive societies become modern
(d) individuals make things for themselves

72. Specialisation and exchange began when men started
(a) big industries
(b) concentrating on their work
(c) producing things for individual use
(d) living in communities

73. Exchange of goods and services becomes necessary because
(a) man is a social animal
(b) reciprocity is the law of life
(c) trade and commerce are means of progress
(d) we cannot produce everything we need ourselves

Passage-IV

I came home from one vacation to find that my brother Ron had brought a dog while I was away. A big burly, choleric dog, he always acted as if he thought I wasn't one of the family. There was a slight advantage in being one of the family, for he didn't bite the family as often as he bit strangers. Mother used to send a box of candy every Christmas to the people he bit. The list finally contained forty or more names. Nobody could understand why we didn't get rid of the dog!

74. Which of the following descriptions fits the dog?
(a) The dog was tiny and delicate
(b) The dog was sturdy and short tempered
(c) The dog was huge and cool
(d) The dog was small and sweet-tempered

75. The dog did not consider the writer as one of the family. What do you think was the consequence of this?
(a) The dog barked at him all the time
(b) The dog drove him out of his own house
(c) The dog behaved with him in an unfriendly way
(d) The dog bit him more than he bit others in the family

76. The Christmas list contained more than forty names. What does this suggest?
(a) The writer's mother had a lot of friends
(b) The writer's family celebrated Christmas well
(c) The writer's dog had bitten at least forty people

(d) The writer's mother sent them candy boxes

Passage–V

A little girl was learning a history lesson with her governess. All the morning she had been reading it over and hearing it explained by her governess, but no good came of either the reading or the teaching. The governess went over the lesson several times, explained the meaning, and for the last time, asked her pupil to read it over. After due time had been given, the girl was examined as to her knowledge of the lesson; but not a single answer could she give correctly. The governess lost patience with her, and threatened to punish her unless she could state where a certain treaty was signed.

77. According to the passage, the little girl read the lesson and heard it explained all the morning because

(a) the girl did not like her governess

(b) the governess could not explain it long enough

(c) the girl could not understand it

(d) the girl read the lesson only once

78. With reference to the passage, consider the following statements :

1. The governess taught the same lesson several times.
2. The governess wanted to complete her teaching work quickly.

Which of the statements given above is/are correct?

(a) 1 only

(b) 2 only

(c) Both 1 and 2

(d) Neither 1 nor 2

79. After reading the whole passage, which of the following impressions do you think correct about the inability of the girl to answer questions correctly?

(a) The dullness of the girl

(b) The incompetence of the governess

(c) The difficulty of the language

(d) The lack of time

80. Which of the following correctly expresses the meaning of 'lost patience with her'?

(a) The inability of the governess to endure further the girl's failure to answer

(b) The governess lost her enthusiasm to teach the girl

(c) The governess felt that the girl cannot be taught the lesson

(d) The governess felt that she was not good enough to teach the girl

Passage-VI

Many doctors flatly refused to believe Jenner when he announced that he had found a preventive against smallpox. They declared vaccination to be a dangerous practice. But the dread of smallpox was in everybody's heart, and people flocked to Jenner to be vaccinated. The Latin word for cow is 'vacca'; it is the root from which the word vaccination was formed. Some of the 'vacca' used by Jenner were not pure and some harms were done; but when supplies of pure vaccine were available, the practice of vaccinating spread all over England and from England to other countries. We hardly hear of outbreaks of smallpox now.

81. The passage describes

(a) how smallpox may be treated

(b) how vaccines were manufactured in England

(c) the dangers of vaccination especially for children

(d) the gradual acceptance of vaccination as a preventive against smallpox

82. Vaccination sometimes proved harmful because

(a) vaccination was a dangerous practice

(b) some of the vaccines used were of a poor hygienic standard

(c) there are physiological differences between cows and human beings

(d) vaccination is given at a very early age

83. People hastened to get themselves vaccinated because

(a) many doctors supported Jenner's claims

(b) fear of the terrible disease drove them to take the risk of vaccination

(c) supplies of pure vaccine had now become available
(d) the practice of vaccinating had spread all over the world

84. Vaccination was intended by Jenner to
(a) cure people suffering from smallpox (b) delay the death of smallpox victims
(c) build up a defence against smallpox germs
(d) prevent cows from spreading the disease

85. With reference to the passage, consider the following statements :
1. Many doctors did not believe that Jenner was a doctor.
2. There are no outbreaks of smallpox nowadays.

Which of the statements given above is/are correct?
(a) 1 only (b) 2 only
(c) Both 1 and 2 (d) Neither 1 nor 2

Antonyms

Direction for Question 86 to 104

Each question in this section consists of a word in capital letters followed by four words or groups of words. Select the word or group of words that is most nearly opposite in meaning to the word in capital letters.

86. DENY
(a) Accept
(b) Proceed
(c) Hold
(d) Promote

87. ACQUIT
(a) Inform
(b) Release
(c) Abuse
(d) Condemn

88. FERTILE
(a) Dry
(b) Useless
(c) Barren
(d) Arid

89. AFFLUENCE
(a) Not being fluent
(b) Poverty
(c) Difficulty
(d) Unhealthy

90. CONFIDENT
(a) Vague
(b) Cowardly
(c) Secretive
(d) Unsure

91. GLOOMY
(a) Cheerful
(b) Forgetful (c) Faithful
(d) Harmful

92. FRUGAL
(a) Excessive
(b) Extravagant (c) Rich
(d) Generous

93. OBVIOUS
(a) Obscure
(b) Obsolete
(c) Indifferent
(d) Difficult

94. FORBID
(a) Defy
(b) Dislike
(c) Permit
(d) Understand

95. HARMONIOUS
(a) Selfish
(b) Aggressive
(c) Mechanical
(d) Discordant

96. INCONSPICUOUS
(a) Open-hearted
(b) Open-minded
(c) Prominent
(d) Smooth

97. FACTUAL
(a) Imaginary
(b) Idealistic
(c) Unrealistic
(d) Verbal

98. ABANDON
(a) Assert
(b) Retain
(c) Produce
(d) Twist

99. ASSENT
(a) Breakdown
(b) Misunderstand
(c) Dispatch
(d) Disagreement

100. FICKLE
(a) Constant
(b) Convenient
(c) Questionable
(d) Faithful

101. DISCREET
(a) Worthy
(b) Wishful thinking
(c) Honest
(d) Careless in behaviour

102. ARTICULATE
(a) Unable to understand
(b) Unable to express oneself
(c) Unable to agree
(d) Unable to live

103. TRIVIAL
(a) Temporary
(b) Delicate
(c) Important
(d) Arbitrary

104. UNJUST
(a) Serious
(b) Self-centred
(c) Fair-minded
(d) Considerable

Ordering of Words in a Sentence

Directions for Question 105 to 120

Each of the following questions in this section consists of a sentence the parts of which have been jumbled. These parts have been labelled P, Q, R and S. Given below each sentence are four sequences namely (a), (b), (c) and (d). You are required to rearrange the jumbled parts of the sentence and select the correct sequence.

105. Now that the office is closed have gone (P)/ the (Q)/ typists (R)/ all (S)

The correct sequence should be
(a) SQRP
(b) RQPS
(c) SRQP
(d) QRPS

106. He gave to the child (P)/ a doll (Q)/ was broken (R)/ whose head (S)

The correct sequence should be
(a) RQPS
(b) PSQR
(c) RSQP
(d) PQSR

107. My father when he was (P)/ at school last year (Q)/ John's fees (R)/ paid (S)

The correct sequence should be
(a) QRSP
(b) SRPQ
(c) RPSQ
(d) PQSR

108. The Prime Minister little chance (P)/ of winning (Q)/ his party to have (R)/ clearly suspects (S)/ the next election.

The correct sequence should be
(a) RSPQ
(b) QPRS
(c) SRPQ
(d) PQRS

109. All the students affirmed positively that (P)/ responded eagerly to the question and (Q)/ the political affiliation of student unions (R)/ interviewed on television (S)/ was undesirable.

The. correct sequence should be
(a) PQRS (b) SRPQ
(c) RPQS (d) SQPR

110. Although the motion until it had been (P)/ from the House (Q)/ received general support (R)/ it

was not carried (S)/ considerably amended.

The correct sequence should be
(a) PQRS
(b) SQPR
(c) RQSP
(d) QRSP

111. The doctor told the patient (P)/ to give an injection to (Q)/ the nurse (R)/ after four hours (S)

The correct sequence should be
(a) RQPS
(b) RPSQ
(c) QPSR
(d) PSRQ

112. The judge lied to the court (P)/ why he had (Q)/ asked the accused (R)/ in spite of his oath (S)

The correct sequence should be
(a) PSRQ
(b) QPSR
(c) PRQS
(d) RQPS

113. His father said and stop (P)/ on trivial things (Q)/ wasting your time (R)/ now get up (S)

The correct sequence should be
(a) SPRQ
(b) PSRQ
(c) QRSP
(d) RQSP

114. The stranger's movements and the police (P)/ him (Q)/ arrested (R)/ aroused suspicion (S)

The correct sequence should be
(a) SQPR
(b) RQPS
(c) SPRQ
(d) RPQS

115. The future is gloomy (P)/ outlook (Q)/ animal (R)/ of this noble (S)

The correct sequence should be
(a) PQSR
(b) QPSR
(c) RPSQ
(d) QSRP

116. The food at the party (P)/ served (Q)/ was delicious (R)/ but not wholesome (S)

The correct sequence should be
(a) PRSQ
(b) QPRS
(c) RSPQ
(d) QRSP

117. In one of the Asian countries as well as (P)/ women (Q)/ wear salwars (R)/ men (S)

The correct sequence should be
(a) PSRQ
(b) PQRS
(c) SPQR
(d) RQPS

118. You won't believe me, to see him (P)/ I went (Q)/ but whenever (R)/ he was out (S)

The correct sequence should be
(a) PQRS
(b) QRSP
(c) SRPQ
(d) RQPS

119. As the car stood up (P)/ to greet him (Q)/ came near the door (R)/ the waiters (S)

The correct sequence should be
(a) QPSR
(b) SRPQ
(c) RSPQ
(d) PRSQ

120. At last had come (P)/ she had been (Q)/ the moment (R)/ waiting for (S)

The correct sequence should be
(a) RQSP (b) QSPR
(c) SQRP (d) QRPS

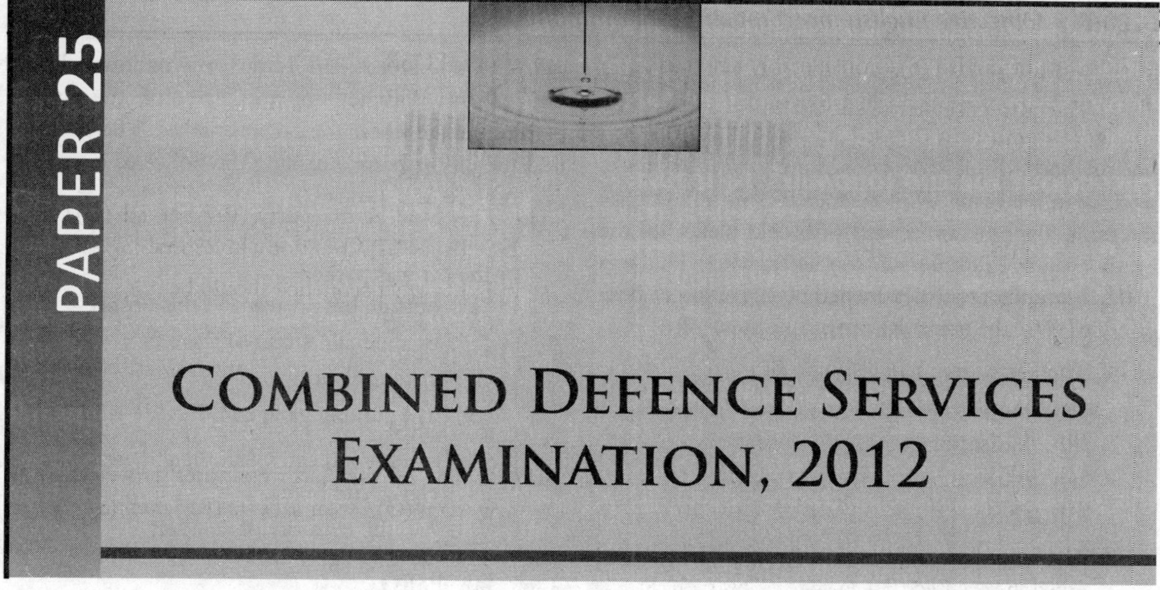

Combined Defence Services Examination, 2012

Comprehension

Directions for the following 17 items :

In this section there are five short passages. Each passage is followed by questions based on the passage. Read each passage and answer the questions that follow:

Passage–1

"Sit down", the Principal said, but Mr. Tagde continued to stand, gaining courage from his own straight-backed stance, because he was beginning to feel a little afraid now.

The Principal looked unhappy. He disliked being forced to perform this sort of an unpleasant task.

"I wish you would consider withdrawing this report", he said.

"I am sorry, Sir, I cannot do that" Mr. Tagde said. He was pleased with his unwavering voice and uncompromising words.

"It will be a very damaging report if put on record". "It is a factual report on very damaging conduct".

"You are asking for the boy's expulsion from school. Don't you think the punishment is too harsh for a few boyish pranks"?

1. Mr. Tagde did not sit down because
(a) he was angry with the Principal
(b) he was in a defiant mood
(c) he did not like the student
(d) he was in a hurry

2. He would not withdraw the report because
(a) he was arrogant and bitter
(b) it was an accurate report
(c) he wanted to create problems for the Principal
(d) he wanted to show his authority

3. The Principal was unhappy because he
(a) did not like to deal with an arrogant person
(b) was angry with Mr. Tagde
(c) could not enforce discipline in school
(d) did not want to expel the boy

Passage–2

It was a bitterly cold night, and even at the far end of the bus the east wind that raved along the street cut like a knife. The bus stopped, the two women and a man got in together and filled the vacant places. The younger woman was dressed in sealskin and carried one of those Pekinese dogs that women in sealskin like to carry in their laps. The conductor came in and took the fares. Then his eye rested with cold malice on the beady-eyed toy dog. I saw trouble brewing. This was the opportunity for which he had been waiting, and he intended to make the most of it.

4. The wind that blew on the night was
(a) mild
(b) pleasant
(c) bitter
(d) sharp

5. The younger woman was carrying the dog as
(a) a necessity
(b) a fashion
(c) an expression of provocation
(d) an escort

6. Which of the following statements best describes the nature of the conductor?
(a) He was dutiful
(b) He was a law-abiding person
(c) He liked dogs
(d) He was unfriendly and malicious

7. "It was a bitterly cold night, and even at the far end of the bus the east wind that raved along the street cut like a knife". This sentence gives us an idea of
(a) a lonely night-bus journey
(b) an unbearable cold night
(c) the wind at the time that was still and cold
(d) the hardship of author's journey

Passage–3

Before an armed robber locked Mary Graves in the sweltering trunk of her car, she dialled an emergency number on her portable telephone and slipped it to her three-year-old daughter. Though confused, the little girl saved the day. She told emergency operators that her mother was locked in the trunk. Although she didn't know where she was, she provided some important clues: she could see airplanes and the sky, according to the transcript of the emergency phone call. The operator called Tampa international airport police, who searched the top floor of the airport parking garage where the car was parked. The operator told the girl to honk, enabling the police to locate the car and free Mrs. Graves.

8. The clues provided by the little girl suggest that the car was parked
(a) outside but adjacent to the airport
(b) by the main street of the city
(c) at the airport
(d) in a parking garage in the side-lane

9. The passage indicates that the girl was
(a) clever and brave
(b) had the maturity of an adult
(c) coy and shy
(d) worried and excited

10. The girl helped the police trace the car by
(a) shouting loudly
(b) making too much din
(c) shrieking frightfully
(d) sounding the horn

11. Through the passage, the writer suggests the importance and utility of
(a) education of little children
(b) parking garages
(c) portable telephones
(d) airports

Passage–4

For days I trudged from one property-dealer to another, from one "to-let" notice to another, with the estimated advance money tucked safely in the inner lining of my handbag, but in vain. At one place they needed a couple, at another a young man, and at another they wished to know my employment status. And I realized that I was a freak called the single woman and the job status being nothing more than a freelance writer with hardly any assignments in hand, only dreams of making it some day. So the dream-house remained far away, gradually turning into a fantasy.

12. The author "trudged from one property-dealer to another" means that the author
(a) had to walk a lot of distance
(b) had to do a brisk walk to save the time

(c) visited several property-dealers without any success
(d) acquired a good knowledge about the property-dealers of that area

13. According to the passage, the author was
(a) a novelist
(b) an independent writer
(c) a publisher of journals
(d) an unemployed person

14. Which of the following statements best reflects the underlying tone of the passage?
(a) People always let out their houses to well employed persons only
(b) People always let out their houses only to couples
(c) Single jobless women find it difficult to rent a house
(d) Women always dream of a house

Passage–5

Martin had many little tricks highly entertaining to his son. On an evening, returning from the market, he would buy a paper mask, the head of a hissing dragon. He would put it on and knock at the door. On opening the door, the boy would be terrified for a moment, but only for a moment, for he would soon remove it and the two would roll with laughter. Tom would, then, go out with the mask and knock at the door for his father to open. Martin had to act as if he was paralysed with fear.

15. Martin played his little tricks because
(a) he was very much interested in them
(b) he wanted to terrify his son
(c) his son got pleasure from them
(d) it was his habit to make tricks

16. Which of the following statements is the most appropriate description of the mask?
(a) It is a mask looking like a dragon with long tail and covering the whole body of Martin
(b) It is a mask looking like the head of a dragon with its tongue hanging out
(c) It is a mask looking like an animal with horns, wings and a pair of ferocious eyes emitting fire
(d) It is a mask looking like the head of a king cobra

17. The father and son rolled with laughter after the
(a) father put on the mask
(b) opening of the door
(c) son saw the mask
(d) father removed the mask

Spotting Errors

Directions for the following 18 items:

Each question in this section has a sentence with three underlined parts labelled (a), (b) and (c). Read each sentence to find out whether there is any error in any underlined part and indicate your answer in the Answer Sheet against the corresponding letter i.e., (a) or (b) or (c). If you find no error, your answer should be indicated as (d).

18. The scientist was seemed (a) / to be excited (b) / over the result of his experiment (c) /. No error.(d)

19. The student could not answer the teacher (a) / when he was asked to explain (b) / why he was so late that day (c). No error (d)

20. John could not come (a) / to school (b) / as he was ill from cold (c). No error. (d)

21. Though she has aptitude in Mathematics (a)/ I won't allow her to take it up as a subject of study for the Master's degree (b) / because I know the labour involved will tell upon her health (c) / No error (d).

22. I am not familiar with (a) / all the important places in this town, (b) / although I have been living here since two years (c). / No error. (d)

23. If I would be a millionaire, (a) / I would not be wasting my time (b)waiting for a bus (c)./ No error (3).

24. Until you begin to make a better use of your time, (a) I shall not stop (b) / finding fault in you. (c) No error (3).

25. Neither of the two boys (a) / is sensible (b) / enough to do this job (c)/. No error. (d)

26. They left (a) / their luggages (b) at the railway station. (c) / No error. (e)

27. You will get (a) / all the informations (b)/ if you read this booklet carefully. (c) / No error. (d) (a) (b) (c) (d)

28. She sang (a) very well (b), / isn't it? (c) No error. (d)

29. He is working (a) / in a bank in New Delhi (b) for the past several months. (c) / No error. (d)

30. There is no question (a) / of my failing (b) in the examination (c). No error.(d)

31. He is going everyday (a) / for a morning walk (b) / with his friends and neighbours (c). / No error. (d)

32. Her relatives could not explain to us (a) / why did not she come for the wedding (b) / as she was expected (c). / No error. (d)

33. He was prevented to accept the assignment (a) / because he was a government employee (b) / and as such barred from accepting such assignments (c). / No error (d).

34. If you repeat this mistake, (a) / I will inform to your father (b) / and do not blame me then (c). / No error (e).

35. Lieutenant Anand was short and muscular (a) / with shoulders that bulged impressively (b) / against his smart uniform (c). / No error. (d)

Sentence Improvement

Directions for the following 14 items:

Look at the underlined part of each sentence. Below each sentence, three possible situations for the underlined part are given. If one of them (a), (b) or (c) is better than the underlined part, indicate your response on the Answer Sheet against the corresponding letter (a), (b) or (c). If none of these substitutions improves the sentence, indicate (d) as your response on the Answer Sheet. Thus a "No Improvement" response will be signified by the letter (d).

36. More than one person **was killed** in the accident.
   (a) were killed
   (b) are killed
   (c) have been killed
   (d) No improvement

37. Not a word **they spoke** to the unfortunate wife about it.
   (a) did they speak
   (b) they will speak
   (c) they had spoken
   (d) No improvement

38. The poor villagers **have waited** in bitter cold for more than four hours now.
   (a) have been waiting
   (b) had waited
   (c) has been waiting
   (d) No improvement

39. If he **had** time he will call you.
   (a) would have
   (b) would have had
   (c) has
   (d) No improvement

40. **All, but her,** had made an attempt.
   (a) All, but she,
   (b) All but her
   (c) All, but her
   (d) No improvement

41. I am used to **hard work**.
   (a) work hard
   (b) work hardly
   (c) working
   (d) No improvement

42. Twenty kilometres **are not a great distance** in these days of fast moving vehicles.
   (a) is not a great distance
   (b) is no distance
   (c) aren't a great distance
   (d) No improvement

43. They were working as **usually**.
   (a) usual
   (b) as usual
   (c) usually
   (d) No improvement

44. He is unlikely to come to the party. But **if he comes** I would talk to him.
(a) if he would come
(b) if he is to come
(c) if he will come
(d) No improvement

45. The passengers **have formed** queue at the booking-counter much before a train arrives.
(a) formed
(b) have been forming
(c) form
(d) No improvement

46. You must complete this work **up to Sunday**.
(a) within Sunday
(b) by Sunday
(c) until Sunday
(d) No improvement

47. **If it will rain**, the match will be abandoned.
(a) If it rains
(b) If it would rain
(c) If it rained
(d) No improvement

48. How long do you think Mr. Kamal **knew** John?
(a) will know
(b) knows
(c) has known
(d) No improvement

49. **I have still to meet** a person who is perfectly satisfied with his job.
(a) am still to meet
(b) am yet to meet
(c) might still meet
(d) No improvement

Ordering of Words in a Sentence

Directions for the following 11 items :

Each of the following items in this section consists of a sentence, the parts of which have been jumbled. These parts have been labelled P, Q, R and S. Given below each sentence are four sequences namely (a), (b), (c) and (d). You are required to rearrange the jumbled parts of the sentence and select the correct sequence.

50. Most of Hitchcock's films
were critically acclaimed on both sides of the Atlantic (P) / earning him both fame and fortune (Q) / and made good money at the box office, (R) / in no small measure (S).
The correct sequence should be
(a) P R Q S (b) P R S Q
(c) Q P R S (d) Q S P R

51. One monsoon evening,
the farmer returned from the fields (P) / when the sky was overcast with threatening clouds (Q) / and found a group of children playing on the road (R) / a little earlier than usual (S).
The correct sequence should be
(a) Q S P R (b) Q P S R
(c) Q R S P (d) P Q R S

52. It must not be imagined
that a walking tour, (P) / is merely a better or worse way (Q) / as some would say, (C) / of seeing the country (S).
The correct sequence should be
(a) R P Q S (b) P R Q S
(c) P Q S R (d) P Q R S

53. It was reported that
the table (P) / belonging to a lady (Q) / with three carved legs (R) / was sold the next day by auction (S).
The correct sequence should be
(a) P R Q S
(b) Q P R S
(c) P Q S R
(d) P Q R S

54. Everything was (P) / after (Q) / plain sailing (R) / we engaged a guide (S).
The correct sequence should be
(a) S P Q R (b) P Q R S
(c) S R Q P (d) P R Q S

55. The boy in the Nehru Centenary Debate (P) / is the eldest son of my friend (Q) / who has won the gold medal (R) / held in the Town hall today (S)

The correct sequence should be

(a) P Q R S (b) Q R S P
(c) R P S Q (d) S P Q R

56. Of paint (P) / two coats (Q) / give (R) / the doors (S).

The correct sequence should be

(a) P S Q P
(b) P S Q R
(c) S P Q R
(d) R S P Q

57. Many of the old sailors (P) / say it is unlucky (Q) / to sail on a Friday (R) / who are generally superstitious (S).

The correct sequence should be

(a) P R S Q (b) P S Q R
(c) S R Q P (d) P Q R S

58. It in the news bulletin (P) / did not feature (Q) / that this matter (R) / was surprising (S).

The correct sequence should be

(a) P S Q R
(b) R Q P S
(c) Q S P R
(d) S R Q P

59. Don't stop him (P) / for an hour (Q) / if you (R) / he will run (S)

The correct sequence should be

(a) Q P S R (b) P Q S R
(c) S Q R P (d) S P R Q

60. In the evenings (P) / she went out (Q) / once a week (R) / shopping (S)

The correct sequence should be

(a) P Q R S (b) R Q S P
(c) Q P R S (d) S P R Q

Ordering of Sentences

Directions for the following 10 items:

In the following items, each passage consists of six sentences. The first and sixth sentence are given in the beginning as S, and S6. The middle four sentences in each have been jumbled up. These are labelled P, Q, R and S. You are requested to find out the proper sequence of the four sentences and mark accordingly on the Answer Sheet.

61.

S_1: A boy tried to discover how wasps find their way home.

S6: These wasps flew straight home.

P : He carried them two miles away and let them go.

Q : First, he marked each of a number of wasps with a white spot.

R : He then put them into a paper box.

S : To do this he carried out a test on them.

The proper sequence should be

(a) P S Q R (b) S R Q P
(c) S Q R P (c) Q P S R

62.

S_1: Rivers have played a great role in our lives.

S6: That was how Sindhu was pronounced by some foreigners.

P : It is famous as the Indus valley civilization.

Q : Communication and trade depended on the rivers for centuries.

R : Who does not know that the very term India originated from Indus?

S : One of the earliest civilizations of the world flourished on the river Sindhu.

The proper sequence should be

(a) S R Q P (b) R S P Q
(c) Q S P R (c) P R S Q

63.

S_1: The next day Hiralal woke early.

S_6: He could find nothing inside them except two letters.

P : Then he began to take out the bags containing the silver coins and the currency notes.

Q : Three of the bags were empty.

R : After washing his face and hands he went back to his bedroom.

S : Suddenly his heart seemed to stop beating.

The proper sequence should be

(a) Q S P R (b) R P S Q
(c) P Q R S (d) S P Q R

64.

S_1: My friend had a dog.
S_6: He took it to the veterinary hospital.
P : He was very much upset.
Q : Two days later it returned home.
R : Its right ear had been torn off.
S : One day he could not find the dog anywhere.

The proper sequence should be
(a) R P S Q (b) P S Q R
(c) S P Q R (d) S Q R P

65.

S_1: A water tap is a device for turning on and off a flow of water.
S_6: The washer is made of a flexible material such as rubber or plastic.
P : The metal parts of a water tap are usually made of brass because brass resists corrosion.
Q : The other part is a washer which is fixed to the bottom of the rop.
R : One is a rod with a handle on the top.
S : It has two important parts. The proper sequence should be
(a) P Q R S (b) S R Q P
(c) P Q S R

66.

S_1: Now these two types of courage, physical and moral, distinct.
S_6: Moral courage is a higher and rarer virtue than physical courage.
P : I have known many men who had marked physical courage, but lacked moral courage.
Q : On the other hand, I've seen men who undoubtedly possessed moral courage but were very cautious about taking physical risks.
R : But I've never met a man with moral courage, who wouldn't, when it was really necessary, face bodily danger.
S : Some of them were in high places but they failed to be great in themselves because they lacked it.

The proper sequence should be
(a) P Q R S (b) P S Q R
(c) P S R Q (c) Q S R P

67.

S_1: Forests have an influence on the climate of a region.
S_6: Thus we see that forests in a region often make the climate cooler.
P : Much of the rain that falls beneath the trees dissolves plant food in the soil.
Q : This gives to the air over the forests a coolness which is felt by balloon-ists and aviators three thousand feet above the earth.
R : The plants absorb all the food and much of the water, but the rest of the water is breathed out through the leaves into the air.
S : This is taken up by the roots of plants and carried upward to the leaves.

The proper sequence should be
(a) Q S R P (b) P S R Q
(c) R S P Q (d) S Q P R

68.

S_1: Albert Edward did very well.
S_6: He then appointed a manager to take care of it.
P : He started looking for a place to open the new shop.
Q : He started his shop with great enthusiasm.
R : He did so well that he began to think of opening another shop.
S : One fine morning he found it on a nearby street.

The proper sequence should be
(a) P Q R S (b) R S P Q
(c) R P S Q (d) P S R Q

69.

S_1: Why do birds migrate in spite of the heavy loss of life on the way?
S_6: The migration of birds thus is a fascinating study, indeed.
P : But birds also migrate during summer.
Q : Primarily they migrate during the summer.

R : Also they cannot endure the summer heat.

S : And the main reason now is not hunger but availability of the nesting sites.

The proper sequence should be

(a) Q P S R (b) P Q R S
(c) R S P Q (d) Q R P S

70.

S_1 : Though hard to please and easily offended, Johnson had a most humane and benevolent heart.

S_6: He got her a job and put her into a virtuous way of living.

P : There he discovered she was one of those wretched persons who had fallen into the lowest state of vice, poverty and disease.

Q : Going home one evening, he found a poor woman lying in the street and took her upon his back and carried her to his house.

R : Soon she was restored to health.

S : Instead of harshly scolding her, he had her taken care of with all tenderness.

The proper sequence should be

(a) P Q R S (b) S R Q P
(c) P R Q S (d) Q P S R

Selecting Words

Directions for the following 21 items :

In the following passage, at certain points you are given a choice of three words in a bracket, one of which fits the meaning of the passage. Choose the best word from each bracket. Mark the letter viz., (a), (b) or (c), relating to this word on your Answer Sheet. Examples Y and Z have been solved for you.

Y. The
(a) boy
(b) horse
(c) dog

Z. was in the school in Simla.
(a) She was homesick.
(b) It
(c) He

Explanation : Out of the list given in item Y, only boy is the correct answer because usually a boy, and not a horse or a dog, attends school. So (a) is to be marked on the Answer Sheet for item Y. A boy is usually referred to as "he", so for item Z, the letter (c) is correct answer. Notice that to solve this kind of items you have to read the preceding or succeeding sentences of the given passage.

Passage

There has been quite some talk in recent times about the status of women in our society,

71. some of it sentimental and some of it, angry. But the status of women
(a) can be
(b) shall
(c) should

72. improved only if we join
(a) ourselves earnestly to achieve the
(b) heads
(c) wish.

73.
(a) goal.
(b) intention.
(c) hands

74. Obviously, it cannot be done merely through
(a) enforcing legislation. It requires an intel-
(b) enacting
(c) passing

75. ligent and sympathetic
(a) presentation
(b) understanding
(c) willingness

76. of each others' problems and a
(a) consent
(b) co-operation
(c) vision

77. to give up pointless claims
(a) of superiority.
(b) about

78. 79.

not (a) by conflict but by peaceful and dispassionate (a) behaviour, in other
(b) through (b) confrontation,
(c) from (c) means,

80.

words, through frank and courteous (a) discussion. The problem can be solved only
(b) bargaining.
(c) argument.

81. 82.

(a) through mutual understanding, and not through insistence on a (a) vital observance
(b) by (b) hard
(c) from (c) rigid

83. 84.

of a code of (a) agreement. If we truly desire a solution to this (a) difficult problem,
(b) conduct. (b) doubtful
(c) rights. (c) small

85.

we should be prepared for (a) one compromise. The system cannot be changed overnight.
(b) a
(c) no

86. 87.

There (a) was a great need for patience in (a) dealing with this complex matter.
(b) is (b) handling
(c) has been (c) tackling

88. 89.

Problems are (a) immensely solved through the application of (a) brain and certainly
(b) best (b) wisdom
(c) rarely (c) theory

90. 91.

not through angry (a) enmity. At every step in our life we (a) understand, then
(b) hostility. (b) compromise,
(c) conflicts. (c) discuss,

why should we take up rigid stand in matters which concern us intimately?

Antonyms

Directions for the following 14 items :

Each item in this section consists of a word in capital letters followed by four words or group of words. Select the word or group of words that is most opposite in meaning to the word in capital letters.

92. PLENTIFUL
(a) Handful (b) Rare
(c) Small (d) Scanty

93. URBANE
(a) Elegant (b) Slow
(c) Crude (d) Foolish

94. FAMOUS
(a) Notorious
(b) Ignorant
(c) Completely unknown
(d) Worthless

95. SPURIOUS
(a) Genuine (b) Authentic
(c) Real (d) Artificial

96. SUCCEED
(a) Achieve (b) Fail
(c) Move fast (d) Lose

97. PROUD
(a) Humble (b) Kind
(c) Gentle (d) Decent

98. LEISURELY
(a) Idly (b) Lazily
(c) Foolishly (d) Hurriedly

99. BARREN
(a) Wet (b) Rich
(c) Fertile (d) Exception

100. CONCEAL
(a) Reveal (b) Show off
(c) Describe (d) Explain

101. ACCEPTANCE
(a) Demote (b) Throw in
(c) Rejection (d) Turn in

102. GRACEFUL
(a) Awkward (b) Ignorant
(c) Slow (d) Disloyal

103. ATTRACT
(a) Severe (b) Repel
(c) Dispel (d) Diminish

104. PROVOKE
(a) Attract (b) Convince
(c) Gratify (d) Pacify

105. VAGUE
(a) Clear (b) Pleasant
(c) Profound (d) Sufficient

Synonmyms

Directions for the following 15 items:

Each item in this section consists of a word or a group of words in capital letters followed by four words or group of words-. Select the word or group of words that is most similar in meaning to the word or words in capital letters.

106. PROHIBIT
(a) Forbid (b) Forfeit
(c) Forsake (d) Forbear

107. DUBIOUS
(a) Dismal (b) Doubtful
(c) Derogatory (d) Devilish

108. ECCENTRIC
(a) Destructive (b) Deceitful
(c) Conformist (d) Unconventional

109. CONTRADICT
(a) Request politely(b) Deny emphatically
(c) Talk abusively (d) Contempt

110. GIVE UP
(a) Abandon (b) Present
(c) Lift (d) Scatter

111. SPECIFIC
(a) Proper (b) Uncommon
(c) Noteworthy (d) Precise

112. ERADICATE
(a) Put up (b) Remove
(c) Soften (d) Suppress

113. PROBABLE
(a) Certain (b) Indefinite
(c) Likely (d) Temporary

114. ADHERE
(a) Act reluctantly
(b) Give allegiance
(c) Waver frequently
(d) React promptly

115. INFER
(a) Conclude (b) Calculate
(c) Debate (d) Suggest

116. HESITATE
(a) Afraid to talk
(b) Unwilling to act
(c) Unwilling to speak
(d) Unable to decide quickly

117. EXPLICIT
(a) Immediate
(b) Plainly stated
(c) Marked
(d) Revealing the secret

118. SUFFICIENT
(a) Adequate (b) Complete
(c) Full (d) Frugal

119. REPRESS
(a) Express (b) Impress
(c) Curb (d) Confuse

120. VINDICTIVE
(a) Cruel
(b) Harsh
(c) Revengeful
(d) Rude

ANSWER KEY

CDS Examination, September 2008

1. (d)	2. (c)	3. (c)	4. (b)	5. (c)
6. (b)	7. (c)	8. (c)	9. (d)	10. (c)
11. (a)	12. (c)	13. (d)	14. (a)	15. (d)
16. (c)	17. (b)	18. (a)	19. (d)	20. (a)
21. (b)	22. (c)	23. (b)	24. (b)	25. (b)
26. (b)	27. (c)	28. (d)	29. (d)	30. (a)
31. (d)	32. (a)	33. (c)	34. (c)	35. (c)
36. (c)	37. (d)	38. (d)	39. (c)	40. (c)
41. (a)	42. (d)	43. (a)	44. (a)	45. (a)
46. (c)	47. (a)	48. (b)	49. (c)	50. (a)
51. (c)	52. (c)	53. (b)	54. (d)	55. (c)
56. (a)	57. (a)	58. (d)	59. (b)	60. (a)
61. (c)	62. (d)	63. (d)	64. (d)	65. (b)
66. (d)	67. (b)	68. (d)	69. (a)	70. (d)
71. (c)	72. (d)	73. (d)	74. (b)	75. (b)
76. (b)	77. (c)	78. (d)	79. (c)	80. (a)
81. (d)	82. (b)	83. (d)	84. (d)	85. (c)
86. (c)	87. (c)	88. (b)	89. (d)	90. (a)
91. (b)	92. (b)	93. (b)	94. (b)	95. (c)
96. (b)	97. (b)	98. (c)	99. (b)	100. (a)
101. (c)	102. (b)	103. (d)	104. (b)	105. (c)
106. (a)	107. (a)	108. (d)	109. (b)	110. (a)
111. (b)	112. (d)	113. (a)	114. (b)	115. (c)
116. (a)	117. (c)	118. (a)	119. (a)	120. (b)

CDS Examination, 2011

1. (b)	2. (b)	3. (b)	4. (c)	5. (c)
6. (d)	7. (c)	8. (b)	9. (c)	10. (b)
11. (d)	12. (b)	13. (a)	14. (c)	15. (b)
16. (c)	17. (d)	18. (b)	19. (a)	20. (a)
21. (c)	22. (a)	23. (c)	24. (d)	25. (c)
26. (c)	27. (d)	28. (a)	29. (b)	30. (a)
31. (c)	32. (c)	33. (a)	34. (b)	35. (a)
36. (d)	37. (d)	38. (d)	39. (d)	40. (c)
41. (b)	42. (a)	43. (c)	44. (b)	45. (b)
46. (b)	47. (c)	48. (d)	49. (c)	50. (c)
51. (c)	52. (d)	53. (c)	54. (b)	55. (b)
56. (a)	57. (d)	58. (b)	59. (b)	60. (c)
61. (a)	62. (c)	63. (a)	64. (b)	65. (c)
66. (a)	67. (c)	68. (a)	69. (b)	70. (c)
71. (a)	72. (b)	73. (b)	74. (a)	75. (c)
76. (b)	77. (a)	78. (b)	79. (b)	80. (a)
81. (c)	82. (a)	83. (b)	84. (a)	85. (b)
86. (d)	87. (c)	88. (b)	89. (a)	90. (d)
91. (c)	92. (a)	93. (c)	94. (b)	95. (d)
96. (b)	97. (a)	98. (c)	99. (b)	100. (b)
101. (b)	102. (b)	103. (d)	104. (b)	105. (a)
106. (d)	107. (b)	108. (d)	109. (b)	110. (d)
111. (b)	112. (a)	113. (d)	114. (a)	115. (d)
116. (a)	117. (c)	118. (b)	119. (d)	120. (c)

CDS Examination, 2012

1. (c)	2. (b)	3. (d)	4. (d)	5. (b)
6. (d)	7. (b)	8. (c)	9. (a)	10. (d)
11. (a)	12. (c)	13. (b)	14. (a)	15. (c)
16. (b)	17. (d)	18. (a)	19. (a)	20. (c)
21. (b)	22. (c)	23. (a)	24. (c)	25. (d)
26. (b)	27. (b)	28. (c)	29. (a)	30. (c)
31. (a)	32. (b)	33. (a)	34. (b)	35. (c)
36. (d)	37. (a)	38. (a)	39. (d)	40. (a)
41. (a)	42. (a)	43. (a)	44. (d)	45. (a)
46. (b)	47. (a)	48. (c)	49. (a)	50. (a)
51. (b)	52. (b)	53. (a)	54. (d)	55. (c)
56. (a)	57. (b)	58. (d)	59. (c)	60. (b)
61. (c)	62. (c)	63. (b)	64. (c)	65. (b)
66. (a)	67. (b)	68. (d)	69. (d)	70. (d)
71. (a)	72. (c)	73. (a)	74. (a)	75. (b)
76. (c)	77. (a)	78. (a)	79. (c)	80. (a)
81. (a)	82. (c)	83. (b)	84. (a)	85. (b)
86. (b)	87. (a)	88. (b)	89. (b)	90. (c)
91. (b)	92. (d)	93. (c)	94. (a)	95. (a)
96. (b)	97. (a)	98. (d)	99. (c)	100. (a)
101. (c)	102. (a)	103. (b)	104. (d)	105. (a)
106. (a)	107. (b)	108. (d)	109. (b)	110. (a)
111. (d)	112. (b)	113. (c)	114. (b)	115. (a)
116. (b)	117. (b)	118. (a)	119. (c)	120. (c)

FREQUENCY ANALYSIS

ABBREVIATIONS USED:

Comprehension / **Comp**, Sentence Completion / **SC**, Sentence Filler / **SF**, Cloze Test/ **CT**, Synonyms/ **Syn**, Antonyms/ **Ant**, Idioms and Phrase/ **IP**, Substitution/ **Subt**, Sentence arrangement/ **SA**, Spelling/ **SPL**, Miscellaneous/**Misc.**, Total Marks/**TM**, Sentence error/**SE**, Sentence Improvement/ **SI**.

CDS Examination, September, 2008

	Comp.	SC	SF	CT	Syn	Ant	IP	Subt	SA	SE	SPL	SI	MISC.	TM
	25				18	20	5		20+15	17				

CDS, Examination 2011

	Comp.	SC	SF	CT	Syn	Ant	IP	Subt	SA	SE	SPL	SI	MISC.	TM
	25				20	19			8+16	15		17		

CDS, Examination 2012

	Comp.	SC	SF	CT	Syn	Ant	IP	Subt	SA	SE	SPL	SI	MISC.	TM
	17			21	15	14			21	18		14		

TREND ANALYSIS

Looking at the questions of 2008, 2011 and 2012 it becomes clear that the pattern is regular. Common items have been set. However, there is a change of items in all three years. In 2008, there was a question on idioms. In 2011 there is an addition of a question on sentence improvement. Likewise, there is a new question on cloze test.

This shows that the setter shuffles among the common items. There is variation in mark distribution also. You may expect the same pattern in future. All these units have been fully covered in the book.

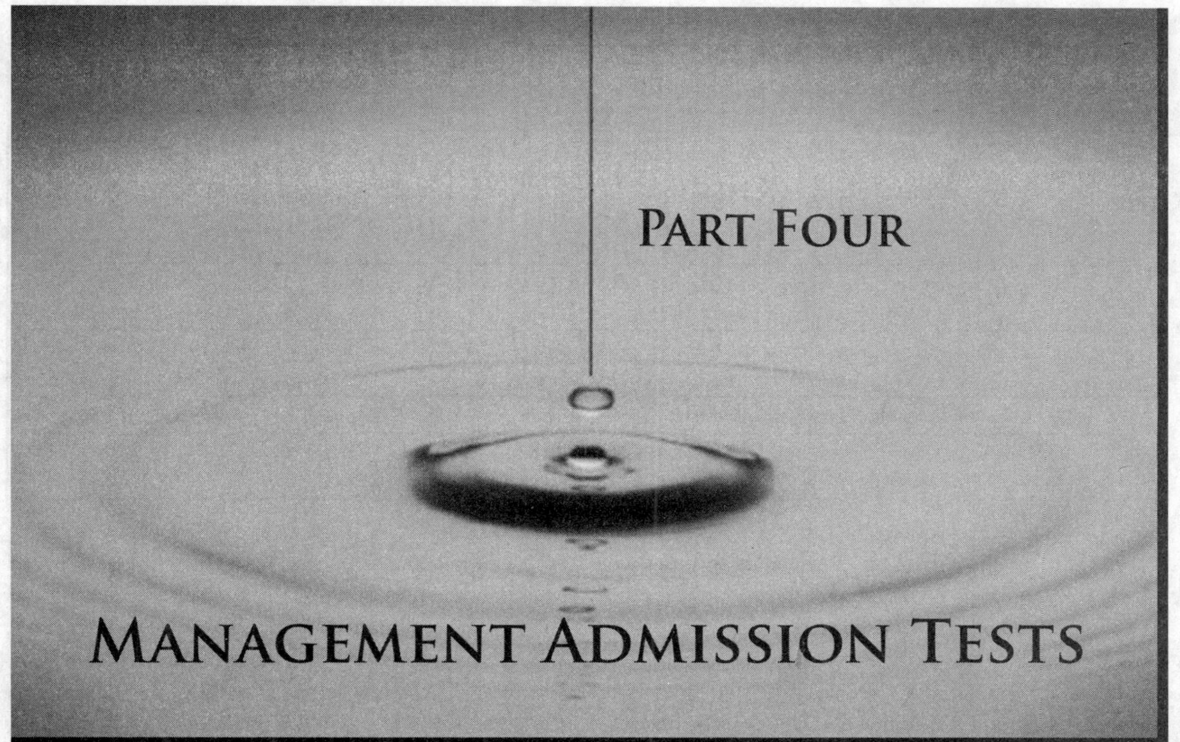

PART FOUR

MANAGEMENT ADMISSION TESTS

Management admission tests in India are complex, eclectic and of various kinds. These tests are conducted by individual institutions, group of institutions, States and several organisations. Some of the popular tests are (or are conducted by) CAT, XAT, SNAP, TISS, NMAT, MICA, IIFT, IRMA, MAT, IBSAT and ATMA. Most recently CMAT has been introduced by AICTE, All India Council of Technical Education. AICTE has now decided to conduct CMAT in foreign countries for facilitating eligible NRIs/PIOs and foreign nationals to appear in CMAT for admission in institutions in India.

Some States also conduct national level tests. They are:

S. No.	*Entance Exam*	*Institute*	*Eligibility*	*Tentative Month*	*Website*
1	MAH-CET	Directorate of Technical Education, Mahrashtra State	45% in Graduation in any discipline	February/ March	www.dte.org.in
2	CUSAT	Cochin University of Science and Technology	Graduation in any discipline	June	www.cusat.nic.in
3	PAM-SAT	GNDU, Amritsar / PTU, Jalandhar / Punjab University, Patiala	Graduation in any discipline	June/July	www.gndu.ac.in www.punjabiuniversity.ac.in www.ptu.ac.in
4	MET-MP	Madhya Pradesh Professional Examination Board	50% in Graduation	July	www.vyapam.nic.in
5	TANCET	Anna University, Chennai	Graduation in any Discipline	May	www.annauiv.edu
6	OCET	Punjab University, Chandigarh	Different Eligibility for Different Course	June	www.puchd.ac.in

S. No.	*Entance Exam*	*Institute*	*Eligibility*	*Tentative Month*	*Website*
7	UP-SEE	UP Technical University	45% in Graduation in any discipline	April	www.uptu.nic.in
8	Orissa JEE	Orissa JEE	Graduation in anyu Discipline	May	www.jeeorissa.com
9	GCET	Gujarat Secondary and Higher Secondary Education Board	50% in Graduation	July	
10	KMAT	Karnataka Private Post-Graduate Colleges Association	Graduation in any Discipline	July	www.kmat-2008.com
11	RMAT	Rajasthan Technical University	50% in Graduation	June	www.rtu.ac.in/rmat/
12	UPMCAT	Uttar Pradesh Technical University	Graduation in any Discipline		

The levels of difficulty of different examinations vary. CAT is the toughest and keeps on making changes every year. However, the book prepares the examinees with a firm background and imparts basic skill of english language required to tackle the test in the objective format. They need to put in specific practice for the CAT exams. Other examinations like MAT, MET, SNAP, IRMA, CMAT etc. vary but they are all fully covered by the book. It is not possible to catalogue the question papers of all examinations and so some representative question sets have been given and the trend analysis of each examination has been provided. These anylses will work as a lighthouse to students.

PAPER 26

MANAGEMENT APTITUDE TEST (MAT), SEPTEMBER 2012

(Conducted by All India Managment Association)

Directions to Questions 1 to 4

In each of these questions choose the option which can be substituted for the given words.

1. To cancel (a law, agreement, etc.) formally or officially
   (a) Terminate (b) Adjure
   (c) Object (d) Abrogate

2. To form a plot of scheme, especially on to do something wrong or wicked or designed to cause harm
   (a) Machinate (b) Conspire
   (c) Fatal (d) Machete

3. Very high-spirited, full of cheerfulness or enthusiasm
   (a) Eccentric (b) Eburmean
   (c) Sporting (d) Ebullient

4. A way of doing something, especially on ordered set of procedures or an orderly system
   (a) Presentation (b) Process
   (c) Method (d) Agenda?

Directions to Questions 5 to 7

A sentence has been broken into four parts with an error in one of the parts. Identify the part that has an error.

5.
   (a) A temple was erected to him
   (b) at the foot of the Capitoline Hill
   (c) at which were deposited the
   (d) public treasury & the laws of the State

6.
   (a) I soon lost sight & recollection of ghastly fears
   (b) in the beauty of the scene as we drove along
   (c) although had I known the language, or rather languages which my fellow passengers were speaking
   (d) I might not have been able to throw them off so easily.

7. As he has refused to accept their summons the police may register a case and proceed under

the provisions of Section 172 (Absconding to avoid service of summons or other proceeding') of IPC.

(a) He has refused to accept the summons and should, therefore, be prosecuted under the provisions of Section 172 of IPC.
(b) The police may proceed to register a case against the absconder and proceed under the provisions of IPC.
(c) He may be prosecuted under the provisions of Section 172 of IPC for not responding to summons by the police.
(d) He will be prosecuted under the provisions of Section 172 ('Absconding to avoid service of summons or other proceeding') of IPC for not responding to police summons.

Directions to Questions 8 to 10

Identify the best way of writing the sentence in the context of correct usage of standard written English.

8.
(a) We can divide the problem into parts in the present case firstly by considering events which are localised on the x-axis.
(b) In the present case we can divide the problem into parts by considering events first which are localised as per x-axis.
(c) By considering first the events which are localised on the x-axis, in the present case we can divide the problem into parts.
(d) In the present case we can divide the problem into parts by first considering events which are localised on the x-axis.

9.
(a) If the constants 'a' and 'b' were known, thus we should have the solution of our problem.
(b) We should thus have a solution to our problem, if the constants 'a' and 'b' are known.
(c) We should, if the constants 'a' and 'b' were known, thus have the solution of our problem.
(d) We should thus have the solution to our problem, if the constants 'a' and 'b' were known.

10.
(a) Excellence will come when the performer takes pride in doing his best.
(b) Excellence comes as the performer will take pride in doing his best.
(c) The excellence will come when the performer will take pride in doing his best.
(d) Excellence comes when the performer takes pride in doing his best.

Directions to Questions 11 to 13

Rearrange the letters of the jumbled word to identify the correct word, and select the option from below which is opposite in meaning to that word.

11. SISPNHAPE
(a) surrender (b) quickness
(c) richness (d) sorrow

12. BRENYA
(a) delight (b) discover
(c) distant (d) direct

13. OSYIN
(a) happy (b) quiet
(c) laugh (d) sleep

Directions to Questions 14 to 33

Study the passages below and answer the questions that follow each passage.

Passage–I

Universal Health Coverage (UHC) has now been widely adopted by Canada and many other developing countries both as a developmental imperative and the moral obligation of a civilised society. India embraced this vision at its independence. However, insufficient funding of public facilities, combined with faulty planning and inefficient management over the years, has resulted in a dysfunctional health system that has been yielding poor health outcomes. Private health services have grown by default, without checks on cost and quality, escalating private out-of-pocket health expenditures and exacerbating health inequity. Out-of-pocket expenditure still remains at 71 percent of all spending, without coverage for outpatient care, medicines and basic diagnostic tests. The High Level Expert Group (HLEG) established by the Planning Commission has submitted a comprehensive framework for providing UHC in India. A health entitlement card should assure every citizen access to a national health package of essential primary, secondary and tertiary care, both inpatient and outpatient. The HLEG is very clear that services included under UHC must be tax funded and cashless at delivery. Contributory social insurance is not appropriate for countries like India where a large segment of the workforce —close to 93 percent—is in the unorganised sector and vast numbers are below or near the poverty line. Increasing the public spending on health is the first immediate requirement. However, even the doubling of public financing will not be adequate to support all the components of a fully evolved UHC. Priorities need to be defined. Clearly, there is no alternative to progressively strengthening public facilities, and thereby reducing people's dependence on private providers. However, the public system may need to "contract-in" the services of willing private providers, to fill gaps in its capacity to deliver all the services assured under UHC. Such "contracted-in" private providers will have to deliver cashless services and would be compensated on the basis of pre-determined cost per package of health services rather than "fee-for-service" for each visit or procedure. In such an arrangement, the private sector acts as an extension of the public, sector where needed, and will not compete for the same set of services for the same people. It is time to recognise that everyone, not just the poor, needs to be protected against rising health costs that can impoverish any family. Apart from improving people's health, adopting UHC is likely to generate millions of new jobs, enhance productivity, and promote equity.

14. It can be inferred from the passage that

(a) better health conditions prevailing in society lead to better impetus for development.

(b) civilised societies usually enjoy better health conditions than uncivilised ones.

(c) morality and development in society are two sides of the same coin.

(d) All these

15. It is implied in the passage that

(a) about 30% of population in India is covered by health insurance.

(b) the private sector health care industry in India has grown essentially because the public healthcare systems are inefficient and/of inadequate.

(c) India adopted 'Universal Health Coverage' as early as in the year 1947.

(d) All these

16. Which of the following statements is true in the context of the passage?

(a) The private health care centres certainly provide better facilities than the government-sun centres.

(b) The government of India proposes to issue health entitlement cards to all citizens for free health care.

(c) The UHC system is fully evolved in India but the government has to pump in more funds to keep it running smoothly.

(d) Implementing the UHC will create employment opportunities.

17. Which of the following statements is not necessarily true in the context of the passage?

(a) Contributory social insurance works best where a large segment of the country's workforce is above the poverty line.

(b) The author of the passage feels that the government should outsource some of the health care-services under the UHC to private players.

(c) Cost of health care is rising rapidly and could severely dent a family's finances.

(d) The primary objective behind issuing of UHC health entitlement cards is to avoid having to pay in cash when citizens avail health care services.

Passage-II

In order to capitalise on the groundwork done for creation of a successful solar market through the launch of the Jawaharlal Nehru National Solar Mission, a recent report has suggested that India now needs to adopt greater transparency, benchmarking and monitoring, strategic approaches to finance, and technology-neutral policies for manufacturing to take the renewable energy mission forward. According to an independent report published by the Council on Energy, Environment and Water (CEEW) and the Natural Resources Defence Council (NRDC), it has been found that India's solar industry is at a crucial stage of its growth and needs strategic nurturing. The report is of the view that a productive solar manufacturing base is an important part of India's aspirations to become a major global solar player. Investing in solar manufacturing now could provide long-term strategic value for India. But to be a dominant player in the global arena, India needs to make prompt, smart and concerted investments in manufacturing. "The National Solar Mission deserves much credit for laying the groundwork for a successful solar market, but a lot of market uncertainty still permeates the solar ecosystem and affects development of manufacturing capacity," says the Director, India Initiative at NRDC. It has pointed out that a range of systemic issues hinder domestic manufacturing in India. "Indian manufacturing is of a smaller scale and more fragmented, leading to higher costs," says the CEO, CEEW. The report finds that the Indian solar manufacturing sector requires systemic improvements in infrastructure, domestic low-cost financing, and raw materials. The director of NRDC said policy makers should also not lose sight of value added industries and job creating potential further downstream. Outlining the priorities, the report states that Government must bring together different financial institutions to strengthen the solar financing ecosystem, which would operate at the strategic level, project level and offer ancillary support (R&D, skill development).

18. Which of the following statements is / are implied in the passage in respect of the solar energy capability building in India?

A. A lot of work has already been clone in this direction.

B. Transparency has been totally lacking with regard to the Indian government's research work done in this field.

C. India could soon be a global player in the area of solar energy.

(a) A only
(b) A & B
(c) A & C
(d) A, B & C

19. Which of the following statements not implied in the passage?

(a) A sound financial strategy is essential for developing a good solar energy market.
(b) Developing a sound solar energy industry, would lead to development of other (related) industries as a spin-off benefit.
(c) The uncertainties in the solar system are affecting the growth of the solar energy industry
(d) Solar energy could play a vital role in India's economic development.

20. According to the passage, the solar - industry in India

(a) is very much dependent on the National Solar Mission for its future growth.
(b) is still in its launch phase
(c) needs governmental support to ensure its progress in the growth path.
(d) All these

21. As per the passage, which of the following factors is/are seen as disadvantageous to the Indian solar industry while competing in the global market?

A. Government's apathy towards this industry.

B. Robust manufacturing practices of the other global players.

C. Lack of adequate capital in the country for channelising into this industry.

(a) A only
(b) A & B
(c) A & C
(d) None of these

Passage-III

Most Indians are not particularly worried about Indian Standard Times (IST), except for those who live in the Northeast where the sun rises around 4 a.m. in summer, and gets dark well before 4 p.m. in winter. Those of us who have to make overseas long distance calls and get into trouble with fractions are not even aware that we belong to a minority (three percent) of regions whose standard times are fractional hours off from GMT. India spans longitudes of 68° at the western end and 98° at the eastern boundary and, as there is a difference of one hour for every 15° of longitude, the two extremes differ by two hours. Thus, when the sun sets at 4 p.m. in Kohima, it sets at 6 p.m. in Porbunder. IST was fixed in 1906 midway at 82.5°, or 5.5 hours ahead of Greenwich Mean Time (GMT). Periodically, there are demands from the Northeast region for a separate time zone so that the clocks there may be advanced by an hour. There is a general misconception among those who worry about saving energy—such as the Planning Commission—that dividing the country into time zones will save "a lot of energy." The savings are almost always described by adjectives, for very few have estimated correctly the amount of savings that may accrue by altering IST or creating two time zones. There is also the practice in several countries, of "Daylight Saving Time" (DST), wherein the time in summer is advanced (or the clocks put forward) by one hour and retracted during winter. This enables people to enjoy sunlight longer in summer and avoid the inconveniences of late sunrises and early sunsets during winter. Our proposal for India is to introduce neither time zones nor DST, but to advance IST by half an hour to being six hours ahead of GMT, once and permanently. Such a suggestion has been made before, but until now no one has computed the energy savings that would accrue as a result, using a correct model and dependable data. Our fairly rigorous method has been vetted by national and international experts and is based on load demand data at five electrical zones of India, provided by the Power Grid Corporation of India. The Bureau of Energy Efficiency provided financial support for the study.

22. It can be inferred from the passage that

A. Time, by clocks across India, would be same at any given point of the day.

B. People in North-East India go to bed well before people in Western India do.

C. People in the North-Eastern part of India work longer hours in summer than they do in winter.

(a) A only (b) A & B
(c) A & C (d) A, B & C

23. Which of the following statements is true as per the passage?

(a) India is amongst the three percent of nations in the world which follow standard time patterns.
(b) India is among the minority of nations whose standard time is at variance with GMT.
(c) Days in North-East India generally begin at 4 a.m. and end at about 4 p.m.
(d) None of these

24. What is the specific misconception of the Planning Commission in respect of energy saving, according to the passage?

(a) Dividing the country into multiple time zones would surely save energy for the nation.
(b) The one and only way to save energy is to divide the country into time zones.
(c) Substantial energy savings could be effected by dividing the country into two time zones.
(d) None of these

25. What is the primary concern of the author in writing this article?

(a) To align the clocks in the five different regions of India, in tune with the respective sunrise and sunset times.
(b) To align IST with GMT.
(c) To ensure that India advances its clock by half an hour only.
(d) That India should implement an effective method of energy savings.

Passage-IV

With the major economies of the United States and the euro zone still showing no let-up from their halting recovery, Indian apparel exporters continue to suffer from tepid demand. They are also, of late, compelled to make do with unpleasant non-tariff barriers (NTBs) such as rigorous standards. Apparently, the most galling one is insistence on fair labour standards. That includes not importing garments/apparel made by child labour or forced labour or prison labour from exporting countries. While no one could fault the new perception of concerns for the vulnerable, the unilateral prescription of what constitutes proper labour practices continues to be a bone of contention.

However, trading countries have braced themselves to face down any challenges with some of the exporting countries voluntarily taking on themselves the onus of putting in place a code of ethical standards so that their merchandise does not get jettisoned in the overseas markets on this count. Though India's merchandise exports overshot the target by a couple of billion dollars to reach $303 billion in 2011-12 fiscal year, the country could not achieve the target of $32.3 billion of textile and clothing exports as it fell short by a substantial value. Still, India ranks as the sixth largest exporter of apparel with a global market share of 3.25 percent, after China at 37 percent, the EU at 28 percent, Hong Kong at 7 percent, Bangladesh at 4.5 percent and Turkey at 3.6 percent. For a country that boasts of being the largest producer of King Cotton, the position behind tiny countries such as Bangladesh and Hong Kong has more to do with several domestic disabilities such as high cost of finance, lack of flexible labour policy and infrastructural impediments. Added to these travails is the emerging concern over and apprehension of India's apparel not making it to the traditional global markets if the orchestrated campaign for labour standards gets strident and stringent. Incidentally, the US and the European Union (EU) together account for 80 percent of India's total apparel exports and the retail stores in these countries, which stock up apparel from developing countries, have lately been crying hoarse over alleged harsh treatment to labourers in exporting countries. These concerns presumably arise out of the prodding from their own governments which find protectionist sentiments in times of trouble a facile course to resort to. It is against this sombre scenario that the Apparel Export Promotion Council (AEPC) worked out a comprehensive compliance code for ethical sourcing for the apparel exports from India. This stems from both a conviction, and recognition of the crucial linkages between ethical trade and economic growth.

26. What is the meaning of the word 'tepid' as used in the first sentence of the passage?

(a) reduced (b) decreasing
(c) erratic (d) rising

27. It is implied in the passage that

A. United States has put in place certain barriers to imports from countries using child labour in their manufacturing units.

B. only some of the exporting countries are really concerned about "ethical standards".

C. there cannot be one standard global definition for what constitutes fair labour practice.

(a) A & C (b) A & B
(c) A only (d) A, B & C

28. It can be inferred from the passage that

(a) AEPC is as concerned about fair labour practices as are the developed nations.
(b) India fell short of its target for exports in 2011-12.
(c) India is the world's largest producer of textiles made of King Cotton.
(d) the US and EU are not really concerned over the fate of labourers in the developing countries.

29. It is implied in the passage that

(a) the US and EU together account for four-fifths of the imports.
(b) India has set up AEPC, to expressly work out a code of ethics for Indian textile producers.
(c) economic growth is certainly dependent on ethical trade practices.
(d) China is one of the major importers of textiles as are the US and EU.

Passage-V

The tussle between coal mining and nature conservation has been long standing. But things have risen to a new level with the Group of Ministers (GoM) being setup to consider the various issues around coal mining. They have recently written to Chief Secretaries of all the coal-bearing states asking them to reapply for permissions to mine in very dense forests. However, environmental scientists and civil society groups worry about the GoM's decision to dilute the environmental safeguards currently in place and open up all forests to mining. They argue that there is an important need for some mechanism to be put in place that recognises certain forests in the country as being critical and, therefore, not open to mining. Their first argument for forests is the various "ecosystem services" that humans derive from these forests. Hydrological, nutrient and nitrogen cycles help plants and food crops to grow. Carbon cycles regulate global climate. These cannot be replaced by afforestation programmes and artificial forests. Ecological scientists have estimated the net value of some of the more easily quantifiable ecosystem services to be around US $33 trillion a year; or more than twice the global GDP. They argue that any industrial projects that involve the destruction of forests must also factor in these ecological costs. Another concern is the large number of tribals and other forest dwellers who directly depend on forests for their livelihood. The current resettlement and rehabilitation policy for such people, in Madhya Pradesh for example, consists of one-tenth of an acre of land and the promise of one member of the household being employed in the mining project or thermal power plant after its completion. A body of work by the World Bank has highlighted the inadequacy of most of these rehabilitation packages. It argues that actual costs of displacing people are considerably more. These must be factored into the "real" costs of large development projects. Non-Government Organisations and activists across the board all accept the urgent need for India to produce more energy. But they express serious reservations about India locking itself into a carbon intense development path.

30. It is implied in the passage that
- (a) the coal minister and environment minister are constantly in a tussle in the GoM meetings.
- (b) Coal reserves have been discovered in several very dense forests that were earlier thought to be lacking in coal resources.
- (c) a great many tribals depend on forest produce for their livelihood.
- (d) None of these

31. Environmental scientists are worried about
- (a) civil society groups as the latter generally tend to rake up issues only to target the former.
- (b) the GoM's decision to pour cold water on safety regulations.
- (c) the potential loss of livelihood of tribals due to coal mining projects.
- (d) the relaxing of norms to allow coal mining in all forests.

32. Which of the following statements is not implied in the passage?
- (a) Need for energy production has been felt only lately in India.
- (b) Government of India's rehabilitation packages more or less suffice to help resettle the tribals from forests.
- (c) India has got blocked in its development path.
- (d) Afforestation programmes and artificial forests adequately make up for destruction of existing forest areas.

33. Rehabilitation packages offered by the government to tribals displaced from forests due to mining activities
- A. vary from state to state.
- B. include instant employment for at least one member of the family.
- C. do not take into account all the costs of displacing people.

(a) A & B (b) B & C
(c) A & C (d) A, B & C

Directions to Questions 34 to 36

Fill in the blanks.

34. Television serials are characterised by a/an ______ story line and______ plots and sub-plots.
- (a) unending, convoluted
- (b) infantile, simple
- (c) uniform, emotional
- (d) extempore, routine

35. If mankind has to survive for long, it must ________ and deliberately renounce the fruits of ________ and whirling technology.
- (a) willfully, wild
- (b) honestly, responsible
- (c) sincerely, labour
- (d) effectively, sliding

36. Pipes are not a safer ________ to cigarettes because, though pipe smokers do not inhale, they are still ________ getting lung and mouth cancers.
- (a) preference, not free from
- (b) answer, responsible for

(c) alternative, prone to
(d) rejoinder, involved in

E. As a result, today we know more about acid rain and its effect than ever before;'

(a) ABDEC (b) DACEB
(c) CEBAD (d) BADGE

Directions to Questions 37 to 40

Choose the order or the sentence/marked A, B, C, D and E to form a logical paragraph.

37.

A. The more fundamental and far-reaching a scientific theory, the more speculative it is likely to be.
B. But speculation is its very life-blood.
C. A mature science tries to arrange facts in significant patterns to see the relationship between unrelated aspects of the universe.
D. Idle speculation has no place in science.
E. It is erroneous to believe that science is only concerned with pure facts.

(a) DBAEC (b) AECBD
(c) BDCEA (d) AECDB

38.

A. But this time a curious philosophy has emerged.
B. However, it seems that a regulatory solution is yet far away.
C. It says that the more we know about a problem, the more uncertainty is introduced and the more it needs to be studied.
D. The recent debates on acid rain have pitted the environmentalists head to head against industry.

39.

A. Seconds later, the glaring object swept past and he thought he had outmanoeuvred it.
B. While flying over enemy territory, Jones received the warning of an oncoming missile.
C. He was proved wrong when he saw the vertical tail fins on fire.
D. Without wasting time, he slammed the throttles forward and made the plane roll into a high speed turn.
E. Hardly had he responded to the message when he actually saw whatever he dreaded most.

(a) EDGBA (b) BCDEA
(c) DAECB (d) BEDAC

40.

A. A film director has to translate the given scenario into visual medium.
B. A novelist works in the written word.
C. Whereas the film director works in pictures, in visual movement.
D. The pictures may be supported by speech and sound.
E. But primarily the film is a pictorial art

(a) ABCDE
(b) CDEAB
(c) BCDEA (4} EDCBA

ANSWER KEY

1. (d)	2. (b)	3. (d)	4. (d)	5. (a)
6. (c)	7. (d)	8. (d)	9. (b)	10. (d)
11. (d)	12. (c)	13. (b)	14. (d)	15. (b)
16. (d)	17. (c)	18. (a)	19. (c)	20. (d)
21. (d)	22. (d)	23. (b)	24. (c)	25. (c)
26. (a)	27. (d)	28. (c)	29. (b)	30. (c)
31. (d)	32. (d)	33. (b)	34. (a)	35. (a)
36. (c)	37. (a)	38. (b)	39. (d)	40. (c)

FREQUENCY ANALYSIS

Substitution	04
Error	03
Sentence Improvement	03
Comprehension	20
Sentence Completion	03
Sentence Arrangement	07 (3 + 4)
Total	**40**

TREND ANALYSIS

The questions are of regular type. The emphasis is on comprehension; it has 20 questions. All other items are usual and have been set in a regular way. A careful reading of the book and regular work with the practice sets will be of help to students.

PAPER 27

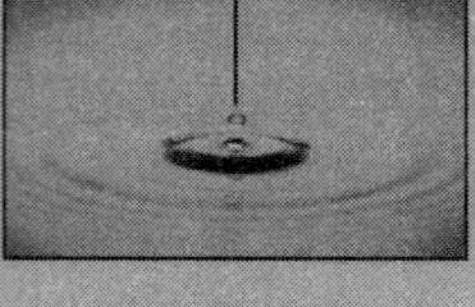

MBA ADMISSION TEST, NOVEMBER 2012

(Conducted by Institute of Rural Management, Anand)

Directions to Questions 1 to 10

In the following passage there are blanks each of which has been numbered. Five words are suggested, one of which fits the blank appropriately. Find out the appropriate word in each case.

Recently I visited Moscow, a Russian city **...(a)...** man/war memorials. There is a huge park in Russia **...(b)...** as Peace park. In the middle of the park **...(c)...** a pillar on which the different battles fought by the Russians have been mentioned along with the names and the places. As I was standing under a tree my eyes **...(d)...** on a young couple who had just been married. I started wondering **...(e)...** they had come to this monument on their wedding day. They walked up to the monument, **...(6)...** down a bouquet, bowed their heads in silence and walked away. I was **...(7)...** to know what was going on, so I asked the tourist guide. "Oh, it is a **...(8)...** in Russia", he said, "every couple must visit an important national monument nearby on their wedding day. It is a mark of gratitude. Our forefathers have **...(9)...** so much for the country. The newly married couple needs to **...(10)...** they are free and living in a peaceful country because of their ancestors' sacrifices. They must ask for their blessings."

1.
(a) with (b) erected
(c) dedicated (d) has
(e) built

2.
(a) identified (b) mentioned
(c) known (d) call
(e) title

3.
(a) placed (b) located
(c) constructed (d) seen
(e) stands

4.
(a) notified (b) go
(c) recognise (d) fell
(e) drew

5.
(a) about (b) why
(c) what (d) if
(e) where

6.
(a) dropped (b) presented

(c) laid (d) arranged
(e) kept

7.
(a) curious (b) puzzled
(c) hasty (d) disappointed
(e) surprised

8.
(a) usual (b) normal
(c) custom (d) rituals
(e) practise

9.
(a) gave (b) remember
(c) honoured (d) sacrificed
(e) abandoned

10.
(a) wish (b) remember
(c) achieve (d) remind
(e) dream

Directions for Questions 11 to 15

Each/sentence below has blanks, each blank indicating that something has been omitted. Choose the word that best fits the meaning of the sentence as a whole.

11. She saw many mobile phones before ______ for this one.
(a) Buying (b) settling
(c) choosing (d) thinking
(e) finding

12. Most of these banks will be______ branches in our city.
(a) cutting (b) seeing
(c) opening (d) initiate
(e) making

13. Most of the teachers were______ at the function.
(a) absent (b) attending
(c) assemble (d) present
(e) gone

14. I think it ______ benefit your health______ take a glass of water before meals.
(a) should; to (b) will; for
(c) may; to (d) can; to
(e) will; to

15. We had to ______ for a very long time before receiving a reply from them.
(a) Wait (b) stay
(c) be (d) look
(e) chase

Directions for Questions 16 to 21

Rearrange the following six sentences (A), (B), (C), (D), (E) and (F) in the proper sequence to form a meaningful paragraph; then answer the questions given below them.

(A) This has come to them through a peaceful revolution underpinned by an extraordinary transformation of legal rights.
(B) But promising equality, of course, is not the same as delivering it on the ground.
(C) Women across the world enjoy greater opportunities and freedom than ever before.
(D) Nearly 140 national constitutions also now specifically guarantee gender equality.
(E) Despite real advances, there sadly remains an immense gap between these welcome legal guarantees and everyday life for women.
(F) Almost every country has signed international conventions signalling their commitment to outlawing discrimination against women.

16. Which of the following would be the First sentence?
(a) A (b) B
(c) C (d) D
(e) E

17. Which of the following would be the (Sixth) Last sentence?
(a) C (b) D
(c) E (d) F
(e) B

18. Which of the following would be the Second sentence?

(a) A (b) B
(c) C (d) E
(e) F

19. Which of the following would be the Fourth sentence?
(a) A (b) B
(c) C (d) D
(e) F

20. Which of the following would be the Third sentence?
(a) B (b) C
(c) D (d) E
(e) F

21. Which of the following would be the Fifth sentence?
(a) A (b) B
(c) C (d) D

Directions for Questions 22 to 35

Read the following passage to answer the given questions based on it. Some words/ phrases are printed in bold to help you locate them while answering some of the questions.

The quality of national statistics produced by the Central Statistics Organisation and the National Sample Survey Organisation has **kicked up some dust**. "We are handicapped by the reliability of some of the basic data that we need to use in policy calculations," Reserve Bank of India governor said on Tuesday.

Dodgy data is a handicap for decision makers. Consider the conflicting signals about the extent of the economic slowdown and especially the state of investment activity, two parameters that are key inputs for the central bank when it decides on interest rate policy. Or : The extent of poverty in India or new job creation in recent years has led to immense debates partly, because the numbers put out by government statisticians are not fully trusted. They presented a rosy **picture**.

So, there is little doubt, that the system to collect various social and economic data needs to be **overhauled**, something that has been discussed at least since January 2000, when the National Statistics Commission headed by C. Rangarajan was set up. Yet, it is a mistake to condemn the entire statistics machinery in a **sweeping** verdict. Let's **face it** : India is not China.

A first step is to identify two sets of problems—knowledge and staffing—and then try to fix them.

Consider the knowledge problems. First, the data collection system at the state level is in a **shambles**. The 13th Finance Commission has already provided grants worth Rs. 616 crore, or Rs. 1 crore per district, to improve statistical systems at the state and district levels, especially the latter. Second, the indexes used to capture high-frequency data such as inflation and industrial production need to reflect the changing composition of consumption and production in a high-growth and fact-changing economy such as ours. Third, new initiatives will be needed to understand trends in subjective well-being and happiness among Indians as well as to build new **measures** of national progress such as green accounting (to capture environmental degradation and the depletion of non-renewable resources).

However, the most immediate problem to be solved is the immense shortage of staff. The minister for statistics and programme implementation spoke last week about the talent crunch because of low salaries. Young statistics grads have skills that are in great demand from the financial sector, consumer firms and market research agencies. They are no longer interested in government jobs.

22. Which of the following can be inferred about the figures of extent of poverty provided by Government statisticians?
(a) Those were Type
(b) The figure did not have government approval
(c) Those were under-estimates
(d) Atleast regarding poverty the figures were correct
(e) Those were either over-estimates or underestimates

23. Which of the following is one of the suggestions given to improve the situation?
(a) The Central Statistics Organisation and the National Sample Survey Organisation may be merged
(b) Another National Statistics Commission may be set up

(c) India should adopt data collection and statistical methods adopted bv China
(d) The indexes should reflect the changing trends
(e) Graduates other than Statistics specialisation may be appointed

24. Which of the following has not been indicated as the area in which the data was considered to be conflicting?
(a) Extent of inflation
(b) E,xtent of poverty
(c) Extent of economic slowdown
(d) Extent of new job creation
(e) Extent of investment activity

25. Which of the following is the meaning of the phrase "kicked up some dust" as used in the passage?
(a) settled the issue
(b) cleared the air
(c) removed some confusion
(d) kick-started an initiative
(e) None of these

26. "India is not China", what is being conveyed through this phrase?
(a) India followed China's model of sample survey
(b) China followed India's model of sample survey
(c) Both the countries follow same method of sample survey
(d) India's population is still less than that of China
(e) None of these

27. Which of the following has been suggested as one of the new measures of assessing national progress?
(a) Industrial progress
(b) Extent of depletion of non-renewable resources
(c) Grant allocated for improving statistical systems
(d) Rate of inflation and industrial growth
(e) None of these

28. Which of the following can be inferred from the information given?
(a) India has about 600 districts
(b) India has about 38 States and UTs
(c) The national statistics is used only by Reserve Bank of India
(d) It has come to light only recently that basic data may not be reliable1
(e) Shortage of staff problem is there in all government departments

Directions for Questions 29 to 32

Choose the word which is most nearly the same in meaning of the word printed in bold, as used in the passage.

29. shambles
(a) non-existent (b) stalled
(c) incomplete (d) fake
(e) disorder

30. overhauled
(a) rejected (b) improved
(c) assured (d) assessed
(e) overtaken

31. dodgy
(a) incomplete (b) difficult
(c) dump (d) unreliable
(e) inclined

32. measures
(a) ideas (b) controls
(c) standards (d) issues
(e) capabilities

Directions for Questions 33 to 35

Choose the vvord(s) which is most opposite in meaning of the word(s) printed in bold, as used in the passage.

33. rosy
(a) gloomy (b) expected
(c) missing (d) leading
(e) unrealistic

34. sweeping

(a) insignificant (b) casual
(c) unverified (d) limited
(e) minority

35. face it

(a) accept (b) reflect on
(c) ignore (d) give in
(e) find out

Directions for Questions 36 to 50

Read the following passage to answer the given questions based on it. Some words/phrases are printed in bold to help you locate them while answering some of the questions.

How important are laws and reservations for gender equality? Are "green buildings" a way forward to help reduce global warming? How inclusive are India and Pakistan for their respective citizens, and why? What can we do to reduce the Rs. 3.65 that the nation spends to deliver a rupee's worth of foodgrains to the poor?

Continually **caught up** in urgent distractions, Indian politicians don't spend nearly as much time as they should **contemplating** important; policy issues.

A good way to stimulate it, and greater appreciation of current international policy debates, is to encourage participation in serious academic forums. One such is the annual India Parliamentary Leadership Programme at Yale University, co-developed with FICCI. Involving days of gruelling research-backed presentations by some of the best academics in the world, and the kind of candid discussions that can only happen away from the spotlight, it is about as far from the typical junket abroad as possible.

So what about mandating gender equity by legislation? India has long **made heavy weather** of legislating quotas for women. Despite much energetic campaigning for it— and I say this as a supporter of the idea—the proposed legislation has always got stalled in acrimonious disputes. What may come as a revelation to some is that while affirmative action for women in politics does help gender equity, there is something that helps far more. It turns out that the maximum positive impact on a nation's level of gender equity is linked to the percentage of women in the workforce. The **corollary** is obvious: far more gains could be achieved by shifting tactical focus to less controversial legislative proposals that counter bias in the workplace.

What about climate change, and does it help to promote "green buildings"? A surprising analysis shows most such constructions are larger than their conventional counterparts and, while consuming less energy per square foot, actually consume more energy per capita. Another emerging trend, that of decentralising energy generation with "energy self-sufficient" buildings, may also be counterproductive. Reprocessing of biomass for on-site generation, supplementing localised solar and wind generation, ends up multiplying "urban heat islands". One reason for these contradictions, at least in the developed countries, could be industry-driven standards that boost energy consumption.

On the subject of inclusivity, the discourse in India has focussed on economic equity. Political inclusion is taken for granted in the world's largest democracy. But it is important to remember what works, in order not to trip up on future challenges. For instance, India and Pakistan have certain obvious similarities and differences, but some less obvious aspects can be illuminating. It is commonly known that unlike in India, the percentage of minorities in Pakistan has sharply declined after partition; what is less well known is that a clear majority of India's minorities, 55%, believes the system is fair. One of the reasons for India's greater success in nation-building—apart from obvious secular, democratic principles—is the much greater tolerance of regional diversity.

Two examples highlight this. First, the ethnic composition of the two countries' armies is telling. While both countries started out in 1947 with three-fourths of their armies being from the Punjab, India has consciously and gradually brought it down to a third; Pakistan's army continues to be less representative, with an estimated 55-65% from Punjab, which has had repercussions for both its internal harmony and foreign policy. Second, despite initial reservations, India under Nehru accepted the demand for multiple official languages, and indeed linguistic basis for statehood. By contrast, Pakistan under Jinnah and his successors treated the more populous east's demand for Bengali to be an additional national language (besides Urdu, which was the mother tongue of only 5% of the population) as **treasonable.**

On the subject of economic inclusivity : despite decades of hand-wringing on how to optimise poverty alleviation efforts, many Indians are still shocked to hear that the country spends Rs. 3.65 for every rupee of foodgrains it delivers to the poor. Surely there must be better ways to do this? Many economists have been advocating at least one radical alternative: direct cash transfers to the poor. Yet, despite successful implementation in other countries, for years this idea did not get the attention it deserved in India. Fortunately, at long last it seems to be getting political **traction.** The government is now on the verge of launching much-delayed pilot projects.

India continues to grapple with the problems of a developing country, while being thrust into new roles **commensurate** with its growing economy and global stature. On both fronts it would be well served by a conscious effort to expose its policymakers to the best minds at home and abroad.

36. Which of the following is recommended by the author?
- (a) Policy makers should interact more with national as well as international academicians on important policy issues
- (b) If India handles the four issues indicated, most of the problems will be solved
- (c) International expertise and research-backed presentations are better than the national ones
- (d) Mere candid discussion does not help the cause, there should be a detailed action plan
- (e) Academic forums only can provide a better solution to most of the problems

37. Which of the following is most similar in meaning to the phrase 'made heavy weather of as used in the passage?
- (a) Created more hangover than needed
- (b) Only talked and no follow up action
- (c) Always went wrong like weather forecasting
- (d) Exaggerated the difficulty of something to be done
- (e) Had a hangover of an important issue

38. Which of the following is not one of the major area/issue raised by the author?
- (a) Delivery cost of subsidised foodgrains to the poor
- (b) Fallacies about green buildings
- (c) Gender equality
- (d) Political inclusion of citizens
- (e) Need for cooperation between the neighbouring countries

39. Who seems to be the focal group needing better appreciation and research-based information on the critical issues?
- (a) General Public
- (b) Parliamentarians
- (c) Grass-root level workers of different schemes
- (d) Women
- (e) Academicians

40. According to the author, more representation of women in which of the following will be more beneficial at national level?
- (a) Parliament
- (b) Education
- (c) Workforce
- (d) Legal Services
- (e) International Services

41. Which of the following goes against the "green buildings"?
- (a) The cost of construction is higher
- (b) Per square foot energy consumption is higher
- (c) Per capita energy consumption is less
- (d) Such constructions are smaller than conventional buildings
- (e) None of these

42. Which of the following is not true regarding the issue of inclusivity as explained in the passage?
- (a) The percentage of minorities in Pakistan has declined after partition
- (b) Two-third of Indian Army's composition is from states other than Punjab
- (c) India has shown much more acceptance and inclusion of regional diversity compared to Pakistan
- (d) 55% of India's total population feels that Indian system has been fair to the minorities

(e) India followed the Policy of creating states on the basis of language

43. "On the subject of inclusivity, the discourse in India has focussed on economic equity". Which of the following represents best paraphrasing of the above sentence, as used in the passage?
(a) Whenever we talked about economic inclusion, the political inclusion was not considered
(b) When it comes to inclusion, there has only been a lip-service and no political will
(c) We have been more concerned in our discussions on the need for economic inclusion
(d) Discourses on economic equity have helped the subject of inclusivity
(e) All subjects under inclusion were only discussed and not implemented

Directions for Questions 44 to 48

Choose the word(s) which is most nearly the same in meaning of the word(s) printed in bold, as used in the passage.

44. contemplating
(a) providing (b) considering
(c) scheming (d) containing
(e) discoursing

45. telling
(a) arguing (b) defending
(c) impressive (d) tiring
(e) revealing

46. caught up
(a) involved (b) detected
(c) distracted (d) pick up
(e) pay

47. corollary
(a) practice (b) resultant
(c) hint (d) action
(e) reference

48. traction
(a) opposition (b) path
(c) trace (d) acceptance
(e) non-interference

Directions for Questions 49 to 50

Choose the word(s) which is most opposite in meaning of the word(s) printed in bold, as used in the passage.

49. treasonable
(a) moralistic (b) untenable
(c) patriotic (d) unrealistic
(e) offensive

50. commensurate
(a) disproportionate
(b) illegally
(c) uncommon
(d) unmeasurable
(e) characteristic

ANSWER KEY

1. (a)	2. (c)	3. (e)	4. (d)	5. (b)
6. (c)	7. (a)	8. (c)	9. (d)	10. (b)
11. (b)	12. (c)	13. (d)	14. (c)	15. (a)
16. (c)	17. (c)	18. (e)	19. (a)	20. (c)
21. (b)	22. (c)	23. (e)	24. (c)	25. (c)
26. (e)	27. (e)	28. (d)	29. (e)	30. (b)
31. (d)	32. (c)	33. (a)	34. (a)	35. (c)
36. (a)	37. (d)	38. (e)	39. (c)	40. (c)
41. (d)	42. (a)	43. (c)	44. (b)	45. (c)
46. (a)	47. (b)	48. (d)	49. (c)	50. (a)

FREQUENCY ANALYSIS

Cloze Test	10
Sentence Completion	05
Sentence Arranement	05
Comprehension	16 (8 + 8)
Synonyms	09 (4+ 5)
Antonyms	05 (3 + 2)
Total	**50**

TREND ANALYSIS

The questions are of regular type. There is no trend for innovation. Common items have been set. There is emphasis on comprehension and vocabulary. The pattern is simple but the level of questions is not simple or moderate. It is of good quality and needs thorogh preparation.

PAPER 28

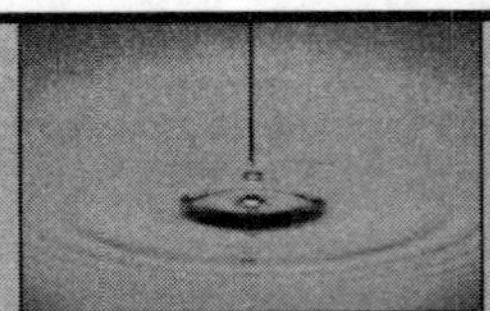

AIMS TEST FOR MANAGEMENT (ATMA), FEBRUARY 2012

[Association of Indian Management Schools (AIMs)]

Directions to Questions 1 to 5

Read the following passage carefully and answer the questions given below it. Certain words are given in bold in the passage to help you locate them while answering some of the questions.

In our life there may be several occasions when.we may have differences with others. Two human beings cannot exactly be the same in physical structure or in mental make-up. Variety is there n all nature and it adds up to the beauty of nature. So, variegated opinions are always more beautiful and charming. They add taste to dull and **desolate** human life. They are the essence of democratic thinking. Regimentation, uniformity and similarity are the attributes of a dictatorial and fascist attitude.

There have been great cruelty and persecutions in the world in the name of religion, nation, race and caste. Innocent people have been tortured and maimed. Even little children and women hme not been spared. Ever since creation of the world, poor animals have borne the brunt of human wrath. We must all realise that this world is the only place where all of us have to live. We have no other world where we may run away. The best course for us is to adopt the policy of "Live and Let live". This is what great men like Buddha and Guru Nanak have taught us.

We should not forget the fact that God is one creator of this universe. He has created all kinds of creatures in this world. They are all supposed to live in peace and harmony. Man is the crown of all creations. He claims to be the only civilised creature. At least he should learn and follow the policy of universal love, peace and brotherhood. Narrow parochial, linguistic, racial, religious and even national aspirations should be given up. Let there be one Warld Government, one World Citizenship. The policy of "Live and Let Live" is the dire need of the time.

1. What is the central quality of democratic thinking ?

(a) Beautiful and charming elements present in the nature

(b) Similarity and oneness in thinking

(c) Peaceful and harmonious living

(d) Different opinions expressed by people.

2. Which of the following is most OPPOSITE in meaning of the word "desolate" as used in the passage ?

(a) Cheerful

(b) positive

(c) Lkind
(d) sensitive

3. What enhances the beauty of nature?
   (a) Similarity of human beings in physical structure
   (b) Positive attitude and mental make up of human beings
   (c) Individual differences and variety in human species
   (d) Individual's exposure to different M situations.

4. What according to the author, must we realise?
   (a) We have to live together in this world
   (b) Democracy is the best form of government
   (c) Race and caste considerations should be banished
   (d) Dictatorial attitude may yield dividends in certain circumstances

5. What policy should a man follow?
   (a) To satisfy his aspirations and needs
   (b) Democratic attitude of mind
   (c) Avoiding regimentation and uniformity
   (D) Universal love, peace and brotherhood

Directions to Questions 6 to 10

Read the following passage and answer die questions given below it. Certain words in the passage are given in bold so as to help you locate them easily while answering some of the questions.

Comfort is now one of the causes of its own spread. It has now become a physical habit, a fashion, an ideal to be pursued for its own sake. The more comfort is brought into the world, the more it is likely to be valued. To those who have known comfort, discomfort is a real torture. The fashion which now decrees the worship of comfort is quite as imperious as any other fashion. Moreover, enormous material interests are bound up with the supply of the means of comfort. The manufacturers of furniture, of heating apparatus, of plumbing fixtures cannot afford to let the love of comfort die. In modern advertisements they have found a means for compelling it to live and grow. A man of means today, who builds a house is in general concerned primarily with the comfort of his future residence. He will spend a great deal of money on bathrooms, heating apparatus, padded furnishings, and having spent he will regard his house as perfect. His counterpart in an earlier age would have been primarily concerned with the impressiveness and magnificence of his dwelling—with beauty, in a word, rather than comfort. The money our contemporary would spend on baths and central healings would have been spent on marble staircases, frescoes, pictures and statues. I am inclined to think that our present passion for comfort is a little exaggerated. Though I personally enjoy comfort, I have lived most happily in houses devoid of everything that Anglo-Saxons deem **indispensable.** Orientals and even South Europeans who know no comfort and live very much as our ancestors did centuries ago seem to go on very well without our elaborate apparatus and padded luxuries. However, comfort for me has a justification; it facilitates mental life. Discomfort handicaps thought; it is difficult to use the mind when the body is cold and aching.

6. Why would manufacturers of various devices not permit comfort to die?
   (a) They want to manufacture more and more comfort goods
   (b) Manufacturers are mainly interested in creating new things
   (c) Emphasis is on producing beautiful things
   (d) Their prosperity is closely linked with the people's desire for comfort

7. Why does the author value comfort?
   (a) It helps to project one's image
   (b) It helps to protect your values
   (c) It facilitates mental life
   (d) It encourages a blend of materialistic and spiritual thinking

8. What is the author's prediction about comfort?
   (a) The value of comfort will increase
   (b) People will value more spirituality thus reducing the value of comfort
   (c) People will desire simple life style
   (d) The advertisements wUl play down the comfort aspect of goods

9. Choose the word which is MOST OPPOSITE in meaning of the word 'indispensable' as used in the passage.
   (a) Unattractive
   (b) Avoidable
   (c) Favourable
   (d) Unelegant

10. What change according to the author has taken place in the attitude to comfort"?
   (a) It is taken for granted in the modern way of living
   (b) It has become now an ideal to be pursued for its own sake
   (c) It is now believed that discomfort handicaps thought
   (d) It is thought that comfort helps body and mind to function effectively.

Directions to Questions 11 to 15

Read /the following passage carefully and answer the questions given below it.

Right of entry to education, an ample teaching-learning environment, a suitable curriculum and an empowered and all-encompassing faculty are four essential prerequisites of an education system that seeks to enable social transformation. While educational reform since the 1980s was strongly focussed on the first two elements, the late 1990s brought the role of the curriculum into national focus. The critical link that binds these four critical elements together—the activity of the faculty continues to be cast aside, by political ideologies of most hues, contemporary curriculum reform efforts and the professional practices of the faculty.

Far-reaching educational initiatives of both the Left and the Right have recognised the potential power of the faculty. In multiple experiments, they have used this dormant force to build committed institutions and cadres of faculties dedicated to their particular causes. In many instances this has led to extreme politicisation of the college faculty. In others it has led to the education of a generation of students in half-truths underpinned by the personal beliefs, sectarian concerns and folk pedagogy of faculties who have had little access themselves to education and training in related areas.

Over the last decade or so, educational reform has included, apart from access, a focus on developing alternative text materials and the training of faculty to handle these materials, without directly engaging with the issue of curriculum revamp. At the turn of the 20th century, a major national curriculum redesign was initiated following the change of political regime at the centre. The subsequent development of college programme came under wide public scrutiny and debate. Issues of equity, inclusion and exclusion, learner medley religious identity and communalism gained considerable importance in the curriculum debates that followed. For instance scholars argued that, "...the curriculum, while loud on rhetoric, fails to address the quality of education that students of underprivileged and marginalised group's experience". Several other critics described the revised curriculum as a retrogressive step in education that sought to impose the religious agenda in the garb of a national identity.

The subsequent change of national government in 2004, led to the curriculum review in 2005 underlining a new political interest in the role of education in national development, its role in social mobilisation and transformation directed specifically at questions of caste and gender asymmetry and minority empowerment. Deeper than these politically driven initiatives, however, the professional need for curriculum review emerges from the long ossification of a national education system that continues to view faculty as "dispensers of information" and students as "passive recipients" of an "education", sought to be "delivered" in four-walled classrooms with little scope to develop critical thinking and understanding.

11. Prior to 1990 what was not the agenda of the educational reforms?
   (A) An appropriate curriculum
   (B) Well-managed admission process
   (a) Only A
   (b) Only B
   (c) Both A and B
   (d) Either A or B

12. Which of the following best describes the phrase "passive recipients" as used in the passage?

(a) The users of the educational system
(b) The political ideology of right and left patties
(c) Well-framed curriculum guiding the teaching/learning process
(d) Free access to education system

13. Revamping of the text material was the main focus in
(a) Early eighties
(b) Late nineties
(c) Evolving curriculum framework
(d) 21st century

14. To facilitate social transformation, which of the following has been identified by the author as one of the factors?
(a) A committed political ideology
(b) Support of the well-framedi curriculum
(c) A strong administration system
(d) Carefully planned education delivery

15. What hampers the critical thinking ability of college going students?
(a) The emphasis on rot« memorisation and recalling the facts of education based on real experience
(b) Lack of political will to develop these abilities
(c) Absence of focus while designing curriculum framework
(d) Ignoring die active role of faculty and the student.

Directions to Questions 16 to 20

In each of the following sentences there are two blank spaces. Below each sentence there are four pairs of words denoted by numbers (a), (b), (c) and (d). Find out which pair of words can be filled up in the blanks in the sentence in the same sequence to make the sentence grammatically correct and meaningfully complete.

16. The______on some of the towns has created _____ among the resident of the other part of the country.
(a) Attack_____ambition
(b) Raid_____awareness
(c) Bombardment______panic
(d) Spell_____satisfaction

17. His ______hasyielded him the______ fruit.
(a) Fate______undesirable
(b) Efforts______unwanted
(c) Action______viable
(d) Perseverance_____desired

18. Liberalisation has removed all the legal______ and______ flood-gates for multinational companies.
(a) Hurdles______awarded
(b) Barriers______opened
(c) Obstacles______guarded
(d) Manipulation______closed

19. His______ contribution to the Tsunami relief fund was ______ by his staff members.
(a) Meagre ______ admired
(b) Spontaneous ______ nullified
(c) Negligible ______sanctioned
(d) Generous ______ appreciated

20. ______to the popular belief that every astrologer nurtures blind faith in fate, our astrologer believes in ______
(a) Contrary_____ action
(b) According ______thoughts
(c) Bowing ______ present
(d) Proving ______forecasting

Directions to Questions 21 to 25

In each of the following questions an idiomatic expression and its possible meanings are given. Find out the correct meaning of the idiomatic expression and select the number of that meaning as your answer.

21. A wet blanket—
(a) A man who is always drunk
(b) A wife who is cold to her husband
(c) To wear black and white clothes
(d) A person who ends conversation

22. To catch a tartar—
(a) To deal with a person who is more than one's match
(b) To catch a dangerous person
(c) To trap a wanted criminal with great difficulty
(d) To meet with disaster

23. To burn one's fingers—
(a) To have a buring sensation at the tips of one's fingers.
(b) To undergo suffering heroically for one's principles.
(c) To behave as if one is very great and important
(d) None of these

24. To end in smoke—
(a) To die of cancer caused by smoking
(b) To end without providing any practical result
(c) Die in a burning house choked with smoke
(d) None of these

25. The green eyed monster—
(a) The creature of the sea
(b) An animal with green eyes
(c) Personal jealousy
(d) To get into trouble

ANSWER KEY

1. (d)	2. (a)	3. (c)	4. (a)	5. (d)
6. (d)	7. (c)	8. (a)	9. (b)	10. (b)
11. (b)	12. (a)	13. (d)	14. (d)	15. (d)
16. (c)	17. (d)	18. (b)	19. (d)	20. (a)
21. (d)	22. (a)	23. (d)	24. (b)	25. (c)

FREQUENCY ANALYSIS

Comprehension	15
Sentence Completion	5
Phrases	5
Total	**25**

TREND ANALYSIS

The question pattern is simple. The emphasis is on comprehension. Two other items are sentence completion and phrases. The questions are tough. The book covers all the items fully.

PAPER 29

Himachal Pradesh Combined Management Aptitude Test, June 2009

(Conducted by Institute of Management Studies, Shimla)

Directions to Questions 1 to 5

In the following questions, four alternatives are given for the idiom / phrase printed in bold. Choose the alternative which best expresses the meaning of the idiom / phrase.

1. We are **looking forward** to a good monsoon this time

(a) announcing (b) visualising

(c) expecting (d) predicting

2. One could achieve success only through **conscious efforts.**

(a) efforts after consulting others

(b) skilled efforts

(c) efforts after gaining consciousness

(d) efforts made with critical awareness

3. It would perhaps be appropriate if the Supreme Court deals with the centre with just a **heavy hand** as it is doing with the states.

(a) like a dictator

(b) sternly

(c) ruthlessly

(d) penalising

4. The thief **took to heels** when he found that the watchman had seen him.

(a) ran away

(b) challenged

(c) resisted

(d) surrendered

5. Old men cannot enjoy **animal spirit.**

(a) youthful stamina

(b) monstrous attitude

(c) animal - like energy

(d) demonic instinct

Directions to Questions 6 to 10

Choose the word nearly similar in meaning to the given word.

6. EXTRAORDINARY

(a) unusual (b) wonderful

(c) rare (d) beautiful

7. PROJECTED

(a) discussed (b) needed

(c) estimated (d) achieved

8. MARGINAL
(a) austere (b) severe
(c) insignificant (d) adverse

9. FAULT
(a) defect (b) offend
(c) blame (d) imperfect

10. DIRE
(a) pessimistic (b) alarming
(c) futile (d) fraudulent

Directions to Questions 11 to 15

Choose the word most nearly opposite to the given word.

11. POTENTIAL
(a) unlikely (b) incapable
(c) unable (d) ineffective

12. INIQUITOUS
(a) immoral (b) godly
(c) virtuous (d) just

13. FINISHED
(a) completed (b) interrupted
(c) began (d) rough

14. ADMIRING
(a) rejecting (b) disapproving
(c) harmful (d) frightening

15. PROMPTLY
(a) later (b) behind
(c) lately (d) relaxed

Directions to Questions 16 to 20

In the questions below a group of words has been given for which you have to find the correct substitute from the following options.

16. Hard to understand
(a) abstruse (b) clumsy
(c) delusive (d) lucid

17. Occurring at the same time
(a) consecutive (b) subsequent
(c) concurrent (d) adjacent

18. Wandering from one point to another
(a) wanton (b) discursive
(c) nostalgic (d) lunatic

19. That produces the desired result
(a) efficacious (b) deliberate
(c) astounding (d) noteworthy

20. Speaking or writing several languages
(a) scholar (b) lexicon
(c) polyglot (d) vivid

Directions to Questions 21 to 30

In each question a sentence is given with a part printed in bold. That part may contain a grammatical error. Replace that part with the four choices given below.

21. The famous playwright has been in the sick bed **from the last** one week.
(a) for the past
(b) for past
(c) since past:
(d) for last

22. Rural area people can cope well with physical strains as they are used to **working hardly.**
(a) work hard
(b) the working hard
(c) hardly working
(d) hard working

23. The famous engineers **are working** on this project right from the day they arrived here.
(a) had been working
(b) have been working
(c) would be working
(d) will have been working

24. He has not written any book since his mother **had died.**
(a) died (b) have died
(c) has died (d) was dead

25. In quick time she got acquainted with the new **environment**
(a) In enough time (b) In small time
(c) In no time (d) On time only

ANSWER KEY

1. (c)	2. (d)	3. (b)	4. (a)	5. (a)
6. (a)	7. (c)	8. (c)	9. (a)	10. (b)
11. (a)	12. (c)	13. (c)	14. (b)	15. (a)
16. (a)	17. (c)	18. (b)	19. (a)	20. (c)
21. (a)	22. (d)	23. (b)	24. (a)	25. (c)

FREQUENCY ANALYSIS

Idioms and Phrases	5
Synonyms	5
Antonyms	5
Substitution	5
Sentence Improvement	5
Total	**25**

TREND ANALYSIS

The questions on English Language are of regular type and have been placed in a straight forward manner. The level is just above moderate and can be solved easily.

PAPER 30

MANAGEMENT ENTRANCE TEST (MET), JUNE 2011

(Conducted by Punjab University)

Each of the following idioms has four responses (choices). Choose the correct meaning of the idiom.

1. Mad as a March hare :
(a) insane
(b) intoxicated
(c) as mad as I could be
(d) slightly touched in the brain

2. To mince one's words :
(a) to take back one's word
(b) to repeat one's word
(c) to speak candidly
(d) to speak hesitatingly

3. To have an edge on :
(a) to cut with a knife
(b) to threaten to wound
(c) to be slightly better
(d) to be in a dangerous situation

4. To go by the board :
(a) to be wholly destroyed
(b) to be honest
(c) to be dishonest
(d) to disguise oneself

5. To grease the palm :
(a) to lubricate
(b) to water the palm plant
(c) to cut down a tree
(d) to bribe

6. A close shave :
(a) a lucky escape
(b) a clean shave
(c) a well-guarded secret
(d) a narrow escape .

7. To be at loggerheads :
(a) to have tough encounter
(b) to be at enmity or strife
(c) to face stiff opposition
(d) to tax one's mind and body

8. A pipe dream :
(a) a pleasant, dream
(b) a bad dream
(c) an impracticable plan
(d) a foolish idea

9. To lose one's head :
(a) to go mad
(b) to become nervous

(c) To become confused and over excited
(d) To lose, the balance

10. To lose face :
(a) To look angry
(b) To be humiliated
(c) To be helpless
(d) To look vacant

Out of the four alternatives giver below, choose which is the correct Passive or Active Voice of the each given sentence.

11. I saw him conducting the rehearsal :
(a) He was seen conducting the rehearsal.
(b) I saw the rehearsal to be conducted by him.
(c) He was seen by me to conduct the rehearsal.
(d) I was the rehearsal being conducted by him.

12. His pocket has been picked:
(a) They have his pocket picked.
(b) Picking has been done to his pocket.
(c) Picked has been his pocket.
(d) Someone has picked his pocket.

13. A stone struck me on the head:
(a) I was struck by a stone on the head.
(b) My head was struck by a stone.
(c) 1 had been struck by a stone on the head.
(d) I was struck on the head by a stone.

14. You must look into this matter:
(a) This matter has been looked into by you.
(b) This matter may be looked into by you.
(c) This matter should be looked into by you.
(d) This matter into looked by you.

15. Please help me:
(a) You were requested to help me.
(b) You are being requested to help me.
(c) You are requested to help me.
(d) You have been requested to help me.

16. Rama dare not disobey me:
(a) I am not dared disobey by Rama.
(b) I dare not be disobeyed by Rama.
(c) Disobey me is not dared by Rama.
(d) None of these

17. One expects better behaviour of a man like you:
(a) Better behaviour is expected of a man like you.
(b) Behaviour of a man like you is expected better one.
(c) A man like you is expected better behaviour.
(d) None of these

18. They made many attempts to contact, us:
(a) Many attempts were made by them to be contacted by us.
(b) Many attempts to be contacted were made by them.
(c) Many attempts were made by them to contact us.
(d) Many attempts had been made by them to be contacted.

19. Did he call anybody for help?
(a) Was anybody called by him for help?
(b) Was help for anybody called by him?
(c) Was he called to be helped?
(d) Was help called by anybody for him?

20. You must look into this matter:
(a) This matter has been looked into by you.
(b) This matter may be looked into by you.
(c) This matter should be looked into by you.
(d) This matter is looked into by you. Out of the four given alternatives choose the one which correctly stands for each expression.

21. A small enclosure for cattle, sheep, poultry etc.
(a) Cellar (b) Sty
(c) Pen (d) Disperse

22. A process involving too much official formality
(a) Nepotism (b) Diplomacy
(c) Red tapism (d) Bureaucracy

23. The place where public, government or historical records are kept
(a) Coffer (b) Pantry
(c) Scullery (d) Archives

24. Gradual recovery from illness
(a) Hysteria
(b) Amnesia

(c) Superannuation
(d) Convalescence

25. A person who believes that pleasure is the chief good
(a) Stoic (b) Hedonist
(c) Epicure (d) Sensual

26. Mania for stealing articles
(a) Logomania
(b) Nymphomania
(c) Kleptomania
(d) Hypomania

27. An animal story with a moral
(a) Fable (b) Tale
(c) Anecdote (d) Parable

28. Simplest and smallest form of plant life, present in air, water and soil; essential to life but may cause disease
(a) Virus (b) Amoeba
(c) Bacteria (d) Toxin

29. A group of military officers holding the power in a country, especially after a coup d'etat
(a) Clique (b) Junta
(c) Mafia (d) Coterie

30. A person who rules without consulting the opinion of others
(a) Democrat (b) Bureaucrat
(c) Autocrat (d) Fanatic

Out of four alternatives given below, choose the one which is opposite in meaning to the each of the word:

31. LUSCIOUS
(a) Dry (b) Sour
(c) Ugly (d) Stale

32. GORGEOUS
(a) Desperate (b) Plain
(c) Fashionable (d) Sumptuous

33. IMPERVIOUS
(a) Penetrable (b) Hidden
(c) Tolerable (d) Gentle

34. PARSIMONIOUS
(a) Generous (b) Frugal
(c) Crude (d) Stingy

35. DISSUADE
(a) Incite (b) Persuade
(c) Advise (d) Instigate

36. ASSISTANCE
(a) Instance (b) Persistence
(c) Remittance (d) Hindrance

37. ABHOR
(a) Detest (b) Condemn
(c) Love (d) Entertain

38. ARID
(a) Barren (b) Marshy
(c) Juicy (d) Wet

39. AUTHENTIC
(a) Real (b) Dependable
(c) Spurious (d) Unpleasant

40. BASTARD
(a) Legitimate (b) Illegal
(c) Handicapped (d) Abnormal

Choose the clause that correctly completes the sentence.

41. His professional ability proves that he is cut _____ to be a doctor
(a) out (b) up
(c) down (d) come

42. Now government servants have the day _____ every Saturday.
(a) out (b) off
(c) since (d) for

43. In accordance with the advice of a doctor she is _____ diet.
(a) on (b) at
(c) off (d) against

44. You're out of breath_____
(a) are you running
(b) have your run
(c) have you been running
(d) has you run

45. There's somebody walking behind us. I think_____
(a) we are following
(b) we are being followed
(c) we are followed
(d) we are being following

46. I'm tired. I'd rather ____ out this evening. If you don't mind.
(a) not going (b) not to go
(c) don't go (d) not go

47. Where_____? Which hairdresser did you go to?
(a) did you cut your hair
(b) have you cut your hair
(c) did you have cut your hair
(d) did you have your hair cut

48. Jim doesn't speak very clearly
(a) it is difficult to understand him
(b) he is difficult to understand
(c) he is difficult to understand him
(d) it is difficult for understanding him

49. The problem of communal harmony cannot be glossed _____ by government
(a) at (b) on
(c) over (d) above

50. Cooperation between friends stems _____ mutual consideration.
(a) in (b) out
(c) from (d) with

ANSWER KEY

1. (c)	2. (d)	3. (c)	4. (a)	5. (d)
6. (d)	7. (c)	8. (c)	9. (c)	10. (b)
11. (a)	12. (d)	13. (a)	14. (c)	15. (c)
16. (d)	17. (a)	18. (c)	19. (a)	20. (c)
21. (c)	22. (c)	23. (d)	24. (d)	25. (b)
26. (c)	27. (a)	28. (c)	29. (b)	30. (c)
31. (c)	32. (b)	33. (a)	34. (a)	35. (b)
36. (d)	37. (c)	38. (d)	39. (c)	40. (a)
41. (a)	42. (b)	43. (a)	44. (a)	45. (b)
46. (d)	47. (d)	48. (a)	49. (c)	50. (c)

FREQUENCY ANALYSIS

Idiom	10
Voice	10
Substitution	10
Antonym	10
Comprehension	10
Total	**50**

TREND ANALYSIS

The questions are simple but preplexing. Normally qestions on comprehension, spotting errors, sentence improvement and sentence arrangement are asked. Here the idoms are of the regular type, questions on "Voice" also have been asked. Each item carries ten marks. The level is just above moderate and slightly tough. All items are covered in different chapters of the book. A careful reading of the theory chapters and a regular work at the practice set will be of help to the students.

PAPER 31

Symbiosis National Aptitude Test (SNAP), December 2012

Directions to Questions 1 & 2

Choose the correct option to fill the blank for correct grammatical use.

1. She is a close friend of______.
   (a) my (b) I
   (c) me (d) mine

2. He took care of her_______ she was restored to health.
   (a) when (b) before
   (c) after (d) till

3. Choose the correct option.

   The man _____ his appearance completely since then.
   (a) is changing (b) changed
   (c) has changed (d) is changed

4. From the options below, choose the word with the incorrect spelling :
   (a) Diarrhoea
   (b) Diaper
   (c) Dichotomy
   (d) Dias

5. Choose the word spelt correctly :
   (a) superintendant
   (b) seive
   (c) alloted
   (d) dissipate

Directions to Questions 6 to 9

Fill in the blanks with the correct pair of words.

6. He lives _______ Bengaluru ______ 115, Richmond Road.
   (a) at, in (b) in, at
   (c) at, on (d) in, on

7. 'Aurally challenged' is a _____ for the______.
   (a) metaphor, blind
   (b) euphemism, deaf
   (c) simile, disabled
   (d) synonym, dumb

8. If error is a ____, fault is_______.
   (a) defect - a mistake
   (b) mistake - a defect
   (c) slip - an inaccuracy
   (d) blunder - to blame

9. The man has _____ the rules of ethical conduct; he is_____ a beast.
   (a) flaunted - literally
   (b) 'ignored - basically
   (c) broken - as
   (d) flouted - virtually

Directions to Questions 10 to 11

Which punctuation mark is missing in the following sentences?

(a) inverted commas
(b) semicolon
(c) comma
(d) hyphen

10. Part of Australia is known to the natives as The Outback.

11. I know that you want to learn to drive Rima but you are too young.

Directions to Questions 12 to 13

Select as/option the word closest in meaning to the given word.

12. Veracious
    (a) False (b) Varied
    (c) Image (d) Truthful

13. Perturb
    (a) Stipulate
    (b) Turn around
    (c) Disturb greatly
    (d) Compatible

Directions to Questions 14 to 15

Choose the option that is the closest in meaning to the phrases in bold.

14. He was a king who ruled his subjects with a high hand.
    (a) Sympathetically
    (b) oppressively
    (c) democratically
    (d) generously

15. I racked my brains to solve this difficult problem.
    (a) I read a large number of books.
    (b) I consulted several people.
    (c) I used my commonsense.
    (d) I subjected my mind to hard thinking.

Directions to Questions 6 to 7

Select the most appropriate meaning of the underlined idiomatic phrase.

16. I was supposed to give a speech to my English class, but I got cold feet and I didn't go.
    (a) My English class-room makes my feet feel too cold.
    (b) My feet got cold so I didn't go.
    (c) I got too nervous and I didn't
    (d) It was winter time and I had no socks for my feet.

17. Take care of what you say! You will have to eat your words!
    (a) You have no food to eat.
    (b) You will have to take back what you have said.
    (c) You are not good with your language.
    (d) None of the above.

18. Which two sentences convey the same idea?
    1. Shouldn't: they have checked your rickets?
    2. I wonder if they should have checked your tickets.
    3. 1 want to know if they checked your rickets.
    4. They should have checked your tickets.

    (a) 2, 3 (b) 1, 2
    (c) 1, 4 (d) 2, 4

Directions to Questions 19 to 21

Choose a single word which is opposed to the meaning contained in the sentence.

19. He was magnanimous and his benevolence made him give to charity.
    (a) mean
    (b) cruel

(c) snobbish
(d) tyrannical

20. Biannual is
(a) once in two years
(b) every7 year
(c) twice a year
(d) after every two years

21. Choose the odd one out :
(a) temporal
(b) ephemeral
(c) transient
(d) eternal

22. Choose the correct option :

If 'inter' means between as in interstate, 'intra' as in intravenous means
(a) into
(b) onto
(c) within
(d) without

23. Match the parts of speech (in bold) to their usage (down) :

1.	Adjective	5.	The fire engine came rushing down the hill.
2	Preposition	6.	He has seen the ups and downs of Me.
3.	Noun	7.	Down with the tyrant!
4.	Verb	8.	The porter was hit by the down train.

(a) 1-8, 2-5, 3-6, 4-7
(b) 1-6, 2-5, 3-8, 4-7
(c) 1-5, 2-6, 3-7, 4-8
(d) 1-5, 2-7, 3-6, 4-8

Directions to Questions 24

Match the items in column I with those in column II. Choose, the correct answer combination given below :

24.

I		II	
1.	As deaf as	5.	gall
2.	As bitter as	6.	an eel
3.	As unpredictable as	7.	a post
4.	As slippery as	8.	the Weather

(a) 1-7, 2-7, 3-8, 4-5
(b) 1-6, 2-5, 3-6, 4-7
(c) 1-8, 2-8, 3-5, 4-6
(d) 1-4, 2-6, 3-7, 4-8

Directions to Questions 25

Match the parts of speech (in bold) to their usage.

25. ABOVE

1.	adjective	5.	Rain comes from **above.**
2.	adverb	6.	His conduct is **above** suspicion.
3.	noun	7.	Look **above** the mantel piece.
4.	preposition	8.	The **above** information is for the public

(a) 1-8, 2-7, 3-8, 4-6
(b) 1-7, 2-6, 3-5, 4-8
(c) 1-5, 2-5, 3-6, 4-5
(d) 1-6, 2-8, 3-7, 4-7

Directions to Questions 26 to 28

Choose the segment with the error. If there is no error choose 'd'

26. Idli and Sambar (a)\make the breakfast (b)\ in the South. (c)\ No error (d)

27. Your account should (a)\ have been credited (b)\ with three months' interest. (c)\ No error (d)

28. Choose the sentence where the underlined word is used appropriately.
(a) **Who's** car are you planning to borrow?
(b) **Whose** planning to have a birthday party?
(c) He is the person **who** you met at the junction.
(d) Does he know **whom** to call about the hotel reservations?

Directions to Questions 29 to 30

'a' if the first sentence is correct
'b' if the second sentence is correct
'c' if both sentences are correct
'd' if both sentences are wrong

29.

1. Can you imagine his forgetting his own birthday?
2. Can you imagine him forgetting his own birthday?

(a) (b)
(c) (d)

30.

1. Recently I read about a unique wedding that took place in the newspaper.
2. Recently I read in the newspaper about a unique wedding that took place.

(a) (b)
(c) (d)

31. Complete the given sentence by choosing the correct phrase.

You cannot succeed unless

(a) you do not work hard.
(b) you shall not work hard.
(c) you will work hard.
(d) you work hard.

32. Re-arrange the scrambled segments in logical order to make a complete sentence.

1. to places where more opportunities are available
2. and so there is a great demand for English
3. for professional and economic growth
4. because it takes one outside one's own community
5. English is the language of opportunities

(a) 1, 2, 5, 3, 4
(b) 5, 4, 1, 3, 2
(c) 3, 1, 4, 2, 5
(d) 2, 1, 3, 5, 4

33. Choose the best construction :

(a) If you would have taken care you wouldn't have got typhoid.
(b) If you took care you wouldn't have got typhoid.
(c) If you take care you wouldn't have got typhoid.
(d) If you had taken care you wouldn't have got typhoid.

Directions to Questions 34 to 35

Fill in the Blanks

34. At times, we are all ____ to be mistaken.

(a) apt
(b) likely
(c) considered
(d) able

35. He hardly cares,____?

(a) does he
(b) doesn't he
(c) will he
(d) won't he

Directions to Questions 36 to 37

Identify the figures of speech in the following sentences.

36. As proud as a peacock.

(a) Metaphor (b) Simile
(c) Apostrophe (d) Epigram

37. Death lays his icy hand on kings.

(a) Personification
(b) Exclamation
(c) Simile
(d) Anticlimax I

Directions to Questions 38 to 40

Read the passage carefully and answer within the context.

"A Way to Deal with Frozen Feelings"

Every child experiences all that happens around him with total awareness. In the first seven years the child's brain is like a sponge, taking in all sensory inputs and building his idea of his surroundings. As long as the environment is safe, the child learns with incredible speed. However, when the environment is scary or stressful, the child unlearns past learning just as rapidly.

In the early years of every child's life, whenever there is shock, violence, fear or pain, these intense emotions are imprinted deeply into memory. Whenever the same activity or situation is repeated, the nervous system and body subconsciously re-experience the memory of that trauma.

Any emotional situation that takes us out of the present and into the past means that whenever the same kind of emotion crops up later in out-life we return to the past for our reference point. If that point was at age three, we find ourselves behaving like a three-year-old. We feel childish and we behave childishly. Our feelings are the cause of this 'glitch' in our learning process. We know we should be able to make a positive change, but that doesn't change anything.

The process of change need not be traumatic. We couldn't have done any better because we didn't know how to. But we should realise that was then and this is now! We can choose to choose again. It's up to us. It's our movie!

38. The "Frozen Feelings" being talked about are about,

(a) negative childhood experiences
(b) childhood learning patterns
(c) inability to learn as an adult
(d) None of the above.

39. A 'glitch' is

(a) a ditch
(b) uneasy emotions
(c) sudden malfunction or breakdown
(d) learning patterns

40. Identify the correct statement, based on the paragraph.

(a) The process of change needs to be traumatic
(b) We feel childish and we behave childishly.
(c) Both the sentences are incorrect,
(d) Both the sentences are correct.

ANSWER KEY

1. (d)	2. (d)	3. (c)	4. (d)	5. (d)
6. (b)	7. (b)	8. (b)	9. (d)	10. (a)
11. (c)	12. (d)	13. (c)	14. (b)	15. (d)
16. (c)	17. (b)	18. (a)	19. (a)	20. (b)
21. (a)	22. (a)	23. (a)	24. (b)	25. (a)
26. (b)	27. (d)	28. (d)	29. (c)	30. (b)
31. (d)	32. (b)	33. (d)	34. (b)	35. (b)
36. (b)	37. (a)	38. (b)	39. (b)	40. (b)

FREQUENCY ANALYSIS

Sentence Completion	3
Spelling	2
Sentence Completion with Pair of Words	4
Punctuation	2
Synonyms	2
Phrases	2
Idioms	3
Antonyms	2
Odd man out	1

Meaning	1
Usage	1
Matching	2
Error	2
Appropriate use	1
Error with variation	2
Sentence Filler	3
Sentence Completion	2
Figures of Speech	2
Comprehension	3
Total	**40**

TREND ANALYSIS

The latest question paper of 2012 of SNAP shows that there are various types of questions. This variety may puzzle students at the first sight. But there is no cause for concern. The idea is to test the understanding of English language, its grammar, vocabulary, sentence skill, fill in the blanks, phrases and idioms, figures of speech, etc.

The point to observe is that if you are clear with the concepts and have solved practice sets, you will have no problem. Just concentrate and all will be well. The level is not higher than what you find in P O or A A O examinations, only the presentation is perplexing. Be calm and use effectively the knowledge you have gained from this book.

PAPER 32

National Institute of Fashion Technology

FASHION MANAGEMENT FEBRUARY, 2013

Directions to Questions 1 to 5

In these Questions keyword is followed by four choices. Choose the one nearest to it in meaning.

1. LOATH
   (a) Tired (b) Unwilling
   (c) Sickly (d) Spirited
2. PROPENSITY
   (a) Quality (b) Aptitude
   (c) Liking (d) Natural tendency
3. CORRUGATED
   (a) Confirmed (b) Wrinkled
   (c) Rough (d) Sifted
4. ETYMOLOGY
   (a) Ancient script
   (b) Foreign language
   (c) Word derivation
   (d) Words
5. SCEPTICAL
   (a) Bigoted
   (b) Unconvinced
   (c) Convinced
   (d) Dissenting

Directions to Questions 6 to 10

In these questions, a keyword is followed by four choices. Choose the one opposite to it in the meaning.

6. COARSE
   (a) Dead (b) Fine
   (c) Dirty (d) Cloudy
7. SLENDER
   (a) Stout (b) Ugly
   (c) Smart (d) Filthy
8. BENEVOLENCE
   (a) Beg (b) Merciless
   (c) Depriving (d) Deny
9. EFFICIOUS
   (a) Useful (b) Skilled
   (c) Useless (d) Unskilled
10. FELICITY
    (a) Thankful (b) Unhappiness
    (c) Happiness (d) Regards

Directions to Questions 11 to 15

Fill in the blank space of the sentence so that it becomes meaningful.

11. He was frightened _____
(a) to be killed.
(b) to being killed.
(c) for being killed.
(d) of being killed.

12. Capitalist society ______ profit as a valued good.
(a) which regards
(b) regarding
(c) regards
(d) was regarded

13. Kicking the buffet is a humorous _____for drying.
(a) dictum
(b) euphemism
(c) incantation
(d) addedum

14. Mr. Gupta ______ his son for breaking the window pane.
(a) coerced
(b) relegated
(c) expropriated
(d) chastised

15. Diseases are easily ______ through contact with infected animals.
(a) transferred
(b) transported
(c) transmitted
(d) transplanted

Directions to Questions 16 to 20

Choose the option which best expresses the meaning of the underlined idiom/phrase in the sentence.

16. He is a **queer fish**. I have failed to understand him.
(a) funny person
(b) sensitive person
(c) strange person
(d) quarrelsome person

17. He knew she was dead but **was completely at sea** about the cause of her death.
(a) anxious
(b) confused
(c) ignorant
(d) certain

18. It is clear that the ideas of both reformers **ran in the same groove**.
(a) promoted each other
(b) clashed with each other
(c) advanced in harmony
(d) moved in different directions

19. He **burnt his fingers** by interfering in his neighbour's affairs.
(a) got rebuked
(b) got himself insulted
(c) burnt himself
(d) got himself into trouble

20. When the police came, the thieves **took to their heels**.
(a) were taken by surprise
(b) took flight
(c) took shelter in a tall building
(d) unconditionally surrendered

Directions to Questions 21 to 25

A word has been written in four different ways out of which only one is correctly spelt. Choose the correctly spelt word.

21.
(a) tariff (b) Tarriff
(c) tarif (d) tarrif

22.
(a) sattellite (b) satellite
(c) sattelite (d) satelite

23.
(a) beligrent (b) beligerent
(c) belligrent (d) belligerent

24.

(a) bouquete (b) bouquet
(c) boquet (d) bouquette

25.

(a) aliennate (b) allienate
(c) alienate (d) alienatte

Directions to Questions 26 to 30

A sentence has been broken into four parts. Choose the part that has an error.

26.

(a) It was on that particular ill-fated
(b) voyage that a Lusitania was
(c) torpedoed by a rogue submarine
(d) and sunk with all hands

27.

(a) One way route is
(b) a mean of
(c) reducing traffic
(d) in congested areas of Delhi.

28.

(a) Again, I always go to sea as a sailor,
(b) because they make a point of paying me
(c) for my trouble, whereas they never pay passengers
(d) the single penny that I ever heard of.

29.

(a) He was roused by a
(b) touch in the shoulder, and a
(c) request from the man with the keys to
(d) follow him into the office.

30.

(a) If you can't change the environment
(b) and you won't move, you will
(c) become a failure, just so tropical plants
(d) fail when transplanted to the Thar desert.

Directions to Questions 31 to 50

Study the passages below and answer the questions that follow each passage.

Passage-I

Urbanisation is a positive phenomenon provided the cities are able to harness its potential. A recently published UN-Habitat global report on human settlement shows that not many cities in the developing countries such as India have managed to do this. Indian cities struggle to manage the swelling numbers: they tend to have inadequate infrastructure, poor mobility, and a lack of affordable housing. The challenge they face is two fold—efforts to distribute growth across urban centres have been inadequate and the urban planning practices are outdated. Much attention is paid to mega cities, leaving the smaller cities largely unattended. Of the 5,161 urban centres, as the Eleventh Five-Year Plan points out, only 1,500 have some form of plan to manage their growth. With quality of life suffering in the smaller cities, more people tend to move to the metres, burdening them further. Although, the need for developing small and medium-size towns was highlighted as early as 1988 by the first National Commission on Urbanisation, not much has happened on that front. As for the bigger cities, the additional attention and the presence of a master plan have not necessarily meant improvement. Managing a city through a single unified master plan has failed to deliver. The reason for this, aside from poor implementation, is that the plans are conceptually flawed. Indian cities are complex composites. Alongside the formal city exists a large and an equally important informal city inhabited by the poor. Even the formal city is composed of many parts such as the historical core, the colonial enclave, and new areas of post-Independence growth. Notwithstanding these differences, the master plan tends to paint the city with a single brush, favouring the new formal areas and ignoring the informal. This has fragmented cities further and skewed development in favour of new areas. The recommendations in the UN-Habitat report do offer a way forward. The suggestion to implement the strategic spatial planning system should be immediately adopted. Unlike the master plan, such innovations recognise the intra-city differences better and help focus on priority aspects or areas. They should help eventually to mitigate spatial inequalities, integrate infrastructure, and evolve compact city forms that will optimise travelling within the city. Simultaneously, the institutional framework for planning should be strengthened with an emphasis on people's participation and regional networking. Earnest implementation and regular monitoring of the plans are equally vital for reaping the benefits of planning,

31. It is implied in the passage that
(a) cities in some of the developing countries such as India have not been able to reap the real benefits of urbanisation due to lack of proper planning.
(b) urbanisation is not a desirable. phenomenon.
(c) urbanisation offers the solution for all the problems that smaller cities face.
(d) None of these

32. What, according to the author, are the main components of a 'formal city'?
(a) The historical core, the colonial enclave and the newly-developed areas,
(b) Pre-independence and post-independence areas.
(c) New city and old city.
(d) Planned city and the unplanned city.

33. Which one or more of the following factors is/are recommended by the UN-Habitat report as essential for planned urbanisation and growth.
A. The master plan proposed by the first National Commission on Urbanisation.
B. The strategic spatial planning system.
C. A strong institutional framework for planning, encouraging people's participation.
(a) A only
(b) B & C
(c) A, B & C
(d) A & C

34. The caption that aptly sums up the contents of this passage is
(a) challenges of urbanisation—the strategic way forward.
(b) the phenomenon of urbanisation—boon or bane?
(c) urbanisation—a monster out of control
(d) None of these

Passage–II

The Genetic Engineering Approval Committee's recommendation that Bt brinjal be commercialised is a significant marker in the country's slow and somewhat hesitant embrace of agri-biotechnology. The nod has come a full seven years after approval for the country's first transgenic crop—Bt cotton. But Bt brinjal is the country's first approved genetically modified (GM) food crop and the decision of the GEAC, the high-level committee under the Union Ministry of Environment and Forests, may be read as an affirmation of a key principle. It is that transgenic seeds wi1l be approved for commercialisation as long as they adhere to the bio safety and other requirements demanded by the regulatory process. This may well spur the process for clearance of other transgenic food crops at different stages of the regulatory and approval process. It is imperative that Union Minister for Environment and Forests, who says he will study the GEAC's recommendation in depth before giving a final stamp of approval, bases his decision solely on the body of scientific data culled from Bt brinjal trials. He should ignore the huge pressure from organisations that have no time for the scientific evidence while claiming to speak for the environment and the public. It is not just the 'organic' movement but also the pesticide industry lobby that is viscerally opposed to Bt crops, which acquire a pest-resistant character with the introduction of a gene derived from a common soil bacterium (bacillus thuringiensis). Introduced commercially in the United States in the mid-1990s, genetically modified crops have expanded substantially in recent years. An estimated 125 million hectares were under such cover in 2008 in 25 countries, including China, Brazil, Egypt and Australia. Even in GM-phobic Europe, seven countries, including Germany and Portugal, grow genetically modified maize commercially. It is nobody's case that the massive spread of agro-biotechnology is proof of its safety. India's regulatory process must continue to put transgenic plants through a battery of rigorous tests—for toxicity, allergenicity, bio safety, agronomic worth, and so forth—before recommending commercial release. It is also important that the country addresses issues such as labelling GM products through an independent regulatory process that commands public confidence. Legislation must be speedily introduced to set up a national Biotechnology Regulatory Authority, as recommended in 2004 by a task force led by eminent agricultural scientist M.S. Swaminathan. In a country where agricultural productivity and food security are vital issues, agri-biotechnology holds great promise. We need to regulate its application, not allow it to be strangled by misconceived or motivated campaigns.

35. Which of the following statements pertaining to Bt brinjal is not implied in the passage?
(a) It is the country's first transgenic food crop.
(b) GEAC has approved its commercialisation.
(c) Its approval process by GEAC took seven years.
(d) Its approval for commercialisation could trigger off the approvals for several other transgenic food crops by GEAC,

36. Which of the following captions is most apt for this passage?
(a) Agri-Biotechnology : Signifies the dawn of a new era in food crops.
(b) The coming of age of Agri-Biotechnology in India.
(c) GEAC—rendering yeoman service in the area of Agri-Biotechnology.
(d) Agri-Biotechnology : a global phenomenon.

37. Which country or group of countries is/are generally averse to the concept of genetically modified foods as per the passage?
A. India B. Europe
C. U.S.A.
(a) A & B (b) A only
(c) B only (d) A, B & C

38. Which one of the following statements is not true?
(a) Certain sections in India are opposed to the concept of agri-biotechnology due to vested interests.
(b) Agri-Biotechnology holds great promise for India where agricultural productivity and food security are vital issues.
(c) India has begun to give agri-biotechnology its due importance lately.
(d) European countries have collectively shunned agri-biotechnology in toto.

Passage–III

A leading Indian industrialist in a recent article on ways to strengthen India's economy has drawn attention to the problems of inflation and industrial sickness among other things. One of the main reasons for industrial sickness in our country has been the fact that business and industrial managers have not been able to look beyond the immediate future. They have been too preoccupied with their attempts to report favourable results for the current year higher profits and larger dividends to the shareholders. The planning horizon has hardly ever exceeded five years. Investments have been inadequate for new plants and towards diversification and expansions. Modernisation and asset creation have seriously lagged behind. In business, growth is needed for survival; one has to grow if one does not want to be wiped out. This is particularly true today with liberalisation of imports and increasing competition. Moreover, growth and higher productivity create employment and higher employment creates larger markets both for industrial and consumer products. It was Henry Ford who brought home the need for he creation of a larger and a more stable middle class, that is, a larger number of people who can afford more and more of goods and services. Even after six decades of Independence our industrialists have not been able to shed the petty shopkeeper's mentality and our highly educated management has tagged along merrily and without concern.

39. Which of the following short- comings of Indian industrialists has been highlighted by the author?
(a) They invest unreasonable high amount on diversification and expansion.
(b) They are more concerned for immediate net gains than for developmental activities.
(c) They are reluctant to maintain the shopkeepers' mentality.
(d) They are less concerned for payment of dividends to shareholders.

40. The leading industrialist attributes industrial sickness mainly to
(a) lacunae in Five-Year Plans.

(b) preoccupations of managers with matters unrelated to business.

(c) higher profits and larger dividends to shareholders.

(d) lack of foresight among managers.

41. The planning horizon has hardly ever exceeded five years implies

(a) planning should not be for a period of less than five years.

(b) the planning process is very time consuming.

(c) the planners are not inclined to think of future.

(d) five-year period is too short for successful implementation of plans.

42. In order to improve the condition of Indian industries, the industrialist should do all of the following except

(a) giving up the narrow mentality which very small shopkeepers generally have.

(b) striving to earn long term profits.

(c) encouraging competition from industrialists within the country and from abroad.

(d) resorting to long-term planning for industrial growth and expansion in diverse fields.

Passage–IV

The public distribution system, which provides food at low prices, is a subject of vital concern. There is a growing realisation that though India has enough food to feed its masses two square meals a day, the monster of starvation and food insecurity continues to haunt the poor in our country. Increasing the purchasing power of the poor through providing productive employment leading to rising income, and thus good standard of living is the ultimate objective of public policy. However, till then, there is a need to provide assured supply of food through a restructured, more efficient and decentralised public distribution system (PDS). Although the PDS is extensive-it is one of the largest such systems in the world—it has yet to reach the rural poor and the far off places. It remains an urban phenomenon, with the majority of the rural poor still out of its reach due to lack of economic and physical access. The poorest in the cities and the migrants are left out, for they generally do not possess ration cards. The allocation of PDS supplies in big cities is larger than in, rural areas. In. view of such deficiencies in the system, the PDS urgently needs to be streamlined. Also, considering the large foodgrains production combined with food subsidy on one hand and the continuing slow starvation and dismal poverty of the rural population on the other, there is a strong case for making PDS target group oriented.

The growing salaried class is provided job security, regular income, and social security. It enjoys almost hundred percent insulation against inflation. These gains of development have not percolated down to the vast majority of our working population. If one compares only dearness allowance to the employees in public and private sectors and looks at its growth in the past few years, the rising food subsidy is insignificant to the point of inequity. The food subsidy is a kind of D.A. to the poor, the self-employed and those in the unorganised sector of the economy. However, what is most unfortunate is that out of the large budget of the so called food subsidy, the major part of it is administrative cost and wastages. A small portion of the above budged goes to the real consumer and an even lesser portion to the poor who are in real need. It is true, that subsidies should not become a permanent feature, except for the destitute, disabled widows and the old. It is also true that subsidies often create a psychology of dependence and hence is habit-forming, killing the general initiative of the people. By making PDS target group oriented, not only the poorest and neediest would be reached without additional cost, but it will actually cut overall costs incurred on large cities and for better off localities. When the food and food subsidy are limited, the rural and urban poor should have the priority in the PDS supplies. The PDS should be closely linked with programmes of employment generation and nutrition improvement.

43. Which of the following is the main reason for insufficient supply of enough food to the poorest?

(a) Mismanagement of foodstocks.

(b) Absence of proper public distribution system.

(c) Production of food is less than the demand.

(d) Government's apathy towards the poor

44. What, according to the passage, is the main purpose of public policy in the long run?

(a) Reducing the cost of living index by increasing supplies.

(b) Providing enough food to all the citizens.

(c) Good standard of living through productive employment.

(d) Equalising per capita income across different strata of society.

45. Which of the following is true of public distribution system?

(a) It has improved its effectiveness over the years.

(b) It has remained effective only in the cities.

(c) It is unique in the world because of its effectiveness.

(d) It has reached the remotest corner of the country.

46. What should be an appropriate step to make the PDS effective?

(a) To make it target group oriented.

(b) To increase the amount of food grains per ration card.

(c) To decrease the allotment of foodgrains to urban sector.

(d) To reduce administrative cost.

Passage–V

Educational planning should aim at meeting the educational needs of the entire population of all age groups. While the traditional structure of education as a three-layer hierarchy from the primary stage to the university represents the core, we should not overlook the periphery which is equally important. Under modern conditions, workers need to rewind, or renew their enthusiasm, or strike out in a new direction, or improve their skills as much as any university professor does. The retired and the aged have their needs as well. Educational planning, in their words, should take care of the needs of everyone. Our structures of education have been built up on the assumption that there is a terminal point to education. This basic defect has become all the more harmful today. A UNESCO report entitled

'Learning to Be' prepared by Edgar Faute and others, asserts that the education of children must prepare the future adult for, various forms of self-learning. A viable education system of the future should consist of modules with different kinds of functions serving a diversity of constituents. And performance, not the period of study, should be the basis for credentials. The writing is already on the wall. In view of the fact that the significance of a commitment of lifelong learning and lifetime education is being discussed only in recent years even in educationally advanced countries, the possibility of the idea becoming an integral part of educational thinking seems to be a far cry. For, to move in that direction means such more than some simple rearrangement of the present organisation of education. But a good beginning can be made by developing open university programmes for older learners of different categories and introducing extension services in the conventional colleges and schools. Also these institutions should learn to cooperate with the numerous community organisations such as libraries, museums, municipal recreational programmes, health services etc.

47. According to the passage, the present education structures assume which of the following?

(a) All people can be educated as per their needs.

(b) Present educational planning is very much practical.

(c) Education is a one time process.

(d) Simple rearrangement of the present educational system is a must.

48. What should be the major characteristic of the future educational system?

(a) Different modules with same function.

(b) Same module for different groups.

(c) Rearrangement of various course contents.

(d) None of these

49. According to the author, educational plan should attempt to

(a) encourage conventional schools and colleges.

(b) decide a terminal point to education.

(c) overlook the people on the periphery.

(d) fulfil the educational needs of everyone,

50. According to the author, what measures should open university adopt to meet modern conditions?

(a) Develop various programmes for adult learners.

(b) Open more colleges on traditional lines.

(c) Overlook the people on the periphery.

(d) Fulfil the educational needs of everyone.

ANSWER KEY

1. (b)	2. (d)	3. (b)	4. (c)	5. (b)
6. (b)	7. (a)	8. (b)	9. (b)	10. (b)
11. (d)	12. (c)	13. (b)	14. (d)	15. (c)
16. (c)	17. (b)	18. (c)	19. (d)	20. (b)
21. (a)	22. (b)	23. (d)	24. (b)	25. (c)
26. (b)	27. (b)	28. (d)	29. (b)	30. (b)
31. (a)	32. (a)	33. (b)	34. (a)	35. (a)
36. (b)	37. (a)	38. (d)	39. (b)	40. (d)
41. (c)	42. (b)	43. (b)	44. (c)	45. (b)
46. (a)	47. (c)	48. (c)	49. (d)	50. (a)

FREQUENCY ANALYSIS

Synonyms	05
Antonyms	05
Error	5
Comprehension	20
Sentence Completion	5
Idioms	05
Spelling	05
Total	**50**

TREND ANALYSIS

The questions are of regular type and they have been placed in a straight forward manner. There is no tendency to deviate or innovate.

Candidates should expect this pattern. The book covers all the units in detail.

PAPER 33

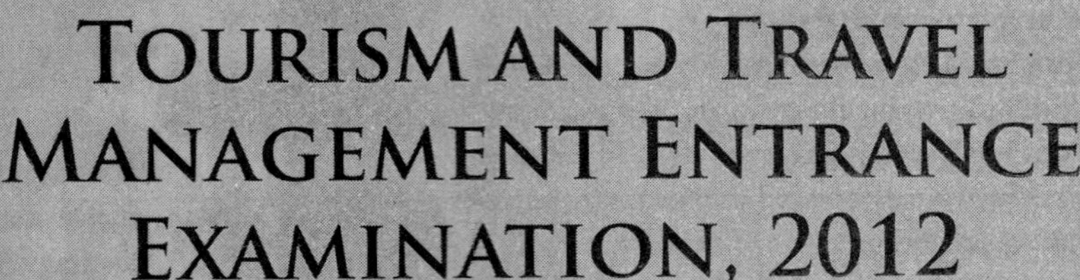

TOURISM AND TRAVEL MANAGEMENT ENTRANCE EXAMINATION, 2012

(Conducted by Indian Institute of Tourism and Travel Management (IITM), Gwalior (Ministry of Tourism, Government of India))

Directions to Questions 1 to 8

Read the /following passages carefully and answer the questions given below each passage.

Passage–I

For almost seventy-five years, Indian films have been a popular form of entertainment for generations of cinema fans in the Southern Caribbean country of Trinidad and Tobago (T&T) where almost one half of the population is of Indian origin. For these children of the Indian diaspora, Bollywood movies and films songs have provided an enduring cultural connection to an ancestral land that has given them a unique identity in the cultural mosaic of the Caribbean. Today, this largely cultural connection is undergoing dramatic transformation as T&T joins hands with India in a major initiative designed to transform its small but well-respected community of film producers into an industry. The launch of the Trinidad and Tobago Film Company (TTFC) in 2006 brought a new organisational dynamic to T&T's fledgling film industry. Charged with the mandate to develop the local film industry, the TTFC began the process of pursuing collaborations and creating an enabling and supportive environment for film production. Over the years, the TTFC has found willing partners in its mission to grow the industry including a close collaboration with the Indian High Commission based in Port of Spain. Along with strategic partnerships, T&T also offers a flexible and diverse film location with climate conditions for every mood, and natural backdrops for every scene. The islands of Trinidad and Tobago have exerted a special magic over film producers for over fifty years. In more recent years, world renowned producers have found Trinidad and Tobago to be not only an exquisite tropical location but an untapped source of powerful literature that is available for adaptation to film. Among the first :o take the leap from print to the screen was Mystic Masseur, a novel by Trinidad and Tobago's Nobel Prize winner V.S. Naipaul, which was adapted for film by distinguished producers Ivory-Merchant in 2001. Dulha Mil Gaya (2010) starring Sushmita Sen, with a special appearance by Shah Rukh Khan, was the first Bollywood feature film to be shot,in the Caribbean. Half of the scenes were filmed on the island of Tobago with the. rest in Amritsar and Mumbai, India. This pioneering film initiative will open the door to a new phase, in the long-standing cinema connection between India and the Indian diaspora in Trinidad

and Tobago. Today, the increasingly global appeal of Indian films has expanded the market across ethnic lines in Trinidad and Tobago, with Hindi soap operas on cable-TV being added to the daily viewing menu of audiences in every demographic The opportunity for co-operating with one of the world's largest and most successful film-producing countries is an exciting prospect for Trinidad and Tobago as it gets ready to launch a powerful range of initiatives designed to position itself as the premier Caribbean destination for international film-makers, and a quality producer of films for the domestic, regional and international markets.

1. It can be inferred from the passage that
(a) T&T is a regular destination for holiday travellers from India.
(b) Festival of Indian films is regularly held in the Caribbean.
(c) Many Indian citizens who love films are resident in T&T.
(d) None of these

2. Which of the following statements is/are true?
(a) The film industry in T&T is of recent origin.
(b) The Nobel Prize winning author V.S. Naipaul is from the Caribbean.
(c) T&T has had many good literary writers.
(d) All these

3. What are the benefits accruing from the launch of TTFC?
A. The film producers of T&T have access to better infrastructure and facilities for film making.
B. The individual film producers of T&T have easy access to the Indian High Commission based in Port of Spain.
C. V.S. Naipaul's literary work got adopted for a film.
(a) A only
(b) A & B
(c) A & C
(d) A, B & C

4. Which of the following statements about Indian films is/are 'not' true, in the context, of the passage?
(a) Indian films were being shot in the Caribbean islands for more than 50 years now.
(b) The islands of T&T hold a special charm for film makers from all over the world.
(c) People of Indian origin based in the Caribbean still relate to India culturally.
(d) T&T is collaborating with India in a big way for the betterment of its community of film producers/

Passage–II

Earliest historical evidence from Mehargarh (north-west Indian subcontinent) shows beginning of civilisation in India at around 6500 B.C. It is the earliest and largest urban site of the period in the world. This site has yielded evidence for the earliest domestication of animals, evolution of agriculture; as well as arts and crafts. The horse was first domesticated here in 6500 B.C. There is a progressive process of the domestication of animals, particularly cattle, the development of agriculture, beginning with barley and then later wheat and rice, and the use of metal, beginning with copper and culminating in iron, along with the development of villages and towns. It has been suggested by some historians that an 'Aryan Invasion' of the Indian subcontinent took place around 1500-1000 B.C. However, current archaeological data do not support the existence of an Indo-Aryan or European invasion into South Asia at any time in the pre- or proto-historic periods. The people in this tradition were the same basic ethnic groups as in India today, with their same basic types of languages. Two important cities were discovered: Harappa on the Ravi river and Mohenjodaro on the Indus, during excavations in 1920. The remains of these two cities were part of a large civilisation and well developed ancient civilisation, which is now called by historians as Indus Valley Civilisation' or 'Sarasvati Civilisation'. Late Harappan (Sarasvati) Civilisation 3100-1900 BC shows massive cities, complex agriculture and metallurgy, sophistication of arts and crafts and precision in weights, and measures. They built large buildings, which were mathematically-planned., The city planning in those ancient cities is comparable to die best of our modern cities. This civilisation had a, written language and was highly sophisticated. Some of these towns were almost three miles in diameter with thousands of residents. These ancient municipalises had granaries, citadels, and even household toilets. In Mohenjodaro, a mile-long canal connected the city to the sea, and trading ships sailed as far as Mesopotamia. At its height, the Indus civilisation extended over half a million square miles across the Indus river valley, and though it existed at the same time as the ancient civilisations of Egypt and Sumer, it far outlasted them. This Sarasvati civilisation was a centre of trading and for the diffusion of civilisation throughout south and west Asia, which often dominated the Mesopotamian region.

5. Which of the following statements is .true as per the passage?
(a) The Indo-Aryans discovered the two cities, namely, Harappa and Mohenjodaro.
(b) The people of Harappa, were well aware of the use, of weights and measures.
(c) Language or script was not a part of the Harappa civilisation.
(d) The Harappa civilisation still remains a mystery with historians.

6. Which one of the following facilities was not a part of the Sarasvati civilisation?
(a) Granaries
(b) Citadels
(c) Rest houses
(d) Household toilets

7. What confirms the presence of civilisation in the site at Mehargarh?
(a) An Aryan invasion around 1,500-1000 B.C.
(b) The presence of copper and iron
(c) Domestication of 'cattle' and evolution of agriculture implying human population.
(d) No, substantial archaeological data is present to confirm civilisation near Mehargarh.

8. The passage could be a part of
(a) A research study at a doctorate level.
(b) A History school book.
(c) An economic text book showing the growth of trade
(d) A book specifically on the domestication of animals as early as 6500 B.C.

Directions to Questions 9 to 18

Fill in the blanks.

9. The mill workers were not ____ with then low wages and non-payment of wages for last three months ______ fuel to die flame.
(a) good, put
(b) satisfied, added
(c) joyful, poured
(d) pleased, directed

10. Though he is reputed for his technical ____ his books were sadly ____of the work of others as he lacked originality.
(a) advice unconscious
(b) skill, independent
(c) knowledge, ignorant
(d) expertise, derivative

11. Nothing is so ____to a nation as an extreme of sell partiality,, and the total want of ____ of what others will naturally hope or fear.
(a) detrimental concern
(b) repugnant, sense
(c) unethical, discretion
(d) fatal, consideration

12. I would like to ____ your attention to the second paragraph of my letter ____ to the terms of sale of the machinery.
(a) invite
(b) withdraw, regarding
(c) react, mainly
(d) draw, pertaining

13. Hence the word sophistry has an unfavourable ____ and means arguing deceitfully attempting to turn a poor case into a good one by means of clever but ______ reasoning.
(a) impact, cogent
(b) denotation, ingenuous
(c) significance, vague
(d) connotation, specious

14. Children are more _____ than adults, it is_____ their quickness in learning a new language.
(a) intelligent, disproved by
(b) adaptable, reflected in

(c) conservative, seen in
(d) susceptible demonstrated in.

15. The candidate's _____ at the polls was _____ as he won with a striking margin.
(a) Claim, unrealistic
(b) victory, overwhelming
(c) image, real
(d) strategy, successful

16. We do not _____ our dreams because they do not _____ with our perceptions of actual life.
(a) adroit, coincide
(b) accept, mix
(c) value, match
(d) believe, agree

17. He was so convinced that people were driven by _____ motives that he believed there was no suchthing as a purely _____ act.
(a) personal, anti-social
(b) personal, eternal
(c) altruistic, praiseworthy
(d) ulterior, selfless.

18. We _____ him with many promises, but nothing would _____ him.
(a) tempted, influence
(b) provoked, desiccate
(c) attracted,. fascinate,
(d) gave, deprive

Directions to Questions 19 to 23

Each question has a group of sentences marked A, B, C, D and E. Arrange these to form a logical sequence.

19.

A. A professional is a person who is paid to undertake a specialised set of tasks and orchestrate them with uncommon skill.
B. It is also used in sport to differentiate amateur players from those paid for their work.
C. Traditional examples of professions included medicine, nursing, law, and engineering but is now more widely used to include many other professions,
D. Hence professional footballer or Professional golfer.
E. In some cultures the term is used as shorthand to describe a particular social stratum of well educated mostly salaried workers.

(a) ACBDE (b) BCADE
(c) CDEAB (d) DBHCA

20.

A. No living being can survive a firestorm.
B. Light, heat, blast and radiation are some of the primary effects of a nuclear explosion,
C. Firestorms deplete oxygen from the environment and create hurricane-like winds, which attract debris and feed the storm itself, causing super-infernos.
D. Immense light and thermal heat (comparable to the interior of the sun) initiate a phenomenon called a firestorm.
E. The word is now used to describe any controversy, as in: there's a firestorm brewing in the city's threat to raise bus and subway fares.

(a) CAEBD (b) BDCAE
(c) CABDE (d) ECADB

21.

A. Astrophysics is the branch of astronomy that deals with the physics of the universe, including the physical properties of celestial objects, as well as their interactions and behaviour.
B. Among the objects studied are galaxies, stars, planets, exoplanets, the interstellar medium and the cosmic microwave background.
C. Their emissions are examined across all parts of the electromagnetic spectrum.
D. The properties examined include luminosity, density, temperature, and chemical composition.
E. The study of cosmology addresses questions of astrophysics at scales much larger than the size of particular gravitationally -bound objects in the universe.

(a) ACEBD (b) EDBCA
(c) ABCDE (d) BEGAD

22.

A. Due to its loyal and protective nature, the German Shepherd is one of the most registered of breeds.
B. Because of its strength, intelligence and abilities in obedience training, it is often employed in police and military roles around the world.
C. As part of the Herding Group, the German Shepherd is a working dog developed originally for herding and guarding sheep.
D. The German Shepherd is a relatively new breed of dog, with its origin dating to 1899.
E. The German Shepherd dog (also known as an Alsatian) is a breed of large sized dog that originated in Germany.

(a) EDCBA (b) DBCAE
(c) ABCDE (d) BECAD

23.

A. Disruption of the ozone layer lets ultraviolet light filter down to the surface of the earth where it can change organisms by mutating their genes.
B. A new theory claims that the explosions, thought to occur when two stars collide, releases tonnes of high energy gamma-ray radiation into space, finally leading to the end of life on planet Earth.
C. Now, they are beginning to connect the timing of these gamma-ray bursts to extinctions on Earth that can be dated through the fossil record.
D. Gamma-ray bursts, massive explosions on the other side of the galaxy, could end life on Earth, say scientists.
E. The scientists have already found that such blasts are contributing to the depletion of the Earth's ozone layer.

(a) DBEAC
(b) CAEDB
(c) EDCAB
(d) ACDBE

Directions to Questions 24 to 28

Choose the word which best expresses the meaning of the word in bold in the sentence.

24. Many species of animals have become **extinct** during the last hundred years.
(a) feeble
(b) aggressive
(c) scattered
(d) non-existent

25. The community is **agog** with speculation about the fate of the money collected.
(a) excited
(b) worried
(c) depressed
(d) annoyed

26. He was drawn into the **vortex** of politics are a very early age.
(a) whirlpool
(b) field
(c) arena
(d) hell

27. He has the **propensity** for getting into debt.
(a) characteristic
(b) quality
(c) natural tendency
(d) aptitude

28. If you lack in **magnanimity**, all your wealth and luxury is useless.
(a) planning
(b) purposiveness
(c) management
(d) generosity

Directions to Questions 29 to 33

Choose the word which is opposite in meaning of the word in bold in the sentence.

29. A **serene** mind can never be the pioneer of a great revolution.
(a) nervous
(b) jocular

(c) earnest
(d) agitated

30. Matter **expands** on heating.
(a) shrinks
(b) reduces
(c) diminishes
(d) contracts

31. She is beautiful as well as **frivolous**.
(a) indecent
(b) serious
(c) insane
(d) rude

32. It is **obligatory** for a common citizen to follow the rules.
(a) optional
(b) superfluous
(c) necessary
(d) advisable

33. Every detail of the painting is **prominent** enough to be seen.
(a) negligible
(b) insignificant
(c) trifling
(d) inconspicuous

Directions to Questions 34 to 38

Choose the option that is the plural form of the given word.

34. Alumnus
(a) alumni
(b) alumnus
(c) alumnuses
(d) alumnus

35. Toe
(a) toes
(b) toss
(c) tows
(d) toe's

36. Brake
(a) brakes
(b) break
(c) braks
(d) brake's

37. Woman
(a) womans
(b) woman's
(c) womans'
(d) women

38. Human
(a) humane
(b) humen
(c) humans
(d) human's

Directions to Questions 39 to 42

Choose the option which best expresses the of meaning of the idiom/phrase in bold in the sentence.

39. It is a matter of gratification for me that he has **turned a new leaf**.
(a) Begun a different mode of life.
(b) Started using his intelligence.
(c) Proved to be a worthy person on his job.
(d) Accepted the new job that was offered to him.

40. He is always **picking holes** in every project.
(a) asking irrelevant, questions on
(b) suggesting improvement in
(c) finding fault with
(d) creating problems in

41. Lokesh always **sets great store** by his father's advice.
(a) laughs at
(b) values greatly
(c) ignores
(d) neglects

42. His boss was always **breathing down his neck**.
(a) abusing and ill-treating him
(b) watching all his actions closely
(c) shouting loudly at him
(d) giving him/Strenuous work

Directions to Questions 43 to 47

A word has been written in four different ways out of which only one is correctly spelt. Choose the correctly spelt word.

43.
(a) sustinence (b) sustenance
(c) sustenence (d) sustinance

44.
(a) achievment (b) acheivment
(c) achievement (d) achievemant

45.
(a) coreander (b) coriander
(c) coriandar (d) coreandor

46.
(a) colaberation (b) collaberation
(c) colaberation (d) collaboration

47.
(a) exagerate (b) exadgerate
(c) exaggerate (d) exeggerate

Directions to Questions 48 to 52

Fill in the Blanks

48. History records seventeen incursions of Sultan Mahmood ____ India.
(a) against (b) into
(c) upon (d) on

49. Your statement is replete ____ contradictions.
(a) by (b) of
(c) in (d) with

50. It is difficult for me to part ____ my belongings.
(a) from (b) of
(c) with (d) off

51. He was sorry ____ what he had done.
(a) over (b) for
(c) at (d) of

52. He was charged ____ murder and brought to trial.
(a) by (b) for
(c) of (d) with

Directions to Questions 53 to 57

A sentence has been broken into four parts. Choose the part that has an error.

53.
(a) The supper party given by Mr. Julius Hershey
(b) to a few friends at the evening of the 30th
(c) will long be remembered
(d) in catering circles.

54.
(a) It was on that particular ill-fated
(b) voyage that, a Lusitania was
(c) torpedoed by a rogue submarine
(d) and sunk with all hands.

55.
(a) One way route is
(b) a mean of
(c) reducing traffic
(d) in congested areas of Delhi.

56.
(a) Again, I always go to sea as a sailor,
(b) because they make a point of paying me
(c) for my trouble, whereas they never pay passengers
(d) the single penny that ever heard of.

57.
(a) If you don't act now
(b) the Himalayan flora
(c) will eventually
(d) be destroyed.

Directions to Questions 58 to 60

Identify the best way of writing the given sentence ensuring that the message being conveyed remains the same.

58.

(a) Altogether, collision between the classes of the old society further, in many ways, the course of development of the proletariat.

(b) Altogether, collision amongst the classes of the old society further, in many ways, the course of development of the proletariat.

(c) Altogether, collisions between the classes of the old societv further, in many ways, the course of development of the proletariat.

(d) Altogether, collisions amongst the classes of the old society further, in many ways, the course of development of the proletariat.

59.

(a) All the preceding classes that had the upper hand, sought to fortify their already acquired status by subjecting society at large to their conditions of appropriation.

(b) All the preceding classes that took the upper hand, sought to fortify their already acquired status by subjecting society at large to their conditions of appropriation.

(c) All the preceding classes that sought the upper hand, sought to fortify their already acquired status by subjecting society at large to their conditions of appropriation.

(d) All the preceding classes that got the upper hand, sought to fortify their already acquired status by subjecting society at large to their conditions of appropriation.

60.

(a) They merely express, in general terms, actual relations that spring from an existing class struggle, from a historical movement going on under our very eyes. .

(b) They merely express, in general terms, actual relations springing from an existing class struggle, from a historical movement going on under our very eyes.

(c) They merely express, in general terms, actual relations sprung from an existing class struggle, from a historical movement going on under our very eyes.

(d) They merely express, in general terms, actual relations that sprang from an existing class struggle, from a historical movement going on under our very eyes.

ANSWER KEY

1. (d)	2. (d)	3. (c)	4. (b)	5. (a)
6. (c)	7. (c)	8. (b)	9. (b)	10. (d)
11. (a)	12. (d)	13. (d)	14. (b)	15. (b)
16. (d)	17. (d)	18. (a)	19. (a)	20. (b)
21. (c)	22. (a)	23. (a)	24. (d)	25. (a)
26. (a)	27. (c)	28. (d)	29. (d)	30. (d)
31. (b)	32. (a)	33. (b)	34. (a)	35. (a)
36. (a)	37. (d)	38. (c)	39. (a)	40. (c)
41. (b)	42. (c)	43. (b)	44. (c)	45. (b)
46. (d)	47. (c)	48. (b)	49. (d)	50. (c)
51. (b)	52. (d)	53. (b)	54. (b)	55. (b)
56. (d)	57. (c)	58. (c)	59. (a)	60. (d)

Frequency Analysis

Comprehension	8
Sentence Completion	15
Sentence Arranement	5
Synonym	5
Antonym	5
Plural Form	5
Idiom	4
Spelling	5
Error	5
Sentence Improvement with variation	3
Total	**60**

Trend Analysis

The question pattern shows variety. Most of the questions are of regular type and have been set in a straight forword manner. However, there are two variations – **Plural Form** and **Sentence Improvement**. There is great emphasis on sentence completion. The level of questions is just above moderate. A careful reading of the book and an intelligent application of the skills taught in the book will help students to a large extent.

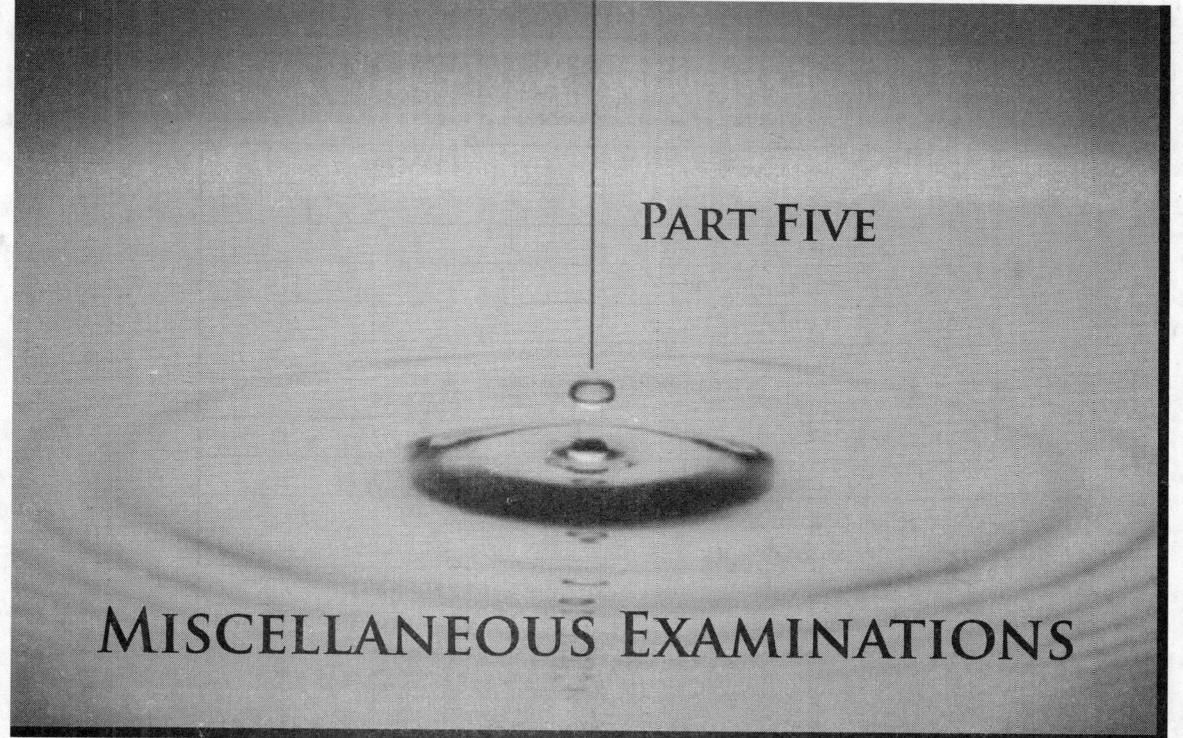

A

Union Public Service Commission (UPSC)

UPSC conducts a large number of examinations. SCRA, (Special Class Railway Apprentice), IES, (Indian Engineering Services) and APFC, (Assistant Provident Fund Commissioner) have English language test in the objective format. English language section contains sixty questions in both examinations. APFC examination has a language component with 25 questions.

Previous years' questions have been provided with answers and trend analysis to acquaint the examinees with the most recent trend and pattern of the test format.

B

Staff Selection Commission (SSC)

SSC conducts examinations for a large number of various types of posts in the different ministerial wings of the government of India. Most important among them are SSC Graduate Level examination, SSC CAPFS, Delhi Police SI, CISF ASI and NCB intelligence officer examination and SSC, FCI examination and SSC Multitasking Staff Examination. These examinations have I and II tiers with English language section as a test component. In Tier I, there are fifty questions and in tier II there are 200 questions. Thus English language forms a very important part of the whole examination.

The examination systems has been comprehensively overhauled recently. Therefore, recent years' questions have been provided with answers and trend analysis to deepen the understanding of the examines and to acqurint them with specific trends of the concerned exams.

PAPER 34

SPECIAL CLASS RAILWAY APPRENTICE EXAMINATION, 2011

Directions to Questions 1 to 10

(i) In this section, a number of sentences are given. The sentences are underlined in three separate parts and each one is labelled (a), (b) and (c). Read each sentence to find out whether there is an error in any underlined part. No sentence has more than one error. When you find an error in any one of the underlined parts (a), (b) or (c), indicate your response on the separate answer sheet at the appropriate space. You may feel that there is no error in a sentence. In that case, letter (d) will signify a 'No error' response.

(ii) You are to indicate only one response for each item in your answer sheet. (If you indicate more than one response, your answer will be considered wrong.) Errors may be in grammar, word usage or idioms. There may be a word missing or there may be a word which should be removed.

(iii) You are not required to correct the error. You are required only to indicate your response on the answer sheet.

Examples 'P' and 'Q' have been solved for you.

P. The young child (a) / singed (b) / a very sweet song (c) /. No error (d)

Q. We worked (a) / very hard (b) / throughout the season. (d) / No error

Explanation : In item P, the word 'singed' is wrong. The letter under this part is (b), so (b) is the correct answer. Similarly, for item Q, (d) is the correct answer, as the sentence does not contain any error.

1. The gardener could not cut the grass today (a)/ because the handle of the machine (b) / has broken a few days ago (c)/. No error (d)

2. He studied in Australia since (a) / two years (b) / and got his doctorate degree. (c) / No error (d)

3. My father does not mind (a) / to be disturbed (b) / while he is reading the newspaper. (c) / No error (d)

4. When the company offered him a purse on his retirement (a) / he refused (b) to agree it. (c) No error (d)

5. The ship sank (a) / before the rescue party (b)/ arrived. (c) / No error (d)

6. When the teacher read my first novel, (a) / he tells a friend that in due course (b) / I should be one of the best writers in the class. (c)/ No error (d)
7. Perhaps you do not know (a) / I am having a car and a jeep (b) / besides a big house in a good locality. (c) / No error (d)
8. The fashion of decorating hats with feathers (a) / declined because too many birds (b) / were slaughtered for their feathers.(c) / No error (d)
9. He stepped (a)/ on the green grass (b) / unmindful of the warning.(c) / No error (d)
10. She was an only child (a) / and indulged at every whim (b)/ by her loving father.(c) / No error (d)

Directions to Questions 11 to 20

In each of the following items, supply the appropriate phrasal verb in the blank to make the meaning clear.

11. Our minds are _____ false ideas,
    (a) clogged in
    (b) clogged about
    (c) clogged with
    (d) clogged for
12. She was _____from the meeting to take an urgent phone call.
    (a) called away
    (b) called for
    (c) called out
    (d) called up
13. I have no idea as to what _____ the change in his attitude.
    (a) brought out
    (b) brought in
    (c) brought about
    (d) brought for
14. Mobile phones with serious faults have been by the manufacturers,
    (a) called out
    (b) called for
    (c) called in
    (d) called up
15. The story is _____ a group of high school dropouts.
    (a) built around
    (b) built with
    (c) built in
    (d) built of
16. I think I have no _____ what she does,
    (a) control for
    (b) control with
    (c) control on
    (d) control over
17. I am _____ hypocrisy more than anything else,
    (a) averse with
    (b) averse to
    (c) averse in
    (d) averse on
18. He always _____ you in his letters.
    (a) asks around
    (b) asks of
    (c) asks about
    (d) asks to
19. You cannot give any decision since you are not _____ all the facts of the case.
    (a) acquainted with
    (b) acquainted to
    (c) acquainted by
    (d) acquainted for
20. His health —— under the pressure of work.
    (a) broke off
    (b) broke down
    (c) broke up
    (d) broke in

Directions to Questions 21 to 30

Each of the following items consists of a sentence followed by four words or groups of words. Select the *synonym* of the word (occurring in the sentence in capital letters) as per the context.

21. His LUCID and melodious prose makes, the subject come alive in our imagination.
    (a) Fluent
    (b) Clear

(c) Musical
(d) Familiar

22. The army RAVAGED a part of the neighbouring country.
(a) Destroyed
(b) Spoiled
(c) Conquered
(d) Robbed

23. He was PERPLEXED by the failure of his scheme, for he had planned it leaving nothing to chance.
(a) Annoyed
(b) Disappointed
(c) Puzzled
(d) Ruined

24. His ANONYMITY has become a blessing in disguise.
(a) Reputation
(b) Publicity
(c) Being unknown
(d) Wrong address

25. We were shocked by the APPALLING conditions prevailing in big cities.
(a) Disturbing
(b) Filthy
(c) Horrifying
(d) Poverty-stricken

26. It was difficult to understand the CAPTION of the picture.
(a) Joke
(b) Definition
(c) Meaning
(d) Title

27. The heavy waves BATTERED the wrecked ship.
(a) Destroyed
(b) Dashed on
(c) Struck hard
(d) Struck off

28. He is an EXTRAVAGANT person.
(a) Hardworking
(b) Good
(c) Extraordinary
(d) Spendthrift

29. The growing use of computers in teaching might one day make teachers REDUNDANT.
(a) Unnecessary
(b) Uninterested
(c) Introspective
(d) Knowledgeable

30. His work was HINDERED by constant interruptions from visitors.
(a) Damaged
(b) Disturbed
(c) Obstructed
(d) Protested

Directions to Questions 31 to 40

Each, of the following items consists of a phrase in the stem, of the item followed by four options (a), (b), (c) and (d). You have to identify from the given options.as to which one. of them correctly describes the phrase.

31. To surround a place with the intention of capturing it
(a) Bivouac
(b) Besiege
(c) Invade
(d) Intern

32. To send back a person from ones' country
(a) Repatriate
(b) Expatriate
(c) Migrate
(d) Emigrate

33. One who is opposed to intellectual progress
(a) Impostor
(b) Chaperon
(c) Prospector
(d) Obscurant

34. A woman with dark brown hair
(a) Blonde
(b) Brunette
(c) Termagant
(d) Coiffeur

35. One who has special skill in judging art, music, tastes, etc.
(a) Connoisseur
(b) Raconteur
(c) Sybarite
(d) Amateur

36. One who devotes his life to the welfare and the interests of other people
(a) Minion
(b) Martyr
(c) Altruist
(d) Fugitive

37. A place where animals are kept alive, and nearly as possible as in their natural state
(a) Vivarium
(b) Orchard
(c) Paddock
(d) Glyptotheca

38. Speech delivered without preparation
(a) Extempore
(b) Flexion
(c) Extensive
(d) Loquacious

39. One who hates mankind
(a) Misanthropist
(b) Misnomer
(c) Misogynist
(d) Philanthropist

40. The period between two reigns
(a) Interregnum
(b) Interval
(c) Interdict
(d) Intercept

Directions to Questions 41 to 50

In the following items, some parts of the sentence have been jumbled up. You are required to rearrange these parts which are labelled P, Q, R and S to produce the correct sentence. Choose the proper sequence and mark in your Answer Sheet accordingly. Example 'Z' has been solved for you,

Z. Some people believe that

the effect (P) / is very bad (Q) / on children (R) / of cinema (S)

Which one of the following is the correct sequence?
(a) PSRQ (b) SPQR
(c) SRPQ (d) QSRP

Explanation : The proper way of writing the sentence is "Some people believe that the effect of cinema on children is very bad". This is indicated by the sequence PSRQ and so (a) is the correct answer.

41. She was born

at 10 a.m. (P) / in India (Q) / in the year 1978 (R) / on 18th August (S)

Which one of the following is the correct sequence?
(a) PQRS (b) QPSR
(c) RSQP (d) SRPQ

42. The highwayman

behind the treetops (P) / when the sun disappeared (Q) / rode to the cottage (C) / where his beloved lived (S) /

Which one of the following is the correct sequence?
(a) PQRS (b) SPRQ
(c) QRSP (d) RSQP

43. She danced

at the town hall (P) / last night (Q) / beautifully (R) / in the concert (S)

Which one of the following is the correct sequence?
(a) PQRS (b) RSPQ
(c) QSPR (d) RQPS

44. My father

shuts out the world (P) / who (Q) / by closing his eyes (R) / is a loner (S)

Which one of the following is the correct sequence?
(a) PQRS (b) SQPR
(c) SPQR (d) QSPR

45. because he detested the food available locally (P) / the refugee (Q) / walking along the deserted streets of the town (R) / thought of the delicacies of his country (S)

Which one of the following is the correct sequence?

(a) RQSP (b) PQRS
(c) RPQS (d) QPRS

46. I believe that

Tendulkar's century (P) / will always remember (Q) / cricket lovers (R) / on Tuesday (S)

Which one of the following is the correct sequence?

(a) SRQP (b) RQPS
(c) PSRQ (d) PRQS

47. It is better to go back to the people for a mandate (P) / if these kinds of accusations go on (Q) / and if the government wants to do something good (R) / even though people do not want another election (S)

Which one of the following is the correct sequence?

(a) SPQR (b) QSRP
(c) QRPS (d) RPQS

48. The newspaper reported that

can never reproduce such a wonder (P) / the rain forest (Q) / is nature's way of telling us that man (R) / for all his ability to create (S)

Which one of the following is the correct sequence?

(a) QRSP (b) QRPS
(c) SQPR (d) QPRS

49. The judge declared (P) / that those people (Q) / will be jailed (R) / who cannot remain silent in the court (S)

Which one of the following is the correct sequence?

(a) PQSR (b) QPSR
(c) SPQR (d) QRPS

50. The first priority before us is

irrespective of their backgrounds (P) / that people (Q) / learn to get on with one another as fellow human beings (R) / understand each other and force bonds of friendship (S)

Which one of the following is the correct sequence?

(a) QSPR (b) QRPS
(c) QPRS (d) RPQS

Directions to Questions 51 to 60

In this section, you have three short passages. After each passage, you will find several questions based on the passage. First, read a passage and then answer the questions based on it, You are required to select your answers based on the contents of the passage and opinion of the author only.

Examples 'I' and 'J' have been solved for you.

Passage (Example)

In our approach to life, be it pragmatic or otherwise, a basic fact that confronts us squarely and unmistakably is the desire for peace, security and happiness. Different forms of life at different levels of existence make up the teeming denizens of this earth of ours. And, no matter whether they belong to the higher groups such as human beings or to the lower groups such as animals, all beings primarily seek peace, comfort and security. Life is as dear to a mute creature as it is to a man. Even the lowliest insect strives for protection against dangers that threaten its life. Just as each one of us wants to live and not to die, so do all other creatures.

I. The author's main point is that

(a) different forms of life are found on the earth
(b) different levels of existence are possible in nature
(c) peace and security are the chief goals of all living beings
(d) even the weakest creature struggles to preserve its life

J. Which of following assumptions or steps is essential in developing the author's position?

(a) All forms of life have a single overriding goal
(b) The will to survive of a creature is identified with a desire for peace
(c) All beings are divided into higher and lower groups

(d) A parallel is drawn between happiness and life, and pain and death

Explanation :

I. The idea which represents the author's main point is "peace and security are the chief goals of all living beings", which is response (c). So (c) is the correct answer.

J. The best assumption underlying the passage is "The will to survive of a creature is identified with a desire for peace", which is response (b). So (b) is the correct answer.

Passage-I

The life cycle of a butterfly is very dramatic and action-packed, because so much happens in so short a time. The most interesting is the caterpillar stage. They are very vulnerable to attacks and use camouflage to protect themselves. Generally their colours help them blend with the surroundings. Also, their bodies have thin lines much like the veins of a leaf. Some caterpillars use the leaf to make themselves invisible. Some of them are even beautiful, especially the ones that are grass-yellow. This shade of green is fabulous but strangely the adult is not so beautiful.

Butterflies have many enemies but most stay away from them because they are very bitter to the taste ! This saves them from many aggressors. The swallowtail caterpillar emits a strong odour to keep its enemies at bay. Some caterpillars simply drop to the ground and climb back up the tree only after the enemy has gone.

51. The life cycle of butterfly is said to be dramatic because
(a) several actions take place at the same time
(b) the changes in its life cycle take place fast
(c) they exhibit different colours and are beautiful
(d) they know art camouflage

52. Which of the following methods are ***not*** used by caterpillar to save itself from the enemies?
1. Making their appearance akin to the leaves
2. Changing the shape of their bodies very fast
3. Giving-off smells that repulse the enemies

Select the correct answer using the code given below :

Code :
(a) 1 and 2 only
(b) 2 and 3 only
(c) 1 and 3 only
(d) 1, 2 and 3

53. The expression 'very vulnerable to attacks' in the passage means
(a) prone to attack others
(b) prone to being overcome by enemies
(c) they provoke others to attack
(d) they are immune to attacks from others

Passage-II

I went into a restaurant, which was already crowded, and ordered my meal. While I was waiting for the soup to arrive, I looked around to see if I knew anyone in the restaurant. It was then I noticed a man sitting at a corner table near the door kept glancing in my direction, as though he knew me. I certainly did not know him, for I never forget a face. The man had a newspaper open in front of him, which he was pretending to read, though all the while I could see that he was keeping an eye on me. When the waiter brought my soup, the man was clearly puzzled by the familiar way in which the waiter and I addressed each other. He became even more puzzled as time went on and it grew more and more obvious that I was well-known in the restaurant. Eventually he got up and went into the kitchen. After a few minutes he came out again, paid his bill and left without another glance in my direction.

54. The narrator observed somebody watching him
(a) immediately after entering the restaurant
(b) some time after he settled down in his seat
(c) while he was eating his meal
(d) when the waiter drew his attention to him

55. The narrator puzzled the man who was watching him because
(a) he was sitting idle without eating
(b) he came to an overcrowded restaurant
(c) he sat without talking to anyone
(d) he appeared to be well-known in the restaurant

56. The man watching the narrator gives us an impression that

(a) he wanted to make friends with the narrator
(b) he intended to observe without being noticed
(c) he wanted to wait until the narrator finished his meal
(d) he was an idler

57. The narrator went into an over-crowded restaurant because
(a) he loved crowds
(b) that restaurant was nearest to his office
(c) the food there is delicious
(d) he is in the habit of going there Regularly

Passage-III

From the first, two facts were obvious: the lady had been quite willing to undergo the wedding ceremony, and she had repented of it within a few minutes of returning home. Obviously something had occurred during the morning, then, to cause her to change her mind. What could that something be? She could not have spoken to anyone when she was out, for she had been in the company of bridegroom. Had she seen someone, then? If she had, it must be someone from America, because she had spent so short a time in this country that she could hardly have allowed anyone to acquire so deep an influence over her that mere sight of him would induce her to change her plans so completely. So she might have seen an American.

58. The writer sees clearly that the bride
(a) wanted at, one and the same time to marry and remain unmarried
(b) agreed to marry on certain conditions
(c) willingly married and then wanted the marriage undone
(d) was unsure what she wanted

59. Soon after the marriage, the bride
(a) became angry
(b) experienced something quite unexpected
(c) grew impatient
(d) fell sick

60. The bride was apparently from America because
(a) her accent was American
(b) she had a casual manner
(c) most of the guests were from America
(d) it was only there she had time enough to develop a strong relationship

PAPER 35

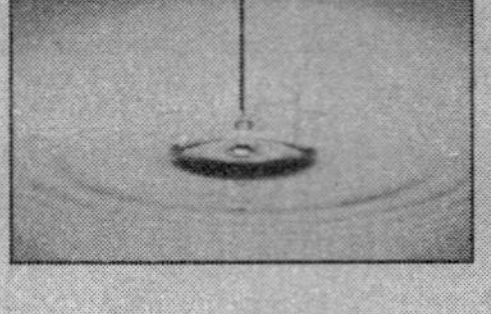

Special Class Railway Apprentice Examination, 2012

Directions to Questions 1 to 10

(i) In this section, a number of sentences are given. The sentences are underlined in three separate parts and each one is labelled (a), (b) and (c). Read each sentence to find out whether there is an error in any underlined part. No sentence has more than one error. When you find an error in any one of the underlined parts (a), (b) or (c), indicate your response on the separate answer sheet at the appropriate space. You may feel that, there is no error in a sentence. In that case, letter (d) will signify a 'No error' response.

(ii) You are to indicate only one response for each item in your answer sheet. (If you indicate more than one response, your answer will be considered wrong.) Errors may be in grammar, word usage or idioms. There may be a word missing or there may be a word which should be removed.

(iii) You are not required to correct the error. You are required only to indicate your response on the answer sheet.

Examples 'P' and 'Q' have been solved for you.

P. The young child (a) / singed (b) / a very sweet song. (c) / No error (d)

Q. We worked (a) / very hard (b) / throughout the season.(c) / No error (d)

Explanation : In item P, the word 'singed' is wrong. The letter, under this part is (b), so (b) is the correct answer. Similarly, for item Q, (d) is the correct answer, as the sentence does not contain any error.

1. The person (a) / who I met yesterday (b) / was my classmate.(c) / No error (d)
2. To me it appears that (a) / Anthropology is the more interesting (b) / of all subjects.(c) / No error (d)
3. A number of Indians have become (a) / software engineers in the USA because of their proficiency in English, (b) / isn't it? (c) / No error (d)
4. Since his arrival in India, (a) / he is visiting as many villages as he can (b) / to acquire a firsthand knowledge of the rural India.(c) / No error (d)
5. It was decided in an emergency meeting of teachers (a) / in the college (b) / to impose on students a fine of five hundred rupees.(c) / No error (d)
6. The honesty (a)/ is (b) / a virtue(c) / No error (d)

7. The committee (a) / could not come to (b) / a final conclusion. (c) / No error (d)

8. Although he is my immediate neighbour (a) / I do not get "help from him (b) / especially when I need it the most.(c) / No error (d)

9. It is impossible (a) / to either predict the future (b) / or forget the past(c) / No error (d)

10. The cattle in the meadow (a) / was terrified to hear unexpected (b) / the roar of a lion which appeared to be wild with anger(c) / No error (d)

Directions to Questions 11 to 20

Each of the following items consists of a sentence followed by four words or groups of words. Select the synonym of the word (occurring in the sentence in capital letters) as per the context.

11. The Minister's ITINERARY has not been announced yet.
    (a) Detailed route
    (b) Series of lectures
    (c) Topic of discussion
    (d) Venue of meeting

12. The decision to hold elections in the four States of the country has been kept in ABEYANCE till the decision of the Supreme Court.
    (a) Guessing
    (b) Confusion
    (c) Suspension
    (d) Consideration

13. What a TEDIOUS lecture we attended yesterday!
    (a) Intellectual
    (b) Exciting
    (c) Ordinary
    (d) Boring

14. He has achieved REMARKABLE success.
    (a) Outstanding
    (b) Strange
    (c) Rare
    (d) Surprising

15. The town is situated in a hot and ARID zone.
    (a) Humid
    (b) Sandy
    (c) Marshy
    (d) Dry

16. The PASSION for uniformity in spelling is unparalleled in the modern age.
    (a) Desire
    (b) Feeling
    (c) Wish
    (d) Ambition

17. The radio APPRISED the public of the safe return of the first space pilot.
    (a) Advised
    (b) Informed
    (c) Instructed
    (d) Revealed

18. He has been very FEEBLE since his illness.
    (a) Unwell
    (b) Thin
    (c) Foolish
    (d) Weak

19. He was INFURIATED by the maddening behaviour of the clerk at the post office.
    (a) Disgusted
    (b) Enraged
    (c) Pacified
    (d) Depressed

20. The medicine did not exactly cure the patient, but it considerably ALLEVIATED his agony.
    (a) Improved
    (b) Increased
    (c) Reduced
    (d) Made pleasant

Directions to Questions 21 to 30

Each of the following items consists of a sentence followed by four words or groups of words. Select the antonym of the word or words (occurring in the sentence in capital letters) as per the context.

21. The CONFRONTATION between the two parties could not be averted.
    (a) Friendship
    (b) Angry disagreement

(c) Reconstitution
(d) Agreement

22. Sometimes even INDUSTRIOUS people fail.
(a) Indolent
(b) Mercenary
(c) Fortunate
(d) Factious

23. A new court has been established to try JUVENILE offenders.
(a) Young
(b) Female
(c) Aged
(d) Male

24. He is disliked by all his colleagues for his ARROGANCE.
(a) Humility
(b) Generosity
(c) Joviality
(d) Decency

25. He got VOLUNTARY retirement on account of his failing health.
(a) Urgent
(b) Compulsory
(c) Premature
(d) Undesirable

26. The land is FERTILE.
(a) Poor
(b) Barren
(c) Deserted
(d) Fruitless

27. For some reasons, the police want to CONCEAL the identity of the detainee.
(a) Reveal
(b) Confuse
(c) Disclaim
(d) Refuse

28. You may not VIOLATE the rules and regulations of the college.
(a) Respect
(b) Study
(c) Comply with
(d) Adopt

29. People GATHERED at his shop.
(a) Dispersed
(b) Spread
(c) Disappeared
(d) Cleared

30. The university's plans were FRAUGHT WITH difficulties.
(a) Burdened with
(b) Designed for
(c) Devoid of
(d) Cause of

Directions to Questions 31 to 40

Fill in the blanks with appropriate phrasal verbs from the alternatives given below under each item.

31. He is ______ making his career in sales.
(a) committed for
(b) committed in
(c) committed with
(d) committed to

32. As she became tired, errors began to ______ her work.
(a) Creep with
(b) creep into
(c) creep off
(d) creep up

33. She seems ______ bad luck.
(a) cursed by
(b) cursed with
(c) cursed for
(d) cursed on

34. Your option on this issue ______ traditional political boundaries.
(a) cuts across
(b) cuts into
(c) cuts off
(d) cuts by

35. Sorry, I am not ______ local places.
(a) conversant to
(b) conversant in

(c) conversant with
(d) conversant into

36. His actions are hardly ______ the tall claims he makes.
(a) compatible with
(b) compatible to
(c) compatible for
(d) compatible on

37. He wanted to ______ his colleagues before reducing a decision.
(a) confer with
(b) confer to
(c) confer in
(d) confer upon

38. The child is ______ calcium.
(a) deficient into
(b) deficient in
(c) deficient from
(d) deficient on

39. Several people have ______ sick today.
(a) called in
(b) called for
(c) called on
(d) called to

40. He was ______ by his aunt.
(a) brought up
(b) brought out
(c) brought off
(d) brought with

Directions to Questions 41 to 50

In the following items, some parts of the sentence have been jumbled up. You are required to rearrange these parts which are labelled P, Q, R and S to produce the correct sentence. Choose the proper sequence and mark in your Answer Sheet accordingly.

Example 'Z' has been solved for you.

Z. Some people believe that the effect is very bad on children of cinema

The correct sequence should be
(a) PSRQ (b) SPQR
(c) SRPQ (d) QSRP

Explanation : The proper way of writing the sentence is "Some people believe that the effect of cinema on children is very bad". This is indicated by the sequence PSRQ and so (a) is the correct answer.

41. I came to India
and when I landed (P) / two words of Hindi (Q) / I could speak, rather badly (R) / when I was twelve (S)

The correct sequence should be
(a) RQPS (b) SPRQ
(c) QSRP (d) PRSQ

42. The only way to learn
is to live a life (P) / automatically develop (Q) / social habits (R) / in which such habits (S)

The correct sequence should be
(a) RPSQ (b) QSRP
(c) PRQS (d) SRQP

43. once you do (P) / and speak out before a group for the first time (Q) / you have taken a big step forward (R) / although it is not easy to get on your feet (S)

The correct sequence should be
(a) SQPR (b) PRSQ
(c) QSRP (d) RQSP

44. We go into the city and
to get a general picture (P) / collect enough samples (Q) / what is going on there (R) / and it tells us (S)

The correct sequence should be
(a) SPRQ (b) RPSQ
(c) QPSR (d) PSQR

45. For five years
for a number of railway companies (P) / Edison worked (Q) / in various towns (R) / as a telegraph operator (S)

The correct sequence should be
(a) PSRQ (b) SPQR
(c) RQPS (d) QSPR

46. In the whole page

he can (P) / point out(Q) / hardly (R) / any mistake (S)

The correct sequence should be

(a) PQRS (b) PRQS
(c) SRPQ (d) RPQS

47. Her mother

when she was born (P) / ten years ago (Q) / threw her (R) / into a dustbin (S)

The correct sequence should be

(a) PQRS (b) RSPQ
(c) PSQR (d) QPSR

48. The Central Leather Institute

for curing and tanning rat skin (P) / has developed (Q) / to make purses and footwear (R) / a new process (S)

The correct sequence should be

(a) SRPQ (b) PSQR
(c) SPRQ (d) QSPR

49. Most people

not realizing how essential judicious exercise is (P) / for good health (Q) / take next to no physical exercise (R) / and are surprised when they fall ill (S)

The correct sequence should be

(a) PRSQ (b) PQSR
(c) RSPQ (d) QRSP

50. she would rather die (P) / where her heart should have been (Q) / than throw herself on the mercy of her sister-in-law (R) / who had a big rock (S)

The correct sequence should be

(a) PRQS (b) PRSQ
(c) PSQR (d) SPRQ

Directions to Questions 51 to 60

In this section, you have two short passages. After each passage, you will find several1 questions based on the passage. First, read a passage and then answer the questions based on it. You are required to select your answers based on the contents of the passage and opinion of the author only.

Examples 'I' and 'J' have been solved for you:

Passage (Example)

In our approach to life, be it pragmatic or otherwise, a basic fact that confronts us squarely and unmistakably is the desire for peace, security and happiness. Different forms of life at different levels .of existence make up the teeming denizens of this earth of ours. And, no matter whether they belong to the higher groups such as human beings or to the lower groups such as animals, all beings primarily seek peace, comfort and security. Life is as dear to a mute creature as it is to a man. Even the lowliest insect strives for protection against dangers that threaten its life. Just as each one of us wants to live and not to die, so do all other creatures.

I. The author's main point is that

(a) different forms of life are found on the earth
(b) different levels of existence are possible in nature
(c) peace and security are the chief goals of all living beings
(d) even the weakest creature struggles to preserve its life

J. Which one of following assumptions or steps is essential in developing the author's position?

(a) All forms of life have a single overriding goal-
(b) The will to survive of a creature is identified with a desire for peace
(c) All beings are divided into higher and lower groups
(d) A parallel is drawn between happiness and life, and pain and death

Explanation :

I. The idea which represents the author's main point is "peace and security are the chief goals of all living beings", which is response (c). So (c) is the correct answer.

J. The best assumption underlying the passage is "The will to survive of a creature is identified with a desire for peace", which is response (b). So (b) is the correct answer.

Passsage-I

Have you ever heard a parrot or a pet talk? Or perhaps you have seen the roadside astrologer who has a couple of parrots in his cage, which, at his command, picks out your fortune card from a pile of cards. You may also have heard of pigeons which, once acted as messengers.

All these make you ask the question : are birds intelligent? Can they learn things? Formerly the biologists thought that birds could not learn anything, because their brains were too small and too simple, compared to the intricate nervous system and brain of higher animals. They can act only by instinct, following certain fixed behavioural patterns. Recent studies have shown that bird behaviour is a combination of instinctive or fixed behaviour and learned or flexible behaviour.

51. The given passage deals with
(a) bird behaviour
(b) the learning capacity of birds/pets
(c) the roadside astrologer
(d) the use of instinct and command by birds

52. The writer evidently
(a) believes that birds are intelligent by birth
(b) suggests that birds can learn by practice
(c) negates the capacity of birds
(d) likes to experiment with pets

53. Formerly the biologists thought birds could not learn anything because
(a) they blindly follow their instinct
(b) they are only interested to eat
(c) they do not have an intricate nervous system
(d) None of the above

54. Recent studies have shown that' birds behave in a particular/peculiar way because
(a) of training and hard-work
(b) they have such unborn, qualities
(c) they listen to the command of their instinct
(d) of their instinctive or fixed behaviour and learned flexible behaviour

55. What can be the most suitable title to the passage?
(a) Birds and other pets
(b) Birds : their instinct and behaviour3
(c) How to train birds?
(d) The brain of birds:

Passage-II

In the early decades of the twentieth century, German was one of the important languages of scientific communication. A scientist did not need the knowledge of any other language to stay abreast of current developments in his/her field. But a recent survey shows that scientists are using German less and less, and are switching over to English. Even in the field of medicine, where on the whole, German till occupies a place of importance, the general trend is towards English.

Greek was the language in which medical treatises appeared. In the Middle Ages, Latin was the language of learning in the countries of Europe. In the eighteenth century, the national languages displaced Latin. In Germany, doctors began to use German. Now, in the last thirty years, there has been a further change. English has become the best, perhaps the only medium, through which communication with a wider audience is feasible.

56. What is the reason for the decline in the use of German as a language for medical writing?
(a) German's defeat in the World War II
(b) The preference of English worldwide with larger audience
(c) The first medical treatise did not appear in German
(d) English is easier than German

57. What was the language in which the first medical treatises appeared?
(a) English (b) French
(c) Greek (d) German

58. In the given context, the author recommends the use of English in medical books because
(a) English has a universal appeal and it keeps abreast of current developments
(b) English has replaced most national languages

(c) most medical journals are published in English
(d) scientists are using less and less German

59. The author suggests scientist wants to stay abreast of current developments in his/her field, he/she must
(a) read medical magazines in all languages
(b) read medical magazines only in English
(c) travel across the globe
(d) learn all national languages

60. The most suitable title to this passage is
(a) English versus German
(b) English as a, medium of communication
(c) Medical science
(d) English as the language of medical sciences

ANSWER KEY

SCRA, 2011

1. (c)	2. (a)	3. (d)	4. (c)	5. (a)
6. (b)	7. (b)	8. (b)	9. (a)	10. (a)
11. (c)	12. (c)	13. (b)	14. (b)	15. (a)
16. (d)	17. (b)	18. (c)	19. (a)	20. (b)
21. (b)	22. (a)	23. (c)	24. (c)	25. (c)
26. (d)	27. (c)	28. (d)	29. (a)	30. (c)
31. (b)	32. (a)	33. (d)	34. (a)	35. (a)
36. (c)	37. (b)	38. (a)	39. (a)	40. (a)
41. (b)	42. (d)	43. (b)	44. (b)	45. (a)
46. (b)	47. (c)	48. (a)	49. (a)	50. (b)
51. (a)	52. (b)	53. (b)	54. (b)	55. (d)
56. (b)	57. (d)	58. (c)	59. (c)	60. (d)

SCRA, 2012

1. (a)	2. (b)	3. (c)	4. (b)	5. (d)
6. (a)	7. (c)	8. (b)	9. (b)	10. (b)
11. (a)	12. (c)	13. (d)	14. (a)	15. (d)
16. (a)	17. (b)	18. (d)	19. (b)	20. (c)
21. (a)	22. (a)	23. (c)	24. (a)	25. (b)
26. (b)	27. (a)	28. (c)	29. (a)	30. (c)
31. (d)	32. (a)	33. (a)	34. (a)	35. (c)
36. (a)	37. (a)	38. (b)	39. (b)	40. (a)
41. (b)	42. (a)	43. (a)	44. (c)	45. (d)
46. (b)	47. (b)	48. (d)	49. (c)	50. (b)
51. (a)	52. (b)	53. (c)	54. (d)	55. (b)
56. (b)	57. (d)	58. (b)	59. (d)	60. (b)

FREQUENCY ANALYSIS

ABBREVIATIONS USED:

Comprehension / **Comp**, Sentence Completion / **SC**, Sentence Filler / **SF**, Cloze Test/ **CT**, Synonyms/ **Syn**, Antonyms/ **Ant**, Idioms and Phrase/ **IP**, Substitution/ **Subt**, Sentence arrangement/ **SA**, Spelling/ **SPL**, Miscellaneous/**Misc**., Total Marks/**TM**, Sentence error/**SE**, Sentence Improvement/ **SI**.

SCRA, 2011

	Comp.	SC	SF	CT	Syn	Ant	IP	Subt	SA	SE	SPL	SI	MISC.	TM
	10	10			10			10	10	10				60

SCRA, 2012

	Comp.	SC	SF	CT	Syn	Ant	IP	Subt	SA	SE	SPL	SI	MISC.	TM
	10	10			10	10			10	10				60

TREND ANALYSIS

The pattern is traditional and similar to that of CDS and All India Engineering Examination. The level is higher than that of Defenee examination. Questions have been asked in a straight forward manner. There is little tendency for innovation. Students may expect a similar pattern in coming years.

PAPER 36

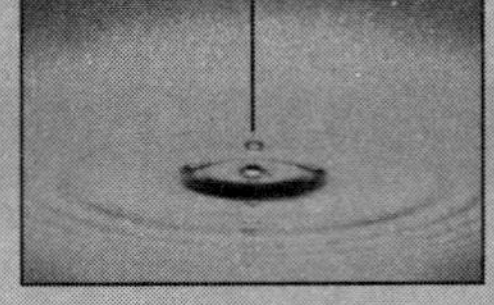

INDIAN ENGINEERING SERVICES EXAMINATION, 2010

Directions to Questions 1 to 10

In this section, you have five short passages. After each passage, you will find several questions based on the passage. First, read the passage and then answer the questions based on it. You are required to select your answers based on the contents of the passage and opinion of the author only.

Passage-I

On the day of the Christmas concert the entire orchestra entered the gymnasium where a large throng of pupils and parents were gathered. The school choir had gathered on the balcony with candles and the orchestra began "Silent Night". Slowly the lights dimmed, leaving us in darkness except for the hundred glimmering candles held by the choir as they softly sang the carol. Slowly, and just as dramatically, the orchestra began to falter—in direct proportion to the dimming of the lights, when the lights faded out completely, so did the orchestra, because no one could read his music. Except for me, for my music was in my head. From a corner of the stage, the sound of my violin filled the gymnasium. The choir and I went through verse after verse. When it was all over, the ovation was positively thunderous.

1. The narrator is
   (a) a priest
   (b) the leader of pupils
   (c) an instrumentalist
   (d) a singer

2. Why did the orchestra begin to falter?
   (a) The orchestra was not led properly.
   (b) The dimming of lights caused it.
   (c) The violin dominated the other instruments.
   (d) There was no coordination in the chorus.

3. How could the choir sing when the lights dimmed?
   (a) They had memorized the songs.
   (b) They could sing in candle light.
   (c) There was some natural light at the choir side.
   (d) The narrator helped them sing.

4. The statements that 'the ovation was positively thunderous' means that
   (a) There was a joyful expression of appreciation by people.
   (b) The audience joined the singers and sang aloud.
   (c) The audience made circles and danced in ecstasy.
   (d) The audience made a noise resembling thunder.
5. How was it possible for the narrator to continue with his music?
   (a) He was at the comer of the stage where he could get light.
   (b) His instrument did not need electric power.
   (c) He played in candle light.
   (d) He did not need to read his music.

Passage-II

Patriotism is easy enough during war. For one thing, people become actively conscious of their country when it is threatened. For another, since everyone or nearly everyone feels it, there is a strong collective emotion flowing trough the country. But when the war is over, the country recedes from the consciousness, and it is rarely even at the back of the mind. The question, "Am I doing any good to the country?" doesn't occur to the mind; and even the question, "Is what I am doing good or bad for the country?" occurs only rarely. A limited patriotism is better than none, but it is not enough.

6. The author says that one reason why patriotism is easy during war-time is that
   (a) war is the only factor responsible for arousing patriotism.
   (b) when the country is in danger, we become conscious of it.
   (c) we become patriotic when we are in a fighting mood.
   (d) patriotism is always in the consciousness.
7. Another reason suggested by the author for the emergence of patriotic feeling during war-time is that
   (a) patriotism is specially required during war-time.
   (b) we become deeply conscious of danger to ourselves during war-time.
   (c) patriotism becomes contagious because one finds a lot of other people feeling patriotism.
   (d) every one feels that he/she should strive to protect the others.
8. When the threat of war is over,
   (a) there is no need for people to be interested in others' welfare.
   (b) people do not consider it necessary to serve the country.
   (c) people tend to become totally unmindful of national interests.
   (d) people are generally anxious to serve the country.
9. When the author says that the country "recedes from the consciousness", he means to say that
   (a) people no longer feel that they belong to the country.
   (b) people do not have the country clearly in the forefront of their mind.
   (c) people are not capable of understanding what is good and desirable for them.
   (d) the moral values which they have so far upheld would disappear from their minds.
10. By a "limited patriotism", the author refers
   (a) the people's attitude of indifference to the welfare of their country
   (b) the attitude of people who love other countries as much as they love their own country
   (c) those who are self-centered and mainly concerned about their own welfare
   (d) the attitude of people who are indifferent to the welfare of their country except during war-time

Passage-III

Most people lead the lives that circumstances have thrust upon them. But Wilson had boldly taken the course of his life into his own hands. At 35, he had quit his job to lead a pleasant life on an exotic island with just enough money to last for twenty five years. Once, fifteen years after he had been on the island, I happened to meet him and enquired about his financial situation. He said, "It will carry me on till I am sixty." "But one cannot be sure of dying at sixty", I said. "Well..." he replied, "it depends on oneself, doesn't it"?

11. According to the author, most people
   (a) do not allow circumstances to affect their lives.
   (b) have fatalistic attitude towards life.
   (c) do not know how to cope with their situation.
   (d) do nothing to change the condition they live in.

12. Wilson's boldest decision was that he
   (a) quit his job.
   (b) saved a lot of money to lead a pleasant life.
   (c) preferred to live in isolation.
   (d) wanted to live without depending on others.

13. "......depends on oneself" suggests that Wilson, at 60, would
   (a) depend on his own resources.
   (b) surrender himself to destiny,
   (c) take way his own life.
   (d) carry on living in the same way.

Passage-IV

A soap opera is a kind of a sandwich, whose recipe is simple enough. Between thick slices of advertising, spread twenty minutes of dialogue, and predicament, villainy, and female suffering in equal measure, throw in a dash of nobility, sprinkle with tears, season with organ music, cover with a rich announcer sauce, and serve five times a week. It may also contain a teaser, a giveaway, a contest offer, or a cowcatcher or hitch-hike for another of the sponsor's products. It is the hope of every advertiser to habituate the housewife to an engrossing narrative whose optimum length is forever and at the same time to saturate all levels of her consciousness with the miracle of a given product, so that she will be aware of it all the days of her life and mutter its name in her sleep.

14. The second sentence of the passage contains the description of a/an
   (a) programme announcement.
   (b) recipe for sandwich.
   (c) advertisement.
   (d) melodrama.

15. Which of the following accurately describes the author's style in the passage?
   (a) Scientific and objective style.
   (b) Romantic style.
   (c) Satirical style.
   (d) Sentimental and melodramatic style:

16. According to the author, the advertisers aim at
   (a) educating and enlightening the housewives,
   (b) brainwashing the housewives.
   (c) selling their wares very cheap.
   (d) offering pure and wholesome entertainment.

Passage-V

Most of you probably did not see Mohan at close quarters. He had amazing qualities. One of these qualities was that he managed to draw out the good in another person. The other person may have had plenty of evil in him. But he somehow spotted the good and laid emphasis on the good. The result was that the poor man had to try to be good. He could not help it. He would feel ashamed when he did something wrong.

17. The author assumes that most of us
   (a) have not seen Mohan.
   (b) have not heard of Mohan.
   (c) are not well-acquainted with Mohan's powers.
   (d) have not observed Mohan's house closely.

18. One of Mohan's greatest qualities was that
   (a) he could completely destroy the evil in another man.
   (b) he could discover the good in another man.
   (c) he always maintained a good life.
   (d) he always kept away from bad men

19. The other man is called poor because
   (a) he usually came from a poor family.

(b) he was always very evil.

(c) he must try to become good and give up his evil ways.

(d) he did not know what to do and was helpless.

20. The other man tried to be good because

(a) Mohan forced him to do so.

(b) he wanted to imitate Mohan.

(c) he was ashamed of doing a wrong thing.

(d) he did not want to remain poor.

Spotting Errors

Directions to Questions 21-30

(i) In this section a number of sentences are given. The sentences are underlined in three separate parts and each one is labelled (a), (b) and (c). Read each sentence to find out whether there is an error in any underlined part. No sentence has more than one error. When you find an error in any one of the underlined parts (a), (b) or (c), indicate your response on the separate Answer Sheet at the appropriate space. You may feel that there is no error in a sentence. In that case letter (d) will signify a 'No error' response.

(ii) You are to indicate only one response for each item in your Answer Sheet. (If you indicate more than one response, your answer will be considered wrong.) Errors may be in grammar, word usage or idioms. There may be a word missing or there may be a word which should be removed.

(iii) You are not required to correct the error. You are required only to indicate your response on the Answer Sheet.

Examples 'P' aid 'Q' have been solved for you :

P. The young child (a) / singed (b) / a very sweet song (c)/. No error (d)

Q. We worked (a) / very hard (b) / throughout the season(c)/. No error (d)

Explanation : In item P, the word 'singed' is wrong. The letter under this part is (b); so (b) is the correct answer. Similarly, for item Q, (d) is the correct answer, as the sentence does not contain any error.

21. Many a student (a) / in our college (b) / are extremely fond of the new game(c)/. No error (d)

22. During India's struggle for freedom (a) / many brilliant students (b) gave up their studies (c) / by Mahatma Gandhi's call. No error (d)

23. He opposed the scheme at first (a) / but when it was fully explained (b) / he came to our views. (c)/. No error (d)

24. The world we live presents (a) / an infinite variety (b) / of experiences everyday(c)/. No error (d)

25. Any meaningful discussion of national integration (a) / must take stock about the tendencies (b) / which threaten it(c)/. No error (d)

26. The lion told the fox (a) / that he is very weak (b) / and that he had no appetite(c)/. No error (d)

27. The traveler was so hungry (a) / that he gulped all the food (b) / placed over the table(c)/. No error (d)

28. You may have to regret later (a) / if you do not start living (b) / within your mean(c)/. No error (d)

29. She was ashamed (a) / when she remembered (b) / that she did not visit her mother for a year(c)/. No error (d)

30. Tell me (a) / what all you know about it, (b) / before I take a decision in the matter(c)/. No error (d)

Ordering of Sentences

Directions to Questions 31- 40

In the following items, each passage consists of six sentences. The first sentence (S) and the final sentence (S6) are given in the beginning. The middle four sentences in each have been removed and jumbled up. These are labelled P, Q, R and S.

You are required to find out the proper sequence of the four sentences and mark accordingly on the Answer Sheet. Example 'X' has been solved for you :

X. S1 : There was a boy named Jack.

S6 : At last she turned him out of the house.

P : So the mother asked him to find work.

Q : They were very poor.

R : He lived with his mother.

S : But Jack refused to work.

The proper sequence should be :

(a) R Q P S
(b) P Q R S
(c) Q P R S
(d) R P S Q

Explanation: The correct sequence in this example is R Q P S which is marked by (a). Therefore, (a) is the correct answer.

31.

S1: What are the practical results of this modern cult of beauty?

S6: For the facts seem to contradict themselves.

P: These are questions which it is difficult to answer.

Q: The exercises and the massage, the health motors and the skin foods— to what have they led?

R: Do they get something for the enormous expenditure of energy, time, and the money demanded of them by the beauty-cult?

S: Are women more beautiful than they were?

The proper sequence should be :

(a) Q S R P (b) R Q S P
(c) P Q R S (d) S Q P R

32.

S1 : The headmaster looked at the boy more closely.

S6 : Besides, one of his feet had been hurt.

P : Although he must have been about eighteen years old, he wore a child's suit.

Q : He noticed the strange mixture of clothes that he wore.

R : His shoes were too broken and old even for a beggar.

S : It was amazingly short in the arms and legs and yet wide enough for his thin body.

The proper sequence should be :

(a) S Q P R (b) RQSP
(c) Q P S R (d) P R Q S

33.

S1 : There was a dacoit who used to rob rich people.

S6 : He robbed rich people again.

P : Once the police managed to capture him.

Q : He was sent to prison for 10 years, but he managed to escape.

R : He helped the poor and the needy from the money so obtained.

S : The court which tried him found him to be guilty.

The proper sequence should be :

(a) R P S Q (b) R S Q P
(c) R P Q S (d) P'Q S R

34.

S1 : In those days I was an even better walker than I am today.

S6 : Even a small additional weight of food bothered me and I looked for a place to eat and rest.

P : But as the day progressed, and with the warmth of the day, the rate of walking fell.

Q : I walked like the young with quick steps covering eight miles in two hours in the morning.

R : On a particular August morning I set out quite early. It was quite pleasant and cool to begin with.

S : I carried with me enough food to meet my simple needs and was therefore able to keep away from the towns.

The proper sequence should be :

(a) PQSR (b) SQRP
(c) RSQP (d) PSQR

35.

S1 : So the father gave his younger son a third part of all that he had.

S6 : He became poor and returned to the village.

P : Then he left his village and went to the town.

Q : The son sold his share of the land and the animals.

R : Soon all his money was gone.

S : He wasted his money on feasting and drinking.

The proper sequence should be :

(a) Q P S R (b) P Q R S

(c) S P Q R (d) R P Q S

36.

S1 : It was an impulsive decision.

S6 : The train was already on the platform and all the passengers were in a hurry to board the train.

P : Buying tickets, therefore, was no problem.

Q : Four of us, all room-mates in the hostel, decided to travel by train from Gwalior to Delhi and witness the Republic Day Parade.

R : Ashok pretended sickness and prevailed upon the man nearest to the window to buy four more tickets—one for him and three for his 'sisters'.

S : There was a large crowd in the station and a long queue in front of the ticket window.

The proper sequence should be :

(a) P S Q R (b) Q S R P

(c) P Q R S (d) S Q R P

37.

S1 : Abraham went to the great slave market in New Orleans.

S6 : He did not rest until he achieved his goal.

P : From that day onwards he hated the entire slave-trade.

Q : The slaves were auctioned like cattle there.

R : The sight of these miserable human beings made him very sad.

S : He resolved to do everything he could to abolish it.

The proper sequence should be :

(a) Q R P S (b) P Q R S

(c) S R Q P (d) Q P R S

38.

S1 : He was no child prodigy.

S6 : He saw the parade as a movement of people compelled to be machines.

P : When soldiers marched through Munich accompanied by drums and pipes, children enthusiastically joined in.

Q : Indeed, it was a very long time before Albert learned to speak.

R : But when little Albert passed such a parade, he began to cry and told his parents, "When grow up, I don't want to be one of those people".

S : He was always taciturn.

The proper sequence should be :

(a) Q P S R (b) R Q S P

(c) S Q P R (d) Q S P R

39.

S1 : I stopped and looked up at the building.

S6 : Help ! Save me !'

P : I thought I must have imagined the scream.

Q : There were no lights on at all in it.

R : Then I heard the voice again.

S : Everyone seemed to be asleep.

The proper sequence should be :

(a) Q S R P (b) P Q R S

(c) Q S P R (d) R S P Q

40.

S1 : The flight was delayed by a few hours.

S6 : The threat turned out to be a hoax and the plane took off a few hours behind the schedule.

P : The caller had given information about the planting of a time bomb in the plane.

Q : The empty plane was subjected to a thorough search.

R : The passengers were asked to vacate the plane.

S : The delay was caused by an anonymous phone call.

The proper sequence should be :

(a) R Q P S (b) S P R Q

(c) Q R P S (d) P Q S R

Synonyms

Directions to Questions 41-50 :

Each of the following ten items consists of a word in capital letters, followed by four words or group of words. Select the word or group of words that is most similar in meaning to the word in capital letters.

41. BEMOAN
(a) Lament
(b) Pacify
(c) Request
(d) Imagine

42. PROSAIC
(a) Dull and ordinary
(b) Slow and steady
(c) Grand
(d) Precious

43. OMINOUS
(a) Helpless
(b) Humble
(c) Restless
(d) Sinister

44. ELOQUENT
(a) Ambiguous
(b) Graceful
(c) Fluent
(d) Productive

45. FRAIL
(a) Astute
(b) Delicate
(c) Foolish
(d) Immature

46. DERELICT
(a) Derogatory
(b) Depressing
(c) Ramshackle
(d) Sluggish

47. INJUNCTION
(a) Bruise
(b) Injustice
(c) Ruling
(d) Reproach

48. IMPLORE
(a) Entreat
(b) Put into Practice
(c) Interfere
(d) Transmit

49. GROTESQUE
(a) Boring
(b) Gripping
(c) Monstrous
(d) Obnoxious

50. PERINENT
(a) Dependable
(b) Relevant
(c) Remarkable
(d) Sensible

Antonyms

Directions to Questions 51-60 :

Each of the following ten items consists of a word in capital letters, followed by four words or group of words. Select the word or group of words that is furthest in meaning to the word in capital letters.

51. PAROCHIAL
(a) Broad-minded
(b) Contradictory
(c) Paranoid
(d) Overriding

52. FICKLE
(a) Belligerent
(b) Constant

(c) Disinterested
(d) Proud

53. DISGRUNTLED
(a) Contended
(b) Detached
(c) Obedient
(d) Vigorous

54. VIBRANT
(a) Feel aggrieved at
(b) Occasional
(c) Pale
(d) Shabby

55. FORBIDDING
(a) Declaring
(b) Forcing
(c) Exposing
(d) Inviting

56. REPRIMAND
(a) Bequeath
(b) Petition
(c) Praise
(d) Scold

57. LUSH
(a) Cramped
(b) Ridiculous
(c) Rampant
(d) Sparse

58. TENTATIVE
(a) Definite
(b) Outdated
(c) Preliminary
(d) Universal

59. MARVELLOUS
(a) Awful
(b) Contentious
(c) Fictitious
(d) Malicious

60. PASSIONATE
(a) Abnormal
(b) Apathetic
(c) Oppressive
(d) Superficial

PAPER 37

Indian Engineering Services Examination, 2011

Comprehension

Directions to Questions 1-10

In this section there are three short passages. Each passage is followed by questions based on the passage Read each passage and answer the questions that follow :

Passage-I

The shy Mr. Smith was regarded as a kind of luck-bringer among the miners, who took care of him, did all he gently asked of them, built his house and spent hours of their free time assisting him. When in a sentimental mood he first wrote about miners, Smith described them as large, muscular men ; when he met them working underground and unclothed, he was struck by the slightness of their build. They were slim and tough, of the stuff from which swift footballers were made. On big holidays they dressed smartly, but the comradeship among them was such that a dressy young man did not mind being seen with one who neither wore nor owned a collar.

1. The miners regarded Smith :
  (a) with awe, as someone very powerful
  (b) with admiration, as an expert in mining
  (c) impatiently, as a bore
  (d) with superstition and affection, as a source of good fortune

2. Smith's attitude towards miners was one of :
  (a) detachment
  (b) suspicion
  (c) affection
  (d) inquisitiveness

3. Smith had formed false impression of miners :
  (a) bodily structure mining
  (b) mental ability
  (c) capacity for work
  (d) generosity

4. We learn that a miner, when well dressed :
  (a) was like a new man
  (b) was unchanged in his friendship with poor co-workers
  (c) wanted to change his employment
  (d) looked uncomfortable

Passage-2

But I did not want to shoot the elephant. I watched him beating his bunch of grass against his knees, with that preoccupied grandmotherly air that elephants have. It seemed to me that it would be murder to shoot him. I had never shot an elephant and never wanted to (Somehow it always seems worse to kill a large animal.) Besides, there was the beast's owner to be considered. But I had got to act quickly. I turned to some experienced-looking Burmans who had been there when we arrived, and asked them how the elephant had been behaving. They all said the same thing he took no notice of you if you left him alone, but he might charge if you went too close to him,

5. The author did not want to shoot the elephant because he :
   (a) was afraid of it
   (b) did not have the experience of shooting big animals
   (c) did not wish to kill an animal which was not doing anybody any harm
   (d) did not find the elephant to be ferocious

6. The phrase 'preoccupied grandmotherly air' signifies :
   (a) being totally unconcerned
   (b) pretending to be very busy
   (c) a very superior attitude
   (d) calm, dignified and affectionate disposition

7. From the passage it appears that the author was:
   (a) kind and considerate
   (b) a cruel hunter
   (c) a confused and worried man
   (d) possessed with fear

Passage-3

For nearly twenty years I taught boys, lovingly and was being loved in return. When, after twenty-eight years of political work, I returned to education, I might have confined myself to administrative side, but took part in the actual instruction. This I did because I found happiness in it. Modern conditions do not tolerate caste and its monopolies, and the high calling of the educator is open to all.

8. The author suggests that he left leaching after twenty years because :
   (a) he was dissatisfied with teaching
   (b) he wanted to become administrator
   (c) he wanted to lake part in political activities
   (d) he was busy with family and domestic affairs

9. Which of the following types of educational activities did the author take up?
   (a) Educational administration
   (b) Teaching
   (c) Advising educational institutions
   (d) All the above

10. Which one of the following phrases best helps to bring out the precise meaning of the term 'high calling of the educator'?
   (a) The noble profession of teaching
   (b) The serious advice to the teacher
   (c) The difficult work of educational administration
   (d) The high-sounding phrases used to describe a teacher

Sentence Improvement

Directions to Questions 11-20

Look at the underlined part of each sentence. Below each sentence, three possible situations for the underlined part are given. If one of them (a), (b) or (c) is better than the underlined part, indicate your response on the answer sheet against the corresponding letter (a), (b) or (c). If none of these substitutions improves the sentence, indicate (d) as your response on the Answer Sheet. Thus a "No Improvement" response will be signified by the letter (d).

11. She did not ask **any questions from him.**
   (a) any question from him
   (b) him any question
   (c) him for any questions
   (d) No improvement

12. Within a few years most of the fertile land **had underwent** forcible indigo cultivation
(a) had undergone
(b) has underwent
(c) was undergone
(d) No improvement

13. If **a person studied** a period of history, he would have wondered how things had happened at that time.
(a) a person would study
(b) a person had studied
(c) a person could have studied
(d) No improvement

14. No sooner, I saw the tiger, than I ran away.
(a) As soon as I saw
(b) No sooner I had seen
(c) No sooner did I see
(d) No improvement

15. You can almost buy anything in this store. **Can you?**
(a) Isn't it?
(b) Do you?
(c) Can't you?
(d) No improvement

16. Mohan will not be **at home** until eight O'clock.
(a) to home
(b) home
(c) in tome
(d) No improvement

17. He could not **cope up with** the heavy rush.
(a) cope with
(b) cope by
(c) cope upto
(d) No improvement

18. She did not like the movie, **nor I did**.
(a) nor did I
(b) nor I liked it
(c) nor I like it
(d) No improvement

19. Old habits **die hardly**.
(a) die hard
(b) die too hard
(c) die much hardly
(d) No improvement

20. His father wrote to him, "It is high time you **start** preparing for the forthcoming examination."
(a) had started
(b) would start
(c) started
(d) No improvement

Restructuring Passage

Directions to Questions 21-30

In the following items, each passage consists of six sentences. The first and sixth sentence are given in the beginning as S1 and S6. The middle four sentences in each have been jumbled up. These are labelled P, Q, R and S. You are requested to find out the proper sequence of the four sentences and mark accordingly on the answer sheet.

21.
S1 : Of course, it is silly to try to overcome fears that keep us from destroying ourselves.
S6 : The only fears you need to avoid are silly fears which prevent you from doing what you should do,
P : This is sensible
Q : You wait until it is out of the way before crossing
R : You need some fears to keep you from doing foolish things
S : You are afraid of an automobile coming rapidly down the street you wish to cross.

The proper sequence should be :
(a) P R S Q
(b) R S Q P
(c) R P S Q
(d) P Q R S

22.
S : Nobody likes staying at home on a public holiday — especially if the weather is fine.
S6 : It was very peaceful in the cool grass — until we heard bells ringing at the top of the hill.

P : We had brought plenty of food with us and we got it out of the car.

Q : The only difficulty was that millions of other people had the same idea.

R : Now everything was ready so we sat down near a path at the foot of a hill.

S : We moved out of the city slowly behind a long line of cars, but at last we came to a quiet country road and, after some time, stopped at a lonely farm.

The proper sequence should be :

(a) P S Q R (b) Q S P R
(c) P Q R S (d) S P Q R

23.

S1 : There were no finger prints anywhere,

S6 : These conclusions made the detectives think that it was a fake theft.

P : First of all it was impossible even for a child to enter through the hole in the roof.

Q : When the investigators tried to reconstruct the crime, it did not tally with the facts.

R : Moreover, when the detectives tried to push a silver vase, it was found to be double the size of the hole

S : Again, the size of the hole was examined by the experts who said that nothing had been passed through it.

The proper sequence should be :

(a) P Q R S (b) S Q P R
(c) P S R Q (d) Q P R S

24.

S1 : The houses in the Indus Valley were built of baked bricks.

S6 : They led outside into covered sewers which ran down the side of the streets.

P : This staircase sometimes continued upwards on to the roof.

Q : Access to the rooms upstairs was by a narrow stone staircase at the back of the house.

R : The drains were incorporated in the walls

S : The houses had bathrooms and water closets, rubbish chutes and excellent drainage systems

The proper sequence should be

(a). Q R P S (b) Q P S R
(c) S P Q R (d) P S Q R

25.

S1 : For years I looked forward to seeing the Olympic Games.

S6 : It was a great delight to watch the closing ceremony.

P : Athletics interested me most.

Q : It was only last year that my dreams came true.

R : I also liked watching swimming.

S : I flew straight to Los Angeles where the games were being held. The proper sequence should be .

(a) R S P Q (b) Q R S P
(c) Q S P R (d) S R Q P

26.

S1 : We do not know whether the machines arc the masters or we are.

S6 : And if they don't get their meals when they expect them, they will just refuse to work.

P : They must be given or rather 'fed' with coal and petrol from time to time.

Q : Already man spends most of his time looking after and waiting upon them

R : Yet he has grown so dependent on them that they have almost become the masters now.

S . It is very true that they were made for the sole purpose of being man's servants. The proper sequence should be :

(a) R S Q P (b) R S P Q
(c) S P Q R (d) S R Q P

27.

S1 : The 'age of computers' is considered to have begun in 1946.

S6 : And now it is difficult to find a field where computers are not used

P : Those early computers were huge and heavy affairs, with problems of speed and size.

Q : It was only with the introduction of electronics that the computers really came of age.

R : But computer were in use long before that.

S : They had several rotating shafts and gears which almost always doomed them to slow operation.

The proper sequence should be

(a) R P Q S (b) P R S Q

(c) R P SQ (d) P R Q S

28.

S1 : Plastic containers are being used more and more to package soft drinks, milk. Oil, fruit juices, ketchup, etc

S6 : Yet as plastics do not decompose by bacteria or naturally in the air, they are a big threat to the environment.

P : Most people think that this is the right thing to do, as it is economical.

Q : Plastic containers are cheap and light.

R : It is easier to transport materials packaged in them than in glass bottles.

S : They also involve the least transport costs.

The proper sequence should be :

(a) P Q R S (b) P Q S R

(c) Q R S P (d) Q S P R

29.

S1 : A farmer was taking the grist (corn for grinding) to the mill in sacks.

S6 : But the farmer saw that he was none other than the nobleman.

P : It was too heavy for him to lift.

Q : On the way the horse stumbled, and one of the sacks fell to the ground.

R : Presently he saw a rider coming towards him.

S : He stood waiting till he found somebody to help him.

The proper sequence should be :

(a) Q P R S (b) P R Q S

(c) P S Q R (d) Q P S R

30.

S1 : He could not rise

S6 : It was colder than usual

P : All at once, in the distance, he heard an elephant trumpet.

Q : He tried again with all his might, but to no use.

R : The next moment he was on his feet.

S : He stepped into the river.

The proper sequence should be :

(a) Q P R S (b) P Q S R

(c) Q P S R (d) P R Q S

Selecting Words

Directions to Questions 31-41

In the following passages, at certain points you are given a choice of three words in a bracket, one of which fits the meaning of the passage. Choose the best word from each bracket. Mark the letter viz., (a), (b) or (c), relating, to this word on your Answer Sheet. Examples Y and Z have been solved for you.

Y. The

(a) boy was in the school in Simla

(b) horse

(c) dog

Z. (a) She was homesick

(b) It

(c) He

Explanation : Out of the list given in item Y, only boy is the correct snifter because usually a boy and not a horse or a dog, attends school So (a) is to be marked on the Answer Sheet for item Y. A boy is usually referred to as "he", so for item Z, the letter (c) is correct answer. Notice that to solve this kind of items you have to read the preceding or succeeding sentences of the given passage.

Passage-1

31. A university stands for humanism, reason and the adventure of ideas. It stands for the onward

(a) motion of the human race

(b) march

(c) progress

32.

(a) towards higher objectives. If the universities

(b) for

(c) on

33.

(a) finish their duty adequately, then it

(b) discharge

(c) obey

34.

(a) is well with the nation and the people. But if

(b) was

(c) will be

35. the temple of learning itself becomes a home of narrow bigotry and petty objectives,

(a) how will

(b) why

(c) when the nation prosper?

Passage-2

When I got off the plane at Heathrow Airport, 1 had the first taste of English hospitality. For I

36. was immediately bounded off to a hospital. No, not because I was

(a) ill but this was to be found

(b) wicked

(c) senseless

37. by them, And truth to say, it wasn't

(a) materially a hospital, but only the sick, bay at the airport.

(b) factually

(c) actually

38. Someone at the immigration counter had taken it into his

(a) mind that I was too thin and an

(b) head

(c) judgment

39. instant X-ray should be done. Needless to say, I much

(a) respected this extra attention. I would

(b) liked

(c) resented

40. much rather have walked away like the other passengers. The X-ray

(a) took an extra half-hour of

(b) demanded

(c) extracted

41. my time. This did not

(a) excite me as much as the discovery that the famous British sense of

(b) annoy

(c) please

humour was by no means ubiquitous.

Antonyms

Directions to Questions 42-50

Each item in this section consists of a word in capital letters followed by four words. Select the word that is most opposite in meaning to the word in capital letters,

42. RUTHLESS

(a) Benevolent

(b) Obliging

(c) Merciful

(d) Affectionate

43. PROSPERITY

(a) Adversity

(b) Sickness

(c) Hardship

(d) Failure

44. ALIEN

(a) Native

(b) Stranger

(c) local

(d) Foreigner

45. FRUGAL

(a) Careless

(b) Rich

(c) Spendthrift

(d) Poor

46. ADVERSARY

(a) Acquaintance

(b) Friend

(c) Enemy

(d) Competitor

47. AFFLUENT
(a) Greedy
(b) Poor
(c) Needy
(d) filthy

48. CONCEIT
(a) Humility
(b) Pride
(c) Determination
(d) Arrogance

49. AVERSION
(a) Application
(b) Attraction
(c) Contraction
(d) Complication

50. WARY
(a) Careless
(b) Foolish
(c) Ignorant
(d) Quarrelsome

Fill in the Blanks

Directions to Questions 51-60

In this section, each of the following sentences has a blank space followed by four words. Select the word you consider most appropriate for the bank space and indicate your choice in the Answer Sheet.

51. Rainfall in the dessert is not only low but extremely__________ .
(a) interne
(b) erratic
(c) meagre
(d) undesirable

52. If mountains are __________of trees, rains will soon wash fertile topsoil down the slope to end as useless silt below.
(a) stripped
(b) deforested
(c) afforested
(d) shortage

53. China is the most ______ country in the world.
(a) popular
(b) populous
(c) populate
(d) popularized

54. The First film on gypsies was such a success that now they are going to make a _______ .
(a) serial
(b) sequence
(c) sequel
(d) sequential

55. The National Assembly of that country has ___________ this year as "gender equality year".
(a) named
(b) permitted
(c) coined
(d) declared

56. He usually ________ on time.
(a) will arrive
(b) would arrive
(c) arrives
(d) could have

57. "You must taste this new dish."
"All right, but give me just ______."
(a) a little
(b) a few
(c) less
(d) some

58. He is very___________: he believes anything,
(a) fallible
(b) gullible
(c) sensible
(d) credible

59. Pandit Nehru was a lover of nature and a _____ believer in the goodness of the people.
(a) simple
(b) good
(c) powerful
(d) staunch

60. I wish I _________ the answer.
(a) have known
(b) had known
(c) knew
(d) know

ANSWER KEY

India Engineering Services Examination, 2010

1. (c)	2. (b)	3. (b)	4. (a)	5. (d)
6. (b)	7. (b)	8. (c)	9. (b)	10. (d)
11. (d)	12. (a)	13. (c)	14. (b)	15. (d)
16. (b)	17. (a)	18. (b)	19. (c)	20. (c)
21. (c)	22. (c)	23. (d)	24. (a)	25. (b)
26. (b)	27. (c)	28. (c)	29. (c)	30. (b)
31. (b)	32. (c)	33. (a)	34. (c)	35. (b)
36. (b)	37. (a)	38. (d)	39. (c)	40. (b)
41. (a)	42. (a)	43. (d)	44. (c)	45. (b)
46. (a)	47. (c)	48. (a)	49. (d)	50. (b)
51. (a)	52. (b)	53. (a)	54. (a)	55. (a)
56. (c)	57. (d)	58. (a)	59. (a)	60. (d)

India Engineering Services Examination, 2011

1. (d)	2. (c)	3. (a)	4. (b)	5. (c)
6. (d)	7. (a)	8. (b)	9. (b)	10. (a)
11. (b)	12. (c)	13. (b)	14. (c)	15. (c)
16. (c)	17. (a)	18. (a)	19. (a)	20. (d)
21. (b)	22. (d)	23. (c)	24. (b)	25. (c)
26. (d)	27. (c)	28. (c)	29. (d)	30. (a)
31. (b)	32. (a)	33. (b)	34. (c)	35. (a)
36. (c)	37. (c)	38. (a)	39. (b)	40. (a)
41. (a)	42. (c)	43. (a)	44. (a)	45. (c)
46. (b)	47. (b)	48. (a)	49. (b)	50. (a)
51. (b)	52. (b)	53. (b)	54. (c)	55. (d)
56. (c)	57. (a)	58. (b)	59. (d)	60. (c)

FREQUENCY ANALYSIS

ABBREVIATIONS USED:

Comprehension / **Comp**, Sentence Completion / **SC**, Sentence Filler / **SF**, Cloze Test/ **CT**, Synonyms/ **Syn**, Antonyms/ **Ant**, Idioms and Phrase/ **IP**, Substitution/ **Subt**, Sentence arrangement/ **SA**, Spelling/ **SPL**, Miscellaneous/**Misc.**, Total Marks/**TM**, Sentence error/**SE**, Sentence Improvement/ **SI**.

India Engineering Services Examination, 2010

	Comp.	SC	SF	CT	Syn	Ant	IP	Subt	SA	SE	SPL	SI	MISC.	TM
	20				10	10			10	10				60

India Engineering Services Examination, 2011

	Comp.	SC	SF	CT	Syn	Ant	IP	Subt	SA	SE	SPL	SI	MISC.	TM
	10	10		11		9			10			10		60

TREND ANALYSIS

The pattern is simple and traditional. Questions on comprehension, synonyms, antonyms, sentence arrangement, spotting error have been asked. Emphasis has been given on comprehension and Vocabulary.

On the whole it is similar in 2011, but there are certain variations in sentence improvement. Cloze test has been added. The pattern is similar to the pattern of CDS examination but the level is higher than that of defence examination. The level of questions is higher than moderate but slightly lower than that of Bank PO Examination.

PAPER 38

ASSISTANT PROVIDENT FUND COMMISSIONER EXAMINATION, 2012

Directions to Questions 1 to 4

In each of these questions, you find a sentence, part of which is highlighted. You may also find only a group of words which is highlighted. For the highlighted part, four words/phrases are listed below the sentence. Choose the word/phrase nearest in meaning to the highlighted part.

1. I rather like the **quaint** little house at end of the street.
   (a) Old (b) Quiet
   (c) Unusual (d) Haunted
2. If she continues to spend her time in such a **frivolous** manner, she will fail in her examinations.
   (a) Frightful (b) Leisurely
   (c) Non-serious (d) Calculated
3. **Sanguine** as he is in his attitude to life and its problems, he cannot but be noticed wherever he goes.
   (a) Optimistic (b) Enthusiastic
   (c) Realistic (d) Dispassionate
4. One's **remonstration** against social ills has to be consistent to be fruitful.
   (a) Outrage (b) Demonstration
   (c) Protest (d) Criticism

Antonyms

Directions to Questions 5 to 7

In this section, each item consists of a word or a phrase which is highlighted in the sentence given. It is followed by four words or phrases. Select the word or phrase which is closet to the opposite in meaning of the highlighted word or phrase.

5. The advice rendered to him sounded to be quite **sagacious**.
   (a) Stupid (b) Shallow
   (c) Impracticable (d) Insincere
6. The Indian cultural fair was held at Rome in a **grandiose** manner.
   (a) Unobtrusive (b) Unimposing
   (c) Unimpressive (d) Simple

7. His voice sounded **haughty** when I spoke to him over the telephone
   (a) Pleasant (b) Humble
   (c) Soft (d) Cheerful

Comprehension

Directions to Questions 8 to 12

In this section, you have one short passage. Below the passage you will find several questions based on the passage. First, read passage to answer these questions based on it.

Passage

When you buy a car, examine carefully the important features of the model you are considering. Many a buyer of the latest models has got into trouble by buying a car too broad or too long for his garage. Furthermore, a long car is much harder to manoeuvre in traffic and much more difficult to park. Another feature is the comfort afforded. Are the seats nice and durably upholstered? Is there enough glass area to give the driver a good view in all directions, particularly to the rear? It should be remembered that the heavier and more powerful a car is, the more expensive it will be to operate. High powered motors require expensive high-octane petrol. The greater weight means greater tyre wear and enlarged brakes. The old cliche is still true; it is not initial cost but the upkeep which matters!

8. According to this passage, the two factors that the buyer of a new car should keep in mind are
   (a) Its price and size
   (b) Its model and upholstery
   (c) Its size and the comfort it offers
   (d) Its upholstery and glass area

9. The size of the car should be in accordance with
   (a) The money one can afford to pay
   (b) The size of the garage the buyer has
   (c) The width of the road where the buyer lives
   (d) The volume of traffic on the road

10. The writer favours a car with a wide glass area so that the driver can
    (a) enjoy the scene outside while driving
    (b) have a good view of the rear
    (c) roll down the glasspanes to get enough fresh air
    (d) display his beautiful upholstery with pride

11. It is very expensive to maintain a large car because it.
    (a) is heavy
    (b) requires more space for parking
    (c) needs changing its tyres more frequently
    (d) needs more durable upholstery

12. While buying a new car, one should specially consider its
    (a) price
    (b) maintenance cost
    (c) upholstery
    (d) brakes

Directions to Questions 13 to 17

Each of these questions carries a phrase/idiom. Select the correct answer out of the four given choices (a), (b), (c) or (d) which conveys the closest meaning of the given phrase/idiom

13. The world is one's oyster
    (a) One feels that nobody in the world would help him/her
    (b) The feeling one gets when he lands in an unfamiliar country
    (c) One is able to enjoy all the pleasures and opportunities that life has to offer
    (d) When one has an uphill task to perform

14. To go for the jugular
    (a) To work very hard for the success
    (b) To make a fierce destructive attack on the weakest point in an opponent's argument
    (c) To go in for the costliest thing
    (d) To go in for dishonest means

15. To follow the primrose path
    (a) To follow one's objectives very steadfastly
    (b) To go on wandering
    (c) To trek to the mountains
    (d) To go in for pursuit of pleasure or an easy life

16. A bee in one's bonnet
(a) To be very enterprising
(b) To be very timid and shy
(c) To have an impractical idea
(d) To have a particular idea which occupies one's thoughts continually

17. To take a rain-check
(a) To decline an offer but promise to accept in later
(b) To go through the weather report
(c) To proceed on sightseeing
(d) To take to farming as a source of livelihood.

Spotting Errors

Directions to Questions 18 to 22

In this section, in each of these questions, a sentence has three parts marked (a), (b), (c). Read each sentence to find out whether there is an error. If you find an error in any one of the parts (a, b, c), select that part as your answer. If a sentence has no error, then mark your answer as (d) which stands for 'No error' Errors may belong to grammer usage or idiom.

18. Choose only (a) / such friends (b) / that you can trust, (c) / No error (d)

19. While he was digging sand, (a) / a large mass fell (b) / and buried him completely, (c) / No error (d)

20. The book is well printed and attractively bound (a) / making altogether (b) / an attractive volume, (c) / No error (d)

21. A little younger (a) / to myself we, both were (b) / devoted to cricket and boating, (c) / No error (0)

22. He had no sooner (a) / arrived than (b) / he was asked a leave again, (c) / No error (d)

Directions to Questions 23 to 25

In these questions, select the most suitable word from the choices (a), (b), (c) and (d) given below each sentence to fill in the blanks.

23. The Rajputs always fought _____ last man
(a) upto
(b) till
(c) to
(d) for

24. I have been surfing internet _____ the last two hours.
(a) Since
(b) for
(c) from
(d) right from

25. You should be considerate _____ your employees and I assure you of your success in every walk of life.
(a) for (b) to
(c) upon (d) on

ANSWER KEY

1. (a)	2. (c)	3. (a)	4. (c)	5. (a)
6. (c)	7. (a)	8. (c)	9. (b)	10. (b)
11. (c)	12. (b)	13. (c)	14. (b)	15. (d)
16. (d)	17. (a)	18. (c)	19. (d)	20. (b)
21. (b)	22. (a)	23. (c)	24. (b)	25. (b)

FREQUENCY ANALYSIS

ABBREVIATIONS USED:

Comprehension / **Comp**, Sentence Completion / **SC**, Sentence Filler / **SF**, Cloze Test/ **CT**, Synonyms/ **Syn**, Antonyms/ **Ant**, Idioms and Phrase/ **IP**, Substitution/ **Subt**, Sentence arrangement/ **SA**, Spelling/ **SPL**, Miscellaneous/**Misc**., Total Marks/**TM**, Sentence error/**SE**, Sentence Improvement/ **SI**.

Assistant Provident Fund Commission Examination, 2012

	Comp.	SC	SF	CT	Syn	Ant	IP	Subt	SA	SE	SPL	SI	MISC.	TM
	5	3			4	3				5				25

TREND ANALYSIS

APFC exam English language test has undergone changes over the years. The recent trend shows that only 25 questions are given as a part of General I paper .The items set on questions are of regular type. Vocabulary, grammar and comprehension-all three basic units have been covered. Vocabulary test has been given in sentence forms. Phrases have been given in simple, direct form. The level is a bove moderate but not very difficult. A careful reading of the book and practice at the set will be of help to the students.

PAPER 39

Staff Selection Commission (SSC) Examinations Graduate Level Tier I, 2012

Directions to Questions 1 to 5

In the following questions, some parts of the sentences have errors and some are correct. Find out which part of a sentence has an error. The number of that part is the answer. If a sentence is free from error, then your answer is (d), i.e., No error.

1. The new dish (a)/ that I ordered (b)/ is tasting good. (c)/ No error. (d)

2. Increasing racism and hate crimes (a)/ casted a shadow; (b)/ over elections. (c)/ No error. (d)

3. I have got your letter yesterday (a)/ and felt happy to learn (b)/ of your recovery. (c)/ No error. (d)

4. Sam is working (a)/ in a bank in Chennai (b)/ for the past five years. (c)/ No error. (d)

5. People living in low-lying areas (a)/ find it difficult (b)/ to cope up with the floods.(c)/ No error. (d)

Directions to Questions 6 to 10

In the following questions, sentences are given with blanks to be filled with an appropriate word(s). Four alternatives are suggested for each question. Choose the correct alternative out of the four as your answer.

6. His words were hardly.... with that screaming and shouting in the market.

(a) legible (b) eligible
(c) intelligible (d) None of these

7. He was .... angry to speak to me.

(a) so (b) too
(c) that (d) such

8. I wish I.......a pen.

(a) were (b) am
(c) was (d) be

9. Look after your health ...... you should repent later on.

(a) as (b) because
(c) till (d) lest

10. Every year millions of tourists .... the Anna Centenary Library in Chennai.

(a) visiting (b) visit
(c) are visiting (d) visited.

Directions to Questions 11 to 13

In the following questions, out of the four alternatives, choose the one which best expresses the meaning of the given word.

11. repeated
(a) disputed (b) elaborated
(c) explained (d) reiterated

12. revere
(a) condemn (b) reverse
(c) humiliate (d) respect

13. erudite
(a) scholarly (b) unlettered
(c) stingy (d) sloppy

Directions to Questions 14 to 16

In the following questions, choose the word opposite in meaning to the given word

14. grating
(a) musical (b) unmusical
(c) hoarse (d) strident

15. capricious
(a) fanciful (b) reasonable
(c) intolerant (d) indifferent

16. lassitude
(a) pleasure (b) lustrous
(c) lethargy (d) enthusiasm

Directions to Questions 17 to 21

In the following questions, four alternatives are given for the Idiom/Phrase printed in bold in the sentence. Choose the alternative which best expresses the meaning of the Idiom/Phrase.

17. The issues were settled in court, but after a few days it was **back to square one.**
(a) to return to the starting point
(b) to run to the first square
(c) to start and return
(d) to come to a stop

18. Politicians enjoy **blowing their own trumpets.**
(a) to boast about their achievements
(b) to use one's own trumpet
(c) to blow their trumpet loudly
(d) to praise others trumpeting

19. Students must learn to keep their belongings **in apple pie order.**
(a) orderly preparation of apple pie
(b) in perfect order
(c) ordering for apple pie
(d) arranging apples neatly

20. Scientific knowledge is no longer **a closed book** in this 21st century.
(a) an unopened book
(b) a covered book
(c) a mystery
(d) a mysterious book

21. It takes **a month of Sundays** to chop all that wood.
(a) a short period
(b) no time
(c) a long time
(d) a special Sunday.

Directions to Questions 22 to 31

In the following questions, a sentence / part of the sentence printed in bold. Below are given alternatives to the bold sentence / part of the sentence at (a), (b) and (c) which may improve the sentence. Choose the correct alternative. In case no improvement is needed, your answer is (d).

22. He reached the village just when the sun was setting.
(a) When just the sun was setting, he reached the village.
(b) When the sun was setting he just reached the village.
(c) He just reached the village when the sun was setting.
(d) No improvement.

23. He evaded **to pay** income tax.
(a) from paying (b) against paying
(c) paying (d) No improvement

24. The gypsies **had left** the village a few days ago.
(a) have left
(b) would have left
(c) left
(d) No improvement

25. When we bought the house, we could tell that **it was a large, new, compact, tinted house**.
(a) it was a new, large and compact house
(b) It was as new, large and as tinted
(c) it was a new, large, compact and bright house
(d) No improvement

26. Migrant workers can be seen working on many of the building **places** in New Delhi.
(a) sites (b) premises
(c) locations (d) No improvement

27. "Indian English" has come of age and has been accepted as a **legitimate** category the world over.
(a) literate (b) local
(c) illegal (d) No improvement.

28. If they **were knowing** about the crabs, they would not have decided to picnic there.
(a) had known (b) knew
(c) did know (d) no improvement

29. A shrewd man could only see through the trick.
(a) Only a shrewd man could see the trick through.
(b) Only a shrewd man could see through the trick.
(c) Through the trick a shrewd man could only see.
(d) No improvement.

30. As soon as I reached my house, I opened my cupboard.
(a) I reached my house as soon as I opened my cupboard.
(b) As soon as I opened my cupboard I reached my house.
(c) No sooner had I reached my house that I opened my cupboard.
(d) No improvement.

31. Your success for hard work depends on your ability.
(a) our success depends on your ability for hard working.
(b) Your success depends on your ability of hard work.
(c) Your success depends on your ability for hard work. -
(d) No improvement.

Directions to Questions 34 to 38

In the following questions, out of the four alternatives, choose the one which can be substituted for the given words/sentence.

32. Science of human mind and behaviour
(a) Physiology (b) Psychology
(c) Sociology (d) Philology

33. A set of three related works by the same author
(a) Topology (b) Trilogy
(c) Trichology (d) Ecology

34. The study or practice of dancing or composing ballets
(a) Calligraphy (b) Cartography
(c) Choreography (d) Epigraphy

35. Having juicy or fleshy and thick tissues
(a) Succulent (b) Translucent
(c) Dissolvent (d) Dissident

36. One who accepts pleasure and pain equally
(a) Thespian (b) Sadist
(c) Stoic (d) Humanitarian

37. One who thinks or speaks too much of himself
(a) Imposter (b) Enthusiast
(c) Egotist (d) Optimist

38. An exact copy of handwriting or a picture produced by a machine
(a) Original (b) Facsimile
(c) Copy (d) None of these

Directions to Questions 39 to 40

In the following questions, four words are given in each question, out of which only one word is correctly spelt. Find the correctly spelt word.

39.

(a) campagnes (b) campaignes
(c) campaines (d) campaigns

40.

(a) rhythim (b) rhithm
(c) rhythm (d) rhithym

Directions for Questions 42 to 50

In the following questions, you have two [passages with 5 questions in each passage. Read the passages carefully and choose the best answer to each question out of the four alternatives.

Passage –I

The Great Pyramid at Giza is one of the world's most amazing landmarks. Rising high above the Sahara Desert in the Giza region of northern Egypt, the Great Pyramid stands some 450 feet into the burning desert sky and occupies of an area of 13 acres. The rough climate of the Sahara has actually caused the pyramid to shrink 30 feet from its original height. The pyramid was such an amazing feat of engineering, that it remained the tallest structure in the world for over 3,800 years ! The entire pyramid was originally faced with polished limestone to make it shine brilliantly in the sun.

Most Egyptologists, scientists who study ancient Egypt, agree that the Great Pyramid was built around 2560 BC, a little more than 4,500 years ago. It took tens of thousands of workers twenty years to build.

The pyramid contains over two million stone blocks. Although most of the blocks weigh two or three tons, some weigh up to 80 tons !

The Great Pyramid of Giza was ordered built by the Pharaoh Khufu as a magnificent tomb. His vizier (advisor) Hemon is credited with being the pyramid's architect. Khufu's pyramid is actually part of a complex of pyramids that includes the Pyramid of Khafre, the smaller Pyramid of Menkaure, a variety of smaller pyramids and structures, and the Great Sphinx. The Great Pyramid of Giza is the last remaining of the Seven Wonders of the World.

41. Which of these does not house the Great Pyramid?

(a) Giza
(b) Southern Egypt
(c) Northern Egypt
(d) Sahara Desert

42. How many stone blocks constitute the pyramid?

(a) 4,500
(b) more than two million
(c) 3,800
(d) 2,560

43. Most of the blocks in the pyramid weigh about.........tons.

(a) five
(b) eighty
(c) two or three
(d) 4,500

44. Which of the following definitions best describes the meaning of "complex" in the passage?

(a) Pyramid
(b) Materials
(c) Group
(d) Army

45. Which of the following is false?

(a) The Great Pyramid is the last of the Seven Wonders of the World.
(b) Khufu was Heinon's vizier and architect.
(c) The Pyramid took tens of thousands of workers about twenty years to complete it.
(d) Hemon was Khufu's vizier and architect.

Passage - II

One of the American Navy's greatest losses during World War II (was inflicted not by the Japanese, but by the weather. On the evening of 17 December 1944, destroyers, cruisers and aircraft carriers of the Third Fleet Task Force 38 were replenishing stocks of food, fuel and ammunition during a sea rendezvous with support ships when a savage tornado struck the Philippine Sea. One of the commanders said later; 'My ship was riding as though caught in some giant washing machine. We were rolling between heaving cliffs of water, caught in so strong a vice of wind and sea that our 50,000 horse-power engines were helpless.' It was nine hours before he regained control of his ship, after the fleet had bobbed like helpless shuttlecocks, unable to prevent collisions in the sledge hammer waves.

46. The American Navy suffered great losses because of
(a) the aircraft raid
(b) the Japanese fleet
(c) the weather
(d) the landmines

47. Find a word from the passage which means "refilling".
(a) heaving
(b) inflicting
(c) retaliating
(d) replenishing

48. A sea rendezvous means.
(a) a dive into the sea
(b) a swim in the sea
(c) a meeting at sea
(d) sailing in the sea

49. Sledge hammer waves means
(a) waves moving like a sledge.
(b) waves like a big, heavy hammer.
(c) waves hammering a sledge.
(d) waves in which a hammer and a sledge are found.

50. The ships caught in the tornado
(a) are compared to shuttlecocks
(b) had a cargo of shuttlecocks.
(c) scattered shuttlecocks in the sea
(d) traded in shuttlecocks

ANSWER KEY

1. (c) 2. (b) 3. (a) 4. (a) 5. (c)
6. (d) 7. (b) 8. (a) 9. (d) 10. (b)
11. (d) 12. (d) 13. (a) 14. (a) 15. (b)
16. (d) 17. (a) 18. (a) 19. (b) 20. (c)
21. (c) 22. (d) 23. (c) 24. (c) 25. (c)
26. (a) 27. (d) 28. (a) 29. (a) 30. (d)
31. (b) 32. (c) 33. (b) 34. (c) 35. (a)
36. (c) 37. (c) 38. (b) 39. (d) 40. (c)
41. (b) 42. (b) 43. (c) 44. (c 45. (b)
46. (c) 47. (d) 48. (d) 49. (b) 50. (a)

FREQUENCY ANALYSIS

ABBREVIATIONS USED:

Comprehension / **Comp**, Sentence Completion / **SC**, Sentence Filler / **SF**, Cloze Test/ **CT**, Synonyms/ **Syn**, Antonyms/ **Ant**, Idioms and Phrase/ **IP**, Substitution/ **Subt**, Sentence arrangement/ **SA**, Spelling/ **SPL**, Miscellaneous/**Misc.**, Total Marks/**TM**, Sentence error/**SE**, Sentence Improvement/ **SI**.

	Comp.	SC	SF	CT	Syn	Ant	IP	Subt	SA	SE	SPL	SI	MISC.	TM
	10	5			3	3	5	7		5	2	10		50

TREND ANALYSIS

Nine items have been covered, but they are regular units. They have been placed in a straight forward manner. There is little tendency for deviation or innovation. The test is comprehensive and the level is slightly above moderate. The test makes a real test of grammar, vocabulary and comprehension with proper distribution. You can expect the same pattern in coming times.

PAPER 40

SSC GRADUATE LEVEL TIER-II EXAM, 2013

Directions to Questions 1 to 20

In the flowing questions, some parts of lie sentences have errors and some are correct. Find out which part of the sentence has an error and the number of that part is your answer. If a sentence is free from errors, your answer is (d) i.e. No error.

1. The reporter (a)/ was unable (b)/ to illicit information from the police. (c)/ No error. (d)

2. Each of these boys (a)/ play (b)/ games. (c)/ No error. (d)

3. These all (a)/ mangoes (b)/ are ripe. (c)/ No error. (d)

4. The students were (a)/ awaiting-for (b)/ the arrival of the chief guest. (c)/No error. (d)

5. If you hear (a)/ engaged tone (b)/ replace the receiver and dial again. (c)/ No error. (d).

6. Henry asked his wife (a)/what had she prepared (b)/ for dinner that night. (c)/ No error. (d)

7. The news (a)/ I have received (b)/ is not good. (c)/ No error. (d)

8. Who (a)/ arranged (b)/ the chairs. (c)/No error. (d)

9. People who live on (a)/ glass houses (b)/ should not throw stones. (c)/ No error. (d)

10. The library members were asked (a)/ to return back the books (b)/ to the library. (c)/ No error. (d)

11. Raghu came out of the bathroom (a)/with a towel (b)/ in the hand. (c)/No error. (d)

12. Neither the girl nor her parents (a)/ was present (b) to receive the award. (c)/ No error. (d)

13. College girls seldom wear (a)/ sarees these days, (b)/ do they? (c)/No error. (d)

14. Scarcely had (a)/the function started (b)/than it began to rain. (c) /No error. (d)

15. My friend (a)/has invited me (b)/for tea this Sunday. (c)/ No error. (d)

16. He discussed (a)/ the murder case (b)/with his juniors. (c)/ No error. (d)

17. The paintings of natural sceneries (I)/ are selling (b)/ like hot cakes. (c)/No error. (d)

18. I (a)/ go to school (b)/ by walk. (c)/ No error. (d)

19. It is a (a)/ desert (b)/ place. (c)/ No error. (d)

20. You shall get (a)/ all the informations (b)/ if you read this book carefully. (c)/ No

Directions to Questions 21 to 25

In the following questions, sentences are given with blanks to be filled in with an appropriate word(s). Four alternatives are suggested for each question. Choose the correct alternative out of the four.

21. Students of St. Xavier's____ all the prizes.
(a) bear of
(b) bore away
(c) bore on
(d) bear on

22. With danger____ the door, you cannot sit idle.
(a) at
(b) in
(c) of
(d) near

23. My servant ___ with all my money.
(a) have escaped
(b) was run away
(c) has run off
(d) running away

24. The driver was___ injured; he died within an hour.
(a) significantly
(b) fatally
(c) fatefully
(d) vitally

25. Lata Mangeshkar was____ with a natural talent for music.
(a) given
(b) found
(c) endowed
(d) entrusted

Directions for Questions 26 to 28

In the following questions, out of the four alternatives, choose the one which best expresses the meaning of the given word.

26. Logical
(a) Responsive
(b) Rational
(c) Educated
(d) Improper

27. Delusion
(a) Illumination
(b) Ilusion
(c) Ascension
(d) Reality

28. Mastery
(a) Mystery
(b) Weighty
(c) Authority
(d) Weakness

Directions to Questions 29 to 31

In the following questions, Choose the word opposite in meaning to the given word.

29. Persuade
(a) Promote
(b) Pervade
(c) Dissolve
(d) Dissuade

30. Outrageous
(a) Justifiable
(b) Lusty
(c) Jolly
(d) Wicked

31. Efficacious
(a) Productive
(b) Ineffective
(c) Improper
(d) Urgent

Directions to Questions 32 to 34

In the following questions, four words are given in each question, out of which only one word is correctly/wrongly spelt, Find the correctly/ wrongly spelt word.

32.
(a) Prestige
(b) Precipitate
(c) Prerequisite
(d) Premaises

33.
(a) Unnecessary
(b) Unscruplous
(c) Unparalleled
(d) Unprecedented

34.
(a) Endeavour
(b) Endaeypur
(c) Endevour
(d) Endeavore

Directions to Questions 35 to 44

In the following questions, four alternatives are given for the Idiom/Phrase printed in bold in the sentence. Choose the alternative which best expresses the meaning of the Idiom/Phrase.

35. He **broke down** when he heard the news of his son's death.
(a) resigned his job
(b) ceased to smile
(c) stopped working
(d) wept bitterly

36. "Don't try to **throw dust into my eye.** You will not succeed."
(a) You should not try to blind me with dust.
(b) I know how to protect my eyes.
(c) I will not let you blind me with dust
(d) "Don't try to mislead or confuse me."

37. **A man of straw**
(a) A man of no substance
(b) A very active person
(c) A worthy fellow
(d) An unreasonable person

38. We visit the shopping mall **off and on.**
(a) up and about
(b) often
(c) really and truly
(d) once upon a time

39. Life is an event of **give and take.**
(a) adjustment
(b) make believe
(c) always
(d) giving

40. Don't mix with the **bad hats.**
(a) people with bad hats
(b) people of bad character
(c) people selling bad hats
(d) people of poor status

41. The personality development class started with an **ice breaking** session.
(a) having breakfast
(b) starting conversation
(c) introducing chief guest
(d) making speeches

42. He **chickened out** when he confronted opposition.
(a) ate chicken
(b) released chicken
(c) hatched eggs
(d) withdrew

43. Try to **make do** with what you have.
(a) create
(b) do
(c) produce
(d) manage

44. The scientist worked for **donkey's years** to arrive at the formula.
(a) a long time
(b) a short time
(c) for donkeys
(d) for few years

Directions to Questions 45 to 64

In the Following questions, the 1st and the (last sentences are numbered 1 and 6. The rest of the sentence/passage is split into four parts and named P, Q, R and S. These four sentences/

parts are not given in their proper order. Read the sentence/passage and find out which of the four combinations is correct. Then find the correct answer.

45.

1. Many people advised me against opting for English.
P. The reason is I love the subject.
Q. Similarly I chose Political Science.
R. I decided to opt for it.
S. I find Political Science extremely interesting.
6. It was a subject in my graduation as well.

(a) PQRS (b) RPSQ
(c) RPQS (d) SRPQ

46.

1. The availability of electric power
P. would make a tremendous difference
Q. to be improved
R. to the countryside
S. and enable rural economy
6. in various directions.

(a) PRSQ (b) RQSP
(c) QRPS (d) RSQP

47.

1. Most of the diamonds found
P. are high enough to allow
Q. where the pressure and temperature
R. on Earth were formed below
S. the Earth's crust in the upper mantle
6. diamonds to crystallize.

(a) PSRQ (b) SRQP
(c) RSQP (d) RPSQ

48.

1. Computers and mobile phones
P. grammar and reducing
Q. are turning us into
R. lazy writers
S. ruining our spelling and
6. our attention span.

(a) QRSP (b) SPQR
(c) QSPR (d) SRPQ

49.

1. Greed is regarded as
P. possible ruinous and
Q. because it has
R. destructive effects
S. immoral behaviour
6. on the other people.

(a) RQPS (b) SPRQ
(c) SQPR (d) SQRP

50.

1. It is true
P. born to be happy but
Q. we are born
R. that we are not
S. to seek happiness
6. seizing every opportunity.

(a) RPQS (b) QSRP
(c) RSQP (d) PSQR

51.

1. Indiscriminate industrialization resulted
P. as the rural
Q. in cities in search R. in urban migration
S. poor settled
6. of opportunities.

(a) PQRS (b) SRQP
(c) RPSQ (d) PSQR

52.

1. There are some stores
P. that make it easy
Q. who have
R. with reasonable goods
S. for people
6. a limited budget.

(a) PQRS (b) SPQR
(b) RPSQ (d) QPSR

53.

1. The transition from
P. school to college
Q. meet it
R. so one must
S. is demanding
6. without expectations.

(a) SQRP (b) PSRQ
(c) PRQS (d) RQPS

54.

1. The Railways have launched
P. where one can find
Q. on a Google map
R. an online application
S. the exact location of 6, 500 trains
6. on a real time basis.

(a) QRSP (b) QRPS
(c) RPSQ (d) SQPR

55.

1. A man is born alone.
P. good and bad
Q. he experiences the
R. and dies alone, and
S. consequences of
6. his actions alone.

(a) RQSP (b) RQPS
(c) QSPR (d) PQRS

56.

1. In, the first years of his reign, Asoka was an autocrat.
P. The effect over the slaughter on his mind was profound.
Q. He .was successful but thousands were slain in the battle.
R. About the ninth year he decided to conquer Kalinga.
S. This caused a sudden change of his heart.
6. He joined the Buddhist community and became a monk.

(a) RPQS (b) RSPQ
(c) RQSP (d) RQPS

57.

1. Vegetarianism promotes a natural way of life.
P. A vegetarian's life-style is natural and healthy.
Q. Despite its message of universal love and nonviolence, it has not spread.
R. It is best cultivated in the mind.
S. This maybe because it is an inward looking habit.
6. Food and health are closely related.

(a) QSRP (b) PQRS
(c) QRSP (d) PRSQ

58.

1. Optimism is not a deep, complicated philosophy
P. In some persons it is an inborn trait.
Q. In fact, it is always taking a positive and bright view of life.
R. It is more of a genera attitude of life.
S. They are tuned that way by nature and temperament.
6. However in most Cases it is an acquired and natured habit.

(a) RQPS (b) QRPS
(c) PSRQ (d) PSQR.

59.

1. Our life is full of ups and downs.
P. They too had problems in their lives.
Q. When we face failures we are often disheartened.
R. They fought against all odds and achieved success.
S. The lives of great men inspire us.
6. By following them we can overcome crises.

(a) SQPR (b) PSQR
(c) SPRQ (d) QSPR

60.

1. We should plan out leisure carefully.
P. The activity we choose should make us happy.
Q. We should choose some interesting and useful activity.
R. It should increase our confidence.
S. We should then work at it during our leisure.
6. That is the way to be healthy, wealthy and happy.

(a) PRQS (b) QSPR
(c) QRPS (d) QPSR

61.

1. The majority of children world-wide who are out of schools are girls.
P. She marries much1 later in life and has fewer children.
Q. A working woman spends 90% of her income on the family.
R. An educated woman acquires self-respect and confidence.
S. Child mortality drops and fewer cases of mothers die in child-birth.
6. So when you educate a woman the benefits cascade across the society.

(a) PSQR (b) RPSQ
(c) QRPS (d) QPRS

62.

1. Architecture began
P. to build their own shelters
Q. on ready-made ones
R. when early people started
S. rather than relying
6. such as trees and caves.

(a) RPSQ (b) PRQS
(c) RQPS (d) PSQR

63.

1. People are like potatoes.
P. It is only after potatoes have been sorted and bagged that they are loaded onto trucks.
Q. After potatoes have been harvested, they have to be spread out and sorted in order to get the maximum market dollar.
R. This is the method that all Idaho potato farmers use-all but one.
S. They are divided according to size big, medium and small.
6. One farmer never bothered to sort the potatoes.

(a) PQRS (b) QSPR
(c) PRQS (d) QSRP

64.

1. Rani Padmini was a Rajput Queen.
P. Allaudin Khilji invaded India and reached the gates of Chittor, the capital city of the Rajputs.
Q. But, the Rajputs under Rani Padmini fought like tigers.
R. Khilji attacked Chittor again, and rushed into the fort, only to be stunned.
S. Khilji desired to capture Chittor and its beautiful Queen, Rani Padmini.
6. The Rani and the other women had burnt themselves alive.

(a) PQSR (b) PSQR
(c) SQRP (d) SRQP

Directions to Questions 65 to 76

In the following questions, out of the four alternatives choose the one which can be substituted for the given words/sentence.

65. A pole or beam used as a temporary support
(a) Scaffold
(b) Prop
(c) Lean-to
(d) Rafter

66. One who studies the art of gardening ;
(a) Agriculturist
(b) Horticulturist
(c) Gardener
(d) Botanist

67. A remedy for all diseases
(a) Cough syrup
(b) Panacea
(c) Medicine
(d) Inhaler

68. Fear of closed spaces
(a) Claustrophobia
(b) Aquaphobia
(c) Botanophobia
(d) Kleptomania

69. Words written on the tomb a dead person
(a) Epigraph
(b) Epilogue

(c) Epitaph

(d) Etymology

70. A handwriting that cannot be read

(a) Illegible

(b) Inedible

(c) Illegal

(d) Illicit

71. The line when the land and sky seems to meet

(a) Atmosphere

(b) Milky Way

(c) Horizon

(d) Distant land

72. A list of passengers and luggage

(a) Waybill

(b) Wagon

(c) Wirepuller

(d) Whist

73. A person difficult to please

(a) Fastidious

(b) Callous

(c) Sadist

(d) Ferocious

74. A decorative handwriting

(a) Calligraphy

(b) Manuscript

(c) Inscription

(d) Hagiography

75. That which cannot be defeated

(a) Invincible

(b) Invulnerable

(c) Infallible

(d) Indictable

76. Study of the nature of God

(a) Philology

(b) Theology

(c) Humanism

(d) Philosophy

Directions to Questions 77 to 96

In the following questions, a sentence has been given in Active/Passive Voice. Out of the four alternatives suggested, select the one which best expresses the same sentence in Passive/Active Voice.

77. Robin would draw a picture in the competition.

(a) In the competition Robin would have to draw a picture.

(b) A picture in the competition would have been drawn by Robin.

(c) In the competition Robin would be drawn a picture.

(d) A picture would be drawn by Robin in the competition.

78. Who gave you ice-cream?

(a) Who has given you ice cream?

(b) By whom were you given ice-cream?

(c) By whom was you given ice-cream?

(d) Who had given you ice cream?

79. Are you not revising your lessons?

(a) Are your lessons not be revised by you?

(b) Are your lessons not being revised by you?

(c) Are not your lessons revised by you?

(d) Are you not being revising your lessons?.

80. We should not encourage indiscipline.

(a) Indiscipline should have not encouraged by us.

(b) Indiscipline should not be encouraged by us.

(c) Indiscipline should not being encouraged.

(d) Indiscipline should not been encouraged.

81. Our Almighty will bless wise men.

(a) Wise men will be blessed by our Almighty.

(b) Wise men should be blessed by our Almighty.

(c) Wise men have been blessed by our Almighty.

(d) Wise men would be blessed by our Almighty.

82. The Army chief punished his subordinate.

(a) His subordinate is punished by the Army chief.

(b) His subordinate is being punished by the Army chief.

(c) His subordinate was punished by the Army chief.
(d) His subordinate was being punished by the Army chief.

83. One must keep one's promises,
(a) One's promises are kept.
(b) One's promises must be kept.
(c) One's promises were kept.
(d) One's promises must kept.

84. They have cut all the telephone wires.
(a) All the telephone wires will be cut.
(b) All the telephone wires had been cut.
(c) All the telephone wires have been cut.
(d) All the telephone wires shall be cut.

85. I shall write a letter.
(a) A letter is written by me,
(b) A letter will be written by me.
(c) A letter has written tome.
(d) A letter has been written by me.

86. Will Motin be helped by us?
(a) Will Motin help us?
(b) Shall we help Motin?
(c) Shall Motin be helped?
(d) We shall helped Motin?.

87. A letter has been written by me.
(a) I have been writing a letter.
(b) I has written a letter.
(c) I had written a letter.
(d) I have written a letter.

88. I cannot draw this picture.
(a) This picture cannot be drawn by me.
(b) This picture cannot be drawn by I.
(c) This picture could not be drawn by me.
(d) This picture could not be drawn by I.

89. The men had constructed the bridge.
(a) The bridge has been constructed by the men.
(b) The bridge was constructed by the men.
(c) The bridge was being constructed by the men.
(d) The bridge had been constructed by the men.

90. Do not inform the police about the robbery.
(a) The police do not be informed about the robbery.
(b) Let not the police be informed about the robbery.
(c) Let the police be informed about the robbery.
(d) The police need to be informed by the robbery.

91. They have spotted me in the crowd.
(a) I am spotted by them in the crowd.
(b) I will have been spotted by them in the crowd,
(c) I would have been spotted by them in the crowd.
(d) I have been spotted by them in the crowd.

92. He made us work.
(a) We were made to work by him.
(b) We would work by him.
(c) We might work by him.
(d) We have to work by him.

93. Leo Tolstoy wrote 'War and Peace'.
(a) 'War and Peace' was written by Leo Tolstoy.
(b) 'War and Peace' is written by Leo Tolstoy.
(c) 'War and Peace' will be written by Leo Tolstoy.
(d) 'War and Peace' was being written by Leo Tolstoy.

94. Rita rescued three puppies.
(a) Three puppies are rescued by Rita.
(b) Three puppies were rescued by Rita.
(c) Three puppies will be rescued by Rita.
(d) Three puppies are being rescued by Rita.

95. Will he have written a letter?
(a) Will a letter have written by him?
(b) Will a letter be written by him?
(c) Will a letter to be written by him?
(d) Will a letter have been written by him?

96. The doctor advised me to give up sweets.
(a) To me give up sweets was advised by doctor.
(b) The doctor advised to give up sweets me.

(c) I was advised by the doctor to give up sweets.

(d) I was advised to give up eat; sweets by the doctor.

Directions to Questions 97 to 118

In the following questions, a sentence/a part of the sentence is printed in **bold**. Below are given alternatives to the bold part at (a), (b), (c) which may improve the sentence. Choose the correct alternative. In case no improvement is needed, your answer is (d).

97. One of my neighbours will sell his house who is going abroad.

(a) One of my neighbours will who is going abroad sell his house.

(b) One who is going abroad of my neighbours will sell his house.

(c) One of my neighbours who is going abroad will sell his house.

(d) No Improvement

98. There are many species of parakeets in India, the **recognizable** being the Rose-ringed parakeet.

(a) more recognizable

(b) more recognized

(c) most recognizable

(d) No improvement

99. You cannot pass **as long** as you study.

(a) provided

(b) unless

(c) less

(d) No improvement

100. They sat by the river bank with their legs **remaining** in the water.

(a) swimming

(b) dangling

(c) washing

(d) No improvement

101. A buffalo cannot defend a buffalo against lion.

(a) A buffalo cannot defend another buffalo against a lion.

(b) Buffalo cannot defend buffalo against lions.

(c) Buffalo car not defend a buffalo against lion.

(d) No improvement

102. I sat down on the bench to look at the trophy I won as a prize.

(a) I sat down on the bench to look at the trophy I had won as a prize.

(b) I sat down on the bench to look at the trophy I have won as a prize.

(c) I sat down on the bench to look at the trophy I had to win as a prize.

(d) No improvement

103. If the room had been brighter, Shweta would have been able to read for a while before bedtime.

(a) If the room was brighter, Shweta would have been able to read for a while before bedtime.

(b) If the room been brighter, Shweta would have been able to read for a while before bedtime.

(c) Had the room been brighter, Shweta would have been able to read for a while before bedtime.

(d) No improvement

104. I like **tea and I like coffee.**

(a) tea to coffee

(b) tea after coffee

(c) both tea and coffee

(d) No improvement

105. They are **bringing down** the old bridge to build a new one.

(a) destroying

(b) damaging

(c) demolishing

(d) No improvement

106. Maggie took a hot bath because she **was** working in the garden all afternoon.

(a) is

(b) has

(c) had been

(d) No improvement

107. The country faced a rainfall deficit of eight per cent **after the** four month long southwest monsoon.
(a) during the
(b) at the end of the
(c) for the
(d) No improvement

108. Children with disabilities and special needs also have the right to education **just like** normal children.
(a) just as normal children do
(b) even as normal children are doing
(c) along with normal children
(d) No improvement

109. He was **too glad** to, see his friend.
(a) very glad
(b) so glad
(c) to glad
(d) No improvement

110. All his efforts to find his lost child were in **vane.**
(a) vein
(b) wane
(c) vain
(d) No improvement

111. He is so intelligent that he **could** win the quiz competition.
(a) will
(b) can
(c) should
(d) No improvement

112. The demonstration passed away peacefully.
(a) passed out
(b) passed
(c) passed on
(d) No improvement

113. They have not spoken to each other **since** they quarrelled.
(a) for
(b) because
(c) ever since
(d) No improvement

114. I walked back home after the movie **yesterday night.**
(a) last night
(b) previous night
(c) that night
(d) No improvement

115. Last evening I went to the optician and bought **spectacles.**
(a) a spectacle
(b) two spectacles
(c) a pair of spectacles
(d) No improvement

116. He came **despite** of his busy schedule.
(a) nevertheless
(b) but for
(c) in spite of
(d) No improvement

117. The receptionist asked the patient, "Who **recommended** you to Dr. Paulson.
(a) introduced
(b) referred
(c) alluded
(d) No improvement

118. **Seeing that she is very tired,** I walked out of the room and let her sleep.
(a) Seeing that she are very tired
(b) Seeing that she was very tired
(c) Seeing she is tired
(d) No improvement

Directions to Questions 119 to 145

In the following questions, a sentence has been given in Direct/Indirect. Out of the four alternatives suggested, select the one which best expresses the same sentence in Indirect / Direct.

119. Naren said, "Why are you still waiting here, Binod?"
(a) Naren asked Binod why he was still waiting there.
(b) Naren asked Binod that why he was still waiting there.

(c) Naren asked Binod why he is still waiting there.

(d) Naren asked Binod that why you were still waiting there.

120. "Jack fell as he'd have wished," the mother said

(a) The mother said that Jack had fallen as he would have wished.

(b) The mother said that Jack fell as he had wished.

(c) The mother said that Jack has fallen as he has wished.

(d) The mother said that Jack had been fallen as he would haye been washed.

121. "Can you see a woman seated on the bench in a park?" —

Alice asked her.

(a) Alice asked her if she can see a woman seated oh the bench in a park.

(b) Alice told her if she could see a woman seated on the bench in a park.

(c) Alice asked her if she could see a woman seated on the bench in a park.

(d) Alice asked her if she could have seen a woman seated on the bench in a park.

122. The king said, "My force will protect the kingdom."

(a) The king said that his force would protect the kingdom.

(b) The king said that the king's force will protect the kingdom.

(c) The king ordered that our force should protect the kingdom. .

(d) The king commanded that his force will be protected the kingdom.

123. The student said, "Let me come in."

(a) The student told that let he be allowed to come in.

(b) The student said that if he is allowed to come in.

(c) The student requested to let him come in.

(d) The student requested that he might be allowed to come in.

124. He said, "Babies, drink milk."

(a) He said that babies drink milk.

(b) He told that babies should drink milk.

(c) He advised the babies to drink milk.

(d) He said that babies drank milk.

125. I said, "I came here yesterday,"

(a) I said that I came here that day.

(b) I said that go here yesterday.

(c) I said that I had come there the previous day.

(d) I say that I went there the previous day.

126. He said, 'The government is writing letters,"

(a) He said that the government is writing letters.

(b) He said that the government was writing letters.

(c) He said that the government will write letters.

(d) He said that the government wrote letters.

127. He said, "I have passed the examination."

(a) He said that he had passed the examination.

(b) He announced that he has passed the examination.

(c) He said that he had to pass the examination

(d) He said that he has passed the examination

128. The doctor says, "It is better you undergo a surgery next week."

(a) The doctor advised me to undergo a surgery the following week,

(b) The doctor says that it is better I undergo a surgery the following week.

(c) The doctor says that it was better I underwent a surgery the coming week,

(d) The doctor advises that it is better I underwent a surgery the following week.

129. The teacher asked the student when he would submit his assignment.

(a) The teacher said to the student, "When will you submit your assignment?"

(b) The teacher asked the student, "When will you submit his assignment?"

(c) The teacher asked the student, "When would you submit his assignment?"

(d) The teacher asked the student, "When would he submit his assignment?"

130. The Principal asked me whether I had informed the Chief Guest the revised schedule the day before.

(a) The Principal said to me, "Did I inform the Chief Guest the revised schedule the day before?"

(b) The Principal said to me, "Have I informed the Chief Guest the revised schedule the day before?"

(c) The Principal said to me, "Have you informed the Chief Guest the revised schedule yesterday?"

(d) The Principal said to me, "Did you inform the Chief Guest the revised schedule yesterday?"

131. "Don't play on the grass, boys," she said.

(a) She ordered the boys "Don't play on the grass."

(b) She said to the boys that they should not play on the grass.

(c) She told the boys that they should not be playing on the grass.

(d) She told the boys not to play on the grass.

132. "What a terrible storm it is !" he said.

(a) He exclaimed that it was a terrible storm.

(b) He exclaimed that it has been a terrible storm.

(c) He exclaimed that it will be a terrible storm.

(d) He exclaimed that it is a terrible storm,

133. The traveller said, "What a beautiful sight!"

(a) The traveller exclaimed that it was an beautiful sight.

(b) The traveller exclaimed that it was a beautiful sight.

(c) The traveller said that it was beautiful.

(d) The traveller remarked the beautiful sight.

134. The Chief Guest said, "It gives me great pleasure to be here this morning."

(a) The Chief Guest said that that gave me great pleasure to be there that morning.

(b) The Chief Guest said that it gave him great pleasure to be there that morning.

(c) The Chief Guest said that it gives him great pleasure to be here that morning.

(d) The Chief Guest said that it gives him great pleasure to be there that morning.

135. He said, "What a lovely voice she has !"

(a) He exclaimed that she had a very lovely voice.

(b) He exclaimed that she has a very lovely voice.

(c) He exclaimed that she did not have a lovely voice.

(d) He exclaimed that she does not have a lovely voice.

136. He said to me, "Where is the post office?"

(a) He asked me that where the post office was.

(b) He asked me where was the post office.

(c) He wanted to know where the post office was.

(d) He asked me where the post office was.

137. My father said, "Honesty is the best policy."

(a) My father stated that honesty was the best policy.

(b) My father said that honesty is the best policy.

(c) My father said that honesty was the best policy.

(d) My father said that honesty has been the best policy.

138. She yelled, "Please help me."

(a) She yelled at one for some help.

(b) She yelled for someone to help.

(c) She yelled for someone to help her.

(d) She yelled at someone to help her."

139. He asked me why I was late.

(a) He asked me, "Why are you late?"

(b) He asked me, "Why I was late?"

(c) He asked me, "Why you are late?"

(d) He asked me, "Why am I late?"

140. He said that I needn't wait there.

(a) He said, "You needn't wait here."

(b) He said, "I needn't wait there."

(c) He said, "You needn't wait there."

(d) He said, "I needn't wait here."

141. I said to the worker, "How do you like your job?"

(a) I told the worker how he liked his job.

(b) I asked the worker how you like your job.

(c) I asked the worker how he liked his job.

(d) I asked the worker how you liked his job.

142. "I don't know why they haven't signed the papers and accepted the gift," said Crene to me.

(a) Crene told me that he didn't know why they hadn't signed the papers and accepted the gift.

(b) Crene told me that he don't know why they haven't signed the papers and accepted the gift.

(c) Crene told me that 1 don't know why they haven't signed the papers and accepted the gift.

(d) Crene said to me that he didn't know why they hadn't signed the papers and accepted the gift.

143. She said, "I must have a computer to prepare a powerpoint presentation."

(a) She said she had to have a computer to prepare a powerpoint presentation.

(b) She said she should have a computer to prepare a powerpoint presentation.

(c) She said she would have a computer to prepare a powerpoint presentation.

(d) She said she could have a computer to prepare a powerpoint presentation.

144. "Don't hesitate to clear your doubts," the teacher said.

(a) The teacher warned me not to hesitate in clearing my doubts.

(b) The teacher ordered me not to hesitate in clearing my doubts.

(c) The teacher persuaded me not to hesitate in clearing my doubts.

(d) The teacher requested me not to hesitate in clearing ray doubts.

145. He said, "I am glad to be here this evening."

(a) He said that he was glad to be there that evening.

(b) He said he was glad to be here this evening.

(c) He says he was glad to be here this evening.

(d) He asked he is glad to be here this evening.

Directions to Questions146 to 170

In the following passages some of the words have been left out. Read the passages carefully and choose the correct answer to each question out of the four alternatives and fill in the blanks.

Passage-1

The presence of certain **(146)** makes friendship a special **(147)**. A **(148)** friend is consistent and honest. A **(149)** is not **(150)** to give an honest **(151)** and does not say things for the sake of getting **(152)**. A friend provides companionship and continuous **(153)**. There is no room for pride, **(154)** or rivalry in **(155)**.

146.

(a) qualities

(b) qualify

(c) frequencies

(d) degrees

147.

(a) hardship

(b) courtship

(c) scholarship

(d) relationship

148.

(a) true

(b) truth

(c) truthful

(d) truly

149.

(a) befriend

(b) friendship

(c) friend

(d) friendly

150.
(a) fear
(b) afraid
(c) fright
(d) fret

151.
(a) opinion
(b) concern
(c) dominion
(d) suggestion

152.
(a) approval
(b) approve
(c) appear
(d) disapproval

153.
(a) support
(b) supportive
(c) suppress
(d) provide

154.
(a) jeopardize
(b) jealousy
(c) humility
(d) open-mindedness

155.
(a) friendship
(b) friendly
(c) befriend
(d) courtship

Passage-II

(Q. Nos. 156 to 165)

Whenever I **(156)** at the moon, my heart **(157)** with pleasure. I wish I had **(158)** to fly up to the moon, I know if I could **(159)** to become an **(160),** I would be able to go to the moon. Special equipment and a **(161)** training are required to go to the moon. I would have to wear a special **(162)** along with a gas-mask for **(163)**. My space shuttle would be equipped with **(164)** cameras and other scientific **(165)**.

156.
(a) looked
(b) saw
(c) viewed
(d) gaze

157.
(a) fills
(b) filled
(c) field
(d) feels

158.
(a) hands
(b) wings
(c) legs
(d) feelers

159.
(a) grow up
(b) mow
(c) blow
(d) show

160.
(a) astrology
(b) astronomy
(c) astronaut
(d) aristocrat

161.
(a) special
(b) ordinary
(c) common
(d) natural

162.
(a) trousers
(b) spacecraft
(c) space-suit
(d) space formula

163.
(a) breadth
(b) breathing
(c) bathing
(d) breathe

164.
(a) sensitive
(b) touchy

(c) primitive
(d) decorative

165.

(a) accessory
(b) things
(c) intuition
(d) gadgets

Passage - III

(Q. Nos. 166 to 170)

Tennis is a game that gives one plenty of exercise; it develops **(166)** of eye and limb and **(167)** the brain too into **(168)**. A few sets of tennis keep one physically and **(169)** fit. But for the indoors, chess is the queen of games. People say chess is a **(170)** game because only two can play.

166.

(a) movement
(b) swiftness
(c) quickness
(d) agility.

167.

(a) commands
(b) asks
(c) signals
(d) calls

168.

(a) response
(b) play
(c) work
(d) action

169.

(a) intellectually
(b) emotionally
(c) mentally
(d) logically

170.

(a) selfish
(b) mean
(c) carefree
(d) careless

Directions to Questions 171 to 200

In the following questions, you have four passages with 5/10 questions in leach passage. Read the passages carefully and choose the best answer to each question, out of the four alternatives.

Passage-I

(Q. Nos. 171 to 175)

Many of the serious health concerns in modern America can be linked to poor diet. People who regularly consume foods high in sodium, sugar and saturated fats not only increase their chances of obesity, but also increase their risks of developing heart diseases, hypertension, diabetes and several types of cancer. Although some people, who regularly consume unhealthy foods do so knowingly, there is also a significant portion of the population that remains under-educated about proper nutrition. What is more, individuals who live in food deserts — areas in low-income neighbourhoods that lack easy access to healthy, affordable food — may not even have the opportunity to obtain nutritious food. Food deserts are located in high-poverty areas, such as sparsely populated rural areas or densely populated, low-income urban centres. Food deserts most often develop when major supermarket chains either relocate out of these areas or simply refrain from building stores there. Major food retailing chains tend to limit their store locations to wealthier urban or suburban neighbourhoods. This means that those who live in high-poverty areas often also live miles away from fresh meats, dairy products and produce available at supermarkets. Furthermore, fast food restaurants are disproportionately concentrated in low-income areas.

171. The best possible title for the passage is
(a) Supermarket's Contribution to Obesity in America
(b) The Dangers of Fast Food
(c) Food Deserts : The Problem of Poor Diet
(d) Why Processed Food Kills

172. Serious health concerns in modern America are related to
(a) smoking
(b) fast life

(c) poor diet
(d) loneliness

173. Food deserts are
(a) areas having large supermarket chains
(b) low-income areas without access to healthy foods
(c) areas having large-scale plantations
(d) areas not having large number of restaurants

174. Food-deserts are formed when
(a) major supermarket chains are unavailable in some areas
(b) people do not like eating fresh food
(c) people relocate to new areas
(d) most remain under-educated about nutritious food

175. People belonging to low-income group mostly resort to
(a) fresh milk and vegetables
(b) gambling
(c) rash driving
(d) fast food

Passage-II

(Q. Nos. 176 to 180)

Today perhaps your only association with the word 'polio' is the Sabin Oral Vaccine that protects children from the disease. Fifty-five years ago, this was not so. The dreaded disease, which mainly affects the brain and the spinal cord, causes stiffening and weakening of the muscles, crippling and paralysis — which is why I am in a wheelchair today. If somebody had predicted, when I was born, that this would happen to me, no one would have believed it. I was the seventh child in a family of four pairs of brothers and sisters, with a huge 23-year gap between the first and the last. I was told that, unlike the others, I was so fair and brown-haired that I looked more like a foreigner than a Dawood Bohri. I was also considered to be the healthiest of the brood.

176. The narrator of the passage is a patient of
(a) diabetes
(b) cerebral attack
(c) polio
(d) heart disease

177. To say something about the future is to
(a) addict
(b) verdict
(c) predict
(d) protect

178. The narrator was the seventh child in a family that had
(a) nine children
(b) one score children
(c) eight children
(d) twenty-three children

179. Polio, the dreaded disease, mainly affects the
(a) heart and spinal cord
(b) brain and spinal cord
(c) brain and nerves
(d) brain and heart

180. What made the narrator look like a foreigner?
(a) He was fair and skinny
(b) He was fair and brown-haired
(c) He was fair with red hair
(d) He was dark and blonde

Passage - III

(Q. Nos. 181 to 190)

Andaman and Nicobar Islands consist of mainly two groups of islands, with distinctive features of the original residents — Negroid and Mongolese. It is strange to see how these two different groups migrated to these islands so far from the mainland — from India and Myanmar. The aboriginals found in these islands are the Jarawas, Sentinelese, Onges, Shompenites, mainly found in Andaman and the Nicobarese in Nicobar. Of these the Nicobarese in general, and some of the Onges, have accepted the so-called 'modern civilization and learned the use of modern tools and facilities.

They can be seen frequently in the Port Blair market. The aboriginals are looked after by the Anthropological Department of the Government, who make regular visits to their islands and supply them with food and other necessities.

These aboriginals still do not know how to use a matchbox and prepare fire by rubbing two pieces of wood; they also do not know the use of cloth. If the people from the Anthropological Department offer them clothes, they use them only as turbans and not to wrap their bodies.

181. Original residents of Andaman and Nicobar Islands are
(a) Negroid
(b) Mongolese
(c) Negroid and Mongolese
(d) None of them

182. The so-called modern civilization has been accepted in general by
(a) all the aboriginals
(b) the Nicobarese
(c) the Jarawas
(d) the Onges

183. The original residents migrated to the islands from
(a) India
(b) Myanmar
(c) Sri Lanka
(d) India and Myanmar

184. The Jarawas, Sentinelese, Onges and Shompenites are mainly found in
(a) Andaman
(b) Nicobar
(c) Andaman and Nicobar
(d) Port Blair

185. The aboriginals are looked after by
(a) the Government of India
(b) the Anthropological Department of the Government
(c) the Tourism Department
(d) some NGOs

186. The aboriginals are still ignorant of the use or
(a) fire
(b) clothes
(c) matchbox and cloth
(d) matchbox

187. If clothes are offered, the aboriginals use them as
(a) turbans
(b) wrappers
(c) curtains
(d) None of these

188. The aboriginals prepare fire by
(a) rubbing two pieces of stone
(b) using a matchbox
(c) using gas lighter
(d) rubbing two pieces of wood

189. Find out a word which means "to cover'.
(a) turbans
(b) cloth
(c) wrap
(d) prepare

190. Find out a word which is the antonym for 'usual'.
(a) strange
(b) migrated
(c) frequently
(d) regular

Passage - IV

(Q. Nos. 191 to 200)

The habit of reading is one of the greatest resources of mankind; and we enjoy reading books that belong to us much more than if they are borrowed. A borrowed book is like a guest in the house; it must be treated with punctiliousness, with certain considerate formality. You must see that it sustains no damage; it must not suffer while under your roof. You cannot leave it carelessly, you cannot mark it, you cannot turn down the pages, you cannot use it familiarly.

But your own books belong to you; you treat them with that affectionate intimacy that annihilates formality.

Books are for use, not for show. A good reason for marking favourite pages in books is that this practice enables you to remember more easily the significant sayings, to refer to them quickly.

Everyone should begin collecting a private library in youth; one should have one's own bookshelves, which should not have doors, glass windows, or keys; they should be free and accessible to the hand as well as to the eye. Books are of the people, by the people and for the people. Literature is an immortal part of history; it is the best and most enduring part of personality.

191. The above passage is all about
(a) books
(b) games
(c) jokes
(d) magic

192. Which title is suitable for the passage?
(a) Merits and Demerits of Books
(b) The Pleasure of Owning Books
(c) Reading a Book
(d) Books and Thoughts

193. According to the passage, a borrowed book is like a
(a) guest in the house
(b) host in the house
(c) neighbour in the house
(d) relative in the house

194. All the following words mean 'mankind' except.
(a) Homo sapiens
(b) humanity
(c) humankind
(d) humanities

195. Which of the following statements is not true?
(a) Books are for use.
(b) Books are for show.
(c) Books must not be damaged.
(d) Books must be carefully handled.

196. According to the passage, everyone should begin collecting a private library
(a) in infancy
(b) in childhood
(c) in youth
(d) in adulthood

197. According to the passage, books are more enjoyable when they are
(a) in book-shops
(b) borrowed
(c) in the library
(d) personal possessions

198. How should you not treat a borrowed book?
(a) It must be treated as one's own possession
(b) It must be treated with a considerate formality
(c) It must be treated carefully
(d) It must be treated carelessly

199. What are the advantages of marking favourite passages of your personal books? (Pick out the incorrect one)
(a) It enables one to remember facts.
(b) It enables one to remember the significant sayings.
(c) It hinders one from remembering more easily.
(d) It enables one to refer to particular passages.

200. How should, the book-shelves of the private library be?
(a) Should have doors
(b) Should, have glass windows
(c) Should have keys
(d) Should be free and easily accessible

ANSWER KEY

1. (c)	2. (b)	3. (a)	4. (b)	5. (b)
6. (b)	7. (d)	8. (d)	9. (a)	10. (b)
11. (c)	12. (b)	13. (c)	14. (c)	15. (c)
16. (d)	17. (a)	18. (c)	19. (b)	20. (b)
21. (b)	22. (a)	23. (c)	24. (b)	25. (c)
26. (b)	27. (b)	28. (c)	29. (d)	30. (c)
31. (b)	32. (d)	33. (b)	34. (a)	35. (d)

36. (d) 37. (a) 38. (b) 39. (a) 40. (b)
41. (b) 42. (d) 43. (d) 44. (a) 45. (c)
46. (a) 47. (c) 48. (a) 49. (c) 50. (a)
51. (c) 52. (c) 53. (b) 54. (c) 55. (b)
56. (d) 57. (a) 58. (a) 59. (d) 60. (c)
61. (b) 62. (a) 63. (b) 64. (b) 65. (b)
66. (b) 67. (b) 68. (a) 69. (c) 70. (a)
71. (c) 72. (a) 73. (a) 74. (a) 75. (a)
76. (b) 77. (d) 78. (b) 79. (b) 80. (b)
81. (a) 82. (c) 83. (b) 84. (c) 85. (b)
86. (b) 87. (d) 88. (a) 89. (d) 90. (b)
91. (d) 92. (a) 93. (a) 94. (b) 95. (d)
96. (c) 97. (c) 98. (c) 99. (b) 100. (b)
101. (a) 102. (a) 103. (c) 104. (c) 105. (c)
106. (c) 107. (a) 108. (a) 109. (a) 110. (c)
111. (b) 112. (b) 113. (c) 114. (a) 115. (c)
116. (c) 117. (b) 118. (b) 119. (a) 120. (a)
121. (c) 122. (a) 123. (d) 124. (c) 125. (c)
126. (b) 127. (a) 128. (b) 129. (a) 130. (d)
131. (d) 132. (a) 133. (b) 134. (b) 135. (a)
136. (d) 137. (b) 138. (d) 139. (a) 140. (a)
141. (c) 142. (a) 143. (b) 144. (a) 145. (a)
146. (a) 147. (d) 148. (a) 149. (c) 150. (d)
151. (d) 152. (a) 153. (a) 154. (b) 155. (a)
156. (d) 157. (a) 158. (b) 159. (a) 160. (c)
161. (a) 162. (c) 163. (b) 164. (a) 165. (d)
166. (a) 167. (d) 168. (d) 169. (c) 170. (b)
171. (b) 172. (b) 173. (b) 174. (a) 175. (d)
176. (c) 177. (c) 178. (c) 179. (b) 180. (b)
181. (c) 182. (b) 183. (d) 184. (a) 185. (b)
186. (c) 187. (a) 188. (d) 189. (c) 190. (a)
191. (a) 192. (b) 193. (a) 194. (d) 195. (b)
196. (c) 197. (d) 198. (d) 199. (c) 200. (d)

FREQUENCY ANALYSIS

ABBREVIATIONS USED:

Comprehension / **Comp**, Sentence Completion / **SC**, Sentence Filler / **SF**, Cloze Test/ **CT**, Synonyms/ **Syn**, Antonyms/ **Ant**, Idioms and Phrase/ **IP**, Substitution/ **Subt**, Sentence arrangement/ **SA**, Spelling/ **SPL**, Miscellaneous/**Misc.**, Total Marks/**TM**, Sentence error/**SE**, Sentence Improvement/ **SI**.

SSC Graduate Level TIER-II Exam, 2013

	Comp.	SC	SF	CT	Syn	Ant	IP	Subt	SA	SE	SPL	SI	MISC.	TM
	30	5		25	3	3	10	12	20	20	3	22	47	200

TREND ANALYSIS

SSC Graduate Level TIER-II Exam, 2013

The test is very comprehensive as it contains two hundred question. Thirteen types of questions have been set. All units are regular and have been set in a straight forward manner. If the book is read carefully there will be no problem. Questions on voice and narration are new in comparison to the pattern of questions in Bank and Defence examinations.

The level of questions is just above moderate. They can be easily solved. A careful reading of all the units of the book and a regular practice at the sets will help the students.

PAPER 41

SSC, CAPFS, DELHI POLICE SI, CISF, ASI AND NCB INTELLIGENCE OFFICER EXAMINATION, 2013

Directions to Questions 1 to 20

In the following questions, some parts of the sentences have errors and some are correct. Find out which part of a sentence has an error and the number of that part is your answer. If a sentence is free from errors, your answer is (d) i.e. No error.

1. He only wrote (a)/ on one side of (b)/ the paper. (c)/ No error (d)
2. Two small boys and a dog (a)/ comprised of (b)/ the street entertainer's only audience. (c)/ No error (d)
3. There is plenty (a)/ of places for (b)/ improvement in this article. (c)/ No error (d)
4. Pursuant to our conversation (a)/ I now send you a cheque (b)/ for Rs. 1000 as my fees. (c)/ No error (d)
5. It is imperative (a)/ that your passport (b)/ carries your photo. (c)/ No error (d)
6. The case (a)/ does not require (b)/ that he is present. (c)/ No error (d)
7. I am (a)/ debarred (b)/ to attend the meeting. (c)/ No error (d)
8. We seldom (a)/ or ever (b)/ see those forsaken who trust in the Almighty. (c)/ No error (d)
9. He stayed in Delhi (a)/ for one and a half months (b)/ because I insisted on him doing that. (c)/ No error (d)
10. Remember that with the skill (a)/ to write good sentences (b) you will have the flexibility to convey your ideas precisely. (c)/ No error (d)
11. By arresting the local criminals and encouraging good people (a)/we can end (b)/hostilities of that area. (c)/No error (d)
12. A river is any natural stream (a)/for fresh water (b)/ larger than a brook. (c)/ No error (d)
13. He managed (a)/ to open the lid (b)/ by a screw-driver (c)/ No error (d)
14. Such a behaviour (a)/can easily (b)/cause offence. (c)/No error (d)
15. These drugs (a)/have no influence (b)/on the virus. (c)/No error (d)
16. The police is (a)/ on the trail of the criminals (b)/ after a daring robbery. (c)/ No error (d)
17. I like reading (a)/ of history (b)/ as it records our past. (c)/ No error (d)

18. Vinay sat (a)/ opposite to me (b)/ at breakfast. (c)/ No error (d)

19. At the end (a)/ I decided (b)/ not to go. (c)/ No error (d)

20. Man alone of all creatures (a)/ thinks of things as tools (b)/and used them as such. (c)/ No error (d)

Directions to Questions 21 to 25

In the following questions, sentences are given with blanks to be filled in with an appropriate word(s). Four alternatives are suggested for each question. Choose the correct alternative out of the four.

21. I doubt whether it ________ an impact on the readers.
(a) will cause
(b) will have
(c) had have
(d) caused

22. _____from blame, he was released to live the life of a free man.
(a) Evaporated
(b) Exempted
(c) Exonerated
(d) Excused

23. Yogeshwar Dutt put ____ him the Beijing disappointment and a serious injury to realize his Olympic dream with a gutsy show.
(a) beyond
(b) above
(c) behind
(d) over

24. If you ______ of wild animals at night, there will be no trouble.
(a) are aware
(b) take care
(c) are beware
(d) are wary

25. He ____ not have spoken the truth.
(a) did
(b) will
(c) shall
(d) may

Directions to Questions 26 to 28

In the following questions, out of the four alternatives, choose the one which best expresses the meaning of the given word.

26. Glue
(a) Detach
(b) Staple
(c) Unfasten
(d) Stick

27. Pugnacious
(a) Querulous
(b) Ambiguous
(c) Audacious
(d) Quarrelsome

28. Ponderous
(a) Slanderous
(b) Populous
(c) Cautious
(d) Massive

Directions to Questions 29 to 31

In the following questions, choose the word opposite in meaning to the given word.

29. Vilify
(a) Cherish
(b) Invalidate
(c) Glorify
(d) Satisfy

30. Tireless
(a) Energetic
(b) Dynamic
(c) Untiring
(d) Lazy

31. Solitary
(a) Full
(b) Crowded
(c) Lonely
(d) Many

Directions to Questions 32 to 34

In the following questions, four words are given in each question, out of which only one word is correctly spelt. Find the correctly spelt word.

32.
(a) Connoisseur
(b) Conoslseur
(c) Conoiseur
(d) Connoiseur

33.
(a) Rehearsal
(b) Rtehersal
(c) Reharsl
(d) Rehiersal

34.
(a) Gilotine
(b) Guilotine
(c) Gillotiner
(d) Guillotine

Directions to Questions 35 to 44

In the following questions, four alternatives are given for the Idiom/Phrase printed in **bold** in the sentence. Choose the alternative which best expresses the meaning of the Idiom/ Phrase.

35. After a period of two months, Nina has **come out of her shell** and talks freely to her colleagues.
(a) become more confident
(b) exhibited her intelligence
(c) made many friends
(d) helped her companions

36. It is a **breach of etiquette** to break into a conversation when you are not invited.
(a) improper and Impolite
(b) shocking arid strange
(c) harsh and cruel
(d) unavoidable and unjust

37. Such dangerous tendencies should be **nipped in the bud**.
(a) nurtured
(b) observed
(c) taken seriously
(d) eradicated in the initial stage

38. The man **has too many irons in the fire.**
(a) is attempting too many prospects simultaneously
(b) is dealing with too many problems simultaneously
(c) is cooking too many dishes simultaneously
(d) is maintaining too many relationships simultaneously

39. The scenic beauty of the valley **took my breath away.**
(a) surprised me
(b) choked me
(c) made me breathless
(d) made me cry

40. His thoughtless act proves that he is **soft in the head.**
(a) kind and gentle
(b) moved to tears easily
(c) generous and forgiving
(d) stupid or unintelligent

41. Shyam drives now and then just **to keep his hand in.**
(a) to keep himself busy
(b) to keep himself safe
(c) not to waste his time
(d) not to lose the skill

42. Naveen **put his brother's back up** by saying that he was unfit for the job.
(a) supported his brother
(b) annoyed his brother
(c) canvassed for his brother
(d) deceived his brother

43. His performance is remarkable. Let us hope it does riot turn out to be **a flash in the pan.**
(a) merely flashy
(b) gorgeous
(c) a one-off achievement
(d) a painful achievement

44. It seems that he **took pains** to write the book.
(a) suffered a lot
(b) procrastinated
(c) was reluctant
(d) worked hard

Directions to Questions 45 to 64

In the following questions the 1st and the last sentences are numbered 1 and 6. The rest of the sentence/passage is split into four parts and named P, Q, R and S. These four sentences/parts are not given in their proper order. Read the sentence/passage and find out which of the four combinations is correct. Then find the correct answer.

45.
1. Raju and Ali were working on Mr. Dutt's roof.
P. A burglar passed and saw the ladder.
Q. The burglar climbed the ladder and got in through the first floor window.
R. The house was now empty as Mr. and Mrs. Dutt were out playing cards with their friends.
S. When they stopped they left the ladder leaning against the house.
6. He went straight to the bedroom, opened the drawer and pocketed Mrs. Dutt's jewellery.
(a) PSRQ
(b) PSQR
(c) SPRQ
(d) SPQR

46.
1. The students were blockading the residences of ministers in protest against price rise.
P. The students started throwing stones at the police cordon.
Q. At least forty students were injured.
R. They turned violent.
S. The police lathi-charged the students.
6. The injured students were taken to a nearby hospital.
(a) PQSR (b) RPQS
(c) RQSP (d) RPSQ

47.
1. An educator named Rowland Hill of England is considered the Father of Philately.
P. Brazil and two Swiss cantons were next to issue stamps.
Q. The US used its first stamps on July 1, 1847.
R. The world's first postage stamp was issued by Great Britain, in 1840.
S. Two years later, in 1842, stamps were issued by a private postal service in New York.
6. India's first stamp appeared in 1852.
(a) QRSP (b) RPSQ
(c) RSPQ (d)RSQP

48.
1. The king called his three daughters to know who loved him best.
P. Cordelia, the youngest, said that she loved his Majesty according to her duty, neither more nor less.
Q. The king was very delighted to hear the words of Goneril.
R. Regan, the second daughter, said that without the love of her dear king and father, she found all joys dead.
S. Goneril, the eldest, declared that she loved her father more than words could give out.
6. The king asked Cordelia to mend her speech.
(a) RSQP (b) SQRP
(c) SRPQ (d) PSQR

49.
1. In our country internet is becoming more and more popular.
P. In one such cafe one can sit before the computer.
Q. Cyber cafes are opening up like STD and ISD booths.
R. One can ask for the information one needs to know.

S. The cost ranges from Rs. 10 to 20 per hour.
6. One needs to tell the search engine to find the information and it will flash on the screen.

(a) SQPR (b) PRQS
(c) QPRS (d) RPSQ

50.

1. Everyone has a mental picture of volcanoes.
P. This is the crater and it is the mouth of the volcano.
Q. In appearance it looks like a cone-shaped mountain.
R. The lava forces its way up this and overflows to form the sides of the volcano.
S. The top of the cone is rather flat and hollow.
6. Thus the volcano mountain is formed from the lava.

(a) QSPR (b) SPQR
(c) RSPQ (d) QRSP

51.

1. 'The Tower of Babel' is highly symbolic.
P. For Bruegel it also signified the vanity of human endeavour.
Q. The building of Babel, as described in the Bible, was an age old symbol of pride.
R. The landscape is not imaginary,
S. He set the Tower in a 16th century setting.
6. It is based on Bruegel's careful observation of the lands around him.

(a) QPSR (b) QPRS
(c) SRQP (d) SQRP

52.

1. About six men broke into the house of Mr. Roy, a businessman in Salt Lake.
P. Mr. Roy reported the case to the police immediately.
Q. They forced Mr. Roy at gunpoint to give the key of the iron safe.
R. They opened the iron safe.
S. They took away gold ornaments and Rs. 1,00,000 in cash.
Q. The businessmen of the area downed their shutters in protest against this daring robbery.

(a) QPRS (b) QRSP
(b) QRPS (d) RPQS

53.

1. Every family has a crazy streak in it somewhere.
P. He was an enormous man with a large head.
Q. He was also a man of temper.
R. In our family my cousin Mourad was said to have inherited it.
S. Before him was our uncle Khosrove.
6. He was so impatient that he stopped anyone from talking by roaring.

(a) SPQR (b) RQSP
(c) PSQR (d) RSPQ

54.

1. The boy-urchin stood on the pavement outside the shop.
P. He was observing the boy closely.
Q. He looked longingly at all the cakes and cookies in the display window.
R. Leaving his table, the gentleman crossed the street.
S. An elderly gentleman was sitting at a table in a cafe across the street.
6. Walking up to the boy, he tapped him on, the shoulder.

(a) QPSR (b) QSPR
(c) PQRS (d) SQPR

58.

1. 'Vipasana', the ancient form of meditation is charming the Indian elite once again.
P. He feels that 'Vipasana' will relieve one from the tensions born out of frustration and anger.
Q. The Chief feels that this form of meditation is of vital importance as it cools down pent up anger.
R. The Supercop and SIT Chief is the new bee attracted to it.

S. The Additional Director -General of the CRPF recommends that every Indian Cop should undergo this therapy to make India a peace-loving paradise.

6. Now that's the step in the right direction.

(a) SQRP (b) RQPS
(c) SRPQ (d) RSQP

56.

1. The landfill began when refugees from former East Pakistan started settling on the banks of the water body after Partition.

P. The banks are dotted with shops, huts, a garage and heaps of waste.

Q. Restoration work has been started but the whole pond cannot be done because the people cannot be evicted.

R. The encroachment continued even after the influx of refugees stopped.

S. Some local residents allege the shops and huts had been built on land that was originally a part of the pond.

6. The first round of excavation will start soon.

(a) QRPS (b) SPRQ
(c) RPSQ (d) PRQS

57.

1. During the mid 1600s, the Sun King, Louis XIV created a new fad of platform shoes, simply because he had the royal power to do so.

P. The chopines were worn to increase a woman's height.

Q. The platform shoes soon became the symbol of nobility.

R. They were often 24 inches off the ground and ladies had to be escorted through the streets.

S. Also during the time, women in Florence were wearing platform shoes known as chopines.

6. Some historians believe the modern day high heel originates from the chopine.

(a) SQPR (b) RSQP
(c) RSPQ (d) QSPR

58.

1. The Man Booker Prize for Fiction is awarded every year for a novel written by a writer from the Commonwealth or the Republic of Ireland, and aims to represent the very best in contemporary fiction.

P. In 2002, the Man Group became the sponsor and they chose the new name, "Booker".

Q. Great efforts are made to ensure that the judging panel is balanced so that a writer, a critic, an editor an academic and well-known persons are included-

R. Publishers can submit books for consideration for the prize, but judges can also ask for books to be included which they think suitable.

S. The prize was originally called the Booker-McCon-nell Prize, which was the name of the company that sponsored it.

However, when the panel of judges has been finalized, they are left to make their own decisions without any further interference from the prize sponsor.

(a) SPRQ (b) QPRS
(c) SQPR (d) PRSQ

59.

1. Developing the next breed of Jobs, Gates and Zuckerberg is something B-schools are keen to facilitate.

P. It was their technological prowess and creative thinking that created their empires.

Q. However, it is important to note that none of them studied for an MBA.

R. But, not all ideas pioneered by 'techies' reach a global market.

S. Many prospective entrepreneurs still feel there is little reason to do so.

6. Many with technological background lack business acumen and commercial skills.

(a) QPSR (b) QSRP
(c) QSPR (d) PSQR

60.

1. Nehru's books deal with different subjects.
P. But yet again, his books are remarkable for their absence of bitterness.
Q. Yet, through these books, runs a common thread of his vision.
R. All of his classics were written while Nehru was in prison.
S. One finds in these books, a passionate commitment to democracy, his aversion to fundamentalism and his celebration of India's pluralistic culture.
6. There is a deep humanity which illuminates the pages of his books.

(a) QRPS (b) QPRS
(c) QSRP (d) QRSP

61.

1. Yesterday evening a gang of more than fifty armed people robbed the villagers.
P. Angry villagers blocked the highway for several hours to protest police inaction.
Q. It is alleged, however, that the police arrived at the scene of the crime several hours later.
R. While the looting was going on, the police were called repeatedly over the telephone.
S. Many people who tried to prevent the crime were beaten mercilessly by the robbers.
6. The blockade was lifted after the DSP himself arrived and promised action will be taken.

(a) SRQP (b) PQRS
(c) RSPQ (d) QPSR

62.

1. This year there has been a bumper production of crops.
P. They are forced to sell their products at a very low price.
Q. This was due to sufficient rainfall during the monsoon season.
R. This has had an adverse effect upon the farmers.
S. As a result prices of food products have come down drastically.
6. The government has therefore initiated better storage facilities.

(a) QPRS (b) QRPS
(c) QSRP (d) QSPR

63.

1. We have been brought up for centuries to believe in men's superiority.
P. Logically speaking, not all men are superior and some women are superior.
Q. But the reality is, when it comes to mental capacity, a few individuals prove to be superior.
R. It may be true in terms of bone structure, hormones, etc.
S. This logical thought tells us that our conception of male power is wrong.
6. So also our underestimation of female power.

(a) PSQR (b) RSPQ
(c) PQSR (d) RQPS

64.

1. Earlier, travellers found incredible beauty in Nanda Devi.
P. Their dumping of garbage disturbed the ecological balance.
Q. But when restrictions were lifted in Nanda Devi in 1974, a deluge of foreign mountaineers descended upon it.
R. With them came garbage and deforestation.
S. Hence Nanda Devi Sanctuary was made out of bounds for outsiders in 1982.
6. Nanda Devi is the third highest Himalayan peak.

(a) QRPS (b) SQPR
(c) PRSQ (d) QSPR

Directions to Questions 65 to 76

In the following questions, out of the four alternatives choose the one which can be substituted for the given words /sentence.

65. Object which moves around its planet

(a) Stars
(b) Galaxy
(c) Constellation
(d) Satellite

66. One who regards the whole world as his country
(a) Spartan
(b) Alien
(c) Stalwart
(d) Cosmopolitan

67. A foolish person
(a) Smasher
(b) Waif
(c) Simpleton
(d) Invalid

68. To listen secretly to what is said in private
(a) Perturb
(b) Murmur
(c) Impel
(d) Eavesdrop

69. The name of the garment worn by a nun
(a) Frock
(b) Gown
(c) Housecoat
(d) Habit

70. The action of draining something
(a) Extortion
(b) Extinction
(c) Expulsion
(d) Exhaustion

71. Surgical removal of all or part of a limb
(a) Ammunition
(b) Amputation
(c) Emancipation
(d) Annihilation

72. The short remaining end of a cigarette
(a) Stump
(b) Stud
(c) Butt
(d) Scrap

73. An animal story with a moral
(a) Fable
(b) Narrative
(c) Parable
(d) Anecdote

74. Bounding line or surface
(a) Periphery
(b) Circumference
(c) Radius
(d) Edge

75. Identification with the feelings of another
(a) Empathy
(b) Apathy
(c) Sympathy
(d) Antipathy

76. A person who conducts a television show
(a) Director
(b) Conductor
(c) Host
(d) Producer

Directions to Questions 77 to 96

In the following questions, a sentence has been given in Active/Passive Voice. Out of the four alternatives suggested, select the one which best expresses the same sentence in Passive /Active Voice.

77. The Cabinet approved amendments to the Insurance Law Bill pending in the Rajya Sabha.
(a) Amendments pending in the Rajya Sabha, to the Insurance Law Bill was approved by the Cabinet.
(b) Amendments to the Insurance Law Bill pending in the Rajya Sabha was approved.
(c) Amendments to the Insurance Law Bill was approved by the Cabinet pending in the Rajya Sabha.
(d) Amendments to the Insurance Law Bill pending in the Rajya Sabha, were approved by the Cabinet.

78. The major points of the lesson were quickly learnt by the class, but they were also quickly forgotten by them.
(a) The class quickly learnt but forgot the major points of the lesson.
(b) The class quickly learnt the major points of the lesson but they also forgot them.
(c) The class learnt and forgot the major points of the lesson quickly.
(d) The class quickly learnt the major points of the lesson but also forgot them quickly.

79. Will no one tell me what she does?
(a) Shall I be told by anyone what is done by her?

(b) Shall I not be told by any one what is done by her?

(c) Shall not be I told what was done by her?

(d) Does anyone told me what is she doing?

80. Jim would know next to nothing of the events.

(a) Jim was being known next to nothing of the events.

(b) Next to nothing of the events would be known to Jim.

(c) Next to nothing of the events would be known by Jim.

(d) It was next to nothing to Jim of the events that he knew.

81. Are the officers finishing the work on time?

(a) Was the work being finished on time by the officers?

(b) Is the work finished on time by the officers?

(c) Is the work being finished on time by the officers?

(d) Was the work finished on time by the officers?

82. We arranged many meetings and collected many signatures.

(a) We have arranged many meetings and many signatures are collected.

(b) Many meetings are arranged, many signature are collected by us.

(c) Many meetings were arranged and many signatures were collected by us.

(d) Many meetings has arranged and many signatures has collected by us.

83. Who did you laugh at?

(a) Who was laughing at you?

(b) Who had been laughing at you?

(c) Who laughed at you?

(d) Who was laughed at by you?

84. They will help us with money.

(a) We shall be helped by them

(b) We shall help them with money

(c) We should help them withmoney.

(d) We shall not be helped by them with money.

85. They told us to walk on the right track.

(a) We were told to walk on the right track.

(b) We are told to walk on the right track.

(c) We are being told to walk on the right track.

(d) We were being told to walk on the right track.

86. Wild animals live in the dense forest.

(a) In the dense forest lives the wild animals.

(b) In the dense forest lived the wild animals.

(c) In the dense forest is living the wild animals.

(d) The dense forest is inhabited by wild animals.

87. Have you shut the window?

(a) Has the window been shut by you?

(b) Has the window being shut by you?

(c) Are the window been shut by you?

(d) Are the window being shut by you?

88. Messi scored the goal in the 10th minute of the second-half.

(a) The goal is being scored by Messi in the 10th minute of second-half.

(b) In the 10th minute of second-half Messi scored the goal.

(c) The goal is scored by Messi in the 10th minute of second-half.

(d) The goal was scored by Messi in the 10th minute of the second-half.

89. A meeting was proposed to be held.

(a) It was proposed to hold a meeting.

(b) It proposed to hold a meeting.

(c) It proposed that a meeting will be held

(d) Someone proposed to hold a meeting.

90. Nothing can be gained without labour.

(a) We could gain nothing without labour.

(b) We cannot gain nothing without labour.

(c) We should gain nothing without labour.

(d) We can gain nothing without labour.

91. The novels of Tolstoy interest me.

(a) I am interested in Tolstoy of the novels.

(b) I am interested by the novels of Tolstoy.

(c) I am interested in the novels of Tolstoy.
(d) I was interested by the novels of Tolstoy.

92. A big crowd chased him and later the police arrested him.
(a) He was chased by a big crowd and later was arrested by the police.
(b) He was chased by a big crowd and later arrested by the police.
(c) He was chased by a big crowd and later the police arrested him.
(d) He was chased by a big crowd and was later arrested by the police.

93. Boil the water and cool it before you keep it in the fridge.
(a) Let the water be boiled and cooled before it is kept in the fridge,
(b) Let the water be boiled and cooled before it is kept in the fridge by you.
(c) Let the water be boiled by you and cooled by you before it is kept in the fridge.
(d) Let the water be boiled, cooled and kept in the fridge.

94. The drivers considered the speed-breakers a menace to smooth driving.
(a) The speed-breakers were considered a menace to smooth driving by the drivers.
(b) The speed-breakers were considered a menace to smooth driving according to the drivers.
(c) The drivers were considered a menace to smooth driving the speed-breakers.
(d) The drivers were considered speed-breakers by the menace to smooth driving.

95. Every dish which had been cooked by my mother was appreciated by the guests.
(a) The guests appreciated every dish which had been cooked by my mother.
(b) The guests appreciated every dish which was cooked,
(c) The guests appreciated every dish which my mother had cooked.
(d) My mother had cooked every dish which the guests appreciated.

96. It was imagined by some of them that they would inevitably run out of cash.
(a) Some of them imagined that they would inevitably run out of cash.
(b) They imagined that they would inevitably run out of cash.
(c) They imagined that they would not have an immense supply of cash with them.
(d) They imagined that they would run out of cash.

Directions to Questions 97 to 118

In the following questions, a sentence/a part of the sentence is printed in bold. Below are given alternatives to the bold part at (a), (b), (c) which may improve the sentence. Choose the correct alternative. In case no improvement is needed, your answer is (d).

97. He practised **regularly to make his speech perfect.**
(a) perfect to make his speech regularly
(b) regularly to make his speech perfectly
(c) perfectly to make his speech regularly
(d) No improvement

98. He is quick-tempered and **circumspect.**
(a) responsible
(b) prudent
(c) impulsive
(d) No improvement

99. I never miss **any worth seeing picture.**
(a) any picture worth seeing
(b) any picture that is worth seeing
(c) worth seeing picture
(d) No improvement

100. She remained a receptionist **until well in middle age**.
(a) until well in her middle age
(b) well until in middle age
(c) until well into middle age
(d) No improvement

101. It took her a long time to **get past her** failure in the medical examination.

(a) give up
(b) go over
(c) get over with
(d) No improvement

102. The sound was thin and unnatural, and the voices were blurred **by** static.
(a) of
(b) in
(c) with
(d) No improvement

103. Take the next turning but **the one** on your left.
(a) the
(b) first
(c) one
(d) No improvement

104. Many would prefer to be savages if they **may** have the magnificent physique of some South Sea Islanders.
(a) could
(b) can
(c) will
(d) No improvement

105. As soon as she noticed the workmen, she asked them **what they have been doing**.
(a) what have they being doing
(b) what they had been doing
(c) had they been doing
(d) No improvement

106. You should give **ear** to what the teacher says.
(a) an ear
(b) a ear
(c) the ear
(d) No improvement

107. It never rains **though** it pours.
(a) and
(b) but
(c) yet
(d) No improvement

108. It **brings** two to make a quarrel.
(a) wants
(b) needs
(c) takes
(d) No improvement

109. There are a few problems we need to **work out.**
(a) erase out
(b) sort out
(c) throw out
(d) No improvement

110. I wonder when your birthday is.
(a) I wonder about when your birthday is.
(b) I wonder that when is your birthday.
(c) I wonder when is your birthday.
(d) No improvement

111. Men of skill and brain should be India's most valuable **treasures.**
(a) property
(b) genius
(c) export
(d) No improvement

112. To err is human, to **forget** divine.
(a) forego
(b) forgive
(c) excuse
(d) No improvement

113. I search in dictionaries for words the are not included.
(a) forego search through
(b) forgive search up
(c) excuse search
(d) No improvement

114. I don't want **a Mr. John** who works in the Acoounts office: I want the other Mr. John.
(a) the Mr. John
(b) Mr. John
(c) a one Mr. John
(d) No improvement

115. Taking the test, the teacher gave me passing grade.
(a) After I took the test
(b) After the test was taken
(c) When I took the test
(d) No improvement

116. According to me, she is sick.
(a) According to my opinion
(b) In my opinion

(c) According to my view
(d) No improvement

117. There are opportunities for **both the rich and poor**.
(a) both rich as well as poor
(b) the both rich and poor
(c) both rich and poor
(d) No improvement

118. He **meditates upon** revenge.
(a) meditates
(b) meditates for
(c) meditates on
(d) No improvement

Directions to Questions 119 to 145

In the following questions, a sentence has been given in Direct/Indirect. Out of the four alternatives suggested, select the one which best expresses the same sentence in Indirect /Direct.

119. Samuel said to Remiel,
"Where do you usually go swimming?"
(a) Samuel asked Remiel where he usually went swimming.
(b) Samuel said to Remiel where he usually goes swimming.
(c) Samuel asked if Remiel usually went swimming.
(d) Samuel told Remiel where he usually had been going swimming.

120. The Captain commanded his men to stand at ease.
(a) The Captain commanded, "Men, stand at ease".
(b) The Captain said, "These men need to stand at ease".
(c) The Captain said, "You can stand at ease".
(d) The Captain said to his men, "Stand at ease".

121. The policeman said to the violent crowd, "Stop all this or you will be arrested."
(a) The policeman said to the violent crowd to stop all this or be arrested.
(b) The policeman said to the violent crowd that they should stop or else be arrested.
(c) The policeman advised the violent crowd to stop all that or they would be arrested.
(d) The policeman ordered the violent crowd to stop all that or they would be arrested.

122. Suma said to him, "Am I to wait for you forever?"
(a) Suma asked him if she were to wait for him forever.
(b) Suma said to him if she can wait for him forever.
(c) Suma asked him if she was to wait for him forever.
(d) Suma asked him if she had to wait for him forever.

123. "Don't pull the dog's tail," his father said.
(a) His father said that he did not pull the dog's tail.
(b) His father forbade him not to pull the dog's tail.
(c) His father told him to pull the dog's tail.
(d) His father told him not to pull the dog's tail.

124. Yolanda said, "I have to leave the class before 12.30 p.m."
(a) Yolanda said that I have to leave the class before 12.30 p.m.
(b) Yolanda said that she has to leave the class before 12.30p.m.
(c) Yolanda said that she had to leave the class before 12.30 p.m.
(d) Yolanda said that she has had to leave the class before 12.30 p.m.

125. She said to her brother, "Don't be late, we'll be waiting for you".
(a) She said to her brother not to be late for they would have been waiting for him.
(b) She requested her brother not to be late for they would be waiting for him.
(c) She requested her brother not to be late for we would be waiting for him.
(d) She said to her brother that he should not be late for she would be waiting for him.

126. Wardha said to her sister, "How long do you intend to stay here?"
(a) Wardha asked her sister that how long she intended to stay there.
(b) Wardha asked her sister how long she intended to stay there.
(c) Wardha asked to her sister how long she intended to stay here.
(d) Wardha asked her sister how long she intended to stay here.

127. Sachin said, "My grandfather recites the Geeta every morning."
(a) Sachin told that his grandfather has recited the Geeta every morning.
(b) Sachin told that his grandfather recited the Geeta every morning.
(c) Sachin said that his grandfather recites the Geeta every morning.
(d) Sachin said that his grandfather is recited the Geeta every morning.

128. Mr. Gupta said to his son, "Do not take up any responsibility unless you are confident you can do it."
(a) Mr. Gupta advised his son not to take up any responsibility unless he is confident of doing it.
(b) Mr. Gupta advised his son against taking up responsibility without completing it.
(c) Mr. Gupta advised his son to take up the responsibility of completing the task.
(d) Mr. Gupta advised his son not to take up any responsibility unless he was confident that he could do it.

129. The man said to the boy, "It only seems complicated because you're not used to it."
(a) The man told the boy that it only seems complicated because he was not used to it.
(b) The man told the boy that it only seemed complicated because he is not used to it.
(c) The man told the boy that it only seemed complicated because he was not used to it.
(d) The man told the boy it only seems complicated, it is really not so.

130. "It's not my business," said the postman. "Let the government do whatever it has to."
(a) The postman said that it was the government's and not his business to do that.
(b) The postman said that the government did not do what it was expected to do.
(c) The postman said that it was not his business and that the government should do whatever it had to.
(d) The postman said that it was the business of the government to do whatever it had to.

131. The doctor said to the patient. "How do you feel now? Has the pain gone down?"
(a) The doctor asked the patient how he was feeling then and if the pain was down.
(b) The doctor asked the patient how he felt then and if the pain had gone down.
(c) The doctor asked the patient how he had felt when the pain was gone.
(d) The doctor asked the patient how he is feeling now and if the pain has gone down,

132. The teacher said, "Students, we live in deeds, not in years."
(a) The teacher said that we live in deeds, not in years.
(b) The teacher said to students we live in deeds, not in years.
(c) The teacher said to the students that we lived in deeds, not in years.
(d) The teacher said to the students that we lived in deeds, not in years.

133. The teacher said, "Rajiv, come to my desk with your exercise book now."
(a) The teacher ordered Rajiv to come to her desk with his exercise book now.
(b) The teacher ordered Rajiv to come to her desk with his exercise book then.
(c) The teacher ordered Rajiv to go to her desk with his exercise book now.
(d) The teacher said to Rajiv come to her desk with his exercise book then.

134. He told me that I was very happy.
(a) He said to me, "How happy you are"
(b) He said to me, "How you are happy !"

(c) He said to me, "I am very happy!"
(d) He said to me, "How I am happy"

135. He said, "Let me have some tea".
(a) He said to let him have some tea.
(b) He told us to let him have some tea.
(c) He wished that he might have some tea.
(d) He wished that he will have some tea.

136. The mother advised her son to be careful and not to enter into a quarrel with the goons.
(a) The mother advised her son, "Be careful and not enter into a quarrel with the goons."
(b) The mother said to her son, "Do not enter into a quarrel with the goons."
(c) The mother said to her son, "Be careful Do not enter into a quarrel with the goons."
(d) The mother said to her son to "be careful."

137. The porter respectfully assured the lady that he would take care of her baggage while she bought her ticket.
(a) The porter said, "I would take care of your baggage while you buy your ticket, Madam."
(b) The porter said, "I will take care of your baggage while you buy your ticket, Madam."
(c) The porter said, "I would take care of your baggage while you bought your ticket, Madam."
(d) The porter said to the lady, "I would take care of your baggage while you bought your ticket."

138. "The last thing I want for my daughter is a boy who drinks!" said Brinda.
(a) Brinda proclaimed that the last thing she wanted for her daughter was a boy who drank.
(b) Brinda said that the last thing she would want for her daughter was a boy who drank.
(c) Brinda told that the last thing she wants for her daughter was a boy who drinks.
(d) Brinda complained that the last thing she wants for her daughter is a boy who drank.

139. "What's that noise? It sounds like an aeroplane," said Ravi.
(a) Ravi asked what the noise was, adding that it sounded like an aeroplane.
(b) Ravi demanded to know what the noise was, saying that it sounded like an aeroplane.
(c) Ravi asked what the noise could have been saying that it sounded like an aeroplane.
(d) Ravi wondered about the noise thinking that it sounded like an aeroplane,

140. "Is that so?" the Sahib said cheerfully, "Well, I like village folk."
(a) The Sahib cheerfully asked if It was such and said he likes village folk.
(b) The Sahib asked cheerfully whether that was so, adding that he liked village folk.
(c) The Sahib told with cheer that it was so arid asked if he liked village folk.
(d) The Sahib was asking cheerfully if it was so and added that he liked village folk.

141. The client told his lawyer, "I'm going away for a few days. I'll call you when I get back."
(a) The client told his lawyer that he was going away for a few days and would call him when he got back.
(b) The client promised his lawyer that he was going away for a few days and would call him when he got back.
(c) The client told his lawyer that he. is going away for a few days and will call him when he gets back.
(d) The client assured his lawyer that he was going away for a few days and would definitely call him when he got back.

142. "And you believe all this?" asked Sriram, in surprise.
(a) Sriram asked me in surprise if I believed all this.
(b) Sriram asked me in disbelief if I was believing all this.
(c) Surprised, Sriram asked me whether I believed all that.
(d) Srirarn was amazed that I believed all that.

143. They said, "It was raining heavily, when they came out of the theatre."

(a) They said that it was raining heavily, when they had come out of the theatre.

(b) They said that it had been raining heavily, when they came out of the theatre.

(c) They said that it rained when they had come out of the theatre.

(d) They said that it had been raining heavily, when they had come out of the theatre.

144. Looking at the Taj Mahal the tourist said, "What an exquisitely beautiful creation !"

(a) Looking Taj Mahal the tourist told that it is an exquisitely beautiful creation,

(b) Looking at the Taj Mahal the tourist exclaimed in wonder that what an exquisitely beautiful creation.

(c) Looking Taj Mahal the tourist said what an exquisitely beautiful creation it was indeed.

(d) Looking at the Taj Mahal the tourist exclaimed in wonder that it was indeed an exquisitely beautiful creation.

145. "Tomorrow gives me no time !"

(a) Amanda exclaimed that tomorrow gives her no time.

(b) Amanda said that tomorrow gave her no time at all

(c) Amanda exclaimed that tomorrow had given her no time.

(d) Amanda exclaimed that the following day gave her no time.

Directions to Questions 146 to 170

In the following passages some of the words have been left out. Read the passages carefully and choose the correct answer to each question out of the four alternatives and fill in. the blanks.

Passage-I

(Q. Nos. 146 to 155)

The Gandhian movement brought a new **(146)** for Indian women. It helped in women's **(147)**. They now enjoy equality with men (148) all spheres. Legislative reforms ensure this **(149)**. They enjoy equal participation in social, **(150)** and political life. Improved **(151)** for health and education, economic independence and active **(152)** in family and community life **(153)** to compete with men. All **(154)** based on sex have vanished. The modern woman is **(155)** march and nothing can stop her onslaught.

146.

(a) transformation

(b) Beginning

(c) awareness

(d) dawn

147.

(a) liberalism

(b) liberalization

(c) liberation

(d) liberty

148.

(a) in

(b) within

(c) of

(d) from

149.

(a) law

(b) right

(c) legislation

(d) step

150.

(a) traditional

(b) cultural

(c) religious

(d) educational

151.

(a) facilities

(b) infrastructure

(c) service

(d) advantages

152.

(a) responsibility

(b) involvement

(c) participation

(d) relationship

153.
(a) has helped
(b) have helped
(c) helped
(d) will help

154.
(a) distinctions
(b) differences
(c) discrimination
(d) discrepancies

155.
(a) in
(b) into
(c) at
(d) on

Passage-II

(Q. Nos. 156 to 165)

The All India Radio, **(156)** as well as films have the **(157)** of speeding up the process of **(158)** awareness. National Programmes of **(159)** dance and of drama on the broadcast **(160)** i.e. radio and television support the **(161)** of composite culture and of exchange of **162)** and artistic forms between one **(163)** and another. The influence of media, in the **(164)** of a composite culture, may have been **(165)** but it is an important factor.

156.
(a) Star Channel
(b) Doordarshan
(c) Cable TV
(d) Video Compact Disc

157.
(a) capability
(b) ability
(c) tendency
(d) technology

158.
(a) regional
(b) local
(c) national
(d) global

159.
(a) music
(b) magic
(c) health
(d) agriculture

160.
(a) systems
(b) machine
(c) communications
(d) media

161.
(a) view
(b) concept
(c) text
(d) content

162.
(a) culinary
(b) musical
(c) literary
(d) theatrical

163.
(a) country
(b) region
(c) village
(d) school

164.
(a) revolution
(b) transformation
(c) progress
(d) evolution

165.
(a) dear
(b) subtle
(c) appropriate
(d) adequate

Passage-III

(Q. Nos. 166 to 170)

Fragmentation of environment is the curse of modern towns. **(166)** public authorities working together to achieve a **(167)** landscape, they appear to act in blinkered isolation and mutual **(168)** as though the human environment **(169)** best split up into separate bits, with blind disregard **(170)** what the final result looks like.

166.
(a) Even if
(b) Even though
(c) Instead of
(d) In spite of

167.
(a) co-ordinated
(b) clean
(c) beautiful
(d) imaginary

168.
(a) distrust
(b) disrespect
(c) trust
(d) interest

169.
(a) is
(b) were
(c) are
(d) was

170.
(a) from
(b) of
(c) to
(d) for

Directions to Questions 171 to 200

In the following questions, you Have four .passages with 5—10 questions In each passage. Read the passages carefully and choose the best answer to each question, out of the four alternatives.

Passage-1

(Q. Nos. 171 to 175)

A glass bottle that is sent to a landfill can take up to a million years to break down. By contrast, it takes as little as 30 days for a recycled glass bottle to leave your kitchen recycling bin and appear on a store shelf as a new glass container. Glass containers are 100 percent recyclable, which means they can be recycled repeatedly, again and again, with no loss of purity or quality in the glass. Recovered glass from glass recycling is the primary ingredient in all new glass containers. A typical glass container is made of as much as 70 percent recycled glass. According to industry estimates, 80 percent of all recycled glass eventually ends up as new glass containers. Every ton of glass that is recycled saves more than a ton of the raw materials needed to create new glass, including 1,300 pounds of sand, 410 pounds of soda ash, and 380 pounds of limestone.

Because glass is made from natural materials such as sand and limestone, glass containers have a low rate of chemical interaction with their contents. As a result, glass can be safely reused. Besides serving as the primary ingredient in new glass containers, recycled glass also has many other commercial uses - from creating decorative tiles and landscaping material to rebuilding eroded beaches.

171. Recycling glass will help the
(a) industrialists
(b) government
(c) environment
(d) bureaucrats

172. Glass is safe to use as it
(a) has high resistance to chemicals
(b) has low resistance to chemicals
(c) looks very clean
(d) can be cleaned easily

173. The material used for making glass is
(a) soda ash and limestone
(b) sand and limestone
(c) soda and lime
(d) sandstone and tiles

174. People don't mind using recycled glass as it
(a) has high rate of chemical reaction
(b) is made from natural materials
(c) helps create landscaping material
(d) retains its purity or quality to a large extent

175. On the basis of your reading, complete the following statement:

It is important to send used glass bottles to a recycling plant because
(a) they are not biodegradable
(b) they can be reused
(c) they can be sold
(d) they can be used for decoration

Passage-II

(Q. Nos. 176 to 180)

Sleep, as every parent knows, is central to kids' well being. There are three main sleep in children : falling asleep, staying asleep and being too sleepy during the daytime. Every parent experiences at least one of them at some point or the other. Perhaps because of this and because sleepless nights have come to be regarded as normal, we fail to appreciate just how important sleep is for our children's health. In fact, sleep has a major impact on their physical development and growth, Research has shown that children who do not sleep as much as they should are smaller than they ought to be. But the impact of sleep is just not physical.

Sleep also has a profound influence on children's behaviour, emotions and ability to learn. As a result children's sleep disorders are not often recognized as such and they may be referred to hospitals for treatment of behavioural problems. And what is completely counter-intuitive is that many of those with attention deficit hyperactivily disorder (ADHD) also experience daytime sleepiness as revealed by something called a multiple sleep latency test. Another common problem is obstructive sleep apnoea. Children with this respiratory condition will be awake up to 12 hours a day making themselves severely sleep deprived.

176. Children who do not have enough sleep may
(a) have to be taken to the hospital
(b) have problems falling asleep
(c) have healthy growth patterns
(d) be smaller than they ought to be

177. Many children are taken to hospitals for treatment because they
(a) are badly behaved due to lack of sufficient sleep
(b) are not disciplined at home
(c) suffer from behavioural disorders
(d) suffer from respiratory disorders

178. The sleep latency test helps in identifying whether a child
(a) suffers from apnoea
(b) suffers from ADHD
(c) is growing normally
(d) experiences normal sleep pattern

179. Lack of sleep can affect a child
(a) physically and emotionally
(b) mentally
(c) emotionally
(d) psychologically

180. Parents often fail to appreciate the importance of sleep because
(a) they are inexperienced
(b) they are unaware of the importance of sleep in a child's life
(c) the doctors have not told them so
(d) they feel not having regular sleep is normal

Passage - III

(Q. Nos. 181 to 185)

Looking back on those days I myself as a kind of centaur, half **alf bike, forever wheeling luburban streets under the ***nas, on **rny way to football s or the library or to a meet-the little group of us, girls **ys, that came together on ***;e's verandah in the evenings a, night come across the Pro***-len on his after dinner stroll; often as not, he would be ***anied by my father, who top me and demand (partly, it, to impress the Professor) j was off to or where I had ***j sisting, with more than his ***Arce, that I come home right \th no argument. I spent j .trs cycling back and forth **i our house and Ross.

McDowell or Jimmy Larwood's, may friends from school, and the Professor's house was always on the route. I was always aboard and waiting for .something significant to occur, for life somehow to declare itself and catch me up. I rode my bike in slow circles or figures-of-eight, took it for sprints across the gravel of the park, or simply hung motionless in the saddle, balanced and waiting.

181. The boy's father was trying to gain the Professor's approval, hence

(a) he followed the Professor on his evening walks

(b) he pretended to be interested in observing the stars

(c) he boasted to the Professor about his son's riding skills

(d) he would make a display of his parental skills on seeing the narrator

182. The boy's constant bike riding reflects his

(a) longing for a simpler way of life

(b) yearning for something exciting to occur

(c) desire to escape from his father's influence

(d) joy in being young and without responsibilities

183. This text is written from the point of view of

(a) an adult reflecting on his boyhood

(b) a boy recounting his summer holiday

(c) an outsider observing life in the suburbs

(d) an adolescent describing his community

184. 'Was always aboard' in the passage means

(a) was always engaged in adventure

(b) was always on the bike

(c) was always doing stunts

(d) was always the outdoor type

185. The narrator described himself as 'a kind of centaur because

(a) he felt that the bike was a part of him

(b) he enjoyed riding his bike in a reckless manner

(c) he used his bike to escape from his family in the evening

(d) he knew that the Professor was watching him as he rode his bike.

Passage-IV

(Q. Nos. 186 to 190)

Like all visions, this one begins with a dream dream is of a stresses education system throughout India. That where there is stress it is the exception, not arising out of the system but out of some aberration or other. The extension of that dream is that the children, thus growing up free will feel better disposed to arrive at the ultimate point of all living, the giving and receiving of love without limits. That growing up in such an atmosphere they become effortlessly harbingers of peace to the world, which is what it seems India used to be in Vedic times. But whatever about the nation's role in the world tomorrow, what is needed is such relationships as both arise out of and strengthen a deep sense of meaning, of self-confidence, of focus, and above all, of peace.

We want that, for our kids, their reach should exceed their grasp, that the accomplishment of goals be only challenges to greater things, that sensing final arrival is either an illusion or an indication that the dream was itself originally petty. We want that they be open to the impossible, the barely imaginable, the almost magical.

186. How will the world be benefited by the loving nature with which children will grow up and communicate with others?

(a) Children growing up in such an environment will bring tranquillity and peace to the world

(b) They will spread love and lessen differences

(c) They will be able to trigger off fast progress and greater development

(d) A better bonding will be created between individuals and the social environment will be bettered

187. What ideal qualities should be nurtured in our children?

(a) They should understand that maintaining a moderate level of ambition is desirable

(b) They should be idealistic, imaginative, ready to face challenges and reach out to greater goals

(c) They should receive proper education and aim higher

(d) They should become better humans and be very practicable, suppressing all softer emotions

188. Which word or group of words in the passage means 'infinite'?

(a) without limits

(b) extension

(c) exceed their grasp
(d) deep

189. What is the implication for India of a pure and untainted system of education?
(a) That too much of baseness has entered the flawless system
(b) That where we find strain it is a product not of the existing system but of some anomaly or other
(c) That where we find some problem it is because of the individual elements
(d) That the stress-free education system is so perfect, that it can only be conceived in dreams

190. What will be the benefits of children growing up as free individuals?
(a) They will consider their thoughts as the highest and will be eager to confidently share them
(b) They will be practical and will be able to control the intensities of their emotions
(c) They will become more genial, sharing and receiving love without restraint
(d) They will be morally upright as far as worldly life is concerned

Passage-V

(Q. Nos. 191 to 200)

Art both reflects and interprets the notion that produced it. Portraiture was the dominant theme of British painting up to the end of the eighteenth century because of a persistent demand for it. It would be unfair to say that human vanity and pride of possessions were the only reasons for this persistent demand, but certainly these motives played their part in shaping the course of British painting. Generally speaking, it is the artist's enthusiasm that accounts for the vitality of the picture, but it is the client who dictates its subject matter. The history of national enthusiasms can be pretty accurately estimated by examining the subject matter of a nation's art.

There is one type of subject which recurs again and again in British painting of the late eighteenth century and the first half of the nineteenth and which is hardly met with in the part of any other country— the sporting picture, or rather the picture in which a love of outdoor life is directed into the channel of sport. The sporting picture is really an extension of the conversation piece. In it the emphasis is even more firmly based on the descriptive side of painting. It made severe demands on the artist and it must be confessed that painters capable of satisfying these demands were rare. The ability to paint a reasonably convincing landscape is not often combined with the necessary knowledge of horses and dogs in j movement and the power to introduce a portrait when necessary. To weld such diverse elements into a satisfactory aesthetic unity requires exceptional ability. It is not surprising, therefore, that while sporting pictures abound in England, especially in the private collections of country squires, not many of them are of real importance as works of art. What makes the sporting picture worth noting, a history of British painting is the fact that it is as truly indigenous and as truly popular a form of art in England as was the religious ikon in Russia.

191. Artists capable of painting sporting pictures were
(a) rarely found
(b) umpteen
(c) without any aesthetic sense
(d) firmly dealt with

192. The motives that played their part in shaping the course of British painting are
(a) the persistent demand for it and its supply
(b) the artist's enthusiasm for it and his efforts
(c) human vanity and pride of possessions.
(d) the spirit of competition that prevailed then and the encouragement given

193. Persistent demand for portraiture could be found
(a) in the early eighteenth century
(b) in the late eighteenth century
(c) up to the end of the eighteenth century
(d) before the end of the eighteenth century

194. British painting of the late eighteenth century and the first half of the nineteenth century chiefly deals with
(a) a love of outdoor life directed into the channel of sport

(b) a love of country life which cannot be found in any other country
(c) love in the open directed into a sporting channel
(d) love out of doors with enough life in it

195. England has sporting pictures in abundance but
(a) they are not easily available
(b) not many of them are significant as works of art
(c) many of them are of real importance as works of art

ANSWER KEY

1. (a) 2. (b) 3. (b) 4. (a) 5. (c)
6. (c) 7. (c) 8. (b) 9. (b) 10. (d)
11. (c) 12. (b) 13. (c) 14. (a) 15. (b)
16. (a) 17. (b) 18. (b) 19. (a) 20. (c)
21. (b) 22. (c) 23. (c) 24. (d) 25. (d)
26. (d) 27. (d) 28. (d) 29. (c) 30. (d)
31. (b) 32. (a) 33. (a) 34. (d) 35. (a)
36. (a) 37. (d) 38. (a) 39. (a) 40. (d)
41. (d) 42. (b) 43. (c) 44. (d) 45. (c)
46. (d) 47. (c) 48. (b) 49. (c) 50. (a)
51. (a) 52. (b) 53. (d) 54. (b) 55. (b)
56. (c) 57. (d) 58. (a) 59. (c) 60. (c)
61. (a) 62. (c) 63. (d) 64. (a) 65. (d)
66. (d) 67. (c) 68. (d) 69. (d) 70. (d)
71. (b) 72. (c) 73. (a) 74. (a) 75. (a)
76. (c) 77. (d) 78. (d) 79. (b) 80. (b)
81. (c) 82. (c) 83. (d) 84. (a) 85. (a)
86. (d) 87. (a) 88. (d) 89. (d) 90. (d)
91. (c) 92. (d) 93. (a) 94. (a) 95. (c)
96. (a) 97. (d) 98. (c) 99. (b) 100. (c)
101. (d) 102. (d) 103. (c) 104. (a) 105. (b)
106. (d) 107. (b) 108. (c) 109. (b) 110. (d)
111. (d) 112. (b) 113. (a) 114. (a) 115. (a)
116. (b) 117. (c) 118. (a) 119. (a) 120. (d)
121. (d) 122. (c) 123. (d) 124. (c) 125. (b)
126. (b) 127. (c) 128. (d) 129. (c) 130. (c)
131. (b) 132. (c) 133. (b) 134. (a) 135. (c)
136. (c) 137. (b) 138. (a) 139. (a) 140. (b)
141. (a) 142. (c) 143. (b) 144. (d) 145. (d)
146. (d) 147. (c) 148. (a) 149. (b) 150. (b)
151. (a) 152. (c) 153. (b) 154. (a) 155. (d)
156. (b) 157. (a) 158. (c) 159. (a) 160. (d)
161. (b) 162. (c) 163. (b) 164. (d) 165. (b)
166. (c) 167. (a) 168. (a) 169. (b) 170. (d)
171. (c) 172. (a) 173. (b) 174. (b) 175. (a)
176. (d) 177. (c) 178. (b) 179. (a) 180. (d)
181. (d) 182. (b) 183. (a) 184. (b) 185. (a)
186. (a) 187. (b) 188. (a) 189. (b) 190. (c)
191. (a) 192. (c) 193. (c) 194. (a) 195. (c)
196. (d) 197. (c) 198. (d) 199. (c) 200. (a)

FREQUENCY ANALYSIS

ABBREVIATIONS USED:

Comprehension / **Comp**, Sentence Completion / **SC**, Sentence Filler / **SF**, Cloze Test/ **CT**, Synonyms/ **Syn**, Antonyms/ **Ant**, Idioms and Phrase/ **IP**, Substitution/ **Subt**, Sentence arrangement/ **SA**, Spelling/ **SPL**, Miscellaneous/**Misc.**, Total Marks/**TM**, Sentence error/**SE**, Sentence Improvement/ **SI**.

	Comp.	SC	SF	CT	Syn	Ant	IP	Subt	SA	SE	SPL	SI	MISC.	TM
	30	5		24	3	3	10	12	18	20	3	22	46	

TREND ANALYSIS

The test is very comprehensive as it contains two hundred questions. Thirteen types of questions have been set. All units are regular and have been set in a straight forward manner. If the book is read carefully there will be no problem. Questions on voice and narration are new in comparison to the pattern of questions in Bank and Defence examinations.

The level of questions is just above moderate. They can be easily solved. A careful reading of all the units of the book and a regular practice at the set will help the students.

PAPER 42

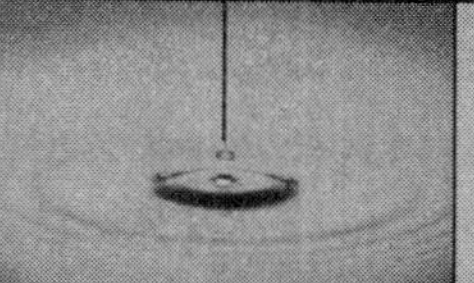

SSC MULTI TASKING STAFF EXAMINATION, 2012

Directions to Questions 1 to 10

In the Hollowing questions, some parts of the sentences have errors and some have none. Find out which part of a sentence has an error. The number of that part is your answer. If a sentence is free from error, then your answer is (d), i.e. No Error.

1. Gulliver's Travels' (a)/are indeed (b)/an interesting book. (c)/ No Error (d)
2. Either Parmeet (a)/ or Jyoti (b)/ have done the crime. (c)/ No Error (d)
3. The streets (a)/ are so wet (b)/it should have rained last night. (c)/No Error (d)
4. Our vacation is (a)/ between 12 May (b)/ to 12 June.(c)/No Error (d)
5. He is very angry on me (a)/because I failed (b)/ to return his book.(c)/No Error (d)
6. The social activist (a)/ was murder (b)/ in cold blood.(c)/ No Error (d)
7. The train will not start (a)/ until the guard (b)/ will blow the whistle. (c)/ No Error {4)
8. I read (a)/ a great deal of (b)/ books.(c)/ No Error (d)
9. The Indians are genetically (a)/ incapable of (b)/ being good or outstanding sportsmen. (c)/ No Error (d)
10. Equator (a)/ divides the earth(b)/ into two hemispheres.(c) / No Error (d)

Directions to Questions 11 to 20

In the following questions, sentences are given with blanks to be filled in with an appropriate word(s). Four alternatives are suggested for each question. Choose the correct alternative out of the four as your answer.

11. The teacher let us________.
    (a) to go early (b) to leave early
    (c) go early (d) early to go
12. Jane is annoyed________.
    (a) on me (b) with me
    (c) against me (d) over me
13. I am not angry___ you, Paul.
    (a) at (b) on
    (c) with (d) against
14. _________ Australian and________ European are there among the tourists. '

(a) An, an (b) The, the
(c) An, a (d) A, an

15. I have been looking for an apartment and I finally found the______ one.
(a) good (b) airy
(c) cheap (d) perfect

16. The youth should believe_____ God.
(a) upon (b) in
(c) on (d) of

17. He was born _____ India.
(a) off (b) in
(c) of (d) through

18. The convict tried his level best to justify himself but the judge looked _____ him and found him guilty.
(a) around (b) at
(c) through (d) to

19. His opponents launched a political _____ against him.
(a) regimen (b) remission
(c) regale (d) tirade

20. What an _____ story! I am not ______enough yet to believe it.
(a) incredible/credulous
(b) incredulous/credible
(c) increditable/believable
(d) unbelievable/creditable

Directions to Questions 21 to 23

In the following questions, choose the word opposite in meaning to the given word as your answer.

21. Barren
(a) frigid (b) fertile
(c) fallow (d) ferrous

22. Hostile
(a) host (b) proud
(c) systematic (d) sympathetic

23. Peril
(a) fatal (b) mortal
(c) uncertainty (d) safety

Directions to Questions 24 to 26

In the following questions, out .of the four alternatives, choose the one which best expresses the meaning of the given word as your answer.

24. Absurd
(a) diligent (b) ridiculous
(c) brisk (d) complex

25. Solitary
(a) sad (b) voluntary
(c) subtle (d) lonely

26. Pacific
(a) extensive (b) peaceful
(c) deep (d) white

Directions to Questions 27 to 29

In the following questions, four alternatives are given for the Idiom/ Phrase printed in **bold** in the sentence. Choose the alternative which best expresses the meaning of the Idiom/Phrase as your answer.

27. Her mother **saw through** the excuse she gave.
(a) revealed (b) detected
(c) viewed (d) hacked

28. She **has a bee in her bonnet** and can say anything.
(a) is a crazy person (b) is a frank person
(c) is a foolish person (d) is a proud person

29. Some people have the habit of working **by fits and starts.**
(a) very seriously (b) excitedly
(c) consistently (d) irregularly

Directions to Questions 30 to 34

In the following questions, a part of the sentence is printed in bold. Below are given alternatives to the bold part at (a) (b), (c) which may improve the sentence. Choose the correct alternative. In case no improvement is needed, your answer is (d).

30. He **makes** excellent portraits.
(a) paints (b) portrays
(c) illustrates (d) No improvement.